GARDENS

OF

COLONY AND STATE

A BOUQUET PAINTED BY JAN BRUEGHEL ABOUT 1650

SHOWING THE WIDE VARIETY OF FLOWERS THEN IN CULTIVATION IN HOLLAND, INCLUDING CROWN IMPERIAL, PEONIES, TULIPS, ROSES, FLEURS-DE-LIS, LILIES, CARNATIONS, AND DAFFODILS, ALL OF WHICH ARE MENTIONED IN COLONIAL RECORDS BEFORE 1700

GARDENS

OF
COLONY AND STATE

GARDENS AND GARDENERS OF THE AMERICAN
COLONIES AND OF THE REPUBLIC BEFORE 1840

INTRODUCTION • MASSACHUSETTS • CONNECTICUT
MAINE • NEW HAMPSHIRE • VERMONT • RHODE ISLAND
NEW YORK • NEW JERSEY • PENNSYLVANIA • MICHIGAN
OHIO • ILLINOIS • FENCES AND ENCLOSURES

COMPILED AND EDITED FOR
THE GARDEN CLUB OF AMERICA
BY
ALICE G · B · LOCKWOOD
CHAIRMAN
SPECIAL PUBLICATIONS COMMITTEE

NEW EDITION PRODUCED BY
SMALLWOOD & STEWART
FOR

THE GARDEN CLUB OF AMERICA
2000

ISBN: 0-917841-01-8

LIBRARY OF CONGRESS CONTROL NUMBER: 00-090371

*"The Garden Club of America is deeply interested in all efforts
to preserve the dignified past for the complicated future."
(Volume 1, Gardens of Colony and State p.441)*

*Published by The Garden Club of America in the 1930s, Gardens of
Colony and State is regarded as one of the most important
reference works in print on gardening in the colonies and the Republic. The
volumes provide a permanent archival and pictorial record of American
achievements and traditions of that period.*

*Realizing the importance of the photographs and information these books
contain, and to mark the approach of the new millennium, The Garden Club
of America is reprinting a limited edition as a gift to the world of horticulture
and landscape design history.*

*We are indebted to those who have advised us on this project, and to
the Executive Committee of The Garden Club of America for support
and encouragement of our efforts to bring these classics to a new and
contemporary audience.*

Jeanne Tansey Will, GC of Morristown, NJ
Marnie Layton Laird, GC of Wilmington, DE

*Co-chairmen of the Gardens of Colony and State
Republication Committee
October 1999*

INTRODUCTION

When was the last time that a garden book illustrated only with black-and-white archival photos and weighing a hefty seven-and-a-half pounds gripped a reader? Each of the two volumes of *Gardens of Colony and State* is just such a page turner. Together they form what their compiler and editor, Alice G.B. Lockwood, calls, in her foreword to Volume I, "the first general survey of the subject." That subject, as the subtitle says, is "Gardens and Gardeners of the American Colonies and of the Republic before 1840." (The 27 states included in the work are those that were both in the union by 1840, and had Garden Club of America clubs by 1930.)

For anyone interested in American history, let alone garden history, this work is important. First, it traces in intimate detail the intense love-affair with the land that powered the European settlement of this continent. (It touches on settlement-era agriculture and subsistence gardening as well as covering ornamental gardening throughout its 220-year time frame.) Second, the sheer extent of documentary research and the hundreds of photographs, plans, maps and reproductions of works of art, especially in the section on fences and enclosures that concludes each volume, maintain the work's position as a design guide for historic restoration. Third, the way this history is done—by many authors, mostly women, in an almost scrapbook or quilt style—has a contemporary noteworthiness. It is now clear that bare-bones garden history—a record of what was designed, what was planted, what was in style—is greatly enriched by the inclusion of material from other fields in a way that has become familiar from the analysis of material culture as a historical tool. In *Gardens of Colony and State* one can find Lydia Maria Child's *The American Frugal Housewife* (Boston: 1832), and George Washington Cable's *The Creoles of Louisiana* (New York: 1889) employed to great effect, for instance.

Lastly, these old volumes have signal importance today because so many of the gardens described have vanished. In fact, that process was well under way when research began on the project in the 1920s, as its garden club chroniclers were well aware. Their pages are filled with sentences like "There is no trace of Mr. Roger's orchards or groves today." Besides the value of the record *per se,* one can add that this refrain adds a haunting sense of loss, nostalgia, and foreboding to a present-day reader's experience. Lockwood and her cohorts were writing only a decade and a half before a wave of garden destruction brought on by post-World War II suburbanization and the disappearance of the staff needed to maintain many of the large estates they described.

Not that *Gardens of Colony and State* is a lament for the past; quite the contrary. There is a double sense of discovery here: the original delight of the garden makers and their visitors, and the no less palpable delight of the writers of the individual garden narratives, such as J.G.D. Paul who, inspired by a 1751 inventory for Rousby Hall, in Calvert County, Maryland, that lists "one lawn sieve and bag, 4 iron-teethed garden-rakes in the greenhouse, 2 pairs old shears, 1 pair better shears," etc., hired a boat to take him across the Chesapeake "in the hope of finding some suggestive ruin." He found nothing of house or garden, he reports, "although the ground was filled with humps and depressions that can only mean old buildings fallen to ruin." (Vol. II, pp.129-32) But it is clear he had a marvellous time, as will the reader.

Another double perception governs a present-day reading of the book: a perception of what "restoration" meant in 1931 and what it means now. The discovery of the very existence of an American garden history followed on the enhancement of the stature of American history in general. Both resulted from the celebration of the nation's centennial in 1876, which formed the original impetus for a Colonial Revival style, first in furniture and architecture, then in gardens. It is possible to look back indulgently at the "restorations" described in this work and see how certain their makers were that their interpretations, mostly made on the basis of documentary sources alone, were valid. Today, restorers and preservationists are more tentative in their conclusions until modern archaeological techniques bear them out.

Today's vantage point and interpretation of the documents and of the gardens themselves differ in many ways from those of Lockwood and her contributors. Contemporary interpretation of what they were up to in writing this book also differs. It is clear this is a work of family hagiography as well as of garden history, a book written for American upper class insiders by themselves. "Garden," for them, could be defined as a domestic layout where members of an elite group could spend their leisure time in a complex more ornamental than useful that expressed their own cultural standards.

One can't help, therefore, noticing who these contributors are: they are not just the well-heeled, well-known amateur gardeners of their day, like Miss Annie Burr Jennings of Fairfield, Connecticut, or Mr. and Mrs. Pierre S. duPont of Wilmington, Delaware, or Mrs. Oakley Thorne of Millbrook, New York, and Santa Barbara, California. They are also the representatives of the families whose names are on 18th-century streets and squares and revolutionary manifestos—Adams, Peabody, Van Cortland, Stockton, Tilghman, Pinckney.

There is a sprinkling of professionals as well, such as the restoration landscape architect, Arthur Shurcliff, creator of Colonial Williamsburg's Colonial Revival gardens, and Mrs. Leah Ellwanger, of the great Ellwanger horticultural dynasty in Rochester, New York. Historians are represented by the redoubtable architectural expert, Fiske Kimball, and by Brooks Adams, author of *Law of Civilization and Decay* (Boston: 1895). And for politicians and statesmen, there is Franklin Delano Roosevelt, soon to be branded a traitor to his own class by many of its members for engineering the New Deal. He contributed a description of his family's old gardens in Hyde Park, New York.

We open the heavy volumes expecting that these people, most of them inspired by an intense desire to reaffirm their status and their background, will claim more than is justified for the continued existence of their old gardens. But in a section of Lockwood's introduction titled "The Life-Span of Colonial Gardens," her practical, knowledgeable gardener's assessment of what survives is a refreshing cold bath for the skeptical modern reader.

She begins: "We often hear of very old plants, and there are a few which reach a century or a little more of actual life, but the great majority of garden things do not live beyond a generation, and if neglected perish very soon." (Vol. I, p. 14) Ancestor worship notwithstanding, and there is plenty of that kind of mythology in the individual contributions, this is intelligent, serious, scholarly history that respects the limitations of its materials.

Alice Gardner Burnell Lockwood, a member of the Greenwich Garden Club, offers nothing personal about herself; surprisingly, there are no dutiful encomia of husband and family (she was the mother of two) for putting up with her as she worked for years on this project. But in fact she and her husband, Luke Vincent Lockwood, a well-known antiquarian, had the same tastes and pursuits and must have contributed much to each other's thought and work: while she was editing the authoritative book about early American gardens, he was writing authoritative tomes about early American furniture and decorative arts. And they must have had fun together in the glory days of hunting for American antiques (let's call it the first half of the twentieth century) making a collection of American furniture, paintings, and drawings fine enough to be sold after their deaths at public auction at Parke-Bernet, New York, in 1954.

The first volume of *Gardens of Colony and State* was originally published by Charles Scribner's Sons in a limited edition of only 1000 in 1931. On publication the book was hailed enthusiastically as "one of the most notable historical garden books ever published, either here or abroad," (*Landscape Architecture,* April 1932) by Theodora Kimball Hubbard, co-author of the standard text on landscape architecture, *An Introduction to the Study of Landscape Design* (Boston: 1917). (Interestingly, Garden Club of America minutes indicate that a delay in publication of the second volume was requested by Scribner's in 1932 "owing to the general financial depression.")

The appearance of *Gardens of Colony and State* could be said to mark the end of an era of fervent garden interest. Beginning in the 1870s and continuing on to the Great Depression, almost every year saw an increased outpouring of garden books of all kinds in England and France as well as in America. Lockwood's voluminous bibliography (a real treasure for historians and serious readers of every stripe) cites *The History of Gardening in England* (London: 1895), by the Honorable Alicia Amherst, a book very similar in ambition, scope and tone to *Gardens of Colony and State*. Other historical works that would have helped direct Lockwood's and her collaborators' researches include Alice Morse Earle's *Old-Tyme Gardens* (New York: 1901) and Frank Crisp's *Medieval Gardens* (London: 1924). Interest in the flamboyant bulge of great new American gardens and estates tied gardens to gentility, as seen in many works of which the most glamorous (and unctuous in tone) is perhaps Barr Ferree's *American Estates and Gardens* (New York: 1904). Regional compendia organized garden-by-garden in the same manner as *Gardens of Colony and State* include *Portraits of Philadelphia Gardens* by Louise Bush-Brown and James Bush-Brown (Philadelphia: 1929) and *Homes and Gardens in Old Virginia,* edited by Frances Archer Christian and Suzanne Williams Massie (Richmond: 1931). Winifred Dobyn's *California Gardens* (New York: 1931) appeared the same year, when Marion Cran, that observant English writer, also weighed in with her acerbic assessment, *Gardens in America* (London: 1931).

It's worth noting that the restoration of Williamsburg, Virginia (which began in 1926), developed during the same years that *Gardens of Colony and State* was conceived and written. Parallels can easily be drawn between the two ventures: they share the same desire to glorify an American past and an imaginative reliance on documentary sources above all.

Thereafter, interest in historic gardens waned in print until the publication of U.P. Hedrick's magisterial *History of Horticulture in the United States to 1860* (London and New York: 1950), and finally the appearance of Ann Leighton's trilogy on American gardens, beginning with *Early American Gardens, "For Meate or Medicine"* (Boston: 1970), *American Gardens of the Eighteenth Century: For Use or For Delight, American Gardens of the Nineteenth Century: "For Comfort and Affluence".*

Gardening is both art and craft. Garden history is a precarious mix of the history of ideas and the listing and description of plants, propagation methods and design elements. Alice G.B. Lockwood was not interested in compiling a history of ideas; she was a descriptive, self-taught historian interested in telling a story, as, for the most part, were her contributors. To that end, the array of primary and secondary historical and horticultural sources they so liberally cite is eye-popping, ranging from the earliest records of the Massachusetts Bay Colony to Liberty Hyde Bailey's *Standard Cyclopedia of Horticulture* (New York: 1925), then the newest, most authoritative reference.

Though they made use of such standard sources, they also drew on memory and oral tradition; on what still stood on the ground around their houses and the houses of their ancestors; on old seed lists (and new research published in general and professional magazines); on travel journals, correspondence published and unpublished, and regional histories; on probate records; and on lists of garden books from libraries both public and private. They commissioned plans and drawings, paying Arthur Shurcliff $650 for a new set of plans of Middleton Place, Charleston, South Carolina, for example. They also drew on their own empirical knowledge—which is probably why Alice Lockwood, in her introduction to the first volume, was able to state so definitely that how old lawns were mowed to perfection was a mystery to her, since "scythes never made a velvety lawn." The materials are assorted and sometimes humble, as are the methods. But the result is an imposing and lively edifice, a storehouse of history.

"So low is the doorway that even one of short stature must stoop to enter," reads the caption for a photograph of the greenhouse at Theodore Lyman's The Vale, in Waltham, Massachusetts, which is as old as any surviving glass house in the country (c.1800). Now, at the second millennium, that greenhouse with its pint-sized door still stands (and still operates) at The Vale, since 1952 the property of The Society for the Preservation of New England Antiquities. *Gardens of Colony and State* still stands as a similar monument, now renewed by its original sponsor, The Garden Club of America, in this much-needed facsimile reprint edition.

MAC KEITH GRISWOLD

MEMBERS AND MEMBER CLUBS OF THE GARDEN CLUB OF AMERICA SUBSCRIBING TO THE SECOND EDITION

PHOEBE ANDREW
in memory of Clarissa Donnelley Haffner
MARY-ELIZABETH (BETSY) ATKINS
ALMA M. ATKINSON

BEVERLY MAURY BAGLEY
MR. & MRS. CRAIG BARROW III
META PACKARD BARTON
CONSTANCE LEEDS BENNETT
MRS. GEORGE P. BISSELL, JR.
presentation to Smithsonian Institution-
Archives of American Gardens
ELEANOR F. BOOKWALTER
MRS. RICHARD P. BOWMAN
MRS. W. WALDO BRADLEY
ALICE CARY BROWN
MRS. JOSEPH BYRAN III
SUSAN PAYSON BURKE
MRS. WILLIAM H. T. BUSH
in honor of Dr. Peter Raven
Missouri Botanical Garden

MRS. R. B. CADWALLADER
MRS. H. AUGUSTUS CAREY
MRS. PETER CARNEY
MRS. WILLIAM M. CARSON
LILIAN S. L. CHANCE
in memory of Lilian Carpenter Streeter
MRS. GEORGE P. K. CHING
MRS. RONALD KINSMAN CHUTE
ANN BOOCOCK COBURN
MRS. J. FERDINAND CONVERY, JR.
MRS. JOHN C. COOPER
MRS. JAMES N. COOKE III
MRS. W. ANDREW COPENHAVER
JOANNE COWAN

MRS. DAVID DALTON
MRS. MURRAY S. DANFORTH, JR.
MRS. J. H. DAVENPORT III

EVELYN SCATTERGOOD DAY
LUCY DAY
ELISABETH DeB. DEANS
ANNA deCORDOVA
MRS. RAYMOND J. DEVLIN, JR.
ALICE McGOVERN DOERING
CAROLINE GREENE DONNELLY
MRS. FORD P. DRAPER. JR.

MRS. WILLIAM L. ELKINS
in honor of Mrs. John R. Young
MR. & MRS. ELMER G. ELLIS
in honor of Elizabeth Peacock Marsh
SUSAN C. EMERY

MRS. LOUIS C. R. FARRELLY
in memory of Mrs. Richard L. Farrelly
MRS. DAVID L. FERGUSON
presentation to Mrs. Christopher Reece
DR. MARY FLEMING FINLAY
DIANA FISH
MRS. JOSEPH C. FRIERSON, JR.
MRS. MARK FULLER
LYNN BOWERS FULTON

MRS. WILLIAM B. GAGE
MRS. ADOLFO R. GARCIA
MARTHA HOOPES PARKE GIBIAN
MRS. FRITZ GRAU
in honor of Dr. Dieter Wasshausen
and Chester B. Locklin
MRS. P. PORCHER GREGG, JR.

MRS. FREDERIK C. HANSEN, JR.
MRS. JOHN M. HASTINGS, JR.
HELEN K. HEEKIN
MRS. JAMES GRANT HELLMUTH
ELIZABETH B. HILL
MARIAN WELDON HILL
MR. & MRS. LOUIS HOOD

AKRON GARDEN CLUB
Ohio
ALAMO HEIGHTS-TERRELL HILLS GARDEN CLUB
Texas
BEDFORD GARDEN CLUB
New York
CAROLINA FOOTHILLS GARDEN CLUB
South Carolina
in memory of Margaret Gardner Alexander
CATONSVILLE GARDEN CLUB
Maryland
CHEROKEE GARDEN LIBRARY
Georgia
COUNTRY GARDEN CLUB
Ohio
DOLLEY MADISON GARDEN CLUB
Virginia
FORT ORANGE GARDEN CLUB
New York
in memory of Elizabeth Platt Corning
presentation to the Albany Public Library
FOX HILL GARDEN CLUB
Massachusetts
GARDEN CLUB OF ALEXANDRIA
Virginia
presentation to The Alexandria Library
GARDEN CLUB OF BARRINGTON
Illinois
presentation to The Barrington Area Public Library
GARDEN CLUB OF CHEVY CHASE
Maryland
GARDEN CLUB OF CLEVELAND
Ohio
in honor of Joanna Bristol
GARDEN CLUB OF DARIEN
Connecticut
GARDEN CLUB OF DENVER
Colorado
presentation to Denver Botanic Gardens
GARDEN CLUB OF EVANSTON
Illinois
presentation to Evanston Public Library
GARDEN CLUB OF THE HALIFAX COUNTRY
Florida
GARDEN CLUB OF IRVINGTON-ON-HUDSON
New York
presentation to The Irvington Library
GARDEN CLUB OF LAWRENCE
New York
in memory of Nancy B. Baldridge
GARDEN CLUB OF MADISON
New Jersey
in memory of Mrs. Ruth V. P. Churchill
presentation to Madison Public Library
GARDEN CLUB OF MORRISTOWN
New Jersey
in honor of Clarissa S. Willemsen
presentation to The Freylinghuysen Arboretum

GARDEN CLUB OF NASHVILLE
Tennessee
GARDEN CLUB OF ORANGE & DUTCHESS COUNTIES
New York
GARDEN CLUB OF PALM BEACH
Florida
GARDEN CLUB OF PRINCETON
New Jersey
presentation to Princeton Public Library
GARDEN CLUB OF TRENTON
New Jersey
GARDEN CLUB OF WILMINGTON
Delaware
presentation to Delaware Center for Horticulture
GARDEN STUDY CLUB OF NEW ORLEANS
Louisiana
GARDEN GUILD OF WINNETKA
Illinois
presentation to June Price Reedy
Horticultural Library, Chicage Botanic Garden
THE GARDENERS
Pennsylvania
presentation to Ludington Library
THE GRASS RIVER GARDEN CLUB
Florida
presentation to The Delray Beach Library
GREEN FINGERS GARDEN CLUB
Connecticut
GREEN SPRING VALLEY GARDEN CLUB
Maryland
presentation to The Enoch Pratt Free Library, Baltimore
GREEN TREE GARDEN TREE CLUB
Wisconsin
presentation to Boerner Botanical Gardens
GUILFORD GARDEN CLUB
Maryland
in honor of Mrs. Frederik C. Hansen, Jr.
HILLSBOROUGH GARDEN CLUB
California
HUNTINGDON VALLEY GARDEN CLUB
Pennsylvania
presentation to Abington Free Library
INDIANAPOLIS GARDEN CLUB
Indiana
presentation to The Holliday Park Nature Center
JUNIOR LADIES' GARDEN CLUB
Georgia
in honor of Mrs. Joseph C. Frierson, Jr.
JUPITER ISLAND GARDEN CLUB
Florida
KETTLE MORAINE GARDEN CLUB
Wisconsin
presented by Maribeth Price
LITCHFIELD GARDEN CLUB
Connecticut
in memory of Doris Hamlin

LITTLE COMPTON GARDEN CLUB
Rhode Island
in memory of Angela Spence-Shaw
LITTLE GARDEN CLUB OF BIRMINGHAM
Alabama
presentation to Birmingham Botanical Society
MEMPHIS GARDEN CLUB
Tennessee
presentation to Library of Memphis Botanic Garden
MIDDLETOWN GARDEN CLUB
Connecticut
THE MONROE GARDEN STUDY LEAGUE
Louisiana
NEW CANAAN GARDEN CLUB
Connecticut
in memory of Catherine Bangham
THE NEW JERSEY COMMITTEE OF GCA
NEW LONDON GARDEN CLUB
Connecticut
ORINDA GARDEN CLUB
California
PISCATAQUA GARDEN CLUB
Maine
in honor of Helen Rollins
in memory of Marion Hosmer
RED MOUNTAIN GARDEN CLUB
Alabama
RIDGEFIELD GARDEN CLUB
Connecticut
presentation to The Ridgefield Public Library
ROCHESTER GARDEN CLUB, INC.
New York
presentation to Rochester Civic Garden Center

SEATTLE GARDEN CLUB
Washington
presentation to Elisabeth C. Miller Library
SHAKER LAKES GARDEN CLUB
Ohio
in honor of Joanna Bristol
SHORT HILLS GARDEN CLUB
New Jersey
SYRACUSE GARDEN CLUB
New York
THE TACOMA GARDEN CLUB
Washington
presentation to Lakewold Gardens
THREE HARBORS GARDEN CLUB
New York
TOWN & COUNTRY GARDEN CLUB, INC.
Wisconsin
presentation to Mead Public Library
WARRENTON GARDEN CLUB
Virginia
WASHINGTON GARDEN CLUB
Connecticut
ZONE III
New York
presentation to Allyn's Creek Garden Club
and Rochester Garden Club, Inc.

With sincere appreciation to:
CATHA GRACE RAMBUSCH
MRS. JOHN LOCKWOOD

ALICE GARDNER BURNELL LOCKWOOD
1874–1954

Looking for ways to channel their gardening energies, a group of young women from Greenwich, Connecticut, all of whom were interested in growing things, "asked the advice of a most erudite matron, a woman who served soup in original Paul Revere porringers, café brûlot in Davenport, and forbade smoking in her dining room." It was 1930 when the young gardeners met with this distinguished lady on the porch of her Greenwich home, called "Riverside," which overlooked her own garden. She advised her younger friends to form a gardening club to be named *Hortulus,* meaning *little garden.* (*Hortulus* History)

The *matron* was Mrs. Luke Vincent Lockwood, who just one year later was a most successful editor and author of the first volume of The Garden Club of America publication, *Gardens of Colony and State,* subtitled *"Gardens and Gardeners of the American Colonies and of the Republic before 1840."*

This two-volume set was born of a recognized need to preserve our early American gardens as a part of our heritage—if not as gardens, then in print and picture. It was a concept that developed from the beginning of The Garden Club of America in 1913, and is reflected in the stated purpose of the organization, "to stimulate the knowledge and love of gardening among amateurs; to share the advantages of association through conference and correspondence, in this country and abroad; to aid in the protection of native plants and birds; and to encourage civic planting."

Members visited each other's gardens—as a way to share knowledge. By 1919, The Garden Club of America had an active Historic Gardens Committee led by Miss Delia West Marble and Mrs. William West Frazier. Committee members collected pieces of American garden history including maps, plans, seed and plant lists, photographs, biographies, family letters, diaries, and ultimately hand-colored glass slides of near and neighboring gardens, especially those gardens thought to be in danger of extinction.

In 1923, The James River Garden Club published *Historic Gardens of Virginia,* a pioneer work in the collection of information about fifty historic gardens. The enthusiastic reception of this book, edited by Edith Tunis Sale, was an impetus to the Historic Gardens Committee to move in the direction of publication.

Interest in gardens was furthered by the exchange between gardening groups of lantern-slides (hand-tinted glass slides). In 1927, slides of American gardens were shown to the English Speaking Union in London, followed by a request for another collection the following season. Individual garden clubs too, were exchanging slides, further stimulating visits to historic houses and gardens and elevating the interest in preservation of these American treasures.

In the *Garden Club of America History—1913-1938,* Ernestine Goodman wrote in 1930: "An interesting Garden Club development which is becoming a national movement is the yearly pilgrimage to historic houses and gardens sponsored by local Garden Club groups, the entrance fees being used to restore old places in danger of being lost by neglect."

This intensified interest and resulting research prompted the selection by the Historic Gardens Committee of an editor, leading to publication of *Gardens of Colony and State.* This editor was Mrs. Luke Vincent Lockwood. Alice Gardner Burnell Lockwood had been serving on the Historic Gardens Committee for some time. She shared her interest in history with her husband Luke Vincent Lockwood (1872-1951), who was an acknowledged and respected antiquarian. Mr. Lockwood is best remembered for his avocation—the history of American furniture. He was the author of *Colonial Furniture in America* and *The Pendleton Collection,* both of which continue to be considered important and collectible.

Mrs. Lockwood volunteered her services not only to The Garden Club of America but also to the Metropolitan Museum of Art, which honored her as a 'fellow in perpetuity.' She was a member of the Greenwich Garden Club in Connecticut. A strong and determined woman, her contemporaries knew her as 'no shrinking violet'.

Alice Gardner Burnell and Luke Vincent Lockwood married in 1897, and lived in Brooklyn where Mr. Lockwood practiced law. They moved to Greenwich, Connecticut, where he was Chairman of the Board of Greenwich Trust Company and much involved in civic endeavors. In 1904, a son Luke Burnell, was born followed by a daughter Jane. Luke B. Lockwood had two children by his first marriage to Dorcas Washburn, which ended in divorce. He then married Marion Miner. Jane Lockwood was a well-respected physician with an interest in wildflowers. After her retirement from the practice of medicine, Dr. Jane continued her wildflower photography and lectures.

By 1919, Alice began her garden at their Greenwich home—"Riverside." Those attending The Garden Club of America's Annual Meeting held in 1927 in the Greenwich area visited this garden. Here is how it was described in the report for that meeting:

"...The parterre garden is so placed as to be seen from the house and the terrace, and is backed by many fine shrubs regularly placed, the trees add to the sense of inclosure without being close. Four wide corner beds surround the square, with four others and a circle in the "Cup and Ball" design. Eight handsome old box bushes mark the paths that lead through the garden and brick edges hold the beds from the reddish gravel paths. The center is of grass with a charming old painted figurehead on a white pedestal, a woman in a shawl and full skirts, holding a rose to her breast. The tones are of pale green, the fashion of the 1850s. A dominating note in the garden was the gray foliage of sedum spectabile and thalictrum glaucum against the soft colors of rows of tall aquilegias. White Sweet William, spirea filipendula and myosotis were used as edgings with ageratum and violas. Iris, dictamnus, digitalis, fine single peonies and hemerocallis gave color, while many clumps of phlox, delphinium and lilies were coming on. While the beds were well planted, there was no crowding and all the excellent material was well grown. From the parterre one came to a wide green space with many stepping-stones pleasingly laid in the grass, to a long pond backed by willows whose dark stems were reflected in the water. Much water-growth adorned the bank and masses of water lilies grew at one side of the pond. Grass walks wound about, with heavy plantings of old, fine shrubs and a few digitalis. The laurel was all in flower and the pink blooms above the masses of ferns were very beautiful. Many small paths with stones led through the wild planting to the little brook dashing over and between the boulders that outline its course from the deep spring that is its source. At that point the shade is deeper, the pool full of lovely green water and one feels in the depths of a truly wild spot. Crossing the stream we returned by another path deeply set in slim trees of shadbush, dogwoods and other native growth, leading back to the pond through a group of large pines with a carpet of needles beneath. It was quite impossible to realize that eight years ago this had been a boggy meadow and that all the stones, all the plant material, and the sort of soil it required, had been hauled to its present position. Vitale and Geiffert made the design but the care and knowledge of the owners has brought it to its present perfection."

In 1931, Volume I of *Gardens of Colony and State* was published. Leila Mechlin, Associate Editor of *American Magazine of Art,* wrote: " The historical facts set forth in this volume give glimpses of what has been, of the zeal and the ardor; the love of nature and beauty, with which our forebears planted and tended their gardens...Also it is noted with pleasure that from first to last the homes of the garden makers are given place with the gardens; and rightly, for house and garden are inseparable, the garden serving as a setting for the house and the house in turn serving as a focal point for the gardens." This was reprinted in The Garden Club of America *Bulletin* of March, 1932.

Alice G. B. Lockwood outlined the format of the books and her method of research in the Introduction to both volumes. She reported in the *Bulletin* of July, 1938, that "these volumes are not garden books in the ordinary sense, but the long history of what were the facts in local conditions, English, or other tradition, which influenced their form, what plants were available, where they came from, who built the houses and the gardens, and many bits of information bearing on garden subjects."

While Volume II of *Gardens of Colony and State* was being prepared, Mrs. Lockwood shared her research difficulties and search for accuracy. She published a series of ten letters written in pursuit of a tidbit of important information about a John Clayton and his botanical garden. Evidently the garden had no gate—it was a dead end. This most enlightening example of how the research team searched for accuracy can be found in The Garden Club of America *Bulletin* of November 1932.

Bradford Williams of Boston reviewed the completed two-volume set of *Gardens of Colony and State* in 1934. He wrote the following:

> "...a new book on one of the arts, and especially a book on gardens, beautifully printed, handsomely bound, and in itself a work of art, is wholly irresistible.
>
> Such a book is the second volume of *Gardens of Colony and State*...It is all the more welcome since its outward aspect is the same in form and size as the earlier volume, its internal arrangement follows the same orderly style, and—most significant of all—the value of its text and illustrations conforms faithfully to the high standards already set under Mrs. Lockwood's able editorial direction."
>
> ...In the North the diversity of local character was reflected in the varying styles of the New England town garden or rural establishment, of the Dutch gardens of New Amsterdam or the Hudson River manor, of the developments in Germantown or on the Schuylkill. In the South as indicated from the many descriptions in the new volume, the diversity was less marked. With two or three exceptions—the gardens of Delaware, which should be included with those of the North, the town gardens of Charleston, which are of a style peculiar to itself, and the monastic establishments of the Southwest, —the gardens of the southern half of the country are more nearly from a single mold...
>
> The point of chief significance in this memorable work undertaken by the Garden Club of America is the fact that we now have for the first time in one place a list of gardens in whose development we can see the history of growth of one of the earliest arts of this country. It is to be hoped however, that the work will not be considered complete as long as the more important of these gardens continue to be threatened by the dangers of insecurity. Who knows how many of these places, significant monuments in the history of the art of American landscape architecture, will have succumbed to economic pressure during the next half century? The people of the Old World show their appreciation of the value of their ancient gardens in a practical way, for historic monuments under private ownership are scheduled for preservation and the enjoyment of future generations. A similar movement should be inaugurated in this country. The publication of *Gardens of Colony and State* is the first step toward this accomplishment." (*Bulletin,* July 1934)

The publication of *Gardens of Colony and State* played a role in recognition of the need to save American gardens—if only on paper or in photographs. Historic preservation and the National Trust became the cry at the time of America's Bicentennial, in 1976, only forty years after the 'sport' of visiting gardens and the 'shows' offered by sharing gardens via glass lantern slides had acted as a catalyst leading to the preservation of historic houses and their gardens.

Many of the glass slides of members' gardens were taken about the time of the publication of *Gardens of Colony and State.* As they resurfaced, in the late 1980s, they were sorted and identified by Helen Rollins to be used to illustrate *The Golden Age of American Gardens* written by Mac Griswold and Eleanor Weller and published in 1991, in association with The Garden Club of America.

These efforts have culminated in a partnership of The Garden Club of America and the Smithsonian Institution. The glass slides are now The Garden Club of America Collection of the Smithsonian's Archives of American Gardens, to which additional slides have been donated. This repository offers opportunities for students to learn from garden history and to recognize the need to document contemporary gardens for tomorrow. Views of the Lockwood garden at "Riverside" can been found in the Smithsonian's Archives of American Gardens.

Republication of Alice G. B. Lockwood's work at this time, underscores not only the value of the original purpose of the two volumes, but also the continuity of interest in preservation of American gardens as an art form.

The formation of The Garden Conservancy in 1989, with Frank Cabot's vision and leadership at its helm, has made it possible for fine American gardens to be saved and made available for public education and enjoyment. The success of The Garden Conservancy demonstrates the growing national support and strength of the historic garden movement and carries this effort into the new millennium.

After her death in 1954, Mrs. Lockwood was remembered *In Memoriam* by The Garden Club of America in the *Bulletin* which listed her accomplishments and included the following:

> "...In the death of Mrs. Luke Vincent Lockwood, The Garden Club of America has lost one of its most distinguished members. For many years she gave of her knowledge and vision and was acting as our Historian until a year ago.... She shared her great knowledge with all people, nor did she hesitate to instruct or correct the uninitiated. Her frankness often bewildered, and her erudition often amazed her friends, but no man or woman who knew her well, but felt the warmth of soul, her humor, her loving spirit. She lived in beauty, not softly, but in knowledge of it. The beauty of growing things, of things made by hands in long past days whether in clay, porcelain, wool or wood, the beauty of prose and verse, such beauty she truly understood and could speak of and write of.
>
> Now we are the richer because through her writing and from our memories we can catch and try to hold on to her interpretations and her wisdom."

JOANNE LENDEN
Historian
The Garden Club of America

FOREWORD

It has been the aim of the editor to present as many facts as possible that bear upon the cultivation of the soil, especially the making of flower or pleasure gardens, and to make no statement or draw no conclusion that is not based upon history. That there is much material not yet discovered and many remnants of old gardens not mentioned is inevitable, but as this is the first general survey of the subject it is to be hoped that it may inspire further research.

During the years that material has been gathered for this history, Miss Delia Marble first acted as Chairman of the Historic Gardens Committee. She was succeeded by Mrs. W. W. Frazier, who did magnificent work in corresponding with representative people in many parts of the country, and gathering valuable material.

The names which follow are of those who acted as zone chairmen at some time in the book's history:

CONNECTICUT	MRS. ROBERT H. FIFE, JR.
MASSACHUSETTS	MRS. WARD THORON
MICHIGAN	MRS. HENRY D. SHELDEN
NEW HAMPSHIRE	*MRS. FRANK STREETER
NEW JERSEY	MRS. ERNEST RICHARDSON
NEW YORK	MRS. F. H. HIGGINSON
OHIO	MRS. WILLIAM S. ROWE
ILLINOIS	MRS. WILLIAM C. EVANS

A LIST OF CONTRIBUTORS

MASSACHUSETTS

MRS. WARD THORON
MISS ETHEL PARTON
MRS. ELIZABETH COLMAN MOULTON NOYES
MISS MARGARET CUSHING
MR. ARTHUR A. SHURCLIFF
MRS. CHARLES F. PERRY
*MR. BROOKS ADAMS
MRS. ROBERT HALE BANCROFT
MRS. JOHN GARDINER COOLIDGE
MR. ALBERT W. HUNT
*MR. JOHN ROBINSON
MRS. GEORGE R. BRIGGS
MISS MARY J. LINTON
MR. ARTHUR LYMAN
MR. GEORGE FRANCIS DOW
MR. EDWARD PIERCE
MRS. F. S. MOSELEY
MRS. A. C. NASON

CONNECTICUT

MISS MARY OLCOTT
MISS ANNIE BURR JENNINGS
MR. GEORGE W. SEYMOUR

NEW YORK

MRS. VIRGINIA E. VERPLANCK
MISS ETHEL WODELL
MRS. F. J. HIGGINSON
MRS. KATHARYN BRUYN FORSYTH
MR. FRANKLIN DELANO ROOSEVELT
HARRIET L. CARTER
MRS. LEAH C. ELLWANGER
MISS ANNE STEVENSON VAN CORTLANDT
MISS SARAH D. GARDINER
MISS CORNELIA HORSFORD

PENNSYLVANIA

MRS. WILLIAM WEST FRAZIER
MRS. DAVID E. WILLIAMS
MRS. CHARLES BIDDLE
MRS. JAMES STARR
MR. CHARLES COLMAN SELLERS
MRS. W. R. WISTER (photographs)
MISS SARAH E. BISSELL
MISS CAROLINE SINKLER

RHODE ISLAND

MISS ALICE BRAYTON
MISS SARAH MORTON

*Deceased.

v

Miss Annie M. Hunt
Miss Caroline Hazard
Miss Maud Lyman Stevens

NEW JERSEY

Mrs. John G. Hibben
*Miss Lucy H. Kean
Mrs. Caroline Bayard Wittpenn
Miss Clara M. Blackwell
Miss Sarah J. Day
Mabel Evans Kearney
Josephine P. Morgan
Elizabeth Breckinridge Field
Mrs. Bayard Stockton

OHIO

Mrs. William S. Rowe

ILLINOIS

Mrs. William C. Evans
Elizabeth M. Moffatt

MICHIGAN

Mrs. Henry D. Shelden
Elsie Sibley Peabody
Dr. Milo Milton Quaife
Helen Muir Duffield
Mr. Charles Monroe Burton

VERMONT

Miss M. L. Johnson

MAINE

Mrs. Walter E. Tobie

NEW HAMPSHIRE

*Mrs. Frank Streeter
Mrs. Edith Wendell Osborn

I should like particularly to acknowledge the assistance of Mrs. Ward Thoron of Boston for the most valuable contributions, and of Mr. George Francis Dow, who has generously given of the result of his profound research in the backgrounds of New England,

Of the Newport Garden Association and of Miss Alice Brayton of Newport and Fall River for the exhaustive study of gardens and gardening in Rhode Island,

Of Mrs. Henry D. Shelden of the Garden Club of Michigan for a most careful search through the records of Michigan's early days for gardens and their makers,

Of all those members of the Garden Club of America who have so generously assisted in many ways the making of this book,

Of Mr. and Mrs. Fiske Kimball who have been most gracious in their assistance,

Of Mr. Charles Knowles Bolton who gave valuable advice as to the use of contributors' material,

Of Miss Margaret McKenny who has acted as my secretary, and whose knowledge and love of the subject, together with patience and hard work, have done much toward the making of the volume.

I should like also to mention here the help derived from the volumes written by that traveler and recorder of the first half of the nineteenth century, John Warner Barber. Were it not for his pen and sketches made on the spot we should know very little today of how New England looked.

I am greatly indebted to the New York Historical Society, and to the New York Public Library, to the Bulletins of the Society for the Preservation of New England Antiquities, whose files are of inestimable value to the student of oldtime New England. The publications of the Massachusetts Historical Society have also been exceedingly valuable. The Bulletins of the Historical Society of Pennsylvania, and publications of the Site and Relic Society of Germantown have been of much assistance.

The list of books given in this volume will show from how many sources our knowledge of gardens is derived.

Alice G. B. Lockwood.

*Deceased.

CONTENTS

ILLUSTRATIONS

INTRODUCTION

MASSACHUSETTS

CONNECTICUT

MAINE, NEW HAMPSHIRE, VERMONT

RHODE ISLAND

NEW YORK

NEW JERSEY

PENNSYLVANIA

MICHIGAN

OHIO AND ILLINOIS

FENCES AND ENCLOSURES

GARDENS

OF
COLONY AND STATE

INTRODUCTION

INTRODUCTION

SEVENTEENTH-CENTURY GARDENS

THE gardens of the first century of colonial settlements of which any record has been found were those of New England, which were all English in tradition; those of New Amsterdam, first under the Dutch, and, after 1674, under the English; and those of Pennsylvania, which were both German and English, for William Penn and all his early associates were English, and the German colonists were both botanists and gardeners. In New Jersey, we find records of gardens before 1700. In California, there were gardens inspired by the Spanish, very early; there were French gardens in Michigan in the seventeenth century. Ohio and Illinois came much later. New England, however, was the source of so many colonial settlements in the north that we shall follow first the records there that give a glimpse of gardens.

The group of English people that changed the wilderness on the eastern coast of North America to an orderly settlement, and as time went on, to towns and villages, came largely from rural England. In the minds of all must have been the English cottage with its paved courtyard, the roses and jasmine over the doorway, and the flowers best known in the first quarter of the seventeenth century, flowers growing in every garden.

Gerard's *Herbal*, which was published in 1597, shows on its title-page what these flowers were. There one may see the roses, single and double, the jasmine, the primrose, the iris, the pink, the crown imperial, the martagon lily, and many other plants less suited to simple gardens. No record of the earliest settlements makes any mention of flowers, and we can only surmise that a way was found, under the greatest of difficulties, to keep the plant or seed which promised beauty when stern necessity no longer demanded every energy.

Perhaps the first record of gardening is a passage from the *Wonder Working Providence of Sion's Saviour in New England*, by Edward Johnson of Woburn:

"The Winter's frosts being extracted from the Earth, they fall to tearing up roots and bushes with their howes, even such men as scarce ever set hand to labour before, men of good birth and breeding, but coming through the strength of Christ to war their warfare, readily rush through all difficulties.

"After they have found a place of aboad they burrow themselves in the earth for their first shelter, under some hillside, casting the earth aloft upon timber; they make a smoky fire against the earth at the highest side, and thus these poor servants of Christ provide shelter for themselves."

Ogilby's notes from America in 1671 make the following record:

"This watery part of the World that almost through all ages lay fallow, hath in these later times been furrow'd by several expert and stout captains, who now by their Art and Industry, have given a good account. . . ."

And as early as 1672 we know from Josselyn's "Voyages" of their pleasant familiar flowers—lavender cotton, and hollyhocks, and satin (We call this herbe in Norfolke sattin, says Gerard, and among our women it is called honestie), and gilly-flowers, which meant pinks as well, and English roses, and eglantine.

For information that would help to provide an historic study of gardening during the first century of colonial development a long and faithful search has been necessary—a search extending to historical societies, patriotic societies, libraries of many kinds, manuscripts belonging to private collections, letters, diaries, and family records—published and unpublished—,books of travel which record impressions made upon visitors during the seventeenth century, garden books of this period, and books dealing with the development of our early settlements, and also many volumes of colonial records.[1]

Perhaps the clearest graphic illustration of the progress of garden form in England, Old and New, during the seventeenth century is to be found in the three plans of an English home reproduced on the next page. They show the contrast between the early part of the seventeenth century, which corresponded with our first settlements, the end of that century, which corresponded with our flourishing town life, and the first quarter of the eighteenth century, when we know gardening to have been a recognized art in the colonies.

It is not strange that we know very little of garden planning during the seventeenth century, for it was inevitable that time, and the profound changes which have taken place over the land since then, should entirely erase the marks of these earliest gardens. But this we know: fruits, vegetables, vines, herbs, and flowers grew together. The only descriptions surviving are those of the probate records of the New England courts, which contain inventories of estates dating before 1700 that make mention of the house and grounds. For example:

Sarah Dillingham, widow, of Ipswich, in 1636 had apple trees with other fruits in the gardens, 30 acres of uplands, 60 acres of meadow, and 6 acres of planting ground near the house.

Henry Fay of Newbury in 1655 wills "his House and Seven acres adjoining—His Orchard and garden and a field of four and half acres."

Mighill Hobkinson of Rowley in 1648 held property described as follows: "His garden, Orchards and Yards and eight acres of Meadow and one of upland at the Farm."

Lawrence Sethwick of Salem in 1660: "My dwelling Houses at Salem, with all the houses, orchards, gardens and appurtenances and the great meadow which lies at Ipswich River fenced in."

Mr. William Walten of Marblehead in 1669 (inventory): "Dwelling House with garden and Orchard—a parcell of land in ye Farm near ye Town."

John Whipple Senior of Ipswich in 1669 (inventory): "The Farm conteyning about 300 acres, the Houses and lands in ye Town conteyning about one hundred acres."

Mr. Thomas Bishop's inventory taken at Ipswich in 1670: "Dwelling house and Six acres of land, Barns, Washhouse, Fences and Garden—1 farm of about 80 acres of land, with dwelling house, barn and Two orchards and 20 acres of land Fenced near to the aforesaid farm."

Henry Short of Newbury in 1673 wills to his dearly beloved wife Sarah "the use of the Littel garden for her own use and Two rows of Apple trees next the English Grass."

Jacob Barne of Salem in 1673 provides his widow with "the priviledge of a garden already Fenced In."

John Collins of Gloucester, in 1675, in his will describes "my housing and lands, orchards and gardens, and all my land and meadow yet ungiven."

Mr. Samuel Symonds of Ipswich (Gentleman) in 1678

[1]A glance at the bibliography will give the best idea of the study given the general background before any conclusions were drawn.

3

provides that his wife shall have "the liberty to take what apples, pears and plums she cares for and what ground she pleases for her garden." He inventories his farm, called "Argilla."

What would such gardens contain and how were they planned? We cannot doubt that they followed the gardening tradition of their time; we may be certain that the lay-out

"My children burnt me at least five hundred trees this spring by setting the ground on fire near them." And in 1648 he traded five hundred apple trees three years old for two hundred and fifty acres of land!

Josselyn tells us in 1673 of the cures practised on ailing fruit trees:

"Their fruit-trees are subject to two diseases, the Meazels,

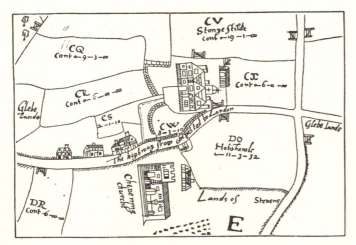

The Chevening Estate-Map of 1613

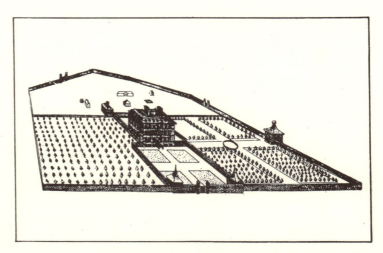

The Chevening Lay-out in 1679

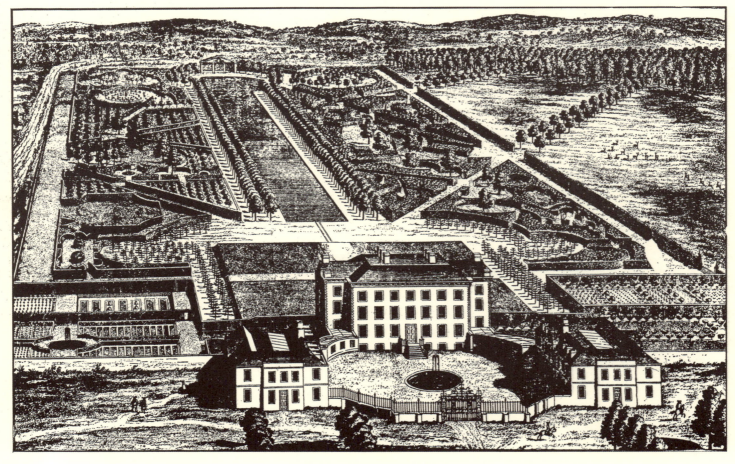

The Chevening Lay-out in 1719

These three plans of the grounds of an English home illustrate a century's progress in garden form in England

was simple but orderly, and that the paths were gravel or grass. For walls, there was earth, planted with such shrubs as were found locally, and stone, where stone was plentiful; as bricks were being made in most of the colonies, brick also must have been used, and of course wooden fences of many kinds.

Fruit trees played a very great part in the gardens of the seventeenth and eighteenth centuries, and it will be observed that all plans for pleasure gardens include sections devoted to fruit trees. This planting probably was largely practical.

As early as 1641, Governor John Endecott of the Massachusetts colony wrote to John Winthrop as follows:

which is when they are burned and scorched with the Sun, and lowsiness, when the woodpeckers job holes in their bark; the way to cure them when they are lowsie is to bore a hole into the main root with an Augur, and pour in a quantity of Brandie or Rhum, and then stop it up with a pin made of the same tree."

So soon then were the husbandman's troubles abroad! Samuel Sewall, that most famous of colonial diarists, tells of his young trees being ruined by his cows.

Dr. L. H. Bailey[1] says that the early explorers found large quantities of peach trees growing in the Creek, Cherokee

[1]Editor of the *Cyclopedia of American Horticulture.*

and Choctaw villages. The seed from these peach trees was undoubtedly obtained from the Florida Indians, who had in turn procured it from the trees planted by the Spanish explorers.

We find no mention of peach trees in early New England, but in Pennsylvania, Delaware, Maryland, and Dutch New York they are often mentioned, especially their beauty when in bloom.

EARLY GARDEN LITERATURE

Two factors that must have influenced most of the early gardens were first, tradition, which means the memory of the home life and its amenities, and second, the reading of the then known literature of gardens.

If you will look through the probate records, which give in detail everything possessed by an individual whose estate was administered, you will often find "a parcel of Books" highly valued in proportion to other things. This indicates that from the very first books, which then were rare everywhere, were an important item in home life. We can be sure that the majority of these books dealt with religion. But next to religion, of necessity came agriculture, and books which dealt with the soil were of great moment; we may consider that there was some book on gardening, in its broad sense, in most households.

GARDEN BOOKS IN THE COLONIES

What books these were can be conjectured, as the garden books then known in England would also have been in use here. The Hon. Alicia Amherst in her *History of Gardening in England* gives a list of books printed in England and available during the years when gardening began in New England. They follow here, with comments:

Gerard's *Herbal* (1597) has already been mentioned. A second edition was published in 1633.

Parkinson's *Paradisi in Sole, Paradisus terrestris*, or "A Garden of all sorts of pleasant flowers—with a kitchen garden and an orchard" (1629). This was the most popular book of the first half of the seventeenth century.

Sir Hugh Platt first published a book on gardening in 1600. The title was *The Paradise of Flora*. A second edition was published in 1660 with the addition of a second part which was called *The Garden of Eden*.

In 1649 Walter Blith wrote a book called *The English Improver, or a New Survey of Husbandry*. He impressed upon his countrymen the advantage of planting orchards, urging them to plant "the vine, the Plumb, the Cherry, the Pear, and Apple."

Ralph Austen in 1653 wrote a treatise on fruit trees called *The Spiritual Use of an Orchard or Garden of Fruit Trees*.

In 1699, London and Wise brought out *The Compleat Gard'ner of J. de la Quintinye*, translated by John Evelyn. They published *The Solitary or Carthusian Gardener* in 1706.

In 1664 John Evelyn published his *Gardener's Almanac*, a most popular work which went through several editions, and appeared with the last edition of his *Sylva* in 1705.

In 1676 was published John Rea's *Flora, Ceres, and Pomona*. In this book we find the approximate size of a garden. The dimensions are much more modest than those of Bacon's "princely garden." Eighty square yards for fruit and thirty square yards for a flower garden are allowed for a nobleman; for a "private gentleman, forty square yards of fruit and twenty for flowers is enough; a wall around of brick nine feet high, and a five foot wall to divide the fruit and the flower gardens, or else pales painted a brick colour. The large square beds are to be edged with wooden rails painted, or box-trees or palisades for dwarf fruit trees."

Most of the designs given are squares, with T- or L-shaped beds, fitting into the angles or along the walls of the garden. These borders were to be about three yards wide. In the corner of each bed were to be planted "the best Crown

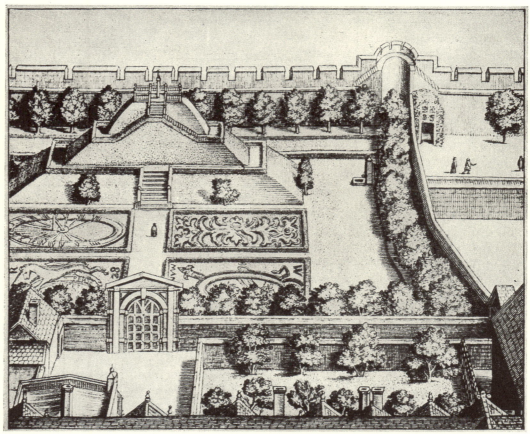

The gardens of New College, Oxford—a seventeenth-century English garden that Samuel Sewall, of Massachusetts, visited and described in letters written from London. He especially remarked the "clock" in topiary work

Imperials, lilies Martagon, and such tall flowers, in the middle of the square bed, great tufts of peonies, and round about them several sorts of cyclamen, the rest [of the beds] with Daffodils, Hyacinths and such like. The straight beds are fit for the best tulips, where account may be kept of them. Ranunculus and Anemones also require particular beds—the rest may be set all over with the more ordinary type of tulips, fritillarias, bulbed iris and all other sorts of good roots. . . . It will be requisite to have in the middle of one side of the flower garden, a handsome octangular somer-house, roofed every way and finely painted with Landskips and other conceits, furnished with seats about and a table in the middle which serveth not only for delight and entertainment but for many other necessary purposes as to put the roots of Tulips and other flowers on, as they are taken up upon papers, with the names upon them, untill they are dried, that they may be wrapped up and put into boxes. You must yearly make your hot-bed for raising choice annuals, for the raising of new varieties and divers kinds.

"These gardens will not be maintained and kept well nourished without a Nurcery, as well as of stocks for fruits as of flowers and seedlings where many pretty conclusions may be practised."

This description of what a garden of 1676 should be sounds to the reader of today as if it had been written recently; the advice as to labels and "hot-beds" and "nurcery" cannot be improved upon. This book was without doubt very widely read, and though we do not find it specifically mentioned, it was available, and can hardly have been unknown in the colonies. We may also reasonably assume that Ralph Austen's treatise on fruit trees was here; we know that the varieties of apples and pears mentioned by him were in New England.

If we add to this list of the Hon. Alicia Amherst the books mentioned in the earliest catalogues of our libraries, we know quite definitely what influences were felt in the world of gardening.

Harvard College in the eighteenth century contained in its library the following books:

The English Improver, or a New Survey of Husbandry, published in London in 1649.
Worlidge's Two Treatises on Husbandry, Cyder, and the Cyder Mill, London, 1694.
L. J. M. Columella, Of Husbandry, translated into English, 1745.
A French book by Du Hamel on the treatment and training of trees and shrubs.
Francis Howe's Principles of Agriculture and Vegetation, 1762.
Philip Miller's The Gardener's Dictionary, 1735.
Stephen Switzer's A System of Agriculture and Gardening.
Thomas Whately's Observations on Modern Gardening, 1770.

The library of Yale college, when the first catalogue was published, held the following:

John Evelyn's Sylva in the 1769 edition.
John Ray's Historia Plantarum, Vol. I, 1686, Vol. II, 1688, and Vol. III, 1704.
John Mortimer's The Art of Husbandry, 1712.
Philip Miller's The Gardener's Dictionary, edition of 1733.

Columbia University, then King's College, New York, had in its early days the following books in its catalogue:

Charles Varlo's A New System of Husbandry from many years' experience, two volumes, published in Philadelphia, 1785.
Addresses to Farmers on interesting Subjects, published in Salem in 1796.
Richard Parkinson's The Experienced Farmer, Philadelphia, 1799.

In the deed of gift of Governor Jonathan Belcher's library (which was the foundation of the Princeton University Library) we find under the date of 1755 two titles listed in this way:

The practical gardner, 2 vols.
Bradley of gardning, 2 vols.

The first books placed in the library of the Massachusetts Horticultural Society appear to have been a donation from one of the founders, Robert Manning, for which the thanks of the Society were presented on the 12th of May, 1829. They comprised the following, evidently long in the colonies:

Forsyth's Treatise on the Culture and Management of Fruit Trees, with Notes by William Cobbett.
New Improvements of Planting and Gardening, both Philosophical and Practical, explaining the motion of the Sap, and Generation of Plants, etc., by Richard Bradley F.R.S., London, 1717.
The Clergyman's Recreation, showing the Pleasure and Profit of the Art of Gardening, by John Lawrence, A. M., rector of Yelverton, London, 1716.
An Introduction to the Knowledge and Practice of Gardening, by Charles Marshall, the first American Edition, in two volumes, Boston, 1790.
Vinetum Britannicum, or a Treatise on Cider and other Wines and Drinks extracted from Fruits growing in this Kingdom, with a Discourse on the Best Way of Improving Bees, by J. Worlidge, Gent., London, 1691.

In 1750 the Redwood Library, of Newport, Rhode Island, contained books which were listed thus:

Gerardes's Herbal
Miller's Gardener's Dictionary
Pomona; or Fruit Garden
Experimental Husbandman, Bradley
Bradley's Gentleman's and Farmer's Guide, Bradley
Modern Husbandman, Ellis
Practical Farmer
Method of Improving Barren Lands
Foreign Vegetables, Thickweise
Compleat Planter and Cyderist
Natural History of Bees

Philip Miller's The Gardener's Dictionary, which we find in the lists of the Harvard and Yale libraries and the Redwood Library at Newport, was reissued many times, and was perhaps as much used as any book of the early years of the eighteenth century. The full title reads: The Gardener's Dictionary, Containing the Methods of Cultivating and Improving the Kitchen, Fruit and Flower Garden, as also the Physick Garden, Wilderness, Conservatory, and Vineyard. The first volume of the 1735 edition contains a delightful plan for a garden, including vineyard, orchard and pleasure gardens. It is here reproduced because it must have been the ideal toward which many a gardener in America strove in the days of its vogue.

Three other English books which were published in London in the seventeenth century, and which were doubtless known in America, were these by W. Lawson:

The Country Housewife's Garden, 1626
Patterns for Knot Gardens, 1626
New Orchard and Garden, 1618

In Boston, in 1710, John Allen printed for Eleazer Phillips The Husbandmen's Guide. It is a small volume divided into four sections, containing "many excellent rules for setting and planting of orchards, gardens and woods, the times to sow corn and all other sorts of seeds."

The Reverend Jared Eliot of Killingsworth, Connecticut, wrote in 1748–9, Essays upon Field Husbandry. Eliot said in his preface that he had examined all available books on this subject published in England and found that differences in climate and plant material made them impractical for New England.

The Reverend Samuel Deane, vice-president of Bowdoin College, published in 1790 his New England Farmer, or Georgical Dictionary, said by a contemporary to be "a system of Husbandry for New England, and gives the best directions for the care of the garden, the dairy and the cellar."

Although these three books must have been well known they do not appear in any of the library lists that we have uncovered.

To bring our survey of early books on gardening up to the terminal date of the period covered by this volume we append a list[1] of garden books published in America (other than those previously listed) before 1840:

Adlum, John; A memoir on the Cultivation of the Vine in America and the mode of making wine; Washington; 1823; Davis and Force.
Agricola, P.; The New York Gardener; White Creek; 1827; published by A. Crosby; G. M. Davison, printer, Saratoga Springs.
Berneaud, Thibaut de; The Vine-Dressers Theoretical and practical Manual; New York; published by P. Canfield; 1829.
Boune, H.; Flores Poetice—The Florists' Manual; Boston, Monroe and Francis; New York, Charles S. Francis.
Breck, Joseph; The Young Florist; Boston; Russell, Odiorne and Co., 1833.
Bridgeman, Thomas; The Florists' Guide; printed and sold by W. Mitchell, New York, 1835.

[1]Compiled from Bailey's Standard Cyclopedia of Horticulture and other sources.

Bridgeman, Thomas; *The Young Gardener's Assistant;* printed by Nichol and Mathew, Brooklyn, 1829.

Buist, Robert; *American Flower Garden Directory;* Philadelphia; E. L. Cary and A. Hoit; 1839.

Cobbett, William; *The American Gardener;* Baltimore and Frederick, Maryland; J. Robinson; 1823.

Dearborn, Henry A. S.; *Monograph of the Genus Camellia, translated from the French of Abbé;* 1838; Breck and Co.

Doyle, Martin; *The Flower Garden, with notes and observations by L. S. Gale;* New York; 1835.

Fessenden, Thomas A.; *The New American Gardener;* T. B. Russell; Boston; 1828.

Forsyth, William; *A Treatise on the Culture and Management of Fruit Trees;* 1802.

Gardiner, John; Hepburn, David; *The American Gardener;* Washington; Samuel H. Smith; 1804.

Green, Roland; *A Treatise on the Cultivation of Ornamental Flowers;* Boston; 1828; New York, John B. Russell, G. Thorn.

Hibbert and Buist; *The American Flower Garden Directory;* Adam Waldie; 1832.

Kenrick, William; *The New American Orchardist,* 1833.

Lelièvre, J. F.; *Nouveau jardinier, contenant les instructions nécessaires aux personnes qui s'occupent de jardinage;* Nouvelle-Orléans; 1838.

McMahon, Bernard; *The American Gardeners' Calendar;* 1806; Graves, New York.

Manning, Robert; *Book of Fruits;* Ives and Jewett; Salem; 1838.

Marshall, Charles; *An Introduction to the Knowledge and Practice of Gardening;* First American from the Second London Edition, considerably enlarged and improved. To which is added an essay on quicklime by James Anderson. Samuel Eldridge; Boston; 1799.

Prince, William; *A Short Treatise on Horticulture.*

Prince, William Robert; edited by William Prince; *A Treatise on the Vine;* 1830.

Rafinesque, C. S.; *American Manual of the Grape Vine;* Philadelphia; 1830.

Squibbs, Robert; *The Gardeners Kalendar for South Carolina and North Carolina;* Charleston; 1787.

Sayers, Edward; *The American Flower Garden Companion, Adapted to the Northern States;* 1838; Boston; Joseph Breck and Co., G. Thorburn.

Thacher, James; *The American Orchardist;* Boston; 1822.

Thorburn, Grant; *The Gentleman's and Gardener's Kalendar for the middle States of North America.*

The Fragaria, or Description of the most improved variety of Strawberries; 1832.

Gleanings from the most celebrated Book on Husbandry Gardening and Rural Affairs Interspersed with remarks and observations by a Gentleman of Philadelphia; Philadelphia; 1803.

The Practical American Gardener; Baltimore; 1819; Fielding Lucas Jr.

The Practical Florist; Compilation; Newburyport; 1823; E. Stedman.

THE EARLIEST HORTICULTURAL PERIODICALS

Before 1840 also, horticultural periodicals[1] had come into existence.

The "Massachusetts Agricultural Repository," first issued in 1793, added a horticultural department in 1821.

The first journal to devote any considerable extent of its space to horticultural matters, however, was the original "New England Farmer," which was established in Boston in 1822, and which was one of the chief instruments in the organization of the Massachusetts Horticultural Society.

A "Floral Magazine" was launched in Philadelphia in 1832 and continued for some time afterward. It included colored plates of ornamental plants. Except for the illustra-

[1]Compiled from Bailey's *Standard Cyclopedia of Horticulture.*

tions it was entirely the work of the two Landreths, who published it. The full title was "The Floral Magazine and Botanical Repository"; published by D. and C. Landreth, Nursery and Seedsmen, Philadelphia.

The "Horticultural Register and Gardener's Magazine," established in Boston in 1835, and edited by Fessenden and Joseph Breck, and "Hovey Magazine" were among the first distinct horticultural periodicals. The former did not long endure, although it was a magazine of more than ordinary merit. The latter was founded by D. M. Hovey and P. B. Hovey Jr., and was called the "American Gardeners' Maga-

This garden plan from Philip Miller's "The Gardener's Dictionary" (1735), the most used book in the colonies, was probably the ideal of many a colonial garden

zine and Register of Useful Discoveries and Improvements in Horticultural and Rural Affairs." It later became the "Magazine of Horticulture," continuing in existence for a third of a century.

An early journal in the new west was Hooper and Elliot's "Western Farmer and Gardener", established in Cincinnati in 1839.

BOTANY AND BOTANISTS

The study of the botany of the New World began very early. Dr. L. H. Bailey has noted several accounts of plant life on the North American continent before 1700. He says that probably the earliest specific work on the products of the New World was that of Nicolo Monardes, which was published in Seville in parts, from 1565 to 1571. An English edition of 1577 was entitled "Joyfull Newes out of the new founde Worlde, wherein is declared the rare and singular vertues of diverse and sundrie Hearbes, Trees, Oyles, Plantes and Stones—also the portrature of the saied hearbes. Englished by J. Frampton." Its picture of the tobacco plant has the distinction of being the first drawing extant of that plant, if not indeed of any plant from America.

It is generally agreed that the *Canadensium Plantarum, aliarumque nondum Plantarum Historia* (1635), by a French botanist, Jacques Cornuti, was the first book on American botany, written on specimens sent to the author from Canada. It seems probable that Thomas Hariot (or Harriott), 1560–1621, was really the first to write on the natural history of America in his *Briefe and True Report of the new found land of Virginia* (1590). Harriott was the friend of Raleigh and was sent by him to America.

Two other Englishmen, John Josselyn and the Reverend John Bannister, added to the existing literature. John Josselyn, who styled himself "Gentleman", visited New England in 1638–9 and again in 1663, remaining as a resident of Boston for eight years. Returning to England, he published in 1672 *New England's Rarities*, which included plants, and in 1674 a second volume, *An Account of Two Voyages to New England*. He gives a list "of such garden herbs as do thrive there, and of such as do not." This list is perhaps the earliest record of its kind. John Bannister in 1680 enumerated *A Catalogue of plants observed in Virginia*. A systematic enumeration of North American plants was not published until 1739, however. It was edited by Gronovius at Leyden, Holland.

Mark Catesby, an Englishman, published the first volume of his *Natural History of Carolina, Florida and the Bahama Islands* in 1732.

John Clayton (1693–1773) was a student of botany all his life and in correspondence with men of science in Europe.

Manasseh Cutler, LL.D. (1742–1823) was minister of the Hamlet parish, then a part of Ipswich, Mass. He is the author of *An Account of some Vegetable Productions naturally growing in this part of America, botanically arranged*. Dr. Cutler is believed to have been the first to suggest a botanical chair in our colleges, and a general herbarium to illustrate the flora of New England. He also published a botanical work containing the descriptions of 370 plants.

Alexander Garden (1730–1791), of Charleston, S. C., a distinguished scholar and botanist, was for a short time professor at King's College in New York. Dr. Howard Kelly records that he wrote to a sympathetic friend: "I know that every letter that I receive not only revives the little botanic spark in my breast, but even increases its quantity and flaming force." Dr. Garden started a nursery and a garden near Charleston, S. C., which will be referred to in another volume, in the South Carolina section.

John Bartram (1699–1777), born in Chester County, Penna., was our earliest naturalist and best known botanist and horticulturist. He was a great lover of all that grew and blossomed, and had a profound influence on his time through his writings and his experiments. His work and his garden are described in the Pennsylvania section.

Humphrey Marshall (1732–1801), cousin of Bartram, traveled widely to study and collect plants, and in 1785 published the *Arbustum Americanum*, a description of the trees and shrubs indigenous to the United States. This was the first book on plants written by a native-born American. Many of the trees planted by Marshall have grown to a great size and are still in a flourishing condition. His arboretum at Marshallton, Pennsylvania, is now one of the most interesting of the old collections of American trees.

Cadwallader Colden of New York (born in Scotland) published about 1744 a treatise on the plants indigenous to the region of Newburgh, where he resided. His daughter, Jane Colden, was a writer on botanic subjects, and was highly spoken of by Peter Collinson to Linnaeus.

John Mitchell was a Scotchman who came to this country in 1700, settling on the Rappahanock River, near Richmond, Virginia. His brief dissertation on the principles of botany was published in 1738, and three years later his *Nova Plantarum Genera* was printed in Nuremburg. In 1763 he refers to the "White Double Daffodil" brought over by the first settlers. This is *Narcissus poeticus, flora plena*.

Adam Kuhn (1741–1817), probably the first professor of botany in America, was born in Germantown, near Philadelphia. He was educated abroad, studying under Linnaeus, and then in London. In 1768, after his return to Philadelphia, he became Professor of Materia Medica in the College of Philadelphia.

John Adlum (1759–1836) established an experimental vineyard in the District of Columbia, and endeavored without success to secure the use of certain public lands in Washington for the purpose of "cultivating an experimental farm."

In 1801, André Michaux, a French botanist, published in Paris an interesting work on the oaks of North America (*Histoire des Chênes de l'Amérique Septentrionale*). In 1803, the *Flora-Borealis-Americana* of the same author, ably edited by Louis Clude Richard, was published in the same city. The latter, though comprising but a portion of the plants of North America, is an excellent work, remarkable for the accuracy and felicity of its descriptive phrases.

Dr. Benjamin Waterhouse (1754–1846), Professor of Medicine at Harvard, read lectures on natural history to his classes as early as 1768, and published the botanical parts of these lectures in the Monthly Anthology, 1804–8. They were reprinted in 1811, under the title of *The Botanist*. The preface of this volume claims these to have been the first public lectures on natural history in the United States.

The first elementary textbook on botany was published in Philadelphia by Professor B. S. Barton in 1803. Prof. Barton taught botany and did much to arouse an interest in plant culture.

Marshall Pinckney Wilder (1798–1886), whose garden was in Dorchester, Mass., was actively interested in horticulture from 1825; he imported many fruits and flowers new to America, and delighted in floriculture. His camellia collection at one time numbered 300 varieties; he also had a notable collection of azaleas. He was greatly interested in hybridization, and as early as 1834 produced a double California poppy. He was a member of the Massachusetts Horticultural Society for fifty-six years.

David Thomas (1776–1859) was a distinguished horticulturist of western New York.

The Horticultural Societies which played such an important part in the development of gardening were largely the outgrowth of Agricultural Associations founded much earlier. The earliest Horticultural Society is that of Pennsylvania, followed shortly by that of Massachusetts, and later by those of New York and Connecticut, and by many other local and state associations. These were the Garden Clubs of their day. But for the interest maintained and supported by them through many indifferent years, our country would have been sadly lacking in horticultural literature and material for fine gardening.

BOTANIC GARDENS

The early establishment of botanic gardens had an indubitable influence on gardening through the introduction of new species and varieties.

John Bartram's garden, about three miles from the city of Philadelphia, was the first botanic garden on this continent, having been established as early as 1732, on five acres of ground which, according to William Darlington in his *Memorials of John Bartram and Humphrey Marshall*, were purchased by Bartram in 1728. Bartram's reputation is so great, and his personality so interesting, that he will be referred to again in the section on Pennsylvania.

William Jackson, a gentleman much interested in horticulture, had an extensive collection of plants at his residence in Pennsylvania in 1777. Though his garden was, strictly speaking, not a botanic garden, it is often so described.

Joshua and Samuel Pierce, of East Marlborough, Pennsylvania, had a specimen garden and an arboretum of evergreens about the year 1800. This also is described in the Pennsylvania section.

David Hosack planned the first botanic gardens in New York in 1801 and called them the Elgin Botanic Gardens. These are described in the New York State section.

and from him received seeds of many Himalayan and other rare and little known plants. A few of the trees planted by Evans are still alive.

NURSERIES AND SEED-HOUSES

The earliest nursery of importance in our country was Prince's Nursery, established on Long Island in 1730 by Robert Prince. It was continued by his son, William Prince, and grew rapidly until the Revolution. After the return of peace it again prospered and offered an unbelievable variety of fruit trees.

Another William Prince, the third proprietor, continued

Dog Rose

Hundred-petal Rose

These and the following familiar garden flowers of the seventeenth and eighteenth centuries are from an eighteenth-century botany

Botanic gardens were in existence in South Carolina about the same date.

The botanic garden at Cambridge, Mass., begun in 1805, was founded largely through the efforts of the Massachusetts Society for Promoting Agriculture, which was also chiefly responsible for the establishment of the professorship of Natural History at Harvard College. The Society contributed $5000 for the garden, and raised more by subscription.

The garden and arboretum planted about 1830 by John Evans, another Pennsylvanian, in Delaware County, about twelve miles west of Philadelphia, contained for many years one of the largest collections of plants in the United States. Evans kept up an active correspondence with Sir William Hooker, the Director of the Royal Gardens at Kew, England,

the work of his father and grandfather by introducing foreign trees and plants of value, and by cultivating new American species and creating new varieties from seed. One of the trees introduced into great popularity was the Lombardy poplar. For fully fifty years the nursery was conducted much less for profit than for a love of horticulture and botany. The catalogues from 1815 to 1850 ranked among the standard horticultural publications of the country.

William Robert Prince was the fourth proprietor. He inherited his father's love of botany and botanized through the entire line of the Atlantic States, in company with Professor Torrey and Professor Nuttall. He was unwearying in his efforts to introduce silk culture into this country, importing both silk worms and mulberry trees to feed them.

We find in Greenleaf's "New Daily Advertiser," Nov. 9,

1798, New York City, the following advertisement of what Prince's Nursery had to offer:

"Fruit Trees. For Sale by William Prince, At Flushing, Long Island, near New York.

"A grand assortment of the best grafted apple trees, pears, plumbs, cherries, peaches, nectarines, and apricots, quince, mulberry and fig trees, a variety of the best currants, gooseberries, raspberries, and strawberries. Lombardy poplars of a large size, horse chestnut, a black walnut, weeping willows, and other ornamental trees, a variety of roses and flowering shrubs and plants. Catalogues of which may be had at messrs. Gaine and Ten Eyck's Printing Office in Pearl Street, where orders left will be attended to, and the trees if required

remarkable camellias of which our country can boast,—such as the Mrs. Anne Marie Hovey, Charles M. Hovey, Charles H. Hovey, and others, for some of which they received the gold medal of the Massachusetts Horticultural Society, and also a first class certificate by the London Horticultural Society. Many of these Mr. C. M. Hovey exhibited in London in person. The camellia-house of Hovey and Company is one hundred feet long, fifty feet wide, and twenty-five feet high, and it contains some of the largest camellias in the country, all planted in the ground."

During the 1830's the Hovey nurseries sent splendid exhibits to the Massachusetts Horticultural Society, of which Charles M. Hovey was for four years president. He was also

Box

Primrose

packed in matts, casks or boxes, so as to be sent to Europe, or to the West Indies with the greatest safety."

The famous Hovey nurseries of Cambridge, Mass., are here described in the words of an account[1] written by Marshall Wilder in 1880:

"In the 1830's Cambridge possessed the most extensive nurseries and plant-houses in New England. Here Mr. P. B. Hovey, with his brother Charles M. Hovey established more than forty years ago the famous nursery of Hovey and Co.

"Their collection of plants contains grand old specimens, which are the result of many years of patience and toil. Some of the Chinese and other palms are fifty years old and twelve feet high. Here was begun the hybridization of plants, by which have been produced some of the most

[1]Chapter on Horticulture by Marshall P. Wilder in *Memorial History of Boston*, edited by Justin Winsor.

the editor of the "Magazine of Horticulture," previously mentioned, for the 34 years of its existence.

Among the nurseries that were prominent from 1820 to 1830 were Bloodgood's and Floy's. The latter issued in 1823 a catalogue of ornamental trees, flowering shrubs, fruit trees, and garden and flower seeds. It contains an astonishing variety of plants, offering among them twenty varieties of camellias. Floy's nursery was in New York, on Broadway, near Art Street. Other nurseries of the time were Wilson's, Parmentier's, and Hogg's, near New York; Buel's and Wilson's, near Albany; and Sinclair's and Moore's at Baltimore.

Of this last group, the nursery of Thomas Hogg was an important establishment. His "Catalogue of the Ornamental Trees and Shrubs, herbaceous and greenhouse plants, cultivated and for sale by Thomas Hogg, nurseryman and florist" numbers sixteen small pages, set in double column, of mere lists of species and varieties, comprising no less than 1,200 entries. They were offered at the "New York Botanic Garden in Broadway, near the House of Refuge." The first Thomas Hogg, an Englishman, procured land in 1822 in upper Broadway (where Twenty-Third Street now is) and began business as a florist and a nurseryman.

The nursery firm of Parsons and Co., on Long Island, was founded in 1838. It was instrumental in distributing great quantities of fruit and ornamental stock during a formative period in American horticulture, and was also a pioneer in several commercial methods of propagation of the more difficult ornamental stock. It was a leading distributor of Japanese plants in the early days.

in New York the city's first seed-house, destined to become the J. M. Thorburn and Company of the present day. It is recorded that in that year he began to sell flowers, later adding potted plants, and issued his first catalogue of four pages. In 1805 he bought a lot of seeds for $15.00 and sold them. He was the author of *The Gentleman's and Gardener's Kalendar*.

Bernard McMahon of Philadelphia did a large business in exporting seeds of native plants, and it is through his work that many American plants came into cultivation in Europe. His catalogue (1804) of seeds of American plants for the export trade contains about a thousand species of herbs, shrubs and trees. He announced at that time that he had

Martagon Lily

Single Carnation

The first nursery in Maine is thought to have been that of Ephraim Goddale, at Orrington, established early in the nineteenth century. Other early nurserymen in Maine were the brothers Benjamin and Charles Vaughan, Englishmen, who settled in Hallowell in 1796. An early nursery in South Carolina was established before the Revolution by John Watson, formerly gardener to Henry Laurens. In Massachusetts there were several small nurserymen toward the close of the eighteenth century, among them John Kenrick of Newton, whose son William wrote *The New American Orchardist*, which was published in 1833 and passed through at least eight editions.

The earliest American seed-house, David Landreth's, was established in 1784 in Philadelphia and was followed by John Make-John's (1792), William Leeson's (1794), and Bernard McMahon's (1800), all of Philadelphia.

In 1802 Grant Thorburn, a native of Scotland, established

"also for sale an extensive variety of Asiatic, South Sea Islands, African, and European seeds of the most curious and rare kinds." McMahon, through business and writing, had great influence on American horticulture. He distributed the seeds of the very important Lewis and Clark expedition; but Landreth is said to have shared these seeds and also those collected by Nuttall. Those were days of enthusiastic exportation of the seeds of American plants.

Louden's *Encyclopedia of Gardening*, an English work published in 1834 which contained descriptions and notes on the United States, has the following to say about our nurseries:

"There have been no royal gardens, no botanical gardens (but in name), no public gardens, to stimulate and instruct those who might wish to cultivate taste or to acquire knowledge of this branch of rural improvement. Four or five public nurseries are all that are recollected of any note, which existed in the states in 1810, and these were by no means profitable establishments. About 1815 a spirit of improvement in horticulture as well as in agriculture began to pervade the country, and the sphere of its influence has been enlarging, and the force of example increasing down to the present time.

"Nursery establishments are increasing in America in number, respectability and patronage. The cultivation of indigenous forest trees and shrubs esteemed for utility, or as ornamental, has been extending, and the study of botany has become more general.

"Prince's Linnaean Gardens at Flushing are the best in the United States. Mr. Stuart says 'The variety of Magnolias in Prince's Nursery is prodigious.' Bloodgood's Nursery and that of Mills and Lawrence, are also at Flushing, and the very complete one of the late Mr. Parmentier at Brooklyn. At Bloomingdale is the establishment of Mr. Floy. Mr. Wilson and Mr. Bridgeman are near New York, and in the city there are extensive seed establishments of Messrs. Thorburn, Mr. Smith, Mr. Wilson and Mr. Kenny."

Of public gardens Louden says: "It is easy to foresee that America will one day be possessed of public gardens far superior to any now existing in Europe. Our grounds for this prediction are, that in America there are no other means by which the grandeur and magnificence of gardening can be displayed; that the Americans delight in doing everything on the grandest scale; and that Nature has bountifully supplied every description of material. Taste and wealth which are now rapidly accumulating, are all that are wanting to realize this view. In the meantime all the old towns have public walks and gardens."

FLOWER SEEDS AND PLANT MATERIAL

The earliest advertisement of plant material that research has disclosed is from the *Boston Gazette*, February 28–March 7, 1719:

GARDEN SEEDS—Fresh garden seeds of all sorts, lately imported from London, to be sold by Evan Davies, Gardener, at his house over against the Powder House in Boston; As also English Sparrow-grass Roots, Carnation Layer, Dutch Goose-berry, and Current-bushes.

Other advertised lists read largely of seeds for the vegetable garden, but a few of them, dated nearly two hundred years ago, are quoted here as of sufficient interest. Occasionally a reference to flower seeds or material has been italicized by the editor.

From the *Boston Gazette*, April 10–17, 1738:

GARDEN SEEDS—Lately imported by Capt. Shepperdson, and to be sold by John Little, in Milk Street, Choice good Windsor and Sandwich Beans, Hot Spur, and Marrow Fat Peas, Raddish seed, Spinage, and Orange Carrot, Sweet Marjoram and Colliflowers, and hard Time Seeds, Large Summer Cabbage, Golded Purslan, Cabbage, Lettice, Parsnip, and *double Marygold Seed;* all of the best sort, and at a very reasonable rate.

From the *Boston News Letter*, April 12, 1744:

GARDEN SEEDS—To be sold by Elizabeth Decoster, at the sign of the Wall-Nut Tree in Milk Street Boston, a little below Dr. Sewall's Meeting-House; English Peas, Windsor Beans, Garden Seeds, Flower Seeds, lately imported, Flower Roots.—and all sorts of the best flower seeds.

It is interesting to note in the preceding announcement that a woman advertised in her own name.

Again the *Boston Gazette*, Feb. 16–23, 1748:

GARDEN SEEDS—To be sold by Richard Francis, Gardener, living at the South end, at the sign of the Black and White Horse, fresh and new imported in the last ships from London, all sorts of Garden Seeds, as follows.—Sweet Marjoram, Time, Summer Savory, Hyssop, Sage, Balm, Dubett, Parsley, and Parsley Dubett, Peppergrass, and single white Mustard, Cucumbers, Musmelion, Watermelions, and all sorts of the best flower seeds.

From the *Pennsylvania Chronicle*, April 12, 1768:

A choice parcel of well-grown English Walnut trees as well as Pear and Apricot and a curious variety of the best and largest sorts from England of grafted Plumb trees fit for transplanting this spring or next fall as well as a great variety of *double Hyacinth roots and Tulip roots*, next season, and most other things in the flower or fruit tree nursery way—[for sale] by Christian Lehman.

From the *Pennsylvania Packet*, February 20, 1781:

General Philip de Baas.
Roots of flowers.

Just imported into this City, immediately from Holland a great variety of the roots of Flowers for the Pleasure Garden; of Bulbous Roots, undoubtedly the greatest variety ever imported in America, such as, Tulips, Hyacinths, Narcessus, Daffadel Lillies, and all other the most admired bulbous flowers now in esteem in the best gardens in Europe; The Bulbs are flowering roots, and in excellent condition; Likewise an excellent parcel of Ranunculus Anemones. Also a great variety of the most admired Flower Seeds, and a complete assortment of seeds for Kitchen Gardens of all sorts. All which was collected last fall out of the most famous gardens in Holland.

Enquire at General Philip De Baas, in Third Street, near Race Street.

Again from the *Pennsylvania Packet*, September 30, 1789:

Peter Crouwels, living out Fourth Street, at the place called Hartsfield, takes the liberty to inform his customers in particular, and the Public in general, that he intends to sell off, at very low prices, from this time until the middle of October next, a great variety of flower roots, as Hyacinths, Lilies, Tulips, Tuberoses &c. Also plants in pots, as Oleanders, Geraniums, of different sorts, Myrtle, Egg Plants, Sensitive, jerusalem Cherries, Passion Flowers, and a great number of others too tedious to mention. He has likewise for sale, a large number of Flower Root glasses of the best kind, and all sorts of fresh garden seeds.

We find advertised in Philadelphia, in the *Federal Gazette* of October 20, 1800:

A few fine healthy Orange and Lemon Trees will be offered for sale at the same time. John Connolly, Auctioneer.

And in the same issue, the following:

> On the premises near the Centre-House Tavern, Market Street, on Thursday, the 6th, of November next, or in case the weather proves unfavorable, on the next dry day ensuing
>
> —WILL BE SOLD BY AUCTION—
>
> The whole nursery stock of John Lithen, deceased, consisting of a great number of fruit trees of the very best and the most esteemed kinds in this country—a great quantity of white and other thorns in excellent order for planting out in hedges. . . .

Flower de Luce

Early type of German Iris. The dark blue, found in many old gardens

"English"; Roses, "double and single" (*Rosa centifolia, Rosa canina*); Scarlet Cross (*Lychnis chalcedonica*); "Several sorts of Sedum"; Star of Bethlehem (*Ornithogalum umbellatum*); Sunflower (*Helianthus annuus*), cultivated by the Indians; Sweet briar (*Rosa rubiginosa*); Tulips, "Fine Tulips"; "Violets of three kinds"; Yellow Day Lilies (*Hemerocallis flava*).

These are the herbs mentioned before 1700:
Balm, Belury, Chives, "Clary," Five Finger, Hyssop, Lovage, Mint, Mustard (single white), Peppergrass, Sage, Sweet Marjoram, Summer Savory, Tarragon, Thyme, Wormwood.

In these years also, four shrubs are named:
Flowering Peach, known as "Double Persica"; Privet,

Florentine Iris

The pale lavender, earliest of its type to bloom. Found in old gardens, North and South

COLONIAL BLOOM

What bloomed in the gardens of the colonies? Even in the rudest and most precarious years, there was surprising variety. In colonial records before 1700, we find mention of the following flowering plants:

"Anemones"; Carnation, or Clove Pink (*Dianthus caryophyllus*); Columbine (*Aquilegia*); Crown Imperial (*Fritillaria imperialis*); Daffodils (*Narcissus*); "Gilliflowers", or Stocks (*Mathiola*); "Grape Flower or Muscary" (*Muscari botryoides*); Hollyhocks (*Althea*); House Leek (*Sempervivum*); Martagon Lilies (*Lilium martagon*); Marigold, double (*Calendula*); Moonwort, or "Sattin flower" (*Lunaria annuus*); Primrose (*Primula vulgaris*); Rose, "blush and *rosa albida*"; Roses,

known as "primworth", "skedge" and "Skedgewith"; White Thorn, (*Crataegus*); and "Flowering currant."[1]

In the next fifty years (1700 to 1750), colonial records add these to our list:

Amaranth; Bachelor Buttons (*Centaurea cyanus*); Bellflowers (*Campanula*); "Candy Tuff" (*Iberis amara*); Devil in a bush (*Nigella*); Flower de Luce (Iris); Fraxinella (*Dictamnus fraxinella*); Jacob's Ladder (*Polemonium*); Lilacs, blue, white, deep purple and Persian; Lily of the Valley, or May Lilies (*Convallaria majalis*); Peonies, white and red; Periwinkle (*Vinca minor*); Southernwood (*Artemisia abro-*

---

[1] We do not know to what this refers, as *Ribes odoratum*, native of the Middle West, was introduced into cultivation at a later date.

tanum); Spiderwort (*Tradescantia*); "Striped Scotch Rose."

In 1736, Thomas Hancock of Boston ordered from London yew trees, hollies, dwarf fruit trees, and espaliers—notably, "100 small Yew Trees in the rough" for topiary work.

The half century following (1750 to 1800) swells the roster.

Mentioned by William Logan of Philadelphia, 1754: Persian Iris, Double China Pinks, Double Larkspurs, and Snapdragons.

Mentioned in Dr. Burnaby's record, Schuyler Garden, Bergen County, N. J., 1759: Aloes, Balsams Peru, Citrons, Limes, Oranges and other tropical plants.

Mentioned by William Hamilton, of Philadelphia, in 1784: Dogwoods, Clethra, Judas trees, Double Oleander, Magnolias, Halesia, Kalmias, Azalea, Rhododendrons, Honeysuckles, Yuccas, Corn Flag (Gladioli), Manulea tomentosa "from South Africa," Double Myrtle, Double Convolvulus, English Ivy.

And the following also appear in diverse records: Double White Daffodils, 1763, (*Narcissus poeticus, flora plena*); Double Hyacinths and Tulip Roots, 1768; Oleanders, 1768; Tuberose, 1768; Passionflowers, 1789; Geraniums, 1800 (five species in the Derby gardens in Salem, Mass.).

The years 1800 to 1840, when gardens were being greatly enriched by importations from Japan, China, Holland and England, show many noteworthy accessions:

Aster, from China (*Callistephus hortensis*); Box (*Buxus suffruticosa*); Canterbury Bell (*Campanula media*); Catalpa; *Chrysanthemum indicum* (from this and from *Chrysanthemum morifolium* through variations and hybridizations have come the highly developed modern Chrysanthemums); *Clematis integrifolia;* Crocus; Fading Beauty (*Scabiosa*); Foxglove (*Digitalis purpurea*); Forsythia; Fringe Tree (*Chionanthus virginiana*); Fuchsia; Garden Balsam (*Impatiens balsamina*); Golden Chain (*Laburnum anagyroides*); *Kerria japonica*; Larkspurs (*Delphinium*); Lemon trees; Mezerion (*Daphne mezereum*); Mock Orange (*Philadelphus coronarius*); Pea (sweet); Poppy (*Papaver*); Rose-colored Hibiscus; Siberian Crab (*Malus baccata*); Snowball Tree (*Viburnum opulus var. sterile*); Snowberry (*Symphoricarpus albus*); "Spirea"; Sweet William or Poetic Pink (*Dianthus barbatus*); Verbena; White lilies (*Lilium candidum*).

Two books of this period may be consulted for details: Roland Green's *A Treatise on the Cultivation of Ornamental Flowers*, covering soil, sowing, transplanting and general management, which was published in Boston in 1828; and Robert Buist's *The American Flower Garden Directory*, written by a nurseryman and florist and published in Philadelphia in 1839. The latter gives full lists of the flowers in fashion and under cultivation at the time this study closes.

The discerning gardener has probably missed from the foregoing lists a number of shrubs often met with in so-called old plantings, shrubs known to have been in cultivation in Europe during colonial times. Although we find no mention of them in records of gardens in America before 1840, the following, for example, may have been here:

Smoke Tree or Rhus Cotinus (*Cotinus coggygria*), cultivated since 1656; Burning Bush (*Euonymus atropurpurea*), introduced into cultivation in 1756; Rose Acacia (*Robinia hispida*), introduced in 1758; Flowering Quince or Pyrus japonica (*Chaenomeles japonica*), introduced in 1790; Wistaria (*Wistaria sinensis*), the purple form, often trained as standard, introduced in 1816.

Certain other shrubs, however, although well known at present could not have been in use in the gardens covered by this study, as they were introduced into cultivation at a later date. For example:

Deutzia (*Deutzia gracilis*), introduced into cultivation in 1840; Weigela (*Weigela florida*), commonest form in old gardens, introduced in 1845; Wistaria (*Wistaria sinensis*) the white form, introduced in 1846; Spirea (*Spirea Van Houttei*), introduced about 1850.[1]

A NOTE ON BOX

In this connection, it is worthy of note that box, though mentioned in garden plantings in England throughout the seventeenth and eighteenth centuries, and doubtless known here, is not included, so far as we have been able to discover, in any garden list of the northern States before 1800. Peter Faneuil and Thomas Hancock of Boston, who ordered many things for the ornamenting of their fine gardens, built before 1740, ordered no box and do not mention it, and in Rhode Island the only reference to box before 1800 is from a traditional source.

There is a tradition that box was brought from Ireland to Pennsylvania in 1763, but neither William Logan in 1754, nor William Hamilton in 1787, mention it in their inclusive garden lists, previously mentioned. The beautiful great box at Boxly (Pennsylvania section) was planted by Jean Du Barry in 1803.

The fashion of the small box-edged bed, so popular in the early nineteenth century, was really a revival of the knot-gardens of the sixteenth century. From 1800 to 1840, immense numbers of these box-edged beds were laid out, and in New England today there are examples of *Buxus suffruticosa* of eight to ten feet in height, and six to eight feet across, which are grown from the border plants of a hundred and ten to twenty years ago.

After box reaches a century of age, it is very difficult to know how much older it is, for the size of the trunk depends upon several factors, such as climate, soil and care.

AMERICAN TREES IN EUROPE

It is interesting to observe that while the colonies were diligently importing shrubs, trees, and flowering plants, the American flora were making their way abroad. There was published in London in 1775 *The English Flora, or A Catalogue of Trees, Shrubs, Plants and Fruits, Natives as well as Exotics*, by Richard Weston. In Chapter VI appears a catalogue of American trees and shrubs then known in Europe. The list follows here verbatim:

Acacia-Gleditsia, Pseudo-Acacia; Allspice-Calycanthus; Andromeda; Arbor-vitae; Ash-tree; Azalea; Beech-tree; Bladder Nut tree; Button wood tree; Cedar tree, white and red; Chestnut tree; Clethra; Cypress; Dogwood; Elder tree; Fir tree; Hickory nut; Hornbeam; Juniper Tree; Judas Tree; Kalmia; Liquidamber; Magnolia; Maple trees; Mulberry Tree; Nettle tree or Celtis; Oak-trees; Pine tree; Plane tree; Poplar tree; Rose-Bay or Rhododendron; Sassafras tree; Snowdrop or Chionanthus; Spindle tree; Sumach tree; Tooth ache tree—Zanthoxylon; Tulip tree; Viburnum; Walnut tree; Winter berry.

THE LIFE-SPAN OF COLONIAL GARDENS

The opportunity to study gardens with a history of a century or more has led to observation as to the life of the actual plants making up their content.

We often hear of very old plants, and there are a few which reach a century or a little more of actual life, but the great majority of garden things do not live beyond a generation, and if neglected perish very soon. Any gardener who observes the life of plants for even twenty-five years finds that most of them must often be renewed. Peonies, dictamnus, hemerocallis, tulips, narcissus, scilla, and lily bulbs some-

---

[1] Dates of introduction from Rehder's *Manual of Cultivated Shrubs and Trees.*

times exceed fifty years, and their progeny go on for much longer. Wistaria vines live a hundred years, but this only with most careful care of the main trunk which decays and falls apart; the off-shoots, self-rooted, of these ancient vines will live, however, as long as the conditions which foster them are present. Roses are known to have lived a century and more, but this again only with care of the old wood. The great majority of very old rose bushes are off-shoots of much older ones. The age to which box lives is a much disputed question. The variety *suffruticosa*, which is the box of most old gardens, doubtless lives two hundred years, and perhaps more, but when such box in New England, where the climate is not too kind, attains a height of six or eight feet with an equal width and a stem or trunk nearly a foot in circumference in one hundred and ten years, one wonders what happens in the next century. Plants of *Buxus suffruticosa* four inches in height planted twenty-three years ago are now twenty-five inches high, eighteen inches across, and have a stem about three inches in circumference.

Lilacs, which live a long time, make an astonishing growth in twenty-five years. Some which were planted twenty years ago are now twenty feet high, and have a trunk like a tree. They require constant watching to prevent the "suckers" from taking too much space, and superseding the main bush. The roots undoubtedly live to a great age, but observation leads to the belief that the very old specimens have died back to the main root more than once.

The most important and interesting garden in America, that at Middleton Place, Charleston, S. C., has been very carefully studied as to the history of its planting. Mr. J. J. Pringle Smith, the owner, believes that not one plant of the original garden of the middle of the eighteenth century is in existence today. The great live oaks alone saw the first years of the garden. The magnificent specimens of camellia are known to have been planted in the late years of the eighteenth century, and the Indian azaleas, now almost trees, in the nineteenth century. Many of the flowering shrubs, now thirty and more feet in height, show that they are off-shoots of great root masses much older than the present growth but not more than a century in age.

What then lives on in the gardens that have a continuous history of a century or more?

Box hedges, bulbs of several kinds, and grape vines attain a century and perhaps more; peonies, fraxinella and lemon lilies stand much neglect and live many years; roses of the hardiest kinds endure at least a generation and with care even a hundred years. But the great majority of garden things do not live as long as tradition would lead us to believe, and as vastly the majority of old gardens have been, at some time in their history, either neglected or deserted, most of what graced them in their early days has long since gone.

We find mention of lawns and well-kept lawns, but how lawns were made and kept many years before lawn-mowers were invented is a puzzle. Sheep could have assisted, but they are not mentioned; "Garden shears" perhaps served, but they seem unconvincing; and scythes never made a velvety lawn.

INSECT PESTS

The life of the gardens of the colonies was probably greatly jeopardized by the devastations of insects. Colonial gardeners were less able than those of today to combat the pests which eighteenth-century notes show to have been of great magnitude. In 1748 Peter Kalm wrote:

"There is likewise a kind of Caterpillars in these provinces which eat the leaves from the trees. They are also innumerable in some years. In the intervals there are but few of them: but when they come they strip the trees so entirely of their leaves, that the woods in the middle of summer are as naked as in winter. They eat all kinds of leaves, and very few trees are left untouched by them; as, about that time of year the heat is excessive. The stripping of the leaves of the trees has this fatal consequence that they cannot withstand the heat, but dry up entirely. In this manner great forests are sometimes entirely ruined. The Swedes who lived here showed me, here and there, great tracts in the woods, where young trees were now growing, instead of the old ones, which, some years ago, had been destroyed by the caterpillars."

In 1791, the February number of the "Massachusetts Magazine" recommended the following:

"To prevent Grubs from ascending fruit trees to deposit their eggs.

"Take a strip of sheep-skin about one inch wide with the wool on it at full length; scrape the rough bark off the tree, and nail the skin around it, keeping the woolly side out."

The New York Agricultural Society heard an address in 1795 by Dr. Mitchell upon the ravages of the Canker Worm, evidently as destructive in orchards then as it is now. He concluded his address with this quotation from Chancellor Livingston:

"The man who has taught us to guard against the ravages of noxious insects will be remembered with gratitude as the benefactor of society."[1]

A century earlier, Josselyn had commented on the "meazels" and "lowsiness" which then afflicted the fruit trees of New England. We have already quoted his description of the refreshing cure for "lowsie" trees.

[1]From the *New York Magazine*, April, 1795.

Drawn on stone by M. M. Tidd from an original sketch by Bowen Buckman, Esq.

New England's lovely prospect in 1820—a view of Woburn, Massachusetts, from Academy Hill

A view along the cross walk in Governor Hutchinson's garden, in Milton, Massachusetts. The garden was laid out about 1743. The gate and arch are modern, but four old trees in the garden, which is described on page 57, are thought to date from the Governor's time

MASSACHUSETTS

In the garden of Theodore Lyman, "The Vale," at Waltham, is the oldest greenhouse in Massachusetts. So low is the doorway that even one of short stature must stoop to enter. The illustration also shows old dwarf box edging and the pear orchard. See page 54

MASSACHUSETTS

THE *Voyages* of Samuel de Champlain, who explored the coast of Massachusetts fifteen years before the Pilgrims landed at Plymouth, records his impressions of the agriculture of the Indians of this region.

Champlain and de Monts sailed into Boston harbor in July, 1605. "Sieur de Monts," says Champlain, "sent three or four men on shore in our canoe, not only to get water, but to see their chief. He came alongside to see us, together with some of his companions. . . . Those that we had sent to them brought us some little squashes as big as your fist, which we ate as salad, like cucumbers, and found very good. They brought us also some purslane, which grows in large quantities among the Indian corn, and which they make no

"We saw two hundred savages in this very pleasant place; and there are large numbers of very fine walnut trees, cypresses, sassafras, oaks, ashes, and beeches. . . . Some of the land was already cleared up, and they were constantly making clearings. Their mode of doing it was as follows: After cutting down the trees at a distance of three feet from the ground, they burn the branches upon the trunk, and then plant their corn between these stumps, in course of time tearing up also the roots. There are likewise fine meadows here, capable of supporting a large number of cattle."

A survey of the earliest records of Massachusetts towns, beginning with Plymouth and including Salem, Boston,

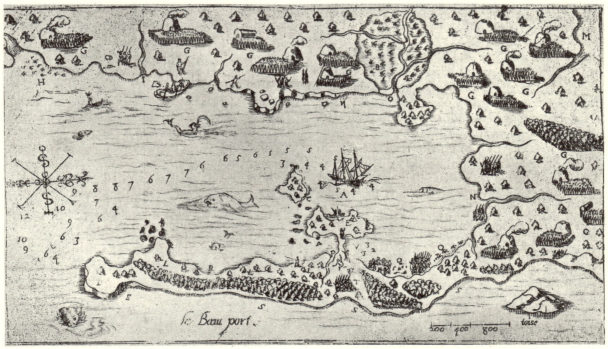

Champlain's map of Gloucester harbor, which he called "Beau port"

more account of than weeds. We saw here a great many little houses, scattered over the fields where they have their Indian corn."

They next explored Plymouth harbor, afterwards visiting Cape Cod. Nausett harbor they called Mallebarre, because of its shoals. Here the friendliness of the natives permitted further observation.

"Before reaching their wigwams, we entered a field planted with Indian corn in the manner before described. The corn was in flower, and some five and a half feet high. There was some less advanced, which they plant later. We saw many Brazilian beans, and many squashes of various sizes, very good for eating; some tobacco, and roots which they cultivate, the latter having the taste of an artichoke. The woods are filled with oaks, nut-trees and beautiful cypresses[1], which are of a reddish color and have a very pleasant odor. . . ."

The harbor of Gloucester, which was visited the next year in the course of a longer voyage, pleased them so greatly that they named it "Beau port." There are interesting details in Champlain's impressions of his visit there.

[1]Probably *Juniperus virginiana*.

Charlestown, Watertown, Roxbury, Dorchester, Cambridge, Newburyport, Marblehead, and Andover, shows that gardens were a fact from the very first. Study leads to the conclusion that these first gardens were largely for food, but it leads also to the conclusion that those gentlemen who were connected with the settlements in Massachusetts, and who had large land holdings for use as farms, could have developed about their town homes gardens used exclusively for pleasure. No exact proof of this can be brought from records, but familiarity with conditions which governed the years from 1640 to the end of the century makes it safe to state that pleasure gardens existed, were used and enjoyed.

From 1700 until the Revolution the building of imposing houses and the laying out of elaborate grounds constantly increased, and we have ample records of many fine homes and gardens. After the Revolution, and notably after 1800, the gardens which were a part of the town land-holdings of the seventeenth and eighteenth centuries gradually disappeared.

Very early, however, we find examples of town and country homes in Massachusetts. John Winthrop had a house and lot in Boston in 1630, and also his farm, "Ten Hills", a few miles out on the Mystic River. We have a map of "Ten Hills", made in 1637. John Endecott had his house and lot in Salem in 1629, and his Orchard Farm of 300 acres at Danvers. In 1659 he had also a house in Boston.

As wealth increased and dangers lessened, houses of increasing importance were built in Boston and in the neighboring towns. Andrew Faneuil built his fine house in Boston and laid out his grounds handsomely between 1700 and 1710. In the 1730's, Thomas Hancock was corresponding with England to get the best advice about the laying out of his grounds. Isaac Royall had, about 1737, a fine country seat at Medford—a portion of the Winthrop "Ten Hills" farm. It was described in 1750 by Captain Francis Goelet as "one of the grandest in North America." At Cambridge in 1706 Lieutenant-Governor Spencer Phips had his country-seat. The Brattles, Vassalls, Olivers, and Apthorps were among those who built important houses in Cambridge and planted gardens of a formal type before 1750. The Davenport farm was laid out and splendidly cultivated at Milton about 1707, and the Smith-Murray farm, also at Milton, about 1734. Mr. Smith had his town house in Boston, on Queen Street. Thomas Hutchinson, whose town house was in Garden Court, Boston, was another wealthy man who had his farm in Milton. Tristam Dalton in the 1760's had a town house in Newburyport, and a large farm on Pipe-stave Hill, above Newburyport.

Indeed, in the records of these holdings there is lamentably little mention of pleasure of any kind, but when Judge Sewall records in July, 1714, that "Mr. Franklyn had me into the garden, and gave me a glass of choice canary," we get a glimpse of a Boston garden evidently for recreation. Later, in 1726, when Judge Sewall was an old man, he wrote to Madam Bridgett Cotton in London: "I miss my old friends and the charming garden and walks which are all vanished." The garden referred to in this letter was in a part of Boston where the opening of new streets was destroying the old gardens.

The Revolution seriously affected many fine gardens, for in Cambridge, Boston, and elsewhere there were those who sympathized with the crown and who were obliged, as feeling rose higher, to leave their homes and go to England or to other English territory. Meanwhile these houses and gardens were used as "quarters" by our army of occupation. Later, some of these gardens were revived, either by members of the original families or by new owners. Thomas Brattle of Cambridge revived his father's garden; Andrew Craigie rebuilt the garden of John Vassall, Jr., and the Apthorp house and garden were restored in 1784. These may be taken as examples of what occurred generally, for throughout the colonies some of the very important men in politics and industry were not in sympathy with the Revolution and accordingly lost their considerable properties.

Charlestown, burned in 1775 by the British army, was rebuilt before 1790, and the gardens restored.

The wave of horticultural enthusiasm which we find all through the young republic from 1800 to 1840 was noticeably strong in Massachusetts, and was directed with admirable intelligence. Such men as John Lowell, Theodore Lyman, Joseph Barrell, Thomas Handasyd Perkins, John Hancock, Peter Chardon Brooks, Governor Gore, Thomas Lee, Thomas Brattle, and many more, all of them active members of the Massachusetts Society for Promoting Agriculture, on their own places were planting the best obtainable ornamental and fruit trees, as well as flowering plants for greenhouse and outdoor culture, and by example and premiums were encouraging such plantings elsewhere. The Harvard Botanic Garden was founded through the efforts of this Society, and one of its members was sent to Europe for a year's study of botanic gardens before assuming the directorship of the garden.

Through the efforts of notable representatives of the group of horticulturists, the Massachusetts Horticultural Society came into being in 1829.

It may be truly said that nowhere in our country was there an equal group of gentlemen who through study and practice contributed so much to horticulture.

PLYMOUTH

"Plymouth was the first town built in New England by civilized men; and those by whom it was built were inferior in worth to no body of men, whose names are recorded in history during the last seventeen hundred years. A kind of venerableness arising from these facts, attaches to this town, which may be termed a prejudice. Still it has its foundation in the nature of man, and will never be eradicated by philosophy or ridicule. No New-Englander, who is willing to indulge his native feelings, can stand upon the rock, where our ancestors set the first foot after their arrival on the American shore, without experiencing emotions, entirely different from those which are excited by any common object of nature."—From Timothy Dwight's *Travels in New England and New York.*

MEERSTEADS AND GARDEN "PLOTES"[1]

The first gardens of Plymouth were those of nature's own planting. In sheltered hollows on the banks of the Town Brook bloomed the trailing arbutus (*Epigæa repens*), with its fragrant clusters of pink and white flowers. The Pilgrim women, homesick and sad at heart after their first dreary winter in their new home, welcomed them with delight in the sunshine of early spring, and called them "mayflowers," in tender remembrance of the may, or hawthorn, of their old homes in England.

Where these wild flowers of the forest bloomed, other flowers, fitfully cultivated by succeeding generations, have lifted their heads for three hundred years, sometimes in plots among tall grass and encroaching weeds, sometimes in well-ordered and flourishing gardens. Always there has been a chain of seed and blossom between us and our forebears on the margin of the Town Brook, or on the terraces above it—terraces which, as a survival of the sojourn of the Pilgrims in Holland, are still called "dykes."

One of the first acts of the Plymouth Colony was to allot land to groups of the settlers. " . . . To greater families we allotted larger plots, to every person half a pole in breadth, and three in width. We thought this proportion large enough for houses and gardens to impale them around."[1]

The records were kept in a series of eighteen manuscript volumes.[2] The first volume opens with a rough plan of the "Meersteads and Garden Plotes of those which came first, layed out in 1620," in the handwriting of Governor Bradford. The illustration on page 22 shows a photograph of the first page of the original records. The term Meerstead—so spelled by Bradford—is still in use in Plymouth, meaning the house lots on Leyden Street, running from the street to the brook. The word *mear* is defined by Webster as a boundary; *merestead* as a farm enclosed by a boundary.

[1]Adapted from a paper by Mrs. George R. Briggs, chairman of Historical Gardens Committee, Plymouth Antiquarian Society.

[1]*Chronicles of the Pilgrim Fathers of the Colony of Plymouth*, Alexander Young. 2d ed., 1841, p. 160.

[2]*Records of Plymouth Colony.*

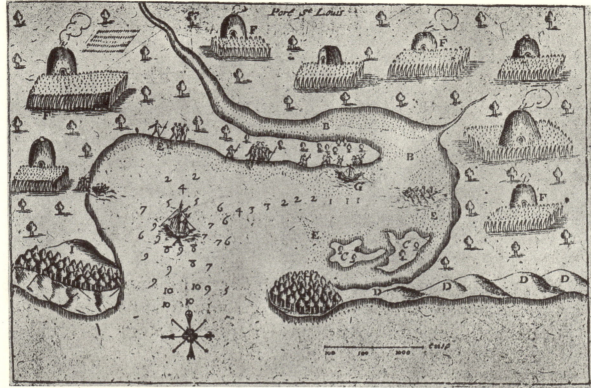

Champlain's map of Plymouth harbor, which he named "Port St. Louis"

The houses were built on a trail which followed the line of the brook, and the "garden plotes" sloped behind them to the edge of the stream. The path ran down from the hill, where Myles Standish had built a fort for the defence of the settlement, to the shore, where the Pilgrims made a landing. This trail was the First Street, now Leyden Street. De Rasieres, a visitor from New Amsterdam to Plymouth, describes this street, still one of the principal streets of Plymouth, as "a broad street, about a cannon shot of 800 yards long, leading down the hill, with a street crossing in the middle, southward to the rivulet, northward to the land. The houses are constructed of hewn planks, with gardens also enclosed behind, and at the sides with hewn planks, so the houses and court yards are in very good order."[1]

After a few years of strenuous labor among many and grave dangers, "the settlement had an air of thrift and prosperity, every house had its vegetable garden, enclosed by palings, and most of the houses had blooming vines running over them."[2]

Sometime between 1629 and 1633, a traveler and observer, William Wood, in his *New England's Prospect*, published in 1634 in London, wrote one of the earliest agricultural accounts of Massachusetts:

"In planted gardens are sweet marjoram, sorrel, perennial yarrow, hempe, and flaxe, besides turnips, parsnips, carrots, radishes, musk mellions, cucumber onyons."

John Josselyn, whose activities have been briefly described in the Introduction, thought the "musk mellions" better than the English ones, but Wood said of the cherry trees, growing wild in the clearings: "English ordering may bring them to be an English cherry, but as yet they are as wild as the Indians." Of the cultivated fruit trees, Josselyn had a much better account to give in 1671:

"The quinces, cherries, damsons, set the dames awork, marmalade, and preserved damsons, is to be met with in every house. Our fruit trees prosper abundantly; apple trees, pear trees, quince trees, plum trees, barberry trees, the country is replenished with fair and large orchards." Josselyn adds further: "House leeks flourish notably, Holli-hocks single and double, of various colors, White Satin, (Honesty) groweth very well, so doth Lavender Cotton, Marygold, Gilliflower will continue for two years, Sweet

Bryer or Eglantine, Violets of three kinds, Patience, and English roses very pleasantly."

The records of the Massachusetts Company show a

Pilgrim meersteads. The site of the first house in Plymouth

memorandum of the 16th of March, 1629, "to provide to send to New England—Vyne planters, stones of all sorts of fruits. . . . Also wheat, rye, potatoes, barley, oats, woad, saffron, lequorice seeds, hop roots, currant plants."

The specific records of the earliest Plymouth gardens are meagre, however, reflecting the extreme simplicity of the life and surroundings. For example:

An Inventory of the Estate of Elizabeth Hopkins, 1659—

[1]Quoted by William T. Davis in *Ancient Landmarks of Plymouth*, p. 156
[2]*Our Pilgrim Forefathers*, Charles Stedman Hanks.

A photograph of the first page of the record in Plymouth

"Gold silver spoons; one garden spot; one cow killed the last year."

August 26, 1646—

"These presents doe witness that Phinias Pratt of Plymouth, Joyner for and in consideration of the sum of 20 pounds sterling, to be paid by John Cooke Junior of Plymouth afforsaid, planter,—doth—sell unto John Cooke, all his house and housing and gardine place and orchard (Excepting the fruit trees now growing therein, or so many of them to be delivered to the said Phinias or his assignes when he shall demand them, so it be in due time) and 50 acres of upland, 2 acres of meadow etc etc to have and to hold the said house, housing, garden, and orchard (excepting before excepted)," etc.

August 2, 1653—

"John Cooke Senior of Plymouth doth acknowledge that for 3 pounds he hath—sold—Thomas Lettice an house and garden plot on which the said house standeth, being scituate in Plymouth in the north street, being next the house and garden plott in which Thomas Lettice now liveth; To have and to hold the said house and garden plott next adjoining unto the garden place or meerstead on which the said Thomas Lettice now liveth."

A Deed of 1653—

"Richard Sparrow doth acknowledge that for—8 pounds—

paid by George Bonum—of Plymouth—planter, he hath sold George Bonum all his house and garden plott on which the house standeth; being scituate in Plymouth in the south street near the mill. To have and to hold the said house and garden spott with all the fence and fences in or upon the said garden spot, with all the fruit trees of any kind on the said meerstead or garden spott;" etc.

From such evidence, we may reasonably conclude that very early the woods and gardens furnished a good store of fruit, vegetables, herbs, and flowers for the industrious and thrifty gardeners of the meersteads, the Pilgrim plots which are among the first of the gardens of the New World, and which are still cultivated after three hundred years.

And indeed, some of the Pilgrim plantings are known to have rounded out two centuries or more of existence. An apple tree planted in Marshfield in 1648 by Peregrine White still survived in 1846. A picture in Russell's "Guide to Plymouth" shows it with a trunk four and one-half feet in circumference, still bearing fruit. A pear tree imported from England by Governor Prince in 1640 and planted on his homestead at Eastham, Cape Cod, was described in 1836 as a flourishing lofty tree. And another pear tree planted in Yarmouth in 1640 by Anthony Thacher produced a fair crop in 1872. (Letter from Amos Otis of Yarmouthport.[1])

[1]*History of Massachusetts Historical Society*, Vol. 1, p. 3.

ELDER BREWSTER'S GARDEN ON THE TOWN BROOK[1]

In the sad and strenuous days of the first winter of the Plymouth Settlement, Elder William Brewster was granted land on the corner of the First Street (Leyden Street) and a cross-way, running down the hill to a ford over the Town Brook.[2] A fresh and flowing spring bubbled up in the midst of the "plotte," and the land sloped to the south on the little hillside by the brook which formed its boundary.

His was one of the seven dwelling houses built in the winter of 1620–21. His garden, and the land close by, which was afterwards divided into other adjoining gardens, is still

Courtesy of the Plymouth Antiquarian Society
Brewster land about the spring where mint grew three hundred years ago, and still grows

cultivated as blossoming "back yards" of the generations who have followed him. Indeed, before Brewster's day the Indians had planted corn on this site for many generations, and the Pilgrims found cleared land along the brook and on the hill. This is one of the earliest records of land known to have been under cultivation for hundreds of years which is still garden ground.[3]

The Brewsters' garden is thus described[4]: "He [the Elder] planted parsley, sweet cervil, sorrel and other pot herbs on one side of his garden path, and on the other side was sage, thyme, spearmint, mullein, fennel and other bitter herbs which every household considered necessary for potions or medicines."

Three hundred years from the bitter winter when Elder Brewster received the grant for his meerstead from the governor of the Plymouth Colony, a descendant of the Jackson family, one of the later owners of the land, conceived

[1]Adapted from a paper by Mrs. George R. Briggs.
[2]*Records of Plymouth Colony*, Vol. I.
[3]Bradford's *History of Plymouth Plantation*, Chap. X, p. 106. Also W. T. Davis' *Ancient Landmarks of Plymouth*.
[4]Edward B. Gregg, *The Founding of a Nation*.

with affectionate zeal the idea of reviving the Brewster "garden plotte."

Below the upper terraces or "dykes" of the meerstead houses, close along the Brook, for the length of several holdings, the land has been cleared of weeds and rubbish, and the Brewster Garden of today has been renewed. Old trees have been rescued and new ones planted, willows shade the spring again, and wild flowers and native shrubs from the Plymouth woods grow on the margin of the streamlet which meanders through the grounds to join the wider brook.

Above the spring, which still flows fresh and free, is a tablet of dedication to Lydia Jackson Emerson, born in Plymouth, wife of Ralph Waldo Emerson, and mother of the donor ; and also to Mrs. Emerson's brother, Dr. Charles Jackson, who gave the service of his life to the merciful alleviation of human pain.

Above, on the bank, the house gardens of the meersteads are blossoming anew. In them, old lilac bushes, pear trees and clumps of peonies are reminders of later gardens than the Brewsters'.

Governor Bradford's house was diagonally opposite Elder Brewster's. He is reputed to have had a trim and tidy garden, but it long ago vanished under the buildings of the modern town.

THE GARDEN OF BARNABAS HEDGE

On the opposite side of Leyden Street from those houses with gardens sloping to Town Brook, stands a large three-storied house with a delicate balustrade and a dentiled cornice. It was built in 1747.

In 1789, when Barnabas Hedge married Eunice Dennie Burr (a niece of Thaddeus Burr of Fairfield, Connecticut), he bought the house, added the third story, and made it his home until he died in 1840. The house and the garden behind it occupy part of the homestead lot of John Howland of the *Mayflower*.

[1]The garden and its first planting was given by Mrs. William H. Forbes of Milton. In 1924 it was taken over by the town.

Robert N. Cram
The door that leads into the Barnabas Hedge garden, Plymouth

Barely can a dandelion push itself between the front wall of the house and the narrow sidewalk, but behind the high board fence at the side lies a quiet and hidden world of scent and color.

A wide gate in the fence opens into a cobble-stoned courtyard, on two sides of which are a small barn and a line of sheds. A white fence with pickets separates the courtyard from the garden, with a gate under a wooden arch and keystone, opening upon a long path which leads down the middle of the enclosure. Narrow flower beds, edged with boards, are on either side of the path, and behind these, on one side, is a long division laid out in raised beds, in circles and segments of circles. Very narrow grass paths separate the figures,—like a parterre, "well contrived and ingenious," which Parkman admired and which succeeded the "Knots" in the old English gardens planned by William Lawson and Gervaise Markham. These raised beds are now edged with grass, but they may have had box borders originally; for in this locality box often winter-kills in borders, while the taller box flourishes. In one of the larger circles is a pear tree; in another a great clump of tall box. The smaller beds have flowers. One finds striped grass, "snow in summer," peonies, wandering Jew, and spirea. At the foot of the garden are more pear trees, a plum tree, and rows of currant bushes.

Courtesy of the Plymouth Antiquarian Society

The gate of the garden of Barnabas Hedge, in Plymouth

Linden trees on North Street, Plymouth, across the street from the Lord garden. They were set out by Colonel Watson in 1765

An apple tree, brought from Fairfield, Connecticut—Mrs. Hedge's old home—bore luscious King apples.

This garden is the only formal one in Plymouth which gives a clear idea of its early arrangement and which has kept its form unchanged.[1]

THE GARDEN OF ARTHUR LORD[2]

The house now belonging to Mr. Arthur Lord[3] on North Street was built in 1802 by David Warren, a descendant of Richard Warren of the *Mayflower;* the land was part of that allotted, and was acquired by John Howland, who also came in the *Mayflower*.

[1]The garden and house are now the property of Mrs. George L. Gooding, whose grandfather, William R. Drew, purchased them from the Hedges.
[2]Described by Mrs. George R. Briggs.
[3]Written before the recent death of Mr. Arthur Lord.

The path through the Barnabas Hedge garden, leading to the house

Photographs by Robert N. Cram

The main path through the garden of Arthur Lord, in Plymouth

The Lord garden lies behind the house and slopes to the sea.   A beautiful old elm hangs over the arched entrance

There is no hint of the garden from the street which slopes down the hill, under great trees, to the sea which shines blue and fresh at its foot. The house stands very near the sidewalk, and the garden lies long and narrow behind it. On one side a wide alley separates it from the neighboring houses, and old trees rise around it on the other sides. Across the street is a row of fine lindens which were set out by Colonel Watson in 1765. The parent trees, from which the row on the street was propagated, were brought from London to Colonel Watson in 1750 by Captain Cameron of Boston, and there is a tradition that they were then small enough to be packed in a raisin box; they are now considered the largest and finest specimens in the country.

In 1839 the house and garden were owned by Dr. Timothy Gordon, and probably dating before his time were the old rose bushes, and a box tree which now has become a sturdy clump without a rival this side of Newport. The blush roses (*Rosa albida*) were brought from England in the very early days of the settlement; they bloomed also in the garden next door when Lydia Jackson was married there to Ralph Waldo Emerson, who once taught school in Plymouth. Some of these roses went to Concord with Mrs. Emerson, and her daughter, Mrs. William Forbes, has taken them to her garden in Milton, where they are called "The Plymouth Rose." There are also a number of very old pear trees in the garden.

When planting this garden anew, Mr. Lord selected flowers which were named in a list published in 1800. There is lavender—brought from Winchester, England—which sometimes, as here, eludes New England winters; brilliant poppies from seed obtained in an old garden in Portsmouth, New Hampshire. Hollyhocks line the fences; lilies and larkspur run riot in early summer, and "sun drops," common in Plymouth gardens, line the courtyards in spring.

Over the long path which leads down the center to the sun dial, against the dark clump of box, are two arches and an old trellised arbor; the path is covered with green moss and the grass in the enclosures is soft and fine.

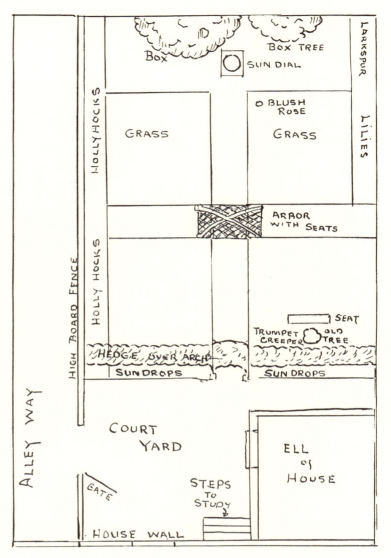

A plan of the Lord garden, in Plymouth

BOSTON AND ENVIRONS

AFTER Plymouth, which will always hold romantic interest for all New England, Boston became the center of the settlement.

Boston in its earliest years is thus described in Wood's *New England's Prospect*, published in 1634:

". . . Boston is two miles northeast from Roxberry. Its situation is very pleasant, being a peninsula hemmed in on the south side with the bay of Roxberry, on the north side with Charles River. . . . It being a neck, and bare of wood, they are not troubled with three great annoyances, of wolves, rattlesnakes and mosquitoes. These that live here upon their cattle, must be constrained to take farms in the country, or else they cannot subsist. . . . This town, although it be neither the greatest or the richest, yet it is the most noted and frequented, being the centre of the plantations, where the monthly courts are kept. Here likewise dwells the governor. This place hath very good land, affording rich cornfields and fruitful gardens; having likewise sweet and pleasant springs. . . ."

Thirty years later the city had taken form. Josselyn's description of it in 1663 remarks "stately edifices," implying a mode of life which would have included pleasure gardens. He says:

"Boston, the chief town in Massachusetts, a colony of Englishmen in New England . . . is built on the southwest side of a Bay large enough for the Anchorage of 500 Sail of Ships, the Buildings are handsome, joyning one to another as in London, with many large streets, most of them paved with pebble stone, in the high street toward the Common there are fair buildings, some of stone, and at the East End of the Town one amongst the rest built by the shore by Mr. Gibs, a Merchant, being a stately edifice, which is thought will stand him in a little less than 3000 pounds before it is fully finished."

John Ogilby's *America*, published in 1671, gives another glimpse of a Boston whose chief citizens would have desired gardens:

"The chiefest part of this City-like town is crowded upon the Sea Banks and wharf'd out with great Industry and Cost, the edifices large and beautiful, whose continual enlargement presages some sumptuous city."

Much later, Timothy Dwight, president of Yale College, wrote of Boston as it appeared to him in 1798, when gardening was well advanced:

"Boston enjoys a superiority to all other great towns on this continent in an agreeable neighborhood. A numerous collection of pleasant towns and villages, almost surround it: the residences, not only of flourishing farmers and mechanics, but also of men, respectable for their polish, learning and worth. The soil is generally fertile, the agriculture neat, and productive; the gardening superior to what is found in most other places; the orchards, groves, and forests, numerous and thrifty. The roads running in every direction, are most of them good, and some of them excellent. Several of them are lined, throughout their whole extent, with almost a continued village. . . . Villas, pleasantly situated, commanding handsome views, exhibiting more lightness and elegance of architecture, and ornamented with suitable appendages, than I have elsewhere seen, adorn at little distances, a considerable part of this region. A singular collection of pleasant rides is opened in this manner to the inhabitants, and of interesting objects, to which these rides conduct them. From the gratification furnished by this source a considerable abatement is made by several slaughter houses, standing on or near some of the roads; one of them near that which passes over the neck. A traveler cannot easily conceive how a people, within and without whose doors so much taste and elegance appear, can be satisfied to pass daily by objects, so deformed and offensive."[1]

All New England then impressed him with its progress in cultivation. In another letter he says:

"A person who has extensively seen the efforts of the New England people in colonizing new countries, cannot fail of being forcibly struck by their enterprise, industry and perseverance. In Maine, New Hampshire, in Vermont, in Massachusetts, and in New York, I have passed the dwellings of several hundred thousand of these people, erected on grounds which in 1760, were an absolute wilderness. A large part of these tracts they have already converted into fruitful fields; covered it with productive farms; surrounded it with enclosures; planted it with orchards; and beautified it with comfortable and in many cases with handsome houses. Considerable tracts I have traced through their whole progress from a desert to a garden; and have literally beheld the wilderness blossom as the rose."

In 1810 Dwight wrote of the gardens of Boston:

"Gardens also of considerable extent and well furnished with vegetables, flowers, and sometimes with fruit trees, adorn many parts of this town. Nothing can give a more cheerful aspect in the midst of a city."

The diary of Judge Samuel Sewall of Boston, published by the Massachusetts Historical Society, is one of the great documents of the New England of the late seventeenth and early eighteenth centuries. It is so largely occupied with very serious concerns that there are few references giving us any hint of gardens, but the following extracts serve to show that Judge Sewall did have some interest in horticulture.

Thursday Oct. 26, 1686. I set Sweet Briar seeds at the pasture of Saunderson's next the lawn at the upper end.

April 15, 1687. Grafted the Button pear tree stock; which dies at the lower end of the garden.

April 13, 1688. Grafted a stock next to Jno. Waits, pretty high out of cows reach, with cions from Mr. Moody's Orange pear, and grafted two apple tree Stocks with Mr. Gardener's

Russetings—the cow having eaten all last year's grafts except one Twigg.

Monday April 2, 1694. Bastian and I set seeds of white thorn at Saunder's pasture, north end.

Dec. 6, 1698. . . . Cherubim's heads set up.[1]

July 15, 1718. Went with Mr. Franklyn to view his walk adjoining to me. He then had me into the garden, and gave me a glass of choice canary.

Tuesday January 21, 1721. . . . Quickly after the wind rose to a prodigious height. . . . It blew down the southermost of my cherubim's heads at the Street Gates.

Feb. 1, 1721. Took down the northwardly cherubim's head, the other being blown down . . . I suppose they have stood there near thirty years. [Actually over twenty-two years.]

Sewall's letter-book contains a letter to Madam Bridgett Cotton in London, dated April, 1726, which says, "I miss my old friends, and the charming gardens and walks which are all vanished." And in a letter on January 24, 1728, to his London agent, Mr. Samuel Stork, merchant, of London, he says, "Desired Mr. Balston to bring over some primrose roots in a box with earth."

[1]These were the ornaments placed on Sewall's gate posts at the south gate of his Boston house.

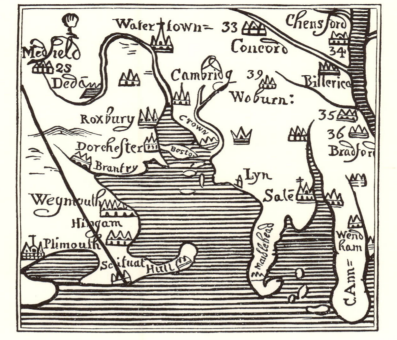

The country in the vicinity of Boston when the first gardens were made. A close copy made by John Warner Barber in 1840 of a map published in "New England's Memorial" in 1667

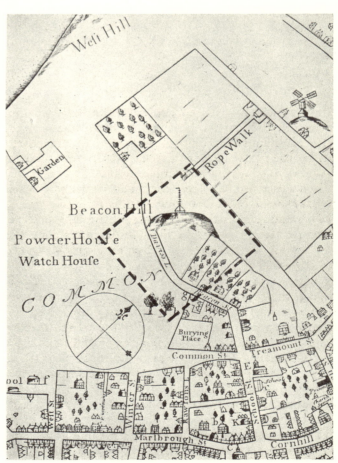

From "Sentry or Beacon Hill and the Monument," by William W. Wheildon

Beacon Hill in 1722, showing the beacon erected in 1635 "to give notice to the country of any danger." It was blown down in 1789 and was replaced by a doric column (shown on page 30) 57 feet high, surmounted by an eagle designed by Charles Bulfinch

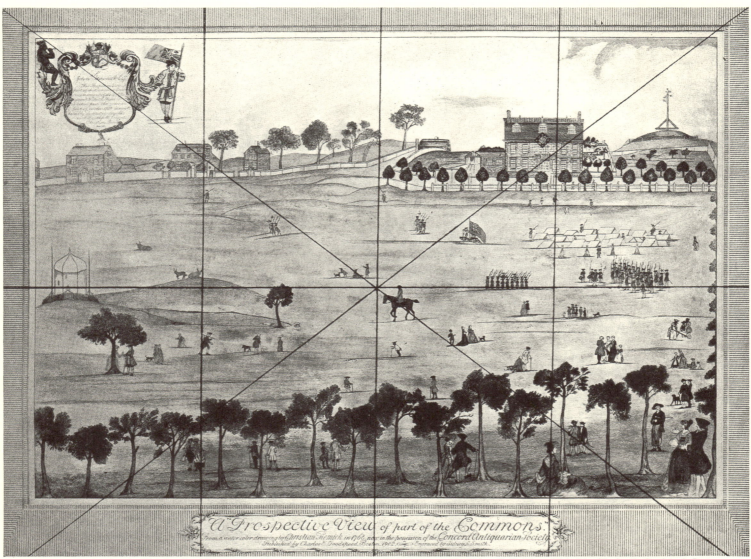

From a water-color drawing by Christian Remick, now owned by the Concord Antiquarian Society; engraved by Sidney F. Smith; published by Charles E. Goodspeed, Boston, 1902

Boston Common in 1764-68, showing the front of Thomas Hancock's house with the hatchment placed there at his death. (Hatchment: the funeral escutcheon placed in front of the house of the deceased, or elsewhere, setting forth his rank and circumstances and depicting the arms, single or quartered.) The illustration shows Beacon Hill and the Beacon at the right, the trees planted by Hancock, the uneven surface of the ground, the elms to the south which were long the feature of that boundary, and the militia in training, with the cows undisturbed

BOSTON COMMON

The land which has been known as the Boston Common for nearly three hundred years was part of a tract granted to the Rev. William Blaxton[1] before Boston became a settlement. In 1634 "the lands of the Common" were purchased by a tax, divided among the "inhabitants." The act provided that it be used for "a Trayning Field and the feeding of Cattell." The right of Commonage was restricted "to those who were admitted by the townsmen to be inhabitants"; none who came after 1664 could have the right of commonage unless "he hier it of those that are commoners." The keeper of the cows was allowed two shillings a cow yearly.

As early as 1640, regulations concerning the Common appear in the court records. From time to time discussion of the problems arising from its use for pasture led to rulings intended to control abuses of various kinds. In a town meeting of 1661 a committee was appointed to look after the trees on the Common. Reference was made in 1678 to six trees, each surrounded by a heap of stones; one of them is mentioned as a walnut, another as an elm.

The Common was probably fenced from the first, but the first fencing of record is that which bordered the Tremont Street Mall in 1733 and the Beacon Street boundary in 1738. Not until 1789 were the malls on Park and Beacon Street laid out by the Town.

As the Common was used for pasture until 1830, an occasional tree was the only planting within the fences. The Great Elm, which stood until 1876, and which was for many

[1]or Blackstone, a survivor of the Ferdinando Gorges Colony.

years fenced and protected, seems to have been there since the beginning. The beautiful row of elms along the Tremont Street Mall, seen in the drawing shown above, was long venerated by lovers of Old Boston. In one of the letters written by John Drayton of South Carolina during a northern tour in 1794, we find this description: "There is a public walk in Boston, called the mall; which is very beautiful. It is upwards of half a mile long; and offers to your choice both a gravel and a turf walk; shaded by beautiful elm trees. A street runs parallel with it on one side; and on the other a large common; where hundreds of cattle feed during the day."

Not one tree of this row of elms survives today.

In 1833 the Common occupied a space of $48\frac{2}{5}$ acres, and an observer of that day records that the malls were bordered with 600 beautiful trees, and were the most beautiful walks in the world. A plan of the city in 1850 gives the appearance of the Common and the Public Gardens, and shows the planting done shortly after 1830. Some of these trees are still standing, and the general plan was much as it is today.[1]

THE PUBLIC GARDEN

Horace Gray was the chief inspirer of the Public Garden. In 1839 he obtained a lease of the land from the city of Boston, and in this same year a circus building was converted into a conservatory containing a great variety of plants and birds.

[1]The facts of this account are drawn from Wheildon's *Sentry Hill*; James H. Stark's *Antique Views of Boston*; Robin Carver's *History of Boston* (1834); and M. A. Dewolfe Howe's *Four Centuries of Boston Common*.

Drawn from nature on stone by Williams and Stevens

Above is a view of Beacon Street and the Common (1804-1811), looking toward the State House. It shows the three-railed fence and the casual paths before the laying out about 1830. The lower view shows the Common and the Public Gardens in 1850, and the planting done about 1830 when the use of the land as pasture was finally abandoned

John Cadness, an Englishman, at this time took professional charge of the gardens. He records that the greenhouses contained a large and very fine collection of plants, especially camellias,[1] Chinese azaleas, ericas, strelitzias, hibiscus, eugenias, and many specimens of Cape bulbs, amaryllis, and pelargoniums, with a fine set of herbaceous calceolarias. There was also a good collection of dahlias and standard roses out of doors.

[1]One thousand camellias from the Marshall P. Wilder collection were given for public enjoyment.

HISTORIC GARDENS OF BOSTON

JOHN WINTHROP'S GARDEN

Did John Winthrop have a pleasure garden in Boston in 1640?

There are only a few references in the correspondence between Winthrop and the members of his family which can be construed to indicate that he did. Bearing in mind the following facts, however, we conclude that beyond a doubt a gar-

From "Sentry or Beacon Hill and the Monument," by William W. Wheildon

This sketch of Beacon Hill and the monument which replaced the Beacon was made on the spot by T. R. Smith in 1811. The monument was taken down in that year despite the protests of many citizens

den for pleasure and not for farm purposes was established by Governor Winthrop at his Boston house thus early.

John Winthrop was a gentleman. He was Lord of Groton Manor in the County of Suffolk, England, and was accustomed to the orderly laying out of grounds which was the rule of the England of his time. His letters to his wife and family show him to have been a most affectionate, thoughtful husband and father, interested in all the details of gracious living. His third wife, Margaret Tyndall, who followed him to New England the year after his arrival, was a well-bred lady whose taste and abilities were high. Winthrop, in writing to her at Chemsey House, Great Maplestead, Essex, addressed his "respects to my lady, your good mother."

So much for the quality and experience of John and Margaret Winthrop.

In July, 1630, John Winthrop writes to Margaret from Charlestown in New England: "I shall expect thee next summer, and by that time hope to be provided for thy comfortable entertainment."

The first year of Governor Winthrop's life in New England was a hard and sad one, but he never lost courage, or his belief that life was good here; he repeatedly states that he would willingly endure again all the first hardships.

Of course, after the arrival of his wife very little correspondence exists; there is only an occasional letter to his son John Winthrop, Governor of Connecticut, and to his beloved Margaret when he is away from her on official business.

In 1637 John Winthrop writes his wife from Newtowne (Cambridge), addressing her in Boston: "And speak to the folkes to keep the goats well out of the garden." We find in his will, made in April, 1641: "I give power to my executors to sell the house I dwell in at Boston and the land beyond Powder Horn Hill . . . and for my dear wife my will is, she should be maintained in a comfortable and honourable condition according to her place. . . . I give to her half my farm Ten Hills during her life." He sets aside to his children "my island called the Governor's Garden, my moiety of the Isle of Prudence in Narragansett Bay, my land at Pullen Point—my lot at Concord, which I intend to build upon and half of my farm of twelve hundred acres upon the Concord River."

So in 1641, when the will was made, his house in Boston

could be sold for the benefit of his estate, and as he gives his wife a half interest in the Ten Hills farm we must conclude that there was a home there for her. There is nothing so far that indicates a pleasure garden. But read the following account of the official visit of three French gentlemen in 1646:

"Being the Lord's day and the people ready to go to the assembly after dinner, Monsieur Marie and Monsieur Louis, with Monsieur D'Aulnay, his secretary, arrived in Boston in a small pinnace, and Major Gibbons sent two of his chief officers to meet them at the water side, who conducted them to their lodgings *sine strepitu*. The public worship being ended the Governor repaired home, and sent Major Gibbons with other gentlemen, with a guard of Musketeers to attend them to the Governor's house, who meeting them without his door, carried them into his house, where they were entertained with wine and sweet meats, and after awhile he accompanied them to their lodgings (being the house of Major Gibbons, where they were entertained that night). Here they did stick two days. . . . The Lord's day they were here, the Governor acquainting them with our manner, that all men either come to our meetings, or keep themselves quiet in their houses, and finding that the place where they lodged would not be convenient for them that day, invited them home to his house, where they continued private all that day until sunset, and made use of such books, Latin or French, as he had, and the liberty of a private walk in his garden, and so gave no offence. . . ."[1]

On that Sunday in 1646, the Governor hastened to receive these three French Catholics officially at his own house. Here, for their comfort, he kept them where they could continue "*private all that day until sunset.*" He left them free to read his books, and have "the liberty of *a private walk in his garden.*" We conclude that the garden must have been enclosed, or it would not have been private.

These French visitors to Boston were men of importance; they could not, because of their religion, comply with the universal custom by attending divine service in the Meeting House of Boston. And so the Governor, who had perhaps the best garden, invited them to enjoy this, together with such books and things of interest as he possessed. They must of course continue private, so that no scandal might occur to the Puritan mind. It seems most unlikely that the walled garden offered for this purpose could have been other than a pleasure garden.

THE HOUSE AND GARDENS OF ANDREW FANEUIL AND HIS NEPHEW PETER

Andrew Faneuil was one of the Huguenots who escaped from France after the revocation of the Edict of Nantes. His name and that of his brother Benjamin, the father of Peter, appear on a list of those admitted from the French nation into the Bay Colony by the Governor and Council on February 1, 1691. They were men of property. The name of Andrew Faneuil appears on the tax list of Boston in that

[1] From *The History of New England, 1630–1649*, by John Winthrop. Edited by James Savage.

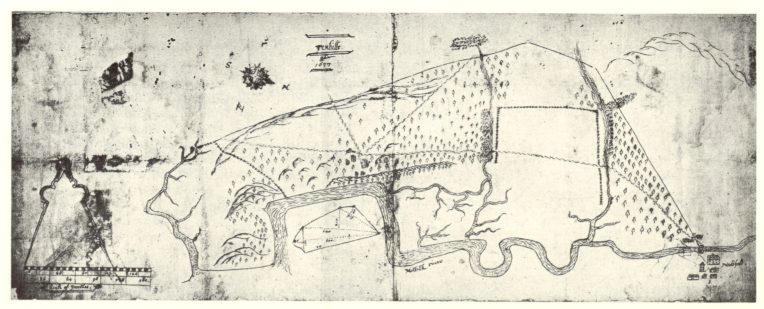

Governor Winthrop's Ten Hills farm, a few miles out on the Mystic River. One of the first plans of an estate in New England

same year; he was soon established in a profitable business and was the holder of large real-estate interests in the city. His mansion-house on the easterly slope of Beacon Hill was erected about 1700. It stood on Tremont Street, opposite King's Chapel Burying Ground, and from an elevated situation commanded a fine view.

Seven acres of garden surrounded the Faneuil house. They abounded in everything that wealth could provide, and we may be sure that they were tended with the greatest skill, as the Huguenots[1] were acknowledged to be the best gardeners, fruit and vine growers in all the world.

Peter Faneuil, from the painting by John Smibert in the possession of the Massachusetts Historical Society

Andrew Faneuil, evidently a man of strong character, piques the interest; we should like to know more about so individual a figure. He designated his nephew Benjamin as his heir on the provision that the latter remain unmarried. When he did marry he was turned out of his uncle's house, and the choice fell on nephew Peter, who thereafter lived with his uncle in great luxury and style as "heir presumptive."

The death of Andrew Faneuil in February, 1738, was an occasion of great importance in Boston and throughout the province. Contemporary reports have it that three thousand pairs of mourning gloves were distributed to friends in attendance at the funeral, and that later two hundred mourning rings were given to the nearer

[1]The Johonnot garden was another famous Huguenot garden in the Boston of this period. Unfortunately no details survive.

friends. The estates were bequeathed to Peter Faneuil. Added to his own acquisitions they made him the Merchant Prince of his day—"the topiniest merchant in all the town," in the words of Thomas Hancock. He lived on in the house built by his uncle, which is thus described in an existing account[1]:

"The Faneuil residence was a magnificent mansion of the time standing back from the street, in the midst of the ample garden with its many attractions. The deep courtyard, ornamented with flowers and shrubs, was divided into an upper and lower platform, by a high glacis[2], surrounded by a richly wrought railing decorated with gilt balls. The terraces which rose from the paved court behind the house were supported by massive walls of brown granite, and were ascended by flights of steps of the same material. One of the ornaments of this tasteful garden was a summer house which resembled an Eastern pagoda, and from the little spire which surmounted it there glittered and whirled about in olden times a gilded grasshopper, for a vane, in imitation of the one upon the Royal Exchange in London."

In his garden, long remembered for its choice fruits and flowers, Peter Faneuil showed that he had tastes and ambitions in keeping with his fortune. He sent to London for gardeners, and set up hothouses, for the cultivation of choice tropical fruits, making himself one of the pioneers in this field in America. He "cherishes the good old-fashioned flowers 'quaint in form and bright in hue,'" and in our mind's eye walks through his seven-acre garden with that satisfied air of self-possession that is reflected in his pseudonym, "The Jolly Bachelor"—a name which he also gave to one of his ships.

In 1740, Peter Faneuil conceived the idea of presenting the town of Boston with the market building for which he is now chiefly remembered. It was completed in 1742, and his death occurred the following year. His mansion and garden then became the property of the Phillips family. The place belonged to the Vassall family during the Revolution, was confiscated during that time, and in December, 1783, was sold by the Commonwealth to Isiah Doane.

[1]*Faneuil Hall and Faneuil Hall Market*, by Abram English Brown, which is also the source of the facts in this account.
[2]Glacis: used as a synonym of terrace.

Western view of Faneuil Hall. From a woodcut made in 1838

The Faneuil-Phillips house, built by Andrew Faneuil about 1700

THE THOMAS HANCOCK HOUSE AND GROUNDS[1]

Very little has been said or written about the first owner of the Hancock house which formerly stood on Beacon Hill, Boston. It was Thomas Hancock who built the house, and his success in business brought him an immense fortune for those days. Except for his wealth and the position his nephew derived from being his heir, it is doubtful if the younger Hancock would have become such a public figure to future generations.

In 1733, Thomas Hancock's partner, Henchman, built for himself a residence on Queen Street, the Court Street of today. It was situated on the south side of the street between Court Square and Tremont Street. Perhaps this made Hancock ambitious to have a home of his own suitable to his increasing prosperity. Shrewd in his purchases, he desired an ample site, in a good situation, not too far from the settled part of the south end of the town, and to be had at a reasonable price. Such a location he found on the southern slope of Beacon Hill.

Thomas Hancock purchased the land in September, 1735, but it was not until the next summer that he began operations. In June, 1736, he asked his associates on the board of selectmen for liberty to grade the street in front of his land. He was given permission to gravel the street, giving it a width of thirty feet, providing he prevented the gravel washing onto the Common and spoiling the herbage. By 1739 the way in front of his house was so much used by carts that he complained of its being spoiled. Although the Common had been railed in on the Tremont Street Mall in 1733, rails were not put up along Beacon Street until five years later. At that time the water ran down from Beacon Hill across the Common and then down Winter Street, to the great inconvenience of the residents.

In the fall he prepared his land for the site of his house. The following record has come down to us:

"I the Subscriber oblidge myself for Consideration of forty pounds to be well & truly paid me by Thos. Hancock Doe undertake to layout the upper garden allys. Trim the Beds & fill up all the allies with such Stuff as Sd Hancock shall order and Gravel the Walks & prepare and Sodd ye Terras adjoining with the Slope on the side next to Mr. Yeomans land, Likewise I oblidge myself to layout the next garden or flatt from the Terras below and carry on the mold thereto belonging and fill up all the walks with Gravel & finish all off Compleat workman like this fall to the satisfaction of said Hancock.

(Signed) WILL^M GRIGG"

"In witness whereof I have hereunto set my hand this 4th day of October 1736

(Signed) NATH^L GLOVER."

William Grigg was by occupation a gardener. But Hancock was not satisfied with native talent in landscape gardening, and so wrote to James Glin (or Glinn), a London gardener or seedsman, as follows:

"BOSTON, Decem^r 20th, 1736.
"Mr. James Glin Sir
My Trees and Seeds of Capt. Bennett Came Safe to hand and I like them very well. I Return you my hearty Thanks for the Plumb Tree & Tulip Roots you were pleased to make a Present of which are very Acceptable to me. I have sent my friend Mr. Wilks a memo to procure for me 2 or 3 Doz Yew Trees Some Hollys & Jessamine Vines & if you

Thomas Hancock, from the painting by Copley in Harvard University

have any Particular Curious Things not of a high price that will Beautify a flower Garden Send a sample with the price of a Catalogue of 'em pray send me a Catalogue of what Fruit you have that are Dwarf Trees and Espaliers I shall want some next Fall for a Garden I am Going to lay out next Spring. My Gardens all Lye on the South Side of a hill with the most beautiful Assent to the top & its allowed on all hands the Kingdom of England don't afford so Fine a Prospect as I have both of land & water. Neither do I intend to Spare any Cost or pains in making my Gardens Beautiful or Profitable. If you have any knowledge of Sir John James he has been on the Spott & is perfectly acquainted with its Situation & I believe has as high an opinion of it as myself, and will give it as great a Carricter. Let me know also what you'l take for 100 small Yew Trees in the rough which I'd frame up here to my own fancy. If I can do you any Service here I shall be glad & be assured I'll not forget your favor which being ye needful concludes Sr."

John James, referred to in the foregoing letter, was clerk of the works at Greenwich Hospital from 1705 until his death in 1746. He worked under Wren, Vanbrugh, Campbell and Ripley. He became master carpenter at St. Paul's Cathedral in 1711 and later became surveyor. In 1716 he was chosen surveyor of fifty new London churches. In 1725 he was surveyor of Westminster Abbey. He designed the church of St. George, Hanover Square, and that at Twickenham; also the manor house opposite the church at Twickenham. He designed and altered many other churches and houses in England up to the year 1736. The most likely period for his visit to Boston was in 1736, when it is not improbable that he was consulted by Thomas Hancock as to the architecture of the house to be erected.

Hancock's importation of shrubs and seeds turned out badly, as may be seen from the following letter to the London gardener:

"BOSTON, June 24th, 1737.

"Mr. James Glinn Sr

"I Recd your Letter & Baskett of flowers & Capt. Morris & have desired Francis Wilks Esq to pay you 26 for them Though they are every one Dead. The Trees I received Last Year are about half Dead. The Hollys all dead but one. most of the Ewe Trees will do well, & worse than all, is the Garden Seeds & Flower Seeds which you sold Mr. Wilks for me Charged at £6-8-2 sterling were not worth one farthing. Not one of all the seeds came up Except the Asparrow Grass, So that my Garden is Lost to me this Year. I Tryed the Seeds both in Town in Country & all proved alike bad. I Spared Mr. Hubbard part of them & they Served him the same I think you have not done well by me in this thing for me to send a 1000 Leagues Lay out my money and be so used and Disappointed is very hard & I doubt not but what you Consider the matter & Send me over Some more of the Same Sorts of Seeds that

From a drawing by J. Davis, engraved about 1850 by T. Illman
The Hancock house (1736), the first house erected on Beacon Hill

return me the money or send me the same sortment of seeds that are good."

From these records we learn that Thomas Hancock, who would "spare no cost or pains" in making his gardens beauti-

Courtesy of the Massachusetts Historical Society
"*View of the Seat of His Excellency John Hancock, Esq., Boston,*" from the engraving by Hill in "*The Massachusetts Magazine*"
for July, 1789

are Good & Charge me nothing for them & if you don't I shall think you have imposed upon me very much & will Discourage me from ever sending again for Trees or Seeds. If you put me up any let them be left at Mr. Wilks. I design to send in the fall of ye Year for a number of fruit Trees to Come next Spring. I am of opinion the Spring will be the best time to bring them to this Country. The Tulip Roots you were pleased to make a present of to me are all Dead. I Conclude Your Humble Servt."

To which we adjoin an extract from another letter:

"That all the Seed he put up for me last Year (Except the Asparagus) was not worth one farthing, not one of them came up, they cost me £6-8-2 it was a great Damage to me & he ought to make me Good, for to send so far pay dear & be Imposed upon at such a Rate is hard to Bare and he must

ful, first employed William Grigg and Nathaniel Glover of Boston to build his terraces and grade his grounds, but, fearing that they might not be all he desired, then consulted James Glinn, landscape architect and seedsman of London. From him he ordered yew trees, hollies and jessamine vines, and inquired about one hundred small yew trees in the rough that he might exercise his own fancy in topiary work. That these yews and hollies would not stand the climate of Boston we are not surprised to learn. The trials of all new enthusiasts were Hancock's as well, as appears in his letter of protest. He also consulted an English architect named John James, who probably visited Boston in 1736.

After Thomas Hancock's death, the place was willed to his widow, who lived there and maintained and enjoyed the garden for some years. At her death in 1777 the property went to John Hancock, who took immense pride in all the

A photograph of the Hancock house made about 1856. The house was torn down in 1863

fine points of the house and grounds, living there until his death in 1793. George Spriggs was gardener for John Hancock, and was evidently authorized to sell fruit trees from the nursery, as we may gather from the following correspondence between Henry Pelham and John S. Copley, which incidentally sheds light on Boston taste in tree planting in the 1770's.

Pelham wrote to Copley from Boston on September 10, 1771:

"I did not intend after so long a letter as that of this date to have wrote so soon but this is to let you know that you can procure Lime Trees from Spriggs, Mr. Handcock's Gardner. He will furnish trees, plant them, and warrant them for 18 Shillings O. T. a peice. This will I imagine be cheaper than they can be procured from New York for, considering Risque, Frieght etc. Spriggs's Trees are four Years old and 12 feet high. If you think proper to have them planted this fall (which I think by all meens would be best) let me know as soon as convenient that there may be a first choice. Mr. Spriggs says he can supply you with every fruit tree, flowering Tree except the Tulip shrub or Bush, that you want. that he will plant them and not receive his pay till it is known weither the Tree lives or not, and that he will supply you as cheap and as well as any Gardner in America. . . .

"P. S. The Tulip Trees are plenty with you and it would be no damage if you was to send some of them by Capt. S.
　　　　　　　　　　　　　　　　　　　　Good Night"

Copley did not purchase lime trees from John Hancock's garden, however, to judge by this extract from his reply, written from New York on September 20th:

". . . Mrs. Copley thinks Locust Trees much better than Lime. I am of the same opinion. the way to Judge is to go at a distance and see if the locust will not be so high that you may see the house under the boughs. I think they will and that the lime will intercept the sight. The Locust is much quicker growth and much cheaper. . . ."

The latest record we find of the Hancock garden is one

made by a Miss Gardner of Leominster in 1862. She wrote that she spent her tenth or eleventh year (1806 or 1807) with her great-aunt in the Hancock house. After describing the house and grounds in general, she continues: "The remainder was a splendid garden, with a summer house. It was laid out in ornamental flower beds enclosed in Box, with a great many box trees and a good variety of fruit trees and several immense mulberry trees." These were the mulberry trees planted by Thomas Hancock in 1736, but the box was of John Hancock's time.

The garden of Thomas and John Hancock is long since gone. The house was torn down in 1863, and Beacon Street is solidly built up where the house and gardens were.

THE HOUSES AND GARDENS OF JOSEPH BARRELL

Joseph Barrell (1729-1804) was a leading merchant whose ships went to the ends of the earth. He was actively interested in horticulture, and through him many new shrubs and plants were introduced from China. The elaborate gardens of his house in Boston are briefly described in the diary of the Rev. Wm. Bentley, who dined at Barrell's home on June 12th, 1791.

"Was politely received by Mr. Barrell who shewed me his large and elegant arrangements for amusement and philosophic experiment. His birds played in a globe of water in which the fish play. . . . He was an adventurer in the first voyage to the back parts of America and has several great curiosities. . . . His house is elegant in all its furniture. His

A southern view of the State House, from a woodcut made in 1838. It was built upon the ground which was Thomas and John Hancock's pasture

garden is beyond any example I have seen. A young grove is growing in the background, in the middle of which is a pond, decorated with four ships at anchor, and a marble figure in the centre. The Chinese manner is mixed with the European in the Summer house which fronts the House, below the Flower Garden. Below is the Hot House. In the apartment above are his flowers admitted more freely to the air, and above a Summer House with every convenience. The Squares are decorated with Marble figures as large as life. No expense is spared to render the whole amusing, instructive and friendly."

In 1792 another house was building for Barrell on Cobble Hill, Charlestown. It became an impressive establishment, evidently the centre of beautiful grounds and gardens, of which, regrettably, we know almost nothing. Timothy Dwight in 1799 wrote: "It is now a beautiful plantation & considering the short period since it was begun, highly improved. The house furnishes one of the best prospects of this charming country."

This Charlestown house, which stood for approximately a century, was one of the first houses built by Charles Bulfinch, the architect, and comprised many notable architectural features, which have no place in this account. Among them might be mentioned an interesting double staircase treatment and an oval parlor projecting on the garden side, in the manner of the design adopted in the same year for the president's house in Washington. Above was a semicircular portico with tall columns. This design was later followed in the famous Elias Hasket Derby house in Salem, which was planned by Bulfinch and modified and executed by Samuel McIntire.

Joseph Barrell and Charles Bulfinch were two of the twenty-eight gentlemen who petitioned to have the Massachusetts Society for Promoting Agriculture incorporated. An Act of the Legislature passed March 7th, 1792, established the incorporation.

Joseph Barrell. From the pastel by J. S. Copley in the Worcester Art Museum

KIRK BOOTT'S GARDEN

Some time during the year 1797, Kirk Boott, merchant of Boston from 1783 until his death in 1817, bought of Thomas Bulfinch "three fourths of an acre of land extending a little East of Bowdoin Square to Bulfinch Street and back to Ashburton Place," then known as "Bulfinche's Pastures," although this same property, as early as 1695, had "comprised a house and garden" of which one John Newgate was the owner.

On this site in 1804 Kirk Boott placed his house and garden.

Joseph Coolidge, second, had already built "his large mansion" on the west corner of Bowdoin Square in 1791. George W. Lyman's "Recollections" of other nearby gardens are: "At Green and Chardon Streets was Mr. Samuel Parkman's estate with a large garden and on Green that of Mr. Samuel Gore and on Bowdoin Square and Chardon the estate of Gov. Gore garden and land, and the estates of Joseph Coolidge second and Kirk Boott."[1]

Kirk Boott had admired Boston from that day in early June when he "landed on Long Wharf . . . after a quick voyage being only five weeks from Gravesent and from the Lizard 26 days, two or three weeks sooner than the general run of vessels." That very day he walked in a garden belonging to his lodging house, and "saw kidney beans a foot high, cucumbers more than that long, things are forwarder than with us . . . peas have been in a week. . . . The Landlady asked me if I would chuse a rose. . . . Three or four were brought me and pleased I snuffed their fragrance. Boston is an irregular place but stands very pleasantly, the entrance to the town is beautiful indeed—O England, what hast thou been doing to lose this country, this land so fine, so fertile!"

A year or so later, Kirk Boott journeyed on horseback through Lynn, Salem, Beverly, Newburyport, etc. Although he was told that he had "seen estates as good as any in America," he remarked that "in Nursery and Gardens and outward accomplishments . . . houses seem to want much. 'Tis true here are gardens but they are kept in a slovenly manner without taste or neatness. . . . The rich luxuriance of England is never to be seen here, but in viewing America, it should never be judged by that standard."

The front of Kirk Boott's lot in Boston was enclosed partly by a low picket fence and partly by the house extension, while high walls encircled the rest of the "Estate." Flower beds surrounded the house on three sides, and a wide border lay along the Bulfinch Street wall to the south, extending its whole length.

Against the rear of the house were placed trellises on which were grown fruits espaliered; behind was the greenhouse and several "frames," with a stable on the extreme southwest.

[1]Except for Kirk Boott's garden, extant records afford no knowledge of the details of these gardens.

Wide rectangular beds divided by paths made up the rest of this garden.

Gardening was indeed one of Kirk Boott's chief pleasures. His son wrote: "My father was often in his garden and about his frames by four o'clock" (A.M.). The following extracts from Kirk's letters to his sister in England give some idea of the plants which he cultivated with such loving care.

December 16, 1805 ". . . . My greenhouse has flourished and I have roses, jasmines, geraniums and stocks in bloom, and Rory's bulbs are shooting above the earth, but as yet I have had nothing to put my skill to the test. The season has been uncommonly mild, but ere January shall be past Jack Frost will give us trouble enough. If that bold intruder can be kept out, I promise myself much pleasure in it [greenhouse] during the latter part of February, March and April; at which time we have but little vegetation. I have taken great pains to keep lettuce alive through the winter and have more of it now than I ever had in St. Peter's parish."

And again on April 15, 1806, he wrote:

"Winter yet bears her sway, the frost is yet in the ground, little or no ploughing or gardening done, scarcely any vestage of spring appearing. My greenhouse has flourished beyond my expectations, and what pleases me much is that I have found my skill equal to the care of it. Lettuces in abundance I have preserved and have had salads thro' the winter. Yesterday I gathered about a bushel and gave them to my friends."

June 3, 1807 ". . . . The products of earth are very backward but we expect to have them in great abundance, fruit trees never exhibited a more promising appearance. We have a greater plenty of fruits than you have and some kinds in greater perfection, such as Apples, Pears and Peaches. I have my doubts whether Strawberries and Cherries are not better with you than here, Gooseberries, Currants and Plums are decidedly better with you. . . . Send me a receipt to preserve apricots."

June 10, 1809. "Our chief pleasure is in our family and among our flowering plants. Flora has decked our parlor windows for four months past in the most gay and beautiful manner. She is now about transferring her beauties to the open garden. I have more than one hundred rose trees of the best kinds just bursting into bloom, from the Moss down to the Scotch Mountain, the Cluster, Monthly Red, the Cabbage, the Province, Pompon, De Meaux, Burgundy, Blanford, Violet, White Musk, etc., etc., etc. From the first dawn of vegetation I have a succession of flowers. The modest Snowdrop, the golden Crocus, Daffodils, Narcissis, Hyacinths, Cowslips, Tulips etc. Those from Derby never blow but with the most pleasing association of ideas. The Common Weeds of my garden are the greenhouse Geraniums, Balsams, Coxcombs, Botany-Bay, Xeranthemums, Palms-Christi, China Asters, Lavatera, Convolvulus, Mignonette, etc. . . . The White Hawthorne is now in full bloom."

Dr. Francis Boott's comments upon this letter add a few more plants to the list.

"My father's taste in flowers was the true one. It had no ostentation about it, and the familiar 'weeds' of his garden were his delight. His roses, stocks, Persian Iris, and Lily of the Valley were the pride of his Garden, as the Heath and Geraniums were of his greenhouse. His salads and cucumbers were the height of his pride as a vegetable grower and I re-

A view of Boston from the road to Dorchester, published in 1776 by J. F. W. Barres Esq.; drawn by W. Pierrie and engraved by James Newton

member with pleasure the Sunday mornings when he called me up early to be his messenger to his friends."

Dr. Boott also informs us that "the seeds for the garden were always imported from England from Minier's in the Strand."

That other and rarer plants found their way to this Bowdoin Square garden is gleaned from the *Memorial History of Boston*. In the chapter on Horticulture, Marshall P. Wilder wrote in 1881:

"Another garden, which was spread around the present site of the Revere House was that of Kirk Boott, an eminent merchant. . . . Here fifty years ago were fruit trees and vines; and foreign grapes and other tender fruits which now succeed only under glass grew in the open air. Here was also a greenhouse with a choice collection of plants.

"Some of these were obtained from the Duke of Bedford and others in England through the acquaintance which Dr. Francis Boott (celebrated Botanist in London) had with such growers.

"The collections of Amaryllises and Orchids were the best in the country, the latter having been the first attempt in New England in the culture of this tribe of plants. Here, forty years ago, was a magnificent specimen of the Phaius grandiflora (now Bletia Tankervilleae) then a rare plant."

An interesting note from the same source tells of the final destination of the collections of amaryllises and orchids:

"Mr. Boott (Kirk II) presented these to the Hon. John A. Lowell, from whence some . . . went to . . . Edward S. Rand, of Dedham, and to which he made a large addition by importation from Europe, and were finally given by him and his friend James Lawrence to the Botanic Garden at Cambridge." The latter had its origin about 1801.

The life of Kirk Boott's Bowdoin Square garden was about 35 years. Samuel A. Drake wrote in his *Landmarks of Boston*:

"Before the work of demolition began in Bowdoin Square, it was the seat of many elegant old time estates with . . . gardens and noble trees of which but a solitary specimen here and there is left. The Revere House, from which Webster harangued the citizens, is on the ground and residence of Kirk Boott."

Over one hundred years have elapsed since Kirk Boott's life on earth ended. His house passed out of the family, and in 1847, on what is the "garden front" of the picture, were planted the back buildings of an hotel. Then the picket fence along Cambridge Street was removed, the city pavement crept to the foundation walls, and left no trace of the gay flower beds that stretched each side of the graceful iron railings. The beautiful entrance porch, with its dignified old door, was in place as late as 1919. Then a devastating fire so gutted the old building that shortly afterwards it was razed.[1]

CAMBRIDGE

Newtowne, now Cambridge, on the Charles River, is mentioned by Wood in his "New England's Prospect" in 1633:

"This is one of the neatest and best compacted towns of New England, having many fine structures, with many handsome contrived streets. The inhabitants, some of them are very rich, and well stored with cattle of all sorts, having many hundred acres of land paled in with general fence, which is about a mile and a half long, which secure all their weaker cattle from the wild beasts. . . ."

The first house in Newtowne was that of Governor Dudley, built in the spring of 1631. The town was from the beginning a thriving venture, even though the original plan of making it the seat of government was not carried out. After the founding of Harvard College in 1637, the name was

[1]Adapted from a description by Mary Newbold Reed, great-granddaughter of the owner of the garden described. The sources of information are: Family letters found in the old homestead in Derby, England, many years after Kirk Boott's death, and notes on these letters by Dr. Francis Boott, his son; "Gleaners" articles from the Boston Transcript, published in 1855, by Nathaniel I. Bowditch; *The Crooked and Narrow Streets of the Town of Boston*, by Annie Haven Thwing; *Landmarks of Boston*, by Samuel A. Drake; "Horticulture in Boston," by Marshall Pinckney Wilder, and "Recollections of the Garden and Open Grounds of Boston, and a few notes," by Mr. George W. Lyman, both to be found in the *Memorial History of Boston*, edited by Justin Winsor in 1881.

changed to Cambridge, in honor of the university in Cambridge, England.

In the middle of the eighteenth century, Cambridge was a favorite resort for wealthy Royalists, who built stately houses, surrounded by gardens and pleasure grounds.

THE JOHN VASSALL-CRAIGIE-LONGFELLOW HOUSE AND GARDEN[1]

One of the largest houses of the Cambridge of this period was built by John Vassall, Jr., on Brattle Street. An iron chimney-back dated 1759 undoubtedly indicates the year in which the house was constructed. As John was married in 1761 to Elizabeth, daughter of Robert Oliver, the house presumably was built in anticipation of the marriage.

Implicit in the history of the house is that alternation of care and neglect which has been the lot of so many colonial gardens.

For a number of years John Vassall lived quietly in Cambridge and interested himself in public affairs. When the Revolution came he was exiled as an ardent Loyalist. His estates were declared confiscated by the act of the Continental Congress in 1778.

During the winter of 1775 Washington made his headquarters in the house, sending for Mrs. Washington to join him. She made the journey from Mount Vernon in a chariot with four horses, with black postilions in scarlet and white livery. After the evacuation of Boston in 1776 Washington left the headquarters, and there was no one in the house until it was bought in 1781 by Nathaniel Tracy of Newburyport.

Later the estate was bought by Dr. Andrew Craigie, who lived there from 1793 until his death in 1819. He was one of the first members of the Massachusetts Society for Promoting Agriculture. In his day the place was the centre of a large farm and had an important garden, with greenhouses.

From the Craigie estate the house passed in 1843 to Henry Wadsworth Longfellow, who was deeply interested in the old grounds and gardens and made every effort to keep and restore all that was possible of its past.

The Vassall-Craigie-Longfellow house (1759) was a great place in the Vassall and Craigie days. It was Washington's headquarters while he was in command of the army in Cambridge. See also page 433

left his wife heavily involved in debt, however, and the land was gradually disposed of, until at the time of Longfellow's occupancy there remained but eight acres. The pond, west of the house, was planted romantically. It lay close to Brattle Street beyond the field where Longfellow's daughters built their houses. Since Longfellow's death in 1882, the estate has remained in the possession of the family.

THE BRATTLE HOUSE AND GARDENS

A few paces west of Brattle Square, on the south side of Brattle Street, still stands the Brattle house, shorn now of all that once made it beautiful, but surrounded by traditions of the charm of the grounds of which it once formed a part.

The earliest owner of the estate was Simon Crosby, who came from England in the *Susan and Ellen* in 1634. Later the place came into the hands of the Brattle family, and in 1727 General William Brattle began to build the house.

General William Brattle was a Tory, and during the Revolution retired to Boston. The house fell into the hands of the patriots, becoming the headquarters of Major Mifflin. General Brattle died at Halifax, Nova Scotia, in 1776. Before his death he gave a bill of sale of the property to his son, Thomas Brattle, then in England.

When the war was finally over, Mrs. Katharine Wendell, General Brattle's daughter, came to look at the house where she was born, now empty again. She was a woman of strong character, and it was because of her efforts and her friendships with the patriots that the Brattle property was not confiscated. Her brother, Thomas Brattle, born in 1742, returned after the popular indignation against his father

From "Beautiful Gardens in America," by Louise Shelton. Photograph by The J. Horace McFarland Co.

Longfellow's garden, in Cambridge

The original Vassall estate had comprised one hundred and fifty acres, and even in Dr. Craigie's time the hill now occupied by the observatory (Harvard Observatory) was part of the garden. On that hill was a spring from which water was carried to the house by a small aqueduct. Dr. Craigie's death

[1]Facts from *Historic Guide to Cambridge,* Hannah Winthrop Chapter D. A. R.

had subsided, and took possession of the estate. He enlarged the grounds and further beautified them; he built a green-house, one of the first in the country, and a bath for the Harvard students on the river. When he died in 1801, universally lamented, his property went to the heirs of his sister.

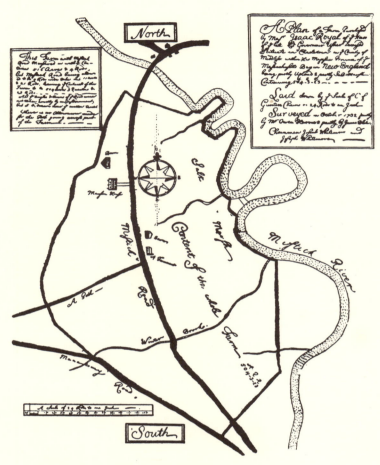

Plan of the Isaac Royall farm in Medford

We find the following account in the Rev. Wm. Bentley's diary[1] under date of Oct. 1, 1792:

"Upon my return I visited Mr. Brattle's Gardens . . . at Cambridge. We first saw the fountain and canal opposite to his house, and the walk on the side of another canal in the road, flowing under an arch and in the direction of the outer fence. There is another canal which communicates with a beautiful pool in the park. . . . The garden is laid out upon a pretty considerable descent and formed with terrace walks abounding with trees, fruits, and the whole luxury of vegetation, and is unrivalled by anything I have seen of the kind. The parterres are in fine order in the garden. The dairy room was the neatest I ever beheld. It was in stone and on the sides surrounded with a white Dutch tile in the excess of neatness. The Repositories for the several fruits were in fine order, the barns, yards, and all agreed with the same good order. . . ."

A few years later A. M. Holmes wrote a *History of Cambridge* which was published in 1801. This is his description of the Brattle gardens:

"The gardens of Thomas Brattle Esq. are universally admired for the justness of their design and for the richness,

[1]Vol. I, p. 398.

variety, and profusion of their production. In no part of New England probably is horticulture carried to higher perfection than within his inclosure. A mall adjoining his grounds, made in 1792 and shaded by handsome rows of trees, is a work of neatness and taste.

"During this summer a bath was erected at the brick wharf, principally for the benefit of the students of the University. It was made under the superintendence of Thomas Brattle Esq. and happily unites ornament with utility."

A much later description of the gardens is that of Marshall P. Wilder[1]:

"Thomas Brattle . . . returning from exile in 1783, took possession of his patrimony, the house which now bears his name, and began to improve his grounds according to the taste of a century ago; and from that time until his death in 1801 his garden, possessing a profusion of fruit and flowers, was the boast of Cambridge. His house was built by his father in 1742, when was planted, probably, the square of English lindens which so long formed a green canopy around it, but which have all fallen, the last one disappearing about fifteen years ago. Mr. Brattle with a native taste for horticulture, and with observation of foreign lands, no doubt laid out his grounds in the latest styles of Europe, having a spring of pure water, a marble grotto, a pond for gold-fish, and a parterre for aquatic plants, and a lower level where the University press now stands. His lawn was so velvet-like that it was said it could not be improved by combing it with a fine-tooth comb."

Thomas Brattle was a charter member of the Massachusetts Society for Promoting Agriculture.

COLONEL HENRY VASSALL'S HOUSE AND GARDEN

This house, called the Vassall House since 1763, is still standing on the easterly corner of Brattle and Hawthorn Streets. The western end of the house with its eight-foot-square stack chimney, the bricks of which are laid with

Isaac Royall Jr. (1719-1781) and his family. From the painting by Feke now in Landell Hall, Harvard University

pounded oyster shells instead of lime, may have been built by William Adams, to whom the homestead lot was granted March 12, 1635.

The plan of the house is entirely different from any other colonial house in Cambridge, and it is evident that additions

[1]*Memorial History of Boston*, edited by Justin Winsor.

have been made at various periods.

In 1741, John Vassall, Sr., sold this estate to his brother, Colonel Henry Vassall, who in 1742 married Penelope Royall of Medford, and brought her to this house. It is thought that in 1747 Henry Vassall built the brick wall on Brattle and Ash Streets which was moved back thirty feet when Brattle Street was widened in 1870, necessitating the cutting down of one hundred of the tall acacia trees that had been the Vassall hedge. This wall, which was a landmark, was surmounted by a coping formed of heavy boards like an inverted V.

The garden, which is south of the house, was stocked with fine fruit trees, brought from England and France. Of these only one ancient purple mulberry, still bearing fruit, is now to be seen. No trace remains of the hawthorn hedge that once bordered the west side of the present Hawthorn Street.

The west front of the Royall house, Medford, showing the garden entrance, and the garden wall and fence which are said to be faithful reproductions of the originals. The summer-house shown below once stood at the end of the path

THE CAMBRIDGE BOTANIC GARDEN

The Botanic Garden at Cambridge was established through the patronage of the Massachusetts Society for Promoting Agriculture, which in 1805 gave a liberal subscription for the founding of a professorship of Natural History at Harvard College. The Botanic Garden was the natural outcome. One of the members of the Society was sent abroad for a year's study of botanic gardens before assuming the directorship of the Garden.

When the Massachusetts Horticultural Society was founded in 1829, its first report states that "the plants were furnished by the Botanic Gardens at Cambridge and others." The Society's reports for the years 1834-5-6 include varied and most important lists of plants under cultivation in the Garden during these years. New varieties were introduced, and the influence exercised by the Cambridge Botanic Garden played an important part in the world of horticulture.

MEDFORD

ISAAC ROYALL'S HOUSE AND GARDEN

Colonel Isaac Royall bought in 1732 a large tract of land in Medford, a part of which was land that had been set off a century earlier to Governor Winthrop's Ten Hills farm.

Colonel Royall was one of the merchants who by successful trade, largely with Antigua, had amassed a considerable fortune. His fine house, three stories in height, stands today practically as it was built, with fine interior woodwork and good architectural detail throughout. Twenty-seven slaves were brought from Antigua, and their quarters still stand near the house—the only slave quarters remaining intact in New England.

We do not know just what the design of the garden was beyond the main path, and nothing remains of the trees or plants of the Royall days. But that it was a handsome and dignified lay-out we may be sure, as Captain Francis Goelet said in 1750 that it was one of the grandest in America. The garden was planned with its main path on a direct axis with the main entrance. Thus the door on the east front looked along the hall, through the door on the west front and across a paved courtyard, through the gate in the garden wall, and down the main path to a mound about five hundred feet from the west front. This mound was surmounted by a

summer-house, shown in the illustration. The graceful ornament that surmounted the summer-house was a weather-vane swinging on a metal rod. It was a "Flying Mercury," about five feet high, carved of wood and originally gaily painted. The mound upon which the summer-house stood was ap-

Isaac Royall's summer-house, photographed before it was destroyed. The mound on which it stood was west of the house, on a perfect axis with the front door and the gate in the wall. The "Flying Mercury" weather-vane atop the summer-house was carved of wood in the eighteenth century

proached by two terraces in which were set stone steps.

This garden was the scene of much gayety until the shadow of the Revolution fell on the Royall household. Isaac Royall, Jr., who had succeeded his father in 1741, was devoted to colonial life and had been most generous to his town and Commonwealth. By education and association he was a Tory, however, and sadly left his home, going to Halifax and later to England. He died in 1781. The property was held by the government until 1806. Up to 1905 it saw many changes in ownership. It is now restored and cared for by the Royall House Association. The battered remnant of the figure which surmounted the summer-house is preserved in a closet of the house.

ROXBURY

JOHN LOWELL, "THE ROXBURY FARMER"

JOHN LOWELL was born in Newburyport, a descendant of one of the first settlers.[1] His father, John Lowell, "the Judge," lived there until the Revolution and then moved to Roxbury, where he developed a large place which he named "Bromley Vale." When he died in 1802, his oldest son, the John Lowell of horticultural fame, inherited Bromley Vale.

This younger John Lowell, who is called in the family "The Roxbury Farmer", is a towering figure in the gardening and horticultural history of Massachusetts. He was a member of the Massachusetts Society for Promoting Agriculture, which had for him, through his parents, the closest associations: his mother, born Russell, was the daughter of the Society's first president, and his father had been the second president. The younger John Lowell was also one of the founders of the Massachusetts Horticultural Society, and his contribution to the spread of the influence of that organization is so important that it seems of interest to trace his activities in the Society, in phraseology borrowed largely from its History.

On the 24th of February, 1829, a meeting of sixteen gentlemen was convened for the purpose of instituting a Horticultural Society. The Hon. John Lowell was chosen Moderator. At the second meeting on the 24th of March of that year, it was voted that a committee be chosen to propose a list of honorary and corresponding members, and that Henry A. S. Dearborn, John Lowell, John C. Gray, Samuel G. Perkins, and Joseph G. Joy compose this committee.

The resultant lists of honorary and corresponding members are quoted in connection with this brief sketch of John Lowell's activity, since we must regard their high quality as an index of the breadth of vision and range of contacts of the man who made them possible. The First List of Honorary Members bore these names:

Adams, Hon. John Quincy, late President of the U. S.
Aiton, William Townsend, Curator of the Royal Gardens, Kew.
Abbott, John, Esq., Brunswick, Me.
Buel, J., Esq., President of the Albany Horticultural Society.
Bodin, Le Chevalier Soulange, Secrétaire-Général de la Société d'Horticulture de Paris.
Bancroft, Edwin Nathaniel, M. D., President of the Horticultural and Agricultural Society of Jamaica.
Barclay, Robert, Esq., Great Britain.
Coxe, William, Esq., Burlington, N. J.
Collins, Zaccheus, Esq., President of the Pennsylvania Horticultural Society, Philadelphia.
Coffin, Admiral Sir Isaac, Great Britain.
Dickson, James, Esq., Vice-President of the London Horticultural Society.
Davy, Sir Humphrey, London.

[1]Richard and Percival Lowle, who had been merchants of Bristol, are recorded as living in Newburyport as early as 1642.

De Candolle, Mons. Augustin Pyramus, Professor of Botany in the Academy of Geneva.
Eliot, Hon. Stephen, Charleston, S. C.
Grieg, John, Esq., Geneva, President of the Domestic Horticultural Society of the Western Part of the State of New York.
Héricart de Thury, Le Vicomte, Président de la Société d'Horticulture de Paris.
Hosack, David, M. D., President of the New York Horticultural Society.
Hopkirk, Thomas, Esq., President of the Glasgow Horticultural Society.
Hunt, Lewis, Esq., Huntsburg, Ohio.
Jackson, Andrew, President of the United States.
Knight, Thomas Andrew, Esq., President of the London Horticultural Society.
Loudon, John Claudius, Great Britain.
La Fayette, General, La Grange, France.
Lasteyrie, Le Comte de, Vice-Président de la Société d'Horticulture de Paris.
Madison, Hon. James, late President of the United States, Virginia.
Monroe, Hon. James, late President of the United States, Virginia.
Michaux, Mons. Andrew, Paris.
Mentens, Lewis John, Esq., Bruxelles.
Mitchell, Samuel L., M. D.
Mossemann—Esq., Antwerp.
Palmer, John, Esq., Calcutta.
Powell, John Hare, Powelton, Pa.
Prince, William, Esq., Long Island, N. Y.
Rosebery, Archibald John, Earl of, President of the Caledonian Horticultural Society.
Sabine, Joseph, Esq., Secretary of the London Horticultural Society.
Shephard, John, Curator of the Botanic Garden, Liverpool.
Scott, Sir Walter, Scotland.
Turner, John, Assistant Secretary of the London Horticultural Society.
Thacher, James, M. D., Plymouth, Mass.
Thorburn, Grant, Esq., New York.
Vilmorin, Mons. Pierre Phillipe André, Paris.
Vaughn, Benjamin, Esq., Hallowell, Maine.
Van Mons, Jean Baptiste, M. D., Brussels.
Vaughn, Petty, Esq., London.
Welles, Hon. John, Boston, Mass.
Willick, Nathaniel, M. D., Curator of the Botanic Garden, Calcutta.
Yates, Ashton, Esq., Liverpool.

The First List of Corresponding Members ran as follows:

Adlum, John, Georgetown, D. C.
Aspinwall, Col. Thomas, U. S. Consul, London.
Appleton, Thomas, Esq., U. S. Consul, Leghorn.
Barnett, Isaac Cox, Esq., U. S. Consul, Paris.
Carr, Robert, Esq., New Jersey.
Gardiner, Robert H., Esq., Gardiner, Maine.
Gibson, Abraham P., Esq., U. S. Consul, St. Petersburg.
Hall, Charles Henry, Esq., New York.
Hay, John, Architect of the Caledonian Horticultural Society.
Landreth, David, Esq., Philadelphia.
Landreth, David, Jr., Esq., Corresponding Secretary of the Pennsylvania Horticultural Society.
Maury, James, Esq., U. S. Consul, Liverpool.
Miller, John, M. D., Secretary of the Horticultural and Agricultural Society, Jamaica.
Mills, Stephen, Esq., Long Island, New York.
Newhall, Horatio, M. D., Galena, Illinois.
Offley, David, Esq., U. S. Consul, Smyrna.
Ombrose, James, Esq., U. S. Consul, Florence.

John Lowell, "The Roxbury Farmer" (1769-1840), was the most important force in the horticultural world of Massachusetts. From the painting by Stuart now in the possession of Mrs. John Lowell, widow of the great-grandson of John Lowell

Parker, John W., Esq., U. S. Consul, Florence.
Payson, John L., Esq., Messina.
Prince, William Robert, Esq., Long Island, New York.
Prince, Alfred Stratton, Long Island.
Smith, Daniel D., Esq., Burlington, New Jersey.
Smith, Caleb R., Esq., New Jersey.

From 1810 to 1822, the Hon. John Lowell was a member of the Corporation of Harvard University. His time, his acquirements, his exertions and his means were at the call of the best interests of the University. Where money was required, he subscribed liberally himself, and—a harder task—induced others to subscribe. The Botanical Department, which had been founded in a great measure by his father, was organized and furnished with a Professor. The Botanical Garden was laid out and planted. In all these operations and others, Lowell was "confessedly the principal agent, alert and unwearied."

In 1829, on Saturday, September 19th, the First Anniversary Festival of the Massachusetts Horticultural Society was held at the Exchange Coffee House. The dining hall was tastefully ornamented, and the tables were loaded with orange trees in fruit and flower, brought from Mr. Lowell's greenhouse. On this occasion, the forty-second toast, by T. Brewer Esq. of Roxbury, was tendered to "The Hon. John Lowell—the Maecenas of New England Horticulture. Himself a Patron, and his premises a Pattern of correct and scientific cultivation. . . ."

In 1830, at the Second Anniversary Festival, held Friday, Sept. 10th, at the Exchange Coffee House, John Lowell exhibited "a plant in flower of Musea coccinea; this plant had never been flowered before in this country."

In 1831, at the Third Annual Festival, William Prince, Sr., proprietor of the Linnaean Botanic Garden, gave the following toast: "The Hon. John Lowell—the distinguished patron and benefactor of Horticulture." At this meeting Mr. Lowell exhibited "a fine specimen of Erythrina picta, and Justicia picta—rare plants. And also a fine plant of the Banana Tree (Musa sapientum) with other rare and choice plants. . . ."

At the 1835 Festival he exhibited "a splendid Orange tree, laden with fruit; the Sweet Lime tree, an exceedingly rare plant; a fine specimen of the elegant Gomphocarpus:

Gloxinia maculata and speciosa, Plectranthus fruticosus, Ardisia solanacea, Justicia picta, Begonia argyrostigma, with many other ornaments of the greenhouse; and amongst a variety of cut flowers were the Canna speciosa, and the rare Strelitzia regina. . . ."

The *American Gardener's Magazine* of September, 1835, printed the following description of John Lowell's garden, Bromley Vale:

"This place is one of the oldest as well as one of the finest in our vicinity. The labours of Mr. Lowell have long been appreciated by the agricultural portion of our community. It is to him we are indebted for the introduction of many of our most esteemed fruits; and through his exertions they have been widely and extensively disseminated.

"In the greenhouse Mr. Lowell is trying the experiment of inarching off the young wood of camellias as practised by the English gardeners. . . . We here observed an extremely vigorous plant of the Ipomaea insignis in beautiful bloom; it was received from the Hon. and Rev. Wm. Herbert. From the axil of every leaf arises a panicle of flowers; they are of a rich purplish red. In the hot-house, Asclepias curassavica, Gloxinia speciosa[1], a plant of Cyrtanthus obliquus, with a spathe of flowers two feet high; also plants of Gloxinia maculata.[2]

"In the garden we observed various plants; Canna speciosa in the border in front of the greenhouse, Gomphocarpus arborescens, one of the Aclepidadaceae, upwards of ten feet high, and covered with bunches of white flowers; a species of Cassia, with brilliant yellow flowers, a fine plant of Poinciana pulcherrima, (Pride of Barbadoes) which was raised from seed last season, and Erythreina picta.

"We omit many other things deserving of mention. . . .

"One plant, however, we would not forget; this is the Nelumbium speciosum, the famous lily of the oriental waters. The plant is growing vigorously, and we should not wonder if it flowered in the course of the Fall. Mr. Lowell is not certain whether it is the white or blush variety, having received seeds from Dr. Nathaniel Wallich, curator of the Botanic Gardens at Calcutta, and an Honorary Charter Member of the Massachusetts Horticultural Society.

"There is also here quite a collection of Ixias, Tritonias, gladioluses etc. and a fine display may be anticipated in March and April."

We quote a note from a visitor to John Lowell's garden in 1838, who saw "Cacti to the number of twenty or more, which were brought from the West Indies, and many varieties of orchids." This collection of orchids was accounted the second in Massachusetts. Mention was also made in the note of the new and "truly elegant Clematis Sieboldii which flowered at Mr. Lowell's last summer." A study of the variety of plants cultivated at Bromley Vale is full of interest for the gardener of today.

John Lowell died in 1840. The following account[3] of a visit to him in his old age may best close our record of him:

". . . About two years since, we had the pleasure of visiting the seat of Mr. Lowell . . . whom we found in a green old age, still enjoying, with the enthusiasm of youth, the pleasures of Horticulture and a country life. For the encouragement of those, who are ever complaining of the tardy pace with which the growth of trees advances, we will here record that we accompanied Mr. L. through a belt of fine woods (skirting a part of his residence), nearly half a mile in length, consisting of almost all our finer hardy trees, many of them apparently full grown, the whole of which had been planted by him when he was thirty-two years old. At that time, a solitary elm or two, were almost the only trees upon his estate. We can hardly conceive a more rational source of pride or en-

joyment, than to be able thus to walk, in the decline of years, beneath the shadow of umbrageous woods and groves, planted by our own hands."

Bromley Vale with all its beauty is entirely gone, and Roxbury, which celebrates its three hundredth birthday in 1931, is now a part of greater Boston.

BROOKLINE

In the late eighteenth century, Brookline had already come to be regarded as "the garden of Boston," in the phrase of the Rev. William Bentley, whose diary records a visit there in 1791. He wrote:

"This little town of fifty families supplies a great part of the vegetation for that celebrated market, and is in a high stage of cultivation. . . ."

The years of teeming horticultural development from 1800 to 1840 brought into being in Brookline some of the finest gardens in the country, and made it a centre of gardening progress. In 1844 Andrew Jackson Downing wrote that "the whole neighborhood of Brookline is a kind of landscape garden." He added:

". . . there is nothing in America, of the sort, so inexpressibly charming as the lanes which lead from one cottage or villa to another. No animals are allowed to run at large, and the open gates with tempting vistas and glimpses under pendant boughs give it quite an Arcadian air of rural freedom and enjoyment. These lanes are clothed with a profusion of trees and wild shrubbery often almost to the carriage tracks, and curve and wind about in a manner quite bewildering to the stranger who attempts to thread them alone, and there are more hints here for the lover of the picturesque in lanes than we ever saw assembled together in so small a compass."[1]

THE GARDEN OF THOMAS HANDASYD PERKINS[2]

Especially notable in the early years of the nineteenth century were the Brookline gardens and greenhouses of Colonel Thomas Handasyd Perkins, a member of the Massachusetts Society for Promoting Agriculture. His natural taste for horticulture had been stimulated by the distinguished examples of gardening he had observed during residence in France and other foreign countries. In 1799 Colonel Perkins purchased the estate in Brookline and began the erection of a house, the laying-out of the grounds, and the rearing of greenhouses and glass structures for the cultivation of fruits and flowers. Until the establishment of the imposing conservatories and fruit-houses of his nephew, John Perkins Cushing, at Watertown, his place was considered more advanced in horticultural science than any other in New England. For half a century the highest level of gardening was maintained at an expense of more than $10,000 a year. Colonel Perkins employed experienced foreign gardeners, and frequently received trees and plants from abroad, displaying their products at the exhibitions of the Massachusetts Horticultural Society.

Perhaps the best view of Colonel Perkins' gardens, grounds, and greenhouses can be had through the eyes of those members of the Horticultural Society who visited the estate and recorded their findings.[3] Under date of January 20th, 1835, we read:

"This is an elegant residence, the large specimens of Pinus strobus, Abies canadensis, balsamifera and alba with others of their species, give the grounds a gay and lively appearance even at this dreary season of the year. There are several

---

[1]The forerunner of the modern greenhouse *Gloxinia*, which is really a *Sinningia*.

[2]The true *Gloxinia*, now little known in cultivation, being apparently unknown in the American trade, and only found in collections of rare plants in Europe. The flowers are white with a yellow-spotted throat.

[3]From *A Treatise on the Theory and Practice of Landscape Gardening, Adapted to North America*, by Andrew Jackson Downing, 1841.

[1]From the 2nd Edition (1844) of *A Treatise on the Theory and Practice of Landscape Gardening, Adapted to North America*, by A. J. Downing.

[2]Now the Shattuck garden, the sixth generation of direct descendants of Thomas Handasyd Perkins being in possession. The facts of this account are drawn from *The Memorial History of Boston*.

[3]"Calls at Gardens and Nurseries," in the *Magazine of Horticulture*, Vol. I, p. 73.

Photographed by Robert N. Cram

In the garden of Thomas Handasyd Perkins, Brookline. Old blue-green Chinese tile atop an ancient brick retaining wall covered with English ivy, with hybrid rhododendron in the foreground, and a venerable catalpa tree beyond

large clumps of the above which serve to break the view of the garden from the mansion, and the ride to the pleasure grounds winds away from the left of the garden through a grove, so dense that you but now and then catch a glimpse of its zigzag direction. . . . We entered the greenhouse from the garden by passing through the back shed, the other entrance being closed up till open weather. . . . The [main] entrance to the greenhouse . . . is by the avenue leading from the house under a grove of pines, cedars, and hemlocks, into and through two peacheries.

"In the greenhouse we found Mr. Cowan rearranging and cleaning up the plants, as they often need it during the winter.

"The first object which struck us, as in Mr. Cushing's, Mr. Lemist's and Mr. Wilder's greenhouses, was a magnificent plant of the double white Camellia, with above twenty fully expanded flowers. We did not know until these visits that there were so many large specimens of this beautiful plant in our vicinity, but we find them as plenty as the China rose. This plant was in the center of the house, and was surrounded by a large number of new and valuable varieties, which for vigorous growth and healthy appearance we have never seen

Photographed by Robert N. Cram

A greenhouse built in 1834, in the Thomas Handasyd Perkins garden, Brookline. To the left are espalier pears against a high brick wall.
Old box bushes are to be seen at the right

Photographed by Robert N. Cram

The old box walk, bordered by box bushes eight feet high, in the Thomas
Handasyd Perkins garden

equalled. Among those that now show the color of their buds and will open in a few days, are Camellia japonica, imbricata, rosa sinensis and gloriosa. Mr. Cowan has upwards of two hundred seedlings two to three years old. There is here a plant of the Enkianthus quinqueflorus belonging to the natural order Ericaceae; it was imported by Colonel Perkins three years since from the celebrated establishment of the Messrs. Loddiges, and is the only specimen in the country; it cost—*six guineas*. It is just showing its pink buds which hang in pendulous umbels, and will be open in a few days.[1] A large specimen of Strelitzea augusta, also very rare, is growing finely. Eriostemon cuspidatus is throwing out its spikes of buds. There are fine plants of Telopea speciosissima."

In September, 1835, the visitors noted in the garden the annual and other flowers blooming profusely. "The dahlias do not flourish very well. . . . A few very fine flowers were open."

In January, 1837, another visit was made and the camellias observed:

"We found very few plants in bloom. Some camellias were just beginning to expand. . . . Mr. Cowan's seedling camellias which we have before mentioned, have made a vigor-

[1]*Enkianthus quinqueflorus or campanulatus.* Drawings and specimens of *Enkianthus quinqueflorus* were first brought to England under the name of *Andromeda arborea* in 1794. Living plants were received in this country in 1832. It has quite recently been again introduced into our gardens by Mr. Ernest Wilson of the Arnold Arboretum.

ous growth. . . . This fine tribe seeds freely, if the flowers are impregnated, and a great number of plants have already been raised in the vicinity of Boston. We may look forward to the time when as beautiful varieties may be produced here as have been raised by Mr. Floy and others in New York."

In 1836 Colonel Perkins had two extensive ranges of glass houses, each about three hundred feet in length. One was devoted to the forcing of peaches and grapes. The axis of the central house was much higher and was devoted entirely to flowers. Connecting high brick walls were used for the general operation of the garden. In 1837 two new forcing houses were added, the length of the two being "upwards of one hundred feet." Colonel Perkins always sent exhibits to the shows of the Massachusetts Horticultural Society. Here are descriptive notes from some of the Society's reports:

(Exhibit) "Hon. T. H. Perkins: a bunch of very fine Dahlias."

1835. Annual Exhib. at the Odeon, situated in Federal Street, Boston, Sept. 16th and 17th—

"T. H. Perkins, from his magnificent and spacious glass houses in Brookline—Peaches: Noblesse, Early York, French Gallane, Grosse Gallande: also Red Roman Nectarines, all

Thomas Handasyd Perkins (1764-1854), from the portrait by Gambadella

very beautiful. Grapes: White Passe Musque, Black Lombardy, White Sweetwater, Black Frankendale, White Muscat of Alexandria, Black Hamburg, White· Syrian, Black St. Peter's, White Frontignac, Black Frontignac, Grizzly Frontinac, Black Cluster or Mennier, Barcelona Long White. These were beautifully arranged in clusters of different colors alternate, and with a fine effect. Such a variety of superior kinds has never been displayed, we believe, at any former exhibition. All were grown by the skill of Wm. H. Cowan. From the same sources a rare and new variety of squash. . . ."

Report of the Committee on Flowers and Plants—

". . . Col. T. H. Perkins, Brookline. A handsome frame work of flowers, on which grapes from his house were suspended; also a specimen of the flowers of Phaseolus Caracalla, a rare greenhouse plant of singular appearance and delightful fragrance."

Thomas Handasyd Perkins was an outstanding figure among those American gentlemen who were influenced by travel and the consequent familiarity with horticulture and landscape gardening to develop fine country estates from 1800 to 1840, when all over our country a great revival in interest in gardening was evident.

Photographed by Robert N. Cram

An ancient brick wall in the Thomas Handasyd Perkins garden, Brookline. To the right are an old box bush and espalier pear; to the left an arbor-vitae hedge and flowering dogwood

Courtesy of the Arnold Arboretum

Rhododendrons and pond in the garden of Holm Lea. In the early nineteenth century this was the Brookline garden of Thomas Lee

THE GARDEN OF SAMUEL G. PERKINS, BROOKLINE

The Perkins family were all distinguished gardeners. Marshall P. Wilder left the following description[1] of the garden of Samuel G. Perkins (1767–1847), a brother of Thomas Handasyd Perkins, and like him an active member of the Massachusetts Society for Promoting Agriculture.

"Next to be named are the garden and fruit-houses of Samuel G. Perkins which were presented to him by his brother, Col. Perkins. The spot was selected on account of its being situated between the Colonel's [Thomas Handasyd Perkins] and the beautiful estate at Pine Bank of James Perkins, an elder brother . . . and as a favorable place where Samuel might indulge his natural taste, and exercise the skill which he had acquired in horticultural science by residing in foreign lands, and by his acquaintance with experienced cultivators of both fruit and flowers. His fruit-houses were two hundred feet in length; and in and around them were grown the choicest varieties of grapes, peaches, and plums; there the Golden Nectarine was produced by him from the stone. Mr. Perkins was the introducer from France of the Duchesse d'Angouleme pear, the Franconia raspberry, and other fruits."

The following letter from Augustus T. Perkins gives an interesting sidelight on the zeal of Samuel G. Perkins as a gardener:

"He attended personally to the pruning and cultivation of his trees; and his success was greater than that of his brother. He usually wore a button-hole bouquet in the lapel of his coat and was fond of surprising his brother with superior fruits. One day he came with a basket of gorgeous grapes,

[1]From *Memorial History of Boston*, edited by Justin Winsor.

peaches and apricots, and said, 'Brother Tom, I know you love fine fruit, and fearing you do not often get it, I have brought you something.'

"'Thank you, Brother Sam, I try to be contented with what I have, and certainly should be, if you were not always bursting in and giving me something that makes me envy you.'"

Contemporary with John Lowell, Samuel G. Perkins was "The Roxbury Farmer's" staunch ally in promoting horticultural activities.

THE GARDENS OF THOMAS LEE: AFTERWARDS "HOLM LEA," JAMAICA PLAIN

Thomas Lee was a charter member of the Massachusetts Horticultural Society at its founding in 1829, and hardly a report read by the Society from that time until 1840 fails to make mention of fine specimens, new varieties, or rare plants exhibited by Mr. Lee. In the report of 1837 was published a most interesting article describing Mr. Lee's experiments with native trees, shrubs and plants. It comments upon his success with the native orchids, and remarks especially his extensive planting of rhododendrons, kalmias, and azaleas, as well as of the northern and southern magnolia. His principal contribution to horticulture, however, lay in his experiments with plants and trees hardy in Massachusetts.

In 1835 the *American Gardener's Magazine*[1] thus described a visit to Thomas Lee's gardens:

"This beautiful place is situated near Jamaica Pond and is nearly thirty acres in extent. . . . The past spring he [Thomas Lee] has set out in different parts of his grounds, a

[1]No. IX, September, 1835.

"Sevenels," in Brookline, the garden of the late Miss Amy Lowell, who inherited the house of her grandfather, John Amory Lowell, son of John Lowell of Bromley Vale, Roxbury. (See page 40)

large number of single red camellias, Arbutus unedo, Rhododendron ponticum, English laurel etc. with the anticipation that they can be made to endure our climate. Each side of the Avenue from the road to the house, he has set out a hedge intermixed together, Kerria japonica, Scotch and other roses for nearly a hundred feet. These are set in double rows, on a banking that rises three or four feet from the avenue. They are all growing vigorously. . . . Here are some of the finest examples of our indigenous forest trees, oaks, beeches, ashes etc. Mr. Lee is already known to our readers as a great admirer of hardy plants and as having made great exertions to naturalize many of the kinds which have generally been called 'tender.'"

Andrew Jackson Downing visited the garden in 1844. He wrote: "Mr. Lee has here formed a residence of as much variety and interest as we ever saw in so modest a compass, about twenty acres."

The place was purchased by Ignatius Sargent, the father of Professor Charles Sprague Sargent, the distinguished arboriculturist. During Prof. Sargent's life there it became the famous "Holm Lea."

DORCHESTER

MARSHALL PINCKNEY WILDER AND HIS NOTABLE GARDEN, "HAWTHORN GROVE"

In Dorchester, at what is now Washington and Columbia Streets, suburban drabness has obliterated "Hawthorn Grove," the richly flowered garden of one of the most important figures in the history of American horticulture. For at least three generations previous to 1832, this place had belonged to the influential Sumner family of Roxbury, but

Another view of the garden of the late Miss Amy Lowell

Photographed by Robert N. Cram

The Ingersoll-Gardner house, "Green Hill," built about 1800 in Brookline, has a magnificent old grapevine trained on the columns

in that year it was sold to a remarkable young man who had been born at Rindge, New Hampshire, in 1798, and at the age of 27 had come to Boston to enter a counting-house. His affairs prospered, affording him means to expand his interest in horticulture. In 1830 he joined the Massachusetts Horticultural Society, then recently founded. Two years later he acquired the Dorchester garden, and almost immediately the horticultural experiments of Marshall Pinckney Wilder became matters of record. Soon his garden at Hawthorn Grove was one of the wonders of the horticultural world of his day.

In 1835 Wilder's collection of camellias included extensive importations from England and France and offered greater variety than any other in Massachusetts and probably in the entire country. He exhibited these, and his other treasures of flowers and fruits constantly. His energy was prodigious in growing and hybridizing flowers, fruits, and shrubs, and in experimenting with all the fresh importations from Europe, Africa, South America, and China.

The early records of the Massachusetts Horticultural Society give a picture of what Wilder grew at Hawthorn Grove and what interested the horticultural world between 1835 and 1840. We cull a few phrases from the Society's reports of Wilder's exhibits:

1835: "About forty varieties of beautiful autumnal roses."

From D. Appleton & Co.'s "Cyclopædia of American Biography"

Marshall Pinckney Wilder

1836: "Eighty-six specimens of the Dahlia" . . . "Twenty-six specimens of seedling pansies."

1837: "Beautiful acacias and other plants, in all about 70 specimens" . . . "An importation of twenty-one of the newest varieties [of camellias] from China, England, Germany, Belgium, Italy, within the year."

1838: "A hundred or more [rhododendrons and azaleas], some of great rareness" . . . "A fine group" of "those anomalous and leafless vegetables the Cacteae" .. "About twenty pots [of geraniums], with three or four seedlings of his own" . . . "A dozen or more species of the more curious tropical orchideae" . . . "The best display of roses," also "24 hardy varieties."

The Society soon recognized Wilder's leadership. In 1839 and 1840 he was vice-president, and from 1841 to 1848 president of the Society. Until his death he served successively on all the important committees.

Wilder founded the American Pomological Society and was its first president. His services to agriculture also were outstanding. As one of the greatest figures in the horticultural world of his time, his activities received national and international recognition. Several years before his death in 1886, he wrote the chapter on horticulture in Justin Winsor's

Courtesy of "White Pine"

The Fairbanks house at Dedham, built in 1636, is the oldest house in America with the possible exception of the shell and adobe houses of Florida and California. The sun-dial of Jonathan Fairbanks is preserved. It is inscribed with the initials "I F" and dated 1650

Memorial History of Boston. It has been an invaluable source of information for this present study of gardens in Colony and State.

As 1840 is the terminal date of this study, our interest centres on an account of Hawthorn Grove as it was a few years after Wilder acquired it. In 1835 and 1836, the *American Gardener's Magazine and Register* published extensive descriptions which can only appear here in a brief digest. We learn that Hawthorn Grove consisted of about fifteen acres, which, "with the exception of a large orchard and the garden, is now . . . grass land. The house is very pleasantly situated, and partly surrounded by evergreens." Much space is devoted to a detailed recital of the contents of the greenhouse as observed in the course of various visits; evidently camellias, acacias, amaryllises, dahlias, rhododendrons—to select only a few from a lengthy list—were grown in the widest variety; there is frequent mention of exotics and rare importations, some of them seen in the Wilder greenhouse for the first time.[1]

One finds an exhaustive description of the new greenhouse

completed in 1835; its plan and arrangements are minutely set forth, and commended to other horticulturists as model. We learn that Mr. Wilder was planning the erection of other buildings, and that the greenhouse was eventually to become a forcing-house, "to include a peachery, grapery, and, perhaps, a pinery." In 1836 he was making arrangements for a show-house for the effective display of the "most magnificent and rare species and varieties when in full bloom. . . . Mr. Wilder is one of the first to introduce a system, which we have long wished to see carried to its greatest perfection. . . ."

We are afforded a glimpse of the garden in the year 1836. "In the garden Mr. Wilder has made many alterations:

"Central part of Dorchester and Milton Village" in 1840

new walks have been laid out, and the fence on the north side removed so that it now includes three or four acres. A fine collection of pear trees has been planted, as also a good assortment of other kinds of fruit trees, particularly plums. Some of the young trees, of the Dutchess d'Angouleme, produced several very large pears this season. A spot of ground has been marked out, on which a rosary is to be planted: already many

---

[1]A study of the unabridged descriptions of Marshall P. Wilder's greenhouse and garden will be for the reader a revelation of the amazing range and variety of what was flourishing in Massachusetts gardens during this remarkable period of horticultural activity. *The American Gardener's Magazine and Register,* Vol. I, pp. 72, 349, 460 (1835); Vol. II, pp. 68, 201, 419, 454 (1836).

excellent sorts occupy part of the ground and additions are to be made another season. In front of his dwelling house, are planted, in the flower borders, a great number of tree roses: these have made a very vigorous growth the past season and will probably bloom finely the coming spring: among the number are several of the most beautiful varieties of the mosses. We hope that the tree roses will be more cultivated; they have a grand effect when in full flower.

"We here saw a bed of very fine pansies; they were raised from imported seeds, but among them we observed some of considerable elegance. . . . Not more than two or three are deserving of names, but they all form a handsome group, standing, as they do, in a small bed upon the turf. A row of them also runs parallel with the box edging, near to it, the whole length of one of the borders."

QUINCY[1]

THE ADAMS MANSION AND GARDEN

The land on which the "Old House" stands was purchased in 1730 by Major Leonard Vassall, who built the mansion and eventually sold the place in 1787 to John Adams. The

The Adams Mansion, Quincy. From a stereograph made about 1870, in the collection of the Society for the Preservation of New England Antiquities

latter in 1792 became a charter member of the Massachusetts Society for Promoting Agriculture, and was president of the society from 1805 to 1813. The garden was laid out by the Vassalls, and looks today much as it did then. Abigail Adams, the wife of John Adams, speaks of it in a letter written when the house and grounds were bought. The rose bush which she planted in 1788 can still be seen, although it has been transplanted from where she placed it under the Long Room windows.

After the death of Abigail, the wife of Charles Francis Adams, minister to England during the Civil War, the Old House—as it came to be called—was used by Brooks Adams, her son, as a summer home, and also for a long while by his brother, Henry Adams, while the latter was writing his *History of the United States.* Brooks Adams died in 1927. Living in the house where three generations of his forebears[2] had lived before him, he was the last of the family to remain in Quincy. It was his pleasure to keep the place and its many

associations alive. In front of the main doorway there are now flagstones set in the wooden piazza. These Brooks Adams discovered half buried in the ground underneath; he reset them so that they might serve again their original purpose in the days of the Vassalls. The rest of the piazza is unchanged, but the chestnut trees that stood along the wall and by the gates in John Adams' time, though well remembered still, have long since died and been removed.

During the last years of his life, Brooks Adams often expressed the hope that the Old House might be preserved by the family after his death as he had kept it. His known desire is largely responsible for the present arrangement, which gives the place into the charge of trustees to be maintained as an Adams Family Memorial.[1]

Brooks Adams had written for this survey the following account of his recollections of the old garden:

"The Old Place"

One of my earliest memories, when I may perhaps have been four or five years old, clad in a little checked frock, was standing at the right hand corner of the panelled-room, and looking through the window at the garden path, which seemed to me to be very long. The whole garden then looked large, but now I estimate it at 135 feet by 200. It had probably been laid out by Leonard Vassall, by whom it was sold to John Adams in September 1787.

The garden then undoubtedly held fruit trees and vegetables, as our New England people were sternly practical in the early days. My brother Henry has told, in his autobiography, how his grandfather John Quincy Adams used to send him out to pick up fruit, which he would leave on his mantelpiece in the room in which I am now writing, for the seed, for the old gentleman loved trees. At all events he set out, at the beginning of the nineteenth century, hickories, oaks, and the like[2], which have no place in a garden, and are only adapted to a forest or at best a grove. All of these trees have now gone on account of age, the last one having fallen perhaps twenty years ago. I well remember certain of the fruit trees which stood in front of my mother's window; there was also an old peach tree which belonged to the age when peaches still grew in New England; then there was the cherry tree which used to be a great temptation to us boys. I perfectly remember when we would pull off our shoes and climb that tree, and how my elder brothers wrote on the stairs of the farm house, which then stood just behind the house, "Henry greedy cherry eater," though I do not remember that Henry ate more than the rest of us.

My mother did more for the garden than any one else ever did, or thought of doing. She learned all she knew from her father's garden, that of Mr. Peter Chardon Brooks, who lived in Medford. Most of the best gardens, in those days, lay in the south, but Mr. Brooks had one of the best in this part of the country. My mother, who loved flowers dearly, acted under many limitations, but she finally laid out the garden almost as it exists now. The pictures which accompany this article show several walks, with box on either side. The flowers are bright colored between.

The York roses which Abigail Adams set out grew near the garden wall then, but being shaded by the large trees, gradually withered, until at last I had to interfere and transplant them to where the sun shone, for everything must have the sunshine; and since, they have grown and blossomed abundantly.

After the last horse-chestnut tree, the largest I ever saw, was blown down, I built a wall with two gates. Originally, as appears by a picture taken in 1798, there was one front

[1]Quincy, traditionally the "Merry Mount" of Thomas Morton, that gay worldling of the Gorges party, was set off from the older town of Braintree in 1792.

[2]The successive owners from the time the place first became Adams property in 1787 were John Adams, 1735–1826; John Quincy Adams, 1767–1848; Charles Francis Adams, 1807–1886; Brooks Adams, 1848–1927.

[1]The facts of the foregoing account are largely drawn from *Old-Time New England,* The Bulletin of the Society for the Preservation of New England Antiquities.

[2]Undoubtedly John Adams, prominent in the Massachusetts Society for Promoting Agriculture, was planting these trees under the impulse of the Society's activities.

door; a second was added by John Adams. The original door was approached by a short walk, flanked by six lilac trees, two of which still live in spite of their great age. The rest have died. The old stones of the piazza remain; I dug them up from where they had been buried when the house was improved almost out of rec- ognition.[1]

BROOKS ADAMS.

John Quincy Adams, the second owner of the garden and the sixth presi- dent of the United States, was actively interested in horticulture. Andrew Jack- son Downing dedicated to him his book on landscape architecture, a tribute which was acknowledged in the follow- ing letter[2], hitherto unpublished:

A. J. Downing Esq'r,
    Newburg, New York.
Dear Sir,

I have received a copy of your ele- gant work on Landscape Gardening and Rural Architecture for which and for the honor done me by the dedi- cation, I offer you my warm and thank- ful acknowledgments.

Its subject is at this time so peculiarly interesting to me that I regret much the necessity which calls me to a scene where I am to expect any thing but the enjoyment of the beauties of Nature. My compulsive absence from my own residence the full half or more of every year will I hope not ultimately deprive me of the pleasure of submitting to you some remarks respecting the cultivation of fruit

Mrs. Abigail (Smith) Adams, 1744-1818, wife of John Adams. From a portrait painted by Gilbert Stuart in 1800

[1]By John Adams, about 1800.
[2]Now in the possession of the Massachusetts Historical Society. John Quincy Adams was then a member of Congress for Massachusetts.

and forest trees *from the seed*, suggested by the first perusal of your descriptions. My departure this day for Washington leaves me now only time to repeat my thanks and with my affectionate regards to Mrs. Downing to wish you all the happiness that a Paradise on Earth can bestow.

Your friend and Kinsman,
JOHN QUINCY ADAMS.

WATERTOWN

BELMONT, THE COUNTRY-SEAT OF JOHN PERKINS CUSHING

In the early years of the nineteenth century, the country-seat which later under John Perkins Cushing became perhaps the foremost horticultural show- place in New England was the property of Eben Preble, merchant of Boston, a brother of Commodore Preble. From him it passed to Nathaniel Emory, who married Preble's daughter in 1808; then, about 1830, to R. D. Shepard, and a few years later to Cushing. In 1880 Marshall P. Wilder wrote[1] of this nephew of Thomas Handasyd Perkins:

"Mr. Cushing was a great lover of the works of nature; and with lavish ex- penditures he improved this estate, in the highest sense of the word, by laying out of the grounds and by the erection of numerous plant and fruit houses. He contributed largely to the exhibitions of the Massachusetts Horticultural Society, and opened his grounds once a week to the public in the summer season, making his place the most famous at that time for horticultural progress in New England."

[1]*Memorial History of Boston*, edited by Justin Winsor.

To the left is a walk in the Adams garden leading towards the library built by Charles Francis Adams, minister to England during the Civil War. To the right is the rose bush first set out by Abigail Adams in 1788

The Adams garden in Quincy, as it is today. "The Old House" in the background was built before 1787

which offers a yet wider prospect, . . . returns to the rear of the garden. . . .

"The garden behind the house is an enclosed square measuring 300 feet each way, level, and formally divided by broad gravel paths, as shown upon the plan. A conservatory and two long graperies, behind which are the potting-sheds and plant-houses, front up-on the northern side of the garden, while two Peach-houses and many well-train-ed Pear-trees occupy the east and west walls. Most of the ground is smoothly grass-ed. There are two large masses of Rhododendrons mixed with similar shrubs; at the sides are long beds of perennials and foliage plants, and grouped upon the grass near the angles of the walks are specimens of such trees as the Flowering Magnolias, the Red-flower-ing Horse-chestnut, the Weeping Elm, the Swamp Cypress, the Ginkgo, the Oriental Spruce, the Swiss Stone Pine. . . ."

After Cushing's death in 1862, the estate became the property of Samuel R. Payson, who maintained it in admir-able fashion. Its appearance when Wilder described it in 1880 —it then embraced some 200 acres—must have been sub-stantially that of Cushing's day.

". . . Its fine avenues bordered with old oaks, walnuts, and tulip-trees (one of the last is eighty feet in height) with other ornamental trees, rhododenrons, azaleas, and different shrubs, make it one of great interest. Here is a large conserva-tory, sixty feet wide, with fourteen other houses devoted to the cultivation of certain classes of plants, fruits, and vege-tables. Among these houses may be named a large greenhouse, two pelargonium, two orchid, one palm, one azalea house, with several others devoted to grapes, peaches, nectarines, figs and vegetables.

"The lawn to the south of the house is magnificent, con-taining about twenty acres, on and around which are some of the finest purple beeches in the land. On these premises are several gnarled old oaks and a deciduous cypress of great age, and also a park well stocked with deer."

Andrew Jackson Downing also wrote of Belmont with great enthusiasm. There is special interest, however, in a description[1] written by Charles Eliot more than forty years ago. Several excerpts are quoted here:

"The house is approached through a wood of trees which arch overhead to form a handsome informal avenue within which the road curves very gently. . . . The house is a sub-stantial structure of brick, with verandas built of stone. Its rooms command a view of the ten acres of lawn, on one hand, and of the interior of the wood, on the other. Over the tops of the trees at the foot of the lawn appears the shining dome of the State House on Beacon Hill, five miles away.

"A broad walk leads eastward from the house to a point of view which commands Fresh Pond and the intervening . . . farms. Six Purple Beeches stand in a row beside this path near the house, but formality ceases at the view point, and the walk wanders off along the brink of the gentle eastward slope, passes among scattered oaks of large size and around the small deer-park, and after sending off a branch to a knoll

[1]Written for *Garden and Forest* in 1889.

WALTHAM

THEODORE LYMAN'S GARDEN, "THE VALE"

The following account of "The Vale" is written by Arthur Lyman, the great-grandson of the first Theodore Lyman.[1]

"The first one hundred and fifty acres, farm and woodland, were bought in 1793 by Theodore Lyman. He bought about three hundred more acres in the next few years. The estate has now about three hundred acres in all.

"The house was built by McIntire of Salem and his original plans are in the Essex Institute, Salem.

"Theodore Lyman created the place and the garden. He 'brought over a celebrated English gardener by the name of Bell. He (Bell) began by laying out and grading the grounds, which took several seasons to finish, but when completed they were in their time the finest illustration in the country of modern landscape gardening.'[2]

"He had a deer park and had swans on the pond in front of the house. He must have planted the foreign trees and surely he had great taste for landscape gardening. I believe some of our large camellia trees in the greenhouse go back to that time.

"The westerly greenhouse, now a grape-house, is of great age,[3] and the garden paths are in part based on it and on the very old peach wall of brick, about eleven feet high, which bounds the garden on the north for a distance of about 500 feet, running easterly from the greenhouses and following the curves of the hill behind it. This is also confirmed by the location of three very old hawthorns, a very old purple beech and a still older white pine. My father never told me of any changes in the paths, and he lived there after the death

[1]The owners of the garden have been Theodore Lyman, 1793 to 1839; George W. Lyman, his son, 1839 to 1880; Arthur T. Lyman, his son, 1880 to 1915; Arthur Lyman, his son, 1915; all distinguished horticulturists.

[2]Marshall P. Wilder in *Memorial History of Boston*.

[3]"The first greenhouse was built about 1800 and divided into two parts, in which were raised pineapples, bananas, and other tropical fruits, and among the ornamental plants the yellow mimosa (acacia), which was then considered very elegant."—Marshall P. Wilder in *Memorial History of Boston*.

Photographed by Robert N. Cram

Two views of the oldest purple beech in Massachusetts, which stands in the Lyman garden, at Waltham. Above, one sees it across the sweep of lawn, with the old greenhouses and two ancient English hawthorns. The tree appears in a nearer view below

of my great-grandfather, Theodore, in 1839, until he died in 1915. There have been no changes since I knew the place except in connection with the change of the lines of the north piazza of the house. Fifty years ago the paths looked as if they had always been as they then were.

"The original heating system of the grape house was by wood fires built in arches of brick at the base of the heavy

against which the peach trees were trained flat, is planted with a succession of old-fashioned perennials. In my grandfather's time and until about twenty years ago, a box hedge, four feet high and nearly the same width, ran the length of the brick wall. It was unusually large for this northern climate but unfortunately it was killed one winter from end to end.

Photographed by Robert N. Cram
In the garden of Theodore Lyman, "The Vale," at Waltham. This is another view of the very old greenhouse shown on page 18

north brick wall, the heated wall slowly giving out its heat to the house. These arches and the flue still exist, though needless to say they are not used for their original purpose. Mr. George F. Stewart, my gardener, knows nothing of the same sort in this country although he knew of a somewhat similar one on Sir George Thompson's estate in Scotland. He has a deep interest in antiquarian research and a love and knowledge of many rare old fashioned flowers.

"Another interesting little greenhouse still in use (and still useful) stands by itself on the high corner of the back garden. The smoke and heat of a small fire in the west end is carried in a long flat horizontal flue to the chimney at the east end. I understand it is the only one of its ancient type in use in this country.

"The garden has large stretches of grass with narrow borders of flowering shrubs along the paths. At one corner stands a late flowering magnolia, and under it is a mass of snowberries. These two and their predecessors have been there many years. On the south, screening the house, and bounding the garden along the driveway to the stable for about 350 feet, is a massed stretch of very fine rhododendrons. Some plants are over 15 feet high. The border of varying width along the front of the greenhouses and the old peach wall,

"At the easterly corner of the greenhouse stands a very old purple beech, hardly a shadow now of what it was when I was a boy but still impressive with its great gnarled trunk. It must have been one of the earliest of these imported beeches. Dr. Asa Gray told my father that this beech was the largest he had ever seen in the United States or in Europe. Under it there are still the beds of lilies-of-the-valley and myrtle.[1]

"Another fine purple beech, probably the offspring of the old one, stands in the garden with a spread of about 80 feet and a still larger one stands on the lawn.

"A great native white pine, badly damaged by storms in recent years, stands at an angle in the wall, where there is a lovely old garden house with a door opening through the peach wall onto the back garden and the high land with its paths through the woods and glades. We think it saw the building of the farm which is now the garden, and knows and could tell you all we want to know, for its 100 feet overlook the whole home place.

"The garden was not planned to make the house the principal feature of the place nor to make a mere setting for the house. The house and the garden lie naturally together as

[1]These beds were referred to in an old letter of Arthur T. Lyman's.

Photographed by Robert N. Cram

The ancient colonial garden-house, built in an angle of the brick garden wall in the Lyman garden, has perennial borders at either side, a huge white pine to the right, and a weeping willow to the rear. A door opens through the brick wall onto the back garden and the high land, with its paths through woods and glades. At the right is a view of the perennial border against the wall; the path leads towards the purple beech

The garden of Governor Hutchinson, at Milton. Looking through the end of the grape arbor along the central garden walk

both do with the sunny lawns, the winding pond, the wooded knolls and hills, and the distant fields and meadows."

About 1840 Downing wrote of "The Vale" as follows:

"Waltham House (The Vale) about nine miles from Boston, was 25 years ago, one of the oldest and finest places, as regards Landscape Gardening. Its owner, the late Hon. T. Lyman, was a highly accomplished man, and the grounds at Waltham House bear witness to a refined and elegant taste in rural improvement. A fine level park, a mile in length, enriched with groups of English limes, elms, and oaks, and rich masses of native wood, watered with a fine stream, and stocked with deer, were the leading features of the place at that time; and this, and Woodlands (the seat of the Hamilton family) were the two best specimens of the modern style, as Judge Peters' seat, Lemon Hill, and Clermont, were of the ancient style, in the earliest period of Landscape Gardening among us."[1]

[1]From *A Treatise on the Theory and Practice of Landscape Gardening.*

MILTON

In 1928 Milton celebrated its two hundred and fiftieth anniversary as a town, having been set off from Dorchester in 1678. The natural lay-out of its land is extremely beautiful, being very hilly, with wonderful slopes to the south. Governor Belcher bought land for his country place here about 1728, and lived here in style. Governor Hutchinson's great place was not far away from Belcher's.

The Diary of John Rowe of Boston for the years 1759 to 1779 makes mention of the fine country seats in Milton and of the great entertainments given by Governor Hutchinson. Robert Carver in his history of Boston, published in 1834, says that Milton had country seats and villas in every direction. Present-day knowledge affords a description of only the garden of Thomas Hutchinson, last of the colonial governors.

Photographed by Robert N. Cram

An ancient brick garden wall in the Governor Hutchinson garden. In the foreground are old box bushes, a weeping willow, and a perennial bed

GOVERNOR HUTCHINSON'S GARDEN, AT MILTON

Unquety (or Unquity or Uncataquissit) is the name Governor Hutchinson used in writing of his beloved place. His fine house was demolished in 1872, but the garden, a plan of which—made in 1919—shows the position of some of the oldest trees, is still a thing of beauty. Marshall P. Wilder said that when he visited the garden in 1881 it had fallen into sad disrepair, but today it is in the possession of Mrs. Albert W. Hunt, and is charmingly restored and admirably cared for.

Mr. Albert W. Hunt has written the following description of the garden:

"In Milton, Massachusetts, eight miles from Boston, is the garden laid out about 1743 by Thomas Hutchinson, the last Royal Governor of Massachusetts. On a hill with broad views across the Neponset River to Boston Harbor and the sea and to the west, a clear sweep to the Blue Hills, he bought some hundred acres for his country place. There he built a house with stables, farm house and gardener's cottage, and to the west of the house laid out his garden.

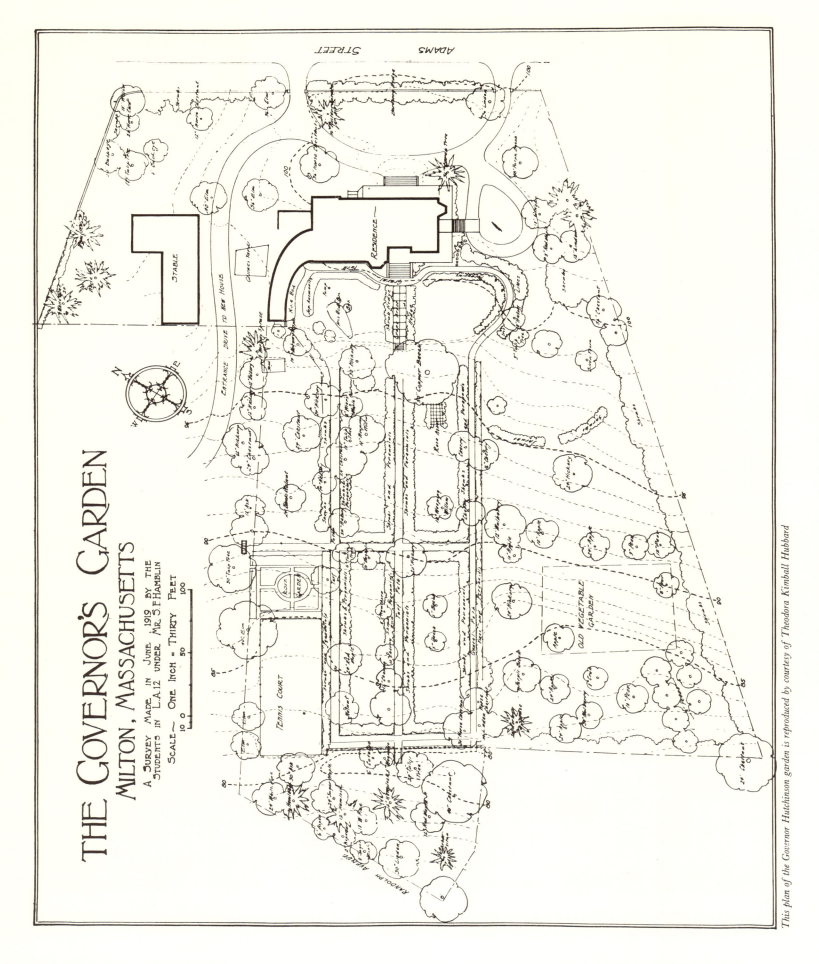

THE GOVERNOR'S GARDEN
MILTON, MASSACHUSETTS

A SURVEY MADE IN JUNE, 1919 BY THE
STUDENTS IN L.A.12 UNDER MR. S.F.HAMBLIN

SCALE — ONE INCH = THIRTY FEET

This plan of the Governor Hutchinson garden is reproduced by courtesy of Theodora Kimball Hubbard

"The farm house still stands in greatly remodeled condition, and the gardener's cottage too, though both are no longer part of the original estate which was confiscated at the time of the Revolution, and later divided and sold. The main house was torn down and a Victorian mansion built on the same foundation about 1870—all that remains of interest architecturally is a wing added after the governor's day, and called the 'Slaves' Quarters,' built on a curve with a brick wall on the garden side and an interesting architectural treatment in wood on the opposite side.

"A persistent local tradition has it that from the cellar of the Governor's house there was a tunnel that ran to an opening in the banks of the Neponset River at the foot of an open field in front of the house. A bricked-in opening on the river side of the cellar keeps that tradition alive, though there has never been found any proof of the existence of such a tunnel.

"We know that Governor Hutchinson took great pleasure and pride in his garden, that he had orchards, planted trees, and even sent back slips from England for it; that he was in-

Photographed by Robert N. Cram

Looking along the central walk in the Governor Hutchinson garden

terested in his grapevines and built a ha-ha at the foot of the garden.

"As gardens go it is a simple garden, though at the time it was laid out it must have been an unusual garden for New England, consisting of three long parallel paths, intersected by a single cross path, all bordered with flower beds on both sides of the paths.

"There are today many old trees and shrubs and a number of box bushes unusually large for this part of the country. An enormous copper beech, and an old Halesia tree in the garden, and on the river side of the house a large European larch and a European linden with a horse-chestnut tree, said to be the largest in eastern Massachusetts, are thought to date from the Governor's time, though there is no record of his having planted them.

"In early spring the large clumps of winter aconite, the great sweep of the scilla and chionodoxia that follow, carry the garden through a succession of bulbs, until the greatest beauty comes in the blossoming of the tulips. Another notable moment is when a large bed of long established Japanese anemones blooms in late August and early September.

"As an example of a simple early colonial garden that has

Looking in the opposite direction along the central walk in the Governor Hutchinson garden, toward the house and the end of the grape arbor

survived with little change to the present day, it still has an interest. And with its long green paths shaded with old trees, screened with flowering shrubs and bordered with bright blossoms, it has an atmosphere that can come only to a garden that has been cared for, loved, and lived in by successive generations for nearly two hundred years."

SALEM AND ENVIRONS

OUR first glimpse of the bounty of the soil of Salem we owe to the Rev. Francis Higginson, who arrived in 1629. He describes first a harbor some distance away: ". . . We had a westerly wind which brought us to a fyne and sweet harbour . . . where there was an island, wither four of our men with a boat went, and brought back agayne ripe strawberries and gooseberries and sweet single roses. Thus God was merciful to us in giving us a taste and smell of the sweet fruit as an earnest of his bountiful goodness to welcome us at our first arrival. This harbour was two leagues and something more from the harbour at Naimkecke [the Indian name—usually spelled Naumkeag—for the settlement at Salem] where our ships were to rest, and the plantation is already begun. . . .

"June 29 . . . We passed the curious and difficult entrance into the large spacious harbour of Naimkecke. And as we passed along it was wonderful to behould so many islands replenished with thicke wood and high trees, and many fayre greene pastures . . . though all the Countrey be as it were a thicke Wood for the generall, yet in divers places there is much ground cleared by the Indians, and especially about the plantation. . . ."[1]

A hint of the gardening efforts of the Salem colonists in these first years is to be found in a letter which came to Governor Endecott in 1629. On Sept. 13th, 1628, Endecott wrote a letter[2] to the Company in England making certain requests while reporting conditions. This letter failed to reach Mr. Cradock, the governor of the Company, until February 13th following. An answer was sent to Endecott dated

"In Gravesend the 17th of April 1629
". . . We take notice that yo[w] desire to have Frenchmen sent yo[w] that might bee experienced in making of salt & plantinge of vynes. Wee have enquired diligently for such, but cannot meete wth any of that nation. Nevertheless, God hath not left us altogeather unprovyded of a man able to undertake that worke, for that wee have entertained M[r] Thomas Groves, a man comended to us . . . for his . . . skill in many things very usefull. . . . His salarie costs this Companie a great some of mony. . . . Wee have also sent . . . grayne for seede, both wheat, barley & rye, in the chaff, &c. As for fruit stones and kernells, The tyme of the yeare fitts not to send them now, soe wee purpose to do it p o[r] next . . ."

William Wood in his *New England's Prospect* (1633) comments on the good yield of Salem soil.

"Foure miles Northeast . . . lyeth Salem, which stands on the middle of a necke of land very pleasantly having a South river on one side, and a North river on the other side; upon this necke where the most of the houses stand is very bad and Sandie ground, yet for seaven yeares together it hath brought forth exceeding good corne, by being fished[3] but every third yeare; in some places is very good ground, and very good timber and divers springs hard by the sea side. . . ."

A century later Captain Francis Goelet, under date of Oct. 21, 1750, notes the Salem gardens.

"Consists of abt. 450 houses, Several of which are neat Buildings but all of wood, and Covers a Great Deal of Ground; being a convenient Distance from Each Other, with fine gardens back of their Houses."[4]

And in the last years of the eighteenth century a French traveller who passed through Salem termed the road from Portsmouth to Boston "an uninterrupted garden. The road is in every part better than any I have ever seen in America. It would be considered a delightful road, even in the most beautiful districts of France and England."[1]

SALEM'S HISTORIC GARDENS

There is today a considerable group of gardens in Salem all a hundred or more years old; in several instances they have been described by their present or late owners. Before we proceed with the historic gardens of Salem, however, we might well introduce a figure who was important to them and who will be frequently encountered. He is thus described in the *History of the Massachusetts Horticultural Society:*

"The first regularly educated gardener of whom we have any account in this vicinity was George Heusler, a native of Landau in the Province of Alsace, Germany. He had been employed in the gardens of several German princes and of the

At top is John Warner Barber's drawing of a "southern view in the central part of Salem," showing a part of Washington and Court Streets. The Court House is seen in the center, and to its right the City Hall. Below is his drawing of a "western view of Washington Square, Salem," showing the arch designed by McIntire and erected in 1805. It is a characteristic example of McIntire's work for ornamental purposes

King of Holland, and came from Amsterdam to this country in 1780, bringing professional diplomas and recommendations. Soon after his arrival, he commenced the practice of his profession in the employment of John Tracy of Newburyport. In 1790 he removed to Salem, and continued his vocation on the farm of Elias Haskett Derby in Danvers (now Peabody), and in many of the gardens of Salem, Danvers, and other towns of Essex County, until nearly the time of his decease, which occurred April 3, 1817, at the age of sixtysix years. As early as 1796 he gave notice that he had choice

[1]The foregoing extracts are from an early manuscript in the possession of the Massachusetts Historical Society.

[2]Not extant.   [3]Fertilized with fish.
[4]*Voyages and Travels*, an abstract of the stay of Captain Francis Goelet in Boston. New Eng. Hist. and Gen. Register, 1770.

fruit trees for sale at the farm of Mr. Derby. The latter gentleman had, just before, imported valuable trees from India and Africa, and had a very extensive nursery of useful plants in the neighborhood of his garden. Mr. Heusler was highly esteemed as an intelligent, upright, kind-hearted, and religious man; and to him the community are largely indebted for the introduction of many valuable fruits, and for developing a taste for gardening."[1]

RELICS OF JOHN ENDECOTT: HIS ORCHARD FARM, SUN-DIAL AND PEAR TREE, IN SALEM FARMS OR SALEM VILLAGE, AFTERWARDS CALLED DANVERS[2]

In September, 1628, John Endecott landed at Naumkeag, (renamed Salem ten months later) as the official representative of "The Company of the Massachusetts Bay in New England." He was accorded the title of Governor. With him were other colonists, in small number. A few scattered survivors of a previous company they found here on arriving.

The following June came the Rev. Francis Higginson, who kept a journal during this voyage for "the satisfaction of loving friends". His words describing his arrival (June 30) were: "The next morning the governour came aboard to our ship and bade us kindly welcome, and invited me and my wiffe to come on shoare and take lodging in his house, which we did accordingly."

Besides the account of the voyage from which the above is quoted, Higginson wrote also, under date of July 24, 1629, a description of the region about Naumkeag and of its conditions, entitling it "New-Englands Plantation". This was published in London in 1630. In it he wrote of the early settlement:

"When we came first to Nehumkek we found about halfe a score Houses, and a faire House newly built for the Governor . . . There are in all of us both old and new Planters about three hundred, whereof two hundred of them are setled at Nehumkek, now called Salem . . . We that are setled at Salem make what hast we can to build Houses, so that within a short time we shall have a faire Towne. . . . Our Governor hath already planted a Vineyard with great hope of increase. . . . Our Governor hath store of greene Pease growing in his Garden as good as ever I eat in England. . . ."

No sooner had these energetic men put up their first houses and surrounded their town with palisades, than they laid out farms for themselves, beyond the too narrow limits of their defenses. In the allotment of these lands the leaders, and often also the ministers, were given by far the largest lots and the choicest sites.

John Endecott's grant, from the general court, is dated July 3, 1632, and is thus described in the ancient record of that date: "There is a necke of land lyeing aboute 3 myles from Salem, cont. aboute 300 ac. of land, graunted to Capt. Jo. Endecott, to enioy to him & his heires for ever, called in the Indean tonge Wahquaine-sehcok, in English Birch-

The sun-dial made in London for Governor John Endecott and calculated for Salem, Massachusetts, as the inscription on the side of the gnomon shows. On the other side of the gnomon appears the word "Salem." The dial is now the property of the Essex Institute, of Salem, by whose courtesy these photographs are reproduced

[1]*History of the Massachusetts Horticultural Society, 1829–1878.* By Robert Manning. Felt's *Annals of Salem,* 1844.

[2]The facts of this account, which is written by Louisa Hooper Thoron (Mrs. Ward Thoron), are drawn from *New-Englands Plantation* (by the Rev. Francis Higginson), London, 1630; "Journal of the Voyage," kept by the Rev. Francis Higginson, Mss., Mass. Historical Society; Massachusetts Bay Colony Records (ancient); Salem Town Records (ancient); Register of Deeds, Essex County (ancient); Probate Court Records for Suffolk County (ancient). The foregoing are quoted in histories, notably the reprints by the Mass. Historical Society, Historical Collections of the Essex Institute, and Sidney Perley's *History of Salem,* written in 1924. Other sources for facts are *Memoir of John Endecott,* by Charles Moses Endicott, privately printed at Salem, 1847; *Diary of William Bentley,* Vols. II, III, IV; Letters—three originals in the possession of the Massachusetts Historical Society; Transactions of the Mass. Horticultural Society; information supplied by the Arnold Arboretum.

Photographs by courtesy of the Arnold Arboretum

To the left is one of the suckers of the Endecott pear tree as it appeared in September, 1923, when in fruit. To the right are the suckers in blossom, as photographed by Mr. E. H. Wilson, of the Arnold Arboretum, in May, 1925, after the ground around them had been cleared and cultivated. The fence was later replaced

wood, bounded by three rivers, south, north & east [elaborate description omitted], bounded on the west with the maine land."

"Orchard" was the name that Endecott gave to this farm. It was not his only farm, but it was the one he loved best. That it prospered, tradition affirms and records, though few, confirm.

In Governor Endecott's will, dated May, 1659, Orchard Farm is the first item mentioned:

"Imprimis I give to my . . . Wiefe Elizabeth Endecott all that my ffarme called Orchard lying wth in the bound^s of Salem together wth the Dwelling Howse, Outhowses,

Courtesy of the Arnold Arboretum

Pears from the suckers of the Endecott pear tree, photographed in September, 1923

Barnes, stables, Cowhowses, & all other building & appurten^ances thereunto belonging & appertayning. And all the Orchards nurseries of fruit trees[1], gardens, fences, meadow & salt marsh thereunto appertayning. And all the feeding

ground` & arrable & planting ground^s there, both that wch is broken up & that wch is yet to break up. As also all the timber trees & other trees for wood or other uses. . . . during her naturall life. . . .

"Also I give unto her . . . my howses at Salem & the ground belonging unto them. . . ."

To his elder son, John, he gives at least two other farms, and to his younger son, Zerubbabel, he gives at least two more. These sons were also to inherit Orchard Farm at their mother's death.

Thus, with some diminutions, Orchard Farm descended in the Endicott family from father to son, until in 1796 Capt. John Endicott, sixth in descent from the Governor, was in possession. Here on a day in September came that remarkable character and diarist, the Rev. William Bentley, the Samuel Pepys of Salem. This is how he records the visit:

Sept. 21, 1796: "After dinner took my compass & pencil, & went for a walk . . ." He reached Danvers and Orchard Farm, recorded who had bought parts of it from the heirs, then continued thus: "A third division on the S. W. is yet retained by the heirs of Endicott. We visited this man who was of the [sixth] generation from the Gov. At the door we found the Gov.'s dial which was in copper a very fair impression, & in the highest order. It was marked 'William Bowyer, London, Clockmaker, fecit. I. 1630. E'. (the initials of the Gov.'s name). On the gnomon on one side 'Lat. 42,' & on the other 'Salem'. . . . We then passed into the Cornfield to find the Site of the old Mansion, . . . gone before the

[1]The Company in London, in their letter of April 17th, 1629, wrote to Endecott: ". . . Wee are disappointed of the pvisions ordered to have bin sent yo^w for yo^rselfe and Mrs Endecote; but, God willing, they shall come by the next." On May 28th, 1629, they wrote a second letter: "Wee send yo^w also herew^th a pticuler . . . of what goods cattle, or other pvisions wee now send upon these 3 shipps [ships named] . . . amongst w^h wee have remembred yo^w, the Govno^r there, wth certaine necessaries pmised by o^r last; and if in ought wee have bin now wantinge, wee shall, upon notice from yo^w, see the same supplyed by o^r next." A memoir of John Endecott by Charles Moses Endicott, privately printed in Salem in 1847, cites the first quotation and remarks: "It is . . . believed that at this time Mr Endecott ordered the fruit trees which afterwards constituted his orchard upon the farm granted him in 1632 . . ." In a footnote in this memoir is the following reference: "Hazard's Coll. We find in May 1629, a Committee was appointed to 'consider what provisions are now fit to be sent over to Capt. John Endecott and his family, and provide the same accordingly.'—Comp. Rec. in Eng." *Memoir of John Endecott*, by C. M. Endicott, p. 23.

memory of any persons living." They thought they found the site. "There is a fine prospect in front, & a gentle descent to a little creek, in which the Gov. kept his Shallop. Tradition says there was a walk to this place with damson trees & grape vines so thick that a person might walk unobserved. These have all been gone many years. This place was called the Gov. Orchard as he planted early Trees around his house. There is only one Tree left, which bears the Sugar Pear, & by tradition was planted in 1630. It is in front of the site of the House, it rises in three trunks from the ground, & is considerably high. It is much decayed at the bottom, but the branches at top are sound. I brought away some of the pears & engaged such as remain, to be brought to my house to send to the Governour of the Commonwealth."

Again and again Bentley's curiosity and his antiquarian flair led him back to this spot.

August 22, 1800: "I visited the antient site of the House of Gov. Endicott & plucked some pears from the antient Tree which he planted in 1631 . . ."

Oct. 3, 1800: "Mr Endicott with me & brought some pears from the Tree which Gov. Endicott planted in 1630. . . ."

Oct. 24, 1801: "In the afternoon I visited the Old Spot which was the first Choice of our old Gov. Endicott. . . . The old dial was broken & the pears from the old Tree were all rotten . . ."

July 26, 1802: "Mr Corné of Naples, an Italian Painter in the town . . . rode with me to the estate of Gov. Endicott. . . . The old pear tree of 1630 hung still full of pears. . . . The dial lays in the Closet as the boys threw stones & broke off the gnomon."

Sept. 25, 1802: "In the afternoon I went to Endicott's to borrow the dial of the Governour as it is a great curiosity. I was very desirous to obtain it. . . ."

In October, 1806, Bentley's diary records a visit from Captain Endicott, who brought "some pears from the Old Endicott Tree which tradition & public opinion assigns 176 years of age. It stood without any sensible injury in the violent storm of Oct. 1804, when some of its younger neighbors fell victims to the fury of the wind. It continues to yield many bushels & I am every year supplied from it. . . ."

Bentley continued to show such persistent interest in the ancient sun-dial that undoubtedly he persuaded Capt. John Endicott at last to let him purchase it.

On April 17th, 1810, he records the price he paid for "the Dial belonging to the first Gov. Endicott & the first ever used in our Colony & the oldest now to be found in all America. . . . The Son of said John consented that I should possess the Dial."

An amusing correspondence with John Adams, the former President, had started up in the previous autumn on the subject of the old pear-tree and the dial. This is how the correspondence began. Bentley recorded in his diary—

Sept. 30, 1809: ". . . I passed to Quincy. . . . I called upon Pr. Adams but found him to have gone abroad to dinner & left him some of the Endicott pears from the Tree of 1630 with my name & directions, *to the Man worthy to eat with our forefathers.*"

Oct. 10, 1809: "Received a letter from President Adams on the subject of the Endicott Pears. After an apology I informed him of the Dial as fixing the Age of the Tree near which it was placed.[1] I informed him of my wish to preserve portraits of our Eminent men. I feel too much cannot be done to encourage the patriotism of John Adams or to express the public gratitude."

April 11, 1810: "I went up to the Endicott farm & ob-

tained from Capt. John Endicott a number of twigs from the Old Endicott pear tree for President Adams, & sent them carefully put up to him at Quincy."

The Massachusetts Historical Society has the original letter that Bentley wrote of this date to John Adams. It begins:

"Salem 11 April 1810

"Sir.

"Agreeably to your request, I accompanied Capt. John Endicott, senior, . . . yesterday [sic.] to the Pear Tree, & received from the Tree the twigs which I have sent by a careful hand, to be sent directly from Boston to Quincy. . ."

Evidently, soon after this, Bentley made Adams a present of a fancy picture of the old Endicott pear tree, showing the trunk and lower branches, but hiding its top behind a wreathed portrait of Adams himself!

John Adams thanks him as follows:

"Quincy May 1810

"Dear Sir,

"I received from our Quincy Stage under the direction of Mr Thayer a Box of Scions from the Endicott Pear Tree carefully preserved and in admirable order for which I pray you accept my best thanks. I have engrafted a number of Stocks which have taken very well according to their present appearances and have distributed others to several Gentlemen in this and the Neighbouring Towns. Mr Norton of Weymouth who loves Endicott Divinity full as well as you and I do . . . cannot be indifferent to the name of Endicott. . . .

"I last night received by Mr Thayer our Stagedriver your favour of the Eleventh, for which I thank you. The Portrait of the Endicott Pear Tree is beautiful in the highest degree. . . . The tree has died at the top as Dean Swift and his melancholy Oak did. The Ladies say that the little Urchin of a Cupid who upholds the wreath, a little fat broadfaced squareheaded spright, resembles me more than the Portrait he holds in his hand. . . ."

On Sept. 29th, 1815, Bentley, in recording the damage after a great gale, wrote: "Gov. Endicott's Pear Tree of 1630 was much injuried."

May 5, 1819: "Saw the Endicott tree for the first time since it was inclosed, and heard for the first time of the conversation about rendering the settlement upon it and near it an incorporation under the name of Endicott."

Thus Bentley continued to help call the attention of his contemporaries and their descendants to the persistence of fruit-bearing in an old pear tree of known great age.

In December, 1819, Bentley died. He bequeathed the old dial to Capt. Charles Moses Endicott, who deposited it in safety in the East India Marine Society. In 1867 it was turned over from there to the Essex Institute.

In Vol. I of the Transactions of the Massachusetts Horticultural Society, one reads that at their ninth anniversary William Lincoln of Worcester devoted several paragraphs and more of his address to Gov. Endecott as a horticulturist, and to a description of the pear tree as it looked in 1837. Then it consisted of three parts: the main tree and two ancient suckers. Since then the main trunk has decayed away, but the suckers persist in bearing the sugar pear. In 1925, Ernest Wilson photographed these for the Arnold Arboretum. In 1930 the suckers were still bearing fruit.

Except between 1839 and 1862, the homestead of Orchard Farm has continued in the possession of descendants of Governor Endecott.[1]

---

[1]Bentley's letter to John Adams is shown here in full in a photostatic reproduction. It points out that Governor Endecott had said that the date on the sun-dial (1630) fixed the age of the tree. This indicates that both tree and sun-dial stood first in the Governor's garden in Salem and were transferred to the farm after it was granted to Governor Endecott in 1632. According to family tradition the tree was brought from England in the *Arbella* with John Winthrop in 1630. The reader will observe that Bentley made several obvious errors in transcribing dates.

[1]The list of Endicott owners runs as follows: John Endecott, 1588-1665-6; Zerubbabel Endecott, 1635-1683; Samuel Endecott, 1659-1694; Samuel Endecott, 1687-1776; John Endicott, 1713-1783; John Endicott, 1739-1816; Samuel Endicott, 1763-1828; William Putnam Endicott, 1803-1888; William Crowninshield Endicott, 1826-1900; William Crowninshield Endicott, 1860—; George Endicott. The last-named received the farm by deed a few years ago.

The letter which the Rev. William Bentley wrote to John Adams on October 10th, 1809. It is now in the possession of the Massachusetts Historical Society, by whose courtesy it is reproduced here

ELIAS HASKET DERBY'S HOUSE AND GARDEN IN SALEM,
       AND HIS FARM AND GARDEN AT DANVERS

The third quarter of the eighteenth century marks the period when Salem was the leading mercantile center for New England. Trade with the East and West Indies and Europe founded many fortunes, and handsome residences and fine grounds were the usual result of travel, means, and leisure. We find no definite record of Salem gardens until the late years of the century, when the Derby family, who were leaders in ship-building, ship-owning, and the banking business which developed from the trade, were outstanding characters. It is reported that Richard Derby, the founder of the

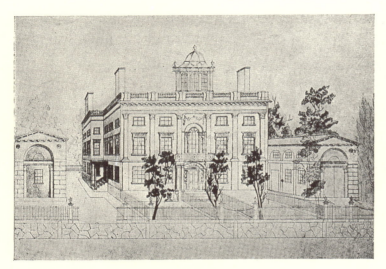

A study by Charles Bulfinch in 1795 for the Elias Hasket Derby house, in Salem. From the original drawing in the possession of the Essex Institute

family fortunes, had a fine garden in Salem as early as 1760, but no description of this has been preserved.

Richard Derby's oldest son, Captain John Derby, followed the family tradition and took to the sea, while the second son, Elias Hasket Derby, became his father's partner in the management of affairs on shore, and succeeded to the business in 1783. Elias Hasket Derby, who was one of the charter members of the Massachusetts Society for Promoting Agriculture, built for himself a house in Salem on Essex Street, at the corner of Washington, which was finally finished in 1799 and was remarked for its elegance by all visitors. The grounds and gardens were developed under the supervision of Samuel McIntire, the architect, and Heussler (or Heusler), the Alsatian gardener. The plan of this garden and of the summer-house and greenhouse are shown in the accompanying illustrations.

Charles Bulfinch had submitted plans for this house, but it appears that McIntire finally took charge. Apparently he modified the plans but slightly, for the drawing done by

Bulfinch, shown here, resembles markedly the sketch of the building made in 1797 by Robert Gilmor of Baltimore when he visited Mr. Derby. He says, "The principal merchant here, Mr. Derby, has just built a most superb house, more like a palace than the dwelling of an American merchant."

Elias Hasket Derby died the year this house in Salem was finished.

Mr. Derby's farm was in Danvers, and there is reason to think that these grounds had been somewhat developed by previous owners before he came into possession. We know at any rate that Mr. Derby took a deep interest in the garden of his farm, and when Samuel McIntire became the dictator of architecture in Salem he was employed at Danvers to develop a superb summer-house and other embellishments for the garden. The Reverend William Bentley, who was then the minister of the principal church in Salem and whose journal is often quoted for descriptions of gardens and grounds, makes an entry under the date of June 22, 1790.

"I went to ride . . . into Danvers. Saw the garden of Mr. E. H. Derby. The Dutch gardener[1] was very attentive. The principal garden is three parts, divided by an open slat fence painted white. . . . It includes $\frac{7}{8}$ of an acre. We ascend from the house two steps in each division. . . . The passages have no gates, only a naked arch with a key-stone frame of wood painted white above 10 feet high[2]; going into the garden they look better than returning; in the latter view they appear from the unequal surface to incline toward the Hill.

"The strawberry beds are in the upper garden, & the whole divisions are not according to the plants they contain. The unnatural opening of the branches of the trees is attempted with very bad effect. Beyond the Garden is a spot as large as the Garden which would form an admirable orchard, [it is] now improved as a kitchen garden, & has not an ill effect in the present state. The Gardener has only come this year, & is not accountable for the arrangement. It was extremely neat. . . . The house is lined with a superb fence, but is in itself a mere Country House, one story higher than common with a rich owner."

In 1794 Mr. Derby erected in this garden the summer-house planned by McIntire, which was remarkable for its elegance. This lovely example of McIntire's work may now be seen in the garden of the late Mrs. Wm. Endicott.[3]

The Reverend Mr. Bentley visited Mr. Derby's garden in April 1797, and wrote in his diary:

"The hothouses were in good forwardness & the gardens were all ready for spring. We went to get a few trees and obtained such as were excellent from the nursery. Every year the arrangements are more extensive and more happy. The

[1]George Heussler.
[2]See the arch in the illustrations of the Peirce-Nichols garden, pages 69, 70.
[3]See page 79.

Published in the Bulletin of the Boston Public Library, April, 1892
"View of Mr. Derby's house at Salem," a drawing made by Robert Gilmor, "a gentleman of Baltimore," in 1797, when the house was already standing

Drawings by McIntire for the Elias Hasket Derby place on Essex Street at the corner of Washington, in Salem

From the Derby papers.   Reproduced by courtesy of the Essex Institute

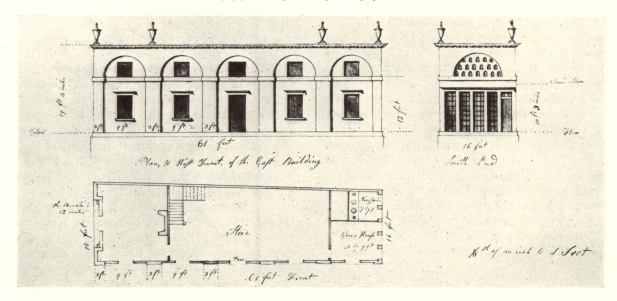

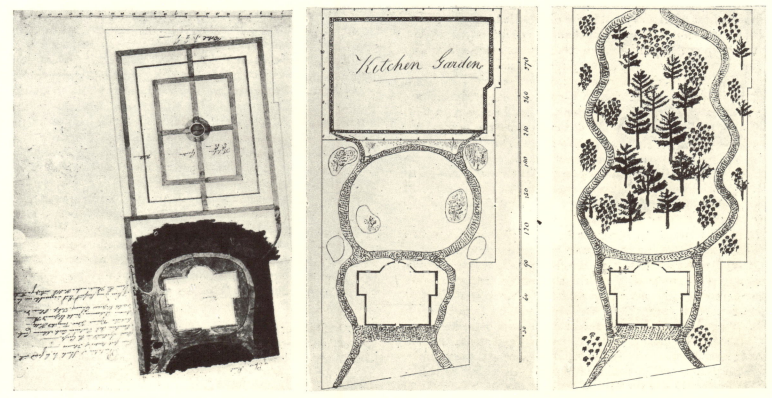

At top is McIntire's drawing for "stove" and greenhouse; at the left his drawing for the lay-out of the grounds.   The other two drawings show his alternative plans

At the right is McIntire's drawing for a summer-house, undoubtedly for the kitchen garden.   The drawing to the left is probably for the rear of the summer-house

importations from the Isle of France did not succeed. Many were dead before they reached the Garden."

Two years later he sadly records:

"Aug. 8, 1799. This evening died Elias Hasket Derby, the most eminent merchant that has ever been in Salem. His industry, his manners, his economy, exactly conformed to the best character of this place. . . . His property is far beyond anything ever known in Salem."

The Reverend Mr. Bentley continued to visit the garden at the farm after it had passed into the hands of Elias Hasket Derby's son. He observes on June 19, 1800:

"Stopped at Mr. Derby's garden in which we experienced the utmost attention of Mr. Heussler, the Gardener. He first fed us with Cherries, and Strawberries, and then exhibited the Luxuries of the place. We saw Lemons growing in the Hot House. A great variety of the Aloe plant was shown to us. We were shown 5 species of Geraniums. We saw the prickly pear in flower, and received some of the flowers. I brought away a specimen of the Roof House Leek which was a beautiful specimen."

From the foregoing notes by the Rev. Mr. Bentley we have learned that garden at the Derby farm in Danvers contained seven-eighths of an acre; that it was divided into three sections, with terraces ten feet high, and that each division was marked at the main path by an arch ten feet high, painted white; that a fine summer-house was a prominent feature. We learn also that the garden divisions were fenced with an open slat fence, painted white. As the kitchen garden is especially mentioned, we must conclude that it was separate from the flower garden. But alas, nothing is said of the flowers; only strawberries and cherries are mentioned. In the *Salem Gazette* of Oct. 21, 1796, however, Geo. Heussler offered for sale at the Derby farm in Danvers, tulip roots and fifty sorts of pink roots, as well as twenty varieties of peach trees, seven kinds of nectarines, and many kinds of cherries, plums, pears and apricots.

Again the Bentley diary:

"Oct. 24, 1801. . . . We passed to Col. Derby's farm. . . . He has added nothing to what his father had done. Autumn appeared everywhere but in the hot house, where we saw Oranges & Lemons & the Lemons in high perfection. We passed through the new road which the workmen are now employed to finish through the farm (leading to his sister's, Mr. West's property) and confess the almost complete state of this most beautiful avenue. Through the great pasture we passed to the house[1] erected by Mr. West, and executed in the taste and under the direction of his wife, the eldest daughter of the late E. H. Derby."

In April, 1805, Bentley writes:

"It is now ascertained that the Derby farm at Danvers, bought of Major Epes and improved by Mr. E. Derby and since in the possession of his Son, is actually sold to the Crowninshield family. The price named is $19,000.00 for the farm, Buildings, stock, Utensils, and all things as they now stand."

"June 26, 1805. This day visited the farm lately purchased by Jacob Crowninshield[2] of the Derby family in Danvers. The strawberries were in great perfection and plenty. We fed and came away richly laden. The family were with us on the occasion."

"June 7, 1807. This evening I spent with Hon. J. C. Crowninshield at his farm in Danvers in company with several other gentlemen. We were handsomely refreshed from the luxuries of a Garden which the heirs of Mr. Derby have sold him."

"April 30, 1808. On Friday last died at Washington Hon. Jacob Crowninshield aet. 38."

[1]The house was called "Oak Hill" by its former owner, the late Mrs. J. C. Rogers. The architect was McIntire, and the woodwork is now owned by the Museum of Fine Arts, Boston.

[2]Mr. Crowninshield had sailed as Captain in command for Mr. Richard Derby's ships, and later became a successful merchant and banker in Salem, and an eminent public servant. The Crowninshield and Derby families are related by marriage.

Thus ends the record of one of the notable gardens of the late eighteenth century in Massachusetts. The modest farmhouse still stands, but no trace of the garden remains.

SOUTHFIELDS: THE GARDEN OF E. HERSEY DERBY

In *A Girl's Life of Eighty Years Ago* we read a contemporary account of the house and garden at "Southfields" of Ezekiel Hersey Derby, a son of Elias Hasket Derby, and like his father an active member of the Massachusetts Society for Promoting Agriculture. He was also a member of the Massachusetts Horticultural Society. The house was designed by McIntire and the garden laid out by Heussler. The following entry is dated July 6, 1802, shortly after the garden had been laid out:

"We returned home, and Mr. Hersey Derby asked if we should not like to walk over to his house and garden—we readily consented as I had heard much of the house. The evening was calm and delightful, the moon shone in its greatest splendor. We entered the house, and spacious entry . . . and at the further end of the entry a door opened into a large magnificent oval room; and another door opposite the one we entered was thrown open and gave us a full view of the garden below. . . . I expected every moment that the wand of the fairy would sweep all from before my eyes and leave me to . . . wonder what it meant. You can scarcely conceive of anything more superb. We descended into the garden, which is laid out with exquisite taste; an airy irregularity seems to characterize the whole. At the foot of the garden there was a summerhouse, and a row of tall poplar trees which hid everything beyond from sight, and formed a kind of walk. I arrived there and to my astonishment found thro' the opening of the trees that there was a beautiful terrace the whole width of the garden; 'twas twenty feet from the street, and gravelled on the top, with a white balustrade around; 'twas almost level, and the poplar trees so close that we could only occasionally catch a glimpse of the house. The moon shone full upon it, and I really think this side is the most beautiful though it is the back one. A large dome swells quite to the chamberwindows and is railed around on top and forms a delightful walk . . . the magnificent pillars which support fill the mind with pleasure."

From this account we can only conclude that there was a graveled terrace with a white balustrade the whole width of the garden; that the Lombardy poplar, the fashionable tree of the period, was placed as a thick screen; that at the foot of the garden there was a summer-house, and that the whole effect was beautiful.

"Southfields" as it was in 1855 is described in the following account by one who was familiar with its later history.

"In my boyhood the Hersey Derby estate, its owners and its equipments had reached the condition of gentle—one might almost say genteel—decay. The Derby Farm as it was locally called, was the turning point in the afternoon or summer evening walks of Salemites before tennis, golf or even croquet, had come to occupy their leisure, and being just one mile from Essex street, it served the place of a pedometer for those who took their exercise systematically.

"Ezekiel Hersey Derby died in 1852 at the age of eighty years, leaving the farm to his daughters who seemed even then to the youthful mind to be elderly ladies altho' no older than my own children are now. They are elegant in their oldtime dress and manners and in their surroundings and maintained an establishment in quiet dignity and in keeping with somewhat reduced means and the increased cost of living just preceding the panic of 1857.

"The estate, which has for many years previous been in the possession of the family, was laid out by Mr. Derby with its gardens, greenhouses, shrubbery and orchards in 1802 when he was about thirty years of age, from plans made by George

The Halliday Historic Photograph Co., Boston

The Peirce-Nichols Garden in Salem

The path through the garden of the Peirce-Nichols house, which was built for Captain Jerathmeel Peirce by McIntire in 1782. The entrance to the garden is through a wide, arched passageway (shown on the following page) which runs through the outhouses across the paved court from the house. The path descends sharply down several terraces and flattens out at the end of the garden. A fine old mulberry tree is seen at the left of the path. In addition to the illustrations on the following page, there is also a view of the gateway of the Peirce-Nichols house on page 429

Courtesy of the Essex Institute
The paved courtyard of the Peirce-Nichols house in Salem. House and outbuildings represent the work of McIntire's
early and best period

Photographed by Robert N. Cram   *Halliday Historic Photograph Co., Boston*
The unique entrance to the garden of the Peirce-Nichols house. Through the arched passageway one sees the end of the garden, where the North
River used to flow, and where Captain Peirce's ships used to lie. At the right is a view of the arch in the garden

Heussler, whose admirable work in landscape gardening made Essex County famous in his day. Mr. Derby had just inherited what was then considered a handsome fortune from his father, Elias Hasket Derby, who died in 1799, but, unlike other members of the family, took to the land instead of the sea for an occupation.

"The Derby Farm had been famous for half a century, but was in its decline when as a small boy I made my first visit there. It must have been in 1855 when a friend of ours, who was much interested in the development of our own garden, which had just then been re-made, took me over there one summer afternoon.

"We walked about the old garden and orchard and inspected the big barn, the front of which was decorated with a load of hay carved out of wood in low relief with carved festoons on each side and a circular many-paned window above in the gable end. The 'Derby girls'—they were always 'girls' to their old Salem familiars—still kept some cattle and a pair of most respectable, veteran horses that took them about town in the family coach in summer and in winter in the 'booby-hut' sleigh, the sole survivor of its type in Salem.

"By the barn to the north was the flower garden with its remaining perennials and some persistent tulips and the last surviving feature of its original glory, a pond about thirty feet in diameter, still inhabited by the descendants of the goldfish that, with the night-blooming cereus, were the wonder of the town when they were first introduced. Beside the pond was a fine old southern bald cypress with a forked top, the most northerly of its species, which, remaining until within a very few years, finally succumbed to the march of improvement (?) when a new street could not be deviated a few feet from a straight line to save this precious relic of the past.

"The grounds about the house were shaded by groups of trees—tulip, magnolia, horse-chestnut, European ash and some others, which left to themselves had formed a little grove about the entrance yard. Opposite the house, across Lafayette street, was the shrub-bordered path, a narrow roadway, or pleached alley, which led to the shore of the inner harbor beyond, which had become a thicket."

With that strange tendency of civic bodies to oppose private tree-planting in the public streets, the Selectmen of Salem frowned upon E. Hersey Derby's plan for lining Lafayette street with elms, although the street itself had been laid out one hundred feet in width through Derby's efforts. In this instance, however, it may have been fortunate, for being a determined man, he proceeded to plant the elms on both sides of the street, but within his own property, which extended upon it for a long distance, so that the trees grew and flourished safe from the bumps of wheels of carelessly driven carts and the gnawings of hungry horses.

The elms were planted in 1808, and many of them are still standing. All but one seem to have been American elms, the single exception being an English elm, opposite Willow Avenue—the only one known in a Salem street.

Some years later than the time of the ramble above recorded the entire estate was taken over by a syndicate and the Miss Derbys moved into town, gave up the ancient "booby-hut" and the venerable horses, and lived out their lives amply provided for from the proceeds of the sale of the farm.[1]

[1]The facts concerning the Derby family and their gardens are drawn from the following sources: Derby papers, Essex Institute; Merchant Ventures of Old Salem, Robert E. Peabody; "Notes on Derby Houses," from the Architectural Record and the Pennsylvania Museum Bulletin—Fiske Kimball; "The Wood Carver of Salem," by Frank Cousins; The Diary of the Reverend William Bentley; A Girl's Life of Eighty Years Ago, the Journal of Eliza Southgate Bowne; Journal of Robert Gilmor.

THE GARDEN AT EIGHTEEN SUMMER STREET[1]

This garden is a part of the original grant of land to Philip Veren, a wealthy seventeenth-century citizen of Salem. After numerous transfers, the lot, in 1805, still in its original[2] dimensions of 80 x 125 ft., came into the possession of Captain Tobias Davis, "master mariner," who immediately remodelled the house and probably made the first real garden. Capt. Davis was the owner until 1841 when he removed to Pernambuco, South America, and sold the property to Benjamin Fabens, whose heirs transferred it to Mrs. Lucy Pickering Robinson, who owned the adjoining estate. She had long gazed wistfully upon the old garden, which had become almost a forest with trees and overgrown shrubs; most of these, however, were soon removed, with the exception of some old lilacs and a Saint Michael's pear tree, which survived a number of years.

Just what Captain Davis's wife had in her garden or how it was laid out there is no record to tell. Probably it had a central path running east and west about where it is today.

The house at 18 Summer Street, Salem. Part of it was built in 1718, and a later part in 1805

The garden of 1851 was laid out by an old Scotch gardener (How many gardens are due to the Scotch gardeners!), William Weeks, short of stature and of temper too, but well grounded in the principles of gardening. There were gravel paths and rectangular beds, subdivided into little diamonds, triangles and circles, edged with dwarf box. Box flourished in those days; and for twenty years after, a dozen Salem gardens vied with each other in their box borders. They have all disappeared, however, and box-edgings cannot now be kept in even passable condition. Why it is so, no one seems to know, but in the 1850's and 1860's, by frequent subdividing and replanting, a good, even box-edging was always possible.

A list of plants to be found in the garden for the first ten years would be too long to use here, for many things were tried, but there are recalled the old double pink, the damask, the yellow and the white Scotch roses; the single moss, and the sweet and interesting striped pink and white "York and Lancaster," a variety of the rose of Provence, it is said, for if not carefully watched and reverts taken out, it will return to a simple pink rose. There was the tall Chinese tamarix, found also in another old Salem garden, but rare elsewhere and far better than the half-hardy, shrubby sort abundant in gardens at the south; the purple and white lilacs, the only

[1]This description was written by the late John Robinson.
[2]The word "original" here refers to the size of the lot when it was sold in 1715.

The garden at 18 Summer Street, Salem, photographed before 1904

An arbor covered with rambler roses in the garden at 18 Summer Street, photographed in the summer of 1910

lilacs then obtainable except the Persian variety; syringas, or mock-oranges; lemon and orange and tiger lilies, and a fine row of the candidum lily, which like the box seems to have disappeared from Salem gardens where it was formerly abundant. Honeysuckles, red and yellow, and the deliciously fragrant open-mouthed variety, besides the "trumpet honey-suckle," as it was called—which is not a lonicera but belongs to another family, tecoma—climbed over trellises at the back fences, while the queen of the prairie and the king of the prairie and Baltimore belle roses mounted high on the end of the old barn. Who cultivates these roses now?

The herbaceous perennials and annuals were selected from that excellent authority and home gardener's Bible of the day, Breck's *Book of Flowers*, and included larkspurs, the two monkshoods, dark blue and the variegated, of which Breck cautions his disciples to beware because of their active poison-ous natures; dracocephalum, now called physostegia, holly-hocks, foxgloves, Canterbury bells, ragged-robin, the single convolvulus and the double, called "California rose," calen-dula, then known as "pot-marigold," ten-weeks stocks—nine-tenths of which came single—and "China-asters" from which the poorer ones were pulled up as they flow-ered, for then seeds were saved and the garden's sup-ply of annuals was raised in cold frames—and won-derfully successful these were, too—, while a con-tinual exchanging of plants among neighboring and often more distant gar-dens increased the variety and enabled the garden to be maintained at tri-fling cost.

The "summer-house," an eight-sided arbor of white pine lattice-work, copied from one in an older garden, and covered with vines, was kept in existence until it actually dropped to pieces after sixty years of service. Early Crawford peach trees were impaled on fan-shaped trellises against the north garden fence, and dwarf winter nelis, Flemish beauty, duchess, long green and Bartlett pears, and black tartarian cherries, occupied the centers of the beds until they either outgrew their quarters or died from disagreement with the quince stock on which they were grafted.

Each spring the house plants journeyed out to summer in the garden—the very prickly cactus speciosissimus and its less ferocious relative with lighter red flowers; the old red and yellow striped abutilon; the agapanthus, the unusual blue flowered lily, which blossomed annually and immediately divided itself in two, one section of which was given to a friend; the orange and lemon trees in large pots, which blossomed occasionally, but which never succeeded in pro-ducing fruit over half an inch in diameter; the rose geranium and the pink "Lady Carington," with a daphne odora, some old varieties of fuchsia and an amaryllis, com-pleted the collection.

Of course there were eschscholtzias, portulaccas, balsams, pansies, poppies, verbenas and the like to make the garden bright, and if the scheme of planting was a little irregular, the garden was no less enjoyable, for it was worked over and picked from in the freest manner possible.

When the home gardeners grew older and stiffening knees made the devotional attitude required for weeding more

difficult, and the box edgings had become unsightly, to re-lieve the situation grassplots were substituted for most of the little formal beds and the garden was practically left to the one-day-a-week visits of the journeyman gardener who be-fore had only done the spading, shrub trimming, and other heavier work. In the half-century of the garden, too, most of the quince stock pear trees had gone, and the espaliered peaches with their fan trellises had followed; the Isabella grape vine arbor had given way to posts with rambler roses, and a comfortable, tight-roofed and cushioned garden rest seat, in a more secluded spot, succeeded the decayed summer house. Newer varieties of lilacs hedged the line of the adjoin-ing neighbor's lot, and hardy teas and hybrid perpetuals were added to the rose beds, without, however, discarding the old friends of 1850.

It has amused the owner to devise ways of planting by which the garden, small as it is, should be made to appear much larger. By using trees and shrubs, properly propor-tioned, keeping the paths in number and of a size to corres-pond with the beds, and by planting out-fences and buildings

A coop of pigeons, whose ancestors had occupied the attic of an adjacent barn since 1825, was given a hooded entrance which made a pleasing break in the long roof line

and thus visually absorbing neighboring lots, a fair measure of success has been attained.

For a century, the garden has had for a corner background the benefit of a large horse-chestnut, with branches reaching nearly to the ground. This tree was planted in 1825, when ten years old from the seed.

A coop of pigeons, whose ancestors, since 1825, had oc-cupied the attic of a barn on an adjoining lot, was rearranged so that a hooded entrance made a desirable break in the stiffness of the long roof line. The ablutions of the pigeons in a great Sumatra oyster shell, holding a full bucket of water, placed at the end of the path, add picturesqueness of a rather unusual character to the garden.

And so, growing older with its owner and changing with the fashions from period to period, the garden has become a resting place instead of a working garden.

THE DEVEREUX-HOFFMAN-SIMPSON GARDEN

The garden at 26 Chestnut Street dates from about 1816. Humphrey Devereux, the first owner, built the house, but sold it when he failed in business.

The second owner was Captain Hoffman, a Swede, edu-cated at Andover. He married a Miss King of Salem. He was

Tilford's Studio

A fine old pump, dating from about 1810, in the Devereux-Hoffman-Simpson garden, Salem

a shipmaster and rich merchant in South American trade, and had a passion for horticulture. His Scotch gardener, Hugh Wilson, came to this country with Peter Henderson. Peter Henderson drifted to New York and started the great seed-house which still bears his name. Wilson was engaged by Captain Hoffman and took care of his garden for fifty years.

Originally there was additional land on Hamilton Street, where stood the gardener's house and four large greenhouses. One was filled with grapes; another with peaches. Some of the peaches were in tubs. In the peach-house a net was kept under the fruit. Captain Hoffman had a stick with

Photographed by Robert N. Cram

The Devereux-Hoffman-Simpson garden offers an excellent illustration of the fact that "though the old designers of gardens realized the value of formality in design . . . yet they seem to have thought it unnecessary to center the garden on a particular window or door of the house." See the full text on page 96

Photographed by Robert N. Cram

This delightful summer-house in the Devereux-Hoffman-Simpson garden has paths crossing through it in both directions. Captain Hoffman's old camellia-house, seen in the rear, has long been used for grapes

which to rap the trees, to see how ripe the fruit was; he would let nobody do this but himself. The greenhouse in the present garden was twice as large as it is now, and contained camellias. After Captain Hoffman's death the camellias were given up and grapes were planted.

One of the notable features of the place is a fine pump, over a century old.

Wilson and Henderson kept up their friendship, and more than once Henderson came to Salem to make addresses on horticultural subjects. Wilson retired at the age of eighty-two and his place was taken by Lewis Dow, also Scotch, who has worked on the garden for more than thirty years, first for Captain Hoffman's widow, and then for Dr. Simpson, the present owner of the property.

Two views of Miss Laight's garden, laid out in 1810 at 41 Chestnut Street, Salem. The arched gate through which one looks from the house terrace along the main path, in the illustration at the right, is very old. At the left is a view along the path in the opposite direction

THE ROBERT MANNING FRUIT GARDEN

In 1822 Robert Manning bought about three acres of land in a part of Salem then called Northfields. The next year he began his garden, and the year after, 1823, he built his house. His family have lived there ever since; a descendant is there today, at 33 Dearborn Street.

Robert Manning was an enthusiast in regard to trees, especially fruit trees, and pear trees most of all. He imported many trees and scions from France and other countries, and devoted himself to comparing, testing, and identifying the various kinds. It is said that he had a thousand varieties of pears. He had a large correspondence with horticulturists

his garden. He called his place "The Pomological Garden." It did not have any formal laying out. A walk ran through the middle from the house to the farther end, where there was once a hedge of crab-apple trees. Along the walk was a row of apple trees, all of which have disappeared. One, a bell-flower apple, is especially remembered for its beauty; the branches, spreading wide and resting on the ground, formed an arbor. Only a hollow stump covered with wood-bine remains, but it still has vitality enough to send up suckers. There is another of the original apple trees, in a dilapidated condition, and two or three pear trees which probably date from the beginning of the garden. One of these is a Dearborn's Seedling, named for the first president of the Massa-

Photographed by Robert N. Cram

Miss Huntington's garden on Chestnut Street in Salem dates from about 1832. This photograph shows the inner yard and gate to the garden.
Barrier entrances such as that shown here were most characteristic of Salem, but are now disappearing

both in this country and in Europe. One who is remembered was Dr. J. B. Van Mons of Belgium.

Manning was a charter member of the Massachusetts Horticultural Society in 1829, and served continuously on its committees until his death. The beginning of its library was made by a gift of some of his own books.[1]

A historical sketch of the Society says of him:

"Robert Manning . . . was unquestionably the best informed and ablest pomologist in the United States, and it is doubtful whether there were many in any country who were his equals in that very interesting and important branch of Horticulture. . . ."[2]

In 1838 Manning published *The Book of Fruits;* in the opening remarks he gives some account of his plans in establishing

[1] See page 6.
[2] "Historical Sketch of the Massachusetts Horticultural Society." H. A. S Dearborn. 1850. (Dearborn was the first president of the Society, 1829–34.)

chusetts Horticultural Society. A large acacia tree and a rose-bush with single white flowers are still there. On the house grows a honeysuckle set out by Robert Manning's wife in 1825, the spring after her marriage. An elm tree set out in the same year on the street in front of the house still flourishes.

After Manning's death in 1842, his sons took up the care of the garden. The older of them, another Robert Manning, then only fifteen, had assisted his father and had been trained by him for the work. He continued to send fruit to the exhibitions of the Massachusetts Horticultural Society, at one time sending 280 varieties of pears and 118 varieties of apples. He also exhibited fruit at the American Institute in New York, receiving some books as prizes, and at one time a silver medal for 100 varieties of pears shown. He became librarian and secretary of the Massachusetts Horticultural Society and editor of its publications. He wrote a history of the Society. He was editor of Tilton's "Journal of Horticulture," and was one of the founders of the American Pomological Society.

This second Robert Manning was interested less in fruit trees than in the more ornamental trees, shrubs and vines. He added the virgilias, wistarias, catalpas, pawpaws, per-

The garden is but a shadow of its former beauty, but is still pleasant and interesting. Even now in the early spring the ground is blue with scilla and chionodoxa flowers. Later, blue and yellow violets abound, and maiden-hair and several other native ferns grow luxuriantly. Sometimes a space two

Photographed by Robert N. Cram

The path in Miss Huntington's garden

simmons—both American and Japanese—, two or three kinds of nut-trees, three kinds of pyrus japonica, a fringe-tree, several kinds of syringa, lilacs, and spirea; also tamarisk, witch-hazel, a Christmas rose, and a fig tree, which, when protected through the winter, grew five or six feet tall and ripened figs. There are fine climbing hydrangea and some actinidias—one having edible fruit. At one time there was a good collection of hardy perennials, some of them given by Francis Parkman.[1]

[1]"Ex-President of the Massachusetts Horticultural Society, who has become almost as widely known for his experience in hybridizing plants as for his historical writings."—*Memorial History of Boston*, edited by Justin Winsor, Vol. IV. Chapter on "Horticulture," etc., by M. P. Wilder. p. 624.

or three feet across is carpeted with ladies' delights. It is sometimes gay with large clumps of pink and scarlet poppies, coreopsis, bachelors' buttons, and hollyhocks. All these are self-planted.

In 1828, Robert Manning built a house next his own for his sister, who was the mother of Nathaniel Hawthorne. Undoubtedly Hawthorne spent many hours in this garden.[1]

[1]Sources: *The Book of Fruits* by Robert Manning; *Memorial History of Boston*, edited by Justin Winsor; *Reports of the Massachusetts Horticultural Society* (1829–42); *History of the Massachusetts Horticultural Society*, by Robert Manning; *The Lure of the Garden*, by Hildegarde Hawthorne; *Old-Time Gardens*, by Alice Morse Earle.

An avenue of elms planted by Joseph Augustus Peabody in 1817 at "The Farm" in Danvers

DANVERS

THE GARDEN OF JOSEPH PEABODY, KNOWN AS "THE FARM"[1]

This estate was purchased in 1814 by Joseph Peabody, and the avenue of elm trees which is still in existence was planted by his son, Joseph Augustus Peabody, in 1817. At this time the avenue was a public highway.

In the autumn of 1814, George Heussler, gardener of Elias Hasket Derby, laid out the planting in the front of the house.

[1]Facts from an article by William C. Endicott in the Massachusetts Horticultural Society's Year-Book for 1927. Since 1814 the owners of the property have been Joseph Peabody; George Peabody, his son; Mrs. Wm. C. Endicott, daughter of George Peabody; Wm. C. Endicott, her son.

The garden was originally planned around a tree which stood on a mound in the center of the plot. In the early thirties a storm destroyed this tree, and a tulip-tree was planted to replace the old one. This later tree became famous as a specimen, but was killed in the winter of 1920–21. When cut down it was ninety-eight feet high, fifteen feet in circumference, and five feet in diameter.

The buckthorn (*Rhamnus*) hedges, of which there are three, were planted nearly a hundred years ago; the arbor-vitae hedge on one side of a path known as "The Lover's Walk" is a fine specimen of a hedge and must also be nearly a hundred years old.

The summer-house built by McIntire for Elias Hasket Derby's farm, as it now appears in the garden at "The Farm" in Danvers, the property of Mr. W. C. Endicott. It was moved here about 1901 from its original site some three miles away on the Derby farm in Danvers

A little summer-house at the end of the old garden, with a gilded pineapple atop, was designed about 1840 by Francis Peabody, the son of Joseph Peabody.

In 1901 the late Mrs. W. C. Endicott purchased the summer-house designed by Samuel McIntire for the garden of Elias Hasket Derby and moved it to this garden. It was so well built that though it was moved several miles, the structure was undamaged. This summer-house has two stories, with an open passage through the ground floor leading to the rose garden.

When the summer-house was moved there were four carved urns on the roof, and a carved figure of a man whetting a scythe (as shown in the illustration). There had originally been a figure of a milkmaid, but this had been removed. This figure was found, however, and was used as a model for a new one which now stands as formerly on the roof.

The garden has been greatly enlarged and beautified by the present owners, who have made an effort to develop shrubs and trees suggested by the Arnold Arboretum.

The garden at "The Farm" in Danvers, the property of Mr. W. C. Endicott, was originally laid out by George Heussler

Photograph by T. E. Mott and Son

In the garden at "The Farm," in Danvers.   The small summer-house ending the central path on the upper level, seen at the left, was designed by Francis Peabody about 1840

T. E. Mott and Son

The house at Hale Farm, Beverly, viewed from across the sweep of lawn. The three old English beeches are to be seen at the left, and the garden and borders at the right

BEVERLY

HALE FARM

Hale Farm has remained continuously in possession of descendants of the original seventeenth-century owner, the youngest representative being ninth in direct descent from the Rev. John Hale (1636–1700). This chain of unbroken family ownership, now approaching three hundred years in duration, is a remarkable record. The line of descent runs as follows:

Rev. John Hale (1636–1700), Dr. Robert Hale (1668–1719), Col. Robert Hale (1703–1767), Elizabeth Hale (1725–1767), Capt. Robert Hale Ives (1744–1773), Elizabeth Ives (1767–1801), Thomas Poynton Bancroft (1798–1852), Robert Hale Bancroft (1843–1918), Elizabeth Hope Bancroft (1895–), Robert Hale Bancroft Winsor (1922–).

Mrs. Robert Hale Bancroft, widow of the eighth owner and now in possession, has written the following account of the horticultural history of Hale Farm.

"In 1664, Rev. John Hale came from Charlestown to be the first settled minister of the first 'gathered' church in Beverly. He lived in the parsonage built for him on Watch Hill until 1694 when he built himself the second parsonage— the present house—which is across Hale Street from the first

The "West Path" from the house to the "Long Walk," at Hale Farm. In the foreground is the tulip-tree

The "Long Walk" at Hale Farm, Beverly, viewed from the Hale Street end

The house at Hale Farm, Beverly, framed by one of the old apple trees. In the background is the gable end of the barn built in 1824

parsonage. He, his son, Dr. Robert Hale, and his grandson, Col. Robert Hale, added many acres to their land and were prominent in the town and commonwealth. Where they had their garden is not known; certainly they supplied themselves and their families from their broad acres.

"Thomas Poynton Bancroft (1798–1852), sixth in descent from Rev. John Hale, and the seventh owner of Hale Farm, made a great interest of the garden and trees, and owned many books on farming and horticulture. The land to the west of the house was laid out for a flower, vegetable, and fruit garden in regular divisions with gravel walks edged with box. The flower garden was nearest the house where still stands the big tulip-tree, and was laid out in rounds and diamonds edged with box, the last of which died in 1922. With the growth of many trees the old garden gradually disappeared. There are still large clumps of 'Rose of Sharon' and Lilies-of-the-valley. Numerous clumps of 'narcissus poeticus' bloom on the lawn.

"An English gardener spent all his time on the garden, and it was Mr. Bancroft's great pleasure to carry the produce of his garden to his friends and neighbors. In his day, two huge hollow-trunked willows stood at the yard entrance, but they were blown down in the gale of September, 1869. An ancient buttonwood tree then stood in the wall on Hale Street. This tree in its prime soared above everything about and was a well known mark for vessels entering Beverly Harbor. The oldest tree on the place, still standing, is an elm over the farm house on Hale Street, at the corner of the Common. In 1840, no one living remembered it as a young tree. (At that time there were one hundred acres in the place. Now, in 1924, the house lot is seven acres, with about four acres more divided from it by streets.) All the other trees, except the large elms and one or two apple trees, were planted about 1846. Among these are three splendid English beeches on the south lawn, where there is room for the spread of their great branches, which sweep the ground.

"For the last fifty years or more, there have been wide borders of perennials near the house, backed by shrubs and trees and in places by trellices[1] covered with flower grapevines. These have always been clipped to make a hedge-like background.

"The present flower garden, dating from 1900, lies to the south. It is 90 feet by 60 feet, with shrubs and trees on three sides and open only to the west. At the east is a clipped grapevine.

"The house stands about 20 feet back from Hale Street, with an old elm at the small gate which opens on a gravel path to the front door. There is a driveway into the yard where is the side door of the house; and 45 feet across the yard is the barn built in 1824, when the very old barn was burned. Still further along Hale Street is the barnyard entrance. Both yards have fine trees and large lilacs."

[1]Wire fences.

One of the three fine English beeches on the south lawn at Hale Farm, Beverly. They were planted about 1846. Just under the low limbs, the trunk of this tree is 15 feet 8 inches in circumference. The limbs extend 45 feet from trunk to tip

Photographs by T. E. Mott and Son

The beech walk at Hale Farm, looking toward Hale Street and the boundary wall

NEWBURYPORT AND ENVIRONS

IN THE narratives and observations recorded by travelers between 1605 and 1799, "Newberry" is first mentioned by name by Thomas Lechford in 1642, in his "Plain Dealing: or Newes for New England." Edward Johnson's "Wonder Working Providence" in 1652 gives us a glimpse of a town "scituate . . . neere upon the wide venting streame of Merrimeck River—this Towne is stored with meddow and upland, which hath caused some Gentlemen, (who brought over good Estates, and finding then no better way to improve them) to set upon husbandry."

Samuel Maverick in "A Briefe Description of New England" observed of "Newberry" in 1660 that "the Houses stand at a good distance each from other a field and Garden between each house. . . ." And in 1671 John Josselyn set down for his "An Account of Two Voyages to New England" the following picture of "Newberrie" and its environs:

"Eight miles beyond . . . runneth the delightful River Merrimach or Morrumack, it is navigable for twenty miles and well stored with fish, upon the banks grow stately Oaks, excellent Ship timber, not inferiour to our English.

"On the South-side of Merrimach-River . . . is situated Newberrie, the houses are scattering, well stored with meadow, upland, and Arrable. . . ."

The Marquis de Chastellux in 1782 described it in recording his travels as a "pretty little town," and an Italian traveler, Luigi Castiglioni, in 1785 remarked its "very pleasant surroundings." George Washington's Diary sets down his impressions of his visit in 1789, in the course of his tours through New England, but aside from finding it "pleasantly situated," gives no hint of gardens or agriculture. That indispensable diarist, the Rev. Wm. Bentley, usually so critically observant of gardening activities, fails likewise to enrich our view of historic gardens in his observations on Newburyport in 1793.

A passage in Timothy Dwight's *Travels* affords us much the best background for our study of the historic gardens of Newburyport:

"Newburyport . . . lies on the Southern shore of the Merrimac. The town is built on a declivity of unrivalled beauty. The slope is easy and elegant; the soil rich; the streets, except the one near the water, clean and sweet; and the verdure, wherever it is visible, exquisite. . . . High Street, which lies in the rear, and almost on the summit of the acclivity, is remarkably handsome; and commands a noble prospect. . . .

"The houses taken collectively, make a better appearance than those of any other town in New England. Many of them are particularly handsome. Their appendages, also, are unusually neat. Indeed, an air of wealth, taste, and elegance, is spread over this beautiful spot with a cheerfulness and brilliancy, to which I know no rival. . . .

"The wealth of this town is everywhere visible in the buildings and their appurtenances. Several of the inhabitants are possessed of large fortunes. . . .

". . . From the tower of the church, belonging to the fifth Congregation, a noble prospect is presented to the spectator. . . . [Here follows a description of the view inland and towards the sea.] . . . Immediately beneath, is the town itself; which with its Churches and beautiful houses, its harbour and shipping, appears as the proper centre of this circle of scenery; and leaves on the mind a cheerfulness and brilliancy, strongly resembling that, which accompanies a delightful morning in May.

"There are ten public schools, supported in this town. . . .

"Nothing which hospitality or politeness could dictate, or refined intelligence express, was wanting to make our stay agreeable."[1]

HISTORIC NEWBURYPORT GARDENS[2]

Newburyport in its ancient prime was a city of greenery and gardens; to that there is ample testimony both in local chronicles and in those of outside visitors. As time went on, the interests of its more enterprising garden-lovers moved them to join the activities of county and state organizations and to organize in 1833 a Horticultural Society of their own. Many flower and fruit shows were held, sometimes as often as once a fortnight throughout the summer. From a much earlier date the citizens individually took pride in their

Robert N. Cram

A typical Newburyport street—Fruit Street, looking into High Street

trees, their fruits, and their flowers. Even the busy housewives of the simpler homes of the Newburies had their dooryard plantings of cinnamon roses and tawny lilies, tansy and Bouncing Bet, whose escaped descendants still persist in many a country byway. The sea-captains, it is known, brought home bulbs and seeds from Europe; probably also trees and shrubs from our southern coast ports. There were assuredly men among them used to the shipboard care of such things, for Manasseh Cutler of Ipswich, clergyman, gardener and botanist, who imported them often, records several times in

[1]From *Travels in New England and New York*, by Timothy Dwight. Letter XLI. Vol. I.
[2]Adapted from an account written by Miss Ethel Parton.

his diary the despatch of such freight for Newburyport, or its arrival there by schooner from Washington. His clerical visits brought him in touch with Newburyport gardens as well as churches.

In May 1781, he visited one of the most notable of Newburyport gardens, that begun by Patrick Tracy and continued and improved under his son John. The ample colonial house of the Tracys, now owned by Mr. Willis S. Johnson, still stands in beauty and dignity unimpaired, and there is a garden gay with bloom at one side; but the garden of the founders, which once occupied a terraced slope at the rear, is no more; even the terraces have disappeared.

"At Mr. John Tracy's; viewed the garden; very fine," wrote Manasseh Cutler appreciatively. "He gave me a large assortment of flower seeds."

It was when John Tracy's estate was at the height of its prosperity that he received the visit of a group of distinguished Frenchmen, of whom one, the Marquis de Chastellux, has left an account. It was night when he arrived, but:

"I went, however by moonlight to see the garden, which is composed of different terraces. There is likewise a hothouse and a number of young trees. The house is handsome and well-furnished, and everything breathes an air of magnificence accompanied with simplicity which is only to be found among merchants."

At the time of this visit the garden had been for a year under the care of an expert gardener whom Tracy had imported from Europe. This was George Heussler[1], the Alsatian gardener who, when the declining fortunes of his patron "cast the poor stranger unpaid upon the world," soon redeemed his fortunes in Salem, where he was placed in charge of the famous Derby gardens. There, as in Newburyport, he was the first man of education and training to follow gardening as a profession.

The mansion next door to Tracy's possessed an interesting garden which was not established, however, until the house had passed out of the hands of his brother-in-law into those of that widely renowned eccentric, the self-styled "Lord" Timothy Dexter, who proceeded to adorn both house and grounds in what he conceived to be a lordly and imposing manner in accordance with European fashion. Two open-mouthed lions guarded the door; minarets and a cupola decorated the roof; in front, a curving open colonnade swept from the entrance in both directions. There were about forty columns, each fifteen feet high, and two arches. Perched on the top of each column was the statue of some distinguished man—Washington, Adams, Jefferson, Nelson, Napoleon, and others—including, in the most conspicuous position, one of Dexter himself, with the inscription, "I am the first in the East, the first in the West, and the greatest philosopher in the known world." All these images were executed by a young ship-carver and gaudily painted. To this extraordinary assembly he added a still more extraordinary feature: he had his own tomb prepared in the basement of an elegant summer-house, well lighted and ventilated and surrounded by shrubbery. When it was completed he arranged a mock funeral—or, rather, the funeral rehearsal of a prospective ceremony which he could not hope to enjoy—in which his elegant but empty coffin was borne in procession from the house to the garden-tomb. Jonathan Plummer, a doggerel rhymester employed by Lord Timothy as "poet laureate", in the course of a lengthy eulogy upon his patron wrote:

"His tomb most charming to behold
A thousand sweets it doth enfold;
When Dexter dies shall willows weep
And mourning friends shall fill the street."

Unfortunately only the willows wept at the anticipatory obsequies; his wife did not—an omission in her role of widow

[1]Previously encountered in the study of Salem gardens.

which her lord, during the carouse following the ceremonies, effectively remedied by a beating.

Although in such an amazing garden attention was naturally attracted from the more usual features, Dexter spent large sums on native and imported flowers, shrubs, and fruits. He had fine currants, gooseberries, and other small fruits, and such "a noble orchard" of cherries that he customarily employed an armed guard when they were ripening. But his grounds were open to the public and he was lavishly generous with fruit and flowers to any who would earn them with sufficient cómpliments.

This unique garden flourished during the eight years from 1798 to the death of Dexter, who was not buried in his summer-house tomb after all, the city authorities refusing their permission. The images were then sold at auction, the growing garden fell into neglect and practically perished, and the house passed through various hands until it was purchased in 1852 by Dr. Elbridge G. Kelley, who replanted and redesigned the estate anew. From that date the Dexter Place, now owned by Mr. George A. Learned, has enjoyed nearly seventy-five years of consecutive good planting and garden care. But of all Lord Timothy Dexter's cherished embellishments nothing remains but the great gilt eagle surmounting the cupola of the house.

Another interesting garden belonged to Tristram Dalton, the first senator from Massachusetts, at Pipestave Hill, in West Newbury. Manasseh Cutler visited this garden also, on June 8, 1773:

"Took a view of Mr. Dalton's country-seat—very elegant. Went up to the walk on the top of the house where he had a most extensive and agreeable prospect."

It was in October, five years later, that Brissot de Warville, the later Girondist leader who was guillotined in the French Revolution, visited the Dalton place. In his "New Travels in America," he wrote:

"We left Portsmouth on Sunday and came to dine at Mr. Dalton's, five miles from Newbury on the Merrimack; this is one of the finest situations that can be imagined. It presents an agreeable prospect of seven leagues. This farm is extremely well-arranged; I saw on it thirty cows, numbers of sheep, etc. and a well-furnished garden. Mr. Dalton occupies himself much in gardening, a thing generally neglected in America. . . . [His household] presented me with the image of a true patriarchal family, and of great domestic felicity."

THE WHEELWRIGHT GARDEN

The estate numbered 75 High Street was for many years, and in its greatest glory, known as the "Wheelwright Place."[1]

The house was built about 1797 by Captain Ebenezer Stocker, and the original lot comprised an acre and a half of land, doubled by subsequent purchase. The house is of the Georgian type of architecture, square and three-storied, interesting still because of its interior carving, landscape paper, staircase and hall. The entrance door is at one end of the hall, and directly opposite is a door leading into the garden and the beauty of lawn, shrub and flower.

William Wheelwright, who created the garden, was a lover and close observer of flowers, delighting in their beauty, variety and fragrance. The effective arrangement and admirable combination of colors as seen in parterres filled him with delight. A close personal friend of his, Henry V. Ward, not a landscape gardener, designed this somewhat elaborate garden.

A gardener by the name of Armstrong ably executed the plans, and later an Englishman trained in his own country, Thomas Capers, had charge of the gardens and the greenhouse for nearly thirty years.

One of the interesting features of the estate is the unusual lie of the land; one ascends a gentle slope of 90 feet before one

[1]Ninety-nine years in the Wheelwright family; there were several owners before this.

An old photograph of the Wheelwright garden, Newburyport, showing the lay-out of a garden of the 1840's, in the days when the Newburyport Horticultural Society was giving fresh inspiration to garden owners and garden lovers. Note the miniature replica of the Old South Church surmounting the summer-house

reaches the house; then on a plateau of considerable extent are placed the house, lawns and flower garden. A steep descent, terraced either side of a flight of steps, leads to the vegetable garden and pasture, and beyond, on a precipitous hillside, is the apple orchard of an acre. This makes a view of wondrous beauty in apple-blossom time, and lends distinction and charm to the view from the house and upper garden.

The street frontage is approximately 105 feet, widening as it recedes; like most Newburyport gardens, the length of this garden many times exceeds its breadth.

In front of the house is a terraced lawn, bordered on three sides by a buckthorn hedge; what was once a magnificent elm divides its huge bulk between the lawn and adjacent sidewalk. Spruce trees, a rowan tree, horse-chestnut, lilac bushes, hydrangea, and what was then a recent importation, a weigelia, add to its adornment.

The formal design of the flower garden was contained in a large circle cut in the grass, broken by straight paths to the house and summer-house. The central design was in the form of a Maltese cross, outlined with box; between its arms were small circles, box-bordered; outside were complete circles alternating with segments of a much larger circle, all of which were bordered with box.

On either side of the path leading to the summer-house were long beds of roses: moss roses with their delicate mossy covering, others of the early pink varieties, and a rose which William Wheelwright imported from England, a rich velvety crimson, with patches of purple in the petals of the bud; as the rose unfolds it becomes purple suffused with red and retains its velvety appearance. Among the flowers which have survived the vicissitudes of time may be seen the grape-hyacinth, daffodil, narcissus and tulip; the iris, the lemon lily, columbine, ratinella, oriental poppy, peony, funkia, and yucca.

The summer-house, built of wood, by a curious architectural combination was surmounted by a weather-vane replica in miniature of the Old South Church, where the Wheelwright family attended worship.

Apples from the orchard were of such a fine variety that Mr. Wheelwright had them sent to him in England. Peaches were of the most luscious kind. One day the gardener, who was allowed to sell some of the fruit, brought a basket of peaches, packed with the utmost care, to a rather superior grocer. (This was before the days of fruit stores and the grocer sometimes dealt in choice fruits.) As fifteen cents apiece was the price asked, the grocer refused, but a gentle-

Photographed by Robert N. Cram

The box-edged parterre in the Moulton garden, Newburyport

man somewhat interested in horticulture who happened to be present bought them and sent them to Boston, where he received twenty-five cents for each peach. This was fifty years ago, which indicates the quality of the fruit.

In 1888, by deed of gift, the house and grounds became the property of the Newburyport Society for the Relief of Aged Women. Obviously a charitable society would not have the funds to keep such an elaborate type of garden up to its highest possibilities. Its greenhouse has gone, an addition to the house in the rear has cut into the plan of the flower garden, and it has been sadly altered. Many of the trees and shrubs have died and have been only partially replaced, but the land is intact and there is enough of its pristine glory left to make it a pleasure and resource for the household and an object of interest to its garden-loving visitors.

THE MOULTON GARDEN[1]

The land was purchased by William Moulton on May 12, 1732 (as per Registry of Deeds at Salem, Massachusetts), and was owned and occupied by descendants of the same name to the sixth generation. The land has been one hundred and ninety-two years in the Moulton family.

On this land, in the year 1800, Joseph Moulton and his son William built the double house, now numbered 89 and 91 High Street, Newburyport, Massachusetts. They were silversmiths; much of their work is now preserved in museums and regarded as rare works of art.

Later, Joseph Moulton, son of William, occupied the home

[1]Written by Mrs. Elizabeth Colman Moulton Noyes.

Robert N. Cram

The skeleton of the summer-house (1840) at the end of the central walk in the Moulton garden

of his grandfather, 89 High Street, and about 1840 laid out the garden as it is now. The work was done by an English gardener named Clifford. Six latticed arches spanned the walks. The summer-house which he built still furnishes a resting-place among the trees. Two bird-houses on high poles are a part of the garden's attraction.

The flower garden lies next the house and is laid out in formal beds with box borders. The box has always been re-

The total length of the garden is 192 feet, 8 inches; the flower garden measures 67 feet in width; the lower, or fruit portion, 96 feet.

COLONEL EBENEZER MOSELEY'S GARDEN[1]

True to the Georgian type, the house at 182 High Street has a wide hall running through it, and, standing at the front

The Moulton garden, the property of Elizabeth C. Moulton Noyes, as it is today. It was laid out in its present form about 1840

newed by separation, therefore descendants of the original plants remain and are still in fine condition. The lower garden was first planted with apple trees, but as pears were considered a rarer fruit, these trees were taken up and replaced by pears.

A long box-bordered path leads to Moulton's Lane; over the gate is a lovely arbor-like arch. On either side of this path were currant and gooseberry bushes. On the right, a long trellis supports Rogers (or Salem) Blood, Isabella and Niagara grapes; a smaller trellis, the Delaware. All were planted with the garden and are still bearing quantities of fruit.

In the garden still stands a very large rhododendron which is even older than all the rest. Every May hundreds of purple blossoms delight the eye.

A bed of rose-trees yields quantities of flowers. These plants are so old we cannot know their names. The Damask, so delicate and lovely, has gone; also a rose with pink and white striped petals; but Moss, Scotch, Prairie, and Baltimore Belle, with its bunches of twelve beautiful white buds tipped with pink, are still there. Many of these rose-trees are ten feet high. One of these yields a single rose of most delicate pink with golden center. There is the Dutchman's-pipe vine with its queer brown blossoms. At one time an arbor-vitae wigwam was planted. It grew to great height and the tops of the trees were tied together, forming a nice play-house for the children. For several years a row of bee-hives added quaintness.

door, the eye is carried beyond the hall itself, across a twelve-foot veranda curtained with honeysuckle, along a hundred feet of ancient sunbaked brick, to the garden itself. Here, through an arch covered with vines, one looks down the first and second terraces to a distant summer-house, with a canopy of the big scentless Prairie rose planted a hundred years ago. The summer-house stands against a high brick wall whose grapevines make a background for bright hollyhocks. This marks the end of the garden walk and a vista of over two hundred and seventy feet.

The walk is bordered on either side by such fine and familiar flowers as have proved themselves in New England. The same soil feeds the heavenly blue larkspur, the sweet-williams of richest hue and the monkshood with its stately growth, as in the days of long ago. Around the whole garden, next to the walls, are the old-time shrubs—syringas, lilacs, mock oranges, and the old-fashioned honeysuckle bushes.

Another summer-house where four paths meet gives shelter from the hot rays of the summer sun, and on its lattice grows a wild grapevine. These grapes were much prized and were used for jelly served with game on my great-grandmother's table.

The house was built in 1811, but owing to the War of 1812 and the consequent heavy taxes and lack of commercial

[1]Written by Mrs. A. C. Nason (née Moseley), the owner.

A rose-covered arch in the Moseley garden, Newburyport.   To the right is the summer-house at the second terrace, covered with wild grapevine

prosperity, soon had to be sold. Shortly after that it was bought by Col. Ebenezer Moseley, an eminent member of the Essex Bar, Yale 1802. His portrait, with that of his grandfather, Rev. Samuel Moseley, chaplain to the royal governor Hutchinson, still hangs in the hall of his old home.

Col. Moseley[1] came from a family much identified with

[1]Known locally as "Squire Moseley."

horticulture and forestry. He was president of the Essex Agricultural Society from 1833 to 1836, and he was also president of the Newburyport Horticultural Society. In the Report of the anniversary festival dinner of the Massachusetts Horticultural Society for the year 1833 we find this:

"14 Toast. By the Hon. Ebenezer Moseley, President of the Newburyport Horticultural Society, present by invitation of

A wintry view of the summer-house at the end of the Moseley garden

Robert N. Cram
The doorway leading into the Cushing garden in Newburyport

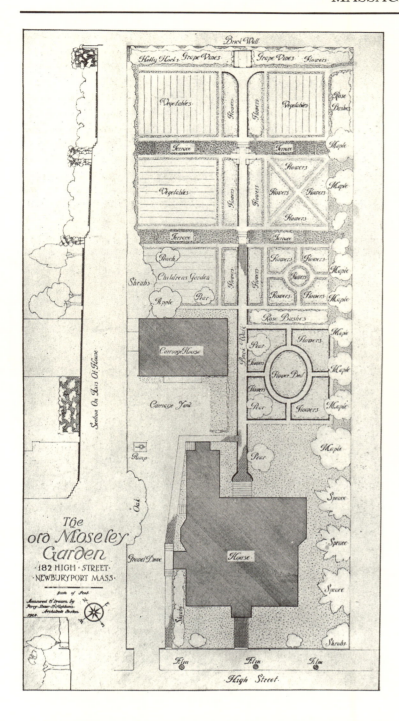

The old Moseley Garden
182 HIGH STREET
NEWBURYPORT MASS.

Robert N. Cram

The central walk in the Cushing garden, Newburyport. A board fence shuts out the traffic of High Street

the Massachusetts Horticultural Society. 'Education. That moral culture which eradicates the weeds of bad principles,'" etc.

He was very fond of the cultivation of the soil and nothing interested him more than the propagation of new varieties of fruits and flowers. It was he who laid out this garden and stocked it with fruit trees and plants. His wife devoted constant care to it as well, and she knew and loved every flower. In the 30's Mrs. Moseley writes to one of her friends: "The bulbs are in full bloom and look beautifully, the hyacinths however are not as handsome as last year, but the polyanthus are superb." She writes elsewhere of her dahlias. At that time there was great rivalry in growing dahlias.[1]

When President Monroe visited Newburyport on July 12, 1817, and was received with an address of welcome by Col. Moseley, the procession moved up High Street to the Mall under a great arch made from flowers from Mrs. Moseley's garden and other gardens in Newburyport. On this Mall are still standing the trees given and planted by Col. Moseley.

Unfortunately one of the most charming and doubtless oldest features of the garden has now gone, but by almost a miracle it lasted into the time of the great-grandchildren. It was a high circle of box. In June, when its dark green encircled a host of the Madonna lilies, it was indeed a thing lovely to behold; but there is a good deal still which has

[1]"Mexican Georginas" they are called in the earliest reports of the Massachusetts Horticultural Society, 1829–33.

weathered the generations: the tree peony, now so seldom seen, the spicy fraxinella, and a specimen of the York and Lancaster rose brought with some lavender in 1794 from a great-great-grandmother's lovely garden which still is kept up in Surrey, England.

THE CUSHING GARDEN[1]

The estate 98 High Street came into the possession of John N. Cushing, Esq., in 1818, by purchase from the widow of Captain William Hunt. The latter bought the land from Elizabeth, the widow of Jonathan Moulton. The house was built by Mr. Hunt, but for 106 years has been owned and

[1]Written by Miss Margaret Cushing.

Robert N. Cram

An ancient pump (about 1810) in the rear yard of the Cushing property

Above is the vine-draped front door of the Cushing house, Newburyport, viewed from the street. To the right is the view down one of the inviting paths in the garden

occupied by three generations of the Cushing family.

Captain Hunt, a skilled navigator, undoubtedly brought ideas from his foreign travels which added much to the attractiveness of the house. He died before its completion.

At first the garden was a playground for the children and then was used to raise fruits, flowers and vegetables for the family. Its shape is a parallelogram, and the dimensions are 145 feet by 40 feet. The main part, box-bordered, contains many shrubs, fruit trees and small fruits, also a variety of grapevines.

It is well remembered by the family that the first Indian peach trees were bought with the understanding that the stones should be returned to the nurseryman. These peaches are small and grey outside, but inside are of a rich crimson color and unequaled for preserving.

A part of the small vegetable section is still used to raise sweet corn that one member of the family, in the early part of the nineteenth century, succeeded in producing by crossbreeding and fertilization. Every year since then enough seed corn has been saved to insure a supply for the family table during the next summer. The corn is not marketable, having small kernels on short ears, but easily makes up in quality what it lacks in quantity.

In 1830 Mr. Cushing's eldest son, Caleb, brought from France the designs much used in gardens there; namely, flower beds in the form of circles and triangles, bordered with box. He was much interested in botany, and there are still in this collection plants and shrubs which he brought from the different forests of New England and planted here when he was a student in Harvard College. There are white rose bushes that are over one hundred years old, taken from

the garden of an ancestor. Of these there are two varieties; one is the double old-fashioned white rose; the other, like a large Cherokee rose or eglantine, is single and has a large golden centre.

Each generation of Cushings has contributed something. A shad bush from Virginia, planted about one hundred years ago, still thrives and delights the owners, especially in early summer, when all kinds of birds come to feast on its sweet berries. Another member of the family planted bloodroot and adder's tongue taken from the neighboring meadows of Newbury; these bloom every spring. And later, in the present generation, our most beautiful fern, the maiden-hair, was brought from the nearby woods to find a new home here.

In the westerly corner there is growing a holly bush[1] brought from Abbotsford many years ago, and associated with Sir Walter Scott. Its clusters of yellow flowers among the dark and shining green leaves in the spring, and its blue berries in

[1] Probably *Mahonia aquifolium*—Editor.

Cross-walk in the Cushing garden, leading to the house

the autumn, are added beauty spots. Like the Walking Fern, our holly has transplanted itself from place to place, so now our next-door neighbor is the proud possessor of a holly bush.

Serving as a background and partial boundary wall is a brick building which was considered old more than a century ago. Clinging vines help to make it an integral part of the view and the historic association gives a quaint flavor, for here, in 1804, Jacob Perkins, Esq., printed bank notes by a new process of his own invention, which was adopted in this country and abroad. Mr. Perkins was a relative of the family and had an international reputation as an inventor. Doubtless in his spare minutes he too looked out on this old garden with pleasure.

The older members of the family remember the hives of bees at the head of the garden, and at the foot the martin pole and house. The return of the martins was eagerly looked for by the children as a sure sign of spring.

gardens, orchards, and hilly verdant country backed by the green of venerable Norway spruces.[1] The "American Pilot" calls this cupola a landmark for mariners along the coast.

The Academy was the favorite school for boys and girls of Newburyport. Here, in the hall on the second story, Ralph Waldo Emerson addressed the Lyceum; nearly all of the Lyceum meetings were held in the Academy.

In 1842, John Osgood and Charles J. Brockway converted the Academy house into a dwelling for two families.

Behind the house, the two gardens, opening into each other almost as one, differ materially in plan.

WEST GARDEN. The first John Osgood, who drew with facility and who knew and loved plants, doubtless designed his own garden. A plan of it is in his sketch book. Loudon's *Encyclopedia of Gardening*, Cobbett's *American Gardener*, and G. W. Kern's *Landscape Gardening* were among his books.

The central walk and garden-house in the West garden of the Osgood-Brockway house, Newburyport

Flowers and fruits grown here were frequently found worthy to be shown, in the past, at the annual Horticultural Exhibitions of Newburyport.

The most striking features in the spring are flowering fruit trees—peach, pear, and plum—and the borders of crocus and the forsythias, which in full bloom form a line of gold across the front of the house and garden. In midsummer, roses, lilies and fleurs-de-lis predominate, while in the autumn, phlox, marigolds, and chrysanthemums come into full flower. Christmas roses burst into bloom just before the snow flies.

Like all other beloved gardens, this one, apart from its material utility, has been the source of spiritual inspiration. Many notable personages have visited this house and admired its garden. Among them are John Quincy Adams, Daniel Webster, Caleb Cushing, Rufus Choate, Jefferson Davis, John Greenleaf Whittier, Franklin Pierce, and a long line of public men of the nineteenth century.

THE OSGOOD-BROCKWAY GARDENS

The yellow brick house at 83–85 High Street, opposite the head of Fruit Street, was built in 1807 for the Newburyport Academy. Seaward from its octagonal cupola, there is a view of blue water and strips of sandy beaches; landward are

Thomas Bradley, an English gardener, worked here, as he did in nearly every other garden in Newburyport.[2]

Originally, the beds nearer the house were divided into four parterres, box-edged. The cross paths and circles were entered through arches covered with clematis. A wooden fence with square posts separated them from the house and oval lawn, and a broad path and shrouding vines formerly enclosed the whole garden. Now, four straight beds, box-edged, lie along the central path from the house. A bower of delicate vines marks the center, to the right of which grows a tall arbor-vitae. This tree seemed to a little girl seventy years ago as tall and large as it is now. With the summer-house, it was probably the nucleus of the garden.

The end of an old barn, grey-shingled and covered with purple wistaria and clematis, woodbine and akebia, adds picturesqueness throughout the summer. The clematis, peonies and roses, larkspur, iris and columbine are planted all together. The box and arbor-vitae, mock orange, mignonette, heliotrope, and sweet alyssum borders fill the garden in June with color and fragrance. Great zinnia heads and rows of marigolds make it gay in September; and always the birds flash among the flowers and pour out their song.

[1]Planted by Nathaniel S., brother of John Osgood, "to hide the cemetery."
[2]As told to the writer by Bradley's son (born in 1855), who helped his father.

A panoramic view of the East garden of the Osgood-Brockway house, Newburyport

Summer-house in the Osgood-Brockway gardens

of flower plots symmetrically laid out and bordered with box. Mr. Arthur A. Shurcliff, who visited the gardens in 1898, wrote for the *New England Magazine*[1]:

"The [East] garden . . . is in a remarkable state of preservation. It lies near the house, upon a gently sloping hillside, and it is broken by terraces which are mounted by short flights of steps. It is surrounded by a high close fence heavily clothed in vines, and no one could imagine from without that such a garden existed; it is as much removed from the street and its traffic as a room in the house itself. Old-fashioned flowers of all kinds flourish in it."

Notes in a journal kept by Mr. Shurcliff when he visited the garden show what these flowers were. We quote his list:

Periwinkle	Foxglove	Phlox subulata
Gaillardia	Poppies	Deutzia crenata
Hybiscus	Peonies	Monkshood
Honeysuckle	Canterbury Bells	Snapdragons
Clematis	Bee-balm	Bachelor Buttons
Rudbeckia	Sweet William	Campanula
Sweet Briar Rose	Mignonette	Dahlias
Iris	Bloodroot	Sunflowers
Gladiolus	Lemon and Tiger Lilies	Deutzia
	Rhododendron	Morning Glories

The article in the *New England Magazine* continues:

"An arbor makes it a pleasant resting place even at high noon. There is every evidence that the garden is regarded by the household as a part of the establishment necessary to their daily life, and there is no suggestion that it is a place for display or that it is a fanciful ornament."

The long main path terminated in a grape arbor beyond which was the wild flower garden and apple orchard on the rising slope, a playground for several generations of children; a great oak tops the hill. Lines of currant and gooseberry bushes and quinces grew among the vegetables. A pump on the back lawn supplied water through a long chute.

A broad cross path under overhanging mock oranges leads from the West to the East garden. A picturesque fence[1] between the two has gradually come down; in its place fragrant old syringas and rhododendrons line the path. A "Strawberry Bush" is here too.

EAST GARDEN. The garden attached to the east side of the house was the more elaborate of the two. It was laid out in 1856 by Thomas Bradley, the English gardener at Indian Hill, but the eccentricity of some of the beds to accommodate fruit trees shows that a few choice pear and peach trees survived from an earlier lay-out. There are terraces here; the top level is ornamented and diversified by an arrangement

---

[1]This fence was similar to one a neighbor had seen in Baltimore: boards surmounted by spindles topped with a fine rail.

[1]"Some Old New England Gardens," *New England Magazine*, December, 1899.

Photographs by Robert N. Cram

*The Osgood-Brockway gardens, Newburyport. Above is a view toward the house from near the summer-house in the West garden.
Below is one of the paths in the East garden*

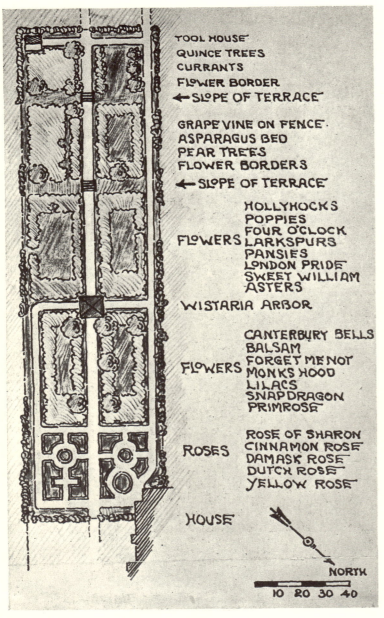

TOOL HOUSE
QUINCE TREES
CURRANTS
FLOWER BORDER
← SLOPE OF TERRACE

GRAPE VINE ON FENCE
ASPARAGUS BED
PEAR TREES
FLOWER BORDERS
← SLOPE OF TERRACE

HOLLYHOCKS
POPPIES
FOUR O'CLOCK
FLOWERS LARKSPURS
PANSIES
LONDON PRIDE
SWEET WILLIAM
ASTERS
WISTARIA ARBOR

CANTERBURY BELLS
BALSAM
FORGET ME NOT
FLOWERS MONKS HOOD
LILACS
SNAP DRAGON
PRIMROSE

ROSE OF SHARON
CINNAMON ROSE
ROSES DAMASK ROSE
DUTCH ROSE
YELLOW ROSE

HOUSE

NORTH
10 20 30 40

*A plan of the East garden of the Osgood-Brockway house, Newburyport,
reproduced here with the kind permission of Mr. Arthur Shurcliff*

Mr. Shurcliff's unpublished journal offers an interesting
generalization, based upon this garden as a type:

"A few of the more common flowers cultivated are mentioned on the accompanying plan. It is worthy of notice that
few of the modern and extravagant double forms are to be
found among them. The rose garden is pretty in design, and
as it is the most elaborate portion of the garden, it is fittingly
placed near the house. The walks which separate the beds
are bordered with neat box edgings. This garden may fairly
be called a type of the old-fashioned garden. The long narrow
plan, the central walk, the terraces, the presence of flowering
fruit trees in the flower borders, the arbor, and the seclusion
of high border screens are to be found in nearly every example.
Although the old designers of gardens realized the value of
formality in design and its direct relation to the rectangular
lines of the house plan, yet they seem to have thought it unnecessary to center their gardens upon a particular window or
door of the house. They placed them where convenience
dictated, and considerations of economy in the uses of their
land often prevented an axial relation of house and garden.[1]
The garden was always made to adjoin the house, however,
and anything approaching informality as a chief motive in
the design was avoided."

Briefly, the chief characteristic of this garden is the terraces: "wonderful neatness; pretty design, very small box
borders not more than 6″ high, and old-fashioned flowers
along the two lower terraces. The vines on the house and

[1]The Devereux-Hoffman-Simpson garden in Salem (see page 74) offers
a good illustration of this peculiarity of design.

fences are clematis, wistaria, grape, woodbine,—a low growth
wonderfully free from massy tangles."

The East garden has been little changed; it has become
only more deep-rooted with the years.

THE PIERCE–PERRY GARDEN[1]

Unlike the majority of its neighbors on the upper side of
High Street, Number 47 stands close to the road. The street
line, measuring 115 feet, is one of the short sides of a parallelogram a quarter of a mile deep, a characteristic of estates on
the west side of High Street.

The buildings—house, stable and lean-to—conceal the
garden. This disposition made possible the unusual arrangement of rising terraces cut into the slope immediately behind
the house, giving the effect of a slightly sunken garden.
Across a stone-paved courtyard is a venerable hedge of
arbor-vitae. An arch cut through this hedge on the axis of
the front hall and terraced walk gives a lovely vista. House,
courtyard, hedge and garden were planned with an unerring
eye and stand unaltered in their essential design.

The garden comprises a parterre and two terraces. Flower-
beds bordered by box are shaded here and there by fruit-
trees and shrubs, under which may be found old-fashioned
perennials and annuals. One side of the parterre is arranged
in formal beds of curved lines about a central oval; the other
has three rectangular beds. A flight of steps leads to the first
terrace, on the right of which grow, just off the path, a plum
tree, quinces, and a venerable apple tree with large out-
spreading branches. On the left is the herb-garden, behind
which are a sweet cherry tree (*Prunus avium*), rhododendrons,
peonies and old roses. A flight of eight steps leads through a

[1]Written by the owner, Mrs. Charles F. Perry, chairman of the Historic
Gardens Committee for Newburyport. Owners: Pierce, 1809; Knapp, 1832;
Perry, 1898.

Robert N. Cram

*A flagged court in the angle of house and outbuildings through which one
enters the Pierce-Perry garden, Newburyport. A perfect out-of-door room*

Photographs by Robert N. Cram

The Pierce-Perry garden in Newburyport comprises a parterre and two rising terraces cut into the slope behind the house. The photograph to the left shows the view along the main walk, illustrating the terrace treatment. To the right is the view from the second level toward the house

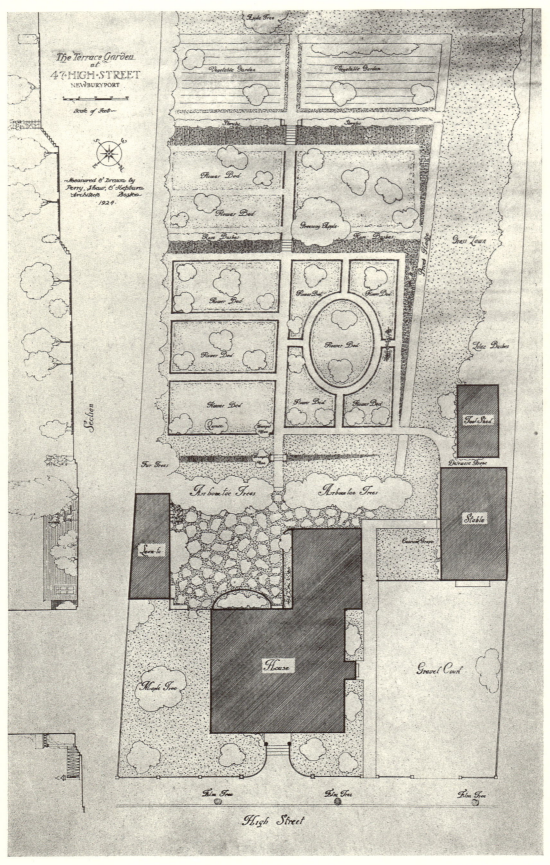

A plan of the Pierce-Perry garden, the property of Mrs. Charles F. Perry

vine-covered latticed arch to the upper terrace where the vegetable and fruit gardens are. A sturdy hedge of Japanese privet planted more than eighty years ago bounds the garden on the north and west, while a border of Douglas-fir trees on the south serves the purpose of a screen.

The slope between the hedge and lilac border on the north line behind the stable remains grass-grown and ungraded.

An attractive feature of the garden is the creeper-covered latticed arch at the top of the upper terrace steps, which is repeated some hundred yards back at the very top of the ridge and still upon the axis of the walk. Beyond the hedge-border of the upper terrace, all effort for formality ceases except for the retention of the axis line of the garden walk; at present,

some of the fruit trees have disappeared and a lawn remains, bordered on two sides by early grape arbors. Behind the orchard is a steep slope covered by a dense growth of hemlock and pine; standing against this background, at the foot of the slope, is a tree most unusual for this latitude, a *Magnolia acuminata* (cucumber tree) fifty to sixty feet high, in full vigor.

Beyond the upper latticed arch the view opens towards the east. A very early orchard stands here, dominated until 1920 by a splendid white-oak, a patriarchal tree in the youth of the old men of today; for many generations a "Crow's Nest," built in its branches, afforded a glorious view beyond the spire of the old Newbury Church, of the River Merrimack, the sand-dunes of Plumb Island, and the ocean.

A general view of the gardens and terraces of the Pierce-Perry garden, Newburyport, looking up the hill from the roof of the house

Photographs by Robert N. Cram

The pattern beds of dwarf box on the lower terrace of the Pierce-Perry garden

Photographs by Robert N. Cram

Two old summer-houses in Newburyport gardens. To the left is one dating from about 1820 which stands in the Thurlow garden; the grapevine obscures the curved roof lines and the slender point which supports the mackerel weather-vane. This summer-house is virtually identical in design with that which stands in the adjoining Wheelwright garden. The summer-house shown on the right stands in Mrs. Barrow's garden and dates probably from about 1840

Photographed by Robert N. Cram
The garden of Indian Hill Farm, West Newbury. Looking west along the broad garden path, which runs between deep borders flanked by high hedges of arbor-vitæ

WEST NEWBURY

INDIAN HILL FARM[1]

There is something seemingly remote in the situation of Indian Hill in the township of West Newbury; approached as it is by winding roads that, leading to it, appear to lead away from it. And finally reaching it through a country of rocky pasture land, most typical of New England, one experiences a sensation, on turning suddenly at the top of a short, sharp grade, in coming upon the long, low house of latticed casements—a house so much more suggestive of old England in Elizabeth's time than of New England at any time. And being to a certain degree in character with the days when Elizabethan Englishmen were engaged in adventuring to the new country of the west and establishing the dominion of the Anglo-Saxon over the native Indian, there is a significance in the idea of a little English Manor House transplanted from burnished fields (though this is mere, but almost inevitable, fancy) and set amongst these rugged lands, while facing squarely and imperturbably the Indian brave whom Major Poore, with a feeling for the epic, brought from his place as figurehead of the ship *Black Hawk* many years ago and fixed in perpetual ambush, from whence with raised tomahawk he ferociously threatens the house a few hundred yards away.

And yet in this region there were friendly Indians, for the land came through a deed from the Chief Great Tom to the Commoners of Newbury, and from them to John Poore in 1654. A house was probably built by this first John Poore of Indian Hill at this time, but all trace of it is lost. The present house was begun in 1688, and has been added to in one generation and another. The idea of the main house, as it now stands, was brought from England by Benjamin Poore, the father of Major Poore, after he had made a visit to Bishop Poore of Salisbury. Major Poore at a later date added a wing

[1]Written by Mrs. F. S. Moseley.

whose features were suggested by Abbotsford. He called its interior the "Continental rooms," designing them, however, as a receptacle for objects of early American interest.

In keeping with the remodelling of his house on an English plan, Benjamin Poore in the spring of 1833 employed James Lowe, an English gardener, to make a new garden on the side of the hill; the description of which comes from Miss Ellen Poore (the sister of Major Poore), whose memory of the place must have gone back for over eighty years—and with whose death the Poore family, except on the distaff side, ends.

"The entrance was through a rustic, thatch-roofed porch. From that two walks divided to the right and left, with box hedges and shrubbery a third of the way up the hill. There the box-hedged flower-beds began, with grape trellises at the back of each border. Little cross-walks connected the two paths. In the centre of the garden was a rustic circle, covered with honeysuckle, inside of which were rustic chairs, a sofa, and also four flowerbeds with box edges. Where these met in the centre stood a rustic vase filled with flowers. The flowers in the garden were the crocus, tulip, narcissus, daffodil, princes' feather, tassel flowers (little bunches of red tassels), ladies' delights, that became almost like weeds, single zinnias, all kinds of marigolds, wild chandelier lilies, balsam (touch-me-not), single asters, and many others. The seeds and bulbs for the garden were supplied by Thorburn of New York, while the trees and plants were, in most cases, imported from England.

"At the top of the garden stood the gardener's house (back of the ash), and at the left of this were the flower-beds in hearts and rounds, with cherry and mulberry trees planted about them. The garden was divided by a hawthorn hedge from the orchard, and the vegetables were raised behind the grape trellises before mentioned."

Among the fruits raised at Indian Hill, cherries seem to have been particularly abundant, being in their season heaped in great mounds.

Photographed by Robert N. Cram

The eastern end of the long perennial borders in the garden of Indian Hill Farm, West Newbury, showing the arbor-vitæ hedges

Photograph by H. Troth

Another view in the garden of Indian Hill Farm, the property of Mrs. F. S. Moseley

In 1849 the garden began to be gradually cut down until it reached its present form of a broad and single garden path running between very deep borders that are flanked by high hedges of arbor-vitae. Through a series of what might be called floral anterooms, short and winding paths lead—some between flower borders, others between ancient hedges of lilac—to that straight path which mounts the hill. This, passing under an occasional rustic shelter, terminates rather steeply at last in a large and airy summer-house, where, on the further side, the ground suddenly falls away into a green and rolling country, over which the eye roves from stone wall to wine-glass elm.

Descending into the garden again from this point, the white church steeples of Newburyport rise into view from the town, ranged against the river and the sea. One moves down the path between high rows of foxgloves in June, or through late summer brilliancy in August or September, framed by a long row of chestnut trees, planted in 1824 by Major Poore.

Beyond these trees rises the summit of the hill that gives its name to the place, identified for miles around by its divisions into pasture land on one side and forest on the other. Over this pasture only white cattle grazed in Major Poore's day. They must have been a striking feature in the landscape, where one descends the few stone steps that lead from the garden to a wide, open space which gives a view of the hill; while nearly at its foot the big barn, the vine-covered turret of the farmer's wing, and the house itself lie clustered, describing many turns and angles, under their red roofs and gables.

And the hostile Indian, long since enchained in honeysuckle and trumpetvine, rests powerless to disturb the peculiar quiet of the scene, in which perhaps the only movement is that of the amenable little red man, who, serving as a weathervane above the clock tower, forever shoots his arrow *with the wind* that blows serenely over Indian Hill.

Two views of the old Abbott homestead, "Happy Hollow" (1685), in Andover. A perfect example of vanishing New England

OTHER HISTORIC GARDENS

ANDOVER

ACCORDING[1] to Colony Records for 1634, "Newtown [Cambridge] men being straightened for ground sent some men to Merrimack to find a fit place to transplant themselves" and in the same year it was ordered by the Court that "the land about Cochichewick (Andover) shall be reserved for an inland plantation."

This land was purchased from Cutschamache, the Sagamore of Massachusetts, by Mr. Woodbridge for £6 and a coat, on behalf of the inhabitants of Cochichewick, and the purchase and grant were confirmed by the Court in 1646 when the town was incorporated by the name of Andover. The first settlement was in the neighborhood of what is now known as North Andover Center where settlers lived near each other for convenience and safety on small holdings generally of six or nine acres, according to the rates paid, which were allotted to them for their homes. There was also granted to them in the neighborhood, plow land in small lots, land of easy tillage, swamp and meadow land for hay, and woodland, often at a distance. These grants were made by vote of the town and all householders and free holders had the right to vote. The earliest list of settlers extant, written on a leaf in the town records, undated but evidently ancient and presumably nearly correct, begins as follows: "The names of all the householders in order as they came to town: Mr. Bradstreet, John Osgood, Joseph Parker, Richard Barker, John Stevens." There are eighteen more and probably all of them were in Andover before 1644.

The garden of the Stevens house, North Andover, the property of Mrs. John Gardner Coolidge. A front view of the house is shown on page 425

THE STEVENS HOUSE AND GARDEN

John Stevens lived undoubtedly on his allotment in the little town and the land on which the present house stands was granted to him as plough land, pasture or even woodland, for it contains all three; this land has remained in the hands of his direct descendants to this day, and has passed down from father to son, in unbroken succession, until the present generation. It is not known when the first house was built on this spot, but the land came to Deacon Joseph Stevens (1655–1743) on the partition of his father's property, and he probably lived here as his descendants have done ever since. The present house was built just before 1800, and is incorporated with a house of considerably older construction. It has been altered and restored but is unchanged in its essentials. The land now going with the house and garden is

[1]This account and the description of the Stevens house and garden are written by Mrs. John Gardner Coolidge (née Stevens), owner and direct descendant of the John Stevens who settled in Andover in 1644 or earlier.

The charming old well, covered with old wistaria, in the garden of Mrs. John Gardner Coolidge, North Andover

in the neighborhood of 100 acres of plough land, pasture and woodland. It has varied slightly from generation to generation; some parts of the original grant were cut off from the main body to provide homes for members of the family and subsequently passed into other hands.

With regard to the garden of earlier days: it was at the side of the house and its site is marked by some very old lilac trees, syringas, quince and pear trees, cinnamon roses, day lilies and lilies-of-the-valley and early spring flowers. There is a very old grape vine covering this end of the house.

The garden was moved about forty years ago to the old orchard along the side of the great barn, and directly in view from the morning room. High privet hedges enclose it. There is a wide grass path in the centre, bordered on either side by perennials and shrubs. A pair of ancient apple trees have been left and young ones have been set out. Beyond the garden is a sunny meadow, fringed by distant woods.

PRINCETON

THE GROUNDS OF MOSES GILL

In the late eighteenth century, there existed in Worcester County, at Princeton, a large landed estate, the property of the Hon. Moses Gill. The place was so highly regarded by contemporaries that an historian of the time adjudged it "being attentively considered . . . not paralleled by any in the New England States, perhaps not by any this side of Dela-

"View of the seat of the Hon. Moses Gill, at Princeton, in the County of Worcester, Massa^ts," surviving in slightly mutilated form from "The Massachusetts Magazine" of 1792. In 1766 this country was forest wilderness

ware." The owner, born at Charlestown in 1734, had married Sarah Prince, the daughter and only child of Thomas Prince, then pastor of the Old South Church in Boston. From 1775 onward Gill was one of the Judges of the Court of Common Pleas for the county of Worcester.[1]

The Gill estate evidently included an extensive garden, and a surviving drawing shows an elaborate lay-out, but no details have come down to us. The historian quoted above, the Rev. Peter Whitney, who wrote in 1793 a *History of Worcester County*, describes at some length the aspect of the place, and gives us the impression that its owner greatly furthered horticultural progress in his locality. We know him to have been in 1796 a member of the Massachusetts Society for Promoting Agriculture. Says the historian:

"His elegant and noble seat is about one mile and a quarter from the meeting-house to the south. The farm contains upward of 3000 acres. The county road from Princeton to Worcester passes through it in front of the house which faces to the west.

"The buildings stand upon the highest land of the whole farm; but it is level around about them for many rods, and then there is a very gradual descent. The land on which these buildings stand is elevated between 1200 and 1300 feet above the level of the sea as the Hon. James Winthrop Esq. informs me.

"The mansion house is large being 50 by 50 feet with four stacks of chimneys; the farm house is 40 by 36 feet; in a line with this stand the coach and chaise house, 50 by 36 feet, this joined to the barn by a shed 70 feet in length—the barn is 200 feet by 32. Very elegant fences were erected around the mansion house, the orchards and the gardens.

"The prospect from this seat is extensive, and grand, taking in an horizon to the east, of seventy miles at least. The blue hills of Milton are discernable with the naked eye sixty miles, as well as the waters of the harbour at Boston, at certain seasons of the year.

[1]Facts from *History of Princeton*, compiled by Francis E. Blake.

"When we view this seat, these buildings, and this farm of so many hundred acres, now under a high degree of cultivation, and are told that in 1766 it was a perfect wilderness, we are struck with wonder, admiration and astonishment.

"The honorable proprietor hereof must have great satisfaction in contemplating these improvements, so extensive, made under his direction, and, I may add, under his own active industry. Judge Gill is a gentleman of singular vivacity and activity, and indefatigable in his endeavors to bring forward the cultivation of his lands—and the county which he has so greatly benefited, especially by the ways in which he makes use of that vast estate wherewith a kind Providence has blessed him."

ABINGTON

THE GARDEN OF ELIHU HOBART

An elaborate garden of the 1830's was that at Abington, adjoining the residence of Elihu Hobart. The *Ladies' Magazine and Literary Gazette* of November, 1830, printed the following description of it:

"The location of the residence, of which a lithographic view is herewith presented, is 22 miles from Boston, and 18 from the 'landing of the Fathers.' It was erected in 1830. Attached to the premises is a garden (comprising little more than an acre) well secured by a fence of stone and wood, and surrounded by a variety of ornamental trees. The number of fruit and ornamental trees, and shrubs, in this enclosure, and immediately around the dwelling, exceeds five hundred.

"In the laying out of this garden, the proprietor has attempted some improvements, which consist, in part, of elevations, or embankments of the straight or circular formations, and avenues, at convenient distances; with the two principal ones running so as to cross, at right angles, a circu-

The residence of Elihu Hobart at Abington. From an illustration in the "Ladies Magazine and Literary Gazette," 1850

lar embankment (in the centre of the garden) of 22 feet in diameter. On the margin, or outer surface, of this embankment, is a circle of ornamental trees. In other parts, the trees (both fruit and ornamental) are so interspersed as to make straight, and circular shaded walks, whenever they shall have attained sufficient growth."

THE CONNECTICUT RIVER VALLEY

To the grand-daughter of Thomas Jefferson, Eleanora Wayles Randolph, whose wedding journey from Monticello to Boston in 1825 included a tour of New England, the Massachusetts of the Connecticut River valley was a fertile, fruitful land, which from the top of Mt. Holyoke resembled "one vast garden divided into parterres." She speaks especially of the village gardens.

"Round Hill, Northampton, former residence of Geo. Bancroft." This drawing, dating from before 1840, shows the sort of country viewed by Eleanora Wayles Randolph

New Bedford in 1807. From a painting by William A. Wall

The garden of William Rotch, Jr., the father of Sarah Arnold, shows how charmingly the Grand style found its reflection in the gardens of New Bedford

"I should judge from appearances" she wrote in a letter,[1] "that they [the New Englanders] are at least a century in advance of us [the Southerners] in all the arts and embellishments of life; and they are pressing forth in their course with zeal and activity which I think must ensure success. It is certainly a pleasing sight, this flourishing state of things. The country is covered with a multitude of beautiful villages; the fields are cultivated and forced into fertility; the roads kept in the most exact order; the inns numerous, affording good accommodations, and travelling facilitated by the ease with which post carriages and horses are always to be obtained. Along the banks of the Connecticut there are rich meadow lands, and here *New* might, I should think, almost challenge *Old* England in beauty of landscape. From the top of Mount Holyoke, which commands, perhaps, one of the most extensive views in these States, the whole country, as you look down upon it resembles one vast garden divided into parterres. There are upwards of twenty villages in sight at once, and the windings of the Connecticut are every where marked, not only by its clear and bright waters, but by the richness and beauty of the fields and meadows, and the density of the population on its banks. The villages themselves have an air of neatness and comfort which is delightful. The houses have no architectural pretensions, but they are pleasing to look at, for they are almost all painted white, with vines about the windows and doors, and grass plots in front decorated with flowers and shrubs; a neat paling separates each domain from its neighbor."

[1]From "An American Wedding Journey in 1825"; Being the story of the marriage of Eleanora Wayles Randolph and her wedding journey from Monticello to Boston, as gathered from letters in the possession of descendants and for the most part hitherto unpublished. By Harold Jefferson Coolidge, in the *Atlantic Monthly*, March, 1929.

NEW BEDFORD

THE ARNOLD GARDEN

At the height of its glory, the one-time whaling center of New England held a garden famous in its day—that of James Arnold, whose gift to Harvard University later brought into being the Arnold Arboretum. New Bedford was bright with gardens in that romantic time, so ably evoked by Mr. Edward T. Pierce, Jr., of the Buzzard's Bay Garden Club, in the following paper, which he has called

"Gardens Harpooned"

"All these brave houses and flowery gardens came from the Atlantic, Pacific and Indian Oceans. One and all, they were harpooned and dragged up hither from the bottom of the sea."

So Melville's brilliant figure holds in perpetual bloom the gardens of New Bedford. They were a unique and early flowering of the nation's genius, grounded upon the astounding profits of the whale-fishery. How congenial to his intricate imaginings would have been the prophecy that there, in the most "opulent" of the parks and gardens which he saw—the estate of James Arnold on the County Road—lay the germ of the Arnold Arboretum, that splendid institution whose works should be known throughout the United States, and even beyond those oceans which had been its spiritual parents. The fact is that James Arnold's gift to Harvard University led to the creation of the magnificent garden of trees and shrubs called by his name. The gift was made after the town officials of New Bedford, with frugality far exceeding their vision of public benefit, declined to accept as a gift and to maintain part of the splendid estate as a public park.

The garden had been open, and was much enjoyed by the townspeople in a day when "diversion" was imperfectly understood. Today nothing of it remains; man as a group has thrown away the beauty that as an individual he created.

To see the spiritual kinship of certain Baroque exuberances among the real beauties of "Arnold's Garden" with the scientific devotion and esthetic success of the Arboretum, a modern eye must put on the vision of a Great Age . . . an age when the young republic had a world to conquer. It had no steam nor electricity, little science and less art; its needs

Above is a drawing from Downing's "Landscape Gardening and Rural Architecture" showing the Arnold grotto as it once was. The photograph below was taken in the days of its desolation

were Gargantuan, but its ingenuity was no less so, and its faith was infinite. The Quaker and Puritan of New England, whose crippling repressions are a matter of concern to a critical and uncreative age, rebounded from their rocky shores and pushed out the limits of the known world. They gave to the world two objects of great usefulness and singular beauty—the whale boat and the clipper ship. Ashore, the wood, the stone, the soil of the New World felt their hand. They left their impress upon hill pasture, salt-meadow and door-yard. So consistent, so unified was it, throughout innumerable instances, that it is accepted as a landscape style. Such was the first or Colonial chapter. New Bedford's rise was microcosmic. The Golden Age, its period of mansion and garden building, was an interlude, a single victory in the conquest. It had the flush of success, the shortness of a triumph. It was a manly pouring out of pent-up feelings; relief from yesterday's hardship, pride in the exploit of today and . . . happy indifference to the morrow. It had no time to work out esthetic forms suited to its own vari-colored life, but part, at least, of its energy, its love for new ways, new places, has found fitting expression in the splendid new plants which have been revealed to garden lovers on the hillsides of the Arnold Arboretum.

Against the background of orchard, vine and grove, which might be felt to represent the Colonial heritage of the Arnold estate, was a parterre suggestive of the Grand style, a maze in the English manner, and a hidden grotto with a ceiling of shells. These say most plainly that nothing is impossible in a Golden Age, not even a sport of Italian Baroque in the garden of a New England Quaker. Water, as an element in garden design, was pretty much ignored at New Bedford. Fish-ponds and fountains may well have seemed anti-climactic in these gardens which were won on blue water in the chase of the spouting whale. The Baroque had been devoured but not assimilated, else the architectural wonders of the whale himself, so impressive in *Moby Dick*, could never have escaped the arbor-builders.

James Arnold was a successful merchant, a man of vigorous intellect and a student of classical literature. A lover of trees and gardens, he wished—like an Englishman of similar cultural background—to create a manor. He desired, not only to raise flowers and fruit and trees, but to create beauty, and foster the love of it in his friends and fellow-townsmen. The Arnold mansion was built in 1821. The land on which it stood was part of a large farm. The cleared land bore magnificent trees, elms, lindens and a very fine old oak. There were also woods on the estate and some swamp land. The garden was nearly twelve acres in extent, surrounded by a wall of cut stone eleven feet high, which sheltered two graperies and a greenhouse. Beyond were fruit trees. James Arnold was especially interested in growing peach trees in espalier form.

If the background was practical and rural, the foreground was urbane, even cosmopolitan. For James Arnold and his wife travelled three years in Europe, collecting things for their home, and making the Grand Tour at a time when few of their countrymen could have done so. The flower garden, with box-bordered beds in fancy pattern, had for setting wide lawns, a little grove, vine-covered arbors and fruit trees. Generous in extent, its decorative designs filled a sunlit space between the green distance and the stately brick mansion. The broad paths among the beds, and the box-bordered walks beside the lilacs were often trodden by crowds of gay people. Villagers danced round the maypole on the lawn. The "quality" overflowed the great house at a costume party. "Patrician," was Melville's word for this life of a century ago. In harmony with the fortunes of the town, the Colonial dooryard became by a sea-change the parterre of a manor. No less ambitious was a reproduction of the famous maze at Hampton Court in England. Unique, however, was the hidden grotto, well befitting one who had made the Grand Tour. Utilizing a group of twisted trees and some adjacent rocks, this singular edifice managed to conceal itself almost completely in foliage. It endured until lately, outliving the planting which gave it charm, and the men and women who had found playful retreat at its rustic chairs and tables. The photograph shows it as a pathetic survival, exposed to the cold eye of an unsympathetic generation. But it was a notable grotto in its time, rejoicing even in a roof of plaster encrusted with a mosaic of sea shells.

Many distinguished visitors, the Adamses (who described the event in their diaries) among them, enjoyed the garden. It was nationally famous. In A. J. Downing's works on landscape gardening and rural architecture there is an echo of contemporary opinion: "There is scarcely a small place in New England where the pleasure grounds are so full of variety, and in such perfect order and keeping, as this charming spot; and its winding walks, open bits of lawn, shrubs and plants grouped on turf, shady bowers, and rustic seats, all most agreeably combined, render this a very interesting and instructive suburban seat."

John Quincy Adams, in phrase not unlike Melville's, bears witness that New Bedford had other splendid estates. "We were taken," he says in 1835, "to see the street which has lately risen like magic, and which presents more noble looking

The garden in Nantucket given by Zenas Coffin to his daughter, Mary Coffin Swift. It was laid out about 1820, and is now owned and cared for by Mrs. Humes

mansions than any other in the country." The Adamses were not given to over-enthusiasm. Among the many that were built, and the few that endure with something of their former magnificence, is the estate created by William Rotch, Jr., father of Sarah Arnold. The house, which was properly regarded as one of the finest, stands in a neighborhood where noble trees, overarching broad lawns, attest that an earlier generation loved them. The garden, in the accompanying illustration, shows how charmingly the Grand style found its reflection in the gardens of New Bedford, the intricate design of its walks and box-bordered beds showing a kinship to the Arnold parterre.

There is another gorgeous picture which Melville has saved from forgetfulness—that of the town as a whole:

"In summertime, the town is sweet to see; full of fine maples—long avenues of green and gold. And in May, high in the air, the beautiful and bountiful horse-chestnuts, candelabrawise, proffer the passer-by their tapering upright cones of congregated blossoms. So omnipotent is art; which in many a district of New Bedford has superinduced bright terraces of flowers upon the barren refuse rocks thrown aside at creation's final day."

NANTUCKET ISLAND

Nantucket, as late as 1780, was very little developed and was almost without important houses. In that year, J. Hector St. John de Crevecœur, in his *Letters from an American Farmer*, spoke thus of the island:

"Sherborn is the only town on the Island, and contains 530 houses . . . .

"The town stands on a rising sand-bank. . . .

"The town regularly ascends toward the country, and in its vicinage they have several small fields and gardens. . . . There are a good many cherry and peach trees planted in their streets and in many other places; the apple tree does not thrive well, they have therefore planted but few. There are but few gardens and arable fields in the neighborhood of the town, for nothing could be more sterile and sandy than this part of the island; they have, however, with unwearied perseverance, by bringing a variety of manure, and by cow-penning, enriched several spots where they raise Indian corn, potatoes, pumpkins and turnips.

"Quayes is a small but valuable tract, long since purchased by Mr. Coffin, where he has erected the best house on the island. By long attention, promiscuity to the sea etc. this spot has been long manured, and is now the garden of Nantucket."

Quincy's record of a few years later says of Nantucket:

"It exhibits no marks of elegance or splendor. I took a walk about the town. The houses, with but one or two exceptions, are built wholly of wood, and have but two stories. By far the greater number are without paint, and with those which have it, red is the predominant color. They are built generally upon the street, and a few are ornamented with poplar trees of a small growth. The streets are without pavements, and of a light sand. . . . At dusk we went to the Town Gate and saw a herd of three hundred and fifty cows returning from pasture, under the care of two herdsmen. . . . The almost total want of trees, houses, and fences, in the interior part of the island, makes the road very uninteresting to a traveller. Once in every two or three miles a single farmhouse appeared.

"The cultivated land had a most wretched aspect. The spires of grain looked weak, and the land turned up by the plough had the appearance of a sand heap. Upon examination I found the soil superior to its promise.

"We dined at Dr. Easton's, a practitioner of physick, a native of Newport, removed for the sake of his profession. Mrs. Easton is the daughter of Mr. Coffin. They were very friendly and polite. Their house and establishment are in style as elegant—by which name, however, it can scarcely be called—as any upon the island."

After the development of the whaling industry, Nantucket

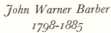

John Warner Barber
1798-1885

He drove about the country in a one-horse cart, sketching from nature for his series of histories, the first of which appeared in 1827. The portrait repro-
duced above, the frontispiece to his "History of the Western States," is based on a photograph. To Barber's efforts we owe much of our knowledge of the
appearance of the countryside in the early decades of the nineteenth century; his drawings have preserved many graphic details which would otherwise have
been lost. His sketch of the "southern view in the central part of Northfield" in 1838, shown to the left and right above, depicts as flourishing trees the
street elms first planted about 1800. Other views of the Massachusetts of about 1840 are shown on this and the opposite page

The historic Washington Elm, at Cambridge, as it appeared to
John Warner Barber in the year 1838

This "western view of Coleraine (central part)" shows how the fields
and pastures looked from the village street in 1840

Both the "north view of Congregational Church, Longmeadow" (right) and the "southern view of Deerfield" in 1838 (left) show the thriving
elms which New England towns began planting along their streets in the early nineteenth century, and which are now passing away

Central Part of Northampton (left)

"*The view shows the appearance of the Court-House, the First Congregational Church, and other buildings, as seen from the road in a north-eastern direction. The Congregational Church is the building seen in the central part of the engraving.*"

Central Part of Pittsfield (right)

"*This view shows the appearance of the Common, as seen from near the western side. The Congregational Church is the first building, with a spire, on the left; the next the Town-House; the next eastward is the Episcopal Church; the other buildings near are connected with the Medical Institution. The ancient elm, one hundred and twenty-six feet in height, is seen rising in the central part of the Common.*"

Court Square in Springfield (left)

"*An eastern view of the Court-House, Congregational Church, and some other buildings around Court Square, in the central part of Springfield. A part of the Hampden Coffee-House is seen on the right.*"

It is interesting to note that Barber's drawing of 1838 shows a fenced Common.

Main Street in Worcester (right)

"*A view taken at the south-western entrance of the Main street. . . . The old South Church and the Town-House appear on the right. A number of private residences are seen on the left. . . .*"

In addition to the elms within the walls, planted probably about 1800, Barber's drawing shows recent tree planting on the right.

grew in wealth and importance, and many charming little gardens in the fashion of the early nineteenth century were to be seen throughout the villages.

THE HENRY COFFIN HOUSE AND GARDEN[1]

Nantucket in 1832 was a prosperous whaling port of some 9000 souls. To it in that year returned Henry Coffin, scion of a family whose history spells distinction in the annals of the Island. Tristram Coffin, the first of the name, came to Nantucket as a sturdy pioneer with a little band of Englishmen who, like himself, were seeking homes and possible fortunes. It was Tristram's son Peter who built in 1686 what is now known as the "Oldest House." Peter built the house for his son Jethro, and the house still stands on Sunset Hill. So the generations have passed, and the family Tristram founded lives on in the numerous branches that cover the island.

In 1830 Zenas Coffin, father of Henry, was one of the largest shipowners on the Island, and it was in one of his whaling ships that Henry journeyed overseas in pursuit of health. He visited England and the Continent, finally stopping at Madeira for some time. The diary he kept then lies in his desk in the Main Street house; in it are long lists of trees and plants then new to him, many specimens of which he sent back in barrels to his Island home for the garden that was to be. For, growing in his mind, was the vision of a stately Georgian house surrounded by an English garden.

Three years later, with health restored, the house finished

[1] Written by Miss Mary J. Linton.

and the garden begun, Mr. Coffin, with his wife and infant son, took possession of the new home.

The Coffin house, like most of those built at that period, was placed on the street line. The grounds extend to a street in the rear on the line of which stood the greenhouse. Laburnum trees planted eighty years ago still bloom each spring, and the ivy tumbles in great cascades over the mellow brick wall at the rear, shrouds the tall chimneys on the house and fairly smothers the old chaise-house. The house is still kept fragrant with flowers from the old borders, and fruit trees that have long outlived him who planted them still yield their increase.

Some years after Mr. Coffin's return from Madeira, the Governor of that island was the guest of honor at a dinner given at the Main Street house, and expressed his amazement at the fruit (figs, peaches, plums and grapes) that loaded the table, and all from his host's garden. For seventy years Henry Coffin lived in and loved his garden. He died at the age of ninety-three.

As the years passed, the garden was given over to fruit-growing, largely grapes and pears, many varieties of the latter being sent yearly to the Nantucket Horticultural Fair, where a first prize was always awarded them.

To Henry Coffin the Island owes its abundant ivy. With the help of his friend, Prof. Emerson of Harvard, Scotch larches were brought over to be "tried out". With the larch trees came, all unbidden, the seeds of the heather now so carefully guarded and tended. And to this lover of his town, Main Street owes the magnificent elms that tower above its colonial roofs, making the street the shady delightful thoroughfare that it is.

New York Historical Society Collections

An old print of Holme's Hole (now Vineyard Haven), Martha's Vineyard

CONNECTICUT

A Connecticut village "in garden form". An old view of Windham

CONNECTICUT

INDIANS AND PLANTERS

"ITS surface is generally beautiful and sometimes magnificent. Its soil is strong and fertile," wrote Timothy Dwight, eighteenth-century traveler.

And Connecticut, with its hundred mile shoreline indented with fine harbors, its mountains rising to two thousand feet, its picturesque lakes, rivers, and waterfalls, well deserves all the praises of the enthusiastic early travelers.

Sometime before 1636, John Oldham explored this part of the country, and gave such a good account of its resources that a number of the settlers in Massachusetts decided to end their dissatisfaction with the autocratic government of that colony by going "west." These people established a trading-post on the Connecticut River near Windsor. Later other colonists, many of them Puritans, settled New Haven, and in 1639 settlements were begun at Stratford and at Fairfield.

So far as is known, the planters in every case purchased their land from the Indians. The terms "old field" and "old Indian field," frequently occurring in the records, are believed to refer to land which had been cleared by the Indians for cultivation before the arrival of the whites, who naturally took advantage of all that had been of profit to their predecessors.

Although, as Osborn says in his *History of Connecticut*, the country was considered a wilderness, with no roads except Indian trails, it was not entirely a forest, but abounded in these open, roughly cleared tracts, which had been cleared by the Indians and were suitable for growing what crops were needed. Some had been cleared for cultivation, and others had been burned over to make easier the taking of wild game. The colonists immediately planted these open spaces, the tidal marshes, and the lowlands. At first their agricultural efforts were far less successful than those of the Indians. William Wood in his *New England's Prospect* (1634) says that the Indians "exceed our English husbandmen, keeping it so cleare with their Clamme-shell hoe as if it were a garden rather than a Cornfield, not suffering no choaking weede to advance his audacious Head above their infant Corne, or an undermining Worme to spoil his Spurnes." Besides the "Clamme-shell," the Indians also used a hoe made of the shoulder-blade of a deer or a tortoise shell, sharpened upon a stone and fastened to a stick.

Corn for food, says Osborn, was the first crop planted by the settlers, as taught by Squanto, an Indian who had been to England and had returned. The corn seed which they planted

> "One for the bug
> One for the crow
> One for the rat
> And two to grow"

did grow and yield prodigiously, and the people soon understood the reverent feelings that the natives had for its marvelous productivity.

The Indians knew that their maize was not indigenous to that part of the country, and had many legends in regard to its origin. Roger Williams wrote of their tradition as to the source of both beans and corn: "These birds [crows] although they doe the corne some hurt yet scarce one native amoungst an hundred will kill them, because they have a tradition that the Crow brought them at first an Indian Graine of Corne

in one eare and an Indian or French Beane in another from the great Cantanowite field in the Southwest from whence they hold came all their corne and Beanes."

Wood recorded an amusing picture of the value attached to the crop by the Indian women, who performed all the agriculture:

"Their corne being ripe they gather it and drying it hard in the sunne conveigh it to their barnes, which be great holes digged in the ground in form of a brass pot, seeled—wherein they put their corne, covering it from the inquisitive search of their gourmandizing husbands, who would eat up their allowed portion, and reserved Seede if they knew where to find it."

Osborn gives the following account, generally accepted by botanists, of the origin of maize, or Indian corn:

"It is a development for which we are indebted probably to some ancient civilization in Central or South America, a development vastly more valuable than those of a modern plant wizard. We know the Mayas reached their highest civilization in the years between 455 and 597 A. D. They planted corn, beans and pumpkins. Among their records are pictures of the Maize-god, planting corn. . . . Other pictures show attacks by worms and birds suggesting that the pests are as old as the plants." Undoubtedly the seed corn was passed from tribe to tribe, eventually reaching the east coast of America.

COLONIAL GARDEN TOOLS IN CONNECTICUT

The colonists' farming tools were no better than those of the farmer of Julius Caesar's day; in fact, the Roman ploughs were probably superior to those in general use in America eighteen centuries later.

The only plough in use up to the nineteenth century was an unwieldy, heavy, wooden affair. The harrow was wooden also, with wooden pegs. This clumsy plough was the only tool used with draft animals; sowing, cultivating and harvesting were all done by hand. Carts with one or two horses were occasionally used, but for heavy work oxen were preferred.

The smaller farm tools were either brought from England or made locally; these were rakes, forks, ax-helves, shovels with wrought iron edges, flails, baskets, and yokes. These tools, moreover, were of a kind designed for tilling soil long under cultivation, and not for subduing forest land or scrub growth.

The following list from Isham and Brown's *Early Colonial Homes* gives an actual record of tools in the possession of the Hon. Theophilus Eaton, governor of New Haven Colony. It is from an inventory taken in the Twelfth month, 1657.

A pr. of garden Sheares, 3 Sickles and 5 hooks, 3 hoes, 2 sithes, 2 stone axes, with brick axes and trowels.

A surveying Compass and Chain, 3 mattocks, 2 Shovells, 2 pitchforks and a spade,

A plow and Plow irons.

But in spite of weak tools and a stubborn, rocky soil, the colonists' first crops grew. Besides their fields of maize, Osborn says, they soon had wheat, to which they were more accustomed, as well as gardens filled with homely herbs and a variety of vegetables, which Josselyn describes in his *New England's Rarities*—and filled also, we presume, with "English roses very pleasantly."

We also read in the colonial records of the State entries telling of early and fruitful activities in spite of a harassing warfare against the encroaching forest and marauding Indians:

"May 1, 1637   General Court at Hartford

"It is ordered that there shall be an offensive war against the Pequot etc.

"It is ordered that Windsor shall provide 60 bush. of corn etc. Hartford 4 bushells of oatemeal, 2 bush. of pease, 1 bushell of Indian Beans."

Also from the records of the General Court at Hartford:

"It is ordered that every family within this plantation shall procure and plant this present year at least one spoonful of English hempseed in some soyle."

Then, in a much later record but still in the seventeenth century, we find that Governor Lute (John Allen, Secretary) reports that the commodities of the country are "wheat, peas, Barley, Indian corn, Hemp, Flax, etc."

From the *Colonial History of Hartford* we learn that a "house lott" consisted of two acres, and that soon the probate records describe the average householder's estate as "A parcel of land on which standeth with other outhouses, yards and gardens."

This last record is dated 1640. Although at that time Josselyn found no apple or pear trees except on "the Governor's[1] Island," nevertheless on his second voyage, thirty years later, he says the finest trees prospered abundantly. He then saw "the country replenished with fine and large orchards, consisting of apples, quinces, cherry, plum and barberry."

THE FIRST RECORDED ORCHARD

Perhaps the most particular account is that of the orchard of Henry Wolcott in Windsor. This was in bearing before 1649. Summer Pippin, Holland Pippin, Pearmain, Belly Bonds (Belle et Bonne), and London Pippin are varieties of apples named. Wolcott also sold orchard trees, both apple and pear, as early as 1650.[2]

And by 1661 orchards seem to have been quite common, if we may judge from the Book of Records of Original Grants and Deeds of Home-lots to the first settlers.

Ephraim Lockwood on Dec. 30th, 1661, bought the home-lot of Jonathan Marshe, "for and in consideration of one mare and sucking colt." Surely the mare must have been of Arabian stock, for Lockwood received in exchange "a house, with the shelfes, dress-boards &c., also the yards, hovells, and tenn fruit trees, growing upon the orchard, and also the home lot containing one acre more or less." In 1665, Thomas Ward sold to Ralph Keeler his "dwelling house" reserving among other things "the younger nursery trees."

First the field and then the orchard, which, in the colonial records, is spoken of as a garden. E. Stanley Welles says[3]:

"Gardens included both fruit trees and flowers as well as vegetables, for such was the English idea of a garden, and our forefathers brought it over with them to the new land." Mr. Welles goes on to say: "Of course the original settlers of Hartford, Windsor and Wethersfield had gardens just as soon as it was practicable, probably a plot of ground in the rear of the home, rudely enclosed so that animals, either wild or domestic, might not 'damnifye' the crops."

As early as 1639 we find a pretty note from George Fenwick Esq., the founder of Saybrook Colony, to Gov. John Winthrop of the Massachusetts Colony:

"I am lastly to thank you kindly on my wife's behalf for your great dainties—we both desire and delight much in that primitive employment of dressing a garden, and the taste of such good fruits in the parts gives us good encouragement."

[1]Governor Winthrop.
[2]Osborn, *History of Connecticut.*
[3]*Beginnings of Fruit Culture in Connecticut.*

THE FIRST RECORDED GARDEN

For the first specific record of gardening in Connecticut we are indebted to the researches of Mr. William B. Goodwin of Hartford, who has noted from colonial records that Lady Fenwick came from Apsley Hall and Worminhurst Manor in Sussex to New Haven in July, 1639. Her equipment included "seeds for a garden, grafts of apple, pear, and plumb trees and English Fruit bushes." A letter from Colonel Fenwick to John Winthrop describes certain "seeds and grafts they might be in need of."

There is reason to believe that this garden stood on the late site of Yale College. This is all we know of Lady Fenwick's garden, for three hundred years have completely erased all traces of it.

WINDSOR'S PALISADO GREEN

From Henry Stiles' *History of Ancient Windsor* we get a record of an early orchard of importance. It lay within the Palisado Green, which is the veritable shrine of Windsor history and romance. We give here a plan of the "Ancient Palisado Plott." This ancient fortification once protected our forefathers from the Indians, and was the forerunner of many a modern park.

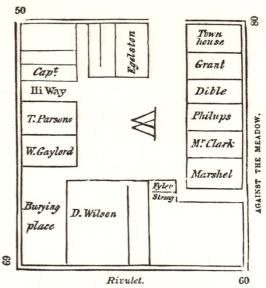

A plan of Windsor's Palisado Plot

Here stood the Town House, located where the present Congregational parsonage stands. The Town House Lot was originally Nicholas Denslow's, who resided thereon during the Pequot War. He sold it to Captain Samuel Marshall, who "dabbled in real estate" in 1654, and Marshall sold it to the inhabitants of Windsor for a town house. In the deed it is described as his "dwelling house, barn, orchard and land about it one acre more or less, with a wood lot of twenty acres," which said inhabitants were "forever fully and freely to enjoy for the benefit and entertainment of a minister successively."

Matthew Grant, who occupied the adjacent lot, was appointed by vote to see to the preserving of the house and orchard, and when any fruit came to ripeness the townsmen were to have the disposing of it for the benefit of the town. Indeed, the orchard seems to have been a more important matter than the house, and hence the property is frequently designated as the "Town Orchard."

One can see from the sentence in regard to the "benefit and entertainment of a minister" that the reverence for religion and learning was ever uppermost in the minds of the early settlers. The following record, dated 1642, gives additional testimony, and in substantial form, of this reverence:

"The proposition for releife of poor schollars att Cambridge was fully approved of, and thereupon it was ordered that Joshua Atwater and William Davis shall receive of every one in this plantation whose heart is willing to contribute there-unto, a peck of wheat or the value of itt." So far away from the seat of learning, and struggling against so many odds, but yet willing to give of the gold they had wrested from the soil to help the "poor schollars"!

But these were the same people who in the Blue Laws, never suffered to be printed, said: "No one shall run on the Sabbath Day, *or walk in his garden*."

The accompanying plan of the Palisado Plot was copied from a larger one in the ancient records of the town of Windsor. The book from which it is taken, entitled *A Book of Towne Wayes in Windsor*, appears to have been first written in 1654. The plot is thus described:

"26th. To return again to the Common wayes from the ferry at the rivulet, it ascends up upon the side of the bank to the house that was Capt. Mason's and bounds west by the fence that was John Strong's —on the top of and east by Samuel Marshall's at the foot of the bank, and then turns to the gate, and is to be three rods in breadth between John Strong's garden on the south, and Henry Clark's on the north. And seeing that I am entered into the pallasadow, I will speak a little of the original of it; about 1637 years, when the English had war with the Pequot Indians; our in-habitants on Sandy Bank gathered themselves together from their remote dwellings, to provide for their safety, set upon fortyfying, and with palazado, which some particular men resigned up out of their properties for that end, and was laid out into small parcells to build upon; some 4 rods in breadth, some five, six, seven, some eight—it was set after this manner; [Here in the record, the foregoing plan is inserted.] These dwel-ling places were at first laid out of one length, but differed as afores^d. Also on all sides within the outmost fence, there was left two rods in breadth for a common way, to go round within side the Palazado, and when divers men left their places and returned to their lotts for their conveniences, some that staid, (by consent of the town) enlarged their gardens. Some had 2, some 3, some 4 plats to their propriety, with the use of 2 rods of breadth round the outside, every one according to his breadth, only with this reserve concern-ing the two rods, that if in future time there be need of former fortification to be repaired, then each man should resign up to the two afores^d. two Rods for a way onley for common use. Note, that in the west corner of the afores^d. plott there is reserved for a common Burying Ground, one particular parcel that is six rods in breadth, all the length on one side, and on one end take it together, it is eight rod in breadth, and eighteen in length.

"There goeth out of the palazado toward north west a high way two rods wide; when past the house plotts it is larger. Also from the Palazado, runs a way north easterly, called the common street, and is to be four rods wide."

TIMOTHY DWIGHT ON TOWN-PLANNING

To the description of the Palisado Green as an example of early town-planning in Connecticut, we adjoin these observations[1] by Timothy Dwight, toward the close of the eighteenth century:

"The town-plot is originally distributed into lots, containing from two to ten acres. In a convenient spot, on each of these,

[1]From *Travels in New England and New York*.

a house is erected at the bottom of the court-yard; (often neatly enclosed;) and is furnished universally with a barn, and other convenient out-buildings. Near the house there is always a garden, replenished with culinary vegetables, flowers, and fruits, and very often, also, prettily enclosed. The lot on which the house stands, universally styled the home lot, is almost, of course, a meadow, richly cultivated, covered during the pleasant season with verdure, and contain-ing generally a thrifty orchard. It is hardly necessary to ob-serve, that these appendages spread a singular cheerfulness, and beauty, over a New England village; or that they con-tribute largely to render the house a delightful residence."

From "Colonial History of Hartford," by Rev. Wm. De Loss Love

The Isaac Bliss homestead, Hartford, whose sole surviving mark is an ancient elm

HARTFORD

A band of settlers from Cambridge, Massachusetts, founded Hartford in 1636. Their land, purchased from the Indians, was immediately distributed in units of two parts each, one part for the house-lot and one for the farm. Each house-lot consisted of about two acres. To prevent too much waste or unoccupied land, a rule was made that each lot must be built upon within a twelvemonth. A large strip of land was set aside for public use. This land, called "The Commons," before it developed into a market-place served first as the public wood-lot, and then as a grazing-ground.

These Hartford settlers of course brought with them the knowledge of the agriculture of the old country, but willingly planted the Indian maize for their first quick crop. Soon they had rye, barley and oats and many kinds of pease, as well as many garden vegetables, among them the vine-apple or squash, "light, sweet and refreshing," and the pump-kins which—the defense is by Johnson in his *Wonder-Working Providence*—"let no man make a jest at, for with their fruit the Lord was pleased to feed his people to their good content."

They also had orchards of pear and apple trees. The words "outhouses, barns, yards and gardens therein," are of frequent occurrence in all the old records. Nearly one hun-dred years after the founding, an early traveler from abroad speaks of Hartford's "broad streets, trees on the sides and handsome houses." In 1732 there is a record of one of these houses, the Isaac Bliss homestead, whose sole surviving mark is now the Bliss elm in West Bushnell Park. A painting in the possession of the Connecticut Historical Society shows the type of fence which prevailed at that time, and the house surrounded by shrubbery and trees.

The Marquis de Chastellux in his *Travels in North America*

says of West Hartford in 1780: "The houses, frequently dispersed, and sometimes grouped together, and everywhere adorned with trees and meadows, form of the road to Farmington, such a garden, in the English style, as it would be difficult for art to imitate."

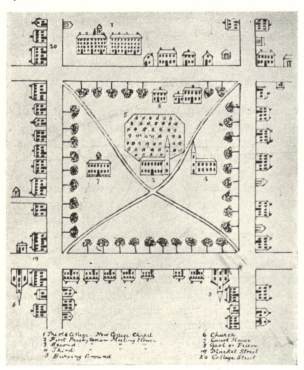

Monte Video, the estate of D. Wadsworth, Esq.

Timothy Dwight also speaks of Hartford in 1821. This is his comment on the difficulty of gardening in the type of soil surrounding the town:

"A dry season bakes the soil into clods, a wet season converts it into mortar. When the difficulties of cultivation are overcome it is one of the richest in the world."

Hartford must surely have had many pleasant gardens, but a patient search in the records of the Connecticut Historical Society and correspondence with many persons who have studied Connecticut history have failed to discover any records of gardens, their plans, or their contents. There is, however, mention of one a few miles away—"Monte Video."

MONTE VIDEO

The estate which was the residence of Daniel Wadsworth, Esq., is thus described by James Stuart, Scottish traveler,

in his *Three Years in North America*, published in 1833: ". . . stands in a very fine situation, not less than 600 feet above the Connecticut River, and its beautiful meadow scenery. The approach to the house is about three miles in extent and is carried over a succession of small hills finely wooded. There is a handsome piece of water near the house, and a hill behind it; from a tower on the top of which is a magnificent view, bounded by the hills of Mass. . . . Advantage has certainly been taken of the natural beauties of the place in laying it out—the road, the piece of water, and the grounds, but nothing about the place is kept up in the handsome style of an English country residence."

NEW HAVEN

In 1638 the town of New Haven was founded under the leadership of Davenport and Eaton, and soon became the republic of New Haven, including Milford and Stamford. Branford, and Southold on Long Island, were later added.

In 1660, Henry Maverick, one of the first white men to settle on these shores, wrote: ". . . this Towne is the Metropolis of that Government, and that Government takes its name from the Towne; . . . many stately and costly houses were erected, the streets layd out in a Gallant forme, a very stately Church; but ye harbour proving not Commodious, the land very barren, the Merchants either dead or come away, the rest gotten to the farms, the town is not as glorious as it was."

But in spite of this early setback, New Haven developed into the beautiful "City of Elms."

NEW HAVEN GREEN

Maverick does not mention the ancient "market place"—now called the "Green"—of New Haven. As early as the year the town was founded, however, this space was surveyed and laid out by John Brockett. As Henry T. Blake says in his *Chronicles of New Haven Green:* "The putting aside of so large a plot for public use was somewhat remarkable for

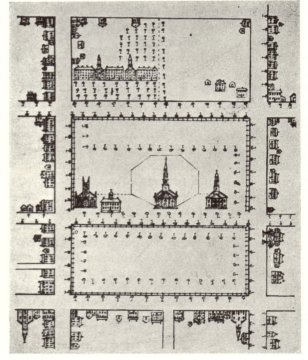

From "Chronicles of New Haven Green from 1638 to 1862," by Henry T. Blake

New Haven Green in 1775, as shown in President Stiles' map   *The Green as it was in 1817, according to Doolittle's map*

those times, and indicates a wise and liberal forethought."

Of course the early settlers of Connecticut came from Massachusetts, and the men who laid out New Haven were doubtless influenced by the Common at Boston. But the New Haven Green has been, to a greater degree than the Common, identified with the important transactions and events connected with the religious, political and civil life of the community. It has especial interest in the history of gardening, for its records through the years can be taken as typical of the development of other New England "Greens," which more than any other thing give character to the New England village.

In those early days the conquest of the forest was the first thought, and by 1649 there was very little of the old timber standing. But not until 1654 do we get any mention of grass. This grass, a welcome relief to the people from the tangled undergrowth of the forest, was immediately coveted, evidently for dooryard planting, for we read that the town-meeting had to make a rule making it a punishable offence to cut sod from "the market place." And we can imagine that it was about this time that the community in general began to take pride in the "Great Square's" appearance. We read in the records that those same people who would have cut the sod now enter protests against encroaching "stink-weed," and the depredations of geese. Doubtless it was easier to uproot the stinkweed than to outwit the geese.

Gradually all the trees were cut down, and up to about 1783 we still see "Market Place" in the records; after that time "The Green" takes its place as the name. Not until nearly a hundred years after the trees were gone did the community come to the realization that as the village pushed back the forest they would enjoy a bit of its shade in their midst. Jared Eliot wrote in 1760: "I observed in New Haven they have planted a range of trees all round the market place, and secured them from the ravages of beasts. This was an undertaking truly generous and laudable. It is a pity they were not mulberry instead of buttonwood and elms."

After these trees were planted the Green constantly increased in beauty, and became closely associated with the life of the people. The trees must have added greatly to the effect of the town in general, for in 1779, at the time of the British

Drawn by John Warner Barber

East view of the Green in 1838

invasion, General Garth declared the village "too pretty to burn." On that occasion beauty was its own protection.

Eliot spoke of the trees being secured from the ravages of animals, but that did not mean that the whole Green had been fenced. Although a number of attempts at fencing were made, it was not accomplished until 1800. Then a wooden fence was placed around the entire area. The posts were squared and pointed, and there were upper and lower rails, which were also squared. This fence stood for forty-six years.

A CITY OF TREES

John Warner Barber says that the original town was laid out in nine squares, each fifty-three rods on a side, separated by streets about four rods in breadth, but that the central square had been left open, and was then the "Green." He adds: "It was formerly used as a burying ground, but in 1821, the monuments were removed to the new burying ground and the ground leveled. It is surrounded on all sides with rows of stately elms, and is considered one of the most beautiful 'Greens' in the United States."

Barber also declared New Haven, except in very dry years, to be remarkably suited for gardens. Its reputation for beauty seems to have been wide-spread over the colonies. Hubbard speaks of the "fair and stately houses wherein they at first out-

Drawn by John Warner Barber

Yale College and the elms in front, in 1838

did the rest of the country," seeming to think that they had "laid out too much of these stocks and estates" in building them. One of the New Haven Historical Society reports says that "the wife of one of the prominent Plymouth settlers returning from a visit to New Haven, was grieved at the 'poor show' which the houses of Boston made when measured with the New Haven houses."

A Dr. Alexander Hamilton traveled in this part of New England before the Revolution. He described New Haven as "a pretty large, scattered town, laid out in squares, much in the same manner as Philadelphia, but the houses are sparse and thin sown." This was in 1744. At that time, this was the Green, according to Dr. Hamilton: "The burying place is in the center of the town, just facing the College which is a wooden building 200 feet long and three stories high, and in the middle part of which is a little cupola, with a clock upon it."

In 1786 Manasseh Cutler wrote in his Journal: "The city of New Haven [Note that it is no longer spoken of as a village] covers a large piece of ground, a little descending toward the sea, with a southern aspect. The streets are tolerably wide, and some of them ornamented with rows of trees." Evidently the beauty of the trees in the Green had had its effect, and the trees in the streets, once so gladly uprooted, had been replaced. Cutler also speaks of another row of trees across the open space. These had just been set out in line with the State House, two large meeting-houses and the Grammar School. He remarked too, that within the square and on the borders of others adjoining there were six steeples and cupolas on public buildings within a very small compass of ground. "The houses in general," he says, "are good, some of them elegant, and a great proportion built with brick. The streets are dry, but very sandy, and *will probably never be paved, as it must be attended with great expense.*"[1]

The indispensable Timothy Dwight, who traveled through New England and New York in 1815, gives a charming picture of the typical New England town, which thirty years earlier Cutler had called a "city":

"The style of building is neat and tidy. Fences and out houses are also in the same style; and being almost universally painted white, make a delightful appearance to the eye, an

[1]The italics are not Cutler's. Three years later, in 1789, when Washington, the newly inaugurated president, made his journey to Boston by way of New Haven he comments not at all on the beauties of the city, much to our regret, and only records that there was a college there under Dr. Stiles.

The Captain Daniel Greene house, built by Ralph Isaacs in 1771

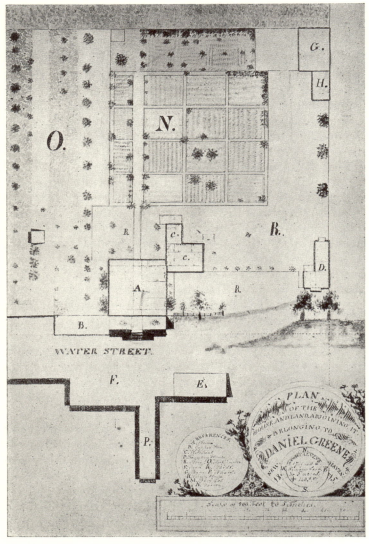

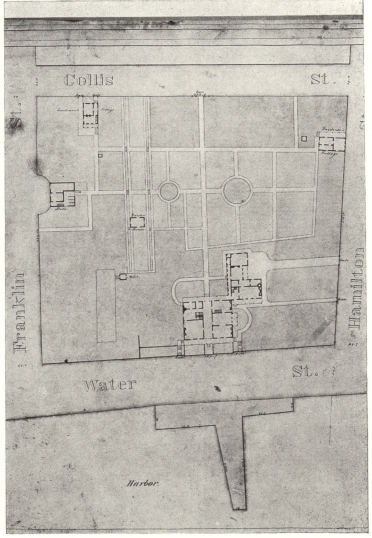

Plan of the Captain Daniel Greene garden in 1815   *"Brewster Place": the one-time Greene garden about 1830*

Illustrations on this page by courtesy of Mr. George D. Seymour

appearance, not a little enhanced, by the great multitude of shade trees; a species of ornament in which the town is unrivalled."

Thus by the early nineteenth century the example of tree planting by the town fathers in 1760 had spread over the whole community.

A score of years later John Warner Barber in his *Historical Collections of Connecticut* allows us one of our rare glimpses of gardens. "Many of the houses have court yards in front, and gardens in the rear," he says. "The former are ornamented with trees and shrubs; the latter are filled with fruit trees, flowers, and culinary vegetables."

Fortunately, the plans of one of these gardens have survived.

THE CAPTAIN DANIEL GREENE HOUSE AND GARDEN

The house was built by Ralph Isaacs, a great Tory, before the Revolutionary War. It was later sold to a Mr. Broome, and then to Captain Daniel Greene, a famous sea-captain who made the money-making voyage to China in the *Neptune*. The plan of the grounds is dated 1815, but faintly dis-

In 1838 Middletown, drawn here by John Warner Barber, followed the style and had planted Lombardy poplars

Drawn by John Warner Barber

A glimpse of a formal garden of about 1832: a southeastern view of Wesleyan University, Middletown

cernible along the bottom margin appears: "House bought by Captain Greene 1795." No doubt the garden was laid out in the form shown in the plan some time before 1815.

The same place is shown in the later plan entitled "Brewster Place"; it was then the property of the celebrated carriage-maker, a descendant of Elder Brewster, and related to the Brewsters of New Haven and New York. Sometime before 1830 or 1832—the date of the Brewster place map—the old garden evidently had been developed along somewhat formal lines.[1]

MIDDLETOWN

In 1650 the lands called Mattabesett by the Indians of Connecticut were visited by a group of settlers and the site of Middletown was decided upon. By the following year

[1]The reproduced photographs of the house and of the garden plans were furnished by Mr. George D. Seymour.

there were thirty-one families in the settlement. In the next hundred years the people of Middletown went through the same vicissitudes that the other settlements of Connecticut had withstood.

In 1786 Manasseh Cutler visited the town and wrote an excellent description of the beauties of that part of Connecticut:

"Middletown is pleasantly situated on the declivity of a hill and extends along the banks of the river. It has an eastern aspect, but does not command a very extended view. It is laid out in oblong squares. The streets are wide, and in some of them are beautiful rows of trees, mostly button-wood, on each side of the street. The houses are in general well built, but, the flat extended caps over their doors, though very convenient, are far from being ornamental. Many of the lots are not yet built upon. At the northern end of the city is a walk of two rows of button-wood trees, from the front gate of a gentleman's house[1] on the bank of the river, by far the most beautiful I ever saw. He permits the people of the city to improve it as a mall.

"The extended tract of country beyond the city, and on each side of the river, is varied with hills and valleys in a high state of cultivation. Extensive fields of grain, lesser fields of Indian corn of the deepest green, plats of grassland and pastures of a livelier verdure, orchards of fruit trees, and groves of woodland form the background of the finished picture.

"It is inconceivable what richness of beauty the whole tract when melted together exhibits."

Apparently the gardens of Middletown were essentially practical affairs. Field's "Account of Middlesex County," written in 1819, says: "We have many good gardens, but the attention of the people has been directed almost solely to the cultivation of those roots and plants which are useful. The state of gardening there is on a level with the state of gardening throughout Connecticut."

In a drawing of Wesleyan University, however, we get a glimpse of a formal garden of about 1832. Here we see the characteristic features—the square beds, the planting against the garden wall, the trees set at intervals, the arch, and the summer-house. Among the meagre records of Connecticut gardens, this is one of the few evidences that this type of garden did exist prior to 1840.

[1]It has been impossible to identify this house.

WETHERSFIELD

THE GARDEN OF THE OLD WEBB HOUSE

The old Webb House in Wethersfield, known from its earliest history as "Hospitality Hall," is one of the interesting houses in Connecticut, both for its historical associations, and for the excellence of its colonial architecture. It was built in 1753 by Joseph Webb, of a well-to-do family of that name, long resident in Wethersfield. In this house was held the conference between Washington, his staff, and De Rochambeau. At that council, the most momentous of the whole Revolutionary War, was planned the campaign which ended with the surrender of Cornwallis at Yorktown.

In 1919 the house was purchased by the National Society of Colonial Dames in the State of Connecticut. It will be preserved by the Society as a memorial of Colonial and Revolutionary times.

The Webb House, Wethersfield, from a drawing made before 1840.
The garden lay behind the house

There are no records of the age of the old garden, but undoubtedly there has been one from the time the house was built. It has now been restored along traditional lines. Iris, peonies, daffodils, funkia, dictamnus and larkspur were laid aside from the old garden, to be transplanted to the new, as well as some fine old shrubs—lilacs, syringas, hawthorns, strawberry shrub, and a favorite grape vine. For the rest, it is intended to make this something of a memorial garden, with plants from the garden of the Ladd House in Portsmouth, N. H. Seeds from Mount Vernon have already been sown and are growing.

NORWICH

Mary E. Perkins' *Old Houses of Norwich* gives an account of the fences which surrounded the gardens and home-lots of the early settlers. They were high fences, the early regulations requiring that those in front should be "a five rayle or equal to it," and "the general fence a three rayle." Later "a good three rayle fence, four feet high, a good hedge or pole fence, well staked, four and a half feet high" was allowed.

In Norwich lived Mrs. Lydia Huntley Sigourney, whose somewhat sentimental poetry and prose won for her a wide literary reputation in the first half of the nineteenth century. She was interested in gardens from the days of her childhood, when she helped her father in his garden. One day she helped him to plant two apple trees in front of his house. When some of his friends protested that the trees were too utilitarian, he replied: "It is better to fill the space with something useful than with unproductive shade,"—a view which fairly reflected the early attitude of Connecticut toward ornamental gardening. But as his daughter grew up she developed a feeling for beauty in the garden, as evidenced by the following account of an unidentified garden which she wrote in 1824:

"In this department of the town was the mansion of Madame L——. It raised a broad, dignified front, without other decoration than the white rose and the sweet briar rearing their columns of beauty and fragrance quite to the projection of the roof. In front was a court of shorn turf like the richest velvet intersected by two paved avenues to the principal entrance, and enclosed by a white fence, resting upon a foundation of hewn stone. On each side of the antiquated gate waved the boughs of a spruce intermingling the foliage and defying in their evergreen garb, the changes of climate.

"The habitation which faced the rising sun had on its left and in the rear of its long range of offices, two large gardens for vegetables and fruit. A third, which had a southern exposure, and lay beneath the windows of the parlor was partially devoted to flowers. There in quadrangles, triangles and parallelograms, beds of mould were thrown up, and regularly arranged, according to what the florists of that age denominated 'a knot.' There in the centre, the flaming peony reared its head like a queen upon her throne, surrounded by a guard of tulips—deep crimson, buff streaked with vermilion and pure white mantled with a blush of carmine. Lilac, snowball, lily, rose, snow-drops, daffodils, violets, hyacinths, blue-bells, guinea hen flowers, Ragged Lady, batchelor buttons, mourning-bride and monkshood, larkspur, sweetpeas and fumitory, also grew there.

"A broad walk divided this garden into nearly equal compartments. The western part, covered with rich turf, and interspersed with fruit trees, displayed at its extremity a summer-house, encircled by a luxuriant vine, and offering a delightful retreat from a fervid sun. . . .

"Near the same region was a nursery of medicinal plants—sage, hoarhound, tansy and bitter rue and wormwood. Also balm and peppermint. Large poppies were scattered here and there, and hopvines."

FAIRFIELD COUNTY

In Fairfield County we find hints and occasional glimpses of more elaborate gardens. An advertisement in a Bridgeport newspaper for June 28, 1800, conveys an impression of gardens well-kept and well cultivated.

For Sale

That beautiful situation, late the property of Thaddeus Benedict Esq., situate at Newfield (Bridgeport) landing containing fifty-five rods of ground under the finest improvement and cultivation as a garden, with a large and elegant dwelling-house; all in excellent order.

In Hurd's *History of Fairfield County* we read of a Danbury garden as the setting for an outdoor wedding in 1815.

"Major Seth Comstock at the marriage of his son made his homestead into a wedding-bower. He had summer-houses, arbors and grottoes put up in the garden. The entire front of the house was changed by the elaborate additions placed thereon, and the premises blossomed into the appearance of a small Paradise. The place was daily visited by Danbury people who were filled with pride and admiration as they viewed it."

THE GARDEN OF THE THADDEUS BURR HOMESTEAD, FAIRFIELD

Fairfield, one of the Connecticut towns settled before 1640, had as its most distinguished citizen during Revolutionary times Thaddeus Burr Esq. Private and historical sources furnish an account of the vicissitudes of his house and garden. The present owner[1] writes:

"There has always been a garden at the Thaddeus Burr Homestead, and a garden of the same type as the present

[1]Mrs. DeVer H. Warner.

The great elm, Wethersfield, was a large tree in 1775

one. A broad path extended toward Long Island Sound from the porch at the southern end of the house and a border of shrubs and flowers and beds with all the old well-known plants. The Burrs entertained very largely and there are frequent allusions in the Diaries and Journals of the time indicating Mrs. Burr's love of flowers, which she was always pleased to give to guests as they came, or as they left the hospitable mansion.

"Fairfield was settled in 1639 and was a prosperous New England village, one of the best known, before, during and after the Revolutionary War. The owner of the Burr Homestead was a prominent citizen, and was well acquainted with the patriots of Boston, John Hancock being probably the most intimate and important of his friends. And it was at the Homestead that John Hancock celebrated his marriage to Miss Dorothy Quincy.

"When Fairfield village was burned in 1779, the Burr Homestead was consumed with the rest of the town, though Mrs. Burr had received a paper from Governor Tryon, granting her protection."

John Warner Barber tells us that in the burning mentioned by Mrs. Warner eighty-five dwelling houses, two churches, "an elegant court house," fifty-five barns, fifteen stores, and fifteen shops were laid in ashes. In Timothy Dwight's graphic description of the plunder and pillage, one can read between the lines the fate of colonial gardens in Fairfield:

"On the 7th of July, 1779, Gov. Tryon, with the army which I have already mentioned, sailed from New Haven to Fairfield; and the next morning disembarked on the beach. A few militia assembled to oppose them; and in a desultory, scattered manner, fought with great intrepidity through most of the day. They killed some, took several prisoners, and wounded more. But the expedition was so sudden, that the efforts made in this manner were necessarily fruitless. The town was plundered; a great part of the houses, together with the two churches, the court house, the jail, and school houses, were burnt. The barns had been just filled with wheat and other produce. The inhabitants, therefore, were turned out into the world, almost literally destitute.

"Mrs. Burr, the wife of Thaddeus Burr, Esq. High Sheriff

The Thaddeus Burr house, Fairfield, as it is today

of the county, resolved to continue in the mansion house of the family, and make an attempt to save it from the conflagration. The house stood at a sufficient distance from other buildings. Mrs. Burr was adorned with all the qualities which give distinction to her sex; possessed of fine accomplishments, and a dignity of character, scarcely rivalled; and probably had never known what it was to be treated with disrespect, or even with inattention. She made a personal application to Gov. Tryon, in terms, which from a lady of her high respectability, could hardly have failed of a satisfactory answer from any person who claimed the title of gentleman. The answer, which she actually received, was however rude and brutal;

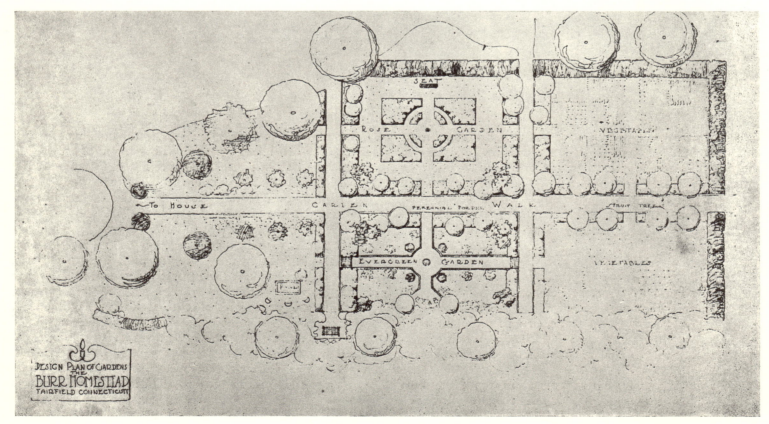

A plan of the present-day gardens of the Burr homestead

The garden of the Thaddeus Burr house, Fairfield
Above: the main path approaching the house from the south.   Below: the fine elm which flanks the main path

The main path, facing the hedge, in the garden of the Thaddeus Burr house, Fairfield
Photographs of the Thaddeus Burr Homestead by J. P. Haley

and spoke the want, not only of politeness and humanity, but even of vulgar civility. The house was sentenced to the flames, and was speedily set on fire. An attempt was made in the meantime, by some of the soldiery, to rob her of a valuable watch, with rich furniture; for Gov. Tryon refused to protect her, as well as preserve the house. The watch had already been conveyed out of their reach; but the house, filled with everything, which contributes either to comfort or elegance of living, was laid in ashes."

Governor Tryon later said in explanation of his action: "The village was burnt to resent the fire of the rebels from their houses, and to mask our retreat."

Dr. Dwight concludes:

"The injuries done to a single family, were an immense overbalance for all the good done on this expedition, either by individuals engaged in it, or the nation in whose service they acted. Particularly that highly respectable pair, Mr. and Mrs. Burr, in the loss of the mansion of their ancestors, and the treasures with which it had been stored through a long succession of years; where the elegant hospitality which had reigned in it; the refined enjoyments which were daily felt, and daily distributed to the friend, and the stranger; the works of charity, which were there multiplied; and the controlling principle; diffused a brilliancy, remarked even by the passing eye; lost more than the whole British nation gained by this devastation.

"The next morning the troops re-embarked; and preceeding to Green's Farms, set fire to the church, and consumed it; together with fifteen dwelling houses, eleven barns, and several stores. Among the houses was that of the Reverend Dr. Ripley; the respectable clergyman of this parish. Here, also, was another proof that burning was the object of the expedition. . . ."

In course of time Mr. Burr rebuilt the mansion, patterning it on the Hancock house in Boston, and erecting a dignified and handsome structure.

The house today stands quite near the old Boston Post Road, and is still surrounded with spacious grounds, shaded by magnificent old trees. A box-bordered walk leads from the street gate to the pillared verandah. At the rear, where Mrs. Burr tended her flowers, the present owner, Mrs. DeVer H. Warner, follows her example, taking pleasure in the marigolds and roses, pinks, hollyhocks, and peonies. There is now an old-fashioned garden, bright with flowers, and the massive arbor-vitae hedge which shields the garden from the east wind dates back generations. Varied vistas of the sea are framed by masses of shrubbery and the graceful foliage

John Warner Barber's drawing in 1838 of the court house, church, and jail in Fairfield, rebuilt on the original foundations and in a style believed identical with that of the buildings destroyed by fire in 1779

of stalwart elms. The old Burr Homestead still keeps the charm which drew to it the visitors of by-gone days.

GREENWICH

Greenwich, now the site of many beautiful gardens, was known as Horse Neck as late as 1789. When Washington passed through on his way to Boston he made no comment upon the village, mentioning only the stony character of the country and the steepness of the hill now known as Putnam's Hill.

There are many records of the early history of Greenwich which tell us much of church and state, but a patient search has failed to disclose any account of the gardens. In support of our belief that the planting of box was largely after the Revolution and well into the nineteenth century, we give here a picture of a box hedge in Greenwich, now over six feet in height, which was planted in 1822. It is *Buxus suffruticosa*, and has at times during its history been badly killed back by severe winters.

STAMFORD

Timothy Dwight's visit to Stamford in 1799 took him to the property of Moses Rogers, on Shippan Point. "This," wrote Dr. Dwight, "is an elegant and fertile piece of ground. The farm itself is a delightful object, with its fields neatly enclosed, its orchards and its groves. Here Mr. Rogers has formed an avenue a mile in length, reaching quite to the

This lovely old box hedge, still flourishing at Clapboard Ridge, Greenwich, was planted in 1822, the date of the building of the original house

water's edge. At the same time he has planted on the grounds surrounding the house, almost all the forest trees, which are indigenous to the country. To these he has united plantations of fruit trees, a rich garden, and other interesting objects so combined as to make one of the pleasantest retreats in the United States."

There is no trace of Mr. Rogers' orchards or groves today.

CASAGMO GARDENS, RIDGEFIELD

John Warner Barber tells us that Ridgefield was called by the Indians "Caudatowa," signifying "high land," because its elevated position afforded a prospect of Long Island for

forty miles. His drawing of the Stebbins house, the site of the present Casagmo Gardens, was made in 1840, when the house was over 100 years old, and was still in the possession of the Stebbins family. We quote from his recital[1] of the Revolutionary history of the scene:

John Warner Barber's sketch of Ridgefield in 1840 shows the Stebbins house, then over one hundred years old, on the right. Both houses had Lombardy poplars, in the fashion of the day, and stone walls and wooden fences as enclosures

"The place represented . . . is perhaps 80 rods north of the Congregational church in Ridgefield, on the north end of the village, on the road to Danbury. It was at this spot that the Americans, under Gen. Arnold, made a stand against the British forces, as they came down from Danbury. . . .

"In order to stop the advance of the British, a barricade was thrown across the street from Mr. Stebbins' house, extending to the place where the house opposite is now built. The place where Gen. Arnold's horse was shot, and where he killed the British soldier who was advancing towards him, is seen on the left of the engraving, the man and the boy are seen standing on the precise spot. Many of the dead and wounded were carried into the house of Mr. Stebbins, and the floors were literally covered with blood; a number of the wounded died in the house. Fifteen of the British and fifteen Americans were buried near the first house now standing south of Mr. Stebbins.' Gen. Wooster received his mortal wound about one and a half miles north, and Col. Gould was killed about eighty rods east of the house; his body was carried to Fairfield. The British encamped over night on the high ground nearly a mile south of the Congregational church, and when they left the place in the morning, they fired a house near by, which was supposed to be a signal for their shipping lying on the coast near the Norwalk Islands."

The following adaptation of a paper by Miss Mary Olcott provides additional historical details and a description of the garden:

"In 1708 a number of men of Norwalk petitioned the

[1]From *Historical Collections of Connecticut*, by John Warner Barber.

General Assembly, then sitting at Hartford, for 'liberty to purchase of the Indians a certain tract of land bounded south by Norwalk bounds, north-east on Danbury and

Casagmo Gardens, Ridgefield.   The entrance

west on York line.' Part of this allotment became the village of Ridgefield, and here in 1721 Benjamin Stebbins took possession of certain acres at the northern end of Main Street, and later his son, Squire Samuel Stebbins, built a house and laid out his colonial vegetable and fruit gardens.

"Squire Samuel Stebbins built his house, thick-beamed and raftered, four-square to the Main Street, facing the south, near what was in those days the 'Pound'—'built ye south side the Rocks in the Street, on ye west side the path near Samuel Stebbins Dwelling House not to contain more ground in it than is equal to Forty Feet Square.'

"These 'Rocks' were the original bank cut through to make the Main Street, and on the 'Rocks' Squire Stebbins grew lilacs which each spring shook out their large purple and white blooms

along the roadside for at least one hundred and eighty-five years.

"Samuel Goodrich ('Peter Parley') wrote to his brother in 1855: 'Master Stebbins' house—from its elevated position at the head of the street, seeming like the guardian genius of the place—still stands . . . embowered in trees, some, primeval elms, spreading their wide branches protectingly over the roof, stoop and foreground, others, sugar maples, upright, symmetrical and deeply verdant.'

"In the course of the two hundred and three years since the allotment, only two families, the Stebbins and the Olcotts, have occupied these acres, although the house and grounds have been the scene of many stirring situations. Here General Benedict Arnold, whose grandfather, Governor Benedict Arnold, is the direct ancestor of Mrs. Olcott, helped hold the British at bay at the Battle of Ridgefield, afterwards escaping to Putnam's camp through the Stebbins cow-path. Here also in the grounds were buried many soldiers, both American and British. They are commemorated by a tablet let into the wall on the street.

"The old house was torn down in 1897, but the site was marked by Mrs. Olcott by an American beech and a cutleaf maple.

"During the lifetime of the old Stebbins house its garden lay eastward and northward from the house, while the flower garden ran on each side of the walk from the front door to the street, as is the New England way, spreading gradually back a little as it slowly grew with the years and ending in a bit of boxwood and shrubbery that separated it from the fruit orchard, of which a few old gnarled trees still remain.

"In 1912 the road in front of the homestead was widened and the long row of white and purple lilacs had to be moved. This was done successfully, including a host of seedlings. And they now stand just within the stone wall which protects the new garden. This new garden was also built in 1912, and in it, beneath the entrance gateway and in the wall of the second terrace, lies the old hearthstone, bearing the date 1721. The original cow-path remains the pathway from the house to the tea-terrace. These gardens are of a formal type, and are divided into three terraces, the first two of which are on the site of the old vegetable gardens of Revolutionary times.

"In addition to the garden on the site of the old one, there

Casagmo Gardens, Old Road of the Revolution, Ridgefield

Casagmo Gardens, Ridgefield
Above: looking toward the residence.   Below: the second terrace

Surmounting Putnam's Hill, Greenwich, in this drawing by John Warner Barber in 1838, is a typical salt-box house with tall locust trees around it. This is the steep, rocky road commented on by Washington in 1789

is another for vegetables and cut flowers, which bears the name 'My mother's garden,' as being especially beloved by each lady of the house. It has as guardian an ancient walnut tree, at least one hundred and fifty years old, while in the park below is the dying stump of a noble American beech, which shows by its rings that it must have been a large tree long before the Revolutionary War."

NEW CANAAN

John Warner Barber's drawing of New Canaan shows how the typical New England village was built around an open spot or green. In this green we can still see the stumps, although New Canaan, incorporated as a town in 1801, had been in existence nearly twenty-five years when the drawing was made. Barber says in explanation of his sketch:

"The surface of the township is mountainous, containing spines or ridges, composed of rock and stone, which extend from north to south through the town. The soil is a hard,

The Episcopal Academy, Cheshire, showing tree planting in the characteristic New England manner of 1820

gravelly loam, being stony, but tolerably well timbered, and generally good for cultivation.

"The following is an eastern view of the central part of New Canaan. The building on the extreme right, with a square tower, is the Episcopal church, recently erected; the building seen standing nearest to it, is the town house. The Congregational church, with a spire, is seen on the left. The building was erected in 1752, and is the second house of worship; the

first stood a little south. The Methodist church is about half a mile south of this place. The building with a small steeple or tower, appearing in the central part of the engraving is the New Canaan Academy, established in 1815."

This locality in 1796 inspired another of Timothy Dwight's vivid pictures of the Connecticut countryside:

"The verdure, which here overspreads a great part of the whole region, is of the finest tint; and produces the most cheerful sense of fruitfulness, plenty and prosperity. Trees, remarkable for the straightness and thriftiness of their stems, the length and beauty of their boughs and branches, and wherever of sufficient age, for their height also, whether standing singly or in groves, or in extensive forests, variegate the slopes and vallies; and cover the summits of the hills. Handsomer groves, it is presumed, cannot be found. Orchards everywhere, meet the eye. Herds of cattle are seen grazing the rich pastures, or quietly ruminating in the shade. Neat farm-houses, standing on the hills; a succession of pretty villages, with their churches ornamented with steeples, most of them white, and therefore cheerful and brilliant; lend

East view of the central part of New Canaan

the last touches of art to a picture, so finely drawn by the hand of Nature."

Dwight also speaks of the magnificent growth of white pines which once clothed the hills of Connecticut. One was measured by a Mr. Law, and found to be 247 feet in length. The width of the boards which we see in the oldest houses attests the great size of these trees. It is interesting to note that Dwight felt even then that the forests were being very generally destroyed. He says (1796): "A few years ago such trees were in great numbers along the northern part of the Connecticut River—but it is probable that the next generation may never see a white pine of full size, and may regard an exact account of this noble vegetable production as a mere fable."

THE GREAT FROST AT GREENFIELD HILL

The spring of 1793 evidently brought a devastating frost to the gardens of Connecticut. Timothy Dwight recorded the following:

"A Mr. Bradley of Greenfield Conn. in the year 1793 planted very early, some cucumbers in the North-western corner of his garden; where the ground was completely sheltered by a close fence on the northern and western sides. At the same time he planted others in the middle of his garden. The great frost, on the morning of May 13th., destroyed all the former; while the latter entirely escaped. This frost was more severe than any other, at so late a season, within my knowledge. In many places it killed the leaves of forest trees, and in some, the rye, then in blossom, and the spear grass.

"My own garden on the Greenfield hill declined easily toward the East; yet its position was such, that the western fence, being an open one, it was brushed by the winds from the North-West even more effectually than most grounds, which decline toward that point. Accordingly, I never lost a plant by a white frost, during the nine years of my residence on that spot.

"As nearly every such frost is produced by the North-West wind it is evident that plants, from which the dew is swept away by the wind will escape; while those, which by being sheltered from its current retain the dew, will be destroyed."

This frost described by Timothy Dwight, which killed the leaves of forest trees on May 13, 1793, may be contrasted with the weather of the week of May 2–9, 1930, when the temperature ranged from 86 to 90 degrees. Leaves developed from bud to full growth during that week.

Two men gave actual inspiration to this work of tree planting—James Hillhouse of New Haven and Lyman Beecher. It is said that a number of young men were so inspired by one of Lyman Beecher's sermons, that to show their public spirit they went to the woods and dug trees and planted them along the streets.

THE JOHN COTTON SMITH GARDEN, SHARON[1]

The house to which the ancient garden is attached is high and broad, and on the western and southern sides runs a piazza high in front, but needing but one low step where the ground rises in the rear.

This garden was the delight of its owner's heart. When Mrs.

Drawn by John Warner Barber

East view of Litchfield from Chestnut Hill

LITCHFIELD COUNTY

TREE PLANTING IN LITCHFIELD

The township of Litchfield was called by the Indians "Bantam." In 1718 it was purchased of the Colony of Connecticut by a company, who divided their purchase of ten miles square into sixty shares, under the name of "proprietor's Rights."

Barber, who sketched it, described it as an elevated township, diversified into hills and valley. "Great Pond, now called Bantam lake is a beautiful stretch of water, the largest lake in the state."

The Marquis de Chastellux visited Litchfield in his travels through America in 1780. At that time Litchfield had, he said, about "fifty houses near each other, with a large square, or rather area in the middle."

In the present day the trees of Litchfield are its pride, but when Oliver Wolcott Jr., returning from Yale, began to set out trees, one of the old inhabitants remarked sadly, "We have worked so hard in our day, and just finished getting the woods cleared, and now they are bringing the trees back again."

That was about 1790. Evidently public sentiment soon began to change, for in the *Monitor* for January 3, 1798, is the following:

"Would it not be a regulation well deserving the attention of the General Court, to require every town to plant the sides of the public roads with forest trees? The planting of quick-growing trees of Willow, Lombardy Poplar, Balm of Gilead etc. certainly deserves attention. Even the elms, ash-trees, button-woods and maples well pay for planting by their growth."

John Cotton Smith came to her husband's home in Sharon, the garden had only been sketched in. It was only two years after the close of the War of the Revolution, and the times were not only dark, but the immediate future seemed darker in outlook. But even before the outbreak of the war deep terraces had been cut in the sloping hillside. Two fish-ponds affording restful pauses in the downward path of the rapid brook had been made and were already shaded with borders of young willows.

Imported vines of several varieties and fruit-trees of all the usual and some unusual sorts had been planted in the orchards behind the house as well as in the future garden; but of flowers there were not many until 1785. The bride, who had the inborn love for them that is nearly always found in persons of Holland descent, brought seeds, roots, and slips to sow and to plant in the formal way in which she had always seen them arranged in the garden of her "Father Everton" and "Grandfather Bloom," the one in the western part of the present town of Amenia, New York, and the other near Pleasant Valley.

The garden contained probably about two acres of rich ground, defended from animal intrusions, but not from friendly observations, by a moderately high fence of yellow pine pales attached to cedar posts, with every picket top cut by hand, finished to resemble a clover-leaf, the whole painted a mossy green.

The ground of the garden sloped steeply to the brook and was according to the fashion of the day formed into a series of terraces connected with steps. About two-thirds of the distance back from the fence which separates the lowest of the terraces from the highway ran a very broad gravelled

[1]Adapted from "An Ancient Garden," by Helen Everston Smith, in *The Century*, May, 1906.

and flower-bordered walk from the house on the north to
the brook at the south where a vine-covered and latticed
arbor, provided with seats, filled the double purpose of a

Barber's drawing of the south view of Gov. Smith's house in Sharon

resting-place and a foot-bridge over the brook where it
merrily fell from the fish-pond to the copse beyond.

No box-borders were allowed on the premises—the odor
being objectionable to the owner—but along the outer edge of
the garden ran a hedge of English hawthorn, kept closely
trimmed.

Directly in front of the house, about sixty feet from it, and
extending across something like 100 feet ran a low stone
terrace wall connecting the highway sidewalk by a wrought
iron gate at the foot of stone steps with the flagged walk lead-

*Barber's drawing of Plainfield (above) about 1840 shows trees on the
village street, and the typical carefully squared and walled fields. His
sketch of Manchester (below) illustrates the tree planting of 1820*

ing to the front piazza. A lilac hedge edged this wall and is
still in existence. It is not too high to shut out the view of rolling hills and vale, but high enough to make a screen from the
highway.

The big squares forming the tops of the terraces were
planted in vegetables. Vegetables and fruits grew luxuriantly,
and quantities of red, purple and white grapes were raised
for the manufacture of home-made wines.

There was also the important "garden of herbs"—camo-
mile, feverfew, saffron, valerian, sage and many others. To
gather and dry the herbs was one of the housewife's many
summer duties, and so was the manufacture of them into
cordials, wines and waters for refreshment and toilet purposes.

Our Gardener, in a small diary which she kept for many
years, frequently refers to "a busy Morning in my Still
Room," and mentions raspberry vinegar, blackberry brandy,
wild-cherry cordial, and rose-water for flavoring.

Around every large square of vegetables in the garden ran
broad walks, and between the vegetables and the walks were
narrow borders of flowers.

Mrs. Smith writes in 1798: "Donning my galoshes, for it
was wet after last night's downpour, I had Silvy put the
Camp-stool under the big willow, where I could watch the
men and oversee the work on the new Asparagus bed. You
know the old is nearly choked with roots and after giving
Papa and Uncle Paul all the roots they wanted I thought I
would have an extra bed made for ourselves. It is a good

*The home of Nathan Hale, Coventry, as drawn by Barber. The maple
trees planted in ordered rows must have followed the fashion of 1820*

thing to have a plenty of, for our neighbors, as well as our
own folks, for everybody likes it and few have."

This asparagus bed had borders of daffodils, narcissus,
white and yellow jonquils, blue-eyed myrtle and stately
crown-imperials. It is now covered with soft green turf, but
is still gay with the old-time flowers.

The bulbs which renewed themselves for over a century
in that old garden are said to have descended from still older
ones from Flüssingen, in the province of Zeeland in the
Netherlands, the home of Mrs. Smith's ancestors. Guelder
roses, artemisias, and Canterbury bells also grew there; foxgloves, cockscombs, marigolds and monkshood, asters and
balsam, pride-of-the-meadow and phlox, stocks—called
"stuck jellies" by "Caius Tite" the negro servant—moss
pinks, and sweet-williams, petunias, larkspurs, columbines,
poppies, pansies, lavender, valerian, gourds, sweet peas,
geraniums, cowslips, primroses, Marvel of Peru, and red
and white peonies, here and there; while along the brookside smiled the purple fleur-de-lis. But the pride of the garden
was the roses, "ten varieties," besides one considered as
"surpassing fine, being very double, and a pure soft white,
bearing very abundantly; the sweetest and best of all my
flowers, only the hateful rose-bugs do spoil them so."

The shrubs and flowering trees of the old time still remain,
many of them in the spots where they were set out. The
heavy-scented syringas and bushes of purple and white
lilacs from fifteen to twenty-five feet in height look freely
in at second-story windows to which they have been over a
century in climbing. The soft blooms of the snowballs
still whiten in June, and the clove-scented flowering currants
still linger by favored banks.

Many of the old locusts have crashed to earth, but their
descendants wave their feathery green each year, and the

The Green or Common in Sharon, as it is today

A view of Wethersfield Common, looking south, in the winter of 1930. In 1771 John Adams considered it the finest common next to that of Hadley, Mass.

The old "Glebe" house (1771) at Woodbury.   A typical dooryard, showing the lilacs against the house and the great button-ball tree before the door

old horse-chestnuts still stand, flowering as freely as of yore. And the stiff, angular limbs of the ghostly button-balls still defy the summer lightning and the winter storms.

AGRICULTURAL SOCIETIES[1]

"A Society for Promoting Agriculture in the State of Connecticut" was formed by persons from several towns at Wallingford on Aug. 12, 1794. Its members were invited to make experiments in the various departments of agriculture; the constitution of the Society contemplated the free communication of that information. This Society was probably the first of the kind to be organized in the United States. A library was started in 1807. In 1809 it was named The Agricultural Society of the State of Connecticut, later The Agricultural Society of New Haven.

The Hartford Agricultural Society was founded and incorporated in 1817, suspended in 1831, and resumed in 1840.

The Horticultural Society of New Haven was organized in 1830 and incorporated in 1831. This Society still exists (1925).

Other Agricultural Societies were established as follows: Litchfield County, 1839; Windham, Fairfield, and Middlesex Counties, 1840.

The Hartford Horticultural Society was organized in 1849. For a time it held weekly exhibits of fruit and flowers from June to October.

An address delivered in September, 1835, before the New Haven Horticultural Society on the cultivation of native plants in gardens is interesting for its revelation of the growing appreciation of the value and beauty of native plantings.

[1]Facts from *The History of Connecticut*, edited by Norris Galpin Osborn.

This address was given by Professor Charles Upham Shepherd, whose love and understanding of the flora of Connecticut is shown by the following quotations:

"But I wish to dwell for a few minutes on the native plants and trees which abound in our immediate vicinity, and which are worthy of being introduced into flower-gardens and door-yards. They are the more deserving of notice that when once established they require no protection against climate, but maintain their footing with true New England hardihood.

"For early spring we may cultivate several of our willows whose blossoms appear even before the snows depart, and whose rich shiny foliage is an ornament through the whole summer. The fleecy shadbush will be a fit accompaniment for the willow, and we may add to them both, the large flowering dogwood. In warm and concealed situations, as beneath the arms of low-branching firs and evergreens, we may have beds of the spring anemone, the liver-leaf, the trailing arbutus, and the checker-berry; in more open, though still sheltered places, it will be easy to cultivate the conspicuous wake-robins, the yellow and purple lady slippers, and the spotted dog-tooth violet."

Professor Shepherd speaks also of the purple clematis, bloodroot, and columbine. And as shrubs that bloom in the late spring and early summer he mentions, "the large white clusters of the lantern bush, the rich purple flowers of the false honeysuckle, the inimitable blows of the laurel, the large white corymbs of the elder, the globose heads of the button-bush, the upright spikes of the fragrant clethra, and the tasseled blooms of the rhododendron. . . ."[2]

[2]By the lantern-bush, Prof. Shepherd undoubtedly meant the American Bladder-nut (*Staphylea trifolia*); by the false honey-suckle, *Rhododendron nudiflorum;* by the laurel, *Kalmia latifolia;* the elder is *Sambucus canadensis,* the button-bush *Cephalanthus occidentalis,* and the rhododendron *Rhododendron maximum.*

MAINE

NEW HAMPSHIRE

VERMONT

A flight of curved grass steps leading to the upper level of the garden of the Ladd house, in Portsmouth, New Hampshire. Steps such as these, though often found in Southern gardens, are a most unusual feature in old New England gardens. The view down these grass steps toward the house is shown on page 144. At the top of the steps and to the right is an old rose bush known to have been there since the garden was first planted in 1763

MAINE

THE broken shore line and numerous rivers of the Maine coast furnished one of the earliest bases for European exploration. Settlements were made in 1604 on Neutral Island, in the St. Croix River; in 1607 at Sabino Point, at the mouth of the Kennebec; in 1608 on

The Edgerton Manuscripts in the British Museum give the first suggestion of established gardens in Maine. The record says that "on Pemaquid River Alderman Alsworth of Bristole settled a company of people in 1625. . . . In 1675 I found Roots and Garden Hearbes, and some old walls there when I

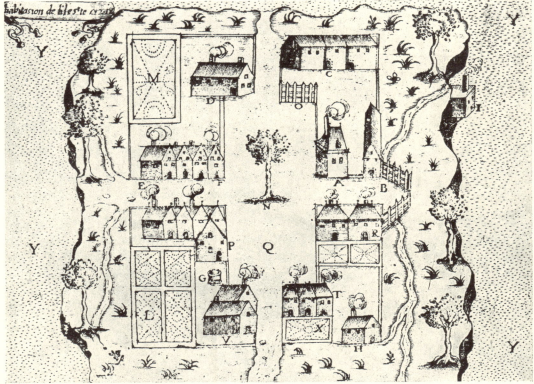

Courtesy of State Street Trust Co., Boston

Champlain's drawing of the short-lived French settlement made in 1604 on an island in the St. Croix River, between Maine and New Brunswick, shows probably the earliest gardens (L, M, X) planted by Europeans in the North

Mount Desert; and in 1623 on Monhegan Island, where Captain John Smith had earlier mentioned a base and even a garden in the summer of 1614. "Yet I made a garden upon the top of a Rockie Ile in 43½, 4 leagues from the Main, in May, that grew so well, as it served us for sallets in June and July."[1]

Massachusetts bought out the land grants of Maine, and was confirmed in her purchases by the charter of 1691. The French, who held the land east of the Penobscot, incited the Indians against the English, with the result that the settlements and towns were sadly ravaged and the colonists harassed for many years. During the Revolution, Massachusetts held the territory as the District of Maine, and not until 1820 did the State of Maine become a member of the Union of States.

The Northwest Country that comprised Maine, New Hampshire, and Vermont had been granted to enterprising colonizers, and much confusion arose among the claimants as to the boundary lines. A magnificent forest of white pine covered the entire section. The colonists are described as husbandmen and planters, but fishing was the most profitable occupation, for it was comparatively easy to barter fish for corn from Virginia and needed stores from England and France. These goods were traded to the Indians for furs, principally beaver.

[1]Smith, *Travels and Works*, II, 720.

went first over, which showed it to be the place where they had been."

OLD GARDENS IN MAINE

The history of the Maine towns and villages that have been examined contains much that relates to their building and government, but lamentably little that gives us any description of their gardens. That gardens there were goes without saying, because the same tastes and customs prevailed in Maine as elsewhere.

From the history of Thomaston and Rockland written by Cyrus Eaton, we learn that the first sidewalks were laid and the first shade-trees planted in 1828, that front yards and other grounds were adorned with beautiful and fragrant flowers and shrubs at the time, and that the Mall was ploughed, leveled and fenced, and bordered with elms. Among the citizens of Rockland who were especially honored, Eaton mentioned S. Dwight "for his taste in laying out and ornamenting his grounds," Casimir Lash "for the introduction of rare flowers," and R. Keith for planting elms and other forest trees.

Maine had no Horticultural Society, but a Pomological Society was founded in 1873.

We have but one surviving historic garden to present. It is, however, one of notable background.

THE WADSWORTH-LONGFELLOW GARDEN, PORTLAND[1]

Few gardens are richer in associations than the Longfellow garden of Portland, Maine, since it links two distinguished American families.

General Peleg Wadsworth, the first owner of the garden,

General Wadsworth built the first brick house in Portland. It occupies the southwestern corner of the land, while the garden extends to the north and rear the length of the lot, some one hundred and fifty feet.

The garden seems to have been kept very simple in design, with one long, straight, bordered path from the trellised

Copyrighted by Frank Forrestall Adams

The Wadsworth-Longfellow garden, Portland

was the maternal grandfather of the poet, Henry Wadsworth Longfellow. Three years after his graduation from Harvard, he married Elizabeth Bartlett of Plymouth, and in 1784, with the purpose of providing a home for his growing family, he bought in Portland a lot of land containing one and one-half acres, located on what is now Congress Street, halfway between Preble and Brown Streets. This lot had a frontage of four rods, and sloped to the north towards Deering Woods and Back Cove, which is a broad inland sea of picturesque setting, as far as Cumberland Avenue of today.

porch, while several narrower lateral paths, extending to the right, enclose beds of flowers or clumps of shrubbery.

In the old days, it held sweet fellowship with the stately garden of Commodore Preble on the east, and on the west with the less pretentious but equally extensive garden of George McClellan. At the present time, Keith's Theatre bounds the Longfellow garden on the north, and the re-modelled Preble Block on the east, while tenement houses line its western side. The theatre and the business block are ivy-grown, and thus present not too ugly a barrier, while a trellis of artistic design, vine-planted and flanked by tall Lombardy poplars, will in time shut out the uninspiring vista.

[1]Adapted from a paper by Mrs. Walter E. Tobie. The garden has been re-stored through reference to old family letters loaned by Miss Mary Longfellow, and also with the aid of the latter's reminiscences.

Because portions of the garden lie for the most part in the shade, the planting there is appropriately of ferns, lilies, Solomon's seal, periwinkle, violets—yellow, blue and white—, aconitum, funkia, striped grass, bleeding-heart, double buttercups, trillium, Jack-in-the-pulpit, widow's tears, scilla, star of Bethlehem and other shadow-loving growths. The sunny beds, however, lovingly harbor peonies of ancestral stock, delphinium, phlox, hollyhocks, poppies, old-fashioned roses, and gay annuals. The Longfellow Garden Club has made it a point to use only old-time garden stock, conforming closely to the planting of a century ago.

After the removal of General Peleg Wadsworth and his family to Hiram, Maine, where he held a large tract of land granted him by the government in return for his valuable military services, the Portland estate became the home of Stephen Longfellow, who had married Zilpah Wadsworth, daughter of the General. At this time the Longfellows had two children, Stephen, and Henry Wadsworth, the future poet, who was then but eight months old.

The old garden appears to have played an important part during the childhood and early manhood of the poet, for he made frequent allusions to it in his journal and correspondence. From this garden, as a child, he often plucked flowers on a Sunday and carried them in his hands as he walked proudly to church beside his mother. Here also were gathered the blossoms that adorned the old First Parish Church on that notable occasion when, in the year 1815, the five children of Stephen and Zilpah Longfellow were christened by the Reverend Ichabod Nichols, pastor of the church for many years. These children were Stephen, aged ten; Henry, eight; Elizabeth, six; Anne, five; and Alexander, just a baby in arms.

Romance was not lacking in the poet's memories of this old home garden, for hither, among other guests entertained by Longfellow's sisters, came Mary Storer Potter, a beautiful Portland maiden of sweet and gracious bearing. This garden meeting led to a warm friendship between the then young professor of Bowdoin College and Miss Potter, who later became his wife. Her early passing was the poet's first great sorrow.

After his second marriage in 1843 to Frances Elizabeth Appleton, "Craigie House" in Cambridge became his home, and his visits to Portland were for the most part limited to summer vacations. But to these he always looked forward with keen pleasure, a pleasure in which the old garden of his childhood figured to no small extent, the garden that brought his "Lost Youth" back again, and "Deering Woods, and the friendships old, and the early loves."

Through the generosity of the poet's sister, Mrs. Anne Longfellow Pierce, who occupied the Wadsworth-Longfellow home until her death in 1901, this much-prized property was deeded to the Maine Historical Society, to be held in trust as a tribute to the memory of the Wadsworth-Longfellow families—surely, a highly treasured link with the past generations that have enriched this world with men and women of integrity, talent and soul.

Copyrighted by Frank Forrestall Adams

Another view of the Wadsworth-Longfellow garden

NEW HAMPSHIRE

THE first settlement in New Hampshire was made in 1623 at Little Harbor (Portsmouth). There were other settlements at Dover, Strawberry Bank (now Portsmouth), Exeter, and Hampton, all before 1640. At Strawberry Bank we get this early glimpse of what must have been the start of a walled garden:

"Mr. David Thompson with the assistance of Mr. Nicholas Sherwill and others with a considerable company built at Strawberry Bank a strong and large House and enclosed it with a large and High Palizado Fence."[1]

OLD GARDENS IN PORTSMOUTH

Portsmouth, the Strawberry Bank of the earliest records, is one of the most beautiful and dignified towns in New England. Its fine houses of several periods are distinguished for their beauty and for the fact that they have not been unduly changed. The houses were usually built very close to the street, and the gardens, like those in Salem and other New England villages, are not visible from the street; they are entered from the door opposite to the street door, or from a door at the side of the house, sometimes known as the "Garden Door."

Portsmouth houses frequently were set up from the public walk by one or two terraces, grassed or walled. Several illustrations of such terraces are shown.

Perhaps the most interesting house in New Hampshire is the Wentworth house at Little Harbor, now the residence of J. Templeman Coolidge. This house doubtless had gardens, but today all that remains are the great lilac trees. There is good reason to believe that these lilacs date back to an addition made to the house in 1750. They are magnificent specimens of their kind, and, as the illustration shows, stand as high as the roof line of the house.

Ancient gardens still in existence in Portsmouth are those belonging to the Ladd house, which retain some of their eighteenth-century design, and that of the Jacob Wendell house, a dooryard garden of the early nineteenth century.

Portsmouth houses frequently were set up from the public walk by one or two terraces, grassed or walled. The photograph of the Reverend Samuel Langson house, to the left, shows a characteristic raised terrace entrance. To the right is the Samuel Lord house (1730), with a double grass terrace

New Hampshire was placed under the protection of Massachusetts in 1641; in 1679 it again became a Royal Province and remained so until the Revolution. In 1775 the State, through its Revolutionary convention, declared for independence and was the first of the colonies to adopt a constitution.

The gardens of the colonists must have suffered severely from the ravages of the savages, for we know that in the late seventeenth century the inhabitants of the New Hampshire settlements were subjected to the cruel barbarity of the Indians; Exeter, Dover and the frontier hamlets were frequently surprised in the night, the houses plundered and burnt, the men killed and scalped, and the women and children either inhumanly murdered or led captive into the wilderness.

THE GARDEN OF THE LADD HOUSE, PORTSMOUTH[2]

The beautiful old colonial house and garden which is now the home of the Colonial Dames of New Hampshire came into their possession in 1912 from the heirs of Alexander Ladd, a direct descendant of the Captain John Moffat who built the house in 1763.

Though situated on busy, noisy Market Street, and surrounded on all sides by shops, warehouses, and dilapidated tenements, it was, when built, in the choicest residence section of the city, with other fine old houses and gardens all about it. The situation is even now beautiful, facing as it does the noble river Piscataqua and looking across to the

[1] *Maine Historical and Genealogical Records*, Vol. I.

[2] Written by the late Mrs. F. S. Streeter, Concord, New Hampshire.

The Wentworth lilacs, at Little Harbor, Portsmouth. The two largest trunks are respectively one foot ten inches and two feet in circumference, measured at a distance of three feet from the ground. The height of the lilacs is about twenty-four feet. Probably planted in 1750, they are the most "historic" lilacs in the United States

rocky, wooded Maine shore on the opposite bank. Even the old gambrel-roofed sail loft in the immediate foreground across the street, and the rotting wharves below, have a picturesqueness all their own.

Nothing is known of the beginnings of the garden; we do not know whose brain conceived nor whose hands executed the plan, but there is no doubt that the garden was laid out when the house was built, for in "good old colony times" the garden was always as much a part of the home as the house, and as naturally taken for granted. As far back as any of the family remember, this garden was always there, and since 1819 we have definite knowledge of it, for in that year Captain John Moffatt's great-granddaughter, Maria Tufton Haven, who had married Alexander Ladd in 1807, came there to live.

In Alexander Ladd's son, Alexander Hamilton Ladd, who fell heir to the estate in 1862, the family love of nature and growing things was developed to an unusual degree, and it is to his skill, care and ardent enthusiasm that we owe most of the beauty of the garden today. We know that he installed the beehives, for he was a devoted and scientific apiarist; that he planted the magnificent wistaria on the garden side of the house and the rare old shrubs throughout the garden; and that to his genius we owe the flight of curved grass steps leading to the upper level of the garden, a most unusual feature in old New England gardens, though one often seen in the South.

The distinctive feature of this garden and one of its greatest charms is its varying levels and terraces. It not only rises from the house in a series of four different levels to its western boundary on High Street, three hundred feet away, but is terraced along the sides also, and the flower beds are built up above the level of the paths in delightful diversity.

The old leaden sun-dial, dated 1770, recently added to the Ladd garden. This and the ensuing illustrations of the garden are shown by courtesy of the late Mrs. F. S. Streeter

The long central path which forms the main axis of the garden of the Ladd house

The long central path forms the main axis of the garden, and originally led directly from a door in the western wall of the house. In later years, however, this entrance was closed, and a garden door was made in the northern wall of the house at the foot of the great staircase. An old brick path now leads west beside the house from this door to

Looking toward the Ladd house from the arbor at the top of the grass steps shown on page 138. Roses and Akebia quinota
are growing over the arbor

the central flower plot, branching south from there to meet the main path, while the rambling gravel path that runs in front of the old office and encircles the lawn at the north where the beehives are, also begins before it. This lawn at the north, the land directly west of the house, and the bird sanctuary are all on the house level.

Ascending to the first terrace by three old brick steps, we come to the second level, the main flower garden, where the large central plot, twenty-six by forty feet, is raised again thirty inches above the level of the surrounding paths and reached by two brick steps in front and by turf steps at either side meeting the narrow turf path that runs through the

center. Old fashioned red roses bloom all along the edge of this first terrace, augmented now by the modern ever-blooming red rose, Gruss an Teplitz (so like the old red Burgundy rose of our grandmothers' day, but far more decorative and fragrant). At the northeast corner of this terrace is a magnificent great *Viburnum opulus*, beautiful in spring with its masses of white bloom, and brilliant in late summer and fall and beloved of the birds, with its hundreds of drooping clusters of scarlet berries. The big central flower plot itself is a mass of pink, white and purple bloom from June to October. Here bleeding heart, pale lavender phlox *divaricata* and columbine begin the pageant, followed by peonies, pyreth-

The central flower plot of the Ladd garden in September. The latticed porch appears in the background, at the right. The trees shown are all pear trees

rum, the old fashioned white dittany with its spikes of fragrant bloom, stately pink and white oriental poppies, white and violet *Campanula persicifolia*, and, in the shade of the pear trees, tall pink and white foxgloves; then early in July come the pure white candidum lilies and pale blue larkspur. As the summer wanes, masses of phlox in shades of lavender, pale pink, and white fill two corners of the bed, diagonally opposite each other, while the rose-pink masses of Rhynstrom and Elizabeth Campbell fill the other two corners. Tall blue and white monkshood takes the place of the foxgloves under the pear trees, speciosum lilies bloom among the peonies, and gladioli and the useful, though prosaic China asters in white, pink, purple and lavender fill up the gaps left by the

passing of the columbines and campanulas. There is not a time during the whole summer when this central plot is not beautiful; it is the center and heart of the garden, seeming to draw to itself and concentrate on this one spot the beauty and fragrance of the whole.

South of this central plot is the wide bed next the latticed porch, raised about a foot above the path and turf-edged. Here are hollyhocks next the porch, tall *Campanula lactiflora*, sweet scented valerian, feverfew, sweet-williams, phlox, peonies, and at either end of the bed beautiful big bushes of the old fashioned white rose, Mme. Plantier, and the lovely pink and white Seven Sisters rose.

Three brick steps lead us from this level to the second,

The path leading to the lawn and house, between the old grape arbor and the central flower plot

The old brick path which leads from the house to the central flower plot

which extends to the foot of the grass steps. The whole length of this path from one flight of steps to the next was originally covered by an old grape arbor with seats along each side, where one could sit to view the garden and smell the spicy aromatic odors arising from the herb garden just south of the arbor, but now only a grape trellis remains, extending all

along the southern side of the path. Along the edge of this terrace just west of the central plot is a long border of lavender iris under the pear trees. West of the iris bed is a raised grass plot in full sunshine, bordered by Persian lilac bushes with peonies and iris growing at their feet.

In the center of this plot is an old leaden sundial dating

Looking toward the house from the extreme west end of the main path. At the right is the kitchen-garden, raised above the level of the path and the flower beds; at the left is an old pear tree

An old spiral rose trellis which stands back of the beehives on the lawn, at the house level

The lawn at the house level, showing the beehives, the old grape arbor, and the curved path from the house to the bird sanctuary

from 1770. This is not original in the garden but was picked up a few years ago in an old shop in New York where its history was guaranteed. The base is of solid lead with a beautiful pattern of acanthus leaves surrounding it, and the dial is of brass, exquisitely chased, and bearing the motto:

> "I stand among ye summer flowers
> And tell ye passing of ye hours.
> When winter steals ye flowers away
> I tell ye passing of their day."

and below, the legend: "Time Flies."

English daisies are planted above its base. It stands there in the sunshine looking as if it had always been a part of the garden.

South of the path, next the herb garden, is a row of gooseberry bushes, and just beyond them a magnificent great cherry tree probably as old as the house, and part of the planting of 1763.

The old grass steps bring us now to the third level, where directly at the top of the steps is the old damask rosebush known as "grandmother's rosebush," the chief treasure and pride of the garden. It is known to have been there since the garden was first planted, and seven generations of brides have taken slips from it to their new homes. As if in response to the romance and sentiment which cluster around it, it blossoms as freely and beautifully now as in its youth, a living witness to the eternity of love and life.

The flower beds upon each side of the path here are in plain sight from the chamber windows of the house and are gay and bright, with annuals chiefly,—gay poppies and marigolds, zinnias and four o'clocks, with a big bed of yellow day lilies and blue larkspur (the Colonial Dames colors) just south of the path.

This path and the land north of it are level from here to the garden's limit, but all the plot south of the path is raised seven or eight feet

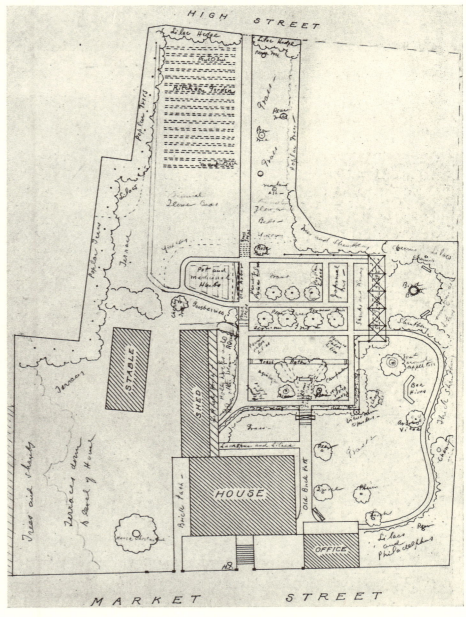

The plan of the Ladd garden. House and grounds are now the property of the National Society of Colonial Dames

The garden of the Ladd house. To the left is the path at the foot of the grass steps which leads north to the bird sanctuary. A glimpse of the herb garden in the right foreground. The beds are raised above the level of the paths, as one sees here. The illustration to the right shows the old grape arbor

Illustration from monograph of the Mentor Association

The beds in the Jacob Wendell garden in Portsmouth are reputed to follow the design of the pieces of an old Chinese puzzle brought home in the early nineteenth century

above the path, edged by a grassy bank, and upon this fourth level, in full air and sunshine, yet unseen from the house, is the kitchen-garden, about eighty by fifty feet. Many fruit trees grow here, peaches, pears, plums and cherries, and the vegetables are unsurpassed. Just at the top of the glass steps stands an old latticed arbor with seats on each side, from which a lovely view of the house and the gay flower beds below is obtained; and behind it old wooden rose-supports bridge the path to the garden's western limit.

The High Street gate is now closed and hidden by tall arbor-vitae trees. Bittersweet vines and clematis climb all over the High Street fence, and in front of it is a tall lilac hedge, marking the western limit of the garden. In former

Professor Barrett Wendell at the entrance to the garden from the house

days the gardener's cottage was situated in the northwest corner facing High Street, as shown in the plan in an irregular plot now cut from the original lot, and in a similar irregular plot on the south boundary was another cottage for servants, but both these parcels of land passed from the possession of the family many years ago.

THE JACOB WENDELL GARDEN[1]

In 1815, Jacob Wendell, merchant, of Portsmouth, bought the house built by Jeremiah Hill in 1789 on the corner of

The Wendell garden. Entrance to the pergola, looking west

[1]Written by Edith Wendell Osborne (Mrs. Charles Devens Osborne), of Auburn, New York.

Pleasant and Edward Streets. The following year he married Mehitable, only child of Mark Rogers, also of Portsmouth. They lived and died there.

Jacob Wendell, the son, eventually bought out the shares of his brothers and sisters in the property, and although he never lived there after reaching maturity, he always retained a keen love and sense of obligation towards what had been home to him. His nephew, James Stanwood, only child of Mehitable, elder daughter of the elder Jacob, lived there all his life, pottering about Portsmouth till 1910, wholly absorbed in collecting *Americana*, good and bad.

At his death it came into the possession of Barrett Wendell, for thirty-five years closely affiliated with Harvard University. From 1911 to 1921, he strove unceasingly, ably seconded by his wife (Edith Greenough), to restore the property to what it had been: the tangible expression of an earlier New England.

That Jacob Wendell, the younger, handed down his strong sense of family obligation is clearly shown in the following extract from the letters of one of his sons, Barrett Wendell. A letter written to an English friend contains this sentence: "June 26th, 1915. Last Sunday the 20th, 35 of my grandfather's descendants came here to celebrate the centenary of his purchase of this house. It was pleasant, I think, for us all."

Behind the house to the south lies a tiny garden, scarcely 50 by 30 feet in size, the irregular flower-beds bordered by narrow wooden supports, and separated by quaint, brick paths, laid in lots of three, suggestive of a basket weave. The garden itself is reputed to be designed after an old Chinese puzzle (still in the house) brought home from an Asiatic voyage in the early part of the nineteenth century, by George Wendell, brother of Jacob, master of a sailing-ship. The pieces of this puzzle, if placed in correct juxtaposition, form a perfect square; each flower-bed follows exactly the shape of one of these pieces. Like the house, the garden had been sadly neglected, and when Professor Barrett Wendell took possession there was little left beyond the shape of the beds, the crumbling paths, a white lilac which had literally grown into a tree, and a decaying pergola, over which a hardy grapevine flourished. A picket fence enclosed two sides of the garden, the pergola the third, and the house the fourth.

Just as in the restoration of the house the first step was the elimination of rubbish, so in the garden the weeds and undergrowth of years had to be removed. Only the magnificent lilac and the grapevine seemed to have withstood half a century of neglect. Professor and Mrs. Barrett Wendell planted only such simple flowers as might have always bloomed there. Care proved fruitful; digitalis and hollyhocks thrive again along the fence; stocks and pansies, heartsease and fuchsias grow sturdily within their narrow confines; close to the house a fragrant honeysuckle entwines its hold upon a trellis flanked by clumps of roseately tinted spirea and serenely nodding dahlias. A trumpet-vine now flaunts its scarlet blossoms above the porch; a wild cucumber unmolested weaves a nebulous covering of green and white among the pickets. The pergola (repaired) bears the weight of more than one grapevine now; woodland ferns grow yearly beneath its shade, and at the entrance there lie the fast-bleaching vertebrae of a whale washed ashore one daren't guess how many years ago.

In the center bed of all, dominating the whole, stands the genie of the garden, a small box tree, fashioning its growth after the wire frame of a Chinaman of high degree, whose living body and terra cotta head and hands are adequately symbolic both of times inanimately past and of ever-living present.

Not a great garden, surely, nor an elaborate one; merely a few square feet of cultivated soil, yielding such posies as they did a century ago, changing annually and yet fundamentally unchanged; the same today, yesterday, and, let us hope, tomorrow.

VERMONT

THE first English settlement was made at Fort Dummer, now Brattleborough, by Massachusetts colonists in 1724.

Massachusetts, New Hampshire, and New York all claimed the territory, and it was not until 1791 that Vermont became a State with a separate constitution. During the Revolution, however, Vermont took an independent position, and made war against England in its own behalf. The names of Ticonderoga and Ethan Allen and his Green Mountain Boys ring clear in American history.

For these 150 years of Vermont's colonial life, the Vermont *Antiquarian* and the Vermont *Historical Gazeteer* fail to give any hint of gardens.

Eleanora Randolph, Thomas Jefferson's grand-daughter, who passed through Burlington in 1825 on her wedding journey, saw in it a lovely village of gardens. She wrote:

"Burlington is the most beautiful village that I have ever seen. It is built on the very brink of the lake, which is here at least ten miles wide, and commands a full view of the mountains and scenery of the New York shore. The streets are wide, not paved, but of a fine white clay which would scarcely soil a fine white shoe. . . . The private houses are among the best I have seen; some are large, well built, and surrounded with handsome gardens and fine trees, others with less pretensions, are extremely neat, and apparently comfortable, with green lots and pretty simple paling."

Vermont had no Horticultural Society until 1908, which perhaps indicates that the gardens of Vermont were farms. A glimpse of the history of the Common at Woodstock and an account of one century-old garden in Woodstock constitute our present knowledge of gardens in Vermont before 1840.

WOODSTOCK

THE LOMBARDY POPLAR IN VERMONT[1]

In Woodstock, in the center of the town, there is a "Green" or "Common" which has been the meeting-place of the townsfolk ever since the first settlers dug their cellar holes on its southern end.

The land was formally taken by the town for park purposes very early, but it was left ungraded and unplanted till about a hundred years ago. Then the citizens became interested in the question of what sort of trees to plant. Deciding to plant elms, they brought in young elm trees from the nearby woods. It was not long before all of them were dead.

The town council then decided to plant Lombardy poplars on the Green. This poplar was the most prized tree in the country at the time, being brought in from Europe in enormous quantities to meet the frantic demand. Poplars were

[1]Written by Miss M. L. Johnson.

also being grown in New England nurseries. One nursery-man, William Tilly of Rhode Island, was making a specialty of poplars and was shipping them all about the country. I do not know where the Woodstock Committee bought their pop-lars, but they were planted and they flourished.

There were people in Woodstock, however, who did not like the poplar tree, and who had opposed its planting. One

a short time; that of Mr. Andrew Tracy, a lawyer, and the originator of the garden; that of Dr. Henry Boynton; and that of Mr. William E. Johnson, grandson of Senator Jacob Collamer, whose home adjoins this place. Mr. Johnson's daughter now lives at The Hedges.

From the street, gravelled paths lead into the garden. They surround a small triangle of grass with a vase of ferns in the

*The Hedges, Woodstock, Vermont. The tallest of the hedges in the garden is seen in the background.
It rises to a height of thirty feet*

night these men of the opposition went to the Green and pulled up all the young and thriving little poplar trees, and threw them into the Ottauquechee River, that delightful river of Vermont which runs with great rapidity through the village of Woodstock close by the Village Green.

After that, the townsfolk seem to have agreed upon maples. These were easily transplanted from the woods about the village. Care was taken to mark the south side of the trees before digging them up, so that they might keep the same exposure in their new environment. Boys living near the Green were told off to water them daily.

On the Village Green of Woodstock those maples are now growing, casting a dense and most welcome shade in August, and turning in October to scarlet and yellow and brown.

THE HEDGES, WOODSTOCK[1]

The house does not stand "somewhat back from the village street," but right on it, and very close to all that goes on in the village of Woodstock.

So close to the street is it, that one of the early owners of the property felt a need of greater privacy and planted the cedar hedges that give the garden personality and charm. He even had a hedge of thick shrubbery along the sidewalk, but that has disappeared.

The house was built in 1809–10 by Job Lyman, and has been changed very slightly. It has a wooden front and "brick ends," and some beautiful hand-carving on balustrade and porch.

Only four families have lived in it—that of its builder, for

[1]Adapted from a description by Miss M. L. Johnson.

center. This was formerly a flower bed. Back of this is a lat-ticed arbor, or summer-house, covered with wild grape, clematis and woodbine, a place where the children love to play.

Passing through the arbor, one comes to the tall hedge of cedar trees. The branches formerly came to the ground, but now have been trimmed out, allowing glimpses of the green lawn and the lower trimmed hedge beyond.

Between these two hedges runs the rose border, where roses bloom in their season and then give place to gorgeous dahlias.

At the end of this path is the lower hedge, carefully trimmed to a height of about eighteen feet. This is thick and broad across the top.

Turning to the right, one finds another opening, and the mountain that stands guard over the village is seen. In this back lawn is a spreading box-elder tree, under whose branches one instinctively longs for tea or a nap. Here is the perennial border, with its peonies, yellow lilies, larkspur, oriental poppies and gas-plant. From this flower bed, the ground abruptly drops to a much lower level, making it the top of a terrace. Below is the vegetable garden, in its way as beautiful as the flower beds. Then comes the Ottauquechee River, a narrow and usually shallow stream that turns and twists its way through the village.

The highest hedge is one running through the grounds at a right angle to the others, and separating these grounds from the Congregational Church next door. The beautiful white spire is seen above the 30-foot hedge, and the hours are sounded by a clear-toned Paul Revere bell.

In these changing times, it is restful to find a house and a garden which have changed so little during their one hundred years of existence.

In the opening years of the nineteenth century, when the merchants of Rhode Island were creating beautiful gardens, Crawford Allen of Providence built for his sister Candace a very fine house set in a most lovely garden. The present owner, Mrs. John Carter Brown, has rearranged the garden a little, but it still remains the best example of a town garden of those early years. *See page 201*

RHODE ISLAND

T. F. McLaughlin, Providence

The "Governor Greene" estate in East Greenwich, Rhode Island, described on page 163, has a number of very ancient garden features. One of them is the "Long Walk," or "Poet's Walk," which extends from the house north along the top of a high terrace faced with fieldstone (to the right of the picture), across the pasture, up through the orchard to the graveyard in another orchard on the hill. There, for 286 years, those of the Gorton-Greene-Roelker line have been laid to rest in graves sheltered from the wind and rain by arbor-vitæ, pine, and Norway spruce, planted long ago

RHODE ISLAND

EDITOR'S FOREWORD

In this detailed study of gardening—in the word's most comprehensive sense—which Miss Alice Brayton has made for the Newport Garden Association, the reader will find what is in effect a history of the life and times of American colonists as reflected in their garden activities, for the problems confronting the Rhode Island colonists were those that all New England had to meet. It is of great interest to the gardener of today to know just what the days brought, what the laws provided, and what the householder accomplished in the first two hundred years of our history, and to trace, in these typical settlements in Rhode Island and the Massachusetts lands about Narragansett Bay, the vicissitudes of New England gardens through the wars and economic changes of two centuries.

THE GARDENS OF THE INDIANS

Years thousand since, God gave command
  (As we in Scripture find)
That Earth and Trees and Plants should bring
  Forth Fruit each in his kind.

The Wilderness remembers this.
  The wild and howling land
Answers the toyling labour of
  The wildest Indian's hand.

—Roger Williams.

THE FIVE TRIBES

AT the time of the colonization of Rhode Island by the white races of Northern Europe, the land had been occupied, no one knows how long, by five—still distinct—Indian Tribes, all of whom were practising agriculture.

NARRAGANSETT

The dominant tribe was the Narragansett, in the "Narragansett Country"; which is, roughly speaking, all Rhode Island west of Narragansett Bay. Their gardening was described by Roger Williams, who settled among them in 1636. He owned a house in Providence, another in Wickford, and some sort of camp on Prudence Island; he spent days together in Portsmouth and in Newport. The Indian Sachems were his personal friends; the common Indians were often his personal servants. His opportunity for observation was unsurpassed.

They were a migratory people, Williams tells us, who spent the summer months on the coast, where they cultivated the land quite extensively, raising corn and beans and artichokes; and growing squash vines, with pumpkins, melons, and cucumbers, in their cornfields, as Rhode Island farmers do today. They grew tobacco—though not the Virginian variety—and in the cultivation of this crop the men helped their wives, every bit of the rest of this Indian gardening being done by the Indian women, all through the Colony, as every contemporary writing Englishman informs us.

Except for their dogs, no Rhode Island Indians had domesticated animals, so once the trees had been deadened, or cut down with stone hatchets and their stumps removed by fire, the Indian women dug up the ground as best they could. Morell, in his "Poem on New England," wrote in 1624:

"Their slender fingers dig the earth and in it lay
Their fair choice corn, and take the weeds away."

Though according to Williams they actually kept it cultivated by means of a primitive hoe fashioned from a long basswood stick and a big clam shell.

They fertilized it with dead fish—herring by the river banks and little mackerel along the shore—a practise still in use on the same ground, as I have seen and smelt, myself, many times. The Indians dug small holes about four feet apart, put a dead fish into each hole, dropped four, five, or six kernels of corn on top of the fish, and covered each hole over with soil very carefully. Which is not the modern method.

All Narragansett land was held in common by the tribe, but it was not cultivated in common. Each family was given about an acre in each of the summer camping grounds of the tribe; more if the family was large; and these "garden spots" were "laid about with stones," or, possibly, enclosed with "hedges." There were variations in planting, but every family raised what we today call Indian Corn. Some authorities say that this corn was hilled, one or two feet high. Roger Williams tells us that the crows pulled up the young corn and that the Indians "put up little watch houses in the middle of their fields, in which they or their biggest children lodge, and early in the morning prevent the birds" etc.

"In the middle of the summer, because of the abundance of fleas which the dust of the house breeds, they will fly and remove on a sudden from one part of their field to a fresh place—sometimes having fields a mile or two, or many miles, asunder; when the work of one field is over, they remove house to the other. But their great remove is from their summer fields to warm and thick woody bottoms where they winter."

The practice of cultivating fields far apart was an English one, as any English country gentleman, or agricultural

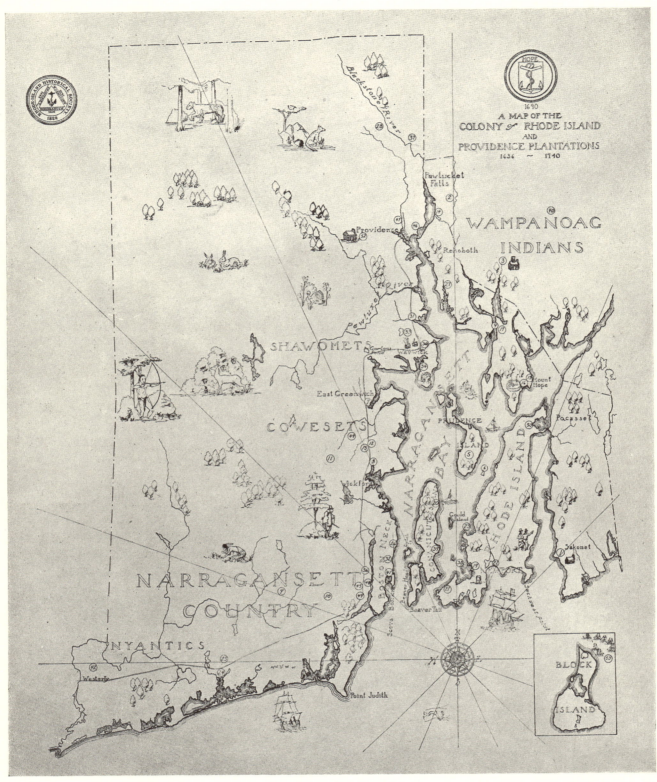

A Map of Colonial Rhode Island

Drawn by Eugene E. Witherell under direction of Howard M. Chapin, Librarian of the Rhode
Island Historical Society.   Copyrighted by the Society of Colonial Dames in Rhode Island

laborer, would have known at that period. The practise of
the Rhode Island planters, of granting house lots of six acres
or so to each planter, and of granting also to the same planter
"planting ground," sometimes of enormous acreage, anywhere and everywhere, all over the Colony, was perfectly
conventional, though puzzling to the modern mind. On this,
Indian and Englishman thought alike, and this common conception of land usage helped them to live together in fairly
peaceful misunderstanding of land ownership, for forty years.

The extent to which the Narragansett Tribe was actually
cultivating the Narragansett Country may be guessed from
the fact that in 1634, before the first white settlement in
Rhode Island, the Narragansett Indians sold 500 bushels of
Indian corn to John Oldham, an English trader, who took it
around from Narragansett Bay to Boston on his ship *Rebecca*.
The Indians had promised Oldham 1000 bushels, "but their

store fell out less than they expected." There is ample proof
that this early cultivation of the soil extended to the islands
off the Narragansett Coast; we find Captain John Underhill
in his *News from New England* (printed in England in 1638),
stating that he went to war against the "Block Islanders"
(Indians of Block Island), and found "much corn and many
wigwams," and that he and forty men "burnt their houses,
cut down their corn, and destroyed some . . . dogs, which
they had left" in those wigwams, to guard the crops. They
found "great heaps of pleasant corn ready shelled; but not
ready to bring it away, we did throw their mats upon it, and
set fire and burnt it. Many well-wrought mats our soldiers
brought from thence, and several delightful baskets."

Even earlier, Gosnold had found, on Martha's Vineyard,
Indians growing "tobacco, very strong and pleasant, much
better than I have tasted in England," as one of his company

wrote in a pamphlet published in 1602. Indeed, all the early adventurers in New England wrote much of this Indian cultivation of the soil, and it seems to be a fact that at the close of the sixteenth century the more fertile portions of Rhode Island and southern Massachusetts were planted ground, with thousands of little gardens covering the outlying islands and the long, indented coast line.

These were of course vegetable gardens. It may be worth noting, however, that although the planting of flowers in a garden as decoration was not—was probably not—an idea ever entertained by any Rhode Island Indian, yet these Indians did plant decorative flowers in their gardens and may have enjoyed them, probably did. The white blossom of the pea vine, the yellow blossom of the squash, we all grow today, and all for the same reason; but the tall pink blossom of the Indian tobacco plant and the brilliant yellow "sunflower" of the Indian artichoke are grown today in Rhode Island gardens for decorative effect; often the tobacco leaf is not used, the artichoke is not always eaten.

The squash vines were no more native to England than were the Indian corn and the Indian tobacco, and Roger Williams first saw the squash in an Indian garden patch. He called it a "vine apple," until he found the Indian name to be "Askutasquash."

WAMPANOAG

Not as powerful as the Narrangansett Tribe, being lately reduced in numbers by a pestilence which did not reach the Narragansett Country, the Wampanoag Tribe of Indians had their chief seat near the confluence of the Warren and Barrington Rivers, in these opening years of the seventeenth century, and cultivated their summer gardens in Bristol, Old Rehoboth, and the Indian villages on the western bank of the Taunton River. Much of this is now Rhode Island territory, but it was part of the original Plymouth Colony Grant, and the Wampanoag gardening is first referred to by Governor Bradford in his "Journal of Plymouth Plantation."

He wrote that in 1621 some Plymouth men went over to Warren, about forty miles away, to buy corn from Massasoit, the Wampanoag chieftain. The Plymouth settlers were starving. "They found but short commons," wrote Bradford. The Indians were going to bed hungry themselves, and had nothing to spare. He added that the soil appeared to be good, but that the "Indians used then to have nothing so much corn as they have since the English stored them with hoes."

It was a Wampanoag Indian, who, earlier in the same year, in April, had shown the Plymouth Planters how to plant their first corn seed—not only how to plant it, but "how to dress and tend it." Also, he told them "except they got fish and set with it (in these old grounds) it would come to nothing."

It was another Wampanoag Indian who emerged from the whole great mass of Indians in Rhode Island, as an individual, with an English name and an orchard—probably a garden—in that name; no tribal affair. According to the Records of Rehoboth:

"May 22, 1665, Sam, the Indian that keeps the cows, was admitted by the town as an inhabitant, to buy or hire house or lands if he can, in case the court allows it." And again:

"May 28, 1689. Voted that Mr. Angier [their new minister, just out of Harvard College] should have a small tract of low land, by the meeting house side, to make a garden plot near the orchard that Sam, the Indian, formerly planted."

But Gookin says it was not unusual, in his time, for many Indians to plant orchards of apples in order to make their own supply of cider. All through the colonies there was restrictive legislation in regard to the sale of "drink" to the Indians; with this very obvious result.

According to Bliss in his *History of Rehoboth*, the earliest settlers in that part of Rhode Island (they were Plymouth men, most of them) not only bought what surplus corn the Wampanoag Indians would sell, but seem to have bargained with the Indians, a year ahead, to supply them with stated quantities of corn and beans. These truck gardens were in the Mount Hope country. It is in these same Rehoboth records that the Indians are said to have enclosed their gardens with hedges—perhaps a peculiarity of the Wampanoags, and perhaps merely a necessity in the Rehoboth Country, where there were few stones in the rich soil along the river bank.

"1645 . . . viewed and laid out that neck of land called and known by the name of Wanomoyset Neck, from the salt water where the Indians had formerly made a hedge, ranging unto the north end of the Indian field and so round about the said Indian Field unto the salt water."

An interesting record, of 1653, is the payment of wampum to the Indians by the settlers of Rehoboth for "damages done upon their corn" by English "hogs and horses." The Indians never could see why they should fence, instead of merely marking out, their gardens, and the Rehoboth planters understood the Indian attitude. Some of the Indians did finally enclose their gardens stoutly enough, and became very good hands at making stone walls, but no Indian can ever have regarded the wandering English sheep and cattle as anything but an intolerable nuisance.

Everywhere throughout Rhode Island, in exchange for the provisions which the early settlers were purchasing in such large quantities, the Indians were demanding the agricultural implements they saw the white men use. Each Indian wanted a hoe and a hatchet. Peleg Sanford's inventory of 1655 betrays the fact that "Trading Hatchets" were—well —trading hatchets. But then, they always are. The trade had reached great proportions at a very early date.

POCASSET—NIANTIC—NIPMUCK

The Pocasset Tribe of Indians, much reduced in numbers by the same pestilence which had so devastated the Wampanoag country, roamed Tiverton, Little Compton, and

The leaf and blossom of the tobacco plant, as shown in an early drawing, and Indian corn

Fall River. They are supposed to have been less advanced in agriculture than their two more powerful neighbors just mentioned, but this is probably because the heavier soil of Tiverton is less amenable to clamshell cultivation.

The Niantics in the lower Pawcatuck Valley and the little tribe of Indians in the upper valleys of the Branch River, called the Nipmucks, had, according to eyewitnesses, small gardens "set about with stones," and grew corn and tobacco for their own uses; but the valleys of the Branch River have a very stony loam and the soil is only fairly fertile. The Nipmucks were a backward tribe; the better gardens of Rhode Island today are not on the old Nipmuck territory.

THE PEQUODS

Over by Westerly, on the Connecticut border, there were other Indians whom the Rhode Island settlers knew only as ferocious enemies of the friendly Indians who sold them corn. These were the Pequods. In April, in 1636, John Winthrop wrote to his father from Connecticut:

"The ground seemeth to be far worse than the ground of the Massachusetts, being light, sandy, and rocky, yet they have good corn without fish: but I understand they take this course; they have, every one, two fields, which, after the first two years, they let one field rest each year, and that keeps their ground continually in hart." It is not uninteresting to realize that these Pequod Indians, flitting about from field to field, letting the ground lie fallow, casually practising rotation of crops, were furnishing data for the development of scientific agriculture, coming slowly, a century later.

These Pequod Indians made another and most unexpected contribution to the development of gardens. Though the Tribe was practically exterminated in the Pequod War of 1637, when the Indians of Rhode Island and the Planters of Rhode Island went into battle side by side as allies of the Colony of Massachusetts Bay, there were a good many Pequod captives. These Pequods became the first actual slave class in Rhode Island, being brought down from the Bay by the planters of 1638, as well as being introduced into Providence in 1637 by the returning soldiery of that young settlement. They were portioned out as spoils of war, and performed the drudgery of the earliest Rhode Island plantations. As gardens and the orderly beauty of gardens are largely dependent upon cheap labor, these Pequod slaves are important in the history of the early gardens of Rhode Island.

An amazing letter written by William Baulston, innkeeper and planter of Portsmouth, to Governor Winthrop, is here quoted, in part, with corrected spelling:

Portsmouth the 22 day of May, 1647.
Honored Sir:—

I am bold to present these few lines unto you in the behalf of Neighbor Captain Morris, that has lately lost his Indian maid-servant.—she having a cousin living with you, therefore my request is that you be pleased to make inquiry for her, and if found, to cause her to be sent home again unto her master, or so much wampum as may purchase either another Indian or blackamoor. For Mrs. Morris is aged and weak, and is in great distress for want of a servant. And also be pleased to understand she (the Indian) was a child of Death, delivered to him (Captain Morris) by the Bay, in time of the Pequod War. Sir, the grounds of her going away I know not, for she was to my knowledge well kept and much tendered, both by master and mistress——

WILLIAM BAULSTON.

In July, in 1637, a gang of captive Pequods were brought into Providence. Roger Williams wrote to John Winthrop:

"Much Honored Sir,—

"It having again pleased the most High to put into your hands another miserable drove of Adam's degenerate seed, and our brethren by nature, I am bold (if I may not offend in it) to request the keeping and bringing up of one of the children. I have fixed mine eye on the little one with the red about his neck, but I will not be peremptory in my choice, but will rest in your loving pleasure for him or any."

The Indian gave the Planter land, crops, and labor.
The Planter gave the Indian hoe and hatchet.
With this exchange, they cultivated their gardens side by side, as the records of Rhode Island state most explicitly, for forty years from the first white settlement within the boundaries of what is now the State of Rhode Island and Providence Plantations.

THE GARDENS OF THE PLANTERS

THE PLANTING OF PORTSMOUTH

RHODE ISLAND'S FIRST RECORDED GARDEN

IN THE Township of Portsmouth, in one of the pleasant meadows which lie between Butt's Hill and the waters of Mount Hope Bay, is all that remains of the first white man's garden on the records of Rhode Island.

It was probably ploughed and planted by the servants of William Coddington in the Spring of 1638, and it was certainly in existence in October, 1639. This is known because on that date the Town Clerk of Portsmouth, trying to make clear a boundary line, refers to the "hieway adjoining to Mr. Coddington's garden." It could not have been planted before 1638, for it was in the Spring of that year, in these meadows just north of the Revolutionary fortifications on Butt's Hill, that the first Plantation on the Island of Rhode Island was made, by a number of Englishmen who came there from Boston under the somewhat unofficial leadership of this same "Mr. Coddington, Planter."

On May 20, 1638, these planters held a town meeting to discuss land allotments. They gave "to Mr. Will. Coddington a houselot of six acres, 8 poles in breadth and 120 poles in

length, lying north and south, the breadth east and west along by the side of the great Pond." Also, "10 acres of plowing ground for Mr. Coddington." It was on the six-acre lot that the first recorded garden in Rhode Island was planted.

"To Will. Baulston, 6 acres on the East side of the Spring" (close by the pond), were allotted at the same meeting. Baulston as well as Coddington planted a garden on his "House stall" of six acres, but we cannot be sure that he did so as early as 1638. It was in 1666 that the Town Clerk mentioned, again quite incidentally, that Baulston had a garden near his tavern. This is the Baulston who was keeping a tavern on Boston Common in 1637, and, in 1647, writing that quaint letter about the Pequod slave. His own labor supply at that time included an English lad named Abel Potter whose stepfather had "placed" Abel with Baulston for a "term of 18 years with the consent of said Abel."

THE EARLY PROBLEM: GARDEN LABOR

These Portsmouth planters who started the settlement in the Spring of 1638 brought with them besides a few actual slaves, many indentured servants, men and women; young boys suitable for farm work, herdsmen, thatchers, blacksmiths, coopers; there is only one trade lacking from the long roll of useful accomplishments—there are no listed "gardiners."

---

¹On the use of the word "planter," we quote the following "answer of the Gov. of Rhode Island to the inquiries of the Board of trade," written in 1680 by Peleg Sanford of Portsmouth: "We answer that we have severall men that deal in buying and selling although they cannot properly be called Merchants, and for Planters we conceive their are about 500 and about 500 men besides."

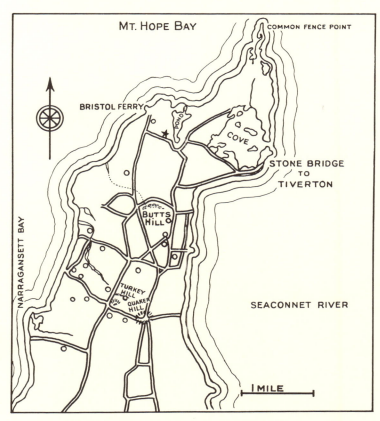

The star in the upper part of the map shows the location of the first recorded garden. The circles show other old gardens mentioned in the text

Though there is extant a letter "of the Governor and Deputy of the New England Company for a Plantation in Massachusetts Bay, to the Governor and Council for London's Plantation in the Massachusetts Bay in New England," dated London, 28th May, 1629, in which it is said that Governor Cradock "has entertained 2 gardnors . . . one of which he is content the Company shall have use of if need be." These men were sent over with other servants on a ship reaching Massachusetts Bay in the early Spring of 1629, one gardener obviously to be a personal servant of the Governor's, but the other at loose ends—he must have lived with the group of Planters who settled Rhode Island a few years later; he may have gone with them to Rhode Island. At any rate, from the letter we know that the New England planters even as early as 1629 did recognize gardening as a distinct vocation and seem to have thought it not at all absurd to bring at least two gardeners into a wilderness.

Nevertheless, it is in a diary written more than a hundred years later, by Thomas Hazard of Tower Hill, that we are told of "John Dye, a gardiner," employed by the day. In 1767, Solomon Drown wrote that Mr. Redwood of Newport employed "a man to take care of his garden," at "100 pounds a year." And I really cannot find, beyond these casual references, any mention anywhere of any man in early Rhode Island who so limited his activities that anybody thought of calling him merely a gardener—with one exception.

There seems to have been one man in colonial Rhode Island who was by profession what we today call a landscape architect.

His name was Johann Caspar Öhlman. He was settled in Newport by 1766, for that was the year he married a Newport girl. As we see by his references, he did not leave his European employers before 1754. It is probable that he was living and working in Newport by 1755, and we know that he spent the rest of his life in Newport, dying some years after the War of the Revolution.

It is possible, and probable, that he worked at first for Abraham Redwood, laying out the formal gardens at the Redwood Farms, although there is no evidence that he did so beyond the fact that they were really laid out with much formality and professional skill, and that the name of Mr. Redwood's gardener, so highly paid as to elicit comment, has

not come down to us. Moreover, the dates of the purchase of the Redwood land, and the immigration of Johan Caspar Öhlman, bear out this conjecture. There is a tradition in his family that he laid out the grounds of "Vaucluse"; there are features in common with the Redwood design; but if he did, it was in his old age, many years after he came to Newport.

The credentials he brought from the old world, were translated in the nineteenth century, and the Rhode Island Historical Society has just printed them. They begin with the name of his former employer:

"His Highness and most powerful Prince, Frederic August, King of Poland, Grand Duke of Lithuania, Reussen, Preussen, Mazovien, Samogitien, Kyovien, Volhinien, Padolien, Padlachien, Lifland, Smolensko, Severien, Schernicovien, Duke of Sachsen, Julich, Cleve and Berg, Engern and Westphalen, Arch-marshall and Grand Elector of the Holy Roman Empire, Landgraf of Thuringen, Markgraf of Meissen, also of Upper and Lower Lausnitz, Burggraf of Magdeburg, Prince-grave of Huneburg, Graf of the Mark Ravensberg, Hanau and Barbey, Seigneur of Ravenstein."

Not only do trained gardeners seem to have been scarce, but the young men who came over as indentured farm servants, or yeomen intent upon the owning of land, were by no means always farm owners or farm laborers in Europe. The Rector of Little Waldingfield in Sussex wrote in 1636 to Governor Winthrop about a nephew of his who was sailing for New England:

"Good sir, put him into some employment; he is both willing and able to work in husbandry, although he has been lately a clothyer."

Symonds wrote in 1637 of a group of settlers:

"They are raw planters as yet, they want experience. While the hard weather lasts, I suppose their work will be to deal in woodwork, as stubbing of trees, clearing of grounds etc. . . . as soon as any open weather comes . . . breaking up of grounds for Indian corn. . . ."

And by 1662 even these men who must be schooled in

The site of the first recorded garden on Rhode Island

Old pasture walls and willows, Portsmouth

husbandry were none too plenty. The demand for servitors was enormous. As one man wrote to a friend in London:—

"If you could procure a likely boy or girl, about 14 years old, you shall do us a very great courtesy. It is said about Yorkshire, or remote places, they may easily be had."

ANOTHER PROBLEM: THE GARDEN WALL

The earliest legislation everywhere in Rhode Island concerned itself however, not with farm labor—there was, after all, plenty of that, such as it was—but with farm fencing.

The houses of the early Planters were built quickly, just shelters for their wives and children. Their real energy was devoted to the problem of separating their crops from their cattle. Within a few weeks in each settlement, it was decided to order each planter to fence his own "planting ground," his own "orchard," his own "Garden," and his own dwelling house if he so desired. The stock was to be permitted to wander where it could, earmarked, of course. Can you say that earmarks have nothing to do with gardens, when you know that Zuriel Hall's cattle were marked with a "flower deluce on the left ear"?

The system continued for a very long time. In 1789, goats were a great nuisance wandering about the streets of Providence. Goats were extremely troublesome on the Tiverton highways, in 1792. Earmarks were still being registered in the Portsmouth town records in the early years of the nineteenth century. And in Cranston, earmarked cattle were permitted to pasture anywhere they could, as late as 1856.

Common pasturage decided upon, walling a garden was imperative. The walls they built and the laws they made about them, are discussed in Mrs. Lockwood's chapter on "Fences and Enclosures."

In certain sections of Rhode Island, the planters surrounded their planting grounds with hedges.

Of what the hedges were to be made, the records do not say. In 1642 "Goodman Borden" had "a Hedge" on his houselot in Portsmouth. So did "Mr. Sanford." Borden must have had a large orchard, for he left his widow "use of 30 fruit trees in orchard that she may choose," and the hedge may have enclosed the orchard. Or it may have separated his fields of Indian corn, rye, wheat, oats, barley, and pease, all enumerated in his inventory. On Martha's Vineyard, Samuel Sewall planted a barberry hedge, about the year 1700, to mark off the Indian Reservation: there being plenty of wild barberry bushes on the Island. In 1744, Dr. Hamilton wrote: "There are whole hedges of barberries in the Narragansett Country." He saw them, when travelling through.

In Pawtuxet, ditches were used to separate the fields and gardens, but they were not common. Occasionally used in Warwick, the records call them "water fences."

THE PLANTING OF PROVIDENCE

THE GARDENS OF TOWN STREET

The second Rhode Island garden of which there is record in authentic documents of the period was planted by Dr. James, in Providence, on Town Street (at Star Street, between Pratt and North Main), probably not later than the Spring of 1639. In 1640, Dr. James sold his "house" and "Garden" to William Field, and the recorded deed is our authority that Providence did have a garden at that early date.

In 1659, John Whipple came to Providence, and bought a house near William Field's, on Town Street by the river (369 North Main Street it is now.)

Ten years later, John Whipple deeded his house and his "garden next the river" to his son Joseph Whipple; his "orchard" also. The Whipples kept a tavern, and in the tavern there were 24 chairs, and six negro slaves, who waited on the customers most certainly, and probably helped the Whipple women in their heavier garden tasks. The Whipple inventory of 1721 included beans, tobacco in the ground, flaxseed in the chamber, hay in the cock, Indian corn in the crib, flax in the bundle, rye, oats, and barley in the straw. Which crop grew in the garden, which on the Whipple planting-ground beyond the village street, no one can say with any certainty. Nor can anyone be sure that this garden was not merely a pleasant place, fenced in against the pigs of Providence, where the customers of the Inn sat down in those 24 chairs and drank the rum served by those six blackamoors, as they watched the little ships come up the river, bringing more rum and more blackamoors to Providence.

An excellent example, from the "Providence Book of Deeds," of a small land grant and the method by which such grants were recorded. It is recorded in 1681 in the "Right of Mr. John Clarke Deceased" . . . "The northwesterne Corner being Bounded with a pine Tree . . . the North Easterne Corner Bounding with an old Walnutt Tree stumpe . . . the South Westerne Corner with a Chesnutt Tree . . . And on the South Easterne part with Three Trees (Viz) a White oake Tree . . . a Black oake Tree . . . and a Walnutt Tree . . ."

Thomas Angell was another Providence planter, living on Town Street by the waterside. When he died, in 1685, he left his widow a "small plot of land adjoining the said house for a little garden." He left her also "conveniency of yard room" and "free egress and exgress for her to pass and repass" to reach her garden gate. Doubtless the large garden was left with the larger part of the house to the eldest son, whose wife would be wanting her own garden for her own use. It was the custom, and, I think, the law. (This Angell garden was on the corner of Thomas Street.)

Joshua Winsor also had a garden between Town Street and the river. He laid it out about 1671, perhaps. His son, Samuel, left his widow, in a will of 1705, "privilege of the house in town, and garden."

It was in the Carpenter garden, on the same street, that Mrs. William Carpenter "soed her seeds." There had been trouble about an official document of the Town of Providence around 1707. "They couldn't find them" as one historian remarks. And "Howlong Fenner said, that Joseph Carpenter

told her, that his grandmother, who was the wife of William Carpenter, had thought it [the document] a piece of waste paper and used it to wrap up garden seeds. . . . When she had soed her seeds she threw away the deed as waste paper."

It is impossible to tell exactly what seeds she had to sow. Inventories of Providence estates, made before 1698, tell us that the planters were growing beans, corn, tobacco, turnips, wheat, flax, apple trees, and peach trees, and they go no further. In 1720, William Crawford, a merchant of Providence, was offering "Seeds" for sale. They are not described. But the tale of the Crawford merchants belongs in another and much later part of this history of gardens in Rhode Island.

THE "HOUSE IN THE WOODS"

Early in the seventeenth century, a few adventurous planters were living in the country outside of Providence Village, and, as we have noted, even the planters with house lots on Town Street, had their "planting grounds" in the "woods beyond the town." Usually they had little houses on this distant property; the "house in the woods" is an expression in the old wills of the period.

These country planters received very large and vague land grants. As they rarely knew their own boundaries, it is immaterial to quote their acreage.

PLANTATIONS IN PAWTUXET

The Arnold Plantation in Pawtuxet had 100 sheep, by 1677, as well as "gardens," "orchards," and negro slaves to cultivate the land. They owned "2 stocks of Bees," so excellent for gardens. Eleazer Arnold, of another Arnold fam-

Drawn by Wm. H. Gibson for "Picturesque America," 1879. Coll. of R. I. Hist. Soc.

The Roger Mowry House

On the outskirts of Providence, there were certain Whipples, living in the house known as the Abbott-Whipple House, or Mowry Tavern (built by Roger Mowry in 1659), who were also a gardening family. In 1714, Ebenezer Whipple deeded his son, John, "my mansion house . . . with orchards and gardens." There was a burying ground "surrounded by tall evergreens," according to a somewhat later observer

The Fenner house, Johnston, a typical "House in the Woods"

ily, owned a house in that direction which is now under the protection of the Society for the Preservation of New England Antiquities. It was built about 1687, and was in 1710 a licensed Public House. By the terms of the license, Arnold had to admit "carters and drovers," and the great tree by the front door of the house, which you can see in the picture, gave shade in summer to the horses and the sheep which the carters and the drovers had to leave outside when they went in to get a drink.

The Eleazor Arnold house in Lincoln, built circa 1687 and now owned by the Society for the Preservation of New England Antiquities, offers a good example of the old practice of leaving a forest tree growing in the dooryard. John Brown, the Providence merchant, retired here for safety when the British occupied Narragansett Bay

Narragansett Country, as well; and his grandson, inheriting the Neck Farm some years later, re-planted 50 acres with native oak, hickory, and chestnut—perhaps the first instance of re-forestation in Rhode Island. This new forest was all cut off in 1850.

There were also many small planters in Swansea. One of these men, Ephraim Pearce, left his widow in 1718, "a garden and 9 apple trees, an acre of land, and clear profit of a cow."

A picture of a typical Swansea house, owned by the Chase family from the earliest days of the settlement, is shown here. The orchard is on the right of the house.

THE EARLY GARDENS OF WARWICK

Down Warwick way, the numerous Greenes must have had early gardens of some sort; but, with the possible exception of those at "Spring Green" and the "Governor Greene House," they are not specifically noted in any seventeenth century record that I can find.

According to the old records, the Indians kept on cultivating their fields in Pawtuxet, up to King Philip's War, having corn lots actually adjoining the corn lots of the Arnold men. Only a ditch separated Indians and Planters, as they hoed their corn side by side. The Indians were notoriously curious, and would throw down their hoes at the slightest pretext, and run over onto the white man's land to see what was going on. They had another annoying little trick, according to Mr. Arnold, of sitting down on stumps to watch the white men at their more complicated garden tasks.

THE GARDENS OF SWANSEA

In the Plymouth lands of Rhode Island, the gardens of the planters began a little later. In 1671, Willett of Swansea, at one time Mayor of New York, left in his will "dwelling house, warehouse, garden, and various parcels of land," including his farm at Wannamoisett, which consisted of 500 acres on both sides of the Seven Mile River. He left 149 sheep and 133 cows, with 22 oxen, so we may assume that his land was actually a working farm, well cultivated. He owned land on Boston Neck in the

"SPRING GREEN"

"Spring Green," enchanting spot, is that part of the huge Warwick plantation acquired in 1642 by John Greene of Bowridge Hall in Dorset, which he did not at once "improve."

A typical old Swansea house, owned by the Chase family since the earliest days of the settlement. The box was eight feet high by measurement in the winter of 1931

For many years it was known by its Indian name, Occupas-suataxet. In 1706, in the will of John Greene, Jr., it is called "Greene Hole," and is said to have orchards and planted ground and a house of sorts. But as a simple farm, its many acres washed by a salt inlet on the south and the waters of Narrangansett Bay on the east, it existed up to the war of the Revolution.

The farm house of 1706 is part of the present mansion, and the elms, planted at each of the corners of the house front, still stand, to show that the early Greenes took thought of beauty and seemliness. The first Greene garden was probably a square planting, southeast of the house. The ground seems quite clearly to retain the marks of an old wall.

During the Revolution, the whole plantation, like nearly everything else in Rhode Island, rather went to pieces.

In 1783, it was sold to John Brown of Providence, whose new town house was the most magnificent residence which had yet been built anywhere in New England. The first thing he did to the old place was to give it a new name—"Spring Green." And he didn't do very much else. For, in most modern fashion, he and his family used the old Greene Farm for week-end parties, driving down from Providence to enjoy the country air.

But a daughter of the Brown family married a Mr. Francis from Philadelphia, about 1785, and these young people, given Spring Green as a wedding present, enlarged the house and laid out pleasure grounds suitable for the formal entertainments of their day. They built verandas, and they planted boxwood about the verandas. They made a shrub walk, since to "walk in the shrubbery" was the genteel exercise in vogue for the young ladies of that incredible past. The shrub walk still exists. It is an eighth of a mile long. It starts from the southeast corner of the house and makes a great loop or curve down toward the water, returning toward the house and ending at the southwest corner. It runs between

Photographed by T. F. McLaughlin, Providence

The well-head in front of the Governor Greene house was built in 1794. On the apex was a gilded weathercock, which from its low and protected situation must have been in a chronic state of uncertainty as to which way the wind was blowing. The well is still preserved, though not now in use

in 1788. She wrote that a garden lay between the house and the "river," and that she admired the garden.

To the north of the house is a spring, covered by an ice-house, quite the oldest ice-house in Rhode Island, they say. Its conical roof and its circular walls are most picturesque. And the young lady from Philadelphia admired the ice-house.

Another unpublished diary, charmingly written by a sweet woman who lived at Spring Green in the early years of the nineteenth century, does not mention any garden at all. It tells of the great peace and beauty of Spring Green when the snow was on the ground.

There never was, perhaps, a great garden at Spring Green at any time in the old days—we do not know. A modern garden blooms luxuriantly on the old grazing land between the house and Narragansett Bay. The property is now the residence of Mr. and Mrs. Frank Haile Brown.

An old drawing of the Governor Greene house in East Greenwich. The right-hand portion was built in 1685

shrubs of various kinds, small trees, even through a rustic grape arbor for a short distance, and it is paved with common gravel. The grass enclosed by this gravel walk may possibly have been at one time terraced, where it slopes to the water. It certainly was cut in two by a path which began in a wooden arbor, directly in front of the southern door of the house, and ran straight down to the clump of thick shrubbery which still marks the southern axis of the old shrub walk. Here another arbor provided seats and shade, from which the view over the salt marshes and the blue waters of the Bay was most charming.

Many distinguished guests were entertained at Spring Green, and they have left grateful accounts of most courteous hospitality. None of them has spoken of the garden of Spring Green. So we depend upon the unpublished diary of a certain young lady from Philadelphia who dined at Spring Green

THE "GOVERNOR GREENE" PLANTATION

"Rhode Island, the land where the exile sought rest;
The Eden where wandered the Pilgrim oppressed.
There Freedom's broad pinions our fathers unfurled,
An ensign to nations and hope of the world."

If you can read with pleasure these verses written in all sincerity by Arthur Ross, a hundred years ago, then you are ready to hear about the Gorton-Greene-Roelker Plantation at East Greenwich, and the gardens on that old plantation; gardens made by persons to whom the words "exile," "oppression," "freedom," meant something; who knew rest in their gardens only after long toil and sacrifice.

The oldest garden feature is the Long Walk. It runs from the house north along the top of a high terrace faced with fieldstone. It is bordered with white lilies and thick shrubbery, green shrubs which bear white blossoms only—the white lilac, the snowball, the mock orange, and the bridal wreath—though the green grass of the walk itself is carpeted with

The Governor Greene house in East Greenwich, as it is today

The parterre gardens of the Governor Greene house

Photographed by T. F. McLaughlin, Providence

The gateway to the graveyard on the Governor Greene estate was erected in 1820. Another view of the graveyard is shown on page 154

purple violets. This was the planting of that young bride from Charleston, Miss Flagg, Ray Greene's wife, who wanted a white garden, a hundred years ago. It was probably a few years later that the Long Walk was called "The Poet's Walk." There Mrs. Greene and Mr. Longfellow used to stroll, at sunset, to admire the view, when he came up for tea. (This was the summer when Henry Wadsworth Longfellow was staying in the Windmill Cottage down the road.) In the late nineteenth century the walk ended in a half circle of arbor-vitae trees. Against this background, William Greene, last male descendant of this branch of the Greene family, had placed a marble bust of his grandfather, the second governor of the State of Rhode Island.

But the Long Walk itself may date back to the days of the original settlement of Warwick. It may be the old "path in the woods," where Samuel Gorton walked up and down, after the work of his farm was done, composing his fiery polemics. All the countryside saw Gorton wearing a path on the edge of the clearing. The little children knew the beaten track he made. And when in the eighteenth century the Rev. Ezra Stiles from Newport asked the people of Warwick Old Town to tell him what they could of Samuel Gorton whose books he knew, they showed him "Gorton's Walk," "where he constantly walked alone by himself," a "holy man," "a man full of thought and study," a pleasant memory in the village which he and his associates had planted on the shore of Narragansett Bay in 1643. It ought to be remembered that "freedom" to Gorton meant an opportunity to cut down a forest, dig out the stumps, plough and plant in the spring of the year, put an earmark on his cattle—an earmark shaped like the tail of a swallow—build with his own hands a little house in which to rear his sons and daughters, and, when the day's work was over, write books.

During the reconstruction after King Philip's War, one of the Gorton girls married a young Greene, and they built the older part of the present Governor Greene House.

The Long Walk, as I have said, runs from this house north along the terrace, across the pasture, up through the lower orchard, to the Gorton-Greene-Roelker graveyard in the orchard on the hill. There at first the apple trees stood all about the gravestones. But later Greenes planted a wall of evergreens around the old graves; arbor-vitae, pine, and Norway spruce. These trees are not too near the graves, nor too far away, but seem to enclose them carefully, and to protect them from wind and rain and the too curious passerby. In 1820 the Greenes built a gateway in the wall of fieldstone which separated their orchard from the country road. The gate is of iron, hung from granite posts, and there is an iron arch over the gate with an iron hook to hold the lantern. A short path bordered with laurel leads from the gate to the oval of the graveyard, as you can see in one of the photographs.

I do not dare to say very much about the formal garden, which lies to the west of the house. I know so little that is definite.

William Greene, son of this Gorton-Greene alliance, was twenty-five years old when he inherited the plantation. He had married a cousin, a Greene girl. These two young people planted new orchards, and built the cider house in which the cider press is worked by horse power—an amazing testimony to the great consumption of cider on the farm. But this young Greene was ambitious, he was full of honest patriotism, he had ideals, and before long he was Governor of Rhode Island, holding office from the King. The old house was enlarged; it became the executive mansion; there was great need of cider, of course.

It is supposed that Mrs. Greene planted the old garden in the new geometric design, much as Mrs. Roelker has it to-day; but in 1758 the estate passed into the hands of the eldest son, another William Greene, who also became eventually Governor of Rhode Island, and it may be that it was this second Mrs. Governor Greene who introduced the more elaborate fashion. This second Mrs. Greene was Catherine Ray, who had been brought up on her father's enormous sheep farm on Block Island, where we will presently observe that gardens did not grow. It is natural to suppose that her ardor for elaborate gardens in the latest fashion would be the greater. We know that the house was enlarged to please her, in 1758. The land was terraced; a retaining wall was built, to give order and form in the immediate vicinity of the house. Steps were cut, leading definitely down to the now distinctly lower meadow where the gardens were. On the upper terrace above the garden the old Long Walk was left, to become, in the language of the day, The Walk in the Shrubbery.

With the coming of the Revolution, the Greenes must have found it most difficult to take sides at all. Unlike most of the Rebels, they had much to lose. Governor Greene had held his office directly from the Crown. But they seem not to have hesitated. For years, their home was a meeting place for all the staunch supporters of the Revolution, who travelled back and forth on the old Post Road which ran through East Greenwich between Boston, Providence, and New York. General Washington came and stayed with the Greenes. Everybody came and stayed with the Greenes. Benjamin Franklin was their intimate friend and frequent visitor. The window where he used to stand and look out over the garden and the woods and shining water, is still pointed out as Franklin's window, and the view that Franklin admired has

not changed in any way. General Nathanael Greene married Mrs. Greene's cousin, a pretty girl from Block Island, right in the Greene's front parlor—that new room built onto the house in 1758. Every resource of the plantation was taxed to furnish entertainment for man and beast, all through the War. Soon after it was all over, William Greene found himself Governor of the State of Rhode Island.

It was then, in 1798, that the Greenes built, as an ornament, the well-head in the front yard. A weather-vane which used to surmount the lattice work has disappeared. The carriage drive which in those days led from the gate in the southern wall to the old front door, has been closed. But the house and the grounds still are much the same as they were in the opening years of the nineteenth century, when Ray Greene brought home his bride from Charleston, to make her "white garden" in the old Long Walk.

The estate is now the property of William Greene Roelker, of the Gorton-Greene-Roelker blood, of course. For 286 years this family has actually worked the farm, kept together the old traditions of gentle living and practical patriotism, and gone to well-deserved rest in the graveyard on the hill.

It is the great American Tradition.

"Cocumsoussuc," the Richard Smith house in Wakefield

"COCUMSOUSSUC"

The "Garden" at "Richard Smith's Trading Post" in Wickford, should be mentioned here. Richard Smith did "put up in the thickets of the barbarians, the first English House among them," in 1637, but he is said to have used his original house only as a trading post until 1659. He leased a great tract of land from the Indians for which he agreed to pay, every midsummerday, a "Red Honey Suckell Grass if it were lawfully demanded." But it is hardly probable that he would have bothered to raise corn and beans around the trading house when he could so easily buy them in trade from the Indian gardens close about him. He must be considered by us as he was, I think, by his contemporaries—an isolated figure, living apart from the other colonists, not remaining long in any one place, closely allied to the Dutch traders who had their trading posts in Rhode Island even before the coming of the first planters in 1636.

In the common peril of King Philip's War, however, the Smith House served as a rendezvous for the Colonial Army during the campaign which ended in the Swamp Fight.

"Visitors are today shown a spot near the house where soldiers killed in the Swamp Fight were buried," among them young Updike who had married Richard Smith's daughter. Wilkins Updike, writing in 1842, said that this grave was in the "southeast part of the garden," and that a tree "called the grave apple tree" was growing on the grave, "broken off in the September gale of 1815." This reference to an apple tree seems to show that the graves were in the apple orchard and not in the garden spot, since apple trees were not planted in gardens; and I can find no other evidence that there was ever a garden at "Cocumsoussuc" in the days of Richard Smith himself.

Mr. Isham writes that this corner of the old orchard where the soldiers were buried "is covered with grass which the cattle will not touch, strangely enough, as it is the famous blue grass of Kentucky."

Though the rebuilt trading post of Richard Smith's still stands, the history of the gardens of his descendants is the history of the Updike Garden, told on page 243 by Miss Annie Hunt.

THE PLANTING OF NEWPORT

As in Providence, the first houselots of Newport were laid out along the waterfront; each seems to have had its garden, and the descriptions vary little. The planters were a small company of men who went out from the settlement of Portsmouth in 1639, with their wives and children and serving-men, to make new homes on the south end of the Island.

JOHN COGGSHELL AND ENGLISH GRASS

By the 24th of May, 1647, Mr. John Coggshell, formerly a silk merchant in London, was writing the following letter to Mr. John Winthrop:

"Honored Sir,   "Newport.

"I have sent you 12 bushells of hayseed. I filled the sacks, because I know you will not repent it, and I also want corn. . . . You may sow this hayseed now if you spread the hills, or upon other ground if you mow down the grass or weeds twice this summer; but upon ground that has been planted (the hills being spread) it will come sooner to perfection and less seed lost."

After the "ploughing fields" had been planted, and the young plants in the gardens, and the young trees in the orchards, were all fenced in, the planters' next concern was proper grazing-land for their stock. The "wild" grass on the edges of the clearing did not make good hay, and there was very little wild grass except in the salt marshes, where it was, naturally, "salt." This they used and were glad to get, but fortunately for their prosperity and for their lawns, they soon succeeded in importing and growing good "English" grass seed. Coggshell seems to have been the first Rhode Island planter to grow this grass on a large scale and to have sold it throughout the Colony.

His efforts were so exceedingly successful that Robert Nichols, Governor of New York, wrote in 1665 to the English Board of Trade that he had found in Rhode Island "the best English grass and the most sheep of any place in the English Colonies."

All honor to John Coggshell!

The reputation of Newport grass continued through the colonial period. In 1773, Cullen Pollock wrote from Edenton to Aaron Lopez in Newport:—

"I should be much obliged to you, also, to procure me 100 li. of Fowl meadow grass seed. I am afraid you will not get it unless you give notice in the papers, but I would begrudge no expense for it; also 50 li. of orchard grass seed such as grows on Mr. Marchant's lot."

GOVERNOR CODDINGTON AND TENANT FARMING

But Governor Nichols also wrote: "in some places they (the Rhode Island men) had corn 26 years together without manuring," which was not so good. And it did happen, allowing for a little exaggeration. Governor Coddington's experience in Newport tells the story.

For Coddington not only planted the first white man's garden in Rhode Island of which we have any record, not only set out in 1639 the first orchard noted in any manuscript of the time, but began, before 1640, what seems to be the first experiment in Rhode Island with tenant farming. Among the Newport land allotments made in 1639, Coddington had been given "6 acres of land for an orchard . . . as convenient as may be to his dwelling house." (On Marlborough Street. It was there in 1832, and a drawing made at that date shows the wooden fence of the townsman enclosing the house and yard, which latter looks quite like a hayfield made from Coggshell's English grass.) And he had also been given a great many other acres of arable land all over the Island. The tenant farmer thus became from the very first a necessity. And the tenant farmer is the natural enemy of good gardening.

Coddington's troubles began very early.

In the Court of the Colony, in June, 1641, there was considered "an action of the case between Mr. William Coddington of Newport against Richard Tew of Newport Cliffs" for "non-performance of a Bargain of Farming."

In December, 1646, in the Court of the Colony, there was tried a case called "The Declaration of William Coddington of Newport in Rhode Island, Gent., Plaintiff, against Jeremy Gould of the same town."

Gould had "indentured and bound himself to keep and maintain himself, his wife, and a maid-servant, and five able-bodied men, kind, good workers, to be of the same farm, and also one to keep the demised goats, and the said Jeremy Gould is to the best of his skill to employ, appoint, and im-

"New Lodge," Newport, the residence of William Coddington, was built between 1641 and 1651

prove the labors of himself and those other eight persons for the best advantage of the said farm."

This delinquent Jeremy had become tenant farmer on this 350-acre farm of Coddington's, in 1642.

It appears from the testimony that he not only did not keep as many farm laborers as he had sworn to, but that he abused and misused the oxen and the horses, let the "fences" get out of repair, and generally wore out the land "for want of good manuring."

He was to have carried "all the corn of the demised into the barns of the demised premises, and there . . . cause it to be thrashed and cleaned . . . divided there by the bushel"— and to have set aside a certain quantity for the use of Mr. Coddington. But he didn't.

Moreover, when Jeremy took the farm, it had as part of its stock "60 female goats and 3 rams," and the "increase" was to have been returned to the home farm of Mr. Coddington. But it wasn't.

THE LAW IN THE GARDEN

There was another Coddington holding of 1643, where a large corn barn was burned in the middle of the winter. Some stock perished, he lost his corn supply, and the clothing of his indentured servants. Did they sleep in the barn? He wrote to his personal friend, Governor Winthrop, "A man's comfort doth not depend on the multitude of those things he doth possess," but I notice that he got the legislature to pass a law making the burning of a corn barn a crime punishable by death. He never found out who burned his barn, however, or how to handle his servingmen; or, indeed, his fellow colonists.

His attempts to market his cows and country stuff are interesting, he being, like Coggshell, somewhat of a trader by disposition. In April, 1647, he wrote to Winthrop:

"I intend to sell 10 ewes, most of them are as we call them, quine ewes, bringing 2 at a time, and few of them old. Two ewes here, in exchange, ordinarily is given for a cow, and the truth is, one ewe is as much profit to me as a cow."

This letter of the Governor of Rhode Island to the Governor of Connecticut indicates the agrarian quality of the period.

Not only the burning of corn in a barn became a crime of the first magnitude, but in 1647 men who cut or took away any corn growing, or robbed any orchard or garden, were to be punished severely. This is, incidentally, evidence that in the thought of these early planters, a corn lot is not a garden, and an apple orchard is not a garden—were such evidence needed.

BLOCK ISLAND

There were plenty of planters who seem to have had no garden plots.

The records are logical. I found but one specific mention of an early garden on Block Island, for instance. And we know that wind-swept Block Island has few gardens today.

> "Lonely and windshorn, wood-forsaken,
> With never a tree for spring to waken
> For tryst of lovers or farewells taken,
>
> Circled by waters that never freeze,
> Beaten by billows and swept by breeze,
> Lieth the Island of Manisees."

So wrote Longfellow, calling by its Indian name the Island of Adrien Block.

As early as 1660, John Alcock had written to John Winthrop:

"Sir, being about to plant and stock Block Island, I do want a 100 or 150 goats."

But the planting was the planting of a people. Dr. Alcock did not settle on the island himself, to be sure. His daughter and her husband, John Williams, did go there, however, and did raise goats and Indian corn. The Rays and the Littlefields had plantations. James Sands ran a sheep farm, mentioned later. William McIntosh and Duncan Ross from the Iron Works at Braintry were foremen on plantations owned by Boston men, a condition not good for gardens, as we have noticed. And I find no mention of any garden until the coming of John Rathbone in 1683. That Rathbone did have a garden is insisted upon by the Historian of Block Island who wrote his book in 1872. He said, "the place where the Rathbone garden spot once was is greener than the adjacent meadow sward." So, when Longfellow wrote:

> "When the hills are sweet with the briar rose
> And, hid in the warm soft dells, unclose
> Flowers that the mainland rarely knows"

I wonder if he was singing of Bouncing Bet, that pretty pink and white flower which escaped from the Rathbone garden, a long time ago, and now grows by every cellar hole on Block Island, in every old orchard, along the sheep runs and the goat paths and the driftways, with unparalleled luxuriance, as though it were cultivated with the utmost care.

The island is not completely without other vegetation.

In 1872 the Block Island Historian saw "quince trees and other imported shrubs and fruit trees, known to have been planted in 1812." I saw those same quince trees, this summer, and they are still bearing fruit. I did not see any other quince trees. "A good deal of plain farming" was being done in the days of the Historian; but not now. "The harrows," he wrote, "had teeth made of ship bolts, the wrecks were so numerous."

I think it is evident that the old Block Islanders did as their records relate: "kept sheep," and didn't bother very much with gardens at any time. Nor can you blame them.

THE PLANTING OF SCITUATE

The poorer people in the seventeenth century in Rhode Island—those with small estates and no occupation aside from their cultivation—no matter how fertile their soil, have, it is true, very often no gardens in their wills and inventories, though each small article, almost each turnip, is set down with care. But they all had orchards, every one.

Today the old Scituate countryside is full of abandoned apple orchards, where the neglected apple trees flower sparsely each spring in a tangle of brush and briar.

It was in 1703 that Mrs. Joseph Wilkinson of Scituate saw a bear in the sweet apple tree in her yard. Mr. Wilkinson was not at home, so Mrs. Wilkinson after watching the bear shaking off the apples onto the ground "where he might devour them," got her husband's gun and "shot him dead. . . . Dropping the gun on to the ground immediately after the discharge, alarmed and trembling, she ran back into the house and shut the door. When Mr. Wilkinson returned home he found the bear dead upon the ground; so that his faithful and resolute wife had not only saved the cherished apples, but had secured some good meat as a supply."[1]

Joseph Wilkinson had come into Scituate about 1703, and had married that Mrs. Wilkinson who shot the bear. He built a fairly comfortable house, the first comfortable house in the town, I should judge, and planted two chestnut trees in the front yard. They were standing in 1877, "magnificent trees, of apparent great age."

According to tradition, Mrs. Wilkinson used to entertain large parties of Indian braves, all by herself, when her husband was away from home, and they would picnic on Wilkinson food in the Wilkinson pasture. This is the famous pasture which was created by beavers. "A beaver dam in the vicinity had caused an overflow of water which rotted the trees so that they fell down and gave an opportunity for the grass to grow." And the grown grass gave the Wilkinsons an opportunity to keep a cow—just like the house that Jack built. This was the "first cow ever brought into the town."

In the Wilkinson yard there were also sheep enclosures, built up against the house, and at night the Wilkinsons used to drive their sheep into the enclosures to keep them from the wolves. "Once in the night they were waked by a bear rolling the logs away to get at the sheep. They were forced to get up and drive him away," according to the local historian. I don't see why Mr. Wilkinson had to.

Not under such conditions, of course, are gardens grown.

And, really, conditions in early Scituate were much like that! Stephen Hopkins, who was born there in 1710, and lived there half his life, wrote the following verses describing the young settlement:

> "Nor house, nor hut, nor fruitful field,
> Nor lowing herd, nor bleating flock,
> Or garden that might comfort yield,
> Nor cheerful, early crowing cock.
>
> No orchard yielding pleasant fruit,
> Or laboring ox, or useful plough,
> Nor neighing steed, or browsing goat,
> Or grunting swine or feedful cow."

[1]From an "Historical Address" delivered in Scituate July 4, 1876, by C. C. Beaman, and printed by order of the Town Council of that date.

He had a very pretty idea of what a garden could mean, "a garden that might comfort yield." There was great need of comfort in Scituate, in his day.

His father, William Hopkins of Providence, had married a Wilkinson girl and moved out onto a small plantation in Scituate at the close of the seventeenth century. One of the sons signed the Declaration of Independence, another planted the first garden recorded in the annals of the town.

By 1877, a road was running between "the old Hopkins house" and that "garden of ancient times." The family burying-ground was still in existence just outside the stone wall of the garden, in a corner of the old apple orchard.

In 1775, James Aldrich bought the old Wilkinson place, and, "having a taste for orcharding," planted fruit trees "for which the soil, climate, and elevation of the land were highly favorable. . . . He became a successful farmer."

In 1777, Mrs. Knight wrote to her husband in the Colonial Army:

"I want you to come home as soon as you can, to see about getting some flax, for it is very scarce to be had."

These are the annals of the countryside.

But I must say that the women of Scituate, first and last, seem to have been a most capable lot. They seem to have had few gardens, to be sure, and the local historian wrote, in 1877:

"There are some good farms in the place, well managed, but the larger number of them are still untilled, or are so much neglected that they are growing up to brush."

PLANT MATERIAL IN EARLY RHODE ISLAND GARDENS

EARLY IMPORTATIONS

What the planters of Massachusetts and Rhode Island (they came over together) brought from the Old World to plant in the first gardens in New England, was not recorded in any definite fashion. But we do know what they meant to bring. The following list was made out by their Agent in London in 1628, "to provide to send for New England":

"Wheat, Rye, Barley, Oates, Benes, Pease, Peach stones, Plum stones, Filbert stones, Cherry stones, Pear kernells, Apple kernells, Quince kernells, Pomegranats, Woad seed, Saffron heads, Liquorice seed and roots, Madder rootes and madder seed, Potatoes, Hoprootes, Hempseede, Flaxseed, Currant plants."

And we know something of what, before very long, was actually growing in the early Massachusetts gardens. The earliest Rhode Island planters came from Massachusetts. It is well to remember, though, that there was a very close connection between the early traders of Rhode Island and the Dutch traders from New York, who had trading posts in the Rhode Island wilderness. Rhode Island was settled in the very years when the Tulip Craze and the export trade of tulip bulbs from Holland was at its height. I think it very certain that there were tulips in the earliest gardens of Rhode Island.

There was a mild revival of this tulip mania in 1733, and the more prosperous planters and the new merchant class probably planted more tulips, as did everybody else.

Letters and diaries of the seventeenth and eighteenth centuries are, however, our best help in our search for what the planters really cultivated from year to year. They confirm our guess, as it were.

In regard to roses, for example, we do know from the historians that the Rev. William Blaxton was growing roses in Boston the year before he began his new plantation near the present city of Providence. They say he brought some bushes with him when he came away. But we get a better knowledge of those early attempts at rose-growing in New England from

a letter written to John Winthrop, Jr., by Joseph Downing, in London, in 1633.

"If you write that you have no roses there, in New England, I will send you over some damaske, red and white, and Province rose plants: all of these, three or four apiece, or more if need be."

HERBS IN THE GARDEN

The importation from England of all the curious herbs used in the medicine of the time was a heavy expense and a great nuisance, even when they throve in the new gardens. The early planters searched the woods and fields for the necessary medical material, for it was quite possible that it might be growing wild in the new world—who knew! Sewall wrote in March in 1676: "In the afternoon Seth and I gathered what herbs we could get, as Yarrow, Garglio, etc." The women were soon growing yarrow in their gardens, for it was dangerous to walk far afield, what with the savages and all, and medicine is always wanted in a hurry. They cultivated white hellebore, too, and horehound.

In 1659, John Davenport wrote to Governor Winthrop: "The candied comfrey roots which my wife sendeth to you are not so white as she desired. The reason, she saith, is because they were boiled with Barbadoes sugar." We can add comfrey to the flowers which grew in the gardens of our seventeenth-century women. "My wife prayeth yourself and Mrs. Winthrop to accept a small token of marmalet of quinces, which she hath made as good as she could." There was also a quince tree in the garden where the comfrey grew.

A bride went down by boat from Rhode Island to her husband's home in Dorchester in Carolina, in 1699. In a letter to her mother she wrote:

"Angelica that we brought with us, is grown out five or six inches long, already. So are some damson trees, the roots whereof we brought over. Currant and gooseberry bushes that we brought with us are green and flourishing. Apple seeds sown by us since we came, came up in January; and are now 3 inches high, some of them. All the other herbs that we brought over seem to take very well and grow here."

APPLE TREES

Before ever they left England, the colonists intended to raise apples in the New World. They brought little apple trees with their luggage. The master of the ship on which some of the first Rhode Island planters came over, wrote to Winthrop who was waiting the sailing of his ship in his lodgings in London:

"Sir:—

"The gardner hath brought to town your trees. They will be put up in two chests."

They wrote back home for more trees. In 1633, Joseph Downing wrote to John Winthrop, Jr.:

"Good Mr. Winthrop—

". . . You wrote to my brother Kirbie to procure you some quodling plants. . . . I have gotten some, and sent them up to London to him for you, and wrote him word how he should put them in an oyster firkin, and how they should be ordered in the ship, when they are at sea, for if the Ship Master hath not especial care of them by the way, in one ten days they will quite wither, and so never grow. I hope, therefore, the Master of the ship will have a care of them, according to the directions to my brother Kirbie, who I make no question will tell him what I write. It is verie late to send them so far now, in regard they are not like to come over to you before May. I am afraid, therefore, that they will decay by the way, though the Master of the ship should see them taken up out of the hold, and set upon the upper deck, 2 or 3 days in the week to take fresh air."

There was also, very early, a brisk exchange of apple trees all over the New England Plantations.

NUTS AND NECTARINES

As early as 1653 the planters were setting out walnut trees; they not only ate the nuts but used the bark in the making of beer.

And by 1735 the culture of rare fruits was being attempted. Governor Belcher wrote a letter to a Boston shipmaster, which is most enlightening:

"Captain Franklyn, . . . You being bound up by the Mediterranean, . . . if you could bring or send me 8 or 10 young almond trees and as many Pisa nectrins it would much oblige me, and anything else curious for a garden. The trees must be grafts (not natural stocks) and very young, not thicker than your thumb. They must be carefully taken up (roots and all) and as carefully transplanted into a good box of their natural earth, and not suffered to be sprinkled with salt water, but duly served with fresh water, and I say the younger they are the more likely to live."

These were the years when Metcalf Bowler was importing apple trees from Persia, and setting them out in his Rhode Island garden.

> "The King of Spain's daughter came to visit me,
> And all for the sake of my little nut tree."

I do believe she did! Now that I know how these men of the early eighteenth century felt about the little trees they sent to the ends of the earth to procure.

There was also much planting of the common pear tree of Europe, very early, in Rhode Island. And as for peach trees, they were everywhere.

There is a delightful story in Fuller's *History of Warwick*, to the effect that a man was fined in Warwick in 1688 for planting a peach tree in his own garden on Sunday.

Though, as a matter of fact, Roger Williams tells us distinctly that a man could plough on Sunday in Rhode Island, if he wanted to. It was in the Plymouth portion of the present State of Rhode Island that agriculture was under the control of the Church. A curious document, just discovered in an old safe, shows that a local citizen was summoned to court and fined for breaking the Sabbath by burning brushwood in Swansea. This was in 1696. And another man was punished for carrying plough irons on the Lord's Day from Portsmouth to Plymouth.

ROSEMARY

In 1668, Peleg Sanford of Portsmouth wrote to his brother in the Barbadoes:

"Loving Brother

"I have laden on board the *New London*, Com. Ralph Parker, 10 barrels of pork, 9 barrels of beef . . . my wife pre-

The John Dockery house in Wakefield, built before 1750, has ancient horse-chestnut trees in the dooryard

sents her kind love to you and would earnestly desire you to send her some rosemary."

It is interesting to realize that these seventeenth-century people sent down to the Barbadoes for rosemary roots. The plant is not hardy in Portsmouth, though it can be potted up for the winter and will do nicely in the sunny window of a farmhouse kitchen.

GARDEN SAUCE

Little by little we can pile up these chance comments, these references in letters concerning graver matters, until we get at last some notion of the garden material in the seventeenth century in this part of the New World. And it is perfectly obvious that the chief purpose of the garden was to provide food. It was of the little towns in Rhode Island that Cotton Mather wrote in 1713, in June:

"It has been a time of great scarcity for corn with some towns in the country; some families have not seen a bit of bread for many weeks together."

In 1699, Fitz John Winthrop wrote to Francis Brinley in Newport:

"Pray give my service to Mrs. . . . And when she has any beets, pray tell her to remember my garden."

In the deserted gardens of Rhode Island I have found plenty of horseradish and carrot. In 1651, John Haynes was writing:

"I send you by this vessel those horseradish roots you mention."

Turnips and onions were grown very early. The onion was always in great demand for exportation. James Brown, the Providence Merchant, wrote in 1735, "Get some onions for me if they are to be had." The slaves on the West Indian plantations were apparently fed on onions grown in Rhode Island, as we know they were fed on pickled fish from Rhode Island waters.

Of the Indian garden products, we know that the planters grew tobacco very largely, especially in the earlier years. They all seem to have used tobacco, men and women. The mother of the Rev. Mr. Comer of Newport set her bed on fire while smoking a pipe. Squash, beans and Indian pease were cultivated as I have said before, and the Indian melons were much prized.

But the habit of setting a high value on imported articles is an old one. When Mrs. Sewall was sick in 1697, Sewall wrote that his little daughter Betty "gets her mother a mess of English beans which she makes shift to eat." He adds that as he was riding toward Braintree from Bristol, he saw a field of "French Barley."

Data on the potato vary. Potatoes were certainly on the list of necessities which the planters compiled in London in 1628. In 1632 a friend of Winthrop's sent him a receipt for a wholesome and savory drink, to which he was told to add "a pretty quantity of potatoe roots which I suppose you have good store of." In 1646 the Governor of Bermuda sent to Winthrop "a token of my respect; one barrel of potatoes and oranges." Potatoes were in Providence inventories in 1734. Yet they were certainly not common in New England before the middle of the century.

There were certain native products of the soil which the Rhode Island planters did not grow because they could get all they wanted in the woods and bogs about them.

According to Roger Williams, the strawberry was "the wonder of all the fruits growing naturally in these parts. . . . The Indians bruise them in a mortar, and mix them with meal and make strawberry bread, but the English have exceeded, and made good wine . . . of their strawberries, as I have often tasted." It is difficult under such conditions to say when the strawberry was first cultivated in the gardens of Rhode Island. By 1733, there were attempts to cultivate a garden strawberry in Boston. Governor Belcher wrote: "One Mr. Travers, an oil man in Fen Church Street, gave me a box of strawberry roots, from Chili in New Spain, which he told me bore strawberries in his garden as big as a Jenniting pear; but I had the misfortune to lose so great a rarity by the carelessness of the shipmaster. If you have any such thing, I should be glad of a few roots."

The cranberry was another important food which we cultivate but which the planters did not, though they used it largely. In the seventeenth century it made an excellent present for the folks back home in England who were always clamoring for "rarities" from the New World. In 1668, Mr. Sewall asked Mr. Crosby, who lived down on the Cape, to send him "a barrel or two of cranberries carefully put up fit to send to England." And in 1676, John Cotton wrote to Increase Mather from Plymouth:

"I am sending my sister a few eggs. By the last boat I sent her some cabbages and cranberries."

The earliest gardens of the planters, however, were long chronicles of failure whenever they tried to raise much besides the cabbage and the turnip and the usual Indian garden truck. It was fortunate that the wilderness supplied so much.

GRAPES

The grape vines which the early planters always seem about to cultivate were intended to produce wine—nothing else. The great abundance of wild grapes in Rhode Island was used for that purpose, and is today. The wine they make is not very palatable. Still, with so much else to do, and so many grapes to be had for the picking, it is no wonder that the early planters set out no vineyards in Rhode Island —nor did they know how to cultivate a vineyard, these Englishmen with Dutch experience. The French Colony who

*Sign of the Bunch of Grapes, which hung
in Providence in 1766*

made their settlement in the Narragansett Country in 1685 were the exception, as I have explained elsewhere.

Yet the growing of the grape was a favorite project. Dr. Child, before his coming over, wrote to Governor Winthrop in 1645:

"Worthy Sir:—

"I received likewise some seeds [sent by Winthrop] which I have delivered to the gardiner of Yorke garden, and Mr. Tredescham, who are very thankful to you for them; and have returned diverse sorts which you shall receive by the hands of Mr. Willoughby. I have sent you 5 or 6 sorts of vines in a cask marked****, with some prime grafts, some pyrocanthus trees, and very many sorts of our common plants, and seeds. I desire you that they (the vines) may be carefully planted with all expedition, and I am confident in 3 years wine may be made as good as any in France, and if I come over this spring, as I hope I shall, I will undertake a vineyard with all care and industry."

Dr. Child had written to Winthrop three years earlier:

"I intend, if I have leisure, to go to Burdeau, from thence to Tholouse, to salute Faber, to procure vines and a vigneron, who can likewise manage silkeworms, if it be possible. I intend to prosecute the planting of vines throughly, to try somewhat concerning silkeworms," etc. He also wrote that he was going to bring over some olive trees, when he came in the spring. Mr. Downing had ordered some, with the idea of introducing the culture of the olive into New England. But I think there were no grape vines in the early gardens of New England, and no olives.

Nor were there any nightingales. Sewall wrote to England to inquire if nightingales would bear the cold of the New England winters, and what would be the cost of a cock and hen nightingale. They seem to have been too expensive.

LATER DEVELOPMENTS OF THE ISLAND FARMS

Like Coddington, the earliest Portsmouth planters accumulated planting grounds in as large acreage and in as many places as they could. When need arose, the scattered meadows and cornfields were given to the married sons and daughters, and new gardens and new orchards were planted around the new house and the new family.

THE SHERMAN GARDENS

Philip Sherman had settled on Common Fence Point with Coddington and the rest. There is no record of a garden in his will of 1681, though he had added 200 acres of farming land to his original holding, and we find him leaving his son Samuel "those 4 Indians which we jointly bought," showing that the Sherman household used Indian slave labor. When

It is interesting to notice that Robert Fish, the village blacksmith, owned a garden at that early period. He left his widow "garden, half the orchard, keep of a cow, swine, geese, fowls, a supply of firewood yearly," as well as beef, pork and Indian corn. His garden and his smithy seem to have been run with slave labor, for he gave his son David his "smith-working tools," and his "three negroes."

The thrice-married Mrs. Lewis Hues had, at one period of her career, in 1691, the use of "the East part of garden" as well as "room in north east end of house."

Robert Bennett left his widow "all the estate she brought with her, a cow, garden, fruit of 10 apple trees, and half the

The old orchard on the Sherman farm, Portsmouth

this son, Samuel, died, the garden came to light, in 1717. He left his widow "choice of rooms in the house," and "use of Garden," and "fruit in orchard" and "a good pear tree." Evidently this pear tree was not growing in the garden or the orchard, but in the "yard." A double row of pear trees from gate to door is an old and interesting use of pear trees which can still be found in Portsmouth.

Benjamin Sherman, a younger son, had married during his father's lifetime, and had been given as a wedding present one of the new grants up the Island. There he built his house and made his garden, and when he died in 1718, he left "dwelling house, orchard, garden, well, and yard around the house," to his three unmarried daughters.

SMALL GARDENS IN PORTSMOUTH

Peleg Tripp bought the old Sisson houselot; when Peleg died in 1713, he left his widow "dwelling house, and a third of the great orchard for life, and my garden." The garden descended for some time in the Tripp family.

dwelling house while widow." This garden was out by the Cory windmill, for Bennett was the industrious apprentice who married the miller's daughter.

Francis Brayton, in 1682, deeded "a garden" and an "orchard" to his son Stephen. In 1691, he gave his other son, Francis, the farm and "garden" which he had bought some years previously from Badcock—that merchant of Westerly whose story is told later in this book. In 1739, this Francis Brayton died. He left a will which reads as follows:

"I, Francis Brayton of Portsmouth in the County of New-port in the Colony of Rhode Island and Providence Plan-tations in New England, yeoman, . . . do for the preventing future trouble in my family make . . . this will. . . . I give and bequeath unto Sarah Brayton, my well beloved wife, . . . all my part and right in the windmill . . . now standing upon the Watch Hill in Portsmouth, with land sufficient within the sweep of the wheel for the convenience and benefit of said mill, together with the little house standing by, together with the sum of four hundred pounds in bills of public credit of New England, the one half of all my silver money, my silver tankard, (etc.). Moreover I bequeath to my said wife one good cow at her own selection, and her election in any one fireroom in my dwelling house, with priveledge in my cellar and fruit out of my orchard both for cider and other use that she may have occasion for, and also the keeping of a cow without any charge to her, to be performed by my son Francis, on the land hereinafter given him, with a sufficiency of good sound firewood to be provided and brought to her door by my said son Francis, and also a plat of ground for a garden for her own use where she shall select; all of which I give her in lieu of her dowry or third of my estate."

There are still traces of an old Freeborn garden by a brookside in Portsmouth, utterly neglected; the house quite gone, the apple trees mere stumps, the gravestones fallen, and the cornfields overgrown with briar. Gideon Freeborn died in the seventeenth century, and left his widow "priveledges in cellar and garden." He was running his farm, when he died, with six negro slaves and an Indian lad.

Near by is "Strawberry Plain Farm," owned by Abraham Anthony. His will of 1688 gives his widow "for life . . . use of all the old buildings of my now dwelling house—garden, fruit of 10 apple trees, keep of a cow, and of a riding beast for life." The Anthonys own this farmstead even yet, and it is literally unchanged.

With all these orchards and little garden spots, it is small wonder that Dr. Hamilton wrote in his *Itinerarium* in 1744:

"Rhode Island is a pleasant open spot of land, being an entire garden of farms, 12 or 13 miles long and 4 or 5 miles broad at its broadest part. . . . The Island is the most delightful spot of ground I have seen in America. I can compare it to nothing but one entire garden. For rural scenes and pretty frank girls, I found it the most agreeable place I had been in thro all my peregrinations."

THE LAWTON GARDENS

As Dr. Hamilton rode all the way up to Bristol Ferry from Newport, and all the way back again, he must have known what he was talking about.

He passed by the Lawton Plantation, in that year of 1744, when we know from the Lawton family records that there were £300 worth of negroes and Indians at work in the fields, and orchards and gardens in a high state of cultivation. We first read of the Lawton gardens when George Lawton's widow receives "the great room, the little closet . . . 6 square feet in the cellar, and the garden," all to be hers while widow.

This plantation went from father to son again in 1706. The Indian labor had disappeared, according to the inventory, and the number of negroes was greater. This was the tendency. Everybody preferred negro labor; it was more docile, though not so inherently intelligent. It was, however, more expensive; though most of these planters were by this time importing their own negroes in their own ships, and landing them on their own wharves; so the actual cost becomes complicated.

The garden is a century old when we lose documentary sight of it. The last record I have is the will of Job Lawton, made in 1773. "My Will is that my wife, Sarah Lawton, have use and improvement of all my real estate, stock of creatures, farming tools, etc. . . . and the improvement of the garden now walled in behind the well, and a privilege in the orchard for apples and cider for herself, and ¼ of an acre of flax, and 30 bushels of Indian Corn yearly," etc. This Lawton farm in Lawton's valley was a redcoat rendezvous only three years later. The apple trees were cut down for firewood, British soldiers were quartered in the house, and all the garden produce eaten at once, of course. When spring came again, there was no one to replant. The Colony had offered every slave who joined the Colonial Army freedom forever if he came home alive. It was not difficult to escape from the Island. Not very many negroes were left to work the fields, only the

women and little children, and the aged, who were too infirm to fight.

Later, the Hessians, in their encampments near by, were a help. The officers used to hire out the Hessian privates as farm laborers, and this seems to have been satisfactory to both the soldiers and the farmers for whom they worked. In the evenings the Rhode Islanders and the Hessian laborers used to take pleasure in listening to the Hessian Regimental Band down by the old mill wheel in the valley.

But the prosperity of the Island ceased with the war, and the Island farms have never quite recovered. I can remember picking great handfuls of purple coronilla in the Lawton garden when I was a girl; it was quite deserted, and the house in the valley was in ruins.

The location of these gardens of the planters of the seventeenth century is easily discovered. Certain portions of the Island of Rhode Island have not been changed at all in the last two centuries. One section, at least, has a number of old farms which are still without connection with the public highway. They can only be approached by lanes and cartways, through meadows where the cattle graze, and where the pasture bars must still be taken down, the wooden gates held back, and replaced, by each traveller who passes from farm to farm. These deeply worn tracks through field and barnyard give an excellent idea of seventeenth century life in one of the most highly civilized parts of Rhode Island. The stone walls mark very clearly the "gardens," "orchards," "yards," etc. of the old plantations. These tracts of land, and the early wills and inventories, give a clear picture of the "gardens" of the planters, and each casual description supports all the others.

The garden was never less than ¼ of an acre, and never more than 1½ acres, in size. It always fenced in, as a separate entity. It was usually fenced with a wooden fence, of rails or paling, in the town, and surrounded by a wall made of fieldstone, in the country. The earliest country gardens had wooden fences when they were first laid out, but this wooden fence was generally changed to a wall of stone within a few years. These gardens had one gate, and one only. This was usually near the "back door" of the house. The house itself never formed any boundary wall of the garden, which lay out a little to catch the sun. A clear space was left all around the house, for "passing." The well was in this clear space, if possible, and it usually was possible because the house was intentionally built beside good water.

Newport, Rh. Isl.

In the eighteenth century every farmstead with an upland pasture had a windmill with great arms outlined against the sky

By the middle of the eighteenth century all the fruit trees, except the apple trees, seem to have been in the garden enclosures, while the lilac bush had become the ornament of the old front yard, as far as I can judge from what now exists, from the memories of old folk who knew older folk, now long since dead, and from documents which tell us something—though they tell us far too little.

At times, to get a level situation, or a southern exposure, a garden would be laid out at the side of the house instead of at the back. Very often there would be two gardens, one at the side and one at the back of the house. Or one would be "below" the other. These people did not enlarge their gardens, apparently, but made "new" ones as needed. And the women of the household actually owned certain parts of the garden, specified parts, which they "used" and "improved," very often with their own hands.

One aspect of the countryside has changed greatly. It is hard to realize that in the eighteenth century every farmstead with an upland pasture had a windmill with great arms outlined against the sky. In these mills the planters ground the corn which every planter grew.

And little brooks which run through so many of the old farmsteads still run over old mill stones which lie below the ruins of a mill house and a dam.

They were hewn in the seventeenth century, between the planting and the harvesting, in the years of the first settlement.

The Planters lived by the grace of wind and water, in old Rhode Island.

THE HARBOURSIDE, NEWPORT

There is not space to mention all of the little gardens which were soon laid out along the Harbourside in Newport and over by the long white bathing beaches of our present day.

Jeremiah Clarke settled in Newport in 1639. In 1652 he died, and was buried on his own homestead. His widow inherited a "dwelling House," "a grass plot next the sea," "a little barnfield," "a great barnfield," "an orchard," and a "garden," all on Thames Street.

Somewhere on this property Clarke had grown considerable tobacco. This widow married again, so she deeds the garden specified, with everything else, to her son, Walter Clarke, claiming the privilege of remaining on the estate till September 29th, "though if the tobacco is not cured" by that date, she may remain longer.

This Walter Clarke became Governor of the Colony. When he died in 1714, his sons made an agreement to provide for their stepmother. "We agree that our mother-in-law, Sarah Clarke, shall have and enjoy during her widowhood, all our deceased father's late dwelling house, with free egress and regress to the street, northerly, where the gate now is, and to the well and garden, with all the garden and land adjoining thereto, with housing and shops built thereon."

In a deed of 1717, Henry Tew of Newport deeded his son Henry "lands in Newport with Mansion House, barns, orchards, and gardens."

In a deed of 1682, Thomas Dungan of Newport sold his "House and garden" to John Bailey.

In a deed of 1704, a trust is created, giving the use of "dwelling house, outhouses, gardens, and orchards" to the wife of Ralph Chapman.

The will of Nicolas Easton of Newport, in 1675, left his widow "dwelling house . . . outhouses, offices, orchards, gardens, barns," etc. This land continued in the Easton family for many years. In 1781, Jonathan Easton estimated the damage done his farm during the late war. He said that he had "one acre of turf taken off, about 2 acres in a fort and cellars and heaps." He had "3 houses burned, one pulled down, a good orchard cut, and upwards of 800 trees cut, near 2000 rails burnt, the only house left, crowded with British Troops for near 3 years." And after the British went, the French Fleet arrived, and camped in his meadow "before it was mowed."

It should be added that the buttonwood trees around the house "crowded with British Troops" were not cut down, for the commanding officer enjoyed their shade.

The house, now owned by Mr. Stephen B. Luce, still stands in Newport, though not in its old location.

THE GARDENS OF BENEDICT ARNOLD

Town records explain so many things. Without them, how could we ever have known that the little stone houses we find set in the corners of old gardens, in the angles of the house yards, without windows or fireplaces, were not tool sheds, but, sometimes, cages for lunatics. They were built out of Christian charity, really, it being felt that a cellar was hardly suitable. There was so much fieldstone, once the forest had been chopped down and the land laid bare, that by the middle of the first century of colonial life the planter began to devise new uses for it, in addition to walls, house-ends, and little houses near the homestead.

Benedict Arnold of Newport built the piers and outer

This seal was used by Benedict Arnold on a document dated October 22, 1686. The arms are three escallops. The use of this obscure Arnold coat so early seems to indicate inheritance and definitely to connect the Arnolds of Newport with the Arnolds of Buckinghamshire

wall of his windmill from this same common fieldstone, and so doing, puzzled all the antiquarians of the nineteenth century. Had he built it on one of the lonely Island farms, close by other farm buildings of the same material, no one would have thought twice about it, perhaps. But a town grew up on the Arnold farmland in Newport, a town of wooden buildings, and the gaunt stone tower seemed alien, old, mysterious. I am putting a picture of the mill into this account because it is the oldest farm building still standing in Rhode Island, and not because it is a romantic ruin, a legend, in a Newport city park.

After the building of his stone windmill, Benedict Arnold bought most of the Island of Conanicut. On this new Arnold Plantation, in the present village of Jamestown, there was laid out the earliest garden on Conanicut of which I can find any record.

According to Dr. McSparren, the early garden owners of Jamestown suffered greatly from drought and worms. But the

In his will, made in 1678, Benedict Arnold desired that his body be buried "in or near the line or path from my dwelling house to my stone built wind mill." It is the oldest farm building still standing in Rhode Island

Arnold Plantation seems to have been large and prosperous.

In his will of 1733, Benedict Arnold, Jr., gave his sister "the use of a quarter of an acre of land in some convenient place near my dwelling house on the north part, for a garden, to be well fenced for her use by the occupiers of that part of the farm . . . and I give her my cow named 'Gentle'."

His directions for making a graveyard are important in a study of the landscape architecture of the period, for we know little of the ideals of the planters, though we know a great deal about what they actually got done.

"I order that the piece of ground where my father and mother lie buried—on the south west corner of my orchard, in form, four square, each side containing 3 rods; be well fenced with a stone wall 6 feet high enclosing the whole, except a suitable gateway to it, and that a suitable gate be placed there, and all of this to be completed within the space of one year next after my decease, the wall and gate to be forever kept in good repair by the occupiers of that part of the farm in which it lies."

Arnold had sold that piece of his farm in Newport which contained his garden to Caleb Carr, who already had a large house lot on Thames Street beside the Arnold property. When Carr died, in 1694, he left his widow his "little house," by Hammett's Wharf, with "the use of the well," the "use of the lower garden to the eastward of the yard which is now fenced with pale . . . to enjoy and improve during the time of her widowhood."

His son John got the Arnold house and garden across the street. In 1715, this son died, leaving to his son, John Carr, "the mansion house" and "the upper garden." He left his two daughters "the new house, one half to each," and the "lower garden, one half to each."

Still later, Samuel Carr left "to my sister, Ann Barker, the westernmost end of the new house built by my father, with one half of the garden adjoining."

GARDENS IN KING PHILIP'S WAR

It is a curious circumstance that all of the territory of present Rhode Island which was not a battle ground occupied by the enemy in the War of the Revolution, had been a battle ground, occupied by the enemy, in King Philip's War, which opened with the firing of the lonely houses of the outlying planters about old Rehoboth, in 1675.

There had been warning enough. In 1665, John Winthrop wrote to Col. Nichols at New York:

"Some English maids at Hadly were with some Indian squaws or maids, gathering berries in the woods, the Mohawks compassed them, and killed and took all the Indians, but did the English maids no hurt, but they were frightened much by it."

They should have been.

The first effect of the war upon the gardens of the planters was their intentional, complete, and wanton destruction, wherever they could be reached by the Narragansett and Wampanoag Indian tribes.

Destruction of the gardens where the actual conflicts took place was of course unavoidable. There was the fight in Almy's "Peasefield" in Little Compton, for a famous example. A man told me that he used to pick up arrowheads in that field, when he was a boy.

And the number of little plantations raided by the Indians, the number of isolated farm houses burnt to the ground, has never been entirely known. Letters like the following give an idea of the situation.

"Honored Sir:—   "Bridgewater, April 17th, 1676

My due respects etc. . . . The 9th of this instant, being the Lord's Day, as we were at meeting, we were alarmed by the shooting of some guns from some of our garrisons, upon the discovery of a house being on fire; which was Robert Latham's. His dwelling house and barn are wholly consumed. The house was deserted a few days before. The corn and the chief of his goods was saved. There was a horse or two killed, three or four carried away, some few swine killed. We sent out a party of men, on the Lord's Night, who found their trackings. One of our men judged there might be ten of them. They followed them by their trackings for several miles . . . but having no provisions with them were forced to leave the pursuit."

"Gentlemen, my respects etc. . . .   "May 23, 1676

Since the damage done at Bridgewater . . . the enemy have killed four stout men at Taunton, and carried away two lusty youths . . . three of the men and two of the youths . . . being securely planting, two or three miles from the town . . . the men leaving 32 fatherless children in a hard world. . ."

It is obvious that the greatest effect of the war upon the gardening of the colonists was the retrenchment of the area they found it possible to plant in the summer of 1675 and the spring of 1676. It was not safe for crops or men outside the limited area of the Island of Rhode Island. It was not surely safe on the Island.

Although the planting acreage was perhaps cut in half, the population which must be fed did not decrease in anything like that proportion. (Although many families perished, as their homes went up in flames, and many men were slain in the actual battles of King Philip's War.) For the greatest number of the women and children who had been living on Block Island, Conanicut, and Prudence were sent at once to their friends in Portsmouth and Newport, where they stayed till the war was over. With them in their flight, they took their flocks of sheep and their cows, of which they had many. These "creatures" required pasture land. Many of the people of Providence, Warwick, Rehoboth, and Swansea also fled to the Island. They had not so much time to rescue their flocks and herds. On June 27th, 1675, Roger Williams wrote from Smith's Garrison House:

"Yesterday, Mrs. Smith, after more, yea, most of the women and children had gone, departed in a great shower, by land, for Newport, to take boat in a vessel 4 miles from the house. Just now comes in Sam. Dyer in a catch from Newport, to fetch over Jireh Bull's wife and children and others from Pettaquomscutt."

The settlers in Tiverton and Fall River were very few, but there were a number of families of squatters and woodsmen who also sought asylum with their relatives in Portsmouth.

The result was the immediate cultivation of all the planting ground on the Island, the use of every acre of pasturage, and the abandonment of every bit of purely ornamental or experimental gardening which may have been going on.

"War gardens" were imperative.

The Portsmouth town records give this glimpse of the thought of the period:

"Voted—whereas several persons by reason of this troublesome time with the Indians, are necessitated (by their being forced from their habitations) for a supply of land to plant on, and this town being willing to afford neighborly charity to men in want and distress, do agree and order that 100 acres, if there be occasion to so much, shall be set or laid out in such convenient places in this Town's Commons as may be most convenient for those that want relief, and so as it may not be prejudicial to any free inhabitant, and what shall be so lent to them, they shall improve by sowing and planting for the time of two years from the date of this meeting and no longer, and then the said land to be freely left, with the fences, to the Town, and not built on."

A letter dated Rehoboth, April 14, 1676, gives the other side of the picture. We know that Rehoboth had been partly destroyed by the Indians, shortly before the letter was written.

"We received your friendly lines . . . and . . . your courteous tender . . . of what accommodations as to houses and what else it hath pleased God still to continue with you, that we, that are several of us houseless and our other substances wasted, might have acceptance and entertainment amongst you. We return you as hearty thanks as if we were in a capacity to entertain your motion—yet it seems most advisable for us yet here to abide. Our removal will be circumstanced with many inconveniences.

"1st: Respecting the considerable quantity of English grain which we now have in the ground, having cast in the more, that we might . . . have some relief, from an early harvest; this, upon removal, we must give up as lost.

"2nd: We foresee, that in probability, before any competant settlement amongst yourselves can be accomplished by us, much of the season of our planting will be past."

The need of food must have been great indeed, when men who had lived through an Indian raid were willing to risk it again on the chance of reaping what they had sown at the peril of their lives.

There was one chance the Rhode Islanders did not take. A man might trust the Indian slaves of his own household, but he did not trust the Indian slaves of his neighbor, during the years of the war. All the Indians were sent off the Island. This meant that, during the days when crops were more needed than ever before, there were no able-bodied men to do the heavier work of the fields. The planters themselves and their negro slaves, apparently, were on the frontiers, fighting for the preservation of the settlements; and for them, also, the Island had to grow the corn, which with chance-met bear and deer and fowl and fish, and the herbs and berries of the woods, was all they had to eat.

By the time the war was over, starvation was very near.

EXPANSION AFTER THE WAR
1677-1700

In 1677, the soldiers came back from the war, and the whole thought and life of Rhode Island experienced an abrupt change.

No young man wanted to live at home; everyone wanted a land grant in the Indian country which few Indians would ever call their own again, and which gave promise of an existence of greater personal freedom than the young man felt possible in the villages of Newport and Portsmouth and Providence. There were few of the first planters left alive; they had been glad enough, perhaps, to settle down, secure at last, on the possessions they had cultivated so carefully for forty years.

Indian captives to work the land were to be had at reasonable prices; each soldier seems to have brought home a few; the towns sold what they had on hand; there were so many that shiploads of them were sent to the West Indies as valuable merchandise—Rhode Island using their purchase money to pay some of the cost of the war.

The earliest exodus into the new country settled Tiverton and Little Compton; then part of the Plymouth Colony, and really settled more largely by Plymouth than by Portsmouth men.

In the records I have found a few gardens made in those last years of the seventeenth century under the same conditions and in the same manner as were the gardens of the earlier Rhode Island settlements of 1636 and 1638.

LITTLE COMPTON

In July, 1654, "William Paybody of Duxburrow, yeoman," bought for 70 pounds the "Dwelling House, outhouses, barns, stables, orchyards, gardens, land, meadows, and pasture"

formerly belonging to Jonathan Brewster, in Plymouth. Paybody was a surveyor, among other things, and he was, a little later, sent over to survey the Plymouth Colony lands of Little Compton. He learned to know them very well, and bought for himself some of the more desirable acres down by the shore. But the growing menace of an Indian uprising—which frontiersmen pretty well understood—probably kept him from settling on his new plantation until after King Philip's war.

About 1685 he and his wife, a daughter of John Alden of the *Mayflower*, moved over with their children, and built a house which is, they say, still standing on that old plantation. Knowing the sort of homestead he owned in Duxberry, it is not assuming too much to say that he probably planted an apple orchard and a garden. They, like the house, still seem to be in existence. Additions and alterations have been made, but I feel pretty sure that we see today the garden spot of Betty Alden, lying out beyond the old house where she spent the last years of her life.

In 1707, William Paybody died. In his inventory he is shown to have owned half of a house (his son had built on to the old one, evidently), all of a barn, 6 pounds worth of books, and a pitchfork worth a shilling.

In 1762, John Peabody sold the farm and the little farm house to Pardon Gray, grandson of Edward Gray of Tiverton. The present owner of the house, Miss Lizzie Gray, is the great-granddaughter of Pardon Gray of 1762, who enlarged the house and planted the yard and garden as we see them today. Miss Gray's recollections are most interesting. She says that the garden has always been southwest of the house, that it never joined the house, but had a stone wall around it on all four sides. It had one gate, facing the house. In her girlhood it was intact. Now it is something of a tangle, and the wall is down. But the old garden flowers persist.

William Almy bought his Little Compton Lands in 1668, March 18, from Robert Bartlett, cooper, of Plymouth, who had owned them since 1651. Six years after Almy's purchase, there took place, in "Almy's Peasefield," one of the famous engagements of King Philip's War. It is possible that Almy, who lived in Portsmouth previous to his purchase, merely planted his new fields across the river with corn and beans and peas without going over to live in that notoriously dangerous country. Any way, this "peasefield" statement, made by Col. Church who took part in the fight, shows that peas, in 1675, were planted in fields by themselves—as we would plant potatoes, and as market gardeners would, I suppose, plant peas today.

Another man came over from Plymouth, a young man with his bride, in 1694. This was Edward Gray's son, and he cleared many acres. At his death in 1721, he left his widow "the use of the new garden." His inventory shows that he had fields of Indian corn and barley, besides cows, sheep, horses, swine, a malt mill, two cheese presses, and six negro slaves. The house and the apple-orchard still stand by the main road in Little Compton. They passed out of the hands of the Gray family only a dozen years ago.

In 1683, the Richmond family of Little Compton, in a deed of that date, mention a garden of theirs which must have been started even earlier. The land where this garden was planted has never been out of the Richmond family since that early date. Young Richmond brought home some Indian captives, as his share of the spoil, and it is a matter for the modern mind to wonder at, that he and all those solitary planters on those remote plantations could and did use these beaten barbarians as farm hands around the place.

Two Woodman brothers planted each a garden. Each left a widow the "use" of the garden he had made.

Samuel Tompkins had no widow; he left his unmarried daughters "priveledge of living in house while single, use of garden" etc.

John Taylor's widow received "all the fruit in the old orchard, half the garden."

A hundred years later, in 1803, the Massachusetts Historical Society printed a description of Little Compton, as it appeared at that date:

"The roads are laid out wide and straight, a laudable practise. Indian Corn is here better than what commonly grows in Massachusetts. An acre often produces more than 40 bushels. Flax, potatoes, oats, hay, and barley, are produced in plenty. Not much rye is raised, on account of its being so

The Betty Alden house (1680), Little Compton

badly blasted, but barley is cultivated with great success. Ten thousand bushels are said to be annually exported. For manure, they are beginning to use seaweed. A common laborer gets from 50 to 80 cents a day. Windmills are everywhere."

So much for Little Compton.

TIVERTON

In Tiverton I have found only two gardens which were surely in existence in this early period, though crumbling walls and the gnarled trunks of ancient apple trees lost in a thicket of briar can be found everywhere by anyone who ventures far from the main roads of the town. And well built, comfortable houses, of late eighteenth century appearance, make it probable that there were the usual garden spots in cultivation before the Revolution. The confiscation of so much Royalist property, the fact that much Tiverton land was owned by Boston men who did not live on their farms, and the rapid changing of ownership, make it probable that elaborate gardening was not done in Tiverton at any time.

One garden quite easily identified was planted by Edward Gray, who had been living on a farm in Plymouth called "Rocky Nook." He bought his Tiverton land from Caleb Loring in 1697. In 1733 he left his widow "the new addition on the east side of the house, the use of 6 rows of apple trees, and the liberty to cut wood, improvement of garden," etc. In 1925 this Gray house was demolished. The orchard still remains, however, and the site of the old garden, close by the cellar hole, is very clearly to be seen, with its old flowers which keep on blooming though quite untended.

The other old Tiverton garden is in flourishing condition, on the hundred-acre farm of Mrs. Edward Marvell, on the Post Road above Nanaquaket Pond.

"Horse high, bull proof, pig tight," is the wall around it, built of stone dug out of the garden soil 239 years ago. Repaired, of course, the old wall must have been, as horse and bull and pig and winter frost have disturbed its balance slightly here and there, but the wall has never fallen into

neglect, and the garden has never been without its growing plants, since the last decade of the seventeenth century, when young William Durfee and his bride cleared off the forest and laid out a proper homestead after the English fashion.

The planting of the garden "with Greens or any kind of Sauce" could not have been any earlier than 1690, nor any later than 1698; as between these dates we know that young William was married, and that his father, old Thomas Durfee, of Portsmouth, on the Island of Rhode Island, gave him this great tract of wilderness as a wedding present, and that he and his bride moved across the Sakonet River, put up a dwelling house, enclosed a garden, set out an orchard of apple trees, and built a stone cook-house together with other stone out-buildings for their negro slaves. The house, the stone out-buildings, the orchard, and the garden, were all built around an oval courtyard — a little plateau sloping toward the east and west and south — and the garden is on the eastern slope, with full exposure to the sun.

By 1698, the Durfee cattle were earmarked and the earmark was registered in the Town Clerk's office; in 1700 William Durfee's eldest son was born on the farm; before the eighteenth century came in the garden must have been in use much as it is today. No garden of earlier date is known in Tiverton, for it was not until the Indian Tribes round about had been crushed and broken in King Philip's War, that the villagers on the opposite Island dared to build new homes for their sons and daughters in Tiverton, across Sakonet River, on the mainland toward the east.

The war was fought to a frightful finish, in 1676. During the war, hordes of painted savages met the Rhode Island farmers in the woods and marshes of this Tiverton shore. Little David Durfee, who toddled through the garden in 1701, must have found Indian arrowheads everywhere when he was a growing boy, and the boys of Tiverton find them still, all over the old farm. For Tiverton was not only an Indian Battle Ground, it was an Indian Hunting Ground, and the deer were so abundant that all through the seventeenth century both Indians and the nearby settlers ate little meat but venison. Though there were bears in the woods, too. As one contemporary wrote in 1690, "Bears, wolves and foxes much molest and damnifie those who live upon the Continent"—the "Continent" being local speech for all

The old stone cook-house on the farm in Tiverton owned by Mrs. Edward Marvell was built of stone dug out of the garden soil two hundred and thirty-nine years ago

Rhode Island not on the Island itself. The garden wall was obviously a very necessary protection.

Even now an occasional fawn in the spring of the year will come down from the woods to nibble young peas in the open field beyond the garden. When Mrs. William Durfee set out the roots and bulbs and little slips she brought from her girlhood home across the river, she did not intend to feed the deer but to cultivate savory herbs and salad plants to serve with the daily diet of venison. She needed a wall against the unfriendly wilderness. She had just one gate in that wall, and a narrow gate it was, opening onto the courtyard behind the dwelling house. The garden could be reached through the

And the song about lavender, "Lavender's green, Lavender's blue." Everybody down Tiverton way knows the Lavender Song, though very few know lavender. It will grow in the garden, but you must dig it up and keep it in the cellar in the winter, if you want true English lavender to flower in June to perfection. Only someone who knows how long horseradish will grow in one spot, can tell how long horseradish has grown in one spot in that garden, for it was there before the memory of man. You may infer that many of the perennials have been "replenished," but the garden design remains the same and there is little difference in the simple garden flowers. The black currant bushes date back, accord-

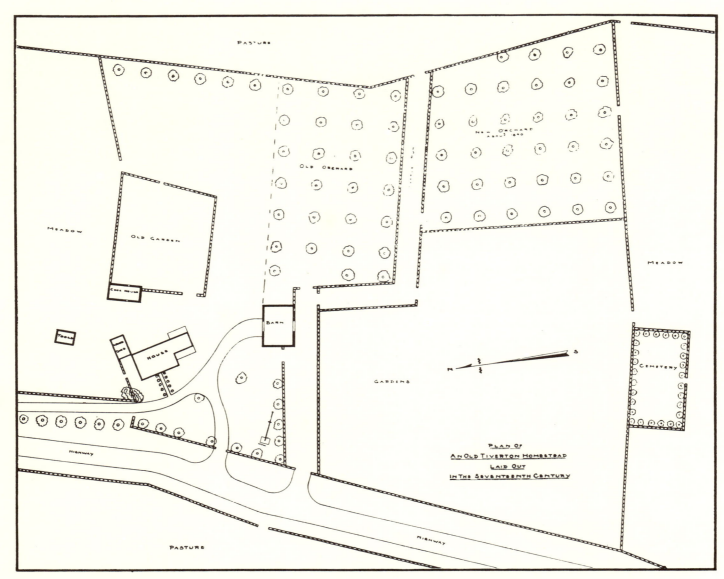

Plan of the grounds of the farm of Mrs. Edward Marvell, Tiverton

stone cook-house, however, and you could then and you can now, sit on the doorstep of that ancient kitchen, with your feet on the grass of the garden and your back to the flame of the open fire. It is just a step from pot to parsley.

Peas and parsley were surely in that early garden, and beans and horseradish and pennyroyal and mint and borage —you can find some of them yet. There was certainly a little row of thyme, that favorite of yesterday which still weathers the winters of Rhode Island, and edges the garden path. One of the old songs they sing to the children of Tiverton—the old, old songs that have come down through three centuries, by word of mouth, from the English settlers—is a song about thyme in a garden.

> "Once I had thyme of my own
> And in my own garden it grew.
> I used to know the place where my thyme it did grow,
> But now it is covered with rue, with rue,
> But now it is covered with rue."

ing to tradition, incredibly far. A very old apricot tree blooms in the garden every spring. It ceased to bear apricots before living man remembers, but we cannot say that it dates back to the seventeenth century, for we do not know how long an apricot tree will live under favorable conditions.

We know that the garden had simple garden flowers from the beginning, because we know that Mrs. William Durfee of long ago fully expected to do the family doctoring from the day she married till the day she died, and she planted her medicines in rows by the garden wall, preparing for contingencies. In the garden to-day grows heartsease for beauty, in the garden yesterday grew heartsease for whooping cough. The effect is much the same, and little David lived through the whooping cough.

He lived through everything, from his birth in 1700 to his death in 1788. He lived through the French and Indian Wars, he lived through the battles of the Revolution, he lived to clear his father's rocky farm away up through the woods to

The garden on the farm of Mrs. Edward Marvell

Another view of the garden, with the old stone cook-house in the background

The graveyard on the farm of Mrs. Edward Marvell, Tiverton

where great granite ledges meet the horizon. He tore down his birthplace and put up on its foundation in 1768 the present farm house which remains unaltered to this date. He was evidently a man with a taste for landscape architecture. The great avenue of elms before the house are planted where they should be, the cemetery he made in a field to the south belongs to the landscape; it is fitted to its purpose. Near the house it had to be, of course; the beasts of the forest would have rifled the graves, otherwise. But a stone wall encloses the acre, cedars planted inside the stone wall form a solid wall of green eighteen feet high, and the little gate of entrance faces the south, where it cannot be seen from the dwelling house. Wild cherries have sprung up in the enclosure. Woodchucks have made homes for themselves among the graves, and there are many graves. Otherwise the place looks as it did in David Durfee's lifetime in the eighteenth century, when he laid away his slaves and his children and was finally himself buried there, at the age of 88.

His wife lived longer. She was 95 when she died and was buried in her own walled graveyard beside her husband.

A beautiful stone, carved from dark slate by one J. Stevens, a stone-carver of Newport, is close by. The inscription is as follows:

In memory of Christiana
Daughter of Captain William Durfee
and
Orpah his wife
who died March 10, 1805
in the 7th year of her age.
Here lies the hopes of a fond mother and the
blasted expectations of an indulgent father.

Captain William Durfee was engaged in the East Indian trade and sailed from Newport on many voyages, leaving his wife Orpah and his little children with his father on the old farm.

The little apple trees set out on the southern slope from the walled garden grew old with the century. They were walled in, like the garden, at first, but the walls are now largely in ruin, and many of the original trees have been cut down, an orchard, called the "new" orchard in the eighteenth century, being used as the orchard proper. Those were the days of Rhode Island Greenings, likewise of cider, made even now on the farm but then liked very hard, and very often, according to report. David's four daughters were married from

the farm in that long period of plenty between the clearing of the land in pioneer days and the disruption of society during the Revolution. Cider from the orchard, mutton from the meadow, young peas boiled with mint from the garden, certainly furnished the wedding feasts, and the four brides wore the garden roses in their hair. Guests came from Portsmouth by boat and from Newport, as well as over from Plymouth and Dartmouth and up from Little Compton and down from Freetown, and the garden paths were gay with home-spun, dyed with garden flowers, as well as with wonderful silks and satins, worn mostly by Newport folks. Departing guests took with them slips from the garden as a matter of course. Though the gardeners of those early days ordered little fruit trees from England as well as seeds in great quantity, their main source of supply was the older gardens of the country, those set out by the pioneer people, and there was really meaning in the slip of lilac or the root of London Pride, which Mrs. Durfee gave away for the asking. To let a guest depart without something from the garden was a discourtesy.

As we see it now, it was also uneconomic. The pretty custom was but one of the folk ways of our ancestors, founded on wisdom. There are gardens you visit today, where the old symbolism is forgotten, where never a blossom is given the guest, but they are not the old gardens of Rhode Island.

The labor of the farm and cook-house was slave labor, of course. All the farms around Narragansett Bay were so run, and with this labor supply the drudgery was done, and the men had time for the fine arts of landscape gardening, grafting, breeding fine sheep and cows and horses, while the women directed the ways of the household—just *directed* them. Of course, it was constant supervision they gave and had to give, but the back-breaking work of a farmer's wife was not theirs till after the Revolution. They had time for experiments in agriculture. Mrs. Durfee, for instance, grew flax in her garden, to see if linen of good quality could be made in New England. She tried new receipts for rose conserves and lettuce cosmetics. She planted a mulberry tree, and raised silkworms.

But in 1775 there was the Revolution at the door. David Durfee was 75 years old, his only child at home—waiting to inherit—was a son too old for service in the Colonial Army, and the grandchildren in the house were all under the age of sixteen. So the contribution of that farm was not man power but food, fodder, and firewood. The Revolution was a garden affair.

The Colonial troops fortified the hill to the north of the garden, and General Sullivan had his headquarters in a farm house up the road. The officers of the army came calling frequently, particularly the quartermaster. The private soldiers came after dark, by way of the garden wall. The orchards were looted, of course.

It was not quite so bad as it seems, though. The Island of Rhode Island across the river was occupied by British troops. They were quartered everywhere, thousands of them. They ate up the cattle, and they cut down the trees for firewood. Even the orchards were sacrificed to the necessities of that bitter winter. Old David Durfee was patriotic, of course. We know that, because the Tories of Tiverton had their farms confiscated after the war was over, and David kept his in the family. But both he and his fellow farmers saw their opportunities. They took firewood across from their forests and sold it at good profit to the suffering people on the Island, to all of the suffering people, we understand. Back wood-lots were cut to the ground, stumps were taken out, dead fish were hauled up from the shore and put to rot on the old fields to increase their yield as new fields were hastily prepared for the corn so badly needed and which would sell at war prices. Horses and wagons were taken by the Colonial troops, it is true, but there was labor left— slave labor—and the farm was made to yield the utmost.

Today the back wood-lots have grown up again. All through the woods you will find stone walls and runways for the cattle, and old stone cellars choked with underbrush. The wilderness is creeping in.

That was the situation faced by the garden at the close of the eighteenth century. Slavery was dead. You read of this and that Tiverton farmer's slave being freed by will after the Revolution, but there were not many of the old slaves left, and a growing sentiment against the importation of new slaves resulted about this time in legislation and a gradual abandonment of the whole system in Rhode Island.

The great size of late eighteenth century families was a help for a while, but the boys went west with the opening of the railroads, and with the death of David Durfee, Jr., in the early nineteenth century, the great days of the garden were over.

Joseph Durfee inherited the old farm, fourth owner since the clearing, and he carried on the garden exactly as he found it till he died in 1851. Then, sad as it seems, the garden succumbed to Victorian Taste, and admitted a yucca. These yuccas are the last word in Victorian elegance in Rhode Island. They came in with cast iron deer and weigela avenues, just after the tiger lily epidemic. The yucca is stiff and improper in New England; yet it is not without charm, since it is of a period; it "dates," and by our yuccas we can tell if our gardens were truly cultivated during the nineteenth century by persons of taste. So our garden admitted a yucca, sent a son to the Civil War, and was tended by the daughters of the house through the nineteenth century.

The present owner follows the good example of her ancient cousin, the Mrs. David Durfee of the eighteenth century, and grows "greens and garden sauce" in the old garden walled against the wilderness. She has day lilies and larkspur down by the garden wall and her little children play under the apricot tree. A few fields are cultivated, there is a pasture for the cattle by the pond, the grass is mowed about the old graveyard, the apple trees are sprayed in the spring of the year. In the old stone cook-house, whose eastern doorway opens on the garden, it is the mistress of the garden herself who makes her own apple jelly at the great fireplace. Labor has left the garden and the hearth, and this old Rhode Island homestead lies, after the centuries, a lovely and a lonely reminder of an older civilization than our own.

The Reynolds house, Bristol

"Silver Creek," the house built in Bristol in 1680 by Deacon Bosworth

BRISTOL

Some time between 1680 and 1708, there came into existence the earliest garden in the contemporary records of Bristol. The following paragraph is a copy of an entry made by the Town Clerk.

"Captain Reynolds departed this life, July 10, 1708, his death being very sudden; for going in from his garden, he sat down about two minutes, then rose up and went in to his lodging room, lay down upon his bed and dyed."

It looks like a sunstroke; July 10th can be very hot in Bristol.

Reynolds was a Boston man who had served under Captain Church in King Philip's War, and had settled with Church in Bristol at its close. Before the war, there had been no English settlement on the Mount Hope lands, although the land had been somewhat extensively cultivated by the Indians for over a century.

We do not know very much about the gardens of these first white settlers; nineteenth-century prosperity wiped out most of the visible remains of the first plantations. We know that Samuel Sewall sometimes stayed with Captain Reynolds when he came down to Bristol to hold Court (Bristol then being Massachusetts Country), and we know that he had a sore throat on one of his trips and "went to bed early at Mr. Sparhawk's, pinned my stocking about my neck, and drank a porringer of sage tea." So we suspect that the Bristol gardens could furnish *Salvia officinalis*. We know that Nathaniel Byfield of Boston got hold of about a quarter of the conquered territory, and went to live for a time in the new settlement. We know that there was a house or so on Poppasquash, for Sewall dined there with the Justices in 1704. But I think there were few permanent settlers and fewer gardens in those early years; with the famous exception of Deacon Bosworth and the garden at "Silver Creek."

"SILVER CREEK"

There is a creek in Bristol which runs like quicksilver through the meadows of the town. It has its rise in Reynolds' Pond. On its north bank at that point where the country highway is about to enter the Main Street of Bristol, Deacon Nathaniel Bosworth built himself a house in 1680. He probably did build himself a house; for he knew the use of tools; he was a cooper by trade, doing fishing and farming on the side. His boat was kept moored to a stake at the foot of the clearing where his new house stood. His cornfield lay off to the right of the house just beyond his orchard of apples. As for fancy garden stuff, whatever his wife and daughters cared to plant and tend with the help of a few captive Indian children, they grew in what they called the "Garden Spot," enclosed by walls of field stone. It lay out toward the south by the side of the creek, to catch the morning sun. And this new plantation in Bristol in New England was named for the old Bosworth farmstead of "Silver Creek" at Market-Bosworth in Leicestershire, England—so they say.

The borders and grass path in the garden of "Silver Creek"

which devastated the New England coast. It was soon after 1750 that Judge Bourne imported rose bushes from France. At least one of these bushes still blooms in the old Bosworth garden spot.

The pleasant ways of Silver Creek were sadly disturbed by the Revolution, and the old garden was curiously injured. Nearly a keg of cannon balls had to be dug up before the garden was fit to plant again, after the war was over. The bombardment of Bristol by the British Fleet seems to have been particularly severe in the Silver Creek neighbourhood.

As early as 1797, more fortunate than other Rhode Island estates of consequence, Silver Creek resumed the old habit of hospitality and comfortable living. Judge Benjamin Bourne came down from Providence to stay in his father's old home, and his friends — Tristam Burgess,

The New England farm house built by Deacon Bosworth in 1680 still stands, enlarged. In the house still live people of the Bosworth blood. Around the house still grow great fields of corn, an orchard of apples, and what few simple garden fruits and flowers the women of the household care to tend. At the foot of the Bosworth lawn the creek still runs up when the tides are high, like quicksilver, through the sweet flag and the cat-tails and the rushes.

But Silver Creek has known days not so peaceful. Changes began when Judge Bourne of Bristol, whose wife was a Bosworth, came into possession. He had some money, and his share of the new eighteenth-century conception of what a gentleman's country estate should look like, of how a gentleman on his country estate should behave. That he should walk in an allée, sit in an arbor, and entertain his friends by exhibiting rare plants and imported trees, was essential to the part.

The Judge imported black horse-chestnut trees from England, and planted a double row of them along the north bank of the creek at the foot of the lawn. The path between the trees became the fashionable allée, and there the Judge and his friends from Providence walked up and down and held their fashionable eighteenth-century conversations. In 1925, some of these chestnut trees were still standing, to be uprooted by that September hurricane

Wilkins Updike, Elisha Potter — were frequent visitors. The Updike and the Potter gardens in the Narragansett Country are famous. The Bosworth house was again enlarged and given a touch of magnificence. The De Wolfs were beginning to lay out their great estates in Bristol. Comparisons were inevitable. It is unfortunate that we have no picture of the days just before the flood of 1815, which destroyed so much.

There had been a storm out at sea, a hurricane which had swept up the coast from the West Indies, driving the waters of the Bay up into the harbor of Bristol, and there piling wave on wave until the salt water of the harbor rushed up the

The front gate to the garden of "Silver Creek."   Another view is shown on page 431

creek and overflowed the banks about the Bosworth farm. For hours the lawns and gardens, and the parlors and kitchens, were many feet deep in salt water. "Up to the window sill" is the description given by one eye-witness. "The grounds were totally destroyed," another authority tells us. But of course they were not—not totally.

In 1836, the house and the remains of the old splendor passed into the hands of James De Wolf Perry, who had married another girl of the old Bosworth blood. Somewhat later, these newcomers planted a narrow border bed on each side of the path leading south toward the creek from the main door of the house.

In 1863, the house and grounds were carefully repaired and restored. The borders were increased in size, until they became three feet wide, as they are to-day. The gravel path, between the borders, was added. This path is now once more a path of close-clipped grass, as it was when the borders were first laid out in 1835. The present owner is sure that in the old garden spot—the Bosworth garden spot of 1680—there are daffodils which go back beyond that new planting of 1835, surviving the flood and the bombardment. It is quite possible.

There are also in the garden grape hyacinth, scilla, iris, day lilies, crocus, tiger lilies, Japan peas, damask roses, lilacs—all of a day beyond the memory of anyone now living.

WARWICK AND EAST GREENWICH

The old Warwick planters, by their wills and inventories, show that they went back to their burnt homesteads and started all over again. New planters took up land grants of

Old boxwood in the garden at "The White Swan," now the estate of Mr. Arthur B. Lisle

the old Indian territory. There was much land speculation all over the Narragansett Country, and a surprising amount of this newly opened territory got into the hands of Boston men, like Sewall, who divided their land into farms and rented it out. Boston Neck is the best example of this state of affairs.

Of the men who really made gardens at the time of the new settlement of the land west of Narragansett Bay, we have noticed the various branches of the Greene family, in an earlier section. There was a William Spencer who built a house and made a garden about 1714. He left his widow, in 1748, "priveledge of garden." And another Spencer garden was laid out in the heart of East Greenwich, where its ruins can still be found in the greater gardens of Mr. Arthur B. Lisle. The Spencers owned that early garden for many years, but on April 14, 1839, Christopher Spencer and Anne Louise Spencer sold their house and their land to John H. Clarke, U. S. Senator for Rhode Island. At that time there was much beautiful boxwood in the garden, and they had recently purchased a fountain, made in the shape of a white swan. Mr. Clarke enlarged the house, and the gardens about the house. So did Mr. Lisle, who later purchased the estate. But the boxwood was left intact, and it is still worth going far to see. The white swan fountain is still a feature of the estate.

In 1741, a planter named Wicks ordered his son, by will, to provide for his mother. He was to "fence her a garden of half an acre . . . she to have what fruit she needs."

In 1746, Anthony Low left his widow "an acre of land for a garden." Low had 500 pounds of tobacco on his farm, and 13 loads of hay, and may be called a practical planter of the period.

The Rufus Barton garden comes to light when we find that a Barton widow got "use of one half of the largest dwelling house, and all of the small house adjoining, and of a small house called the Stone House, with use also of the garden." The first Barton planter had built a "Thatch House" at the head of the Cove before King Philip's War. The "largest house" was built in 1680, for a Barton son who appears to have raised race-horses.

HUGUENOT GARDENS IN FRENCHTOWN

From a *Short Account of the Present State of New England*, written in 1690, I want to quote what I well believe:

"What is most considerable in the Narra-

The White Swan fountain on the estate of Mr. Arthur B. Lisle in East Greenwich

gansett Country is the Settlement of the French Protestants
. . . they have made good improvement, live comfortably,
and have planted great numbers of vines, which they say
thrive well."

Only, they did not "live comfortably."

Potter, in his *History of Narragansett*, written in 1835, says:
"In the course of the persecution which followed this act
[the repeal of the Edict of Nantes] large numbers of Protestants were obliged to leave France. A number of these came
to the Narragansett Country and settled in what was then
a wilderness, which is today called 'French Town.'"

According to Mr. Updike, who published his *History of
the Narragansett Church* in 1847, "they planted an orchard
where they first sat down, of which there are now some
remains on the farm in East Greenwich late belonging
to Pardon Mawney, Esq., which is still called the French
Orchard."

This farm is now the property of a descendant of that Philip
Sherman who planted pear trees in Portsmouth in the seventeenth century. Mr. Sherman says that the last of the old
French apple trees blew down some years ago, but that there
are young apple trees, shoots, now to be found in the same
old pasture up in his back lot by the spring around which
the Huguenots laid out their house lots in 1685.

Wild grape vines smother the stone walls of this Sherman
farm—they may be descended from the grape vines which
the Frenchmen brought from France. And a very old cherry
tree stands in the Sherman dooryard.

The Sherman dooryard is an excellent example of the
dooryards of a hundred years ago, at which time it was
probably planted with the bushes and flowers which grow
there today. The pale fence which ties it to the corners of the
house and separates it from the road which runs by the west
of the house was probably built at the same time. Box trees
which have grown so tall that they completely block the gateway were then planted on each side of the gate. But it is
nevertheless the old garden spot of earliest days, and which
of the old perennials that border the enclosed square of
grass were planted in the eighteenth century, and which in
the time the fence was built, I do not know. A disused path
runs from the blocked gate to the locked west door. Mr. Sherman told me that the garden has not been altered by him or
his, and I doubt if a more perfect example of the unrestored
garden of its period is in existence.

A contemporary reference to the French Settlement is the
letter written by Dr. Ayrault, who was one of the planters.
It bears the date of 1700:

"I had already fenced in 60 acres of land, purchased and
made very good improvements for a large orchard, garden,
and vineyard, and a good house."

His letter is a very good account of the disgraceful events
of 1692, when the jealous and resentful English settlers
pillaged the French crops, let their cattle into the French
gardens, and tore up young vines, hoping to drive the
foreigners out of Rhode Island altogether. The Warwick men
were a wild lot. They were soldiers, mostly, who had fought
for two years in one of the most merciless and barbarous wars
which history has ever recorded. They were colonial born,
all of them, I think. It would seem that they resented the
tidyness, the thrift, and above all, the success of these Frenchmen who came from the French country districts, where the
agricultural methods were much superior to the ways of the
Warwick men. It is also true that the land titles of the Frenchmen were not clear; but that is what the Frenchmen did not
know, and the Englishmen could hardly have been sure of.
No, it is quite understandable! The Warwick women made
their jelly out of wild grapes which grew plentifully all over
the countryside. Why should Frenchmen plant grape vines!
And the fun of the fight, the chance to pillage, the small
boy's urge toward destruction!

But it was unfortunate. For most of those practical French
planters, who were men of good birth and education, left

Rhode Island before 1700 on account of their ill treatment,
and Rhode Island could hardly afford to let them go.

White heather grows today in Frenchtown, and tradition
is sure that it was planted by the Huguenots in 1686. It probably was.

FRENCH FRUIT IN NEWPORT

Dr. Ayrault, who had been a physician in Angiers before
the revocation of the Edict of Nantes, went over to Newport
when the Frenchtown plantation was abandoned, and there
practised his profession. I do not know that he had a garden
in Newport, perhaps he did, indeed most probably. But Mr.
Lucas, "a Huguenot of some wealth and distinction," is
known to have grown pears. He "hired an estate" of Mr.
Robert Gardner "for his residence." He brought with him a
graft of a pear tree, and "reared it in the garden of his hired
house." About the time the pear tree had begun to bear,
Mr. Gardner wanted his house again, and Mr. Lucas left
town; leaving his pear tree behind him on the Gardner
estate. . . . "So the pear, which soon gained a great reputation, was named the Gardner Pear," and the Frenchman
was forgotten. Channing, in his *Early Recollections of Newport*, 1793–1811, recollects the "Gardner Pear . . . incom-
parable for its beauty and flavor." He could also remember that another pear, "the St. Germain," had a marked
flavor. These pear trees were grown in the garden spaces,
in Newport.

BLACKBIRDS IN THE GARDEN

But in these last years of the seventeenth century, when
the Frenchmen came to Rhode Island, the plain farmer was
still a power in the land and sophisticated agriculture—
pomology—all the rest—were not in favor at all. Important
problems of an earlier age still confronted the planters. Like
the Indians, they spent much energy on blackbirds. On April
10, 1697, it was voted in Portsmouth "that every householder
shall kill 12 blackbirds between this and the 10th of May
next, and bring in their heads to some men appointed." It
was still permissible throughout the colony to pay taxes in
Indian corn, barley, oats, or sheep's wool. The cornfield, not
the garden, was still the great concern of the common man.

*The Hazard house, South Kingston, was given to George Hazard (1699-
1746) in 1721, on the occasion of his marriage, by his father*

Those early planters were greatly interested in the birds
and animals they found about them. Blackbirds they did
have to exterminate. But Sewall actually sent a racoon as a
present to a friend in England.

"Sent him a racoon: paid Joseph Marion for taking care of
it on the way: corn and fish good diet for him."

Somebody else sent over an otter, which jumped overboard
when taken on deck for the air. As Roger Williams wrote:

"New England's wild beasts are not fierce
As other wild beasts are."

Yet they, like the blackbirds, were fiercely destructive. The harmless bear, the timid deer, were common garden pests, who could destroy a whole planting in no time.

And what with the blasted rye and wheat, the blighted barley, the apple trees in need of a spraying they never got, and the floral experiments which turned out badly, the look of an old plantation must often have been pretty discouraging.

I should say, however, that of all the dangerous beasts in the New England universe, the Palmer Worm was the worst.

THE GREAT PLANTATIONS OF THE NARRAGANSETT COUNTRY

It was in the eighteenth century, in the old South County, in that Narragansett Country across the Bay, that the last and the greatest of the Rhode Island Planters lived out their legendary lives on their estates of truly magnificent tradition.

Planters in the old sense they surely were; traders of horses, ship owners, dealers in home-woven cloth though they often were besides. They and their wives and children went out into the wilderness after King Philip's War, and took up vast tracts of wooded country; old Indian clearings, ponds, rivers, hills, and valleys; and they ploughed the land with their oxen, and they planted wheat and corn, and they walled in their planted land, and raised great flocks of sheep and innumerable horses all over the enormous grazing meadows round about them. There were not so very many of these great Rhode Island planters; a man who lives in the center of a holding of a thousand acres has few neighbors, and Rhode Island is a small State. Even of the few there were, not all are known to have had gardens of any kind. The Champlains, for example, held 2000 acres for a few years, but there is no record of their planting anything but corn.

We know a great deal about the farm belonging to Robert Hazard. "It consisted of nearly 1200 acres. . . . The best part, 200 acres, was in Boston Neck." Judge Sewall of Boston went over to adjust its boundary line in 1706, and noticed there was good grass on the Neck, and some woodland. By 1745, the state of cultivation can be gathered from the will of Robert Hazard himself. He left his wife "4 cows, a negro woman named Phoebe, one riding mare, six dung hill fowl, 6 geese with the privilege of raising what increase she can, but she shall put them off, all of them, to six, by the last of January yearly." Also, "the improvement of a quarter of an acre of land, where she shall choose it, to be fenced for her use yearly"—obviously, the conventional widow's garden. But in no other record can I find so small a garden plot. Half-acres were common, but quarter-acres on 1200-acre farms are unique, and conspicuous. Another Robert Hazard, in 1762, gave his wife Sarah "the use of the improvement of my garden, annually." Since this is a garden book, we are not concerned with the huge Hazard dairy and the export business in cheeses.

Thomas, son of Robert Hazard, was married in 1744, and his father gave him forty acres on Tower Hill. There he lived for the rest of his life as farmers do. He kept an expense book, which has been published. It appears that he raised oats and sold them to his father. He made 3627 pounds of cheese in 1754, and sold it all; buying "herd's grass seed," at 26 shillings a quart, to seed down his grazing meadows. In 1756 he grew potatoes and turnips. Early in the century for large crops of potatoes, according to agricultural authorities. His onion crop was good in 1767. He sold plums in 1771. He planted English black cherry trees. Authorities tell us that there used to be much fruit grown on the Tower Hill farm, but only cherries, apples, pears, and plums are specifically noted. An authority adds, "some of the trees in their season looked more like pyramids of fruit than trees."

Which remark is exactly what I expect of any person writing of any planter or any plantation in the Narragansett Country in the eighteenth century.

We are told that buttonwood trees bordered the pastures

of Tower Hill. This may be the place to mention that the buttonwood tree is a native of Rhode Island, that unlearned people of literary bent call it a sycamore, which it is not, and that the planters of Rhode Island quite generally used it as a border about pasture lands when pasture lands began to be

An occasional buttonwood tree was left standing in the pastures to give shade to the cattle. All evidence tends to show that cows have been pastured here for at least two hundred years

enclosed. Up to that time, they left occasional buttonwood trees standing about on the farm or in the yard to give shade to the "creatures." The buttonwood is the largest of the Rhode Island forest trees, and it is exceedingly picturesque, especially when its boughs are bare in winter. Possibly most of the buttonwoods in Narragansett and on the Island of Rhode Island were cut down for firewood and fortification during the Revolution, and a blight in 1840 destroyed the rest, but giant buttonwoods of great age and beauty still stand in the pastures about Swansea and Rehoboth.

Of course, not only the Hazards owned these enormous estates, and not only in the Narragansett Country were they to be found. In 1709 Samuel Perry bought 236 acres in the township of Charleston, and soon increased his holdings to a matter of 500 acres, where he raised cattle, sheep, and horses, for the export trade. The Perry homestead is now a museum, and is open to visitors during the summer season. In Samuel Perry's will of 1767, he left two unmarried daughters "the use of three lower rooms in the east part of my new dwelling house for 5 years" and "the use of old garden." The plantation was run by negro labor, as is shown in the inventories of 1716 and 1767.

The whole of Prudence Island was erected into a manorial estate in 1672, and granted to John Paine.

Mr. Sands, of Block Island, owned 400 acres in 1694, with "an orchard." He kept sheep. And he used Indian slave labor. His Indians escaped from Block Island, nobody knows how, and they take up a good deal of room in the old Colony Records.

These captive Indians, while I feel sure they saw nothing unjust in their enslavement, can hardly have been happy about it. I was not surprised to see in the Town Records of Portsmouth that one of the Indian slaves on the Fish Plantation hung himself from the limb of a walnut tree in 1684.

Still, life was none too easy for anyone; even John Crage, a Scotchman, a tailor by trade, was found hanging to the bough of a cherry tree, fastened by his own laced neckcloth, and the Jury called it suicide. In 1688, it was felt necessary to pass a law prohibiting a master from killing intentionally any negro or Indian slave in his possession. The raging discomfort of the slave-owner seems also evident.

I have dwelt upon this question of slave labor to some extent, because the whole system of Plantation life in Rhode Island was founded upon its existence. No free man would endure this monotony of labor by the year, year after year, on an isolated farm. He would not then, he did not have to. There was always free land to the west to be had for the asking. He will not now, he does not have to; there is always better paid labor in the great cities. So only in the eighteenth century, under a system of slave labor which went to pieces during the Revolution, was it possible for the owners of great tracts of Rhode Island soil to become prosperous, even opulent; as they certainly did.

Of the other great planters of the Narragansett Country, there was one named Thomas Gould who owned an estate called "The Mount." He planted "hawthorn, buckthorn, and the prim bush," according to the books.

Two seals used by planters of the Narragansett Country in the eighteenth century

"Dale Carlia House" had a brief period of splendor a century later, when the Niles family named it for a neighbor of theirs who had been a Consul in Sweden. When "Dale Carlia House" passed into the hands of Rowland Hazard in 1818, there was a large orchard north of the dwelling house, containing "Marigold" apple trees, of which some vestiges still remain. The trees and shrubs which are now the sole features of interest about "Dale Carlia" were all planted between 1820 and 1825.

"Hopewell" was a Plantation of 800 acres. It was purchased, improved in 1750, by Matthew Robinson of Newport, who had married a daughter of that French Huguenot, Lucas, who grew pear trees in his hired garden.

The Robinsons had built a "mansion house after the style of the English Lodge," at "Hopewell," sometime before the Revolution. By 1907 only the chimney was left standing, and I believe that today even the chimney has disappeared. In 1842, Updike wrote:

"An afternoon stroll was taken to this spot, and a walk over the grounds . . . there were his rows of box, here his beautiful tall sycamores, there his spacious garden arranged with exotic plants, and on this extended green was his morning and evening walk.

"Mr. Robinson died insolvent at the age of 85. His estate was sold at auction, in 1795."

Still the intangible. We know that the "beautiful tall sycamores" were buttonwood trees, *Plantanus occidentalis*, natives of the surrounding forest, that every farmer in the neighborhood used as shade for his cattle. As for the "exotic plants"—I sometimes feel that the word "exotic" like the word "sycamore" is used by the Narragansett historian from preference. However we do know that there is boxwood, today, around the cellar hole of the ruined house which, once upon a time, is said to have contained one of the finest libraries in Rhode Island.

It seems a little cruel to quote Count Axel de Fersen, yet he was a gentleman, he came to Rhode Island with the French fleet, he had seen much of the world, and his report on the Narragansett Country has at least the merit of having been written to his father in 1780 and sent back home with no thought of its effect upon the planters whom he was describing and whom he evidently liked.

"Sept. 8, 1780

"Vous connaissez les Français, mon cher père, et ce qu'on appelle les gens de la cour, pour juger du désespoir où sont tous nos jeunes gens de cette classe, qui se voient obligés de passer leur hiver tranquillement dans Newport. . . . Nous avons eu ici des chaleurs excessives dans le mois d'août, je n'en ai jamais senti de pareilles en Italie. Maintenant, l'air est plus frais, c'est un superbe climat, et un charmant pays.

"Nous avons été dans le continent, il y a huit jours, avec le général. J'étais le seul de ses aides de camp qui l'ait accompagné. Nous sommes restés deux jours, et nous avons vu le plus beau pays du monde, bien cultivé, des situations charmantes, des habitants aises, mais sans luxe et sans faste; ils se contentent d'un nécessaire qui, dans d'autres pays, n'est reservé qu'aux gens d'une classe inférieure; leur habillement est simple, mais bon, et leurs mœurs n'ont pas encore été gâtées par le luxe des Européens."

Had there been great pleasure gardens in the Narragansett Country it is at least probable that de Fersen would have seen them, would certainly have heard of them, were they still in existence. And had there ever been many ornamental fish ponds, amusing garden houses, pretty parterres, labyrinths, terraces, topiary work, they could not have vanished utterly between 1775 and 1780; though those were the years of havoc on the Island of Rhode Island and of coast raids on the mainland everywhere. Had the slaves uprisen—but they did not; and for the most part the houses, even, were not destroyed, nothing was destroyed; neglect set in—just neglect and poverty; loyalist-Planters and rebel-Planters, all grew poor as the war went on; the plantations were just not "kept up."

It seems to be obvious that although there was wealth and comfort on those old Narragansett Plantations, although the life was a gay and happy one, as life went then, in harder times than ours, there was little ornamental gardening done, little pains taken to elaborate the social customs of the time, the houses of the people, or even the yards and gardens about the houses.

Many acres roughly cultivated, space, a sense of power, the beauty of the unspoiled countryside, were their luxuries. I think it is true that the Planters of Narragansett, even the great Narragansett Merchants, for all their enormous acreage, had few gardens, and the most of those that they had were very simple, very small.

They do not, except for some old boxwood, a patch of briar, a decrepit fruit tree, a tottering wall, exist today in any form at all.

I make this statement with hope of contradiction. I hate to give up the glitter and the tinsel of the past.

THE GARDENS OF THE CLERGY

"WHITE HALL"
THE GARDEN OF BISHOP BERKELEY

WHITE HALL today looks exactly like a farmhouse in a fairy story. You find it by luck, if at all. Tucked away in a fold of pasture land, three miles northeast from Newport, it is not on any highway, but must be reached by a lane of its own choosing, which runs between two pasture walls and stops abruptly at the house it has served, very badly, for nearly two centuries.

White Hall was built in 1729, impulsively, by George Berkeley, Dean of Derry; probably from plans by, certainly under the supervision of, Berkeley's protégé, Harrison, the English architect. It was at once occupied by Dean Berkeley and his pretty young wife, who were on their honeymoon. Together, with Harrison to help them, they laid out the land about their new Georgian farmhouse in the best taste of England in 1729. That taste was very good taste indeed.

The broad front of the house had been built to face the ocean, a mile away to the south. They planted no trees which might interfere with that glorious view of grazing land, great rocks, and blue water. They started an apple orchard on the eastern side of the house, and walled it in with fieldstone; as did their neighbors whom Berkeley, innocent of offence, called "the boors" in a letter he wrote to Sir John Percival. They walled in a small garden close to the house, on the west, where it would get the morning sun, and in that garden they put a cherry tree or two, as well as all the garden flowers of that time and place which they could procure for the spring planting.

In this, Dean Berkeley was no novice. He did know flowers. All of his books and most of his letters contain intelligent references to plants and trees and caterpillars and other garden adjuncts. He once wrote a book on the Flora of Sicily, when he was a young, unmarried man attached to the suite of the English Ambassador to the Kingdom of the Two Sicilies. He lost the manuscript, he thought, during the voyage from Palermo to Naples; or perhaps on Ischia where he went often. He liked islands. He may have done the White Hall garden in the Italian manner!

Unfortunately, no trace of any formal garden planting remains. We find only the garden wall, the garden space, and, here and there, growing in the coarse grass, caraway and chamomile. Those old perennials, Bouncing Bet and Deptford pink, are, to be sure, flourishing in corners, and there is tansy in abundance on the farm, but nobody knows with any certainty that they were ever in Dean Berkeley's garden, old though they are. It is certain however, that from Dean Berkeley's day to this, nobody has ever planted any other garden at White Hall at any time.

To the north of the garden space, the Berkeleys built a little one-room house in which they kept "the library." And there among his books, or walking up and down in the grassy spaces of his garden, three miles from Newport, Dean Berkeley received all Rhode Island.

The Rev. John Comer, a Newport clergyman, wrote in his diary:

"July 14th, 1729. This day Mr. John Adams and I waited on Dean George Berkeley at his house. Kindly Treated."

Of course he was kindly treated. The Berkeleys were very happy and very nice to everybody, that first summer. Their son and heir was born in July, a healthy infant who throve on the milk of the White Hall cows. "The weather," wrote Berkeley, "is delightful," and "I thank God I have two domestic comforts which are very agreeable, my wife and my little son, both of which exceed my expectations, and fully answer all my wishes."

He liked the solitude, too, as men will, when they seek it of their own accord and know it cannot last for long. He found the simple habits of Rhode Island most amusing, and went about a bit, even preaching for Dr. MacSparran occasionally over in the Narragansett Country, sharing Dr. MacSparran's interest in the development of his farm.

All the time, however, he was expecting a royal grant of a large sum of money, from England. When it arrived he was going at once to Bermuda, to be the Founder and President of a College for the education of North American Indians. He had come to Rhode Island because, well, because he had just been married, he liked to travel, he didn't want to wait about in London until the money he felt sure of was actually in hand; and because he had been told, and he believed, that the Island of Bermuda was too small to grow food enough to feed the proposed college, and he thought it would be practical to buy a farm on the nearest mainland and there raise the food and ship it over. He had been told that Indian corn would not grow in Bermuda, and that the North American Indian students would simply have to have Indian corn. Rhode Island was an excellent place to grow Indian corn.

So the Berkeleys, and Smibert who had been appointed Professor of Fine Arts in the proposed college, and Peter Harrison who was to be its architect, came to Newport in January, and stayed in the town while the Dean looked about for a good farm.

The land struck him as exceedingly expensive. But he was in a hurry to plant his corn so that it would be ready to supply his College the coming winter, and in the early spring he bought 100 acres from Captain John Anthony, "out in the woods." He also bought some negro slaves to cultivate the cornfields.

Dean Berkeley named the new purchase "White Hall" in memory of the old palace of the English kings. He had to use much of his own money in acquiring the land, and when April came and no grant from England, he decided to build a modern farmhouse, also with his own money, near the old farmhouse where the farmer was still to live and manage the farm. There the Berkeleys intended to spend the summer, preparing to go to Bermuda in the Fall. With this pleasant dream in the back of his head, and nothing to do but build and furnish his new house, outside and in, Dean Berkeley made his garden in that long, golden summer of 1729.

There is little more to tell. When the cold set in, and the snow covered the garden, and the wind howled about the unweathered house, the Dean, who was a philosopher by profession as everybody knows, tried to forget that the King's grant had not come, and amused himself with writing a really entertaining book. He called it *Alciphron*. It is an account of a series of polite discussions on Atheism, supposed to have been held in the pleasant parlors and the green gardens of Newport. In one of the chapters, Alciphron, the hero, is "seen walking in the garden with all the signs of a man deep in thought." In another, Alciphron and his friends sit "around a tea table, in a summer parlour which looks into the garden." In another chapter the rural philosophers take their tea "in a library which has an arched door opening into a walk of limes."

White Hall in 1837

Sketched by Lieut. Harwood. U. S. N., for Robert Johnson, for use in a book called "Picturesque Illustrations of
Rhode Island and the Town of Newport"

philosopher though he was. And with the coming of the third summer, and again no grant, he gave away his precious books, packed up his household goods, and deeded the whole farm of White Hall to Yale College, glad to get rid of it in fitting fashion, and to go back to the Old World and civilization.

He sailed from Boston.

The English Church made him a Bishop upon his return, and he wrote more books, and became a great man in the great world of his day. The modern critics say that Berkeley is "one of the most admirable writers in the history of English Literature" . . . "one of the most distinguished of all English Philosophers."

White Hall was the creation of an impulse, little more. Made by an artist for love and leisure and the enjoyment of beauty, when the Berkeleys went away it became at once a rented thing.

The published book was amazingly successful, both in London and in the colonies. Dean Berkeley's view of the garden as a parlour, not a pantry, permeates the book, and it impressed the larger colonial public as his use of his own garden as a pleasant meeting place had doubtless surprised and interested the Rhode Island farmers who lived round about him. Perhaps no other man who ever came to Rhode Island had a greater influence on garden architecture. Coming to the Colony from London and the world where fashions rise, he made gardens fashionable. The larger and more important gardens of the eighteenth century in Rhode Island begin with this date.

But the Berkeleys themselves were not very happy, once the book was finished, the winter over, another summer upon them, and again no royal grant. Another child was born at White Hall who did not live. Smibert, realizing, as Berkeley began to, that the Bermuda College was an impossible project, seeing, as Berkeley saw, the North American Indians at work in the fields about him, gave up the dream of teaching the North American Indians the Fine Arts, and began to paint the portraits of such colonial gentry as would employ him. That he could not do at White Hall. So the farm developed that summer without Smibert and Harrison, and it is doubtful if much was done. The second winter seemed to Berkeley unbearable,

The land was starved. The house was used for a few years as a tavern, according to Dr. Hamilton, who wrote in his *Itinerarium* in 1744: "We called at a public house which goes by the name of 'White hall,' kept by one Anthony, about 3 miles out of town, and the dwelling here of the famous Dean Barclay, when in this Island, and built by him. As we went along the road we had a number of agreeable prospects. At Anthony's, we drank punch and tea and had the company of a handsome girl, his daughter." This was, I suppose, the future mother of Gilbert Stuart. She not only came under the traditional influence of the Berkeleys, it

White Hall as it is today

would seem, but she served in a tavern to which all the most brilliant and amusing travellers of the age came at least once—and she waited upon them and heard their talk. This may explain why her son, born in the little snuff-mill in the Narragansett Country, should have acquired the manner of the great world so easily. I said, it *may*.

Andrew Burnaby, a young Englishman just out of college, travelling about to see the world, rode out to White Hall from Newport in 1754, just ten years later than Hamilton. He wrote in his book of travels that he found Berkeley's farm house "most indifferent" though set in the heart of a beautiful country. He noted that Berkeley's bookroom had been turned into a dairy. All traces of splendor, of the charm of gracious living, had already passed away.

During the Revolution, whatever remained of the trees were cut down for firewood, and British soldiers were quartered in the house. They ate up what stock was on the farm, and left the whole place a wreck.

Some tenant, after the war, tidied up White Hall a little, and in the early days of the nineteenth century planted pear trees to border the walk which runs down from the front door to the lane. Someone set out new apple trees in the old orchard, and repaired the stone walls, putting a new wall about the grass plot in front of the house itself. For with the turn of the century, the fashion for the enclosed front yard came in, and the farmhouse gardens were brought around from the kitchen to the front door.

In 1900, White Hall was in a most abandoned state. The house and the tangle about it were unfit for human use. Fowl from the neighboring farm were roosting in the Berkeley drawing room, and pigs had made a pen of the old garden and the bookroom.

Just in time to prevent the house from tumbling down, the Colonial Dames of Rhode Island bought the lease which still had 90 years to run, and took White Hall under their kind protection. They repaired the roof, planted a row of box bushes from Mount Vernon on each side of the front walk, and cleared house and yard effectively. They welcome visitors to White Hall, as Berkeley did, and treat them kindly.

But for some reason—partly atmospheric, I think—the old farm still seems asleep, still under the enchantment of the cruel years of poverty, and the farmhouse itself looks exactly like a farmhouse in some old English fairy tale.

If you go to pick the bitter chamomile, growing in the grass, walk softly. Something might happen.

"THE NARRAGANSETT GLEBE"
THE GARDEN OF THE REV. JAMES MACSPARRAN[1]

About the year 1760 the Rev. Jacob Bailey, a frontier missionary of the Church of England, made a journey through New England. His comments as noted in his journal are not of a flattering kind, but in the village built on Tower Hill he discovered some of the finest gardens in New England. "The people here live in better position than in most parts

[1]Written by Miss Caroline Hazard.

of the government" he writes in his journal. Judge Helme was living in the great gambrel-roofed house near the corner of the post road, and the road leading to the Pettaquamscut. Squire Case kept the tavern and came to greet his guests as they 'lighted from their horses at his door. A little to the south, Thomas Hazard, son of Robert, called College Tom, had planted his orchards of apple and pear, peach and plum trees. Some of his cherry trees were in a pleasant meadow, nearly a mile from his house. There are records of haying, and barley, of corn, and potatoes.

Little remains on Tower Hill of any of these gardens. A splendid mass of purple lilac, which hides a yawning stone foundation on the west side of the road, tells of springtime joy today as it has done for scores of years. Tansy has escaped and waves its frond-like leaves, and beckons with its golden flowers, the direct descendant of the precious roots brought from England with so much care. Harebells grow beside the stone walls, and an orange lily, not of our lovely native American varieties, marks the spot where some forgotten housewife took her pleasure in them.

But there is one place that may still be called a garden. Not on Tower Hill itself, but below that ridge which is the backbone of New England running to sea to appear once more as Block Island, and overlooking the lovely Pettaquamscut lake, the Bass Pond of our forefathers, is the hillside farm bought so long ago, and now called The Glebe, from the fact that it was bequeathed to the church by the owner, the famous rector of St. Paul's parish.

Here Dr. MacSparran built the house which is still standing, and made a garden. It was on the 22nd of May 1722 that he married Hannah Gardner of Boston Neck, Handsome Hannah, as she was called and as Smibert's portrait still shows us. All the world was young with them; he was twenty-five, ordained to the priesthood by the Archbishop of Canterbury only two years before, and she was seventeen. Dr. Goodwin says that it was early in his ministry of thirty-six years that he built his house beneath the sheltering hill which bears his name, but above the road, so that it has to be approached by terraces. By the roadside stands the mounting block, about four feet high, built of rough stones fitted together. A short flight of steps at right angles to it lands on the first terrace, on which is the gate. Stone walls extend on either side, almost masked by a lilac hedge. A straight flagged path leads up a gentle incline to the steps of the second terrace, also walled, and with lilac trees. Up these steps is a broad sunny area with an old pear tree at the north end, and new peach trees, to replace the ones for which the region used to be famous. The stone-flagged path leads on to the third set of stone steps, and the level of the house is reached. It is gambrel-roofed, and of good size. The south ell, which was the Doctor's study, has gone, and the great room in which prayers were read in inclement weather has been divided. Some later tenant removed the great chimney, which was the centre of the house. But it is good to know that the present owner is restoring and preserving the old building with care and intelligence.

In one of these enclosures are mulberry trees, one would

The Rev. James MacSparran, D.D.

From the paintings by Smibert, as reproduced in "History of the Episcopal Church in Narragansett," Updike-Goodwin

Mrs. MacSparran

Glebe House, seen from the open gateway

twenty-three years. For yᵞ great Goodness to us, all this time Lord make us truly and fruitfully thankful and give us yᵞ Presence and Blessing in all times to come.

"My Spouse's head aches. Tom and Harry howing and picking Peas."

A couple of years before, there is a record: "My wife had yᵉ Hysterick last night," but it was "very hot weather these two days past."

A few years later occurred the incident when the Doctor coined a phrase by which his wife is remembered, but one can see she had a righteous occasion for her anger. Hanibal, one of the slaves, had been guilty of a grave offense, and Dr. MacSparran as a just master had to discipline him. "I stript and gave him a few lashes till he begged. As Harry was untying him, my poor passionate dear, saying I had not given him eno' gave him a lash or two, upon which he ran and Harry after him, as far as William Brown's." The chase is described, how the man was caught and how he had "wᵗ [what] is called Pothooks put about his Neck. So it has been a very uneasy Day with us, O yᵗ God would give my Servants the Gift of chastity."

A little later the Doctor writes, "Lord direct me how to manage my Man Hanibal who is headstrong and Disobediant." That same day comes the record "Hanibal whipped." Later he was found conspiring to run away, and was sent to Conanicut, where the Doctor finally directed him to be sold. So strong was the influence of the time! Dr. MacSparran had insisted on the duty of catechising the negroes, declaring them to be Sons of Adam, who had souls to be saved, but the man who had "howed" his beans proving unworthy, he sold him. "Lord pardon my short comings in Duty, and ill Deserts," his diary records about this time.

like to think descended from those of an older day. Clove pinks still bloom, and there are lilies beside the great lilacs. The Diary has no mention of flowers, though it seems as if this terraced garden was meant for them.

Dr. MacSparran records "Stepney payed 3ᵈ per Plant for ye Colli-flowers," and in 1743 on a September day "Ye negroes" were "gathering Beans." In 1745, "Augˢᵗ 16ᵗʰ Broʳ Jnᵒ mowed my Rye. Tom Walmsley cut and topt my stacks with Emblo's assistance, and Harry harrowed." Corn is constantly mentioned, and apples. "All ys week making Cyder" is the record of Oct. 6th in the same year. The good Doctor did not neglect his land, as when a little later, "My two negro's plowing in ye Buckwheat as Manure for English Wheat." And again, "My two negro's howing in ye Buckwheat and sowed turnips to-Day."

The weather is constantly noted and "a fine refreshing Rain ys Forenoon" is recorded, but one can imagine the disgust of the worthy divine who was so good a farmer, when in 1751, "Wednesday July 31st It rained, and my Men are threshing."

Smibert, who was not only an artist but the architect of Faneuil Hall, painted a portrait, now in the Boston Museum of Fine Arts, which shows that Dr. MacSparran made no vain boast when he wrote to his kinsman in Ireland: "I *know* you would be pleased with the person and accomplishments of my *consort*." Among her accomplishments must be reckoned the constant entertainment of a succession of visitors. "Capt. Hill, his wife Anstis & Roland dined with us after church." This was a small party; eight and ten people often came, many of whom "lodged here." They were a devoted couple, as this entry shows:

"May 22, 1745 My Wife and I have been married this Day

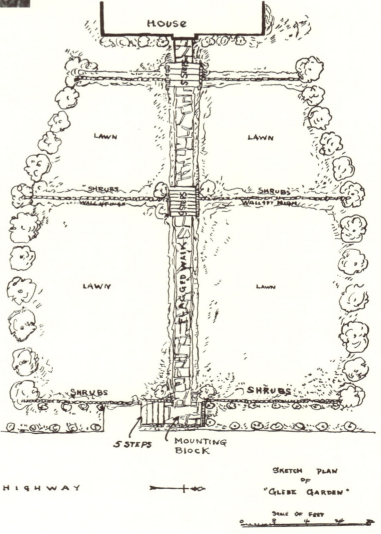

Dr. MacSparran, his "poor passionate dear," all her kinfolk, the many guests—of whom the poor master wrote "so much company is fatiguing to me"—are long since gone. But the horse-block from which they dismounted, the flagged walk leading through the garden, the very lilac bushes which bloomed in the May sunshine are here, the flowers as fragrant this year as they were those years long passed. Here we quite literally walk in a good man's footsteps.

CAROLINE HAZARD

"STUDY HALL"
THE GARDEN OF THE REV. WILLIAM BLACKSTONE

The Reverend William Blackstone, last survivor of Gorges' Colony in Massachusetts Bay, was born in England, educated at Oxford for the ministry, took orders, and for a few years held the living of a village church.

Nobody knows exactly why he came to New England.

Everybody knows that Governor Winthrop found him there, in 1630, living all alone on Beacon Hill. His house stood near a spring, which is called a fountain by some of our earlier historians. They say that on his clearing he had a garden where he was growing roses, and that he had planted an orchard which was bearing apples when he suddenly sold out to Governor Winthrop, in 1634. He then bought a "stocke of cowes." This we know from his contemporaries.

He took those cows and went off all by himself; down along the Indian trail which led to the shores of Narragansett Bay and the Rhode Island trading stations of the Manhattan Dutch.

Nobody knows why he went. Nobody knows what he did when he got there.

At some time between 1633 and the day of his death in 1674, he built some sort of house and planted an apple orchard, on the south bank of what is now called the Blackstone River, where it flows through what is now called Lonsdale, Rhode Island. The land was under the jurisdiction of Plymouth in the seventeenth century, and that particular section lies in the old Attleborough Gore.

Blackstone's inventory is filed with the Records of Rehoboth, and shows that in 1675 he owned 200 acres of land on which were standing both a house and an orchard. No garden is mentioned.

The first reference made to Mr. Blackstone, after his settlement, states that he had "swine." This was in 1635.

In 1636 he wrote to his old friend, the Rev. Roger Williams, who was having trouble with the ecclesiastics of Boston and Plymouth—indeed with all the ecclesiastics—that the country nearby would make a good refuge if he were thinking of "removing."

In 1637, the Rev. Mr. Lechford, an English clergyman who had been in New England getting material for a book of travels, wrote that

"One Master Blaxton, a minister, went from Boston, having lived there nine or ten years. He lives near Master Williams, but is far from his opinions."

But Blackstone's garden, not his opinions, is what I started to discover. I cannot do it. However, I can find a great deal of information about his orchard.

The earliest reference is, "August 12, 1646. Blackston's apples gathered." From that date the orchard can be traced through the pages of the historians up to 1836, when the Rev. Mr. Bliss wrote:

"Three apple trees are now standing, in the south end of Blackstone's meadow, and two of them bear apples. They appear to be very old, but probably grew from the sprouts of those planted by Blackstone."

It was in 1765 that Governor Hopkins had written: "Many of the trees which Blackstone planted, about 130 years ago, are still pretty thrifty fruit-bearing trees." He added: "Blackstone had the first of that sort of apple called yellow sweetings, that were ever in the world, perhaps the richest and most delicious apple of the whole land."

The apples themselves made a last appearance, on the banqueting table at the Centennial Dinner of the Massachusetts Historical Society a few years ago.

The site of Blackstone's garden

Blackstone is said to have had in his house a really large library, which he is said to have brought down with him from Boston.

Because it was the seventeenth century, when conceits were accounted quaint, and wise men were naïvely proud of their wisdom, Blackstone called his lonely dwelling house, with its library of "folios" and "duodecimos," "Study Hall."

The Rev. Mr. Bliss of Rehoboth wrote that he went over in 1836 to look at what then remained of "Study Hall," and the Blackstone plantation. It had been looted and burned by the Indians in 1675, but Bliss found that the cellar of the house and the stoning of the well were still almost entire. He described the "landscape gardening."

"The meadow was divided into 3 tables, elevated one above the other, which appeared to be water formation. The house was on the first table, the well was on the second. A knoll or hillock rose abruptly from the three shallow tables, like a pyramid, on the very brink of the river, to a height of about 60 or 70 feet." This hill, Blackstone called "Study Hill." It was thickly wooded, and commanded a lovely and peaceful landscape, looking down the curving river to the Bay. Perhaps he took his books up there, to be away from the cows and pigs and friendly Indians who hung about the house.

A cotton factory now covers the site of both hill and Hall.

Around the memory of William Blackstone there have grown up delightful legends: that he rode a cream-colored bull from Providence to Boston; that he went about with his pockets full of yellow sweetings, to give to the children of Providence, who had never seen apples before, etc., etc.

It is true that he read the Church of England services, in Providence, occasionally. It is certainly not true that he preached on the street corner, to anyone who would listen, and rewarded his hearers with presents of apples. He was a scholar and a clergyman in the Church of England.

One late historian says that Blackstone grew roses at Study Hall. Another says he "laid out a great park" around his "manor house." Which sounds like nonsense.

It is kinder to leave him in his study, interested in his orchard but thinking the natural beauty of the landscape, the rushing river, the thickets of wild rose, the meadows of blue iris, the woods full of shad bush and laurel and dogwood and pink orchids, the islands and beaches festooned with the wild grape and clematis, garden enough. No, I do not think that the Reverend William Blackstone ever had a proper garden on his plantation. And I know he never did live in Rhode Island. I have just naturally included him with those colonial clergy who lived on the land and knew the ways of wind and weather—fit leaders of a pioneer people—great men, every one.

A TOWN GARDEN
OWNED BY THE REV. DR. STILES

It was on June 2, 1770, that Dr. Ezra Stiles, Pastor of the church in Newport, wrote in his diary, "Sat for my picture. Silk worms hatched."

By that single entry the historian learns for the first time from contemporary evidence that gardens in Newport were being planted with the white mulberry tree, imported from China.

At various dates, in various communities, silk-worm culture was attempted in all the colonies. How early the fad reached Rhode Island I do not know. Field in his *History of Providence* says that there is a white mulberry tree in the yard of Fenner's House in the Woods, in Johnston, R. I. Tilton's *History of Rehoboth*, mentions white mulberries as growing in scattered colonies on old farmsteads in the Rehoboth country. He saw them near the Salisbury place in the Hunt neighborhood and on the T. V. Allen place north of Perryville. I picked white mulberries myself, forty years ago, from a very old mulberry tree growing at the end of Cory's Lane in Portsmouth, and I have seen them in the old gardens of Tiverton. But as far as written record is concerned, Dr. Stiles makes the earliest contemporary reference to the existence in Rhode Island of the silk-worm and his food, the white mulberry trees of China.

Obviously, Dr. Stiles' trees were planted before 1770, since the silk-worms "hatched" that year, in June. The next year we get more details.

"June 4, 1771. I have now 3000 silk worms hatched."

"July 4, 1771. Some silk worms done eating."

"July 8, 1771. Above 3000 silk worms are cocooning. Perhaps 150 remain feeding, and almost satiated."

Silk-worm culture was not a commercial success in Rhode Island. It was abandoned quickly by those who could not afford experimental agriculture. But, as a fad, it was a source of much interest; there were great rivalries.

Dr. Stiles writes, "Oct. 19, 1772. 21 ounces of raw silk raised by my wife."

It would appear from this casual entry that Mrs. Stiles, not the Doctor, fed the little worms with the mulberry leaves, confirming my idea that the parsonage garden was not the Doctor's affair at all. Except in clerical circles, the gardens, as I have noted, were always the woman's to "use" and "to improve," and the Stiles family seem to have lived after the manner of the laity.

Dr. Stiles adds: "This day [the woven silk] is making up into a gown; which my wife gives (after she is done with it) to Betsey or the oldest daughter surviving her; to be preserved as a memorial of her once having a silk gown made from her own raising."

The Doctor's diary has been published, in two large volumes. Only once does the Doctor write, by name, of the garden of the parsonage in Newport, where he lived for many years. He doesn't leave it out as a trivial detail; small

From an original painting in the Redwood Library

The Rev. Ezra Stiles

things interest him very much. For example, he explains carefully that his wife didn't really raise enough silk to make her whole dress; he had to buy her a little more in Philadelphia to put with it.

No, it seems obvious that the garden was his wife's premise, and that she only brought it to his attention when she had something queer to show him, such as satiated silk-worms, or mucilaginous caterpillars. His solitary reference to the parsonage garden, aside from the silk-worm episode, is as follows:

"Sept. 27, 1775. A mucilagenous worm took the Pare Trees in my garden last summer and eat the upper surface of the leaves—so that most of them have dropped off for this month. Now they are shooting out again as in the Spring, and some of the leaves of the second growth this year are at full Bigness. Blossom Buds are on both, and one of the Trees is in Bloom."

THE CLERGY ON THE CAMPUS
THE GARDEN OF THE REV. JAMES MANNING

The campus of Brown University is the home-lot of Chad Brown, Planter of Providence in 1636, Pastor of the First Baptist Church in Providence in 1642.

The old college pump is the well in his yard; the college buildings stand on his planting fields.

On pleasant Sundays in the summer-time, the Baptists of Providence met in the orchard beside the house of Pastor Brown, listened to his sermons, and were edified. Many years later, the descendants of Chad Brown gave the old Brown Plantation to the Trustees of the first Baptist College in America, as a site for the first college building, and today the students of Brown University meet on the site of the old orchard, where Chad Brown lectured to the people of Providence in 1642. It is an old tradition.

Near that first college building, the college trustees built a house for the first college president.

The Rev. James Manning, D. D., who came up with the young college to Providence in 1770, had been college president (and most of the professors) since the opening of the college in Warren, in 1765. He was the son of a New Jersey farmer; he had lived on his father's farm in Elizabethtown until he was 18, and he really was himself a practical farmer, by training and inclination. He seems to have planted the garden spot at once, putting in potatoes, we know. He probably grew melons; he must have grown melons—at that date, everybody grew melons. This is evident, because in June, 1783, the Rhode Island Legislature passed a law, "An Act to Prevent Melon Stealing":

"Whereas, divers persons have wilfully, wickedly, and wantonly, entered into the fields and gardens of many of the inhabitants of this State, and have plucked and carried off the melons growing in the same, and whereas, by the common law, the offense of taking and destroying anything annexed to the freehold is only trespass, which does not sufficiently deter evil-minded persons from such wanton destruction, it is thereby enacted . . . that if any person . . . shall enter into any field, garden, or patch of melons, and shall take and carry away any melons . . . he, she, or they . . . shall be adjudged guilty of theft," etc.

I know of no other fruit which was able to get a whole act of the Legislature for its own particular protection.

Melons had been growing in Providence, however, for many years before Dr. Manning planted the "College

Estate." Another Baptist Clergyman, the Rev. John Comer, of Newport, went up to Providence in 1733 to supply a vacant pulpit. He stayed some days, and was invited to dine with Col. Power. In the Comer diary is this entry: "I was served with a rare water melon from Col. Power's own Garden." The Brown family came into possession of this garden a little later and it is quite likely that Dr. Manning got from the Browns his melon seed as we know he did get the college endowment.

Whatever Dr. Manning planted in his garden had not been long in the ground when the Revolution totally disrupted the life of Providence. Dr. Manning wrote to a friend in later years:

"The College was quite broken up, and the edifice was occupied by a rude and wasting soldiery."

He continued to live in his house on the campus, and to cultivate his garden, with the rude soldiery hanging out of the windows to watch him hoeing his potatoes and putting on the fertilizer. By 1784, Dr. Manning was almost without any income whatever. He was cultivating the garden as a means of livelihood. In a letter he explains the situation.

"At that time I made my own garden, and took care of it; repaired my dilapidated garden walls, went nearly every day to market, preached twice a week and sometimes oftener," etc.

He became ill. In another letter he writes:

"I was taken sick the day after the great snow, with no provisions in the cellar except one hundred weight of cheese, 2 barrels of cider, and some potatoes; with not a load of wood at my door; nor could I command a single dollar to supply these wants. The kindness of my neighbors kept me from suffering. . . . But when a man has hardly earned money, to be reduced to this abject state of dependence requires the exercise of more grace than I can boast of. I have

From a portrait painted in 1770

James Manning

From the "Early History of Brown University," by Dr. Reuben A. Guild

Brown University, showing University Hall, with Dr. Manning's residence on the left

serious thought of removing to the farm at the Jerseys, and undertaking digging for my support."

We know that he did not go back to the Jerseys, but lived through the Revolution and the period of reconstruction when the college opened again, gradually finding less and less time for his garden labors.

He died in 1795. Not long after his death, his house was moved away and new buildings for the growing college were erected on the Manning garden and the orchard and the corn field of old Chad Brown.

There are no gardens on the campus any more.

THE "GLEBE" IN PROVIDENCE
THE GARDEN OF THE REV. ARTHUR BROWNE

When Arthur Browne entered on his pastorate in Providence, he succeeded a certain O'Hara of somewhat extraordinary habits.

The people of King's Church were so grateful for the decent and sensible living of the Rev. Arthur Browne that they gave him a farm of 18 acres, with a dwelling house —situated a mile and a half away from the church in order to be nearer to Rehoboth, where some of his parishioners lived.

He came to Providence in 1730. When he went to Portsmouth, he presented the Providence parish with the rectory and the farm land, "for the repairing and upholding the church of England in Providence." The Browne Farm then became the Glebe Farm, according to the English fashion of speech, as truly as any land could so be called which was not set aside for church uses by the civil government.

The church kept this property until 1794.

In 1738, the incumbent was the Rev. John Checkley. That amazing man says that in the first year of his ministry he visited almost all the Indians remaining in this part of the country, and built a "Barn And Stable" upon the Glebe, "by borrowing money at 12 per cent." He wrote that "the home and glebe are not yet wholly paid for."

He frequently preached in Taunton, and he says that one winter when he was obliged to ride into Taunton very often the snow lay so deep upon the ground that the fruit trees in the "Glebe Garden" did not blossom until the middle of June.

So we know that there were fruit trees in that Rhode Island garden, in the first half of the eighteenth century.

THE CHANNING GARDENS
WILLIAM ELLERY CHANNING'S BIRTHPLACE, IN NEWPORT

William Ellery Channing was born in Newport, April 7, 1780. He lived in a house which had not only one garden but two. His brother wrote a book of recollections in which he says:

"I remember my father's tastes with pleasure. He had two gardens, one of them quite large, and as he sought to have everything which he cultivated of the best of its kind, our table, otherwise simple, was, in this respect, luxurious. He was not satisfied with what contented his neighbors, but introduced new varieties of vegetables into the town."

There were fruit trees as well as vegetables in the Channing gardens, undoubtedly. Channing wrote:

"The greening apple was the great staple, whether for the production of cider or for house use, and had a zest which increased rather than satisfied the appetite. There were peaches too, more luscious than any of Southern growth; and what clime save Newport ever yielded such quinces!"

Channing wrote also of his early recollections of "the black heart or mazzard cherry," "The Gardiner Pear," and "the greengage plum."

The little Channing boys had their bedroom up under the eaves, and the Rev. Dr. Channing in his old age wrote that he could well remember looking out of his window across his father's garden very early in the morning, and seeing the Rev. Dr. Samuel Hopkins still working over his sermon by candle light.

Many years later, when Channing was famous, and did not live in Newport any more, he liked to come back in the summer time, to rest and recapture the ardors of his boyhood, surrounded by the quiet and the charm of the green island which he loved so well. He always stayed with his wife's people, out on the Gibbs' Farm, on the East Road in Portsmouth. George Gibbs, founder of the Gibbs' fortune, had died in 1803, but his daughter kept up the old country place for many years.

There on the Gibbs' Farm he found most beautiful gardens, I am sure; but all that is left of the old planting today are the enormous elm trees on the lawn and some sections of the evergreen allées which run through the Gibbs' meadow land in a most fascinating manner. They were probably a late development of the "winding walks" and the "serpentine walks" of "Malbone" and "Redwood" and "Vaucluse" and "Spring Green," and other Rhode Island estates of pretension; but I can remember the Gibbs' allées very well; I walked in them when I was a little girl, and I think they did not curve or wind very much. They resembled, in fact, their contemporaries, the walks on the Hodgman Estate in East Greenwich, "Fyrtree Hall," which were laid out about 1840.

One of the Gibbs' allées still runs diagonally across a meadow where it seems to have no excuse whatever for intruding. The story goes that Miss Gibbs planted the trees from the side door of her dwelling house to the north door of the Gibbs Memorial Chapel, that she might "walk to church" quite unobserved.

And now Miss Gibbs is dead and her house has been taken away, and the trees close by the church door died, I think. But enough remain to show the pleasant green paths where Channing walked in peaceful meditation, remembering perhaps the gardens and the visions of his youth.

Trinity Church, Newport

THE GARDENS OF TRINITY CHURCH
VESTRYMEN'S PROBLEMS IN NEWPORT

At a vestry sitting in Trinity Church in 1722, it was ordered that there should be put "a post and rail fence at the end of the lane," which is Church Street. In 1732, in April, "William Weston agreed to take 44 pounds for the balance of his account for the fence around the church yard, and gates thereto, in full."

A hundred years later, in November, 1833, the following entry was made:

"On a motion of Edward Brinley to ornament the church yard with trees. Voted, that the wardens be authorized to purchase and have set out as many and such kinds of trees as they may esteem best."

According to Mr. Mason, the Newport historian, "the trees so planted in that rich soil grew apace, and spread out so wide as in time to become objectionable, in that they disturbed the graves and the monuments. They also became a source of complaint from the owners of houses on the north side of Church Street, made damp by the masses of foliage that hung over them. And when it was decided to put around the grounds the iron fence now there, it was found that the trunks of the trees had so pushed across the line as to make any attempt in that direction futile until they were removed. One tree alone was left standing, the elm still seen on the west of the yard in open ground."

Such is the history of the garden close, about the church itself. The Glebe of the Church is another matter.

"August 27, 1752. Voted that there be a committee to collect by subscription a sufficient sum of money to purchase a house and glebe for a minister of the church for the time being."

And there was a third garden with which the vestry had to deal. Nathaniel Kay had left the church his mansion house, where Kay Street now runs, surrounded by outhouses, and a garden, etc.—about seven acres in all. The church was supposed to let the property, and to use the rental to pay a schoolmaster whose duties should be "the free instruction of 10 poor boys in grammar and mathematics gratis," and to "assist the minister of Trinity in all his undertakings."

The church, what with the war and all, had found it impossible to keep the Kay house with the gardens in decent order, and could get little income from the rental of run-down property. In April, 1796, Richard Harrison of New York offered to take a lease of the Kay property for 999 years at an annual rental of 300 silver dollars. The offer was accepted, and the church thought it had got rid of its gardening problem forever.

But Harrison apparently did not repair the Kay mansion. By 1833 the Kay buildings had fallen down, and the garden was back in the hands of the church vestry once more. This vestry appointed a committee "to lease the Kay or Harrison Estate." Mr. Engs offered to lease the ruined garden and the old cellar holes, for the conventional 999 years. He built a new house, in the old Kay garden, southeast of the Jewish Cemetery; and Trinity Church lost that garden at last.

THE TOOL HOUSE

IN MY own garden in Rhode Island, laid out in 1852, there is a tool house, right beside the garden gate. Next to the tool house is the tool shed, where the grindstone has always stood, and where the cider press used to be. It is difficult for me to conceive of a garden without a tool shed or a tool house of some sort, yet I do not think there were many tool houses in the gardens of Rhode Island

kept in the garret—"three sithes in the garret" of Stephen Arnold's house in Providence in 1719; or in the kitchen or in the Great Room where the fire was, so that they would not rust out in wet weather.

It seems probable that the first planters in Rhode Island brought with them far better garden tools than the next generations were able to make or to buy. In an inventory of

Courtesy of the Museum of Fine Arts, Boston, Massachusetts

"The Tools of Husbandry" as portrayed in a tapestry of the sixteenth century. The forms have changed very little, as the following illustrations show

before 1800, and I do not think that they were ever a colonial garden feature.

Not that the colonials had no garden tools. They had a great many. They had them very early. They valued them very highly.

Sometimes, to be sure, the tools were neglected; the inventories of the seventeenth century give more than one plough found in the orchard or the open field—not under cover; but, as a rule, they were cared for most carefully, and the inventories show that the sickles and the spades and the axes were

the year 1641, in Plymouth Plantation, there is listed a "pair of garden sheares" worth 1 shilling 6 pence, a modern garden implement which we do not associate with pioneer conditions. "A little grafting saw" appears in the same inventory. Also "a latin water pot for a garden." The man who owned these garden tools is described as a "Gentleman," although most of his neighbors are listed as yeomen and husbandmen. It is probable that the early "gentlemen" in the various Rhode Island settlements had as many garden tools as English or French gentlemen of the period. It is also probable that

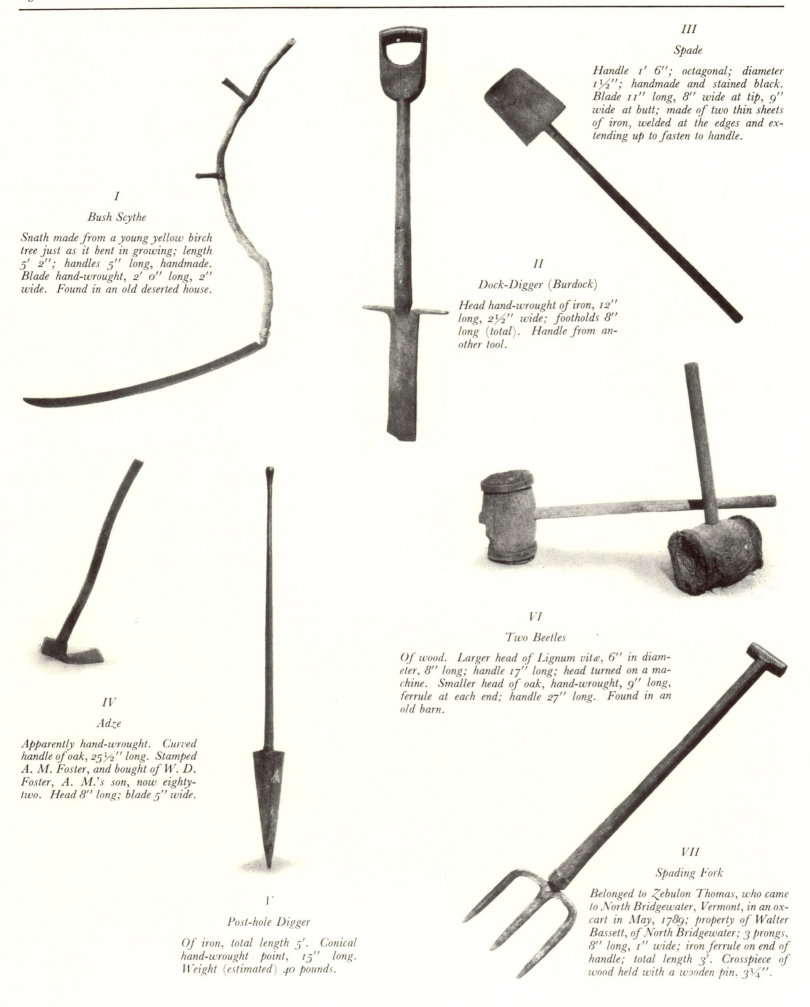

I

Bush Scythe

Snath made from a young yellow birch tree just as it bent in growing; length 5' 2''; handles 5'' long, handmade. Blade hand-wrought, 2' 0'' long, 2'' wide. Found in an old deserted house.

III

Spade

Handle 1' 6''; octagonal; diameter 1½''; handmade and stained black. Blade 11'' long, 8'' wide at tip, 9'' wide at butt; made of two thin sheets of iron, welded at the edges and extending up to fasten to handle.

II

Dock-Digger (Burdock)

Head hand-wrought of iron, 12'' long, 2½'' wide; footholds 8'' long (total). Handle from another tool.

IV

Adze

Apparently hand-wrought. Curved handle of oak, 25½'' long. Stamped A. M. Foster, and bought of W. D. Foster, A. M.'s son, now eighty-two. Head 8'' long; blade 5'' wide.

V

Post-hole Digger

Of iron, total length 5'. Conical hand-wrought point, 15'' long. Weight (estimated) 40 pounds.

VI

Two Beetles

Of wood. Larger head of Lignum vitæ, 6'' in diameter, 8'' long; handle 17'' long; head turned on a machine. Smaller head of oak, hand-wrought, 9'' long, ferrule at each end; handle 27'' long. Found in an old barn.

VII

Spading Fork

Belonged to Zebulon Thomas, who came to North Bridgewater, Vermont, in an ox-cart in May, 1789; property of Walter Bassett, of North Bridgewater; 3 prongs, 8'' long, 1'' wide; iron ferrule on end of handle; total length 3'. Crosspiece of wood held with a wooden pin, 3¾''.

the gentlemen farmers as well as the ordinary husbandmen farmers kept those precious tools in some dry place in the house.

Of course these tools brought over from England and Holland and France by the first planters were worn out and more than worn out, before they were discarded, and it is most improbable that any of them exist to-day. What we do find, sometimes, are tools made in New England, on the more remote farms, in those hard days after King Philip's War, when there was no money left for ordinary men to send abroad for farming gear, and when the agricultural implements made in the small centers of population, for sale, were crude in the extreme and almost prohibitive in price.

I have selected for illustration a few farm-made tools of an undoubtedly early period. They were made on New England farms, where they have been found recently, laid

VIII

Manure Fork or Spade

Handle 4' 8" long, 1⅝" diameter; made from a small oak tree. Iron part 10" long, handwrought. Found in an old abandoned house.

IX

Rake (1830)

Label reads "Handmade by John Pinks." Belonged to Col. Russell in the '40's; after his death sold at auction to W. D. Foster. Tail 6'. Rake 16" wide; head of wood, teeth of wrought iron, 3" long, shaped like short knives.

X

Rake

Of wood throughout, except for two iron braces, 14" long, and six teeth; total length 6' 2"; head 20" long; teeth are driven through the wood and held with nuts; the head, of wood, is 1½" wide and 1¼" thick.

XI

Bucket for Well

About 12" high and 9" across.

XII

Pail

Made from a section of a basswood log, rotted inside, the rotten part pushed out, the outer portion thinned down from within. Bottom set in and fastened with wood pins. Homemade handle added. Homemade hoop at the top. Dimensions: 14" high, 11" wide at bottom, 9" wide at top.

Basswood trees very commonly rot inside, and in former days were cut down, the rotten wood taken out, and containers made like this.

XIII

Cradle

Handle 4' 8": blade 4' long. 3" wide; cradle 3' 7" long, 21" wide.

aside in an old woodshed, or forgotten when the family moved to Ohio. In some way they seem to have escaped the general destruction. They interest me because they illustrate the enormous preliminary labor which the planter could not avoid if he wanted to make even the most simple of gardens in his hand-made world of the eighteenth century.

I have no picture of an axe, it was not really a garden tool. We may take it for granted that the forest trees were cut down

and the stumps were out of the way, before the garden was attempted.

Picture 1 shows a primitive "bush scythe." The snath is made from a young yellow birch tree, just as it bent in growing. The blade is handwrought and the handles are handmade. The dimensions are given here as they are given with each illustration. I show this scythe, because after the trees were felled and the house was built, the garden spot had to

XIV

Flail

Oak (?) handle, turned, 3′ 9″ long.
Flail of oak, handmade, 35″ long.
The usual leather hinge, 2″ wide.
Found in an old deserted house.

XV

Winnowing-Basket

About 4′ long and 2′ wide. It is made of a section of a basswood tree, evidently a large tree and one which had decayed very badly inside. It is somewhat in the form of a very shallow bowl, though to say that it is like a dust-pan in form would be a little more accurate. The handles are made of strap iron and are riveted to the outside of the bowl. The method of use is partially to fill the bowl with beans or grain of some sort that has been threshed but is still mixed with hulls, etc., and stand outdoors when a breeze is blowing, tossing the contents of the basket into the air several times until the air has carried away all the light stuff.

XVI

Corn-Sheller, showing interior and exterior

Made from a section of a basswood tree which had rotted inside. Bark taken off, outside smoothed down; 34½″ high; diameter 24″ more or less; thickness of wall from 2½″ to 3″. 8½″ from the bottom, two stout sticks, 2½″ by 2″, are set in and across. These hold a floor of oak 1½″ thick, made in three parts and held to the crossbeams by pins of wood. In this floor are bored nearly 150 holes each ⅝″ in diameter.

In the upper part was placed corn on the cob, perhaps a bushel at a time. This was pounded with a pestle. The corn, knocked off the cob, fell through the holes.

Length of pestle 31″; Length of head 9″; Diameter of handle 1⅝″; Diameter of head 5½″. Cut from one log, the handle a component part of the head.

XVII

Half-bushel Measure
Diameter 15″; depth 8″.

Peck Measure
Diameter 9½″; depth 4¾″.

have all of its bushes and heavy wild growth cleared away very carefully. This tool was made on the farm to cope with just this condition.

Picture 2 shows a "dock digger," needed at the same time, for the burdock is a stubborn plant, with tough roots, which had to be dug out of the garden spot, most thoroughly, before the planting. It was a very common nuisance.

Picture 3 shows a spade, a common utensil enough. The

handle is of octagonal shape, the blade made of two sheets of iron, welded together at the edges. With this spade, the garden was dug up, and prepared for the planting.

Before the planting, very often, and always before the young growth came up in the spring, every planter saw to his fences. At first, every planter put up a fence of wood—it was the fence most quickly built—and haste was necessary. He took the trunks of small trees and shaped them roughly,

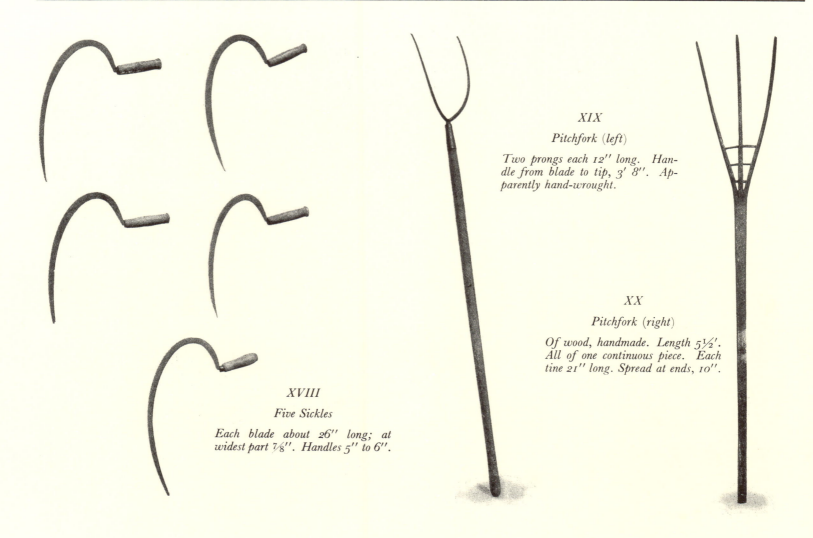

XVIII

Five Sickles

Each blade about 26" long; at widest part ⅞". Handles 5" to 6".

XIX

Pitchfork (left)

Two prongs each 12" long. Handle from blade to tip, 3' 8". Apparently hand-wrought.

XX

Pitchfork (right)

Of wood, handmade. Length 5½'. All of one continuous piece. Each tine 21" long. Spread at ends, 10".

with an adze perhaps, such an adze as is illustrated by Picture 4. The handle is made of oak, handwrought. Before the handle was made, the tool to shape the handle had to be manufactured by hand, and was. The amount of labor on a lonely farm in New England is simply incredible!

Number 5 shows a post-hole digger. It weighs about 40 pounds. Any attempt to dig a post-hole with a spade will convince any man that a post-hole digger must have been an essential part of a pioneer's equipment. Especially when it is remembered that the planter's garden was being fenced from necessity and must have posts set deep enough to stand the charge of a bull or the dead weight of a pressing herd of cattle. There were wild animals, too, such as bears, who would try to pull down the rails.

Number 6 is a picture of two beetles. The larger head is of lignum vitae, the smaller of oak. With these beetles, the fence posts were driven into the ground. And there is hardly any other implement more conspicuous in the old inventories, than are these "beetles" and the "beetle-rings."

Number 7 is a spading fork. This was brought up from Rhode Island to Vermont in 1789, by Zebulon Thomas. He travelled up to North Bridgewater, in May, with all his farming equipment loaded onto an ox cart.

Number 8 is a manure fork, made from a small oak tree. Both handle and iron fork are handmade.

All of these eight implements are really very old. Number 9, a garden rake, is not so ancient. It seems to have been made in 1830. The teeth are of wrought iron. The handle is of wood, made by hand.

Number 10 is another rake, older, with 6 iron teeth which are driven through the wood, and held with nuts. After sowing the seed, raking a garden is rather a garden necessity, and this rake may have been used in the garden as well as in the hayfield.

The watering of a garden is considered essential today. In a dry season, or after transplanting, it does seem unavoidable. I do not know if many of the early planters watered

their gardens. Perhaps not. I know of at least one garden in Rhode Island which never gets watered even in the dryest season, except during the time of transplanting, when the seedlings would surely perish without a bucket or so of water from the well.

Probably the planters managed about that way. In the Plymouth Colony inventory, the gentleman's watering pot was listed as I have noted, but this picture, Number 11, shows the type of bucket which hung in the planter's well, on every homestead; and Number 12 shows the ordinary sort of bucket in which the water, once drawn out of the well, was carried down into the garden, and poured onto the seedlings if they were watered at all. Before the water was carried, the bucket was made right on the farm where it was to be used. The process of making it is described on the page with the picture.

Numbers 13 and 14 are cradle and flail.

Number 15 is a winnowing basket, showing what a husbandman, on a lonely farm, in the remote hills, could devise.

Number 16 is a very interesting corn sheller.

Number 17 shows the usual measures for corn and beans, used everywhere. The corn never grew in the garden, but the quaint old tools by which it was harvested and made ready for the family bread, were farm-made, as were the garden tools, and show, perhaps, why there was not an infinite amount of time left for gardening and things of the garden proper.

Number 18 is a picture of five sickles. Number 20 shows the pitchforks for the hay.

There is one other garden accessory, which I have not pictured here, but it was common, both cheap and abundant. This was the garden basket.

In 1683, an inventory includes both "wicker baskets" and "Indian Baskets." Usually, only Indian baskets are listed. Sometimes, "Indian bowles," or "trays." In 1637 Gov. Winthrop's wife sent an "Indian basket" to Mrs. Tyndall in England. It seems evident and reasonable to suppose that the Indians furnished the colonists with all the baskets they could possibly need, and that baskets were used in the work of the garden whenever such use was practicable. To have plenty of baskets in the tool house is, today, a luxury.

On the shelf of our tool house, there is always a garden-soiled copy or two of some seedsman's catalogue, where directions as to when and what and how to plant can be found, I suppose—I have never read one.

On the shelf in the fire room of the early planter, there was occasionally a book or so on husbandry, on how to make a garden. If the planter planted in New England according to such of those books as I have seen, he didn't do it twice.

By an inventory of 1633, Samuel Fuller appears to have owned a copy of *Goode's Husbandry* worth 6 pence. Elder Brewster in 1644 had a book called *Of the use of Silk Worms*. Of course the Plymouth settlers were not attempting to grow mulberry trees before 1644, and we know that

they consulted the Indians, not *Goode's Husbandry*, when they really wanted to know how to grow some crops. But it is not without interest to see that there was a garden literature in the Plantation of Plymouth in the first years of the settlement of Rhode Island. (Much of the Plymouth Plantation is now a part of the State of Rhode Island—a confusing condition of affairs for any historian trying to keep strictly to Rhode Island material.) I might add that the Brewsters of Plymouth owned a large *Book of Husbandry* worth 10 shillings 6 pence. And that Captain Miles Standish, of all people, owned a copy of *The Country Farmer* valued at 8 shillings.

All this is a century before the establishment of the Redwood Library, and the introduction into the Rhode Island plantations of the books listed on page 221. Always, you see, we had men of letters.

THE GARDENS OF THE MERCHANTS

BEFORE THE REVOLUTION

PELEG SANFORD, Governor of Rhode Island, wrote in 1680, when trying to answer a questionnaire sent out by the English Board of Trade:

"We answer—that as for merchants, we have none, but the most of our Colony live comfortably by improving the wilderness. That the great obstruction concerning Trade is the want of Merchants and men of considerable Estate among us."

The Rev. Jacob Bailey, in 1754, wrote in his Journal, when travelling about New England, "Providence is a most beautiful place."

Between these dates, the merchants, and the men of considerable estate, long wanted, at last arrived, and made Providence, and indeed all the towns about Narragansett Bay, "most beautiful."

MERCHANT GARDENS OF PROVIDENCE

It is curious that even as Peleg Sanford was writing to England that he knew of none in Rhode Island who might properly be called merchants, two of the old planters of Town Street in Providence were asking the Town Council to grant them little spots of land opposite their home lots, on the river bank. They wanted to build warehouses and wharves.

There is, to be sure, evidence of an export trade in Providence, as early as 1652, when flour, tobacco, and peas, grown in the gardens of the Rhode Island planters, were shipped to Labrador. In 1665 William Field of the little Field garden on Town Street was sending some trading venture to the Barbadoes. But it was not till the end of the century that a real merchant came to town—Gideon Crawford, from Scotland.

He was what might be called a professional merchant,

The warehouses of the merchants on Long Wharf, Newport, in the early eighteenth century

The side court of the John Brown house, showing the original marble figures of 1786

recognized as such. By 1690, he was owner of a warehouse lot; between the little gardens of those old planters, Field and Winsor, he had a garden of his own for the use of his wife, Freelove Fenner, a Town Street girl. But he was distinctly a merchant, not a farmer.

In a book of land transactions of the years around 1705, the citizens of Providence appear as "Planter," "Husbandman," "Yeoman," "Weaver," "Servant" and the like. The term most in use was "Husbandman." It does represent more clearly than "planter" exactly what most of them had become by that date. But Gideon Crawford is definitely described as a "Merchant of Providence."

As merchant, he exported rum to the West Indies, and brought back negroes for the slave market. It was lucrative business. He owned a "boat," as he called it, named *Freelove* for his wife. He died young, and this wife of his managed the business while the boys were growing up.

We get a very interesting inventory of the Crawford property at the death of the eldest son, in 1720. There was by this time a special warehouse for the storage of rum, and another for the storage of salt. There was a shop, and a backshop, besides. In searching the inventory for garden supplies imported by the Crawfords, I found listed "in the back shop," sickle, pruning knife, and trowel. They seem to have dealt mostly in dry goods, aside from rum, negroes, and such oddities as "4 doz. brass Jews Harpes"; but in one of the drawers of his main shop, the appraisers found "whetstones" valued at 2 shillings 6 pence, and "seeds" valued at 2 shillings.

In the north warehouse chamber, there was wheat, malt,

rye, beans in a cask, and Indian corn. In the north warehouse proper, they found 80 bushels of oats and 2 bushels of rye, some wheat and hops, and 3 hogsheads of tobacco.

In the family barn, there was hay—naturally—and "Rakes." Oats, also; and somewhere they found "sheepsheares," which would have been expected because the Crawfords had 68 sheep including the lambs. There were also on the place two old plows, a tumbrill with horse chain, and a cart with wheels.

At the time of the death of this Captain William Crawford, we find him owning not only one half of his father's old boat, the *Freelove*, but also a boat called after his own wife, the *Sarah*; the *Sarah* was worth, "with appurtenances, 400 pounds." He had pasturelands and cornfields, "at the neck." He had a new house, furnished with great luxury—it sounds like luxury, anyway. A "Clock in a Case," "6 pictures"—Peleg Sanford's merchants, men of considerable estate, have at last arrived in the Colony.

And all men shared in this more comfortable life.

In the opening years of the nineteenth century, Crawford Allen of Providence built for his sister Candace a very fine house set in a most lovely garden; the house still stands on Benevolent Street near the old Crawford warehouse below the hill. The present owner, Mrs. John Carter Brown, has rearranged the garden a little, but it still remains the best example of a town garden of those early years. A photograph is shown on page 152.

In 1762, the Providence *Gazette* published, on November 27, the two following advertisements which describe the ordinary town and country residences which this new wealth was making possible for many people.

Courtesy of Marsden J. Perry Esq.

The John Brown house, showing the entrance gate and the stone coping with the fence. See also page 432

TO BE SOLD
A FARM IN SMITHFIELD

About five miles from Providence Court House; containing 300 acres, or better; with 3 dwelling houses thereon; one of which is a new house 42 feet front, 56 feet rear, 2 stories high, an entry way of 10 feet wide through it, a garden near it of about an acre, inclosed with pale Fence, and a good well in said Garden; also another well near the kitchen of said house. There is a good barn, cribb, and saw mill on the farm, 3 good orchards of the best fruit trees for cyder; the whole of said farm is fenced in with chestnut rails.

Inquire of

Hiram Paget at his Insurance Office.

TO BE SOLD

A convenient well-finished Dwelling House, 2 stories high, with 5 rooms on a Floor, a very good cellar under the same, and a handsome Garden adjoining, pleasantly situated in the Back Street, [Benefit Street it is called today] directly opposite the Presbyterian Meeting House in Providence. Terms of Sale may be known of William Potter, living at Warwick, who will give an indisputable title.

As the Rev. Jacob Bailey wrote, Providence had, by 1754, two streets of "Painted houses." One of these was of course the old Town Street with the little orchards and the little garden spots, described in the section on The Gardens of the Planters. The other was called Back or Benefit Street. Above the two streets rose a "delightful hill . . . , gradually ascending to a great distance, all cut into gardens, orchards, pleasant fields, and beautiful enclosures."

In the counting rooms of this new merchant class, fortunes had been accumulated which were making it possible for them to build these new houses up on the delightful hill, and to make these new gardens, in which, by the way, they planted everything they could get hold of. There was no need any longer to make the garden pay; they wanted "rarities," regardless of expense, and "rarities" they had. In 1736, John Comer records in his diary that he ate a "rare melon" which had been grown in the garden of Col. Power.

Courtesy of Marsden J. Perry Esq.

A side view of the John Brown house, built in 1786. It is today, as it was in the year of its building, the finest house in all Rhode Island

But perhaps the Rev. Mr. Comer merely meant that it was late in the season for melons; which it was. The melon was not, to be sure, as unseasonable as the "new corn in the ear" advertised "to be sold" by Samuel Chase in the *Gazette* of December 18, 1762. Chase had on hand also "a quantity of Callavancoes or Beans." And it is certainly rare to hear of callavancoes.

The home-lot of Col. Power with its garden where "rare" melons grew became, by the marriage of Hope Power to James Brown, the property of her son, John Brown, greatest of the great merchants of Providence. In 1786, he built a mansion house in the middle of the lot, which is today, as it was in the year of its building, the finest house in all Rhode Island.

The garden, which he mentions specifically in his will, was on the east side of the house. There was, according to the will, a "green yard" on the west side of the house.

The site of the old garden has been obliterated, by the taste of a later day. Old planting about the house still exists, however, and there is still the "green yard." The Estate was purchased in 1901 by Marsden J. Perry. He purchased and transplanted at the same time some very beautiful box borders growing in the old garden at "The Mount" in Bristol. And at the gate of the old Brown mansion he planted a huge boxwood tree, some 15 feet in height and over 30 feet in circumference, which he had found in the ruins of the Roome garden, down in the Narragansett Country.

Another Merchant of that early day was Mr. John Merritt. "A staunch supporter of King's Church" was John Merritt, "an Englishman of ample means and scholarly tastes, who came to Providence, probably from Newport, in or near

1746. He was prosperous, liberal, kindly, a man of culture and experience, yet withal a bit autocratic and hotheaded. His two-hundred-acre estate lay to the east of the present Arlington Avenue, and extended to the banks of the Seekonk. To a later generation it was known as the 'Moses Brown Farm.'. . . His land was well farmed, having two barns, a large coach house, a sheep house, granary, gardens, and orchards. . . . He died in 1770, leaving the best Library in Providence."

In the garden on this farm there was a "Grotto." On May Day, in 1838, the scholars of the Greene Street School in Providence marched out to the Moses Brown Farm, and held May Day Exercises. Margaret Fuller, the Margaret Fuller of Emerson and Concord, had been a teacher in this Providence School that winter, and she composed a poem for the occasion which the children sang to a flute accompaniment:

> "White blossoms deck the apple tree
> Blue violets the plain".

And the King and the Queen of the May were crowned in the "Grotto" in the garden.

THE NARRAGANSETT GARDENS

The most important of these gardens of the Merchant class in the Narragansett Country before the Revolution was that of Mr. Roome, the loyalist, whose estate was confiscated by the colonial authorities and given over to such neglect that within ten years it was nothing but a meadow where the boxwood, "clipped in to shape," stretched up, dishevelled, for any man to rescue if he would.

Mr. Roome was an Englishman, they say, not a colonial, although men of his name were with the earliest Portsmouth planters. He came to Newport from London in 1761, as agent for several London business firms. He secured much real estate in dealing with debtors, and about five years after his arrival he possessed himself of Henry Collins' farm at Boston Neck in the Narragansett Country. (Collins was sold out by Roome under assignment.) He also foreclosed on Collins' town house in Newport. Fortunately Mr. Collins had given away in 1748 "a great part of a lot called the Bowling Green" to the Company of the Redwood Library. It is on this bowling green that the Redwood Library building was erected. It is of this Henry Collins that the Hon. William Hunter of Newport said, in his Centennial Address:

"He has taste; the sense of the beautiful in nature, conjoined with the impulse to see it imitated and surpassed."

Dr. Waterhouse called him the "Lorenzo de' Medici of Newport." Now, the Collins farm in the Narragansett Country consisted of 700 acres. The taste of Mr. Collins being the talk of his day, it is probable that the gardens on this farm taken over by Mr. Roome were really beautiful. But during the eight years of Mr. Roome's occupancy, he so altered the estate, and gave such famous house-parties, that the garden is always known as the Roome garden, and poor Mr. Collins gets no credit at all.

One early writer says that a "stately avenue of buttonwood trees" led to the mansion. Of course that was Collins' work. Buttonwood trees planted by Roome would not have become stately during the few years of his occupancy. But the same authority tells us that this buttonwood avenue (there were so few roads in the Narragansett Country that most of the houses were off in the pastures of their enormous farms, and a cart road had to be run through from house to highway, which could be called an avenue if necessary) ran past "fish ponds, and through flower beds, in the formal arrangements of the time." Some marks of the former fish ponds and flower gardens are said to have been dimly visible in 1907.

Updike tells us that the Roome garden contained "the rarest native and exotic varieties"—of what he does not say. The boxwood that went to Providence is the only vestige that survived the horrors of tenant ownership after the Revolution.

Of course, an English merchant, employed by Londoners, could not have desired a revolution in his trading section of America; his interests were served by a speedy crushing of the colonials; and he appears to have thought that they would be speedily crushed. He worked as an avowed Loyalist, and it is only surprising that he was not killed by the riff-raff which, with nothing to lose by any change of government, swarmed about the camps of the Colonial Army, and harried the countryside in the name of Patriotism.

Roome was soon thrown into prison. His confiscated estate was at first rented to Stephen Boyer for one year for 97 pounds 10 shillings. The next year, 1779, John Gardner took it over. He entertained Col. Angell and other officers of the American Army; as they tell us in their diaries. They write of a very agreeable day, at Mr. Gardner's, but they say nothing about gardens.

The British came over from Newport one night, and stole a considerable number of sheep and cows from the farm. The slaves of Mr. Roome soon disappeared. The government had tried to make them work for the new proprietors, but it couldn't be done.

Then, slaves and cattle stripped from the estate, the government cut down the trees—for firewood, "for the benefit of the Poor." The 700 acres, made into something of beauty by these merchants of Newport and London, civilized, cared for, were soon torn apart. Under the name of the Point Judith Farm they figure in the records of the State for a few years, and finally, dismembered, pass into oblivion.

Judge William Potter "inherited a large landed estate in South Kingston, one mile north of Kingston, and was otherwise wealthy." He had many honors, held distinguished positions, but in 1790 fell under the influence of Jemima Wilkinson. "For her accommodation, he built a large addition to his already spacious mansion. She lived there five years." At last, when Jemima had departed, to form her colony of Disciples in Jerusalem, Yates County, New York (I think he went with her but soon came back), Judge Potter, disillusioned, turned his belated attention to mundane affairs. He found himself deeply in debt. Updike, writing in 1847, says: "Judge Potter was compelled to mortgage his estate—he finally, in 1807, sold it. The late Hon. E. R. Potter purchased the Homestead, but the elegant garden, with pastures, borders, shrubbery, summerhouses, fruit orchard—his ancient mansion, with the high and costly fences, outhouses and cookery establishment, were in ruins, and within a few years, the whole of the buildings have been removed, and a small and suitable house for a Tenant has been built in its place." News must have come to Judge Potter of the wonderful gardens which Jemima Wilkinson was planting in Jerusalem, New York. I wonder how he felt.

MOWBRA CASTLE

In Belleville on the old Post Road, near Wickford in the Narragansett Country, there is standing today a battered wreck of a house called, for no reason I can discover, "Mowbra Castle." At the time of the great land grab after King Philip's War, a certain Phillips of Newport had received a grant of some mythical number of unsurveyed acres in the old planting grounds of the Narragansett Indians. He built the northern part of the house—just as we see it today—in 1709, and then died, leaving a son, Christopher, who added the southern part to the house and "embelished the estate." He went into trade, making enough money to pay for all the embellishments he could think of, and all the later embellishments devised by his son, Christopher, Jr. The garden is said to have been delightful, and there are still traces about the old house of the old planting.

Writing in 1847, Updike tells us of another Mr. Phillips, a

The Phillips house, in Belleville

"Young Ladies' Seminary," Warren, in the year 1834. There was a large garden and "playground for the convenience of physical exercise"

Mr. Peter Phillips, born in 1731, who was a man of considerable property. "He owned the handsomest estate in Wickford, his house was neat and pleasantly situated and his gardens and grounds tastefully arranged. Since his death all has gone to decay." By 1907 it had disappeared altogether. I am told that the estate even in its last days had been locally famous for its beautiful flower garden.

THE MERCHANTS OF WARREN

In Warren, there was much prosperity before the Revolution. The Warren merchant class built a number of substantial brick houses, with the usual garden leading out of the house-yard on the sunny side of the estate. Josiah Quincy wrote in his diary of 1801, "The houses are of two stories, generally painted, and within appear remarkably clean and commodious." Another observer says that the finest residence in town was painted "a peach bloom tint, before 1778." But with the war came stagnation, and the river which was the life of the town for two hundred years is too shallow for modern shipping. The great brick house of old Barney of Barneysville, on the river just above Warren, with its rotten wharves and abandoned pleasure ground, is a derelict of a forgotten past.

THE GARDENS OF THE LAWYERS

These Rhode Island merchants of the eighteenth century employed many lawyers; they seem to have enjoyed doing so. It cost them something.

Lawyer Cole of Providence, for instance, built himself "a house with five rooms on a floor" and laid out about it what he calls a "handsome garden." He says his view is "inferior to no place whatever." The garden is now a part of Tockwotten Park.

A celebrated member of the Rhode Island Bar, James Mitchell Varnum, built a fine house in East Greenwich, before the Revolution, and planted elm trees which still flourish. It still has "spacious lawns" but of the old garden nothing now exists except the "flowering shrubs."

Judge Bull of Newport grew cabbages. His people had lived in Newport since the year of its founding. In the eighteenth century they went into trade. Most profitably—for they

built a new house, and Henry Bull studied Law, and was duly appointed Judge of the Superior Court of Rhode Island, and had time to cultivate a garden, of which we know nothing except what Updike tells us in the following little story:

"When Judge Bull made up his mind to practise Law, he went into his garden, to exercise his talents in addressing the court and jury. He then selected 5 cabbages in one row, for judges, and 12 cabbages in another row for jurors. After trying his hand there awhile, he went boldly into court, and took upon himself the duties of an advocate, and a little observation and experience there, convinced him that the same cabbages were in the court house which he thought he had left in the garden."

But there is another famous lawyer of this period whose career was even more important to a history of the old gardens of Rhode Island. This is that extraordinary man, William Bradford of Bristol. In his youth he had been a practising physician, in Warren. Before 1758 he had moved down the road to Bristol, where, about 1764, he began to practise law.

He owned a house and garden on the northeast corner of Hope and State Streets, and we get a glimpse of this garden while reading a Bristol poet's account of the bombardment of Bristol by the British fleet:

"In seventeen hundred and seventy five
Our Bristol town was much surprised

*   *   *   *

At eight o'clock by signal given,
Our peaceful atmosphere was riven
By British balls, both grape and round
As plenty afterwards were found.

*   *   *   *

But oh to hear the doleful cries
Of people running for their lives.
Women with children in their arms
Running away to the farms."

The residence of General James M. Varnum, built in 1767, in East Greenwich. From a photograph made in 1887

It seems that "a great gap was made in the stone wall near the residence of Governor Bradford, and while that gentleman was climbing the fence which separated his house from his garden, a frolicsome shot knocked into the air the board on which his hand had just rested."

The Governor Bradford house, now the property of Rudolph Haffenraffer

next to his back yard where he made tombstones, conveniently near the graves they were to mark. Notice the standardized size of his garden.

There were doctors, too, whose very calling in the earlier days demanded a garden patch. In 1671, the town of Newport realized this and granted land for a garden to Thomas Rodman, a practising physician. The first recorded garden in Providence belonged to Dr. James, as I stated in the earlier section of this garden history. But aside from the gardens of Dr. Spencer and Dr. Ayrault in East Greenwich (already noted), and that of Dr. Babcock in Westerly, I can find no record of a doctor's garden in the

The Lawyer Bradford had become the Deputy Governor of the State. His garden was evidently a definite enclosure, separated from his house-yard by a fence of wood. There was a gate in the fence, probably, but Bradford didn't have much time.

His house in the town having been destroyed by the bombardment, Governor Bradford in 1783 acquired the confiscated Isaac Royall farm of 368 acres, which lay between Mount Hope Bay and the little town of Bristol, the western portion being the old planting ground of the Wampanoag Indians. There on the slopes of Mount Hope he seems to have lived with some degree of magnificence. He had a celebrated garden, of which traces now remain behind the house. George Washington visited him once, staying a whole week. The house is now the property of Mr. Rudolph Haffenraffer. Great mulberry trees in the corner of the garden still bear delicious fruit every year.

DOCTORS AND OTHERS

There were others besides the lawyers who profited by this greater wealth in the hands of the merchant class. Colonel Zephaniah Andrews, for example. Colonel Andrews was a mason builder, living in Providence. The magnificent house of John Brown, on Power Street, was built under his supervision. He himself lived down by the river. Henry Howland writes:

"In 1806 there was still standing on the houselot of Colonel Zephaniah Andrews; his mansion house, a two story house next above, and on the front a one story shop and a large store house and garden below the mansion. His Estate ran to the channel. At the foot of his garden there were stone steps that led to the water, where the north side of Pine Street now is. From these steps my first fishing was done; with a pin hook. . ."

In 1750, John Anthony Angell was making, in Providence, artistic and expensive tombstones for the wealthy merchants and their families.

We see in the town records that he too had a garden. "Upon the petition of John Anthony Angell, praying that the town would be pleased to grant him the liberty of an acre, or half of an acre, of Town's Land near the burying ground, next adjoining to his own land there, in order to inlarge his garden, on such conditions as the town shall think proper, etc." The town did give him land for a garden, right

White mulberry tree in the garden of the Governor Bradford house

Colony until the nineteenth century, with the gardens of Dr. Eldredge in East Greenwich, Dr. Wilbur in Fall River, and Dr. Solomon Drown in Foster, all of which I have described in their proper place in this long chronicle.

Of course, Dr. Peter Turner built a house in East Greenwich in 1774, but I have never heard that he owned a garden. Last summer I found old herbs growing in the grass in his back yard, but there really should be somewhat better evidence of the herb gardens of our early Rhode Island physicians.

I feel with Anne Royall, who wrote in 1826 that Providence is indeed "a very romantic town." I feel that there should be more to say of the old gardens before the Revolution. But, like Anne Royall, I know there isn't. Like her, I must add one detail of its later charm. "The streets . . . have handsome sidewalks, planted with trees."

This planting the public street with trees is not a very old habit; it came into being because of poverty, I think. Few at the close of the Revolution had money enough to live in luxurious solitude, few in power had the habit of a secluded existence; they were of the common people, for the most part, gregarious always by choice or necessity. It was about 1800 probably that the gardens of Rhode Island came round to the front of the house, grew smaller; two patches, one each side the front walk; and the elm-bordered village street which we knew in our youth, came into existence. That date may be a little early. The Main Street of the village of Fall River was first planted with elms in 1840. Josiah Quincy wrote in his diary of 1801: "We proceeded to Warren. Rows of Cherry Trees, planted in front of most of the houses, give the place an uncommon air of improvement and taste." He was apparently not used to the sight of street planting. Last summer the Town Council of East Greenwich took down, in order to widen the road for motor traffic, a row of magnificent elms, planted just after 1800. There are signs that the majority of Rhode Island people are not willing to keep even the old street planting of the past. But in a few communities, such as the blessed village of Peace Dale, we can still see in all their beauty great elm trees bordering the village street.

The Providence Athenæum, opened in 1838. The sidewalk was built and the trees planted in that same year

A MERCHANT OF WESTERLY

In 1648, in Portsmouth on Rhode Island, there was a young man who could not read or write; yet he was a freeman, owner of a freehold, and he planted a garden beside his house, and he married, and had many children.

Of a restless disposition, he soon sold his freehold to his neighbors; Francis Brayton bought the garden; and the restless young man purchased a thousand acres of land on the very edge of the present State of Rhode Island, in the town of Westerly, in the days when there was no town of Westerly, and the old Pequod Trail, winding through the wilderness from the Narragansett Shore into the colony of Connecticut, was the only roadway to his new purchase.

From the paintings by Blackburn

Joshua Babcock   *Mrs. Joshua Babcock*

Along this Pequod Trail he drove his sheep and cattle, he and his wife and children riding the horses of the Portsmouth farm. On high land, overlooking Pawcatuck River, one mile east of Pawcatuck Village, he built a house, which stands there today. He fenced in a garden by the house, planted an apple orchard, walled in a meadow for the cows, and devoted the rest of the 1000 acres to the raising of sheep. I wouldn't be sure that he didn't keep an acre or so for a wood lot, but as far as the sheep go, they are historic.

His boys grew up on this sheep farm; the eldest son, James, inherited by English law the mansion house and garden and most of the property, but there was enough for all. When James died, in 1736, it was not 1000 but 2000 acres that he left behind him; with innumerable sheep, many valuable horses, and negro slaves to work the whole plantation. James could sign his own name, and in doing so, altered the spelling. From Badcock it became Babcock.

The son of James was Joshua. He was born on the Westerly plantation in 1707. He went to Yale—does it surprise you?—and after he had been graduated, he went to Boston to study law—or was it medicine?—and when he knew that, he went to Europe to study something else, and to travel about until the death of his father made it necessary for him to return to the sheep farm in Westerly.

He immediately started to practice medicine. This was in 1736. He seems to have been an excellent physician, with a great reputation in his day; he owned the largest retail store in Westerly—that was how he made his money. He was certainly a pretty good architect, for he enlarged the old farm house, and did it so well that Field in his *History of Rhode Island* calls it "a fine example of early Colonial architecture," and says it is "admired for its strength and beauty."

Around the house he did much planting; he knew Bishop Berkeley and the theories of his day. He made over the garden of his grandfather into a very fine garden indeed. Updike, writing in 1848, says:

"The family mansion, though dilapidated, is still standing on the old country road one mile east of the village of Pawca-

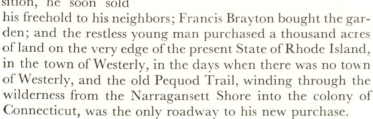

The Babcock mansion, in Westerly

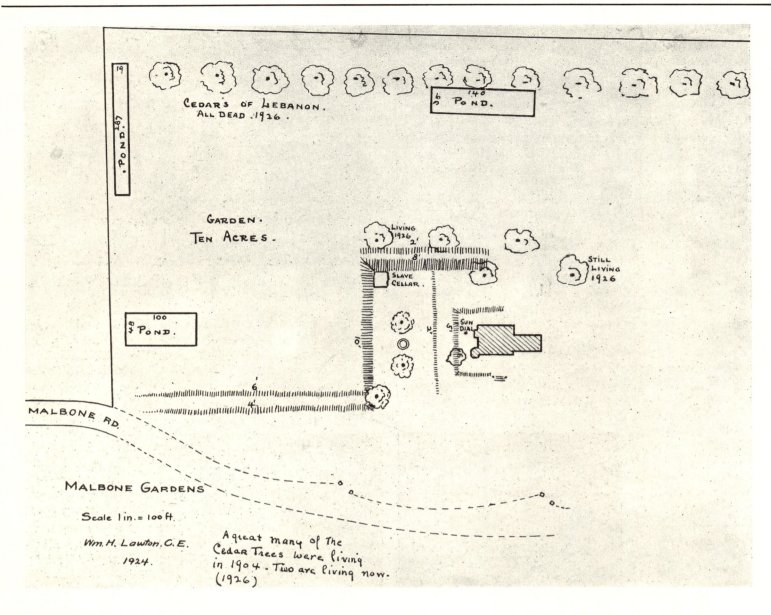

CEDARS OF LEBANON.
ALL DEAD .1926.

POND.

GARDEN.
TEN ACRES.

POND.

SLAVE CELLAR.

LIVING 1926

STILL LIVING 1926

SUN DIAL.

MALBONE RD.

MALBONE GARDENS

Scale 1 in. = 100 ft.

Wm. H. Lawton. C.E.
1924.

A great many of The Cedar Trees were living in 1904. Two are living now. (1926)

tuck in Westerly. The tall box standing on each side of the path leading to the house, the massive gate, the once expensive fences and enclosures, now in ruins,—and the other evidences of departed grandeur—impress on the beholder that this was one of the plantations of the old aristocracy of Naragansett." Aristocracy?

Weedon, writing in 1910, says "the boxtrees line the approach to the front door." Apparently, beyond the boxtrees, there is little that is definitely known of the old planting.

"MALBONE"

There was in colonial Rhode Island in the eighteenth century, one really great country house, comparable only with the manor houses of Virginia and the Hudson.

It was built on the Island of Rhode Island, in 1741, by a Newport merchant, Godfrey Malbone.

One of the Malbones of Princess Anne County, Virginia, Godfrey had come to Newport about the year 1720, and married a Newport girl, Margaret Scott. When the Malbone heir, Godfrey Malbone, Jr., was born in 1724, the Malbone town house, a huge affair facing the Parade, was much in evidence; the Malbone warehouses by the waterside were one of the sights of the town; the Malbone ships were known in every port in the West Indies, at every castle on the coast of Africa; and Captain Malbone was almost ready to settle down and build a country house, after the manner of his kind.

In 1728, Peter Harrison, an English architect, came to Newport in the train of Bishop Berkeley. As the years went by, Malbone saw from his own windows the building of the Redwood Library, the Market, the Synagogue; he even served on building committees with Harrison. It is not unreasonable to think that he engaged Harrison to draw up plans for his new house in the country.

The land he had—about 600 acres, a mile north of Newport, running down the slope of Mianotonomy Hill to the water's edge.

The ancient cedar left standing at "Malbone"

He had the building material also. On a great plantation he owned in Brooklyn, in Connecticut, there was a quarry of pink sandstone, and he thought it a simple matter to get out the stone, send it by ox-cart to Providence, and ship it down the Bay in his own ships to his own wharf at the foot of the long slope of meadow land where the Malbone country house was built, in six acres of formal garden, in 1741.

In 1766, on the seventh of June, it was burned to the ground.

There is no picture of that "Malbone" of pink sandstone,

tance, but is not extraordinary for the architecture, being a clumsy Dutch model. Round it are pretty gardens and terraces, with canals and baisens for water, from whence you have a delightful view of the town and harbour of Newport, with the shipping lying there."

"August, 1744 [A month later, on his return to Newport from Boston]

"I put up at Nicholl's at the Sign of the White Horse, and lying there that night was almost eaten up alive with bugs. . . .

The present-day house at "Malbone," seen from the fish-pond, with a view of the terraces and the site of the old garden

which was the finest house in all the English colonies of its own brief day. There is left only the pink sandstone, the faint outlines of an old garden, an ornamental fish pond, an ancient cedar, a terrace toward the west.

And the tales of the travellers.

In the *Itinerarium* of Dr. Alexander Hamilton occur the following passages:

"July, 1744. [Three years after the building of "Malbone"]

"I went with Dr. Moffatt at ten o'clock to see a house about half a mile out of town, built lately by one Captain Malbone, a substantial trader here. It is the largest and most magnificent dwelling house I have seen in America. It is built entirely of hewn stone of a reddish color; the sides of the windows and the cornerstones of the house being painted like white marble. It is three stories high, and the rooms are spacious and magnificent. There is a large lanthern or cupola on the roof, which is covered with sheet lead. The whole staircase which is very spacious and large, is done with mahogany wood. This house makes a grand show at a dis-

Dr. Moffatt took me out to walk near the town, where there are a great many pleasant walks amidst avenues of trees. We viewed Mr. Malbone's house and gardens, and as we returned home, met Malbone himself, with whom we had some talk about news. We were met by a handsome bona roba in a flaunting dress, who laughed us full in the face. Mr. Malbone and I thought her a paramour of Moffatt's, for neither of us knew her. We bantered him upon it, and discovered the truth of our conjectures by raising a blush upon his face."

"Tuesday, August 21, 1744. [A few days later]

"I walked out betwixt 12 and 1 with Dr. Moffatt and viewed Malbone's house and gardens. We went to the cupola at the top, from which we had a pretty view of the town of Newport and of the sea toward Block Island; and behind the house, of a pleasant mount, gradually ascending to a great height."

This Dr. Hamilton had a fairly good knowledge of the

Another view of the old cedar, the only one still standing at "Malbone"

full of pieces-of-eight and the bones of Spanish prisoners. Oh, yes, they had Spanish prisoners in Newport, lots of them. My great-aunt Susannah had to give up her bedroom to a number, who were temporarily lodged in her father's house, because the jail was full, and they had to be kept somewhere until their ransom was paid.

One of the Malbone privateers was named the *Charming Betty*, and another the *Young Godfrey*, for the children of the house. You can read all about them in Chapin's *Rhode Island Privateers*.

The firm of Malbone ran slave ships also, importing their own slaves from the coast of Africa. The Malbone plantation at Brooklyn was probably stocked with laborers by this method, a whole shipload of the poor things having been taken up there at one time, according to the most unreliable of Rhode Island historians, the Rev. Edward Peterson. You really ought to read his account of the transaction. But it is obvious that 600 acres of farm and garden could have been kept in a high state of cultivation in New England in the eighteenth century in no other way. And "Malbone" was so kept.

important estates in the colonies in 1744; he had travelled widely. He had been a classmate of Dr. Moffatt's at Edinburgh University in his youth. His opinion in regard to the size and magnificence of "Malbone" can hardly be disregarded. And without doubt the gardens about the house had much to do with his verdict, for he thinks, you remember, the architecture of the house itself a bit clumsy—Dutch.

The Malbones lived in state. It would seem from a letter written to Godfrey Malbone by Robert Morris, Captain of the *Duke of Marlborough*, a Malbone ship, that this state was maintained by the most profitable privateering that ever was known.

"New Providence, March 18th, 1745.

". . . the 14th of February about 12, saw a sail off Cape Antons, which we took in about six hours. She belonged to Nanz, came from Logan, and designed to touch at the Havanna. Her cargo is by the manifest about 250 Hds. of sugar, some Indigo, some hides and tobacco. The Captain says she is richer than we expected. . . . I am now bound on a cruise in concert with a snow and a sloop, as you will see by the enclosed, to intercept if possible a fleet of 16 sail bound from Cape Francois. . . ."

He did.

This captured merchandise was brought to Newport and sold from the Malbone warehouses. Theoretically, a duty was paid on every article to the Crown which issued the permit to each ship owner who wished to engage in this irregular warfare. But nobody ever supposed that any such tax could be collected. A little, perhaps—but what would you have? And it is still believed in Newport that Captain Malbone built a tunnel under his gardens, connecting his wharf with his magnificent country house; a secret tunnel, so that he might smuggle ashore the rich prizes of which the Crown conveniently knew nothing. I think it quite probable, and really expect to see the tunnel discovered, one of these days,

The cedar on the upper terrace was blown down in 1919. Long Pond shows in the distance

The most distinguished visitor that "Malbone" ever knew was young George Washington. The following entry occurs in his Expense Book:

"February 26, 1756, Thursday. Rhode Island. By cash to Mr. Malbone's Servants. 4.00 pounds. To a bowle broke 4 pounds.

From Ledger A op. cit. G. Washington"

Unfortunately, no Washington diary for the year 1756 has yet been found, so all we know is that Washington came north that winter to see Governor Shirley in Boston, that he had never been north before, that he lingered a week in New York, seeing the sights, and that he went to Boston by the circuitous route of Newport, arriving in Boston the day after the dated entry I have just quoted.

He could have seen little of the Malbone flower gardens,

for nothing blooms in Rhode Island on Washington's Birthday but the crocus, and there is snow on the ground more
likely than not. But he must have seen the formal garden
spaces, the pink sandstone sundial, the fish ponds, and the
cedars; it is interesting to know that
Washington did see in Rhode Island an
elaborate, formal garden, some years before he laid out the present gardens of
Mount Vernon. How much "Malbone"
influenced the development of Mt. Ver-
·non, I do not know.

It was ten years later that the great
house burned to the ground.

But the travellers still wrote of the gardens of "Malbone" for another seventy
years at least.

The diary of Solomon Drown has this
entry:

"June 7, 1767. [The year after the
burning of the house.]

"Lewis Jenkins and I went up to
Colonel Malbone's House or the Ruins
of his house. There was a fine Garden
and a summer house there. His house was
built of stone and marble. [Already tradition was getting it wrong—it was wood
painted white; to represent marble, perhaps.] It had six chimneys. In his garden
was a fish pond and a duck pond. The
water was drawn out of the fish pond when
his house was burned."

Solomon was right about that fish pond,
for he saw it. You can see it today, for that
matter. And at that, not dried up.

Twenty years later, Dr. Manasseh Cutler
wrote of the garden in his diary:

"October 16, 1787. Mr. Atkinson and I
took a walk to see Malbone's Gardens. The
House was burnt a number of years ago,
but the Garden remains in tolerable order."

Peterson knew the gardens when he was a
boy, about this same date, and in his history
of Rhode Island he wrote:

"The garden, which lay directly in front
of the mansion, with natural embankments,
embracing as it did ten acres, was enchant-
ingly laid out, with gravelled walks, and
highly ornamented with box, fruits of the
rarest and choicest kinds, flowers, and shrubbery of every description. Three artificial
ponds, with the silver fish sporting in the
water, gave to the place the most romantic
appearance. We have often fancied to ourselves in our youthful days, when seated on
the high flight of steps which led to the

*George Washington, a visitor to "Malbone."
From the painting by Charles Willson Peale
in 1772*

spacious hall of this princely mansion, and which commanded an extensive view of the beautiful bay of Newport, of the
magnificent state in which Colonel Malbone must have lived,
far beyond anything of the present day. It is one thing to have
wealth, and another to know how, and
in what manner to appropriate it. There
was at this period, sublime conception
and taste, which enabled gentlemen to
adorn and beautify the Island. No
situation could possibly exhibit a scene
more diversified and pleasing than this;
here the eye wandered from one beauty
to another more enchanting, and when it
seemed to have discovered a still more
superior view, the slightest glance presented another, if possible more inviting
and wonderful,—apparently raised by
the power of magic to captivate the
astonished beholder. This seat was once
the resort of all the gay and great ones of
the Island." Peterson wrote more, much
more. This will perhaps suffice.

George Channing also had early recollections of "Malbone." He was a boy
in Newport in the last years of the eighteenth century. He wrote:

"Saturday afternoons in pleasant

*The present house at "Malbone" as it appeared in 1927. It is built of the
original sandstone of the house of 1741*

weather were generally given to excursions to 'Malbone's
Gardens,' to Miantonomy Hill, and to the 'Block House'
which surmounted it. Although these localities had become
wastes, still the ruins of the famous mansion were peopled
to my imagination which was already kindled by frequent
stories of the almost regal position of the owner of the
estate, and of his sumptuous feasts—the relics of rural
cultivation in and around 'Malbone's Gardens' were to
me full of attractions. The well-defined paths, with their
borders of boxwood, preserved so many years in that
splendid enclosure, were so beautiful in my eye, as to leave
impressions almost as vivid today as in my youthful peregrinations sixty-five years ago."

The *Newport Mercury* of May 24, 1796, carried the following
advertisement:

"Mr. Eugene Mahè respectfully presents his compliments
to the Public and would inform them that he has taken, and

*"Pineapple" from the old gates at "Malbone" (1741); it is
now in the cemetery, Fort Adams*

The church built by Godfrey Malbone, Jr., at Brooklyn, in Connecticut. It was finished in 1771. A service is held here once a year, on All Saints' Day

has now under improvement that beautiful Situation (commonly called) Malbone's Garden,—that he is prepared to entertain, and will, with the most pleasing attention, endeavor to make it agreeable to those who will do him the Honour to call upon him."

The gardens had become commercialized. Yet the glamour was not lost.

Mrs. Cahoon, who published a little book in 1840, called *Sketches of Newport*, had known the gardens in the early years of the nineteenth century, and weaves a description into her little tale.

"They drove directly to Malbone's Garden, into which they obtained admission by the payment of four pence each. The men of the party climbed Mianotonomy Hill. Having finished their survey of the hill, and enjoyed the extensive prospect it afforded, they now descended to examine the celebrated ruins of Malbone House. They found the ladies sociably seated on the lofty flight of stone steps which once conducted to the principal portal of this splendid mansion, where Ellen was employed in a first attempt at sketching from nature, being desirous of conveying on canvass to her friends at New York some faint idea of the beautiful prospect around. The younger children were gamboling among the ruins, or bounding along the garden-walks, in pursuit of wildflowers and butterflies. As the gentlemen rejoined the group, a venerable figure, dressed in the primitive attire of a Quaker, suddenly emerged from the shadow of some trees hardby, bearing in his hand a rake with which he had been employed.

"'A beautiful spot, sir,' exclaimed the Colonel, bowing with polite affability to the aged man, 'a beautiful spot, sir, notwithstanding its formal borders of clipped boxwood and the antique taste, which so strictly required that every "alley should have its brother." From the vestiges of elegance yet remaining, I should suppose the villa must have been superb.'

"'Thou art right, friend, there was no such dwelling in the Provinces,' replied the Quaker, 'but like all earthly pomps and vanities it had but a brief existence. It is melancholy to walk here of an evening, as I sometimes do, and hear the snake hiss, the ivy rustle, and the winds moan, where kind words and glad voices once so gaily echoed.'

"'The proprietor of this villa must have been affluent,' observed the Colonel.

"'He was one of the most opulent in the Provinces, young

man,' was the reply. 'The house on the ruins of which you stand, was the most superb mansion in the Colonies.' He stooped as he ceased speaking and gathered some wallflowers and wild roses that bloomed amongst the ruins and presented them to Ellen, saying 'Let these remind thee through the day at least, young friend, of the melancholy ruin of "Malbone House."'"

A year or so later, in September, 1842, Thomas Hunter wrote to his mother in Brazil:

"One of the most agreeable walks I ever had was the other day to Tomany Hill with Caroline, her two children, and Agatha. . . . Malbone Garden is now owned by Mr. Prescott Hall, her husband's brother, . . . it seems to be filling up.

The tombs of Godfrey Malbone, Jr., and his wife Catherine, née Brinley, in Brooklyn, Conn.

The fish pond is dry, and overgrown, and time has turned the paths and the artificial mounds into almost a level green."

The tales of the travellers have all been told.

The Malbone family did not rebuild "Malbone." Old Godfrey died about a year after the burning of his house. Young Godfrey had already taken his bride, Catherine Brinley, to the Malbone plantation in Brooklyn, in Connecticut, where they lived in a delightful farm house, painted white, built on the slope of a green and lovely hill; where the decline in the West Indian trade, the coming of the Revolution, the loss of the Malbone fortune, hardly troubled them at all. They set out a few apple trees, and a little garden enclosed by a stone wall. They built a church, with white clapboards and long green blinds. There in the churchyard, under the great trees they planted long ago, they lie at peace with all their dignities set out in the good old fashion on entablatures of that same pink sandstone which went to build "Malbone." Once a year the church is opened, on All Saints' Day, and the vicar reads the services for the dead.

But this does not complete the history of the Malbone garden on the six-hundred-acre estate in Newport in Rhode Island.

The Metropolitan Museum owns the Office Book of an American architect named William Alexander Davis. In the book are the plans for a house to be built in Newport, for Mr. J. Prescott Hall of New York. According to the specifications, the house is to be built out of,—of all things—the pink sandstone ruins of "Malbone." Davis notes that the pen drawings and the specifications are worth 75 dollars, and that working details will be furnished for 25 dollars more. The date of these drawings is 1848.

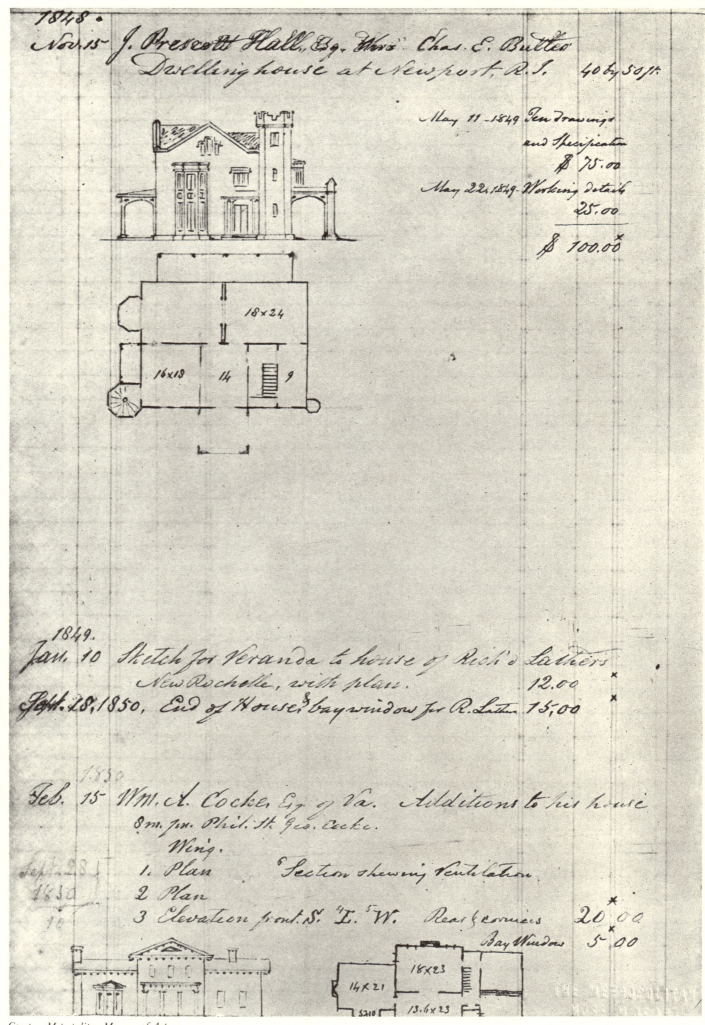

This page from the Office Book of William Alexander Davis shows "Malbone" (above) as it was without the rear wing, added two years later

In 1876, D. Appleton and Co. published *The Art Journal, New Series*, containing an article on "Newport Villas." "Malbone" is described at length—"Malbone" rebuilt.

"Life can offer few more attractions than are combined at 'Malbone,' the charming home of Mr. Bedloe. Fragrant with historical memories, the scene of many an antique revel, it is

"Malbone" in 1878, then the home of Henry Bedloe. The cedar tree on the terrace is shown blown down on page 210

at once one of the most elegant, most comfortable, most agreeable, and perhaps the most historical house . . . in Newport. Mr. Malbone, in his stately villa with its formal statues in box, cut in quaint shape, his pleached alleys, his marbles, his terraces, and his negroes, was a famous man. His dinners were good and frequent; on one occasion he gave one which was perhaps too good, for word was brought him at the third course that the house was on fire. 'Remove the dinner to the lawn,' said he, 'we will finish it by the light of the fire'; and so this male Cleopatra drowned his burning house in Madeira. Years after, the mass of ruins and the alleys of box, and the farm became the property of Hon. J. Prescott Hall . . . who built the present 'Malbone.' It is a handsome castellated house in the Elizabethan style. . . . Out of one of the windows of the diningroom young couples are encouraged to jump through a matrimonial tree, one of those vegetable twins so common in our country, or rather just so uncommon as to be noticed and preserved.

"Mr. Hall, with judicious taste, restored the terraces and the box as far as possible, and restocked the deserted grounds with marble fauns, naiads, hamadryads, and nymphs, after, perhaps, the questionable taste which prevailed in the Versailles period. Time has made these marble visitors grey, so that they compose beautifully with the dark green of the firs, the lawn, and the fine plantations of domestic and foreign trees.

"On the death of Mr. and Mrs. Hall, 'Malbone' became the property of Mr. and Mrs. Bedloe, under whose tasteful management it has constantly been improved. Its brownstone walls are hung with ivy. . . . Other houses are perhaps light and tasteful resting places for a season; 'Malbone' is a —home."

A couple of years later, Mrs. Martha Lamb published her well known *Homes of America.* She wrote that "Malbone" was "one of the Show Places of Newport," and that when Mr. Hall rebuilt "Malbone" he "restocked the ruined grounds with marble fauns, naiads, hamadryads, and nymphs, after the taste of an older period. He kept the banks and the terraces, the hedges of shrubbery and groups of rare trees, which alternated with plots of flowers and artificial lakes."

I know that the Halls were a long time in getting their estate back into shape. The house was built in 1849. In 1852, Peterson still could write: "The site formerly occupied by Mr. Malbone's House, after a period of 84 years, has been improved by J. Prescott Hall, Esq., of New York, who has erected a house for a summer residence; but the glory has departed."

Which is as may be.

This J. Prescott Hall, Esq., was a man of taste. His charming wife, Harriette De Wolf, daughter of James De Wolf of Bristol, was a woman of feeling. Moving with elegance in the polite world of 1840, they represent American society emerging from its orgy of republicanism, its democratic delusion. The towns of the day were full of an architecture which aped that of Greece and the Roman Republic. On the New England hillsides and in the New England fishing villages, local carpenters were still putting up their pretty pillared porticoes. But men of taste no longer had any taste for a republican society. Women of feeling felt themselves pathetically aloof from the common people, who had begun to seem uncommonly well able to look after their own interests, and whose own taste, at last unbridled by necessity to please, was not in the direction of republican simplicity.

The thought of most persons with some leisure and intelligence, in England as well as in the new United States, was turning back to quite another period in quite another civilization. These pathetic aristocrats were remembering with a very strong feeling of regret the days when wealth and power lived, safely entrenched, in a fortified castle with turrets and battlements and donjons and ruins—they wanted estates which should express an aristocratic difference. So, suddenly, America took up the "Gothic." It did not persist. It was never a thing of great beauty, perhaps. But it had charm and character. "Malbone," the new "Malbone," the Gothic "Malbone" of the J. Prescott Halls, is delightful.

The Halls had been fortunate in finding this lovely old ruin of pink sandstone, three miles from "Vaucluse" which belonged to Mrs. Hall's cousin, Charles De Wolf, and just across the Bay from Bristol where all the other De Wolfs had built their great mansions by the waterside. If you remember, this was the day when people actually built ruins in their gardens, to give an air of elegant gloom to the estate. And here was this great ruin covered with ivy, set in a garden full of gloomy box and broken urns and shattered columns. It was really too utterly sweet and romantic!

But by 1875, the renovated estate was in perfect condition, and the "Malbone" of the J. Prescott Halls was known for its quiet distinction and unfailing hospitality throughout the English-speaking world. There is perhaps no other unaltered example of American Gothic left at the present time. That the estate was never changed to conform with later ideas is perhaps due to the fact that with the passing of the Halls there was none too much money to spend on it, and, later, no one who cared to live in it at all, money or no.

It was left again, to moulder as it did, and little children going home from school ran quickly as they passed the tottering gates. It was a haunted place.

In 1905 Lewis Gouverneur Morris, a descendant of the Halls and Bedlows, inherited "Malbone," and every summer he and his wife and little daughters come there to live. Again there is life and laughter at "Malbone," and again the old gardens are coming back into their old beauty, as anyone can see who walks out from Newport along the old roads the eighteenth-century travellers took.

Anyone sitting on the terrace as the sun sinks behind Conanicut, can feel something of the charm which drew old Godfrey Malbone to these fields which lie between Miantonomy Hill and the Bay of Narragansett. Anyone can see the lines of the eighteenth-century garden; and the water, shining through the trees, in the old fish ponds which formed a part of the eighteenth-century design. Anyone can understand why the J. Prescott Halls of the romantic forties bought the lovely ruin, and built from the old stone a watch-tower with a winding stair and crenelated battlement. There is a glamour about the place which is not, I think, due wholly to its romantic past, but something perhaps to the old planting, the old architecture, and surely something to the atmosphere, to the haze which lies at sunset along the Narragansett shore.

THE BOWLER GARDENS

While "Malbone" was still a heap of smouldering ruins, the English Admiralty sent over an agent to make a proper survey of the harbors and coast line of Narragansett Bay. The so-called Blaskowich Map is the result. With the map, the following explanatory letter was forwarded to the Admiralty. It is much the best contemporary account we have of the appearance of the Island of Rhode Island just before the Revolution.

"Newport, in his Majesty's
Colony of Rhode Island.

"My Lord,

"I arrived here after a passage of 60 days from Land's End, and from that time to the present, a period of 2 months, I have been constantly engaged in obtaining the surveys and drafts of this harbor and Narragansett Bay . . . in conformity with your lordship's direction. . . .

"On the Map . . . all the roads are laid down, and the seats of the principal farmers designated. . . .

"The roads of the Island are bordered with a variety of ornamental trees; nearly every farm has its orchard of engrafted trees of every description—suited to the climate. The whole Island is of an excellent soil, and under the highest state of cultivation. In the vicinity of the Town are several fine gardens belonging to gentlemen of fortune and taste; having fish ponds of perch, trout, etc. and their greenhouses and hot houses producing the fruits and plants of every clime.

"Many families of fortune from the West Indies and Europe have taken up their permanent residence here."

However that may be, there certainly were at this time two great gardens which rivalled the gardens of "Malbone." These were laid out for two great merchants, Redwood and Bowler, at their country seats within riding distance of their houses in the town of Newport.

The town house of Metcalf Bowler still stands on the corner of Mary and Clarke Streets in Newport, though the garden which he made in the yard of the house has entirely disappeared, built over by the crowding neighborhood.

The country house of Metcalf Bowler is now a shapeless heap of rotten wood in a large and naked pasture surrounded by the conventional stone wall of the Rhode Island countryside.

He built his town house in his youth, with his first great fortune, the profits of a thriving trade in slaves and rum. As relaxation after the thrill of the counting house, where risks most amazing were taken as part of the day's work, he turned to the cultivation of his garden, and grew roses.

At the height of his career, when he was making so much money he didn't know how much money he was making, when every venture turned out to be no venture, and all his ships came home, he bought 70 acres of farm land in Portsmouth, and turned the old farmhouse into a very fine house indeed. The panelling is now in the Metropolitan Museum in New York. But he bought the place largely that he might make another garden, a larger garden, several gardens— "eleven acres of pleasure gardens." There was not room for all his projects in the town. And actually, he was so rich that

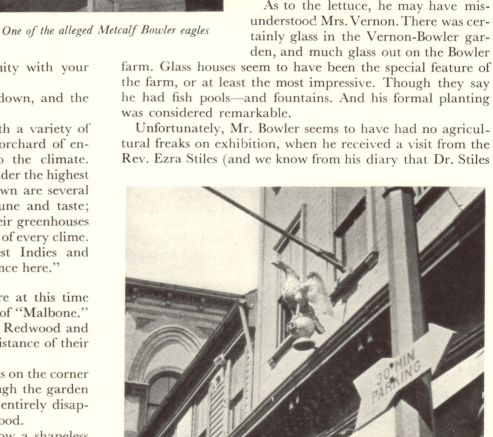

One of the alleged Metcalf Bowler eagles

he felt he could afford to have not only a garden, but a farm. He was so accustomed to making money that he felt he could make a paying proposition of a farm in Portsmouth, Rhode Island. He understood his counting house so well that he felt he could understand turnips and the ways of wind and weather. This is a delusion common to all ages.

In order to be entirely practical, he let his town house to the Vernons of Newport, and lived out on the farm altogether—oh, he neglected nothing, his hobby was ridden to the finish.

These Vernons, by the way, kept up the Bowler garden, and gave dinner parties. The Rev. Ezra Stiles wrote in his diary:

"Jan. 7, 1773. At dinner [at the Vernons'] we ate lettuce, gathered in the garden, growing abroad and not in hot beds, so moderate the season. I saw and measured a branch of Rose Bush of this winter's fresh growth, gathered New Year's Day, above 6 inches long, of which the new growth stalk was above 4 inches, and some leaves nearly full grown."

As to the lettuce, he may have misunderstood Mrs. Vernon. There was certainly glass in the Vernon-Bowler garden, and much glass out on the Bowler farm. Glass houses seem to have been the special feature of the farm, or at least the most impressive. Though they say he had fish pools—and fountains. And his formal planting was considered remarkable.

Unfortunately, Mr. Bowler seems to have had no agricultural freaks on exhibition, when he received a visit from the Rev. Ezra Stiles (and we know from his diary that Dr. Stiles

One of the eagles said to have topped the gateposts of the Bowler Farm is now high up on the façade of an old building on Thames Street

was interested only in the unusual), so we get merely the following entry in the Stiles diary of the day:

"May 9, 1770. Road out with Mr. West to Mr. Redwood's and Mr. Bowler's Gardens, and conversed on metaphysics."

Of course, that is exactly what Bishop Berkeley thought gardens were for, but that Rhode Island Life should become so like Rhode Island Fiction, startles me.

Peterson, in his *History of Rhode Island* (1853), tells us that Mr. Bowler at his country-place had "an elegant garden, filled with every description of fruits and flowers, with artificial ponds" etc. Which is just like Peterson. "Every description," yet no description whatever of even one flower, even one fruit.

He admits that when he saw the farm it was "nothing more than an ordinary place," yet he insists there had been "artificial ponds," a few years earlier, which had entirely disappeared! The gate posts were topped with eagles. One of these heraldic eagles is now high up on an old building on Thames Street, the other in the custody of the Newport Historical Association. (It has not been really proved that these eagles ever did belong to Mr. Bowler.)

Updike repeats what he, too, had been told of "The Bowler Magnificence." He never saw it.

Mr. Bowler "had the most splendid and best cultivated garden, on the Island [of Rhode Island]; his taste for agriculture and gardening, in which he cultivated the best fruits and flowers, exceeded that of any gentleman of his day."

Thomas R. Hazard, not born till after the death of Mr. Bowler, lived in his old age at "Vaucluse," next door to the Bowler farm.

He writes: "On the north [of Vaucluse] lies the old Isaac Chase Farm, which in the olden time was owned and occupied in the summer season by Mr. Bowler, a rich East Indian Merchant of Newport. Mr. Bowler had a beautiful garden and took great delight in beautifying his grounds and hot houses with exotics from all parts of the world."

How they did delight in "exotics"! I wonder if the fact that these merchants of the eighteenth century used "exotic" plants—things ill-adapted to Rhode Island—is one of the reasons why there is nothing in their garden spaces today? Or perhaps, to them, zinnias were exotic, and amaranths were "rare"; whatever was not common in the gardens of Old England and did not grow wild in the woods around New England farms.

The "exotic" of which Mr. Hazard gives a definite description, is the apple tree known today as the Rhode Island Greening.

For what it is worth, I give you an outline of the tale; that Captain Green of the Bowler merchant ships, brought the little apple tree in a porcelain pot, from Persia to Portsmouth, as a tribute to the owner of the Line.

What is true and what Channing in his *Early Recollections of Newport 1795–1811* remembers:

"The greening apple was the great staple, whether for the production of cider or for home use, and had a zest which increased rather than satisfied the appetite."

To carry the greening into our own time, I must tell you of a greening apple tree I saw last week, in full bloom. It was planted 135 years ago, and the owner says that she gathers apples every year from this tree, as her mother and grandmother did before her.

Of the private and personal life of Metcalf Bowler, this is not the place to speak. It is on the public record that he married a wife in 1750, made a trip to New York in 1765, was a Deputy to the State Legislature from Portsmouth in 1770, and was made Chief Justice of the Superior Court of Rhode Island in 1776.

During the Revolution, he is rather a forlorn figure. He remained loyal to the Crown. His letters to Sir Henry Clinton prove him to have been an authorized spy in the pay of the British Government, though in the records of Rhode Island he seems to be a red-hot patriot. And this dirty work didn't do him a bit of good. For the British paid him very little. All commerce was stopped, and his income had come from commerce. The British troops, in spite of his loyalty, were quartered on his farm. And they ruined his garden and cut down

his orchard, and broke his glass houses. And I don't know what they didn't do to his artificial ponds!

At the close of the Revolution he was living in Providence, where he kept a boarding-house and wrote a book.

The book written by Mr. Bowler was not, as I have said, published until 1786, after the war was over. He then most obviously needed the money. He also needed patronage. The copy in the John Carter Brown Library has a dedication to "His Excellency the Governor and Company of the State of Rhode Island."

The book was printed by Bennett Wheeler, in Providence. It is just another eighteenth-century production, by an amateur turned farmer and author, of whom later times were so prolific. But I know of no other such pamphlet published in Rhode Island before 1840, except the little book on agriculture by the Drowns.

Bowler opens his book with a quotation from Virgil, partly in Latin, although he seems to believe that he is writing his book for the farming population of Rhode Island.

"Happy the man, who has his honest will;
Content to cultivate the grateful fields." etc.

Mr. Bowler then addressed a preface:

"To the Candid Reader

"The large and expensive books, filled with copper plates, describing cumbersome and unnecessary instruments of agriculture, have very little promoted the new method of cultivation amongst farmers. One strong common plough and a little swing plough is sufficient to execute the horse-hoeing scheme, but the drill-husbandry, which should always accompany it, requires an instrument of a curious complex nature. This plough makes the channels, numbers out the seed, and covers them at the same time. The intelligent husbandman should procure one of the drill-ploughs, which may easily be purchased ready made (as I am informed) in the City of Philadelphia, but in case he cannot procure one, I advise him to use a hand drill, which with a little more travel will answer the purpose. Considering the great expense of laborers, working cattle, and manure, necessary upon an arable farm, it plainly appears to me that the Grazier hath often a great advantage of the ploughing farmer, therefore I recommend mixing both species of husbandry in the improvement of lands; and have in this publication laid down directions accordingly. Hoping that this short treatise on the cultivation of the soil (the production of some leisure hours) will be of some use to the community. I am, etc."

The Town House of Abraham Redwood. This sketch by Jonas Bergner now hangs in the rooms of the Newport Historical Society

At the close of his book, he prints a "Conclusion," which runs as follows:

"We do not expect that gentlemen should be constantly employed in the common occupation of husbandry, because

Ruined terrace at the Redwood Farm

there are laborers enough to be hired for that purpose; but they may understand the modern method of cultivation, and be able to direct their servants in the execution of every new improvement. Can there be a more useful, more innocent, or a more delightful employment, for the vacant hour.''

THE REDWOOD GARDENS

At his town house in Newport on the Island of Rhode Island, Abraham Redwood, Merchant, is said to have had a botanical garden, the first in New England. Charles Parsons in *Early Votaries of Natural Science in Rhode Island* writes that Redwood cultivated this garden ''for scientific purposes.'' Perhaps he did.

All we really know about that Redwood garden we find in the diary of a fourteen-year-old boy, Solomon Drown.

''June 24, 1767. Mr. Redwood's Garden . . . one of the finest gardens I ever saw in my life. In it grows all sorts of West Indian fruits, viz: Oranges, Lemons, Limes, Pineapples, and Tamarinds and other sorts. It has also West India flowers —very pretty ones—and a fine summer house. It was told my father that his garden was worth 40 thousand pounds, and that the man that took care of the garden had above 100 dollars per annum. It had Hot Houses where things that are tender are put for the winter, and hot beds for the West India Fruit. I saw

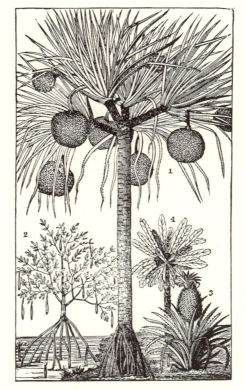

The exotics of the period of Abraham Redwood's glass-houses

one or two of these gardens in coming from the beach.''

This boy Drown grew up to be the great botanist of his day. In his old age he had a botanical garden of his own, out on that farm in Foster which he called ''Mount Hygeia.'' But in 1767 he was making his first voyage down the bay to Newport from his home in Providence, and I doubt if he had ever seen a really fine garden. What is of value in his description is his astonishment at Mr. Redwood's professional gardener, an astonishment we share, for skill in the raising of pineapples under glass was hardly to be expected in colonial New England. There must have been a well trained man in charge of Mr. Redwood's estate in Newport, a man trained in Europe. Fortunately the Rhode Island Historical Society has just published an account of such a man, who came to Newport from the Continent sometime after 1754, bringing excellent letters of recommendation.

It is more than probable that this well recommended man was in charge of the Redwood estate, when Solomon Drown visited Newport in 1767.

That Redwood should have desired to grow West Indian fruits and flowers is not surprising. His father, Abraham Redwood, Sr., a native of Bristol, England, had gone to the West Indies as a young man, and there married Mehitable Langford, a daughter of the Langfords who owned great sugar plantations in Anti-

The Redwood Farm in Portsmouth, photographed from the highway

wards I was informed that the Coins should be of Red Bricks, and have therefore sent 1m of them. I hope it will be of no loss to you as the charge of them is not very great. These things are what I am no great judge of, and if anything should be amiss I hope you will be so good as to excuse it, for I do assure you that I have used my utmost endeavors to get everything in as handsome manner, and as cheap as possible, they being all bought with ready money."

The gates and the red brick gateposts were set up on the Redwood estate on Thames Street, where they remained until the house was torn down in the nineteenth century. They now form the northern entrance to the grounds of the Redwood Library.

Gardens were laid out when the gates were ordered. All the houses on Thames Street before the Revolution had gardens. But the stocking of the Redwood gardens probably proceeded slowly during the next forty years. The difficulty of importing West Indian fruit was perhaps the original reason for attempting to grow oranges and lemons in Newport. In 1731, the Redwoods' agent in Antigua wrote that he had sent up to Newport lemons and oranges and limes (none of which had kept) and that he was now sending a few more which he feared wouldn't keep. Three kegs of tamarinds were also on the ship, and 12 bottles of citron water. The next month, Eliza Langford sent up a keg of tamarinds marked "A.R.," and that same spring, Isabella Langford had sent "a cagg of tamerons" according to her own letter. Tomlinson of Antigua also wrote in 1733: "I have sent you 2 barrels of oranges, but I am very much afraid that they wont keep till the vessel arrives; but the Captain has promised to take all the care that can be."

About this time Abraham Redwood married. He also imported a coach and horses from England, and

gua. On one of these plantations, "Cassada Garden," the little Abraham was born in 1709, and although the Redwoods left Antigua in 1715—they were living in Newport in 1718 when Ann Redwood married John Wanton, Governor of Rhode Island—yet the whole family kept up a close relationship, and Abraham as a boy used to go down there occasionally on the Redwood ships.

Upon the death of his father in 1729, Abraham Redwood, Jr., not yet of age, inherited the sugar plantation, the large house with unfinished grounds on Thames Street, and a number of vessels engaged in the West Indian trade.

These ships went down from Newport with horses and sheep and onions and pigs and apples and lumber, and took the sugar from "Cassada Garden" to Bristol in England, where it was sold, and the ships sent back to Newport with whatever cargoes they could find.

In April, 1729, soon after the death of Abraham Redwood, Sr., the Redwood agent in Bristol, Rowland Frye, wrote that he had shipped "certain Lead and Iron Work."

In July he wrote: "I shall be glad to hear that the Iron Gates and Stone Work are as you directed, the workmen inform me that your directions were not as perfect as could be desired, however that everything was performed in the best possible manner, and the stone work fitted to the gates that there cannot well be a mistake in putting them up. Flower pots are not now in fashion; so that I have sent you two pine apples of a new sort of stuff which wears as well as stone, and comes very cheap; for in stone they would cost above 12 pounds; if you do not like them, they will probably serve for some other place about the house, and I will then send you any sort you please to order. There are 1m. [one thousand] of bricks more than you ordered, but as you did not mention what sort they were to be, I first shipped Grey Stocks. After-

Linden trees at the Redwood Farm, photographed in 1914

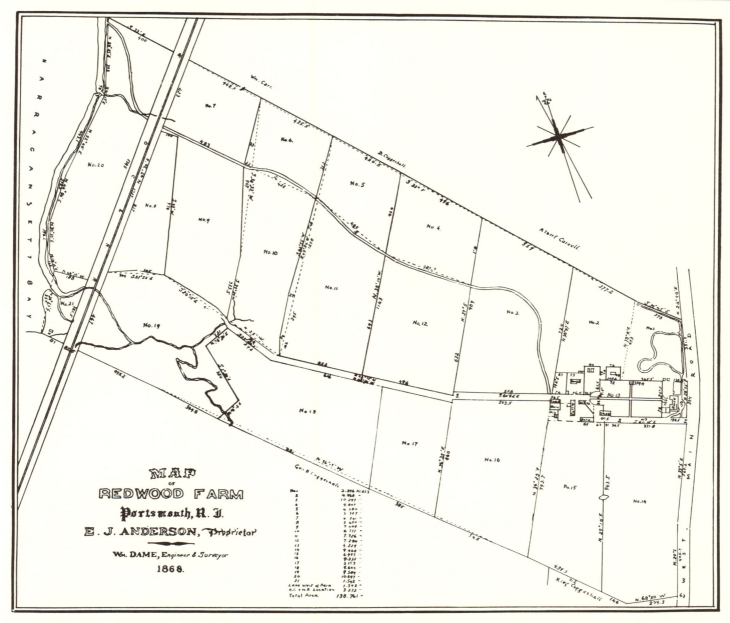

MAP
OF
REDWOOD FARM
Portsmouth, R. I.
E. J. ANDERSON, Proprietor
Wm. DAME, Engineer & Surveyor
1868.

This map of the Redwood Farm is reproduced from a paper now in possession of Mr. Bradford Norman, the present owner of the farm. It shows the entire farm from Road to Bay as the Redwoods bought it from the Coggshells

he tried to import an English coachman. But the Redwood agent wrote that coachmen in England were hard to get and would not go to the colonies. Redwood was advised to try to get one in Boston.

In 1741, Godfrey Malbone, another merchant in Newport, not only set up a coach but laid the cornerstone of a seat in the country. Redwood, far more prosperous than Malbone, was not to be outdone. As "Malbone" was building, Redwood looked about for a plantation, to which he also might drive out in his own coach and four.

In 1743, he bought for 6500 pounds the middle strip of the Coggshell farm on the west road running north from Newport, that farm in Portsmouth where William Coggshell, Planter, had been growing and marketing English grass seed as early as 1647. Redwood had married a Coggshell girl.

He built a house by the highway, of wood, three stories, with dormer windows. All about the house he laid out the grounds with as much attention to detail as I have ever seen.

Anyone can get a good idea of the general plan from the accompanying map, which is a photograph of an original surveyor's blue print, owned by Mr. Bradford Norman, who purchased the Coggshell–Redwood farms, not many years ago.

William Redwood (1734-1784), son of Abraham Redwood, Jr. From a portrait painted by Gilbert Stuart

Abraham Redwood, Jr. (1709-1788), from the copy of Smibert's portrait by Charles Bird King (1785-1862)

These pictures now hang in the Redwood Library

In front of the house, Abraham Redwood planted twelve English lindens. They are often called lime trees, in the old garden books.

Some forty years ago, the town straightened the road, at the request of the Andersons, last of the Redwood blood to

The summer-house from the Redwood Farm as it now stands on the grounds of the Redwood Library

live on the old plantation; so that a little of the original garden planting has been lost. But the great hedges of arborvitae and the stone walls and the terrace faced with stone remain in their original condition. The lines of the formal garden behind the house can still be traced, by the aid of

Photographed by J. Rugen, Newport

The gates of the Redwood Town House (1729) in Newport are now used at the north entrance of the Redwood Library. The pineapples were made in 1729 of "a new sort of stuff which wears as well as stone"

the old plan. Where the garden wall curves toward the western gate of the garden, on an axis with the western door of the house, the stone work is in excellent condition, and shows much skill in the use of the material the architect found at hand. The slope of the ground was carefully considered. There is evident a real sense of style and proportion. Traces of a curving walk of stone can be found in the meadow, north of the house. There are remains of the hedge of lilacs which were apparently used as a border. This walk is shown plainly on the map. In this same meadow there remains the fish pond, another conventional feature of our eighteenth-century gardens. And old fruit trees are growing in the gardens, where they were planted as part of the usual eighteenth-century garden design. Not apple trees, but pear and plum and apricot. The large apple orchard lies beyond the garden wall, to the north of the house.

The well in the yard is of course where it was dug when the house was built, part of the whole design of the great plantation which sloped down to the water's edge, where it ended in a little stone wharf. It was far easier to send goods to the plantation by water in the eighteenth century than by the cart-road running out from town.

The most important feature of the garden was the garden house. It is of most interesting design, and stood until a few years ago, quite close to the dwelling house, where I often saw it in use. Mr. Norman consented to its removal from the old farm, not long ago, as the danger of its destruction by hoodlums was very great. It now stands in the grounds of the

The Redwood Library, Newport

Redwood Library, in the City of Newport. A photograph of the garden house in its new situation accompanies this account.

It was in 1747, as Redwood was laying out his gardens at his new seat in the country, that he was elected a member of the new library society in Newport, an outgrowth of the Philosophical Society of Berkeley's day, to which he had not belonged. It was the intention of the Society to build a library and purchase a collection of books which were to be kept in the new library building and used in common. Collins, an old member of the organization, gave the land on which to build the library, and enough money was raised by subscription to hire an architect, Peter Harrison. But Abraham Redwood, one of their new members, volunteered to send to London at his own expense for all the new books to be placed in the library. So, when the library society was incorporated, it was called "The Company of the Redwood Library," and as the Redwood Library it is known today.

From the point of view of this garden history, it is interesting to read the titles of the books which Redwood ordered from his London agent. Those bearing on gardens are fairly numerous. I give them here. For these books were read by the patrons of the library from 1750 until they were stolen by the British army of occupation, and may well have had an influence on the development of the art of gardening about Narragansett Bay.

Books in Folio

Gerrardes' Herbal, by Johnston
Gardeners' Dictionary, by Miller
Magazine of Architecture, by Oakley
Pomona; or Fruit Garden, Illustrated

Books in quarto

Experimental Husbandman, by Bradley

Classicks

Plinii Epistoloe, by T. Hearne
Pliny's Epistles, by Melmoth
Georgicks of Virgil, by Martyn
Horace, by Mr. Francis
Odes of Horace

Physick

Boerhoave's de Materia Medica

Arts, Liberal and Mechanical

Gentleman and Farmer's Guide, by Bradley

On Husbandry and Gardening

Modern Husbandman, by Ellis
Practical Farmer
Method of Improving Barren Lands

Other Books

Foreign Vegetables, by Thickweise
Gardener's Calendar, by Miller
Compleat Planter and Cyderist
Natural History of Bees
The Columbarian or Pigeon House, by Pointer
Compleat Body of Distilling, by Smith

Peter Harrison, the architect of the Redwood Library. From Louis Sands' copy of the portrait by Smibert

For these books and the books on more general subjects which I have omitted, he paid 500 pounds sterling.

All through the months of the long Newport summers, the Redwoods lived on their new plantation in Portsmouth from 1744 to the death of Abraham Redwood in 1772, much as they had lived on their old plantation in the West Indies. The work of both plantations was done by negroes, imported from Africa in the Redwood ships. When they proved refractory, on the Rhode Island plantation, they were sent down to "Cassada Garden" where life on a sugar plantation made them glad to return to Rhode Island and the care of the cattle and the corn.

The Redwoods imported their own wine, as well, bringing a pipe or so from Madeira every year for their own hospitable purposes.

And every year the travellers who came to Newport were taken out to see the Redwood gardens, and to drink the Redwood wine.

In the Spring of 1770, there are these two entries in the diary of Dr. Stiles:

"April 28. Rode out to Mr. Redwood's Country Seat with Brother Hubbard."

"May 9. Rode out with Mr. West to Mr. Redwood's and Mr. Bowler's gardens; and conversed much upon metaphysics. He has a peculiar notion about sin."

After the war, both the Redwood house in Newport and the Redwood farm fell into neglect. Repaired and in use in 1850, according to Peterson, there is nothing now left of house or garden in the town; and the country seat, though not beyond restoration, is uninhabited.

THE ELDREDGE GARDEN

There is an eighteenth-century garden across the Bay from Newport which apparently has been left in its original condition.

It is difficult to classify this lovely Eldredge garden in East

Greenwich. It is impossible to reproduce it in a photograph because of the dense shade.

Planted about the year 1757, when the old colonial house to which it belongs was built, house and garden were later bought by Dr. Charles Eldredge, who gave it to his son, Dr. James Eldredge, a well-remembered Rhode Island physician. It is now owned by his great-granddaughter, Mrs. William Grainger, of Easthampton, Long Island, and the Rev. Henry M. Saville of Providence.

The plan of the garden, here given, was drawn to scale by Miss House, the present tenant.

The garden is laid out in three terraces, each approached by four irregular flagstone steps. A trumpet vine covers the arbor over the steps to the second terrace. On the third terrace there was once a long row of cherry trees, of which only two now remain.

Violets, both purple and white, really carpet the whole garden. Wandering jew, white funkia, myrtle, and fleur-de-lis seem to be everywhere. The garden paths are all edged with box.

The paths in the yard of the house leading to the garden are of flagstone, flanked by cobblestones in places.

A stone wall (fieldstone without mortar) borders the garden on the south, and the same type of wall is used as a retaining wall on the north. The front yard is enclosed by a wooden fence.

This fern-leaf beech in the grounds of the Redwood Library was planted by Robert Johnston about 1833, and is the finest specimen in existence today. This photograph, taken in 1844 to illustrate "Reminiscences of Newport" by George C. Mason, shows a wall around the grounds which is not now in existence

The Dr. Eldredge house, built in 1757 on Division Street in East Greenwich. Of the two elms, one was English, the other American. The garden lies to the right

done, once and for all time—in the most delightful garden book which I have ever seen. Were it not printed for private circulation only, I would quote it throughout. I do quote just a little.

"Once upon a time, before the days of motor cars and airplanes, and radios and world wars, there was a garden, and a day in June when it was full of roses; great sweet hundred-leaf roses, dark red crisp glorious George the Fourth roses, beautiful yellow-centered single roses, sunshiny prickly yellow roses, tiny Scotch baby roses, and pure white Baltimore Belles.

"It was a wonderful place, that garden, up three steps from the square green yard. That was cool and quiet and shady from the elm branches over head, and cut off from the street by a tangle of lilacs and syringas and such things—but the garden was full of color and sunshine and fragrance and the happy hum of bees.

"There were many paths, very trim and orderly, and every path had box borders and a different interest at the end.

"There were big square tulip beds, riotous with color in

There are old pear trees in the garden, hung with trailing grape vines. There are horse-chestnuts in the back yard. There are two elms in the front yard, one of which is an English elm.

The vegetable house (root cellar) in the garden is exceedingly interesting.

But I did not mean to describe the garden—that has been

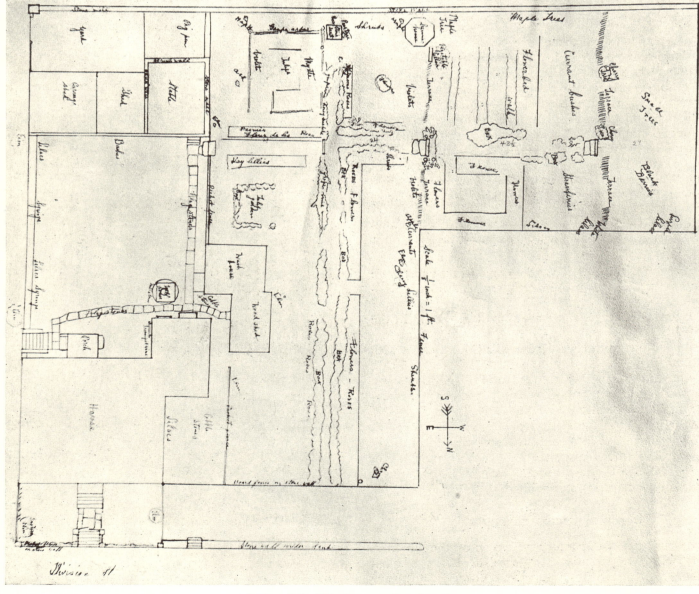

A plan of the Eldredge grounds and garden

The Brenton House, Newport

From the drawing now in possession of the Newport Historical Society, done by E. P. Coe from information supplied by the Society for the Preservation of New England Antiquities, and photographed for this book by Antoinette von Horn. Built for Jahleel Brenton supposedly about 1700 on Thames Street, the house still exists as a ruin. Confiscated during the Revolution because the Brentons were Tories, it became a boardinghouse run by some people named Almy. General Washington stayed there

their day, and there were borders full of myrtle and grape hyacinths and lily of the valley and violets.

"Under the archway in the grape trellis was a long path leading to the left, past the herb garden with its border of larkspur and monkshood, to the stone seat under the Pear Tree, all fragrant with Lemon Balm.

"To the right it ran past the two old box trees, 'Baucis and Philemon,' to the vine covered wall. . . . The box trees were very old, and one of them had a hole in it, in the middle, quite large enough for a play house for a little girl if someone would lift her in."

"HAMMERSMITH FARM"

Another great family of merchant princes was the family of Brenton. With the Revolution they left Newport; for they were all Loyalists, and owned much property which looked good to the Patriot without an acre of his own. But on any map of Newport you will find the Brenton name. And anyone at all in Newport will tell you that, once upon a time, the Brentons owned a great place out on Brenton's Neck, called "Hammersmith Farm," now the property of Mrs. Hugh Dudley Auchincloss, whose garden the whole world goes to see.

William Brenton, by profession a surveyor, was admitted a freeman of Boston, May 14th, 1634. He was an Englishman of some property, whose English home was in Hammersmith, then a delightful country town near London.

He had succeeded in getting from King Charles I the rather singular grant of a certain number of acres out of every square

The present condition of the Brenton house. It was restored after the Revolution to the Brenton family, who sold it because of poverty. Thereafter it changed hands frequently

mile which he should survey—anywhere, apparently, in the New England colonies. Of course, at the time of the grant, there were not many New England colonies. There were no English settlements whatever in Rhode Island. An accurate survey of New England was really needed, but Brenton's commission seems excessive.

He first took up land in Boston, and never gave up his settlement there, returning with his family from time to time. When the Portsmouth settlers went out from Boston in 1638, Brenton was with them, probably to survey the new grants and purchases. When some of the Portsmouth people started a new colony at Newport, Brenton took as his proper share a house-lot of six acres on Thames Street, and planting ground of about 2000 acres besides.

This Brenton grant covered eventually not only Brenton's Neck, but a large part of the meadow land through which the Ocean Drive now runs. He divided it all up into farms—"Hammersmith Farm," "Rocky Farm," "Cherry Neck." Before long he built a farmhouse, on the farm called "Hammersmith." He had a large number of indentured servants, and as one was by trade a thatcher, it is quite possible that the first Brenton house had a thatched roof.

But the garden? I know very little about the Brenton gardens. The colonial records do tell us that the people of Newport in 1668 plucked down 140 rods of fence on Hammersmith Farm, and plucked it down 10 times, just as fast as Mr. Brenton rebuilt it. Which shows that Mr. Brenton was using wooden fencing and was attempting to enclose land his neighbors felt he shouldn't. But that has little to do with the Brenton garden of the early days of Newport.

In 1854, G. Champlin Mason published a book called *Newport, Illustrated by Sketches with Pen and Camera*. He describes Hammersmith Farm as follows:

"A short distance from the first gate, there stands a dark house with brick ends. It is all that remains of one of the most noted dwellings in the early history of the Island. It was built by Governor William Brenton, who then owned nearly the whole neck; and the grounds, through which the road now runs, were adorned with rare and costly plants, gravel walks, groves, and bowers, and all that wealth and a refined taste could obtain in this and foreign lands."

Evidently there was nothing of this to be seen except the "dark house," in 1854.

The only other nineteenth-century description of the estate, as far as I know—and there are none earlier—, was written by a descendant of Governor Brenton. She too writes from tradition. She says, "The estate was ornamented with gravel walks, flowering trees, folding gates with massive pillars, gardens where the box, the fir tree, and the peony, graced the gravelled alleys and the yards of velvet green."

There is not much left of the old farm today. A part of the farm house, greatly enlarged in the eighteenth century, has been destroyed by fire. The great doorstep of slate, the flagged path through the green yard leading to the gap in the stone wall which was once the garden gate, some old garden flowers in the lane which runs through what was once the garden patch, some old trees—there is really nothing more.

The town house of the Brenton family, their winter residence on Thames street, is now nothing but a shell of masonry, falling to pieces. A motion picture house has been built in the front yard, and shops cover the gardens at the side.

"ROCKY FARM"

"Rocky Farm," the Brenton property on the ocean, was never occupied by the Brentons. It was rented by them to various tenants, and used largely for the raising of sheep. When it was confiscated by the government during the Revolution, it was purchased by the Hazard family.

"The enclosures of the gardens and orchards, which were of cut granite, 3 feet wide and 5 feet high," were built by General Alfred Hazard, early in the nineteenth century. The farm buildings, the sheep folds, still standing, are of this same stone. At the front of the old house, General Hazard planted an arboretum, and many of the unusual trees he cherished still remain, though sadly neglected. I am glad to say that the new owner of the property is bringing the place back to its original condition.

Not many years ago there was still a quaint box garden near the house, the beds being planted in the design of a bow and arrow. It is in the stone courtyard of Rocky Farm that daffodils, naturalized nobody knows how long ago, bloom abundantly every spring, as all Newport children know very well.

OCHRE POINT

There were also, in Newport as in Providence, many merchants of less wealth who were making their little gardens all through the eighteenth century. The Taylor family, for example, had a garden at Ochre Point. Across the Seaconnet River they could see, from their orchard, the orchards of the eldest Taylor boy, who had a house and garden down by Taylor's lane, in Little Compton. Ochre Point, by the way, gets its name from the soil, which is really the color of yellow ochre.

The first Taylor came from Scotland to Newport in 1712.

In the restored garden of the Wanton-Lyman-Hazard house, done by a plan drawn by Mr. Norman M. Isham, box edging was used extensively. In the side yard the box encloses white sand instead of flowers

He was nothing more important than a shipwright, but from shipwright to shareholder in a ship or two is not far in a new country, and the Taylors prospered. They lived on Thames Street in Newport, by the Carr garden, and according to an inventory, had a "billiard table" in the yard. Could it have been a bowling green? As trade prospered, the Taylors bought a farm at Ochre Point. In 1763, old Taylor died, and left to his daughter Patience "one quarter part of my orchard and garden belonging to said house as long as she remain unmarried, provided she will live [on the estate] herself." On this Taylor farm was a "Chaise chair and a Chaise House," a press and other utensils "for carrying on the dairy," negro slaves, cattle, wells with "Pumps"—but I cannot find out anything more about the garden.

THE WANTON-LYMAN-HAZARD HOUSE, IN NEWPORT

In 1928, the Newport Historical Society purchased an old house and grounds on Broad Street, with the purpose of preserving a good example of Colonial architecture.

That part of the house on the left of the picture was built in the seventeenth century, when Broad Street was the old Newport Path connecting the Island colonies of Portsmouth and Newport. The main part of the house, with its interesting and typical front steps, is an eighteenth-century addition.

The restoration of the house was placed in the hands of our most distinguished authority on colonial architecture, Mr. Norman M. Isham.

The Newport Garden Association asked Mr. Isham to lay out the grounds of the house in the manner of the eighteenth century.

The plan here given shows the proposed restoration. The picture shows that in the restoration, box edging was used extensively.

House and grounds are now open to visitors during the summer season, and flowers which grew in the garden in the days of the Wantons and the Lymans and the Hazards have been planted again in the box-edged spaces behind the house. In the side yard, the box pattern encloses white sand instead of flowers.

THE BOWERS GARDEN, SOMERSET[1]

On the west bank of the Taunton river lies the little village of Somerset. It is today a curious mixture of small, solid, century-old houses, and unsightly tenements dating from the time when the village had two good-sized iron works. There is nothing to mark it as the scene of past prosperity and grandeur. Part slum, part dignified New England, there is little to suggest that it was once the home of a family interesting for their great wealth as well as their vivid personal qualities. It is here that Jonathan Bowers built the first Bowers house in

[1]Written by Sarah Morton, a descendant of the Bowers family.

Photographed by J. Rugen, Newport
The earliest portion of the Wanton-Lyman-Hazard house was built in 1675

1695; and here that his great-grandson John laid out a garden and squandered a fortune. It is here that Jerathmael, father of John, amassed his wealth and erected his pretentious house. And it is here that the late Captain Daniel B. Eddy, himself a Bowers descendant, built his homestead and another garden, twenty years after John's death.

One cannot write of Jerathmael Bowers without being tempted to philosophize, for Jerathmael was undoubtedly the black sheep of the Bowers family. Yet it was he who threw the family star high into the heavens, where before its sudden fall it shone with a dazzling splendor. As a young man Jerathmael attracted only unfavorable attention. Slighted by his father, who refused to build him a house as he had for his five older brothers, and disliked by the townspeople, it was not until 1760 that he achieved prominence and favor by marrying Mary Shurburne, a Boston beauty who possessed 5,000 pounds in her own right. It was undoubtedly the name of Bowers, even then widely known and considered a passport to distinction and credit, which won him such a distinguished bride, for Jerathmael is described as being illiterate and crafty, with sharp features, possessing no personal attractions whatever. Whether he chose her on account of her pounds or for her beauty which is evident in the remarkable portrait of her by Copley, now in the Metropolitan, we are left to wonder. It was with her pounds, at any rate, that he realized his first ambition and set out to build himself a house which should far surpass those of his brothers in finish and grandeur. And his wife's pounds were probably the foundation on which he erected his fortune. For Jerathmael is later described as being the Caesar of the village, though the youngest of the

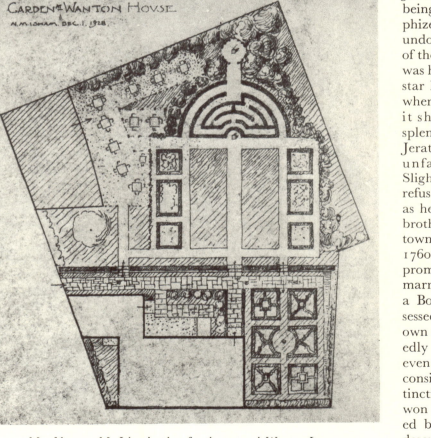

Mr. Norman M. Isham's plan for the restored Wanton-Lyman-Hazard garden

A view of the south side of the Bowers house

The little garden of formal design planted on part of the old Bowers garden by Captain Eddy in 1838

Mrs. Jerathmael Bowers. From the painting in the Metropolitan Museum of Art

family, a money-getter and miser,—the Shylock of numerous communities, and the terror of widows and orphans. His wife, on the other hand, was extremely popular with the people of the village and seems to have been only too willing to spend that which Jerathmael squeezed from the poor. Finding little to admire in her boorish husband Mrs. Bowers was forced to seek her pleasure outside and took to entertaining the gentility of Boston, Newport, and Providence. This, we are told, Jerathmael endured rather than enjoyed. His ideal of social life was copied from the little he knew of the court of Charles II, and frequent acts of his life were far from being in harmony with the American code of social ethics.[1]

It is a relief to turn from Jerathmael to his only son, John, in whom were combined all those attractive characteristics which so enhance the possession of riches. He was the idol of his parents, tall, well-built, of a sandy complexion and fair skin. In due time he also married a reigning beauty, Mary Robinson of Newport. And the two beauties and John led a life of pleasure and gaiety in the house at Somerset, entertaining lavishly day in and day out, spending Jerathmael's money freely while he yet lived.

The garden which John, his wife, and his mother built with

old Jerathmael's money during the latter part of the sixteenth century was undoubtedly one of the finest in New England. It was destroyed following the collapse of family fortunes, and the last of the bricks from its great wall were used in building Fort Adams at Newport. It was on the English style, with terraces and stone-flagged, gravel-lined paths. A few of the terraces still remain. And during the dry season light brown streaks in the grass show where the paths were. It covered, in all, more than an acre of land and is remembered chiefly for its enormous greenhouses, something unusual at that time. In these, pineapples and bananas were grown. Avery P. Slade gives the fullest description of them in his *Sketches of the Early History of Somerset Village*, printed at Fall River, Massachusetts, in 1884:

"John's garden which embraced the land lying north of his father's house, now owned by the heirs of the late Captain Daniel B. Eddy, was conceded to be the finest in New England. It was bounded on the north by the lane leading to the David Bowers house, and was sheltered by a brick wall from ten to twenty feet in height, commencing at Main street and running westerly to Duck pond. On the south side of this wall was constructed costly houses of glass, whose floors and fountains were of marble, and many of the niches were filled with rare vases and expensive statuary. Native summer fruits were here grown in winter. Tropical fruits of the finest flavor daily supplied his table, and the floral department was alleged to have surpassed even the Flora of the tropics. His manor was the constant abode of luxury, fashion and wealth. While the servants were numerous and well paid, the villagers recognized a generous friend in the 'lord of the manor.'"

[1] "Jerathmel Bowers of Swansea, suffered in his rights, properties and possessions during the rebellion in consequence of his loyalty, and from 1776 to 1779 was the perpetual subject of insult and oppression from minute men and committees of correspondence. Early in the political dissentions he was removed by armed men from his wife and children to a prison and closely confined within its walls and was denied intercourse with his family and friends for many months. To the losses from the rebels must be added his losses from the Royal Navy and Army of a ship and cargo, and in 1777-1779 from the encampment of British soldiers on his property on the Island of Conanicut, Rhode Island. This memorial is endorsed: Rejected, May 29, 1786."
—*The Loyalists of Massachusetts: Their Memorials, Petitions and Claims*, by E. Alfred Jones. Published by the Saint Catherine Press of London in 1930.

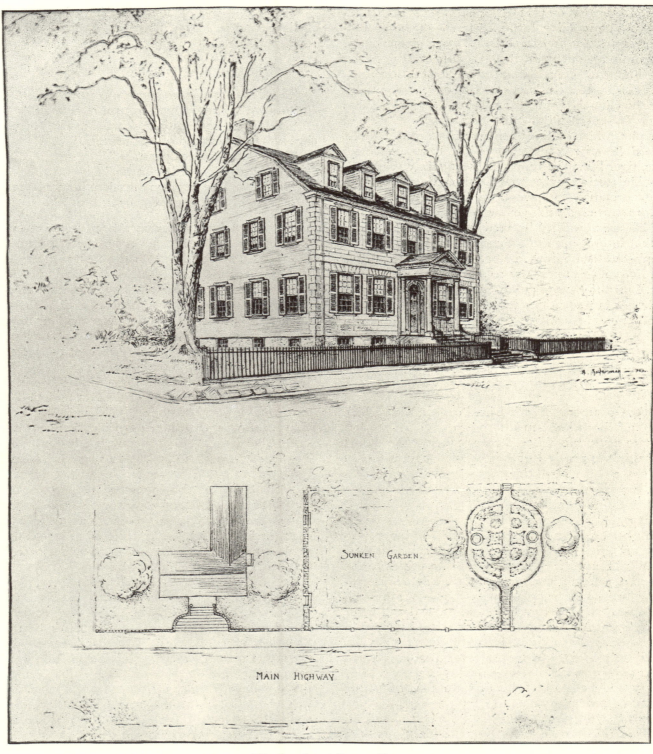

The Jerathmael Bowers House

This is all that is known about what was really an extraordinary garden, but it will, perhaps, be of interest to say a few words about John, whose life was extraordinary for other things than his garden. It was he who challenged a friend to see who could eat the most expensive breakfast and ended his meal by devouring a hundred-dollar bill sandwiched between two pieces of cake. On one occasion he was sent to Boston to dispose of a cargo of tea arrived from Canton on one of his father's ships. On the first night he gambled away the cargo; on the second, the brig. Afraid to return home and face his father's anger, John sailed off to New Orleans, and then up the Mississippi where, for a period of two years, he dwelt with an Indian tribe, marrying the daughter of the chief. His father, on learning his whereabouts from traders, sent word of his forgiveness and begged John to return home, which he did. A few months later a dusky Indian maiden walked into the village of Somerset, carrying a papoose on her back, of which she claimed John as the father. One can well imagine the disturbance produced in the village. And long after the Indian maid had quietly departed bearing generous gifts from John which fully recompensed her for the loss of a husband,

the sewing circle discussed her brief visit. They saw a savage refinement in her manner; they thought her features regular and irresistibly bewitching; in fact, they considered her the peer of any lady in town. And from this came the popular verdict: John's taste was justified. John was certainly one who believed with Horace, 'Dum licet in rebus iucundis vivet beatus' (While time permits live happily in the midst of pleasures).

After Jerathmael's death in 1796 John fairly squandered his inheritance and no one was more surprised than he when in 1804 creditors laid claim to his last penny, for John Bowers firmly believed and frequently avowed, that the ordinary lifetime of a man was not long enough in which to spend his fortune. It turned out otherwise however, for when John was last heard of in 1819 he was serving as supercargo of a ship off Guinea.

And now on the site of his greenhouses stands the homestead of the late Capt. Daniel B. Eddy. And between it and the Jerathmael Bowers house, stands a house erected during the last sixty years. The Bowers' house itself still stands, roomy, reserved, dignified. One can well believe that it and the tall elms around it have memories of a golden age.

It is quite fitting that on part of the old Bowers garden, in front of the Captain Eddy house, there should be an old-fashioned garden built by one of Jerathmael's descendants. This garden was laid out about 1838. Captain Eddy designed it himself with the aid of his compasses while off on a voyage, bringing back with him the bricks for the walks, the granite-rounds for the fountains, and even some of the plants. There are three circles on either side of the center path. These and the garden plots which outline them are still planted with the old-fashioned flowers: columbine, phlox, balm, madonna lilies, irises, tiger lilies, red tulips said to be sixty years old, a semi-double rose brought from Louisiana seventy years ago, violets supposed to have been there always, grape hyacinths, nasturtiums and yellow lilies. The two outer circles, which are now filled in, used to be fountains, and I was told that in order to make these play, someone had to keep pumping water up in the house. I asked the son of the late Capt. Eddy if this really was so and he replied, "It certainly was. I used to have to pump." While the Eddy garden is neither large nor pretentious, it has in a marked degree the quality and atmosphere which characterize all old gardens.

SARAH MORTON

GARDENS DURING THE REVOLUTION

In 1777 the Governor of Rhode Island wrote a letter which contained the following statement:

"This State never raised bread corn sufficient to support its own inhabitants; nearly ¼ of the best plow land is now in possession of the enemy; and other considerable tracts so exposed that the occupiers have not yet dared nor been able to plant them for two years past."

It is obvious that all the gardens of the State were growing food, not flowers, during the Revolution, since the importation of corn, etc., from the surrounding colonies grew increasingly difficult as the war went on. The British troops on the Island of Rhode Island and the French fleet in Narragansett Bay had to be supplied with food—to the small planter who was trying to feed his household it didn't make any difference whether friend or foe demanded the corn in his barn and the apples in his cellar. And it didn't make any difference to the troops that some of the corn was growing in the pastures of the loyalists and some on rebel territory. They were hungry and had to be fed. The Commissary in Chief sometimes left a promissory note.

The Governor wrote that a quarter of the best plow land was in the hands of the enemy. That was Rhode Island—the actual Island. From that base, the farms on the mainland were easily ravaged. Foraging expeditions went up the Bay as far as Fall River and Bristol. They frequently pillaged the Narragansett shore. And we must not forget that the Revolution was fought with horses. Hay was a necessity. The British stole the horses of the farmers and the Colonial Army commandeered them and both armies took the hay with the horses. They had to. It was so important to raise more hay and more corn that the soldiers were allowed to leave their regiments and go home to get in the crops. When not allowed, they went. Knowing the dire need for foodstuffs, it is easier to understand the diaries of Hazard and Freeborn and the rest who remained on their Rhode Island farms during the Revolution. Though their attitude does seem a little detached. These extracts are from the Journal of Joseph Dennis:

"June 29, 1778. Portsmouth. I was at home amowing."

"July 1, I was at home, and the Hessians went away, and the 22nd Regiment came and incampt, and the 43rd regiment took their places."

"July 6, I was at home, mowing."

"July 11, In the afternoon I was at Holder Chase's, reaping of rye."

"July 18, I was at home a reaping of our own rye, and last night there were ten geese stolen from my father."

"July 30, I was at home acarting of grain, and the two Galleys and a frigate down by Fogland was burnt and destroyed."

And these are from the Journal of Thomas Hazard:

"April 20, 1779. Narragansett. Began work in the garden."
"May 7th, Planted corn for cousin Hazard."
"May 21st. Laid out the cornfield. The Regulars landed last night and carried off the negroes."
"May 29th. Planted potatoes."
"June 3rd. Planted our beans."
"June 8th, The regulars burned 2 houses last night."
"June 29th. Set out French Turnips."

The heavy demand for garden produce began as early as 1774, when Boston sent an appeal for food for her poorer inhabitants. Rhode Island had no extra crops, so Tiverton sent 72 sheep, Benjamin Jencks, Pardon Gray, and William Durfee driving them up to Boston. Cranston sent four oxen, driven up by Christopher Lippett and Nicholas Sheldon, while East Greenwich sent 25 sheep and four oxen. Newport had no extra food at all, so she sent about one thousand dollars, by Jacob Rod Rivera. As a contrast, we might notice that Hartford sent 738 bushels of rye.

It was with this obvious shortage of foodstuffs, that Rhode Island faced the beginning of the Revolution. The situation soon became very serious in the cities of Newport and Providence. I suppose that there was literally no pleasure gardens in Rhode Island at all, during the whole duration of the war. The reality was pretty bad. It does no harm to repeat one of the bits of folk-lore current in Newport in 1824:

"Mrs. Guthrie's father was obliged to keep his cow in the house in a little bed-room for fear the English soldiers would steal her. He had to make a garden in his parlor chamber because they robbed him of all he could raise in his garden. So he carried earth upstairs and covered his floor a foot deep, and planted it for a garden."

And there is much traditional history, never yet collected. My own father tells the tale his great-aunt Nancy told to him, when he was a little boy. The British were encamped on the Island, where Aunt Nancy could see them from the farm in Somerset where she lived. The men were coming in from the towns above Somerset, to join the American forces on the north end of the Island. They had to cross at Slade's Ferry, just at the foot of Aunt Nancy's farm. All the men were very thirsty when they reached the farm, and before the end of the day they had drained the well absolutely dry—a very serious thing to happen on a farm, you know. Aunt Nancy could remember the calamity very distinctly.

Nothing to do with gardens? Very much to do with gardens. Rhode Island never, as a whole, recovered from the Revolution, and the lost gardens of the days before the war can never now be brought back to their old beauty. It is too late.

AFTER THE REVOLUTION

NEWPORT GARDENS AFTER THE WAR

The Duke de La Rochefoucauld-Liancourt wrote a careful (and somewhat unusual) account of the condition of the Island of Rhode Island in 1795. That was twenty years after the beginning of the Revolution, and therefore twenty years since any important private residences had been built in the colony or any pleasure grounds had been laid out. It was fully fifteen years since the great destruction of trees on the Island, and new fruit trees had undoubtedly been planted to some extent, but the Island was still practically without timber. For Lossing wrote in 1848 that Rhode Island, approached by steamer from Providence, had showed a "bald appearance relieved only by orchards, which showed like dark tufts of verdure in the distance." And in 1794, John

Drayton, Governor of South Carolina, had written to his family from Newport: "The eye is thrown round for trees, but in vain. The troops of Britain like the locusts of Afric, have withered each tree upon this unhappy Island."

So the Duke writes, in 1795: "This Island exhibits a continued succession of meadows and maize. Barley is likewise produced here in abundance. The breweries of Philadelphia and New York furnish an advantageous market for this last article. Formerly this island was entirely covered with fruit trees and other wood. But these the English destroyed during the war. The soil is light, sandy, and in general unimproved by manure or skillful tillage. The common extent of the farms is 70 acres. Some small number of them contain 200 acres, and 3 or 4, even 400 acres. . . .

"So many [of the Rhode Island young men] are disposed to become farmers for themselves, even without adequate stock, that laborers are not to be procured for any reasonable hire, even in cases of the most urgent necessity. It is a disadvantage also to the agriculture of this territory, that it is everywhere adjacent to the sea. The young people have, in consequence of this, long been accustomed to prefer a seafaring life to husbandry."

the traces of their former inclosures, can be seen. The houses are either desolate or are inhabited in their least ruinous parts by people who, on account of the smallness of their capitals, their dislike to labor, and many other reasons, are much inferior in condition to the people of other parts of New England."

The Merchants, and the gardens of the Merchants, had disappeared. Their houses were "left desolate," and some stand today, still desolate, after 132 years of waiting for their splendor to return—or were used by faithful henchmen of the rebel party, whose services had to be rewarded somehow, of course.

The Overing House is a case in point. Now the property of Mr. Bradford Norman, Lossing wrote in 1848 that it was probably before the war "the most spacious mansion on the Island out of Newport." He made a sketch of it for his *Pictorial History of the Revolution*, and wrote that it was finely "shaded by willows, elms, and sycamores." But it had "fallen into much neglect."

The new land holders had no "old retainers," no "faithful negroes," little furniture, no large ideas of spacious living, no need for much house room. They just "lived in the ell,"

"Vaucluse," last and loveliest of the old country houses of Rhode Island. The façade is now in the Metropolitan Museum

It is quite evident that the first requisite for the maintenance of a pleasure garden, an abundance of labor, was lacking when the Duke wrote his memoirs. The great labor supply of the days before the war had never included Freemen or the sons of Freemen. Agriculture under supervision had been felt for two centuries to be a slave's job. And one of the main causes of the Revolution was the hatred of the landless man and the man of small estate for the great landholder whose wealth was not, of course, produced by the land he held but by the brain which ran his counting house and sent his ships to trade with all the world.

For the landless man, the Revolution was a great success. The class he hated was annihilated. The Royalist fled for his life, which he did not always save. The Patriot was ruined. In both instances, the new government took the property, through confiscation or taxation or legislative regulation—it doesn't matter very much, now, though it must have mattered greatly then, as the intelligent members of the community looked about them, in 1800, and saw what the Duke describes so well:

"Before the War there were many opulent inhabitants on Rhode Island, at present only the ruins of their houses, and

and raised some "garden sauce" out back, letting the great farms and orderly garden spaces go to rack and ruin. Some grew barley for the New York market, most grew Indian corn for their daily Johnny cakes—not much more; and the old farms never came back to their own.

Baron Dubourg, in his diary of 1781, tells the same tale: "Rhode Island must have been one of the most pleasing spots in the world before the war; since, notwithstanding the disasters it has suffered, some of the houses destroyed, and all of its woods cut down, the Island is still a charming residence. The inhabitants are inactive and in consequence not laborious."

Josiah Quincy in his diary of 1800, wrote: "It is 11 miles from Bristol Ferry to Newport—the soil is rich and willing—all the wood upon the Island was cut off by the British during the war, so that there is none at present, but what is of late growth. Marks of improvement are rare. One cannot refrain from believing that this Island has been . . . stagnant for 30 years past."

There was, however, one great exception. The Elams were still able to keep up their Island farm. This is the era of "Vaucluse."

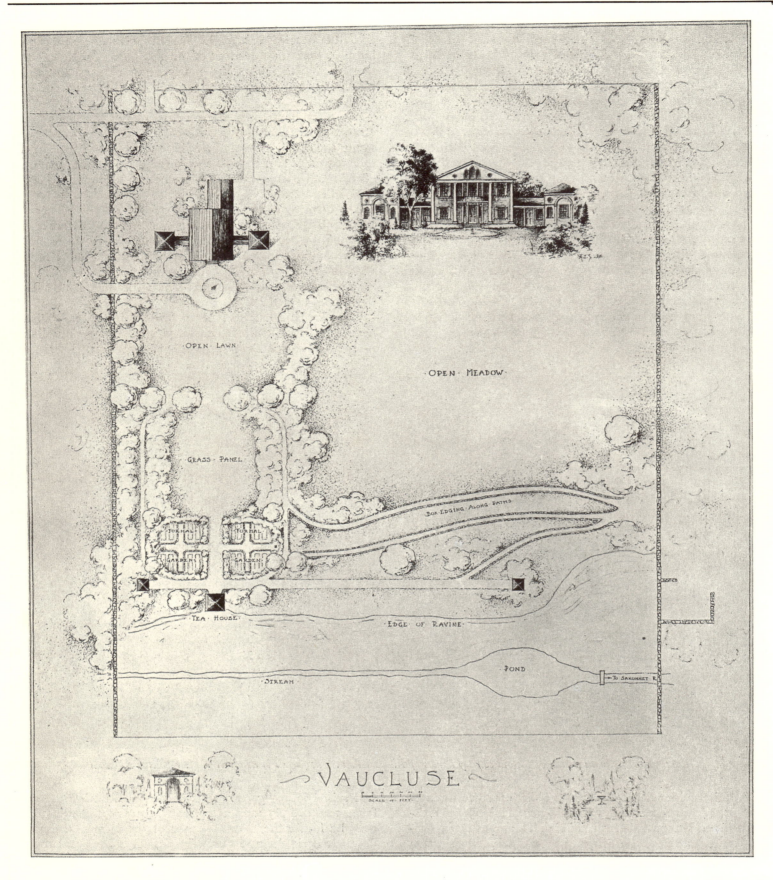

VAUCLUSE

"VAUCLUSE"

In the days of a culture we have forgotten, a splendor now desolate or dead, there were Englishmen, there were colonial Englishmen, living in Newport, Rhode Island, who read leisurely, in their great libraries, the sonnets of Petrarch, bound in calf with tooling and gilding and copper plate. Petrarch, the lover of Laura, was to these men of the eighteenth century a symbol of romance—elegant, eighteenth-century romance. When Laura proved unkind, Petrarch left the gay world of Rome, to bury himself and his elegant sorrow at Vaucluse in Avignon, a place in the country—so read these men in their libraries. There was a fountain in the gardens of Vaucluse, they read, and there were nightingales, and Petrarch in the gardens of Vaucluse wrote out his heart for all the world to read.

They were bewitched by the beauty of words, were those men of old-fashioned culture, and it came to the mind of one of them, a certain Honorable Mr. Elam, how lovely any place in the country might be, if it were called "Vaucluse" and filled with the fragrance of great gardens and the sound of falling water.

There was, moreover, to the melancholy satisfaction of the Honorable Mr. Elam, a pretty girl in Newport who had proved unkind.

So this typical gentleman of his generation, who had, typically, inherited from his Uncle Jarvis some hundred acres of good farm land three miles from Newport, determined straightway to make a "Vaucluse" of his very own. Which he did, for all the world to see.

The place is now a ruin. Where all the world rolled up in coach and four, an occasional trespasser now squeezes through a gap in a wall of fieldstone, and looks, half frightened, at the utter desolation of an eighteenth-century dream. Hauntingly lovely, the falling house and the hedges of box, monstrous and neglected, still look south toward a romantic ravine down which a little brook runs quickly into Seaconnet River and the Atlantic Ocean. But the paths of the formal garden are smothered. I cannot find the "labyrinth with serpentine walks, fit emblem of ancient Troy."

He had one, however, the Hon. Mr. Elam, that first owner of "Vaucluse." In the library in the left wing of his house stood Virgil, flanking Petrarch, with all the leading works on scientific agriculture including Topiary Design. In his garden were the Trojan Maze and the Roman Temple and the marble goddesses all white and new from Carrara. And on his farm there was certainly a plough to figure in the table talks of Mr. Elam, for the War of the Revolution was over, you see, when he acquired "Vaucluse" in 1789, and Mr. Elam knew well the habits of Cincinnatus. You may be sure that the fruit trees he imported that first year from France had some connection with Horace. Though the fact that the British army had cut down every tree on the place, for firewood, might have served as a practical reason for planting, had Mr. Elam ever desired a practical reason for anything.

Eighty thousand dollars did he spend on his house and his formal garden alone, with labor at 25 cents a day and the day from sun to sun. Agents of Mr. Elam ransacked France and England for rare trees and shrubs to make six miles of "Winding walks" in the plain Rhode Island meadows. Most of the trees lived. Anything lives on Rhode Island. Roses were his craze. The borders were full of the roses of France, and today there are briers in the dank undergrowth and sparse hayfields by the ravine.

After a breakfast, well cooked and well served by slaves imported by the Hon. Mr. Elam from Africa for his own use, he would sit awhile in his library and read the Bucolics. Breakfast digested, he would stroll out to look at his "kine," grazing in the green meadows, or to admire his new lambs just imported from the mainland. The British army had

The sun-dial at "Vaucluse"

The sad wreck of beautiful "Vaucluse"

eaten up all the livestock on the Island, and the farm had to be restocked, from chickens up.

In the heat of the day, Mr. Elam would take his Petrarch to the Roman temple looking toward the ocean, and sleep a little after his hearty dinner, until he felt the need of exercise. Whereupon he always had the seventeen acres of formal garden to inspect, besides the one hundred and fifty acres of farmland, all under cultivation.

The Duke de la Rochefoucauld-Liancourt, in his *Travels through the United States of North America*, tells us that the farming of "Vaucluse" was really a serious affair. William Rush of Philadelphia had given him a letter of introduction to Mr. Elam, which was presented in the spring of 1796, and the Duke's impressions of "Vaucluse" are informing:

"Samuel Elam is the only farmer on the Island of Rhode Island who does not personally labor upon his own ground. He is an English Merchant from Yorkshire. He lives in a snug small house. [Remember that a Duke is speaking.] Agriculture is the only business that he now follows. He does not boast of having found it, as yet, very profitable. The stone fences enclosing his fields are higher and better than any I have seen in Massachusetts. His meadows are in a state of improvement and fertility, which is considerably profitable. But the difficulty of procuring laborers stands greatly in the way of all agricultural improvements in these parts. Mr. Elam often meets with a contradictory spirit in his working people, who are apt to think that their toil must make them more skillful in husbandry than their idle master."

We observe that though "Vaucluse" was staged for elegant melancholy, Mr. Elam entertained his friends at times. Not only the travelling Dukes of the period were welcome; to the townsfolk of Newport he gave "princely entertainments," according to George Channing who wrote his *Recollections of Newport* between 1793 and 1811. "His tumblers and wine-glasses were highly ornamented, and bore his initials."

His interest in his garden was not greater than his interest in his cellar, it would seem. They made a certain cider

"Vaucluse"—the desolation of an eighteenth-century dream

from the orchards of "Vaucluse" which could not be told from champagne, even by experts. It would appear from contemporary records that the guests at "Vaucluse" were all experts.

But Mr. Elam, on the whole, a little preferred brandy. In fact, his taste for brandy was like his taste for beauty, unbridled. He made "Vaucluse" loveliest of Rhode Island pleasure places, and he ruined his stomach.

So he died, in that east room whose roof is falling through, his bed by that low window veiled in yellow briar, above the vanished bowling green and marble goddesses and all the rest.

The romantic spirit of Mr. Elam worked so well, the magic of man-made beauty is so great, that "Vaucluse" did not die when Mr. Elam died, but caught the heart of a certain Charles De Wolf of Bristol. Under his care, the gardens grew in beauty until there seemed no more that fancy could devise. So the De Wolfs gave a garden party.

It was the talk of the century. Minute accounts are extant. The language is glamorous, confusing. In plain words, which nobody used about a party in those days, or these, it would seem that Mr. De Wolf hung two hundred kerosene or whale oil lamps from the trees and the shrubs in those gardens, hired a singing orchestra which concealed itself in a honeysuckle arbor, served absolutely unlimited champagne, and gained a reputation as host which has endured. The beauty of the women who attended the party was not strictly to his credit, nor did he plant the "winding avenues" in which the "fair ones," "votaries of Venus," walked. Nevertheless he did well, and increased the glory of "Vaucluse."

In 1837 the estate was on the market. Thomas Robinson Hazard bought it, and lived in it so effectively that to all the countryside it is now known as the "old Hazard Place." There are Hazards in the graveyard and ghostly Hazards haunt the falling house.

In the old library Thomas Robinson Hazard wrote of many things. He has left us a record of the traditions of "Vaucluse" before his day. But chiefly was he concerned with the routing of ancient wrongs, that new quest for perfection not of gardens but of humanity which is our mood in this the twentieth century.

THE JEWISH MERCHANTS' GARDENS

Sometime after the Revolution, Abraham Touro, a merchant of Boston, visited Newport, where he had lived as a little boy.

He found the Synagogue where his father had been a Rabbi closed; the grass was growing rank between the stones of the flagged walk from gate to porch; the street in front of the Synagogue was out of repair; and the ancient burial-place was almost lost in a thicket of briar. There was not one living Jew left in Newport.

Touro cleaned up the cemetery, whose deed bears the date of 1677, and planted it with rare trees and flowering shrubs. In his will of 1822, he gave the city $10,000, the income of which was to be used in keeping both the cemetery and the synagogue in repair; and he left $5,000 toward the upkeep of Touro Street, which connects synagogue and cemetery.

It is hard to realize that long before the time of the Touros, Newport had grown to be an intellectual center of the ancient Hebrew civilization. By 1774, there were in the town at least 300 Jewish families and the wealth of Newport was in their hands. They owned wharves and shops and houses, built between the synagogue and the harbor. They owned many ships. And the sons of the first planters of Rhode Island were in command of these ships. I do not find that these Jewish merchants were ship captains or planters themselves, and I do not think that they were ever greatly interested in gardens.

The following extract from a letter written by Abraham Pereira Mendez, who was living on the Island of Jamaica, to Aaron Lopez in Newport, shows more interest in agriculture than does any other record I can find.

"Savannah la Mar, 11th March, 1768.
"Dear Mr. Lopez

"I received your severall favors per Johnson, Tillinghast, Coddington, Andrews, and Brayton, all which give me infinite pleasure to hear of your being in perfect health in company of all our family to whom you'll be pleased to make my best love. . . .

"The sheep are all in poor order, most of them having the swelling under the throat and the running in the nose which prevented my disposing of them. The horses are in poor order. Some can scarcely walk being old, which is the case of northward horses. The staves are so bad that I cannot get half price for them. I wish instead of those articles you had sent split shads, candles, and fish, which would have turned out to great advantage. The oysters has not a handful in each cag.

"The backwardness of our crops and the great rains we have had, prevented my sending Tillinghast with a full load, as most planters has pre-engaged their first rum. . . . I return you my hearty thanks for your kind present per Brayton, and am sorry times will not permit my sending anything good. You'll be pleased to make my love to dear Mrs. Lopez, my sisters and brothers, more so to my little Jacob whom you'll embrace with 100 kisses for me. I wish I could see that happy day of returning to your dear companies as I assure you I am heartily tired of Jamaica.

"I shall procure the Vine Slips and send per first opportunity, as time will not permit sending that quantity.

"Abraham Pereira Mendez"

Lopez made another attempt to get grapevines. I quote from the sailing orders he wrote out for Captain Hyer.

"Sir,   "Newport, December 2, 1769.
"The Sloop *Industry* now under your command, being ready fitted for the seas, you are to embrace the first fair wind and proceed to the Island of Teneriff. . . . When you return, would be glad you would touch at St. Martin's or Saltertudas. . . .

"P. S. I desire you'll procure me about one thousand good long Vine Slips, which please to see well put up in a cask or box with earth."

Where Lopez expected to plant his vineyard I do not know. He may have contemplated purchasing a country seat, as did the other great merchants of Newport. But whatever might have happened was stopped by the war. The Jewish colony suffered greatly, not all of them removing at once.

They found the war bewildering—as Nazro wrote to Lopez: "Can't by any means see through their (British) policy of burning commercial towns." Mr. Lopez had removed his family from Rhode Island very soon after the war began. His house was occupied by the French allies; as we can see in the following letter, from Moses Seixas, one of the few Jewish merchants who remained in Newport through the war period.

"June, 1781.
"I am of opinion flour will be dull here, now the French Army are gone from hence, all except about 400 which are to remain for the present. Amongst the gone are those which held your house, which was evacuated this morning. I have been to take a view of the house, but such a collection of

Judah Touro

straw, dirt, and nastiness I never before saw in any house that was occupied by any that professed gentility."

Though I can find nothing concerning the planting of gardens by the Jews of Newport, I do find the following observation which implies a garden somewhere. The Rev. Ezra Stiles studied Hebrew under a Rabbi in Newport, and he often went to the Synagogue to observe the beautiful old ritual. On the Day of Pentecost in 1773 he noted in his diary that the whole interior of the Synagogue was hung with wreaths and garlands of spring flowers.

"Gone are the living, but the dead remain,
    And not neglected; for a hand unseen,
Scattering its bounty like the summer rain,
    Still keeps their graves and their remembrance green."

So wrote Henry Wadsworth Longfellow, of Abraham Touro and the garden which he made of the Jewish Cemetery on Touro Street. Mr. Longfellow, this, of Craigie House in Cambridge, one-time traveller in Spain and Portugal, no mere poet but a "summer visitor," writing of an ordered beauty which he understood, made by a people exiled from a land which in his youth he had much loved and somewhat comprehended.

Before his day, in 1842 I think, another of the little Touro children, born in Newport before the Revolution, returned from New Orleans where his fortune and his philanthropy were famous, and substituted for the low wooden fence about the burial ground, a high wall of open ironwork and granite posts, building over the iron gate a massive arch of granite, carved with the ancient symbol of the angel of death.

Photographed by Antoinette von Horn

The gate of the Jewish Cemetery in Newport, probably erected about 1840

Through this gate of iron tracery, the tombs of the Touro family, the "marble" of Jacob Rodriguez Rivera with its date of 22d Sebat, A.M. 5549, and other old gravestones with Hebraic inscriptions, can be seen by any passerby, set in a garden of trees and shrubs and pretty flowers.

A purple wistaria vine of great height and beauty blossoms there on each Memorial Day, trailing its enormous clusters from tree to tree.

THE LATER GARDENS OF BRISTOL, MAINLY DE WOLF

At the close of King Philip's War, Bristol, and that neck of land beyond the little town of Bristol called Poppasquash Point, were for the first time available for purposes of colonization, as I have noted earlier in this survey.

The gardens the Bristol planters made during the colonial period were not elaborate, apparently, and I have described them in that earlier section. The earlier merchants who did business in Bristol, such as Nathaniel Byfield from Boston and the Vassall family of Cambridge, may have laid out gardens of a sort. After forty-three years the Byfields went back to Boston, where it was, of course, more comfortable than in Poppasquash. And the Vassall property was confis-

The oldest drawing of the William De Wolf house, now owned by Miss Middleton and called the Middleton house. It was built by the architect Russell Warren, who also built the Colt house, "Linden Place," in Bristol

A Byfield tomb, in an old drawing

cated by the State in the course of the Revolution.

It is with the spectacular rise of the De Wolf family that the making of pleasure gardens began in Bristol, and the country round about.

We first come across old Mark Anthony De Wolf, living on a small farm on Poppasquash. He had a number of sons; they followed the sea, they served in the ships of the merchant house of Brown—so did most of the sons of the old planters thereabout. But the De Wolf boys developed a most extraordinary aptitude for life on board the slave ships and the privateers of the period. No one could take a ship to Africa, and bring home a greater number of negroes in the hold, with less expenditure of rum. No one could board a ship belonging to the enemy, and get away with more plunder. No

one knew better, for a time, what to do with the high profits which came in. All the De Wolfs had a perfect genius for dramatic living on the sea and on the shore.

So about the year 1800, Charles De Wolf, who was looking after the mercantile end of the business, built a great house in Bristol, near Constitution Street, facing the harbor. The gardens ran down to the water. People who knew the old place say that there was a raised terrace in front of the house, and on that terrace a most beautiful formal garden. In the garden there was a "summer house" a picture of which is shown here.

For when the mansion house was burned to the ground in 1852, the summer-house was removed to the grounds about Captain Gardiner's residence and there preserved most carefully. Later, it has again been moved to "Linden Place" on the main street of Bristol, where it can be seen by any passerby.

It is not uninteresting to remember that Charles De Wolf at one time owned the old Elam place, "Vaucluse", on the Island of Rhode Island, and there lived a few years. The three "summer houses" in the garden of "Vaucluse" may have been built by Charles De Wolf—it is quite possible. If so, they were built before 1829, for in that year he sold the Island property to Peleg Tallman.

The second De Wolf to make a pleasure garden was William. In 1808 he hired a Providence architect, Russell Warren, to draw plans for a great house he erected on Poppasquash Point, on the farm lands of old Mark Anthony himself. This

An old drawing of stumps of the Mazzard cherry on the estate of Wm. De Wolf. This cherry, grown throughout England and France in the seventeenth and eighteenth centuries and now largely gone wild, was universally used for making brandy, and was very early imported into this country for that purpose. It is described in Andrew Jackson Downing's book on fruit

The Susan Reynolds De Wolf garden, laid out shortly after 1798, at "The Farm," Bristol

The main path in the garden at "The Farm"

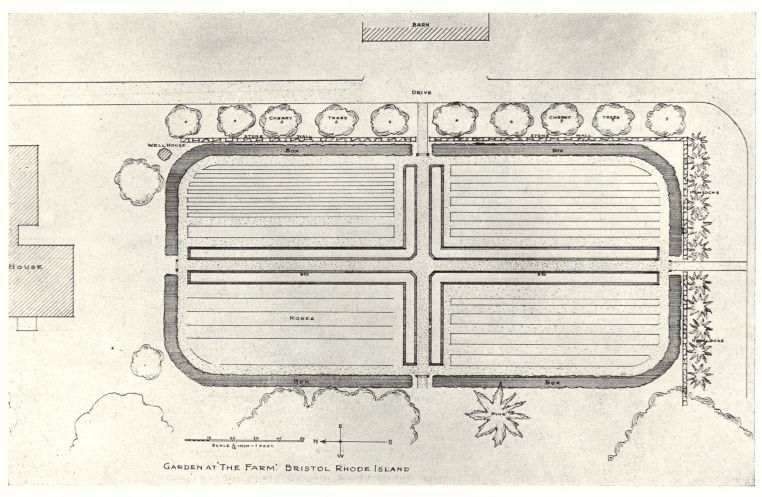

The plan of the Susan Reynolds De Wolf garden

house is still in existence, and the same lawns slope down to the water, and the same fence still fences out the highway on the west. I have given here the earliest drawing of the house built by William De Wolf, and also a view of the house and grounds as they look today, taken by permission of Miss Middleton, the present owner of the property.

It was in 1780 that Claude Blanchard, Commissary in Chief of the French army, was in Bristol on Poppasquash. He wrote in his diary:

"Poppusquash forms a kind of landscape surrounded by trees. The commonest are acacias, pear trees, and cherry trees; the ground is sown with flax and maize, with very little barley and rye. . . . In the afternoon we observed a plant which is very common in this country. The botanists call it Recenus Americana; in France it is found only in the gardens of the botanists. We saw no peculiar plant anywhere else, and much wild chickory and sorrel thorn."

Poppasquash looks much today as it did in the days of the French encampment, and around the Middleton house grow the acacias, the pear trees, the cherry trees, the buttercups, and the Indian corn. Blanchard

would miss the flax — we do not grow flax in Bristol any more.

In 1798, Susan Reynolds, brought up in the old Reynolds garden dating from the seventeenth century, married John De Wolf who had built a big farmhouse a little way out in the country, where the ground rises toward Mt. Hope. Before

The summer-house from the garden of Charles De Wolf, as it appears in its present location at "Linden Place," in Bristol

The William De Wolf house as it is today, photographed by permission of Miss Middleton, the present owner. See also page 430

long the young bride made a large but simple garden to the west of the new farmhouse, and that De Wolf garden is still in existence. A plan of the garden, drawn to scale, and a picture or two, are shown here. The garden paths are bordered with box, and the four gates are of wood, all painted white; these high gateways remind me of the old gateway at "Silver Creek." All through the nineteenth century, the garden was tended carefully, the tiger lily and the yucca added as each came into fashion. By 1900 it had run down a little, as gardens will, and Mrs. Herreshoff restored it most carefully to its original lines and planting. Of the old flowers, there still remain the day lilies, the syringa, the yellow iris with the brown stripes, and the great lilac bushes.

The summer-house which stood in the garden of "The Mount," the mansion of James De Wolf. Photographed forty years ago, it is no longer in existence

The most vigorous of the De Wolf brothers of the earlier generation was Captain James. He was actually the captain of a slave ship before the age of twenty-one. He was a really great privateer, well known in the bloody annals of his time. Before the age of twenty-five, he had made his fortune.

And then, of course, "he took a great interest in agricul-

ture." He acquired a thousand acres of land round about Bristol. He built a "stately mansion" called "The Mount." . . . "From thence in the early morning he strode forth to superintend the cultivation of his fertile acres."

His garden has been entirely obliterated, but many persons now living say it was exceedingly beautiful. The formal flower garden was on the south side of the house, toward Tan Yard Lane, and the flower beds were all bordered with box. In the garden was a charming summerhouse, built on a rock, having a little lead image of King Philip on the apex of the roof, as you can see in the picture taken forty years ago.

"Linden Place," the most magnificent and the latest of the De Wolf mansions, was built by a member of the next generation of the De Wolf family. This was General George De Wolf, son of Charles who built his pretty summer-house in his garden by the harborside. Like his uncle William, he hired Russell Warren, the Providence architect, to make his plans. And the house is today the most important building in Bristol, one of the outstanding relics of our pseudo-Grecian period of architecture. I doubt if it ever had an elaborate garden. In laying out the grounds, brick and marble were called for in the specifications, and the tale is, that the builders went out to Somerset, and bought the dismantled pleasure grounds of Jerathmael Bowers. The Bowers family had lost their money a little earlier in the century than did the De Wolfs, but Bristol and Somerset alike, De Wolf and Bowers and all the rest, went down together in the new world where the qualities which had made them great in an earlier day proved their undoing.

There is in Bristol another survival of the great period when Bristol was more wicked and more beautiful. This is the Babbitt-Morice garden whose history and photographs,

In 1800, Theodore Foster, United States Senator for Rhode Island, and Dr. Solomon Drown, lecturer on Botany in Brown College, bought jointly a farm in the village of Foster.

Dr. Drown went to live on the farm with his family in 1801, and in 1803, at the close of his political career, Foster did the same. They had been boys together, fellow-students in Brown College, and friends through the succeeding years. They had much the same tastes and they developed the farm jointly.

They called it "Mount Hygeia." To various spots on the farm they gave other classical names, even calling the new

The garden laid out by Captain Morice

taken for this book by Mrs. Babbitt's kind permission in the last year of her life, really deserve a separate description.

THE BABBITT-MORICE GARDEN

This garden was laid out in its present form in 1835. Captain Morice bought the house in 1810. He then went back to France and returned with a wife. The two of them, according to tradition, laid out a garden full of little box-bordered beds in the shape of hearts and diamonds and crescents. This garden was destroyed by the big storm which ruined also the garden at "Silver Creek," up the road, and it was in 1835 that the present garden, full of oblong beds, box-bordered, was laid out in its present fashion with gravel walks and fruit trees.

The owner of this garden says that none of the old garden flowers exist, but that the box is the box of 1835.

highway, when it passed through their farm from Providence to Hartford, "The Appian Way."

They wrote verses together, full of classical allusion, and made a garden of curious botanical specimens. There they lived until they died, and were good citizens of Foster.

I do not know if all their little temples to Hygeia and the other deities of Greece have utterly disappeared; it may be that in Foster they can still be found.

In 1824, Field and Maxcey of Providence printed a little book by Dr. Drown called *The Compendium of Agriculture*.

ROSE FARM, PROVIDENCE

Between 1799 and 1803 the Dexter family of Providence built a large square wooden house on land that now forms a corner of Angell Street and Diman Place. At the beginning of the nineteenth century no other house could be seen from

Another view of the Babbitt-Morice garden

this Dexter house, it was so far out in the country. The estate consisted of four acres of land, the dwelling house, a barn, some outbuildings, including a summer-house, some sort of garden. The Dexters soon sold the place to a man from Charleston, South Carolina, who immediately sold it to another Charleston man.

Again it was sold; this time to Alexander Brown, also of

Charleston. Mr. Brown named the place "Bellevue," and he built a wooden fence or balustrade around the roof of his house and had chairs placed about on the flat enclosure. On clear days a beautiful view of Newport was plainly visible down the Bay.

"In 1837 he sold the estate to Mr. John J. Stimson of Providence, whose grandchildren still own the house. Mr. Stimson

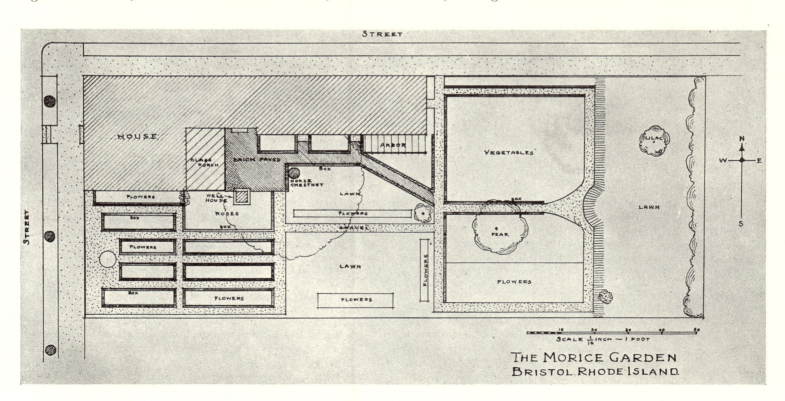

THE MORICE GARDEN
BRISTOL, RHODE ISLAND

The Garden at Lippitt Hill Farm

Lippitt Hill Farm, the old homestead at Hope, Rhode Island, is an inheritance which has never been out of the family. Its present owner is Miss Julia Lippitt Mauran, direct descendant of that Moses Lippitt who bought the land from Peleg, grandson of Roger Williams. His old house still stands, built in 1720. In 1805, his descendant, General Christopher Lippitt, divided the farm and built the generous, wide-roofed old mansion to which the garden belongs.

The garden is a space seventy-five feet by a hundred, on the south side of the house, enclosed in old stone walls. Over these walls riot clematis and woodbine, trumpet vine and roses. Within, the plan is simple—just a border all around, a central bed of damask and yel-low briar roses, a grass plot, and one precious little space reserved for bleeding-heart, polyanthus and other special treasures. At one corner grows an acacia locust with trunk four feet in diameter, which throws an agreeable shade on hot midsummer days, and diagonally across is the tall elm which serves as a support for a huge trumpet vine.

At the far side, an arched gate leads to the picking and monthly rose garden and to the orchard beyond.

Beehives and a few shrubs find a place in this garden. There are lilacs twenty feet tall, but the old box bushes, six feet high, were killed by severe ice-storms a few years ago. Grapevines cover the picturesque outbuildings beyond the garden gate.

had a large garden and extensive orchard in which there were all kinds of fruits including pears, apples, cherries, peaches, quinces and strawberries. Loveliest of all was his rose garden, and because it was so beautiful the name of the estate was changed to 'Rose Farm.' There was an old fashioned summer house in the garden at the end of a box bordered path." Probably the summer-house of the Dexters who built the dwelling house also.

"The summer house was a perfect specimen of the colonial type," according to a local historian. But as it was, probably,

The summer-house at "Rose Farm," now 300 Angell Street, Providence

not built before 1800, this seems odd. It was papered, so they say, with landscape paper, representing alpine chalets surrounded with borders of roses. A large glass chandelier for candles hung from the center of the ceiling, and the windows were protected by panelled shutters.

In 1881 the larger part of the garden was cut up into house-lots.

THE SULLIVAN DORR ESTATE, IN PROVIDENCE

The Sullivan Dorr house was built in 1809–10 by Sullivan Dorr, father of Thomas Dorr of Dorr's Rebellion. It is said to have been built on the model of Pope's villa at Twickenham.

The terraced gardens behind the house were laid out on the land where Roger Williams planted his orchard in the seventeenth century. He was buried in a corner of his orchard, of course, but for years the place of his burial was forgotten.

The terraces are full of old fruit trees, and offer an interesting example of the manner in which ground ascending steeply from the house can be treated.

Anyone who goes to the Dorr estate will probably go into the house to see the lovely mural decorations painted by Michele Felice Corne, about the time the house was built. He was an Italian from Naples, and he did much work in this country in the earlier years of the nineteenth century.

In 1822, he went to Newport, where he lived until he died.

The Sullivan Dorr house

There he bought a house and a little land; he was, according to tradition, the first person in Newport to grow and eat tomatoes.

SOME OLD PEACE DALE GARDENS[1]

In 1789, the first week in May, Nailer Tom (Thomas B. Hazard) records "began to Garden. Went to get Nezer Smith to help me Garden tomorrow but he said he could not. Robert Knowles Plowed my Garden." The next day, May 8, "Worked in Garden, got many sorts of Roots out of Benjamin Rodman's Garden this morning." A few days later, "Thos. Redwood went to John Congdon's after onyons and sott them out." As late as the 25th of June "sott out Cabbages." The fourth of July that year was "generally Foggee. Finished wedeing the Garden." The 30th of July, "Else Congdon dined here, and I gave her some peese and Turnips." In October he took forty bushels of potatoes to the ferry to send to Newport for Rowland Hazard; and the 8th of November, "put my beets in Sellar." So here were onions, cabbages, peas, turnips, beets and potatoes, all grown on the pleasant sloping land which lies a little to the south of the present Peace Dale church, between the church and the High School, on what is now called Columbia Street. This land is still famous for its vegetables and part of it is now cultivated as a market garden. But with these entries of a strictly utilitarian nature, on the 18th of October of that same year Nailer Tom "Sott out six white Rose Bushes in my Garden."

July 13, 1805, Nailer Tom records: "Rowland Hazard and family came from Newport to Benjamin Rodman's house to live," and a few days later, "Warner Knowles began an addition to Benjamin Rodman's house." There are deeds of this year recorded with full description. A pear tree was one point of departure, but the garden wall is more solid, "running easterly to the plain." We therefore have good authority for believing that this house and garden became the home of Rowland Hazard in 1805, when Benjamin Rodman moved across the Saugatucket where Shepherd Tom describes him as grinding corn into Ambrosia.

The house that stood in this garden is the house which Nailer Tom mentions in January, 1790, in which the first Friends' Meeting was held after the destruction of the old meeting-house by fire on Tower Hill. It is still standing, and one can imagine its pleasant long room, with the windows facing the south, large enough to hold a company of fifteen or twenty with ease; its great fireplace opening into the square stone chimney with blazing logs on that January day.

The garden has always been a famous one since the days of its first mention in 1789. Here came Caroline Newbold, brought as a bride by her husband, Rowland G. Hazard.

[1]Written by Caroline Hazard.

The plantation of native rhododendrons was done in her time, the whole west of the house being screened by clumps of rhododendron trees. Here also is the Bloomsdale summerhouse, copied from one on her father's estate at Bloomsdale on the Delaware, a few miles from Philadelphia. She brought with her lovely clematis, with its bell-shaped lilac flowers, which was cherished carefully and grew in this garden and later in the garden of her own planning and planting, when she moved to the house which has now become Holly House.

Great trees in a Peace Dale garden

The lines of this garden are extremely simple: a broad path leading directly south from the wide stone steps of the house with a circular bed blocking its course about fifty feet from the house, the path dividing and going about it to reunite some distance farther and end in a broad cross walk which divides the flower garden and the pleasant shady grove on each side from the vegetable garden lying full to the south, free to the sun.

The great strawberry shrub bush of the older Mrs. Hazard's planting is still there, and the house has been happy in having only sympathetic occupants who have cared for the garden. To it, in the early thirties, Dr. William Ellery Channing

eastward just on the border of what the old deed called the "Plain." The land on the north of the stone wall was described as the property of Rowland Hazard and on that land his father, called College Tom, had some of his orchards, the remains of which I can remember in my childhood. College Tom had the land from his grandfather, old Thomas Hazard of Boston Neck, who made the original purchase from Samuel Sewall, in 1698, deriving his title from John Hull, his father-in-law, one of the original Pettaquamscut purchasers.

On this land, with all its associations and traditions, Oakwoods had already been built, and the second stone house, into which Mr. and Mrs. Rowland Gibson Hazard moved, followed a year or so later. Here Mrs. Hazard was able to have a garden to her mind. Here is the beautiful magnolia tree she set out, and the lines of the old garden are carefully preserved; the square garden which one often sees with a border all about it and a cross walk with a center bed. Her grandson's wife, also Mrs. Rowland Gibson Hazard, has added to and developed it.

A table made from an old millstone, in the garden of Mrs. Rowland Gibson Hazard, Peace Dale

To the north of the formal garden is a broad grass walk, divided from it by rose covered arches. A hedge screens it from the westerly and northerly winds. At the foot of this broad walk is a cross path leading through the hedge toward the Saugatucket, and down a couple of great stone steps which were the doorsteps into College Tom's cheese house. These are carefully marked and dated 1750.

At the south of the formal garden the land falls away and a flight of steps leads to the lower garden. Fruit trees are pleached against this wall and opposite the steps a little Chinese pagoda rises from the rock garden. A cross walk leads to the great table made from an old millstone, with a circular seat around it, and at the other end to the bowling green which leads to the beautiful natural spring bubbling up from the sand glistening white even against the marble

found his way. Miss Elizabeth Peabody came too and there was high converse. In the summer the delightful relatives of Mrs. Hazard came for long visits, which were the custom, for why should one take a journey that lasted for days to turn around and go back again? So for a month or six weeks every summer the house was full of young cousins, and the beautiful sisters of Mrs. Hazard, for she was one of the six daughters of John Newbold. The house might almost be called a six-daughter house, with the fame of old Benjamin Rodman's daughters clinging to it also.

It was in 1856 that this house was left by Mr. and Mrs. Hazard to take up their abode in the new stone house to the

coping. This used to be called the iron spring, and my grand-father, who was a follower of Berkeley in his medical as well as his philosophical views, and believed in the virtues of tar water and especially of iron, thought it had special properties. At certain seasons of the year the iron spring water was always brought to the house as a suitable tonic. This garden, thanks to the old planting which has been done for years, and the beautiful trees which are around it, has the look of age, and is the direct descendant of some of the oldest gardens in this part of the state. In itself it is nearly seventy years old, and has many features which are much older. Under the enthusiastic care of its present owner it is a mass of bloom from early spring to late autumn. Its peonies and campanulas are famous. There are climbing roses and splendid standard roses. In the mild climate of southern Rhode Island the sun is genial, and frost delays. This year, on the 23rd of October, fifty-seven different kinds of flowers were still in bloom. It is a lovely place of rest and refreshment, a joy to all who can spend in it "sweet and wholesome hours."

CAROLINE HAZARD

THE GARDEN OF THE HON. WILKINS UPDIKE[1]

In 1813, Wilkins Updike, having lost his vast ancestral acres at Cocumsoussuc, Wickford, Rhode Island, through endorsing a note for an older brother, came to Little Rest (now Kingston), then the commercial center of the Town of South Kingston. Here he opened a law office and in 1820 built the commodious dwelling house which is still standing. The great front door is entered over a Dutch stoop with its straight-backed seats and the traditional trees—one on either side. Following the general architecture of the times, the bright sunny rooms cluster around an immense central chimney with a generous fireplace in each room. But little space is wasted in the small front entry with its winding stair.

Through the wide front door, hosts of friends were always coming for a cordial welcome. With a genial disposition, a keen wit, and generous hospitality abetted by a wife whose tastes were in sympathy with his own, Col. Updike was a favorite host with his friends, both young and old. He was a lover of the beautiful in art and in nature and gradually the walls of his home were covered with portraits by Copley and Smibert, and many other fine old paintings. It was in the cheerful western room, surrounded by his fine library of valuable old books, that the *History of the Narragansett Church* (that invaluable contribution to Rhode Island history) and the *Memoirs of the Rhode Island Bar* were written. And in this charming home his family of twelve children (all but one) grew to maturity. The crane has never been unhung from the old kitchen fireplace and the great iron handirons and many cooking utensils still bear testimony to the delicious cooking of the days gone by. In the ample garret a little square green platform on castors tells the tale of a large oleander tree, too large to be handled in any other way, but which could thus be moved from one sunny window to another. In those days the oleander tree was a very important winter decoration.

But long ere this, Mr. Updike's beloved garden had been started, wherein he sought relaxation from his busy life as lawyer and author. This garden began directly from the eastern piazza from which ran a broad path for sixty feet, bordered on either side by a box hedge. At the end of this path stood a beautiful white lilac which still rears its dainty head far above surrounding shrubs as if in its old age it is bound to keep its lovely clusters from a desecrating hand. This broad path was met by another at right angles, which, after some distance, having left the flowers behind, ran straight through a vegetable garden. At the intersection of other paths were shrubs: Tartarian honeysuckle, pink and white spirea and the stately althea. The borders on these paths were radiant with flowering almond, yellow lilies, widow's tears, blue bells, bleeding-hearts, marigolds, daf-

[1]Written by Annie M. Hunt.

The Wilkins Updike garden

fodils, narcissus, larkspur, roses, and, of course, those spicy, feathery pinks and sweet williams, and many others. At the extreme edge of some of the borders the modest little English daisy, with its white centers and daintily tinged pink edges always claimed its place as the favorite flower of Mrs. Updike. Lilies of the valley, myrtle, johnny-jump-ups and none-so-pretties still bear testimony to their ancestors, but the most pathetic of the survivors are the homely little mullein and chimney pinks which are so scorned in the wealth of bloom of the present day. Tulips were rare in these old days, and an ardent admirer of an older daughter sent her some bulbs of

Box border in the Wilkins Updike garden

the precious flowers which were carefully planted and their development anxiously watched. The buds duly appeared, but alas for human anticipation! in an unguarded moment a tiny niece strayed near the precious plants and, attracted by the bright colors, filled her little skirt with the unopened flowers! She honestly and proudly took them to her aunt, saying "pretty, pretty." History goes no farther.

At the very end of the long straight path into the vegetable

The trees of "Fyrtre Hall," crowning the hill, are seen from all parts of Narragansett Bay

garden, as if loath to leave the flowers behind, are great clumps of yellow lilies and cabbage and cinnamon roses. This path too was most attractively bordered with red, white, and black currants and gooseberry bushes. Of course, in this vegetable garden were sweet marjoram, summer savory and sage, not forgetting a good mint bed and a great variety of vegetables which amply supplied this large family in summer and winter.

The third generation are enjoying the fruits of Col. Updike's labors, for the dogwood which was set out back of the box border has attained a wonderful size and in the spring is a delight to all beholders. An English hawthorn on the south far out-tops the old house and at blossoming time is a mound of beauty. Purple lilacs meet one at every turn. The Indian currant with its fall burden of crimson berries snuggles up to one of the old stone walls. A beautiful, small, white climbing rose still survives. Here too are great clumps of burnt-orange lilies, the like of which, as garden escapes, have done so much to beautify our roadsides and, with the groups of purple lilac which are so often near them, tell the passerby of a home that has vanished.

ANNIE M. HUNT

FYRTRE HALL, EAST GREENWICH

On the crest of the hill in Warwick, on Division Street which divides Warwick from East Greenwich, there is an old estate of about seventy-five acres which was laid out in its present form at the very ending of the period under our consideration. It is called "Fyrtre Hall" (by its present owner, Mrs. William Hodgman, who bought the place in 1900), because of its long rows of superb firtrees; or, more accurately, Norway spruce trees.

Before 1816, much of this property was part of the Governor Greene estate across the road. After that date the land changed owners rapidly, until it fell into the hands of Josiah Barker, who came to Rhode Island from New Orleans about 1840 and developed the estate, building a large house in the Southern colonial style. Rumor has it that Barker was a

New England lad who went South after an unfortunate love affair, and that his lady, dying many years later, left him this property in her will. It is certain that he planted some of the trees about the house, and probable that he laid out the little box garden on the west, which at one time was surrounded by a hedge of arbor-vitae, and had strawberries in each of the four box beds. Behind the garden, he built a little house for his colored servants, whom he had brought up from New Orleans—typical slave quarters. This house and the remodeled Great House still stand.

In 1856, Thomas J. Hill bought the estate from the Barker family, and planted more firtrees, double rows of them.

The trees of "Fyrtre Hall," crowning the hill, are seen from all parts of Narragansett Bay. Experts in tree lore have pronounced them the finest in New England. Though beautiful in spring, with fresh green on the tips of their branches, in winter after a snow-storm they are at their best.

THE GARDENS OF FALL RIVER

Last to be settled of all the land about Narragansett Bay were the 41 square miles of the territory which is now Fall River.

In the heart of the present city there is a ledge of excellent granite, and boulders of pudding-stone higher than a man's head are still to be found, even beside the main thoroughfares. Bell Rock where the arbutus grows, Cleft Rock with the columbine, Rolling Rock, the Ledge, are familiar landmarks; and the open meadows are still strewn with common fieldstone of every size and shape. Old Indian trails ran through this territory; from Plymouth and Boston to Providence, the Connecticut settlements, Portsmouth, Newport, and the many isolated farms of the countryside. When we read of Robert Gibbs of Plymouth being summoned to court for "fetching of plow irons from Rhode Island on the Lord's Day," we know that he was but one of the thousands of men and women who rode—yes—and walked—along these trails on the ordinary business of their daily lives. All the planters round about knew from observation that the soil of Fall River was full of rocks and far from fertile.

So, apparently, although Fall River was a part of the Plymouth Grant, nobody from Plymouth or anywhere else cared to settle there before King Philip's War. At the outbreak of the war, the whole 41 square miles seem to have been uninhabited, except for a few hunters and trappers and friendly Indians living in their summer encampments by the shore.

During the war, the whole territory was a battleground.

But when King Philip's War was over, all the country round the Bay became desirable. The old settlements were getting crowded. Companies were formed to purchase vacant lands.

Some of the old hunters and trappers in Fall River territory objected. They had squatters' rights. We read of a group of purchasers coming down to the bank of the stream with their legal adviser, to take possession of the land in the fashion of that day and generation. The Court Records of Plymouth say "that David Lake, in the month of May, in the year 1680, near to the river called the

Jefferson Borden, of Fall River

Long double row of Norway spruce trees at "Fyrtre Hall"

Fall River . . . did interrupt, molest, and hinder the said complainants from taking or receiving quiet and peaceable possession of the said lands—which they had right to have—, the said Lake, forceably taking and pulling the turffe and twigg out of the hands of Joseph Church, attorney to the sellars of the said land, which he had cutt up to deliver to the said complainants, the said Lake pretending title in the behalf of himself and others," etc.

It seems very old and far away—the law of Twig and Turf. They were indeed a people of the soil.

And yet, none of these first settlers of the 41 square miles of Fall River seems to have expected to live by farming alone. Each man thought of himself as a planter, and built himself a farmhouse on a farm, but each man had some other project by which he rather expected to support his family. The Reads from Newport came to start a tannery. The Winslows opened a blacksmith shop. Chase was a cooper from over the River, burnt out during the late war. The Hathaways ran a tavern up Assonet way. Other men took shares in schooners, and their sons went off to sea. John Borden and his sons from Portsmouth were interested in using the water power along the stream. Captain Church, from Tiverton, had put up a saw mill, down by the falls of the Quequechan River, near the old foot-bridge. The Bordens took it over.

Of course, as everybody knew, when the saw mill was built, it was safe to start with the new farms—one crop, at least, that from the wood lot, was now sure of a market.

So up came the others; mostly from Portsmouth and Newport, one or two from Taunton, a few from Plymouth, practically all blood relations, wherever they came from—all of a common stock. They came with cows and sheep, with a bag of English grass seed from the old Coggshell farm, with dunghill fowl, and gentle mares with white faces for the women folk. They brought parcels of little apple trees from their fathers' orchards, which they set out at once. The trees are still standing.

To the saw mill was soon added a grist mill, to which the planters brought what corn they could raise on their new farms —those rocky pastures, cleared and worked by the Pocassett Indians a hundred years before. Each planter had some sheep. The Bordens built a fulling mill by the stream.

But not for a hundred years were there more than a dozen houses in the actual village of Fall River. These Englishmen were land hungry, and their farms were scattered far and wide. Their neighbours were the travellers upon the rough cart tracks which ran from door to door.

Of what they grew upon these eighteenth-century farms, we have a very good idea. Their wills and their inventories are most exact. There were ryefields as well as cornfields. They experimented with flax and with mulberries. They had orchards of cherries and orchards of pears as well as the universal orchard of apples, and the Reads had an "orchard for summer fruit." There were many small gardens. In 1752, the village blacksmith left a garden by will to his widow. In 1799, the appraisers decided that the Widow Read be allowed "land for a garden," and must have room in the cellar to "store her Garden Sauce." The precise dimensions of the garden were given, and we learn with interest that she was to be allowed to walk through the house-yard to reach her garden gate.

These countrymen were busy with such detail when round about them the towns were full of people of the merchant class, who were leaving country ways behind them. In Fall River these simple patriarchal fashions were still the way of all their world. Fall River knew no merchant class until the eighteenth century had long gone by. If, as tradition runs, those early planters were of the old-world aristocracy, they had forgotten it. They were Freemen of the village, with nothing to regret, as they gazed at their fields of ripening corn or sat drinking cider in their snug little kitchens.

As for labor in the cornfield, they used negro slaves, as did their neighbors. I do not want to emphasize the fact that the village blacksmith made iron collars for these laborers when it was necessary. But he did.

How many of these old farms there were, nobody knows. Each farmstead had its own graveyard in its own first orchard and the Rev. Orin Fowler wrote that he knew of 21 such burial places, in 1840, right in the village, and believed there must be more. And all about in the old woodland between

century. It is known as the Dr. Wilbur house, and it is curiously similar to the Dr. Eldredge house of East Greenwich. The two houses have the front yard raised high above the street level and enclosed with a wooden fence. And English elms stand in both of the dooryards.

I do not think there was at any time either taste or wealth enough to build a pleasure garden in Fall River during the

This photograph of 1840 shows the house, stable, and orchard of the Richard Borden estate, in Fall River. Today only the elms in the yard fronting on Main Street remain. The mill down on the water's edge was called "The Doctor Durfee Mill"

Fall River and Plymouth, there are today hundreds of these plantations, abandoned a century since. A few of the houses are standing, more have left cellar holes, but in the greatest number of cases the casual hunter of deer or bear or partridge finds only crossing lines of crumbling wall marking out the orchard and the garden and the cornfield, beside an abandoned roadway overgrown with briar.

The village grew very slowly. There is a delightful legend of an eighteenth-century estate stretching from the Watuppa Lakes to the Taunton River, owned by Thomas Durfee, Esquire. He is said to have had a deer park in the English fashion, and great kennels, with French hounds, presented by Lafayette. All we know is that Thomas Durfee was a Freeman of the village, that his farm was one of those long and narrow tracts of land which did stretch from lake to river, and that he was on the side of the colonists from the very beginning of the Revolution. At the close of the war he was bankrupt; Jerathmael Bowers foreclosed the mortgage on his farm, and the Durfee meadow, where the deer park may have been, was known to all the boys in town for the next hundred years as a very good huckleberry pasture.

On the opposite page appears an excellent example of the type of house which the more prosperous inhabitants were building on the main street of the town in the closing years of the eighteenth

eighteenth century. The planter was in possession, the merchant had really not arrived.

It was in 1799 that there was born, on one of the old farms in the woods across the pond, the first and the greatest merchant and manufacturer Fall River has ever known. His name was Holder Borden. He died a bachelor at the age of

The garden of Jefferson Borden, on Crab Pond, in Fall River, photographed in 1835 just before its destruction. The house, not shown in the photograph, still stands. Today the railroad passes through the site of the garden

38, having changed the whole standard of life and thought in the village.

His father died when little Holder was only seven. It was impossible to live on the farm; there was no one to work it. So Mrs. Borden, with Holder and his three baby sisters, moved down onto the Central Street of the town, and opened a boarding house —an inn—a hotel—call it what you will; it was a period of transition.

Holder had the education of the village street. He came in contact, also, with the few travellers who stopped to "oat" or get a drink of rum. By the age of ten, he was earning money. At twenty he was a financier. At thirty, he was building mills, looking about for good men to run them. His activities extended. He became influential in the business circles of Providence.

The first fine garden in Fall River of which we know anything at all was laid out on the north bank of Crab Pond, by Holder Borden's uncle, Jefferson Borden, manager of one of the newly organized Holder Borden industries between Crab Pond and Mount Hope Bay. The photograph, taken of the garden before its destruction, due to the running of the railroad through to Newport, shows what a delightful place Crab Pond must have been.

The Robesons of New Bedford came over about 1825, and built rather magnificent houses, whose terraced gardens of well-remembered beauty rose from Crab Pond to the high hill beyond. But of these gardens nothing remains.

On the opposite page there is a photograph of the homestead of Richard Borden (another manager of Holder Borden

The house built about 1840 in Fall River by Matthew Durfee and his wife, Fidelia Borden Durfee, had a fine garden at the back, with fountains, pools, glass-houses, box-bordered walks, and statuary. The house, torn down long ago, stood on a hill, and the garden, a part of which remains, was on three terraces

The Dr. Wilbur house, on Main Street, in Fall River

The house and grounds of Joseph Durfee and his wife, Sylvia Borden Durfee, now the residence of Mr. James Edward Osborn. From an old print

interests), and in the picture you can see one of the little mills of the period, long ago destroyed by fire. The Borden orchard occupies the center of the picture. Today the Court House stands on the Borden garden, and the house and orchard and all trace of garden planting have been rooted out. Except, of course, the elm trees at the gate.

Holder Borden would doubtless have made a pleasure garden of his own, as all great merchants did, had he lived to the great age they most of them achieved. He did subscribe heavily to the new Fall River Athenæum, following the example of Redwood and Collins and the rest. But his varied interests kept him on the road, day after day, driving fast horses from New Bedford to Providence and back again, linking up Fall River with the communities round about, where the old plantation life had been abandoned long before. His early death left his large fortune unspent.

All that remains of the garden his mother made after his death can be found behind the Public Library on Main Street—great elms, good turf, small creeping things which never do die out. And there is a circle of the old box at "Broadview," transplanted when the garden was abandoned.

The three pretty sisters with their pretty names—Fidelia, Delana, Sylvia—built three houses on the hill, high above the center of the town. They had married very well, in the winter of 1826-1827; two brothers named Matthew and Nathan Durfee, just out of college, and their cousin, Joseph Durfee, a shipwright.

These Borden-Durfee houses with their Grecian porticoes were built in great open spaces, planted carefully with an evident sense of design. Each estate had a really beautiful and large formal garden, full of little granite steps which ran up and down the steeply terraced hillside sloping away from the house to the west. I remember the little granite steps. When I was very young I used to run through the gardens, and in my memory they are interminable. There were pools and fountains, and arbours and trellises, and fruit trees of every kind. There were glass-houses, there were benches of iron, curling around in the shape of a grapevine bearing grapes. Best of all, there were iron deer colored quite naturally, which browsed in an elm-studded deer park, or lay in peaceful repose on close-cropped lawns.

Of the three houses, one remains. An old print shown here

was made soon after the house was built, and the elms were planted in 1843.

This was the home of Joseph Durfee and his wife Sylvia Borden Durfee, whose daughter married William Carr. To-day the little Osborns and the little Burchards, great-great-grandchildren of the builders of the house, play in the old garden spaces.

The Matthew Durfees built the house next door. The photograph shows only the street planting, and does not even hint at the elaborate portico on the western front overlooking the gardens and the bay. A little of the garden planting remains, behind three modern houses which line the street front of the old estate. But the round pool, with its arbor-vitæ border, has disappeared, and the lemon groves and the glass-houses where the fig trees grew are no longer there. Every one knows, however, that Mrs. Durfee took first prizes with her hot-house grapes, at all the country fairs, and built enormous graperies, both hot and cold.

This Corinthian capital from the Nathan Durfee house was taken down to the Cape when the house was demolished years ago

On the opposite page is a reconstruction of the estate of Nathan Durfee and his wife Delana Borden Durfee, as they laid it out in 1838 or 40. They built their house where, in the memory of man, Prospect Street crossed and finished Rock. It was a large and elaborate house, exactly facing the middle of Rock Street, up which you came as you would up a private avenue, and saw, far away, the white Corinthian columns shining through tall elms and many copper beeches. The house was taken down in 1880, Rock Street was carried north, right through the center of the place where the old house used to be, and fifteen houses, with garages and gardens and playgrounds, have been built on the old "Nathan Durfee Estate," which had been hardly large enough for all the fruit and flowers and vegetables and exotic trees which the Nathan Durfees planted in their time.

The plan of the estate here given is drawn to scale, after a careful survey of the premises. The iron bench in the lower left-hand corner is still standing under one of the old elms. The stag at the right can be found on the lawn of a house near by. Some of the apple orchard at the top of the plan is still in a good state of preservation, behind a row of houses west of Rock Street. The garden pool is in the apple orchard —eight curved slabs of granite form its outer edge, which is perfectly circular. The pear trees shown in the formal garden are, some of them, growing in that same garden space today, and two magnificent magnolia trees flower there every spring. The elm trees flourish. The beeches are in excellent condition, though transplanted when the road went through. Of the vegetable garden in the center at the top of the plan, the gardener's cottage just below, the greenhouses on the left between the garden and the orchard in which peaches and apricots and grapes and carnations were grown, there is nothing left.

Mr. Durfee was President of the Bristol County Agricultural Society for a number of years. In his time, at the annual show in 1832, the Society had a special class, with prizes, for growers of mulberry trees, and mulberries and silk were both entered. Without doubt, somewhere on the estate there were mulberry trees. And the lilac bushes and the wistaria vine are still growing in odd corners.

From vestiges of old planting, from an old print, a photograph, an early map of the town, this reconstruction of a fine estate has been quite possible. And those who lived in the old house long ago as little children have remembered much.

What very few remember, is that all this beauty of peace and space and ordered living, this existence in a garden, was made possible in Fall River (as it was at an earlier period in all the villages about the shores of Narragansett Bay) by a few men, traders born, who forsook the meager though possibly more virtuous life of the planter, the life of the farmer and the farm, and, buying and selling, building furnace and factory, brought wealth and taste and more beautiful living to those most fortunate communities where they happened to be born.

It was in 1832 that the local Fall River paper published the following reflections: "It is undoubtedly a fact that in proportion to our population, too many leave the occupation of the agriculturist for other employments. If this arise from its being considered that the occupation of a farmer is not respectable, it is a very great mistake."

GLOOM IN THE GARDEN

On the parlor table, in the great Fall River houses with their Grecian porticoes, there appeared just before 1840 a literature of unusual quality.

It was written by women for women. It was popular; there are still surprising numbers of these books about the town. It was read; that is apparent from the appearance of the books which I have seen. And it was all concerned, from cover to cover, prose and poetry alike, with gloom, gloom in the garden, gloom among the flowers.

As literature, the books are probably worthless, but as commentaries on the gardens of the period, as explanation of the taste which made the gardens what they were, they are worth examining. *Select Poems*, by Mrs. L. H. Sigourney, published in 1838 by Frederick W. Greenough, will serve as an example.

The picture on the title page gives an ideal "flower ar-

Summer-house in an old Borden garden now owned by Mrs. James Buffinton, Fall River

rangement." The vase is the popular parlor ornament. The broken blossoms on the tablecloth give that elegant unstudied appearance, even that note of approaching decay, which polite society absolutely demanded in every form of art. The lyre is the lyre of Mrs. Sigourney, I suppose; her publisher has thoughtfully hung a wreath of laurel on it.

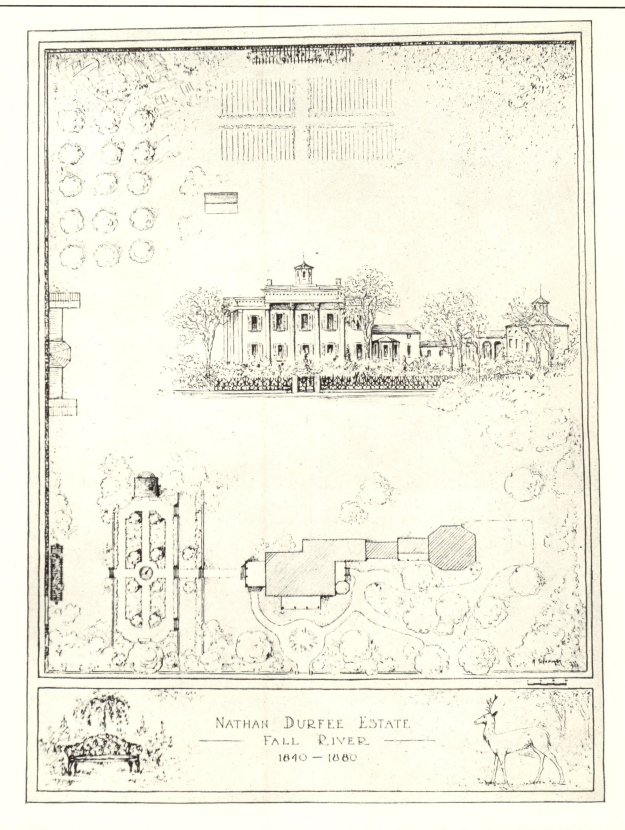

NATHAN DURFEE ESTATE.
— FALL RIVER —
1840 – 1880

On page 294, Mrs. Sigourney writes:

"The flowers, the dear familiar flowers, that in thy garden grew,
From which thy mantel vase was filled, methinks they breathe anew.
Again the whispering lily bends, and ope those lips of rose,
As if some message of thy love they lingered to disclose."

So it seems obvious that the vase stood on the parlour mantel, and that the place of honour in a mixed bouquet was occupied at that period—as it would not be today—by the lily and the rose. Very important adjuncts to the social life of 1838 were these bouquets. The book has a "Poem on Forgotten Flowers to a Bride," which begins:

"We were left behind but we would not stay."

It seems that the bride forgot her bouquet and had it sent after her in a tin box—

"In the snug tin box where we quietly lay."

And the happy destination of the bridal bouquet was to die on the breast of the bride at the close of the journey.

Bouquets made up to take to sick female friends were sometimes composed of roses and myrtle. On page 99:

"I plucked a rose for thee, sweet friend,
Thy ever favorite flower,
A bud I long had nursed for thee
Within my wintry bower.
I grouped it with the fragrant leaves
That on the myrtle grew.
And tied it with a silken string
Of soft cerulean blue."

When the lady reached the sick room, she entered alone and found her friend lying dead on the sofa—

"Here on thy cold unheaving breast,
The promised rose I lay."

To us it is gruesome. In 1838 it was a pleasing conceit.

This picture, which Delana Borden, Holder Borden's sister, and later the wife of Nathan Durfee, embroidered in lovely shades of silk sometime after 1804, shows Holder Borden's mother mourning her husband. The longest side of the embroidery measures about a yard

Evidently that particular bouquet was gathered in a greenhouse. In contemporary eyes, the glory of the gardens about Narrangansett Bay, up to 1840, was always the greenhouse. I imagine—I do not know—that the greenhouse in its early days in New England was not the ugly thing it has become now that it has been perfected. Previous to 1840, perhaps the glass-houses resembled the English orangeries, which were really delightful garden ornaments. Anyway, all important gardens had glass-houses, and all garden observers praised them highly.

As poets do, Mrs. Sigourney in 1836 affected to despise the artificial. Yet she refers to the greenhouse constantly. She cannot leave it alone. She actually wrote a whole poem to

"The Cactus Speciossisimus"

"Thou biddst the queenly rose with all her buds do homage
And the greenhouse peerage bow their rainbow coronets."

Her "Wild Flowers" has the lines:

"Should the greenhouse patricians with withering frown
On your simple vestments look haughtily down"

And she accepts the greenhouse as a necessity in "Autumn":

"Then quick the proud exotic peers
    In consternation fled
And refuge in their greenhouse sought
    Before the day of dread."

It seems probable that a preference for a hardy garden did not exist before 1840, anywhere in New England.

The poem on Autumn is exceedingly interesting, for two reasons. It enumerates the flowers which grew in the New England gardens Mrs. Sigourney knew: "queenly dahlias," "hydrangias," "violets," "lilies," "anemones," "daisy from the vale," "purple lilac," white lilac called "sister pale,"

and "ripened rose"; and it exhibits emphatically the fashionable mood. Opening with

"Has it come, the time to fade?"

it contains such lines as

"I call each sere and yellow leaf
    A buried friend to me."

and ends

"Go let the strange and silver hair
    That o'er thy forehead strays
Be as a monitor to tell
    The Autumn of thy days."

It is a little hard to understand this passion of the young ladies of 1838 for death among the flowers. Yet I like to think of them, the pretty creatures, sitting long hours at their embroidery frames behind their Grecian porticoes, depicting tombstones set in weeping willows, while their swains read aloud from Mrs. Sigourney:

"Death walketh in the forest,—And the worm,
    Coiling itself amid our garden flowers,
Did make their unborn buds its sepulchre.
    —And so I said, if in this world of knells
And open tombs—"

Gloom in the garden. Yes, they liked it. I wonder, however, how much gloom the ladies of 1840 were really able to get into their actual gardens.

The embroidered landscape which Delana Borden worked so beautifully in lovely silken shades of green and brown and raven black, in Fall River, a hundred years ago, is of course the ideal landscape of her girlhood. But in the actual garden of Delana Borden and her kind, beyond much box, some evergreens, a pool or so, I do not think the shadow of romantic grief lay heavily.

THE SPRAGUES OF CRANSTON—MERCHANTS OF CALICO

In 1843, the American nation was shocked by the brutal murder of Amasa Sprague, merchant and manufacturer, of Cranston, Rhode Island. He was shot in mid-afternoon, beside a much travelled path near his new house and ornamental garden. His body when found had been fearfully mutilated, and a gun, broken, lay on the ground by his side.

The Sprague family were early settlers in Rhode Island. The first Sprague in Cranston owned a farm through which a river ran, convenient for a saw-mill, also a grist-mill, both of which he built.

In 1808, a son of his converted the grist-mill into a cotton mill where cotton yarn was carded and spun. This yarn was woven by the neighbors into cotton cloth, and then brought back to the mill to be sold by this new type of farmer-merchant, adventuring in fields unknown.

Before long, William Sprague, 2nd, undertook to print these calicoes, beginning with "Indigo Blues." He was the very first calico printer in America.

How has this to do with gardens? Up to this date, it was at home that the cloth of the household was dyed; it was in the home garden, on the home farm, that the dye stuffs were grown. It has very much to do with gardens when the women of the community cease to look on the flowers of the garden as material for the dye pot.

The merchant changes the character of the garden, always. Not with intention, for to the merchant the garden is an emblem of stability, of old ways, eternal verities, to those who have ventured far. It is curious that to his garden, at the end of the struggle, he and his wealth so persistently come back.

William Sprague made a great deal of money out of this printing experiment. Enough to fix up the farm a bit, enlarge the old grist-mill, and build other cotton mills in Johnston and Natick. Sprague was of the true Rhode Island type, not above raising what he could in farm and garden and selling it at a profit, but relying on his "merchandizing" for money enough to run the farming end of his existence.

At the height of his prosperity, they say, he drove an ox-cart into Providence from Cranston, with a load of ship lumber cut from his own acres.

When he died, in 1836, he left two sons to carry on the cotton business, both of whom had worked in the factory since early boyhood. These boys, as soon as they took over the business, opened a dry-goods shop, where they also sold groceries. Mainly, of course, to the operatives. For the whole countryside was now working for the Spragues, in the Sprague factories, where wages, whatever they were, were evidently more to be desired than the profits of the farm, whatever those profits might have been.

All along the Narragansett shore, little farms were being sold or abandoned, and the small farmer with his wife and children began to "move in" toward the Sprague cotton mills, where the constant building of new factories almost kept pace with the demand for a chance to "work in a factory." And these "mill hands"—all of them farm bred—did not go back to the farm. The innocent manufacturer and country-loving merchant little realized that never again, after 1840, would Rhode Island be a garden country, nor that to these same mill hands the term "farmer" would become a term of scorn—that "hayseed", precious product of Mr. Coggshell in the seventeenth century, would be an insulting epithet applied in scorn to those who still preferred to cultivate the land their fathers were "allotted," two centuries before.

The product of the Sprague Cotton Mills was greater than that of all the other factories in the United States combined.

At the time when we leave them, in the first real enjoyment of their wealth, they are beginning to leave their primitive farm houses and to erect palatial mansions, surrounded by the lawns of 1840—that period when we stop our garden history, as we should.

1840

Since this record of Rhode Island gardens must close in 1840, it can contain nothing contributed to garden history by the summer residents of Rhode Island, who have done so much for Newport and Narragansett.

Quaint as the old gardens of 1860 often are, delightful and quite unknown to the present generation though they may be, these gardens framed by the Norway pine and trimmed with the yucca, are not for this chronicle of an earlier day than yuccas ever knew.

The book must end as Newport and Narragansett stir slowly, coming into life after the dark ages and deserted gardens of the years which follow the war of the Revolution.

The book must end as Providence, after an era of unparalleled prosperity, when wealth and taste seemed without end, was quietly conserving a beauty which time and the taste of Victoria have not entirely defaced.

The book must end as the country districts of the State, never quite recovered from the war, were being still further impoverished by the emigration of the young people who were "going West." The railroads were building and the farmers of Rhode Island were following the railroads. The factories were building, in Fall River, in the Blackstone Valley, in all too many villages of the State. The farmers were moving into town that their children might be near the factories.

The year 1840 is a natural pause in the history of the gardens of the State.

Main Street, Fall River, in 1840. The greater part of the village was then in Rhode Island

The upper and lower gardens of the Van Cortlandt Manor House, Croton-on-the-Hudson, New York. The garden is described on page 271

NEW YORK

The great box trees flanking the gate in the garden of Sylvester Manor, Shelter Island, New York. See page 276

NEW YORK

NEW YORK CITY

WHEN Hendrick Hudson first saw the Island of Manhattan from the decks of the *Half Moon*, the waves broke on rough and rocky shores clothed with a wild and tangled growth of primeval forest. The Indians greeted him as an unknown god, and as he made his way up "The Great River of the Mountains"—as he called the majestic stream which now bears his name—they heaped maize, tobacco and other growths of the country as gifts at his feet.

New Amsterdam in 1659

Hudson claimed the surrounding country for the Netherlands, and wrote in his Journal: "The land is the finest for cultivation that I ever in my life set foot upon." He little knew that vine-draped Manhattan was to be the site of the largest city in the world, and that he was the herald of a mighty nation which was to grow a great portion of the food of all the world's peoples.

THE DUTCH PLANTERS

The Dutch immediately took advantage of Hudson's discovery. By 1621 "The privileged West India Company" had colonized the country, establishing its principal trading-post on Manhattan Island, and calling it Fort Amsterdam.

These early Dutch settlers, homesick for the old country, called their colony New Netherland. They endured a period of trial and privation after their arrival, but owing to the milder climate it was hardly comparable to the severity of the struggle of the English colonists on the rocky coast of New England. The first to arrive came in the fall, and, fearing the stress of an unknown climate—according to Cornelius Tienhoven, Secretary of the Dutch West Indies at Fort Amsterdam—dug themselves cellars, and there lived "dry and warm" the first winter.

But soon the word was sent to Holland that ships bringing settlers should leave in the winter, so that they might arrive in the spring; the newcomers would then be able to get their crops in and build adequate houses for the winter.

Of course these colonists, coming from a land cultivated for so many hundred years that it was almost artificial in character, had much to learn before they could subdue the primitive forests in which, as they wrote, the trees grew "without order as in any other wilderness." Like all the first settlers in America, they took advantage of the example of the natives by raising the easily cultivated crop of maize or Indian corn, but according to Van der Donck in his *Voyages*, they thought very little of the Red Man's method of tilling the land. Van der Donck says:

"All their agriculture is performed by their women. The men give themselves very little trouble about the same, except those who are old. . . . They cultivate no wheat, oats, barley, or rye. . . . The grain which they raise for bread, or mush, or sapaen, is maize or turkey-corn, and they raise various kinds of beans. They also plant tobacco for their own use. Of garden vegetables they raise none, except pumpkins or squashes. They usually leave their fields and garden spots open, unenclosed, and unprotected by fencing, and

take very little care of the same, though they raise an abundance of corn and beans, of which we obtain whole cargoes in sloops and galleys in trade.

"Of manuring, or of proper tillage they know nothing. All their tillage is done by hand and with small adzes which they obtain from us. Although little can be said in favor of this husbandry, still they prefer their practice to ours, because our methods require too much labor and care to please, with which they are not well satisfied."

But soon the land about the Fort and in the surrounding country was laid out into "boweries" or farms, checkered with well cultivated fields. We can but marvel at the industry of these Hollanders who left their land of "dykes and ditches and set up stake and post" in a wilderness, turning it into a garden.

The following translation of a letter written in Dutch in 1626 by Pieter Jansen Schagen and addressed to the State General at The Hague shows how early remunerative crops were produced.

From Barber and Howe's "Historical Collections of New York"

Above is the "Stadt Huys" or City Hall, built of stone in 1642 at the head of Coenties Slip, facing Pearl Street. It was razed about 1700. Below is the Van Kleek house, a stone building of before 1700

"High Mighty Sirs:—

"Here arrived yesterday the ship, the *Arms of Amsterdam*, which sailed from New Netherland. . . . Sept. 23; they report that our people are of good courage and live peaceably. They have the island of Manhattan from the wild people for the value of sixty guilders. . . . They sowed all their grain the middle of May and harvested it the middle of August.

Thereof being samples of summer grain, such as wheat, rye, barley, oats, buckwheat, canary seed, small beans, and flax."

Adrian Van der Donck[1], who came to New Netherland in 1642 and purchased a "bouwerie" on the upper part of Manhattan, gives us a most comprehensive account of the flowers, fruits, and vegetables which he found in the new

"Although the land is full of many kinds we still want settings of the best kinds from Germany for the purpose of enabling our wine planters here to select the best kinds and propagate the same."

Grace Tabor in *Old-Fashioned Gardens* thus quotes Van der Donck's lists of flowers with her own comments:

"'The white and red roses of different kinds, the cornelion roses and stock roses; [may these last two not refer to *Rosa*

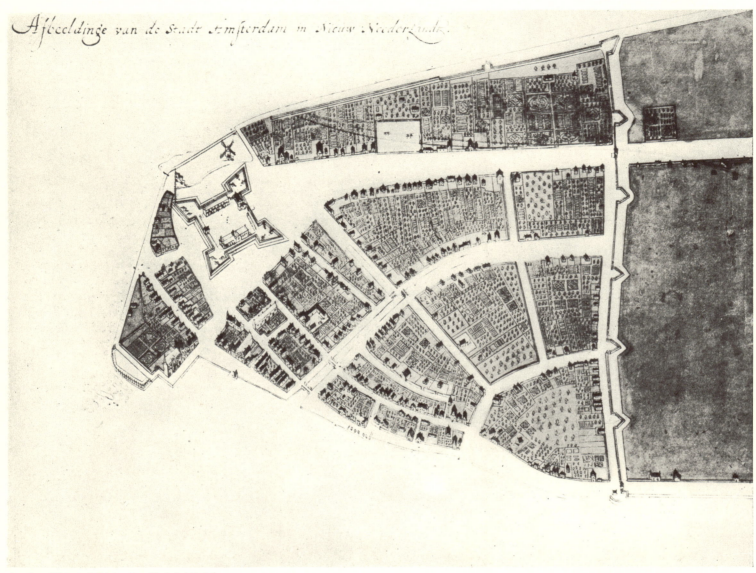

The Castello Plan. The earliest known plan of New Amsterdam, and the only one dating from the Dutch period. Depicting the city in the summer of 1660, it was copied by an unknown draftsman from an original survey by Jacques Cortelyou, now lost; the draftsman probably filled in areas of "waste" land with the formal gardens shown. The drawing here reproduced is owned by the Italian government, and preserved in the Medici Library, Florence

land. The fruit trees brought over from the Netherlands were, he says, ". . . various apple and pears which thrive well. Those also grow from the seed of which I have seen many, which without grafting, bore delicious fruit in six years. . . . The English have brought over the first quinces, and we have also brought over stocks and seeds which thrive well. Orchard cherries thrive well and produce large fruit. Spanish cherries, forerunners, morellas, of every kind we have, as in the Netherlands, and the trees bear better because the blossoms are not injured by the frosts. The peaches which are sought after in the Netherlands, grow wonderfully well here. . . . We have also introduced more cotoons [a kind of peach], apricots, several of the best plums . . . cornelian cherries, figs, several sorts of currants, gooseberries, calissiens and thorn apples; and we do not doubt that the olive would thrive and be profitable, but we have them not."

Of grapes Van der Donck says:

canina—the dog rose—which has always been much used as a "stock" for grafting upon? There is a possible connection in the term "cornelion," this being the name applied to a cornel or dogwood—the cornelian cherry or *Cornus Mas;* possibly he used it in this sense to designate the dog rose] and those of which were none before in the country, such as eglantine, several kinds of gilly-flowers, jenoffelins [no one can even guess what these were], different varieties of fine tulips, crown imperials, white lilies, the lily fritilaria, anemones, baredames [another mystery], violets, marigolds, summer sots [possibly daisies, sometimes called "maudlin wort"], &c. The clove tree has also been introduced; and there are various indigenous trees that bear handsome flowers which are unknown in the Netherlands.'

"By 'the clove tree' he must mean the real spice clove—*Caryophyllus aromaticus.* This is cultivated in the West Indies where the Dutch had long traded, and doubtless they thought it possible that it would grow here."

Van der Donck also mentions native flowers, "as for instance, sun flowers, red and yellow lilies, mountain lilies

[1]Van der Donck's *Voyages.* Van der Donck was called the "Yonker," the Dutch word for gentleman. His estate was called Yonker's land, and from that comes the modern "Yonkers."

View of the city and harbor of New York in 1792. Looking south from Mount Pitt, the seat of John R. Livingston, where Grand Street now is. Brooklyn is shown to left, Governor's Island in the middle distance, Staten Island in the far distance, lower New York to the right. The original unfinished pencil sketch is owned by the New York Historical Society

[martagon lilies], morning stars, and red, white and yellow maritoffles (a very sweet flower), several species of bell flower, etc."

"Morning stars" are a problem; so are the "maritoffles." Grace Tabor thinks that by "morning stars" Van der Donck meant flowering dogwood, which is certainly a charming surmise. Maritoffles she thinks were lady's slippers, literally "Mary's slippers," the wild *Cypripedium pubescens, C. spectabile,* and *C. acaule,* furnishing the yellow, the white and the red, as nearly as Van der Donck could distinguish the colors.

He also lists the vegetables. "They consist then of various kinds of sallads, cabbages, parsnips, carrots, beets, endive, succory, finckel [fennel], sorrel, dill, spinage, radishes, Spanish radishes, parsley, chervil (or Sweet Cicely) cresses, various leeks and besides what is commonly found in a kitchen garden. The herb garden is also tolerably well supplied with rosemary, lavender, hyssop, thyme, sage, marjoram, balm, holy onion (ajuin helig), wormwood, belury, chives and clary; also pimpernel, dragon's blood, five finger, tarragon (or dragon's wort) &c. together with laurel, artichokes and asparagus and various other things."

Elsewhere he says: "No reasonable person will doubt that there are many medicinal and healing herbs in the New Netherlands. A certain chirurgeon who was also a botanist, had a beautiful garden there, wherein a great variety of medicinal and wild plants were collected. . . ."

We feel, after reading the foregoing descriptions, we must agree with Jacob Steendam, the Dutch poet who wrote "Praise of New Netherland," saying:

> "This is the land where milk and honey flow,
>   Where healing plants as thick as thistles grow,
>   The place where flowers on Adam's Rod do blow,
>   This, this is Eden."

By 1656 the settlement was laid out in streets, crooked

enough at that time, and contained about one thousand inhabitants. Of this period it has been written that "excessive land grants had been made to persons who had since failed to take advantage of them. Land lay yet 'unimproved, yea, wild and waste . . . many spacious and large lots, even in the best and most convenient parts of the city' were not built on, the owners holding them for a rise in value or using them as orchards and gardens."

The so-called "city" is shown in the Castello Plan of New Amsterdam, which is the earliest plan of the city, in fact the only one from the Dutch period. The Castello Plan was based upon the Cortelyou survey, ordered June 7, 1660, and was completed just in time to be despatched in the ship which carried Governor Stuyvesant's letter of October 6th of that year, addressed to the directors in Amsterdam and containing the words: "After closing our letter the Burgomasters have shown us the plan of the city which we did not think could be ready before the sailing of this ship."[1]

In reply the directors in Holland wrote:

"We have been pleased to receive the map of the city of New Amsterdam; we noticed, that according to our opinion too great spaces are as yet without buildings—the houses are apparently surrounded by excessively large lots and gardens."

From the records we may assume that Governor Stuyvesant and a few others had parterre gardens in the prevailing style of the gardens of Europe at that time, but we conclude that the cartographer who worked from the Cortelyou survey, being unable to comprehend that there could be so much land allowed to lie "waste," filled it with the formal designs to be seen in all the Old World city plans of that period. It is too bad to dispose ruthlessly of a pretty myth, but we feel that in 1660 the industrious New Netherlander was spending more time in tilling his new fields of Indian corn, and in keep-

[1]N. Y. Colonial Documents, Vol. XIV, p. 486.

American Historical Prints, New York Public Library

Broadway, near City Hall, from an aquatint drawn in 1819. Note the swine in the street

ing up the boundaries of his "bouwerie," than in laying out the geometric patterns which we see in so many of the modern illustrations of that period of New York, even though these pictures had their origin in the elaborate Castello Plan rather than in the imagination of the artist.

New Amsterdam held its name until 1664, when Charles II of England totally disregarded the rights of the Dutch and claimed the province for his brother, the Duke of York. There was peace between England and Holland at that time, and the Dutch, being not entirely satisfied with their colony as a business investment, agreed to turn it over to the English without resistance. They were given most excellent terms, and though a few of the citizens returned to the Old Country, the greater number remained to live in what then became New York. Their sturdy independence, their industry, and their integrity aided greatly in the development of the province under the rule of Great Britain.

From the rare and quaint volume published soon after this date, Ogilby's *America*, we quote the following description of New York at about the time it was transferred from the hands of the staid Dutch to those of the adventurous English:

"It is placed upon the neck of the Island Manhattan looking toward the Sea; encompass'd with Hudson's River, which is six miles broad, the town is compact and oval with very fair streets and several good Houses, the rest are built much after the manner of Holland, to the number of about four hundred Houses, which in those parts are held considerable: Upon one side of the Town is James-fort, capable to lodge three hundred soldiers and Officers; it hath four bastions, forty pieces of Cannon mounted; the Wall of Stone, lined with a thick Rampart of Earth, well accommodated with a Spring of Fresh Water, always furnished with arms and ammunition against Accidents: Distant from the Sea Seven Leagues, it affords a safe entrance, even to unskilful pilots; under the Town side ships of any burden may ride secure against any Storms; the Current of the River being broken by the interposition of a small Island, which lies a mile distant from the Town.

"About ten Miles from New York is a place call'd Hell Gate, which being a narrow passage, there runneth a violent stream both upon Flood and Ebb; and in the middle lie some rocky Islands, which the Current sets so violently upon, that it threatens present Shipwrack; and upon the Flood is a large

Whirlwind, which continually sets forth a hideous roaring; enough to affright any stranger from passing farther; and to wait for some Charon to conduct him through; yet to those who are acquainted little or no danger: It is a place of great Defence against any enemy coming in that way, which a small Fortification would absolutely prevent, and necessitate them to come in at the west end of Long Island by Sandy Hook where Statten Island forces them within the Command of the Fort at New York, which is one of the best Pieces of Defence in the North parts of America. It is built most of Brick and Stone and cover'd with Red and Black Tyle, and the land being high, it gives at a distance a most pleasing prospect to the Spectators. The inhabitants consist most of English and Dutch, and have a considerable trade with the Indians for Beaver, Otter and Rackoon Skins with other Furrs; as also for bear, Deer, and Elke-Skins; and are supply'd with Venison and Fowl in the winter, and Fish in the Summer by the Indians, which they buy at an easie Rate; and having the Countrey round about them, and are continually furnish'd with all such provisions as are needful for the Life of Man, not onely by the English and the Dutch within their own, but likewise by the adjacent Colonies."

THROUGH TRAVELLERS' EYES

As the years went on and New York, in the hands of the English, grew from the village-like fort of New Amsterdam into a thriving city, it naturally became a Mecca for travellers from other parts of America as well as from abroad. From the accounts in the journals of these visitors we learn more of the appearance of the country and of the gardens than is to be gleaned from the colonial documents, or from the meagre histories of those times.

In 1670 Daniel Denton wrote[1]:

"The greatest part of the Island is very full of timber, as oaks, white and red, walnut trees, chestnut trees, which yield store of mast for swine, as also maples, cedars, sarsifrage, Beech, Holly, Hazel, with many more. The herbs which the country naturally affords are Purslane, white Orage, Egrimony, Violets, penniroyal, Alicompane. besides Saxaparila, very common, with many more, yea, in May you should see

[1]From *A Brief Description of New York*, by Daniel Denton, 1670.

the woods and Fields so curiously bedeckt with Roses and innumerable multitude of delightful Flowers, not only pleasing to the eye but smell, that you may see Nature contending with Art and striving to equal if not excel many gardens in England.

"There are divers sorts of singing birds whose chirping notes salute the ears of Travellers with harmonious discord, and in every pond and brook green silken Frogs who warbling forth their untun'd tunes strive to bear a part in this musicke.

"Strawberries were so plentiful that in June when the fields and woods were dyed red with them the country people ... instantly arm themselves with bottles of wine, cream and sugar and instead of a coat of mail everyone takes a female upon his horse behind him, and so rushing violently into the fields, never leave until they have disrobed them of their red colors and turned them into the old habit."

In 1679, after New Amsterdam had become New York, the two Labadist monks, Jasper Dankers and Peter Sluyter, visited the colony.

"... we stepped ashore about four o'clock in the afternoon ... and went out to take a walk in the fields ... as we walked along we saw in different gardens trees full of apples of various kinds, and so laden with peaches and other fruit that one might doubt whether there were more leaves than fruit on them."

And again, speaking of New York in particular:

"Everywhere in New York we were astonished by the abundance and variety of its food supplies—its crop of wheat —and above all its fruits—apples, and pears of wonderful size and quality and still more wonderful peaches, so plentiful they were fed to the pigs. Striking indeed it was between this province and Maryland where the people bestowed all their time and care on the cultivation of tobacco, so the country folk, and especially slaves and bond servants, lived in penury, on coarse, monotonous and often insufficient fare."

In 1748, Peter Kalm, the Swedish botanist, gives us a fine description of the streets shaded by trees vocal with birds and frogs, very different from the canyons of the financial district of the present day, reverberating with motor-horns and traffic signals. Writing in November of that year, he said of New York:

"... in size it comes nearest to Boston and Philadelphia. But with regard to its fine buildings, its opulence, and extensive commerce, it disputes the preference with them. ...

"The streets do not run straight as those of Philadelphia, and [have] sometimes considerable bendings: however they are very spacious and well-built, and most of them are paved, except in high places, where it has been found useless. In the chief street there are trees planted, which in summer give them a fine appearance, and during the excessive heat of that time, afford a cooling shade: I found it extremely pleasant to walk in the town, for it seemed quite like a garden; the trees planted for this purpose are chiefly of two kinds. The Water Beech, Linnaeus's Platanus occidentalis, are the most numerous, and give an agreeable shade in summer, by their great and numerous leaves. The Locust Tree, or Linnaeus's Robinia Pseudo-Acacia is likewise frequent: its fine leaves, and the odoriferous scent which it exhales from its flowers, makes it very proper for being planted in the street near the houses, and in gardens. There are likewise lime-trees and elms, in these walks, but they are not by far so frequent as the others: one seldom met with trees of the same sort next to each other, they being in general planted alternately.

"... Many of the houses had a balcony on the roof, on which the people used to sit in the evenings in the summer season; and from thence they had a pleasant view of a great part of the town, and likewise part of the adjacent water and of the opposite shore. ..."

The tree frogs evidently greatly impressed Peter Kalm. He wrote:

"Besides numbers of birds of all kinds which make these trees their abode, there are likewise a kind of frogs which frequent them in great numbers in summer, they are Dr. Linnaeus's Rana arborea, and especially the American variety of this animal. They are very clamorous in the evening and in the nights (especially when the days had been hot, and a rain was expected) and in a manner drown the singing of the birds. They frequently make such a noise, that it is difficult for a person to make himself heard."

St. John de Crevecœur, the Frenchman, whose so-called *Letters from an American Farmer* give most realistic pictures of life both rural and urban, visited New York in 1771. He speaks of the irregular way in which the city had developed because of the uneven contour of the land, and then adds: "Certain streets have sidewalks on both sides paved with slabs of rock, adorned with plane trees, whose shade in summer is equally pleasant to the passerby and to the houses. Here one finds a union of Dutch neatness with English taste and architecture."

And Timothy Dwight, that cheerful, indefatigable chronicler, says twenty years later (1791): "The Island of Manhattan ... is set with cheerful habitations, with well-stocked gardens, and neat enclosures, while the heights, and many of the lower grounds, contain a rich display of gentlemen's country seats connected with a great variety of handsome appendages. [We have learned that "appendages" means "gardens" in the vocabulary of Timothy Dwight] No part of the United States has such a numerous collection of villas within so small a compass; nor is any ride in the country made so cheerful by the hand of art, as is the first six miles of the Bowery road; and indeed the whole distance to Haarlem Bridge."

And again: "The city of New York is an object, which in this country is singularly splendid; the groves are numerous and fine; the plantations remarkably gay and fertile; and the villas rise in perpetual succession on the shores and eminences; embellishing the landscape, and exhibiting decisive proofs of opulence in their proprietors." Dwight notes that "the streets are generally wider, and less crooked than those of Boston; but a great proportion of them are narrow and winding."

Barber and Howe cite, unnamed, an early English traveller for the following description of the harbor:

"I have never seen the bay of Naples, I can therefore make no comparison; but my imagination is incapable of conceiving anything more beautiful than the harbor of New York. Various and lovely are the objects which meet the eye on every side; but the nameing of them would only be to give a list of words, without conveying the faintest idea of the scene. I doubt if even the pencil of Turner could do it justice, bright and glorious as it rose upon us. We seem to enter the harbor of New York upon waves of liquid gold, and as we dash past the green isles which rise from its bosom like guardian sentinels of the fair city, the setting sun stretches his horizontal beams further and further, at each moment, as if to point out to us some new glory in the landscape."

Mrs. Grant, in her *Memoirs of an American Lady*, speaks also of the beauty of the islands of the harbor. "Staten Island," she says, "rose gradual from the sea in which it seemed to float, and was so covered with innumerable fruit trees in full bloom, that it looked like some enchanted forest."

Mrs. Trollope in her *Domestic Manners and Customs of the Americans* (1832) says: "There is hardly an acre of Manhattan Island but what shows some pretty villa or stately mansion. The most chosen of these are on the North and East Rivers, to whose margins their lawns descend. Amongst these, perhaps the loveliest one is Woodlawn situated in the beautiful village of Blomingdale. Here within the space of sixteen acres, almost every variety of garden scenery may be found."

EARLY GARDENS IN NEW YORK CITY

Explicit records of early gardens during the Dutch period are almost entirely lacking. Van der Donck speaks of a scientific garden containing medicinal plants, but said it had fallen into decay before he carried the people's Remonstrance to Holland in 1664. It is thought that it was revived by Governor Stuyvesant, however, for he sent to the botanical gardens at Leyden for seeds and roots. Perhaps this was the garden owned by the West India Company which was situated on the site of Trinity Church.

GOVERNOR STUYVESANT'S GARDENS

We are able to assert with a good deal of certainty that Governor Stuyvesant and a few other prominent men, including Van der Donck himself, had excellent gardens, though no definite plans remain. Stuyvesant built a mansion

The Beekman House, Sir Wm. Howe's headquarters in 1776, from a drawing in "Valentine's Manual," 1861

of hewn stone, and called it Whitehall. It was located on the street which was eventually named for it, and was surrounded, according to Martha J. Lamb[1], by a garden on three sides, while a rich velvet lawn in front extended to the water's edge, where lay the Governor's barge at the foot of fine cut-stone steps. Upon the north side of the grounds there was an imposing gateway.

Mrs. Lamb goes on to say that the Governor's country-seat, where he and his family usually spent the summer months, embraced the greater portion of the present Eleventh Sixteenth, and Seventeenth wards. It cost him originally 6400 guilders. His house was a great, commodious, comfortable, homelike specimen of Holland architecture. His gardens were remarkably fine, and his land was in a high state of cultivation. It is said that he kept from thirty to fifty negro slaves, in addition to a number of white servants, constantly employed in the improvement of his grounds. The road to the city had been put in good condition, and shade trees had been planted on each side where it crossed the Governor's grounds.[2]

"Near the house," says Mrs. Lamb, "Stuyvesant planted a pear tree. . . . For more than two hundred years it marked the spot where had been the old director's garden. In 1867 it was still living, protected by an iron railing at what is now 13th str. and Third Avenue, but that year it was blown down."

Another garden often mentioned is that of Dominie Bogardus, said to have been laid out by his own hands. It included not only the "sallets" and herbs, but also tulips and

---

pinks, roses, lilacs, jessamine and syringa, all growing in such profusion that it was the pride of New Amsterdam.[1]

GARDENS ON BROADWAY

Broadway was first called Heere Straat, later Breede Wag, and by translation into English became Broadway.

According to *Valentine's Manual*, north of the old Dutch burial grounds and bordering on Broadway were a number of good residences with large gardens and orchards attached, the principal one of these being that of Burgomaster Paulus Van der Grist, a substantial stone house which endured over a century. These orchards and gardens were highly cultivated, extending to the very edge of the North River, and having a front along Broadway of one hundred to two hundred feet.

Indeed, in retrospect we find Broadway to have been, at least on one side, an agreeable thoroughfare of orchards, gardens, and pleasant residences.

Up to 1664 there had been no paving, but within a few years the middle of the street was paved with "pebble stones," and the inhabitants were authorized to plant trees along the sides of the streets. European travelers comment on the streets being enveloped in foliage.[2]

The residence of Abraham Van Nest, from a drawing published in "Valentine's Manual" in 1854

THE ABRAHAM VAN NEST GARDEN

In 1740, Sir Peter Warren, Vice-Admiral in the Royal Navy, and at the same time in command of the British fleet in the port, built a mansion in Greenwich village. This old Warren mansion was for long the most ancient and most notable landmark in Greenwich village. It stood in the center of the block now bounded by Bleecker, Charles, and Perry Streets. Sir Peter used it for a summer home, as his town house was on the Bowling Green. In 1819 it became the property of Abraham Van Nest.

Originally the place extended to the Hudson River, and a double row of century-old cottonwoods formed an avenue all the way down the gentle slope to the water's edge. The house at that time was approached from the west by a circular driveway which made an extensive sweep around the lawn. This beautiful curve always remained defined, even when grass-grown. The house stood in a perfect forest of grand old trees, horse-chestnuts, willows, poplars, sycamores and locusts, forming in some places an impenetrable shade. Besides these were peach, apricot, and cherry trees, always laden in their season with delicious fruit, while a pear tree, standing guard at one corner of the house, could almost thrust its great branches into the upper windows.

---

[1]*History of the City of New York*, by Martha J. Lamb, 1877–81.
[2]Extensive search has not revealed the source of Mrs. Lamb's information about the Stuyvesant garden.

[1]Contemporary records disclose no information about this garden.
[2]The editor has been unable to find the source from which Martha J. Lamb and *Valentine's Manual* secured the above information.

The long garden extending the entire width of the block was in summer days a veritable fairyland of flowers, where hollyhocks, coxcombs, sweet-william, and bleeding-hearts, ragged-sailors and maid-in-the-mist, bachelor buttons and wall flowers, "old man" and mignonette, lilies, clove pinks, phlox, poppies, larkspurs and strawberry shrub, and all the other dear old-fashioned favorites, grew in profusion in their fanciful-shaped, box-bordered beds. During the month of June the garden was literally pink with roses.

In the spring when the grass was studded with golden dandelions, and hedges of hawthorn, syringas and purple and white lilacs were in bloom, and snowballs nodded over the stone sphynx heads at the garden gate, while just below them the lilies-of-the-valley shook perfume from their hundreds of tiny bells, and violets and snowdrops peeped out from every hand, it was all so beautiful, that the remark of a former resident upon revisiting the spot, did not seem extreme, that "when she left it she felt like Eve leaving Paradise."[1]

THE RUTGERS MANSION AND GARDEN

We know that after New York was taken over by the English there was a period of great development both commercial and architectural, and can readily surmise that the garden, so dear to the English heart, kept pace with his growth. Of course hogs ran freely in the streets until 1817, and at the beginning of the eighteenth century only a few of the lower streets were paved, but we know that a number of excellent houses were built, among them the Rutgers' mansion, erected in 1754–5 by Hendrick Rutgers on a farm which was part of Bouwery No. 6.

The Inman homestead, Seventh Avenue at the corner of 25th Street, about 1800

The Rutgers place was representative of the type of house and grounds one would have seen before the Revolution. It was built of brick, said to have been brought from Holland, and stood in the block bounded by Rutgers Place on the north, Clinton Street on the east, Cherry Street on the south, and Jefferson Street on the west. For fifty years after the close of the Revolution it was the home of Colonel Henry Rutgers, personal friend of George Washington and benefactor of Rutgers College. At his death the house passed to a great-nephew, William Bedlow Crosby. It was then surrounded by a block of lawn and garden, with carriage-house, stables, etc. *Valentine's Manual* says that the grounds were handsomely laid out in the geometrical style then in vogue (1825). In 1865 the house was torn down; tenements now occupy the site.[2]

[1]*Reminiscences of the Old Van Nest Homestead*, by Mrs. Ann Van Nest Bussing.
[2]Facts chiefly from *Iconography of Manhattan Island*, by I. N. Phelps Stokes.

THE GOVERNOR'S HOUSE

In these early days New York was often swept by fire. The great conflagration during the British occupation in 1776 obliterated the greater part of the old Dutch landmarks, and many of the points of interest of the English period; with them many gardens must have perished.

Martha J. Lamb says: "The portion of the city laid in ashes during the first years of the Revolution had been rapidly rebuilding since 1788, some of the streets widened, nearly all of them straightened, and raised at an angle sufficient to carry off the water to the side gutters; footwalks of brick had also

From the Bulletin of the Boston Public Library

The Governor's House, sketched by Robert Gilmor in 1797

been made on each side." Another historian adds this to the picture: "The part that was destroyed by fire is almost wholly covered with elegant brick houses."[1]

The most elegant mansion among those built in New York after the fire was the one which stood on the site of the old fort opposite the Bowling Green. It was intended for the occupancy of Washington and all succeeding presidents. After the seat of government was moved to Philadelphia, this house was used by the governors of the state. No details of its garden survive. It was afterwards converted into the Custom House, and later was removed.

New York Historical Society Collections

A large garden surrounded the house erected by Gary Gilbert about 1810 on the east side of Fourth Street, between Christopher and West Tenth Streets

THE GARDEN OF THE RICHMOND HILL MANSION

Beyond the limits of the fire stood the Richmond Hill Mansion, on the southeast corner of Varick and Charlton Streets. In 1789 it was the residence of Vice-President Adams.

According to the *New York Magazine* for June, 1790, it was beautifully situated, "near the City of New York on the banks of the Hudson of which it commands an extensive prospect. The venerable oaks, and broken ground, covered with wild shrubs give it a very romantic air. . . ."

[1]*An Historical, Geographical, Commercial, and Philosophical View of the United States of America*, by the Rev. William Winterbottom, 1797.

Mrs. John Adams left a description of the place as it appeared in 1789. "In natural beauty," she wrote, "it might vie with the most delicious spot I ever saw. . . . The house stands on an eminence; at an agreeable distance flows the noble Hudson. . . . In front the Jersey shores present the exuberance of a rich well-cultivated soil. In the background is a large flower-garden, enclosed with a hedge and some very handsome trees. A lovely variety of birds serenade me morning and evening, rejoicing in their liberty and security."

During the Revolutionary War the Richmond Hill house was occupied by Sir Guy Carleton, Lord Dorchester, and several other distinguished noblemen. Later it was the property of Colonel Aaron Burr. It was torn down in 1849.

An approximate idea of the contents of the Richmond Hill garden and greenhouse can be gained from the list of plants given by T. E. V. Smith in his *New York City in 1789*. We learn that the cultivated shrubs which were sold at that time were shaddock, citron, lemon, olive, lime, and green bay trees; large alotis, large myrtle, box leaf, small myrtle, tea plant, pomegranate, creeping ceres, Arabian jasmine, balm of Gilead, rosemary, and lavender; common, striped, and partridge-breasted aloe, passion flower, oleander, polyanthus, auricula, and carnation pink.

Another large garden mentioned by T. E. V. Smith was that surrounding the residence of David M. Clarkson on Great George Street, between what is now Leonard and Franklin. This two-story house, thirty feet wide, had a garden 160 feet broad on Great George Street and 300 feet deep.

The Richmond Hill house

THE KIPS FARM AND THE COSTER GARDEN

Dr. John W. Francis says: "On the old road toward Kingsbridge, on the eastern side of the island, was the well-known Kips Farm preëminently distinguished for its grateful fruits, the plums, the peach, the pear, and the apple, and for its choice culture of the Rosaceæ. Here our Washington, now invested with presidential honours, went and was presented with the Rosa Gallica, an exotic first introduced into the country in this garden."[1]

The old Coster place at Thirtieth Street and the East River was originally part of this Kips Bay Farm.

The property was purchased April 30, 1805, by Henry A. Coster; in 1835 it was bought by Anson Green Phelps from Coster's widow, who had become the wife of Dr. David Hosack.

During the Coster occupancy of the house and during the later occupancy by Dr. Hosack, the founder of the Elgin Botanic Gardens, the grounds were stocked with choice plants and trees, and came to be regarded as among the finest gardens in America. Before First Avenue was cut through, the bluff was terraced down to the river, and on the lowest terrace was a summer-house and a boat-house.

The place was thus described by Mrs. James Stokes in a letter quoted in *Old New York from the Battery to Bloomingdale*:

"As I now look back on the lovely country home, with pleasant memories of my early years, I think of it as a remnant of Paradise. The garden was filled with the choicest

[1] *Old New York*, by John W. Francis, M. D.

fruit and many exquisite flowers, shrubs and trees. There was a cedar of Lebanon, said to have been brought by Mr. Coster himself from Mount Lebanon. We had also a large Conservatory of rare fruits and flowers."

The house was still standing in 1868, but was soon after demolished.

THE GARDEN OF ALEXANDER HAMILTON

In 1801 Alexander Hamilton built Hamilton Grange, a square, two-story structure which stood on what would now be the south side of 143rd Street, about 60 feet west of Convent Avenue. Hamilton's newly acquired farm extended from the St. Nicholas Avenue of today westward as far as the Hudson River. It was then, as he wrote in a letter to a friend, "about nine miles from town."

Hamilton laid out a garden and embellished the grounds around his home with flowers and shrubbery. Near the southeast corner of the house he set out a circle of thirteen gum trees, naming each after one of the original thirteen states. They were too closely set to attain great size, however, and after a time began one by one to die, their end hastened by the attentions of relic-hunters. The last one was cut down in 1908.

Hamilton's taste for gardening and farming was greatly encouraged by his association with his family physician, Dr. David Hosack, the founder of the Elgin Botanic Gardens, which were situated on the middle road (now Fifth Avenue) between 47th and 51st Streets. In his daily drives to town, Hamilton would stop to compare notes with Hosack, who would give him cuttings and bulbs for his new garden.

Some of Hamilton's letters show the great pleasure he found in his garden. On December 20, 1802, from his retirement "amidst the triumphant reign of democracy," he wrote to another ardent Federalist, Cotesworth Pinckney of South Carolina:

"A garden, you know, is a very usual refuge of a disappointed politician. Accordingly I have purchased a few acres about nine miles from town, have built a house, and am cultivating a garden. The melons in your country are very fine. Will you have the goodness to send me some seed, both of the water and musk melons? My daughter adds another request, which is for three or four of your paroquets. She is very fond of birds. If there be anything in this quarter, the sending of which can give you pleasure, you have only to name them. As farmers, a new source of sympathy has arisen between us, and I am pleased with everything in which our likings and tastes can be approximated."

Pinckney's reply on March 6, 1803, announced the dispatch of "some watermelon seeds and musk-melon seeds by the brig *Charleston Packet* which sails this morning. I formerly sent some to Mrs. Washington, at Mount Vernon, but she told me they did not answer so well as some she got in the neighborhood; perhaps had she planted the seeds from the melons which were produced from the Carolina seed the subsequent year, they would have adapted themselves to the climate and produced good fruit." His letter tells us the names of some of the flowers which found their way into Alexander Hamilton's garden, for Pinckney was planning to send by a later ship "a few seeds of the salvia cocinea, or scarlet sage, which I believe you have not with you, and of the erytherina herbacea, or coral shrub; also a few seeds of the Indian creeper, and some of a beautiful purple convolvulus.

"I will endeavor to obtain some paroquets for Miss Hamilton. I have not seen any for some years; ours are the large kind, by no means equal in beauty to the small African species. . . ."

Letters which Hamilton wrote to his wife in the course of frequent trips to Albany show how intent he was on the progress of his farm. From Claverack he wrote on Oct. 14, 1803:

". . . Let a separate compost bed be formed near the present one, to consist of 3 barrels full of the *clay* which I bought, 6 barrels of *black moulds* 2 waggon loads of the best clay on the Hill opposite the *Quakers plain* this side of Mr. Verplanks (the Gardener must go for it himself) and one waggon load of pure cowdung—Let these be well and repeatedly mixed and pounded together to be made up of hereafter for the Vines.

"I hope the apple trees will have been planted so as to profit by this moderate and wet weather. If not done, let *Tough* be reminded that a temporary fence is to be put up along the declivity of the Hill from the King's bridge road to the opposite wood so as to prevent the cattle injuring the young trees—the fence near the entrance to the Helicon spring ought for the same reason to be attended to—The materials of the fence taken down in making the Kitchen Garden & some rubbish, which may be picked up will answer——"

And two days later, having arrived at Peekskill:

"It has always appeared to me that the ground on which our orchard stands is much too moist. To cure this, a ditch round it would be useful, perhaps with a sunken fence as a guard. But this last may be considered at a future time.

"If you can obtain one or two more laborers, it may be advisable to cut a ditch round the orchard—three feet deep by three feet wide at the bottom. The clay that comes out of the ditch will be useful to give firmness to our roads and may be used for this purpose.

"Yet you will consider this merely as a suggestion and do as you think best after you shall have ascertained whether you can procure any better materials for the purpose. But remember that mere *sand* and stones will not answer."

But despite such close attention, Hamilton's grandson records[1] that "the returns from his farm seem to have been trivial; a few baskets of strawberries, cabbages, and asparagus were sold in 1802, the returns from the same being ₤7.10.2. And the experience of the amateur farmer then seems to have differed but little from that of most of us to-day."

Memoranda left by Hamilton after his death show that his knowledge of gardening, however unremunerative, was nevertheless practical. Some of these notes follow:

"1. Transplant fruit trees from the other side of the stable.

"2. Fences repaired. (Worn away) repaired behind stable. The cross fence at the foot of the hill? Potatoes Bradhursts? Ground may be removed and used for this purpose. Cows no longer to be permitted to range.

"3. The sod and earth which were removed in making the walks *where it is good* may be thrown upon the grounds in front of the House, and a few waggon loads of the compost.

"4. A *Ditch* to be dug along the fruit garden and grove

[1] *The Intimate Life of Alexander Hamilton*, by Allan McLane Hamilton (Charles Scribner's Sons, 1910), which is the chief source of the facts and letters of this account.

Alexander Hamilton at 45, from a painting by John Trumbull

about four feet wide, and the earth taken and thrown upon the *sand hill* in the rear."

Other notes give details for the laying out of a vegetable garden, the arrangement of flower beds, and the planting of raspberries "of the English sort"; then comes a suggestion for a charming bit of planting:

"3. If it can be done in time I should be glad if space could be prepared in the *center* of the flower garden for planting a few tulips, lilies, hyacinths, and [missing]. The space should be a circle of which the diameter is Eighteen feet: and there should be nine of each sort of flowers; but the gardener will do well to consult as to the season.

"They may be arranged thus: Wild roses around the outside of the flower garden with laurel at foot.

"If practicable in time I should be glad some laurel should be planted along the edge of the shrubbery and round the clump of trees near the house; also sweet briars and [illegible].

"A few dogwood trees not large, scattered along the margin of the grove would be very pleasant, but the fruit trees there must be first removed and advanced in front.

"These labours, however, must not interfere with the hot bed."

After the duel and Hamilton's tragic death, his widow strove to keep up the place, but was ultimately compelled by financial pressure to sell it. Today the house still stands, though removed to another site.

Another of the historic mansions of the period which is still preserved is the Gracie Mansion, whose grounds are now a public park. Josiah Quincy wrote in 1805 that they were

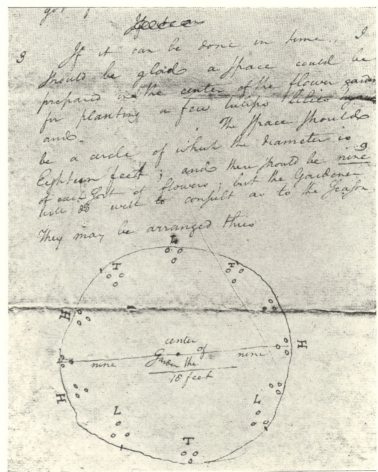

From "The Intimate Life of Alexander Hamilton," by Allan McLane Hamilton

The garden plan in Alexander Hamilton's notes

*The Grange, Alexander Hamilton's home, photographed before it was moved from its original site. The thirteen gum
trees, the last of which was cut down in 1908, are shown at the right*

"laid out with taste in gardens," but every trace of these gardens has disappeared.

"SMITH'S FOLLY": MOUNT VERNON, ON THE EAST RIVER

Colonel William Smith, who married Abigail Adams, the daughter of John Adams, purchased in March of the year 1796 a large property on the East River, the western half of the block bounded by First Avenue, Sixtieth Street, Avenue A, and Sixty-first Street.

Here Colonel Smith, who, from his portrait painted by Mather Brown in London about 1785 and now to be seen at the Adams Mansion in Quincy, Massachusetts, was a very comely and attractive man, as well as a cultivated one, built

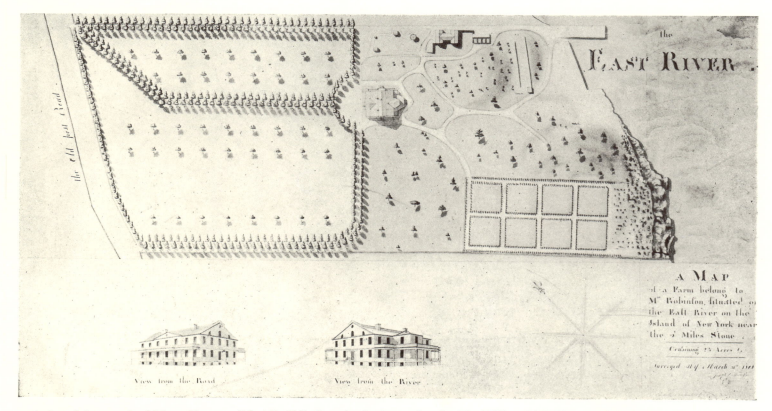

*A plan of the grounds of Mount Vernon or "Smith's Folly," made after its purchase by Mr. William T. Robinson and the building of the carriage
house and stable, still in existence. The plan is now owned by Miss Anna C. R. Dunn of Katonah, N. Y., and is reproduced by her permission*

an "elegant and spacious mansion," which he called Mount Vernon, and further embellished his property by the laying out of orchards and gardens. The plan reproduced here shows that the mansion was approached by a comprehensive driveway, that the house faced the river across an extensive lawn, and that a formal garden, designed as a series of squares, was at the left of the approach from the river.

Colonel Smith, like many another householder and gardener, got in deeper than he intended, and before it was even completed his place became known as "Smith's Folly," and had to be sold to satisfy claims. So the lovely Abigail Adams never lived in "Mount Vernon" on the East River.

In 1798 William T. Robinson purchased the house and grounds, and it was Colonel Robinson who built the stable and carriage house which still stands on East Sixty-first Street. In 1826, after passing through various hands, the mansion was entirely destroyed by fire, and was never rebuilt.

Joseph C. Hart, who owned the place in 1826, converted the stable and carriage house, which was substantially and handsomely built, into a dwelling-house. But still "Smith's Folly" passed from hand to hand; for a while it was a hotel and later was used as the private residence of the Towle family. In 1924 the Colonial Dames of America purchased the house for their headquarters in New York. It is very pleasant to record that though the grounds and gardens shown in the old plan are long since gone, the Society into whose hands it has come have made of it a very attractive and delightful place, having rescued such grounds as remain and planted them, and furnished the house with many beautiful things of the eighteenth and early nineteenth centuries.[1]

THE ROGER MORRIS MANSION AND GARDEN

The property was bought by Colonel Roger Morris from James Carroll, who bought it from the sons of Jan Kiersen, one of the pioneers of the district.

In 1765 was erected the mansion which still stands on Washington Heights, its chief historic ornament and the most impressive example of colonial architecture within New York City. The house built by Colonel and Mrs. Morris was spacious and had excellent proportions. There were extensive grounds and a garden. The house was reached from

The Roger Morris Mansion, now called the Jumel Mansion

the highroad by a driveway lined with trees. The sloping lawn which extended in front is in part preserved to this day. At the rear there was a large formal garden.

During the Revolution the estate suffered greatly. Col. Morris himself wrote that "All the timber upon the farm has

[1]Facts from an article by Joseph Warren Greene, Jr., in the *Bulletin of the New York Historical Society* for January 1927, and *Bulletin of the Society for the Preservation of New England Antiquities*.

been cut down and there is not a panel of fence upon the 100 acres excepting what are around the house and garden."

In 1810 the house was purchased by Stephen Jumel. He and his wife proceeded to restore the Morris Mansion, and laid out the grounds in an attractive manner.

In 1903 the property was purchased by the City of New York, thus happily ending the long career of ownership and sale, of war and confiscation, of poverty and wealth, of romance and legal wrangles, which have made the dwelling a centre of public attraction and historic interest.[1]

GARDENS IN THE SHARPLES DIARY

The diary of Mrs. Ellen Sharples offers this record of a visit which she made with her husband to the "country house" in Greenwich (Village) of Mr. C. Wilkes in 1809:

"We were much pleased with our drive and visit. The houses on the Island were delightfully pleasant, particularly

Mount Washington, residence of Samuel Thomson. Note gazebo in Gothic style at right. About 1840

those situated on the North River. Mr. W. had made his garden very pretty by the pleasing contrast of trees which he had tastefully planted—weeping willows, poplars, maples etc., had grown to a prodigious height in eight or nine years. . . . The porch was decorated with jessamine and woodbine. Had a pleasant drive home by moonlight."

A few days later appears this entry:

"In the afternoon had a drive on the Island; called at Bishop Moor's, who lived in the house we had formerly occupied, not far from Greenwich. . . . We were much struck with the beauty of the house, and the view it commanded of the noble North River. We remarked that we had always fixed upon the prettiest places. We then drove to call upon our old and esteemed acquaintance Mrs. Gates who prevailed upon us to stay and take tea. The view from her house appeared even more beautiful than we had just seen; an extent of cultivated land finely wooded, elegant villas, and ships sailing on the noble East River."[2]

PUBLIC PARKS BEFORE 1840

THE BATTERY AND CASTLE GARDEN

A most comprehensive and well illustrated account of the Battery and Castle Garden is to be found in the study by William Loring Andrews.[3] He tells us that the southwest extremity of Manhattan Island, which had originally been known as Schreyer's Hook, was first laid out as a public park in the late seventeenth century. The Battery was constructed in 1693, and the work of filling the grounds about the fort

[1]Adapted from the account in *Washington Heights*, by Roger Pelham Bolton.
[2]The foregoing extracts are reprinted by permission from *The Sharples: Their Portraits of George Washington and His Contemporaries*, by Katharine McCook Knox, published by the Yale University Press, in which the original Diary of Ellen Sharples was printed by special permission of the present owner, the Royal West of England Academy in Bristol, England.
[3]*The Iconography of the Battery and Castle Garden.*

City Hall Park, probably shortly after 1842

with the object of laying out an esplanade and pleasure ground began at about the same time. In 1734 the Battery was ordered "kept clear of houses from Whitehall Street to Eeld's corner, now Markertfield Street." About 1788 it was decided to remove the old fort and build in its stead what subsequently became the Governor's House.

By 1824 the place had quite lost its martial character. The Corporation then gave a lease on it for a period of five years and it was fitted up as a promenade and place of entertainment. Then began the peaceful and palmy days of the Battery and Castle Garden. The attractions of its "large and dry terrace and parterres of the Battery walk . . . the fine trees . . . the distant hills of Staten Island and New Jersey covered with verdure" made it the favored place of public resort.

Barber and Howe cite an English visitor's description of the Battery before 1836:

"The Battery extends somewhat in the form of a crescent from the termination of Broadway, Greenwich and Washington Streets, on the northwest to Whitehall Street, covering an area of nearly eleven acres, and laid out in grass plots and gravel walks, shaded with trees. The exterior, fronting the harbor, is built up with hewn stone; and on this side is a paved walk, with stone posts connected with a neat open railing. An expensive iron railing, with gateways, extends along the interior front."

Dr. John W. Francis in *Old New York* speaks of the Battery being profusely set with Lombardy poplars.

Robert Gilmor in 1797 described it as "the grand public promenade of the ladies." Mrs. Trollope in 1832 also speaks of the Battery as the principal promenade, ". . . and a more beautiful one no city can boast. It commands a fine view of the magnificent bay, and forms a termination to the splendid street called Broadway, which is ornamented with several handsome buildings, some of which are surrounded by grass and trees."

CITY HALL PARK

City Hall Park, once the site of an Indian village, was first known during the Dutch period as the Vlacte or Flat, and later as the Commons. At this time it was well outside the walls of New Amsterdam, and provided free pasturage for the cattle of the citizens. When the title to the park was given to the Corporation in 1686, the Commons was a wild uncultivated tract on the outskirts of civilization.

The first boundary was the rambling old Post Road, which

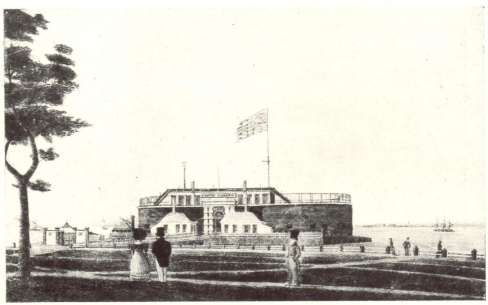

Castle Garden in the 1820's

came down the Bowery and Chatham Road, which is now Park Row, as far as Broadway.

A part of the park called Spring Garden was afterwards a public resort, but in the latter part of the seventeenth and the first part of the eighteenth centuries, this tract was so remote and so unimproved that it was the spot chosen for the hanging of criminals.

In 1785 appears the first record of a suggestion for enclosing the fields with a fence. The suggested plans were approved by the Common Council, "if it could be done without expense. . . ." The fence did not materialize.

In 1792 the first fence was set up, made of posts and rails. In 1797, we see the enclosure for the first time dignified by the name of "Park" on the maps of the period. Early in the nineteenth century the rail fence was superseded by wooden palings; then, as civic pride increased, by an imported iron fence, which was brought from England and put in place in 1821. At this time the southern gateway consisted of four marble pillars, surmounted by iron scroll-work, supporting lanterns. Trees were then set out, and "two ladies gave rose-bushes, the latter surviving vandal-ism about one year." In 1832 the grass plots were surrounded with iron chains on locust posts, and in 1842 amidst great festivities a fountain was installed.

I. N. Phelps Stokes says that the park, consisting of four acres, was "planted with elms, planes, willows and catalpas, the surrounding foot-walk encompassed with rows of poplars. . . . This beautiful grove in the middle of the city combined in a high degree ornament with health and pleasure."

Later Dr. John W. Francis tells us that "the more conspicuous and beautiful trees, the sycamores, the maples, the walnuts, and the Babylonian willows of the growth of ages were cut in City Hall Park."

At the end of the period covered by this book City Hall Park comprised about eleven acres and was surrounded by an iron fence on a plinth of brown free stone; the fountain of that time (1842) threw a jet of water seventy feet in the air.

ST. JOHN'S PARK

"The beautiful park in front of St. John's Church was not only appropriated from the Trinity Church domains, and made the pride of the city, but embellished at the expense of the church corporation," says Martha J. Lamb. E. Porter Belden's *New York, Past, Present, and Future* speaks of St. John's Park as a highly ornamental enclosure of about four acres. . . . "It stands in the name of the corporation of Trinity Church though it is virtually the property of surrounding owners; and its privileges are confined to the proprietors and such others as are permitted on their recommendation to hire the keys at the annual charge of $10.00. It is surrounded by an iron fence, contains a most beautiful fountain, and is more abundantly supplied with trees and shrubs than any other park in the city."

Dr. Francis says that St. John's Park was laid out by Louis Simons, the distinguished traveller and artist, and that a botanical enquirer could find there a greater variety of trees and shrubs than in any other ground of equal size in the known world. This was early in the nineteenth century, long before Central Park was planned, or even thought of.

Mrs. Trollope wrote in 1832: "St. John's Park is of considerable extent, and has lately been thrown open to the inhabitants; it is tastefully and very judiciously planted with the ornamental trees and shrubs indigenous to the country."

The garden adjoining St. Paul's, from a sketch made between 1800 and 1810

BOWLING GREEN

In the seventeenth century the open space in front of the fort at the lower extremity of Manhattan Island was first used as a parade-ground for the garrison. In 1659 it became, and continued to be for many years thereafter, the town's established market-place, called the Marchvelt. In 1732 the Corporation resolved to "lease a piece of land, lying at the lower end of Broadway, fronting the Fort, to some of the inhabitants, in order to be enclosed to make a bowling-green therein, for the beauty and ornament of said street, as well as for the delight of the inhabitants of this city." The lessees were John Chambers, Peter Bayard, and Peter Jay, for one pepper-corn per annum for eleven years. In 1786 it was granted to Chancellor Livingston on condition that he should, "at his own expense, manure the ground, and sow the same with grass seed, and have it well laid down as a green." But this arrangement was short-lived, and in 1795 it was ordered "that the enclosed ground, commonly called the Bowling Green, be appropriated to the governor for the time being." In 1798 it was ordered that John Rogers may have the use of the Bowling Green "on condition that he keep it in good order and suffer no creature to run on it."

The opening of the nineteenth century found the Bowling Green given over to municipal care.[1]

GRAMERCY SQUARE

The name "Gramercy" is derived from Krom Moerasje, "Crooked Little Swamp." The latter was part of Cedar Creek which once flowed from Madison Square to the East River. It was long called "Crommessie" in the Dutch records.

In 1761 it was part of the twenty-acre farm of James Duane, once mayor of the city. His farm was then called "Gramercy Seat."

In 1831 the Square became a private park, presented to the owners of the surrounding sixty lots by Samuel B. Ruggles.

In 1837 a fountain was built, and trees and shrubbery of great variety and beauty were planted under the direction of Charles A. Davis.[2]

PLEASURE GARDENS IN NEW YORK CITY

According to Mrs. Schuyler Van Rensselaer, "The Locust Trees," on the bluff overlooking the North River, back of Governor Stuyvesant's garden, was a favorite trysting and loitering place. Indeed, more than one primeval tree appears to have been preserved within the city limits to shelter the pipe-smoking burgher who might not smoke in his own home. Nutten (Governor's Island) was also some sort of a pleasure ground, and Bowery Village, said Dominie Selyns, writing to Amsterdam, was "a place of relaxation and pleasure whither people go from the Manhattans for the evening service."

Valentine mentions the Cherry Orchard, sometimes calling

[1]Facts from *New York Old and New*, by Rufus Rockwell Wilson, and *Peter Stuyvesant*, by Bayard Tuckerman.

E. Porter Belden's *New York, Past, Present, and Future*, 1849.

Union Square about 1840

it the Cherry Garden, and says it was originally the property of Egbert Van Bursum, the ferryman of New Amsterdam, afterward becoming one of the first public resorts, the property of Richard Sacket. It was celebrated for its fruit.

Sperry's Gardens were established by Jacob Sperry, who came to this country from Switzerland in 1740. He was educated as a physician, but later became a florist. He purchased land in a rough state, and established himself as a horticulturist. In 1803 the property was bought by John Jacob Astor, who leased it to Delacroix, a Frenchman, who remodelled and replanted the gardens and named it Vauxhall. According to Rufus Rockwell Wilson, these Vauxhall Gardens stretched from Fourth Street to Astor Place, and were surrounded by a high board fence. They were laid out in alleys and shaded walks with small boxes fitted up to represent mystic bowers. The Astor Library later stood in the center of the vanished garden.

Niblo's Garden was on Broadway near Prince Street. It was a fashionable place of resort during the summer months, and included in addition to its theatrical attractions, walks bordered with shrubbery and flowers in great variety.

There is mention of another pleasure garden in T. E. V. Smith's *New York of 1789*. We learn there that in 1784 Brissot de Warville wrote: "It is tea that you go to drink in the beautiful gardens of M. Cummings, the Florida garden of New York. This garden is situated on the North River and the view is charming." The garden in May, 1789, passed into the hands of George Leay Craft. Other popular gardens were Perry's, on the west side of Union Square, and Williams', on the east side of Greenwich Street.

THE ELGIN BOTANIC GARDENS

The Elgin Botanic Gardens were founded in 1801 by Dr. David Hosack, professor of botany at Columbia College. They covered nearly twenty acres of cultivated land on Murray Hill between Forty-seventh and Fifty-first Streets

and between Fifth and Sixth Avenues. We quote from a monograph by Addison Brown:

"The development of the garden was pushed forward with the energy and success of an enthusiast. Dr. Hosack's acquaintance with scientific men abroad greatly aided him in obtaining plants, seeds, shrubs and trees from every quarter.

"By 1806 the grounds were well under cultivation, having 2,000 species of plants, and one spacious greenhouse and two hot houses, presenting a frontage of 180 feet. The plots devoted to plants were encircled by shrubs and trees; and the whole ground encircled by a stone wall seven feet high and two and one half feet thick."

Dr. Francis in *Old New York* says that in 1807 the place was "a triumph of individual zeal, ambition and liberality, of which our citizens had reasons to be proud. The eminent projector of this garden, with princely munificence, had made these grounds a resort for the admirers of Nature's vegetable wonders and for the student of her mysteries."

Gray and Torrey were both pupils of Dr. Hosack, and such men as Michaux, Bartram, Doughty, Pursh, and Le Conte met in the gardens to discuss and settle botanical problems. Dr. Hosack was always most generous in his commendation of botanical achievement. He speaks of Frederick Pursh in his preface to a catalogue of plants of the gardens as follows:

"It would be injustice to Mr. Frederick Pursh, who with a knowledge of the science of botany unites a very extensive and accurate acquaintance with the plants of this country, not to notice the very numerous contributions he has made to the collection of the native plants of the United States."

Pursh was at that time curator of the gardens.

After expending much time, energy, and money up to $100,000 on his experiment, Dr. Hosack felt that the State should take over the work. Long negotiations and many disappointments led finally to the purchase of the gardens by the people of the State of New York in 1810. In 1811 they were leased for five years to the College of Physicians and

Surgeons. Then followed a period of neglect and deterioration, though the founder never lost interest in his creation.

The following account of a visit to the garden shortly after it was taken over by the State was published in the form of a letter, and shows the type of petty enmity with which the large-minded, enthusiastic botanist had to contend:

"My sensations were indescribable, tumbled as I was in a moment from the very acme of expectation into the deep Trophonian abyss of disappointment. I do not know whether to vent my execration or my laughter. There never was in the world such a piece of downright imposture as the Botanic Garden, and as it is delightfully called Elgin. Take away from it the 'Orangerie' or Green house which stands at the remote end of it, and it looks more like one of those large pasture-grounds near Albany, in which the western drovers refresh their cattle. . . . It is a lot of twenty acres, with no other buildings but the greenhouse just mentioned, which has two small wings, and two other buildings of about 12ft. square, fancifully called porter's lodges (because there are no porters in them) one of which

David Hosack

is placed at each gate. There is a small culinary garden on the western side, laid out in the common way in Squares; and the east of the grounds are in grass. No fruit whatever is to be found here; no large trees to furnish a retreat from the meriddian sun; no little porticoes, no knolls; nor in fine is there anything which tends to embellish or diversify the grounds. Barring the greenhouse which is like those generally found in private gardens, the tout ensemble of this celebrated Elgin, has, as already observed, the air of a common pasture ground. . . . We visited the interior of the greenhouse. There we found orange and lemon trees, geraniums, two or three coffee and pineapple plants, and all those little quelque choses which are usually to be seen in the gardens of private gentlemen, but nothing whatever of national importance. Such my friend, is what is absurdly called the botanic garden. . . ."

In contrast to this morose and evidently jaundiced view is Dr. Hosack's concept of the ideal botanic garden as set forth in an inaugural address before the New York Horticultural Society in 1824. So many of the points are pertinent to modern botanic gardens that they are here quoted in his language in summarized form:

1st. It should be sufficiently extensive to contain all varieties of fruit trees and shrubs. . . .

2nd. Compartments should be provided for all the esculent vegetables of the table.

3rd. Provisions should be made for the culture of those plants that are most useful in medicine, or are subservient to the arts, or are employed in manufacture. . . .

4th. To those should be added . . . a collection of the most rare and ornamental plants that can be procured. . . .

5th. The whole of this Institution should be surrounded by a belt of forest trees and shrubs, foreign and domestic.

6th. There should be a lecture room and a library.

7th. A Herbarium.

8th. Another advantage which such an establishment should possess, is that of exemplifying the principle of ornamental planting, or landscape gardening.

9th. There should be instruction in Horticulture, pruning, grafting etc.

10th. There should be a professor of drawing employed. . . .

11th. Especial attention should be given to the cultivation of our native fruits.

By 1829 the gardens were in a lamentable state because a short-sighted State had not appropriated sufficient money for their upkeep. Dr. Francis says of the scheme: "Flourishing under its founder, it perished under the neglect of the public."

A century ago, Dr. Hosack's view on the liquor question was evidently that of a moderate. He said in his address: "Among the wants in our domestic economy none are more conspicuous or lamentable than that of some agreeable beverage which, may supersede the use of ardent spirits, the inordinate and extensive use of which has long been among the opprobria of our countrymen." He advised the use of apple, pear, blackberry, currant, raspberry, gooseberry and elderberry in the preparation of such "agreeable beverages."

A cherished but unrealized plan of Dr. Hosack's was to write and publish an American Botany, or Flora of the United States, the illustrations of which were to have been made by James Inderwick and John Le Conte.

Dr. Hosack also developed an estate called Hyde Park on the Hudson. Louden in his *Encyclopedia of Horticulture* says: "The natural capacity of this seat for development has been taken advantage of in a very judicious manner; and every circumstance has been laid hold of, and acted upon, which could tend to beautify or adorn it. The mansion is splendid and convenient. The park is extensive, the rides numerous . . . the pleasure grounds are laid out on just principles . . . and there is an excellent range of hot-houses with a collection of rare plants." Hyde Park was, in the words of James Stuart in *Three Years in North America*, "quite a show place in the English sense of the word."

American Historical Prints, New York Public Library

The Elgin Gardens, from a sepia drawing by Hugh Reinagle, about 1812

THE MANORS OF NEW YORK

DURING the English period a number of great Manors were erected in the State of New York. Some of them succeeded patroonships of the Dutch period, and others were confirmations of land grants made by the crown.

A LIST OF MANORS

The following list of Manors, all granted within a period of three decades, is an indication of the agricultural, and conse-

March 20, 1687; the Manor of Saint George in Suffolk County, granted to William Smith, October 5, 1693; and the Manor of Bentley, sometimes called Billopp Manor, granted to Christopher Billopp, May 6, 1687. Another, called Fischer's Manor, appears north of Newburgh on Cadwallader Colden's Map of Manors and Grants. And another called Queen's Manor, on Long Island, granted to the Lloyd family, is mentioned in early documents about the year 1697.[1]

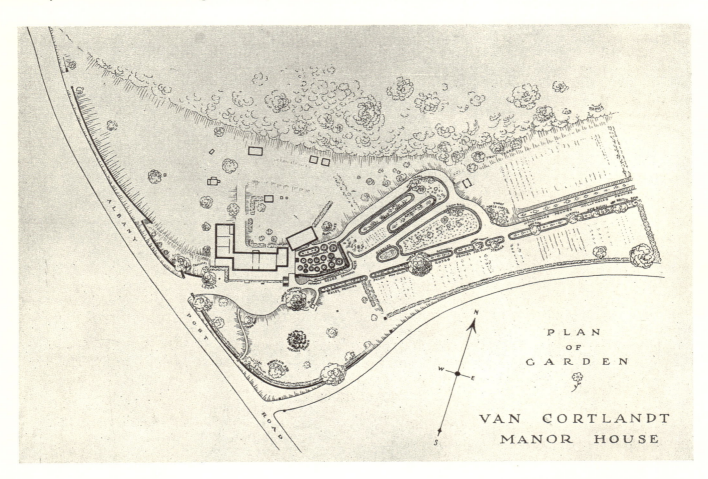

PLAN
OF
GARDEN

VAN CORTLANDT
MANOR HOUSE

quent horticultural, development of New York State in these years:

The Manor of Fordham, granted to John Archer, November 13, 1671; the Manor of Fox Hall, near Kingston, granted to Thomas Chambers, October 16, 1672; the Manor of Rensselaer, November 4, 1685; the Manor of Livingston, granted to Robert Livingston, July 22, 1686; the Manor of Pelham, granted to Thomas Pell, October 25, 1687; the Manor of Philipsborough, granted to Frederick Philipse, June 12, 1693; the Manor of Morrisania, granted to Lewis Morris, May 8, 1697; the Manor of Cortlandt, granted to Stephanus van Cortlandt, June 17, 1697; and the Manor of Scarsdale, granted to Caleb Heathcote, March 21, 1701.

The early records of the State also contain references to at least seven other Manors, the exact status of which it is impracticable to ascertain owing to the loss or inaccessibility of original records. Five of them were the Manor of Gardiner's Island, at the eastern end of Long Island, granted to the Earl of Stirling, March 10, 1639; the Manor of Plumme Island, consisting of Plum Island and Gull Island, granted to Samuel Willes, April 2, 1675; the Manor of Cassiltown (Castleton) on Staten Island, granted to John Palmer,

A FEW MANOR GARDENS

Fortunately, portions of several of the Manor gardens have survived to the present day, and the records contain a few meagre gardening details of several of the others.

PHILIPSE MANOR AND GARDENS[2]

Philipse Manor was one of the several great Manors erected in the State of New York during the English period. It was granted to Frederick Philipse in 1693, by a Royal Charter, in the name of William and Mary. In 1702 the first Lord of the Manor died, leaving his vast estates to be divided between his wife, his three children and his grandson, Frederick. To the latter he gave his house in New York in which he was living at the time of his death, and six other buildings; the island of Papirineum at Spuyten Duyvil creek, with the meadows, King's Bridge, and toll; all the lands and meadows

[1]Lists from *Philipse Manor Hall*, by Edward Hagaman Hall; the American Scenic and Historic Preservation Society, New York.
[2]This description is drawn chiefly from *Philipse Manor Hall*, by Edward Hagaman Hall. It is slightly adapted.

called "ye Yoncker's Plantation," including houses, mills, mill-dams, orchards, gardens, etc.

In 1745, in the midst of his distinguished career, Judge Philipse, the grandson, is said to have enlarged the Manor Hall to thrice its original size, by the addition of the northern extension. By this change the eastern side became the main front. Between it and the old Post Road stretched a velvety lawn with garden terraces and horse-chestnut trees. On either hand were laid formal gardens and grounds, ornamented here and there with valuable trees, choice shrubs, and beautiful flowers. Through these ran graveled walks, bordered with boxwood. To the west of the building the greensward sloped to the river, unobstructed save by the fine specimens of trees, among which were emparked a number of deer. From the roof of the house a superb view could be obtained in every direction.

The well-house of Morrisania

John Jay says of Judge Philipse: "This Frederick I knew. He was a well tempered, amiable man; a kind benevolent landlord. He had a taste for gardening, planting etc., and employed much time and money in that way."

The floral opulence of the gardens of Philipse Manor was the inspiration of this passage in a poem in the true sentimental style addressed "to Mr. Bleecker, on his passage to New York by Ann Eliza (Schuyler) Bleecker, of Tomhanick, near Albany," and written about 1840:

> "The eastern banks are crowned with rural seats,
> And Nature's work the hand of Art completes.
> Here Philipse' villa, where Pomona joins
> At once the product of a hundred climes.
> Here, tinged by Flora, Asian flowers unfold
> Their burnished leaves of vegetable gold.
> When snows descend, and clouds tumultuous fly,
> Through the blue medium of the crystalline sky
> Beneath his painted mimic Heaven he roves
> Amidst the glass-encircled citron groves;
> The grape and luscious fig his taste invite,
> Hesperian apples glow upon his sight,
> And sweet auriculas their bells display,
> And Philipse finds, in January, May."

THE HEATHCOTE OR SCARSDALE MANOR AND GARDENS

Caleb Heathcote, who came from England to America in 1691, bought a large tract of land in Westchester, fronting on Long Island Sound. To these holdings he added lands acquired by purchase from the native Indian proprietors. These lands were erected into a Manor in 1701. Here are now located Mamaroneck, Larchmont and Scarsdale.

At Mamaroneck, on a hill overlooking the waters of the Sound, Colonel Heathcote built his Manor House, with the usual farm houses and outbuildings. It was named Heathcote Hall, and must have been for its day quite a pretentious place. It is described by Madame Sarah Knight, who, journeying from Boston to New York in 1704, speaks of "the Manor-House of Colonel Caleb Heathcote, with its broad lawns, handsome gardens, elegant shade trees, and great deer park after the most approved English fashion."

Heathcote died in 1721. The mansion was burned at the time of the Revolution, and was replaced by a frame dwelling.[1]

---

[1]Facts from an address written for the tenth annual meeting of the New York branch of the Order of Colonial Lords of the Manor in America by the Honorable Chas. B. Wheeler of the New York Supreme Court.

THE MORRIS MANOR, MORRISANIA[1]

Captain Richard Morris purchased land which had been granted by the Dutch in 1639 to Jonas Broncks, the first white settler in Westchester County.

The plantation of Lewis Morris was erected into a Manor in 1694, and was called "Morrisania." It eventually included part of the Manors of Fordham and Scarsdale. The whole of the original Manor, with the adjacent portions of Westchester County, was in 1774 annexed to the City of New York. During the Revolution the family had to flee, and the Manor House and 1000 acres of woodland were burned and laid waste.

In 1790 Congress was memorialized with the suggestion that Morrisania would make an ideal spot for the seat of the Federal Government. Congress preferred the banks of the Potomac, however.

Gouverneur Morris was of this family, and made Morrisania his home.

No details of the garden of Morrisania have been recorded. In 1810 Ellen Sharples paid a three-day visit to the restored Manor House with her husband. Her Diary comments on the magnificence of silver, china, tapestries and other furnishings, and hints at "beauties both of nature and art," but tells us nothing of the grounds.

LLOYD'S OR QUEEN'S MANOR, OF QUEEN'S VILLAGE

A grant was made to James Lloyd by Governor Thomas Dongan, Mar. 18, 1685. This paper enumerated "wood, beaches, marshes, meadows, pastures, creels" etc. The rent to King James was yearly "four bushels of good winter wheat or the value thereof in current money of this province." The Manor was small in size, however, in comparison to the princely estates on the Hudson.

THE GARDEN OF THE VAN CORTLANDT MANOR HOUSE, CROTON-ON-THE-HUDSON[2]

On the north side of the Croton River, a short distance from the Albany Post Road, stands the Van Cortlandt Manor House, built originally as a place of defence against the Indians. The date of its erection is not certain, but it undoubtedly was standing in 1681.

When all dangers from the Indians had ceased, the fort was turned into a dwelling house by Stephanus Van Cortlandt, the first Lord of the Manor.

The old trees stand close to the Manor House, a guardian at either end. The tree at the right, a very old locust, is gnarled and bending, but every year covered with blossoms. Its age can only be guessed. It is probably over three hundred years old, its longevity accounted for by the fact that a spring lies close to its roots. At the eastern end of the house stands the other sentinel tree, a beautiful horse-chestnut. The old apple orchard contained many very large trees. Here grew the Dongan apple tree, planted by Governor Dongan on

---

[1]Facts drawn chiefly from *Order of Colonial Lords of the Manor in America*, by Lucy D. Akerly.

[2]Written by Anne Stevenson Van Cortlandt.

Looking toward the entrance to the grounds, with the old locust tree in the background

from the garden—roses, lilies, peonies, harebells, and sprays of flowering almond and convolvulus. To this son, Pierre, the Manor House was left by his father. He married in 1748 Joanna Livingston, and in 1749 they came to the Manor House to live.

The garden, destined to be the delight of generations, was now more fully developed. To it the young wife added many flowers from her Rhinebeck home, among them white Scottish roses, and small, bright yellow poppies. The white roses vanished during the last century but the yellow poppies still linger, turning up in the most unexpected places. This was the playground and favorite resort of the children, but play was abandoned on one occasion, when the first grandchild was brought, in 1771, by his mother, Mrs. Beekman, to visit her parents. She came riding on a pillion behind her husband, holding the baby in her arms, wrapped in a scarlet cloak. Pierre Van Cortlandt, then ten years old, and his little sister Ann, afterwards Mrs. Philip Van Rensselaer, started for the house up the garden path, each desirous of being the first to welcome the baby and his mother.

one of his visits. It was standing until the middle of the last century, and the fruit was always spoken of as the "Dongan Apple."

The lawn lies in a half circle in front of the house. It is adorned with groups of very old lilacs, and a hedge of Rose-of-Sharon surrounds it. Here gathered the crowds when Whitefield, while on a visit to the Manor House, preached from the verandah.

The "Lady of the Manor" made frequent trips between New York and the Manor House in her coach with its four white horses and outriders, and tradition tells that she often returns to the home that she had loved. In the quiet of the evening, as the twilight melted into darkness, the clatter of horses' hoofs was heard and the sound of a heavy coach. The horses were reined up sharply before the door, the rumbling of the coach suddenly ceased—silence followed.

Near the entrance to the garden stands the sun-dial, engraved by Christopher Colles, with the motto "Noli confidere Noctem." It is mounted on the end of an old roller of sandstone, made for the garden about one hundred and fifty years ago.

There is reason to believe that the garden began to take its present form when Philip Van Cortlandt, at the death of his father, Stephanus, inherited the Manor House. In the hall of the house hangs a portrait of Pierre Van Cortlandt, Philip's son, painted probably in 1730, when he was nine years old. On the left of the little figure stands a large vase of flowers gathered

A bit of the upper garden of the Van Cortlandt Manor House. A more extensive view of the upper garden is shown on page 252

Many distinguished officers visited the Manor House during the Revolution—Washington, Lafayette, Rochambeau, Schuyler, Von Steuben, and others of note. Doubtless the garden was a centre of attraction, and pleasant hours were there whiled away. The war brought many and great

The Van Cortlandt Manor House

The house from the lower garden

The ancient Van Cortlandt locust tree, probably over three hundred years old

Revolution, although an occasional reference in old letters to some episode connected with it shows it was in continuous existence.

In 1836 Colonel Pierre Van Cortlandt came into possession of the Manor House, and in his time the garden was a dream of beauty; flowers bloomed in every available spot, and all he touched grew and flourished. He planned and made the little parterre on the east, into which one steps from the veranda, a picturesque foreground to the older garden. It is placed where two wings of the house connect and is held up by retaining walls of red brick, covered with climbing roses and vines. The beds are circular in form, filled with blossoming plants. From here a path bordered with old-fashioned flowers leads along the terrace to the summer-house.

The older garden has never been altered. It shows no

Pierre Van Cortlandt, from a painting executed about 1730, and now in the possession of Miss Anne Stevenson Van Cortlandt

formal beds nor color schemes; only the flowers which were loved for their beauty or sweetness were planted, and as each generation contributed its share in adding to the interest of the garden, it is full of the spirit and sentiment of the past.

With the melting of the snow, the crocuses and snowdrops appear, and soon after the daffodils, violets, and lilies-of-the valley are to be found at their posts. Then come the pinks, iris, and peonies, with many other treasured flowers, and the roses, a glory in themselves, the York and Lancaster, the centifolia and the damask, filling the air with sweetness. These grow without let or hindrance, falling in cascades of white and pink and crimson, and then great is the loveliness and the charm of the garden.

changes. Lawless bands of Tories infested the neighborhood, and as the father of the family was absent at Kingston, attending to the duties of his office, and the eldest son was serving in the army, it was decided to close the house, and send the mother and the children to a safer abode. The place of refuge was Rhinebeck, where they remained three years, and returned to their home in 1780 to find it a scene of desolation, the house pillaged, and the garden and grounds laid waste. But with energy and diligence, order was finally restored.

Little is known of the garden in the years following the

Sagtikos Manor, at Islip, Long Island

SAGTIKOS MANOR, APPLETREEWICKE, AT ISLIP[1]

Long and narrow, extending eight miles north from the Great South Bay, Sagtikos Manor, an estate of twelve hundred and six acres, and probably the oldest farm under continuous cultivation on Long Island since the reign of William and Mary, is situated about forty miles from New York.

Colonel Stephanus Van Cortlandt received a license to

granddaughter of the fourth Lord of the Manor of Gardiner's Island.

Isaac Thompson was a magistrate for more than forty years, and was active during the Revolution in organizing the militia. He went through many trying experiences during these years of turmoil, but we feel certain that when more peaceful days arrived he had time to develop a garden enclosed by a tight board fence. The spacious music-room now covers this ground, but we know that formerly there grew

The varnish tree at Sagtikos Manor is probably the largest of its kind in the Eastern States

purchase the property from the Indians, in 1692, and built the Manor House the year the patent was obtained from William III, King of England, signed by Colonel Benjamin Fletcher, Governor of New York.

Stephanus Van Cortlandt did not remain many years at Sagtikos, which the Indians called Saghtekoos and the Christians "Appletreeneck." He disposed of the property, preferring to establish himself on the banks of the Hudson, where Van Cortlandt Manor perpetuates his name.

In 1758 the property was purchased by the Thompson family, and in 1772 Isaac Thompson was married to Mary Gardiner, daughter of Colonel Abraham Gardiner, and

[1]Written by Sarah D. Gardiner.

in this sheltered spot parterres edged with box and in May bright with tulips, while later on phlox, hollyhocks, and althea lent their share of brilliant color. There were pinks, mullein, mountain and China; there were roses also, one white rose-bush having been brought by Mary Gardiner from her home at Easthampton. And no doubt the dooryard itself possessed the usual lilacs and waxberry bushes.

All around the house are immense black walnut trees, and opposite the main entrance stands a wonderful specimen of the varnish-tree (*Koelreuteria paniculata*), a native of China. This tree, sixty feet high and six feet in circumference, is said to be probably the largest of its kind in the eastern part of the United States.

The enormous oak at Sagtikos Manor, Islip

In the middle of the field in front of the house stands an enormous oak called Sir Henry's Oak, doubtless from Sir Henry Clinton who during the Revolution often stayed at the Manor House. Perhaps Mary Gardiner Thompson often sat under its shade, her small boys playing beside her, and we can imagine General Washington on his tour through Long Island resting beneath its wide-spreading boughs.

As was usual on these old estates, there was a family cemetery at Sagtikos. It is still in existence, enclosed by a handsome iron fence; the ground is carpeted with English ivy.

There is an interesting epitaph on one of the tombs, that of a little child—

"Thou wert so like a form of light
That heaven benignly called you hence,
Ere yet the world could breathe one blight
O'er thy sweet innocence;
And thou, that brighter home to bless,
Art passed with all thy loveliness."

GARDENS IN LIVINGSTON MANOR

Robert Livingston, who came to America in 1673, obtained on July 22, 1686, a grant of land consisting of a great tract of more than 160,000 acres which he had obtained from the Indians. It stretched for twelve miles along the Hudson, widening out toward the east some twenty miles along the Massachusetts border, embracing large parts of what are now Columbia and Dutchess counties.

Robert Livingston married into the powerful Schuyler family. In 1699 he built his Manor House, which stood for over a century; but it was long before his princely domain had many inhabitants. His second son, Robert, built in 1730, on a cliff close to the Hudson, a large brick and stone mansion, which he called Clermont.

Martha J. Lamb says of the Livingston Manor of later years: "The beautiful estates of the various members of the Livingston family on the shores of the Hudson at this period would have made a village of villas, indeed, if they could have been collected. John R. Livingston competed with his brother, the Chancellor, the honor of having the show place; his stately house covered so much ground, and was esteemed so perfect in architectural symmetry, that drawing-masters made sketches of it, and gave them to their pupils to copy.

"Clermont, the country seat of Chancellor Livingston in 1790, on the shores of the Hudson, with its library opening into a greenhouse and orangery, its half mile of lawns and richly cultivated flower gardens, its blossoming orchards and magnificent forests, was for many a long year the seat of princely hospitality."[1]

Another historian thus describes Arryl House, built by Chancellor Livingston in 1783 near Clermont and overlooking the river:

"The house was built in the form of a capital H. Between the two projecting wings of the river front was an elevated, stone paved terrace, upon which were set orange, lemon and myrtle trees in tubs, after the contemporary French manner. The conservatory ran the whole depth of the house on the south side and here on great occasions the dinner and supper tables were set, the tables being so constructed that large plants rose from their centres. Two skilled gardeners took charge of the conservatory, the greenhouse and the flower gardens."[2]

In the *New York Magazine* for May, 1791, appeared a picture of Henry Livingston's seat at Poughkeepsie, with this description:

From "The New York Magazine," May, 1791

The seat of Henry Livingston, Esq., at Poughkeepsie

"Nature in her kindliest mood has undulated the hills around and smoothed the terrene where the buildings are erected, laved the shore with the majestic Hudson, and made the whole delightful—so it is that no voyager of taste passes it without acknowledging the rural beauties; and none visit it without receiving impressions in its favor."

THE GARDEN AT SYLVESTER MANOR, SHELTER ISLAND[3]

Shelter Island lies between the two arms into which the eastern end of Long Island is divided. Gardiner's Island and Plum Island cut off the force of the ocean from its quiet shores. Literally it is an "island sheltered by islands," which is the translation of its Indian name, Manhansuke Ahaquat-zuwamocke.

It was granted as a Manor, with all the immunities and

[1] Martha J. Lamb, *History of The City of New York.*
[2] *The Manors and Historic Homes of the Hudson Valley*, by H. D. Eberlein.
[3] Written by Cornelia Horsford.

Box-bordered paths in the garden of Sylvester Manor, Shelter Island.   The great box trees are shown on page 254

The later garden at Sylvester Manor

privileges of an English Manor, to Nathaniel Sylvester and his brother Constant on May 31, 1666, by Richard Nicolls, the first English colonial governor of New York, serving under King Charles the Second.

The Sylvester brothers were sugar planters in the Island of Barbadoes. Nathaniel came north in 1652 in his vessel, the *Gulden Parrit*, to get oak staves of which to make barrels in which to ship sugar to England. He remained

founder of the society of the Quakers. He tells about preaching to the Indians in Madam Sylvester's dooryard, and was twice a guest in the house. By that time the box edging (*Buxus suffruticosa*) planted twenty years before must have formed well grown borders to the flower beds and paths. These have now grown to the size of trees about ten feet high. A pretty custom was that of decorating these old box trees with gold leaf when the heir of the Manor brought home his

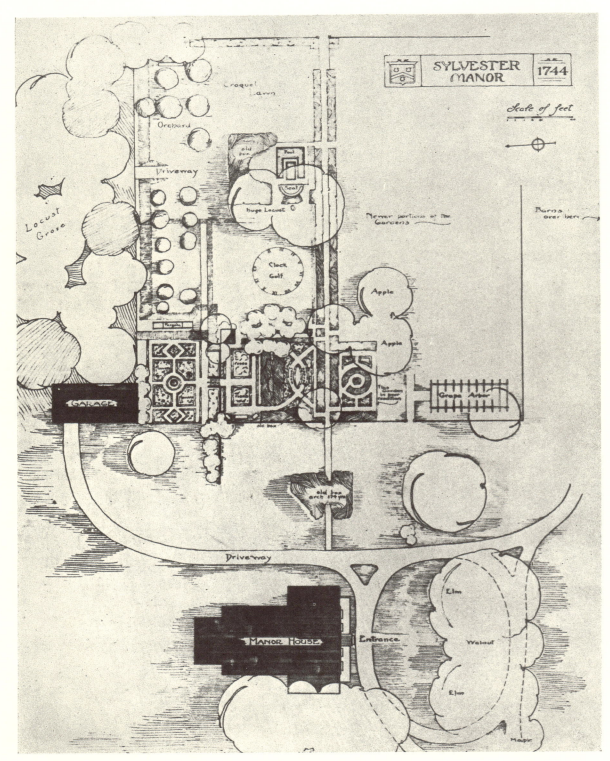

A plan of the grounds of Sylvester Manor, Shelter Island

permanently with his family, and the *Gulden Parrit* plied between the two islands.

The house faces full south. To the west a few hundred yards away flows a lovely tidewater creek. Near the house is a rough stone bridge with a flight of stone steps, built about 1652. This crosses a small arm of the creek. These steps are the old landing place where arriving friends were welcomed and departing guests were sped on their way.

East of the house lies the garden of which I write. This garden of Sylvester Manor was begun in 1652. The first printed mention of it is in the journal of George Fox, the

bride. In the present century, after a hundred and eighteen years, the custom has been revived; "Sylvester" has been lent to various members of the family for their honeymoons, and wreaths of glittering oak and laurel leaves have four times welcomed happy couples to the home of their ancestors.

Beside the Water Garden is another tall box hedge which arches over old flower beds and paths. These can be seen between the branches of the box-trees.

Beyond the garden was a fine orchard.

The most picturesque period in the history of the garden is that in which Massachusetts was persecuting the Quakers.

Nathaniel Sylvester offered these unfortunate people a safe shelter at his island home.

Lawrence and Cassandra Southwick were the most noted of those who, "whipped, despoiled and starved," fled here only to die three weeks after their long journey in an open boat was over. Whether or not their weary feet ever walked through these garden paths, they themselves at least looked down from their sunny windows on the flowers and the trim box edging, and thanked God for peace and freedom at last. Mary Dyer, another Quaker, who visited here, embarked from the steps of the old stone bridge when she sailed for Boston, where she later was hanged from the old elm on the Common.

At this time Benjamin L'Hommedieu, Huguenot, who had come from La Rochelle in France after the Revocation of the Edict of Nantes, was courting a young daughter of the house. It is said that he first saw her in the church at Southold which the Sylvesters attended, and whither they were rowed in a canopied barge by eight negro slaves on Sunday mornings. No doubt these lovers enjoyed to the full the garden, the flowers, and the blossoms on the fruit trees in the sweet spring weather.

From Connecticut came Governor John Winthrop, Jr., and from New York Lewis Morris of Morrisania; from Gardiner's Island, Lieutenant Lion Gardiner, famous in the Pequot Wars, and his friend Wyandanck, the great chief of the Montauk Indians. In one of his letters Winthrop describes the generous entertainments he received here, "which are fit only a colonies' acknowledgment." In 1673 "the commissioners of their High Mightinesses the Lords States General of the United Netherlands, and his Serene Highness the Prince of Orange," arrived in the frigate *Zeehond* under Captain Cornelius Evertson, on their way to Southold to force the claim of the Dutch to the towns on eastern Long Island. They spent the night at the Manor House.

The family burying-ground lay about a quarter of a mile southwest of the house, in a fine oak grove at the head of the creek, and here under the green turf many Quakers lie at rest, their graves marked with modest head-stones. But the family and their beautiful sandstone tables with carved armorial bearings were removed to the churchyard over a hundred years ago.

Exactly what was being done in the garden during the early years of the eighteenth century is not known. In 1735 the first Manor House was replaced by a much larger building. William Prince in 1730 started his nursery at Flushing, and Brinley Sylvester was able to secure near at hand the best that could be bought in the country. According to the custom of the day a wide avenue of cherry trees was planted in front of the house. These trees grew to an immense size, and in the spring when they were covered with their white blossoms, the branches almost sweeping to the ground, were a most exquisite sight, besides giving forth a delicious fragrance.

One of Brinley Sylvester's nieces married Governor Thomas Hutchinson of Massachusetts, whose gardens in Boston and Milton are prominent in the horticultural history of that State. A letter still extant tells about Peggy Sylvester visiting her cousins in Boston, and asking if she might wear stays and have a spinet. That she was allowed to have stays is evident from Blackburn's portrait of her painted about this time. It is more than likely that the Sylvesters wished to emulate their cousins in their beautiful gardens also.

The Sylvester Manor House as it is today

Miss Margaret Sylvester in 1754, from a painting by Blackburn, now owned by the Metropolitan Museum of Art

In 1798 the second William Prince advertised for sale ten thousand Lombardy poplars, and about the same time Lombardy poplars, weeping willows and the exquisite three-thorned acacias were set out here in the French style. A son of the house brought hawthorns for a hedge from Massachusetts, where he visited the Quincys. Part of this hedge is still living at an advanced age.

The nineteenth century saw the end of the Revolution and prosperity reigning again in the land. A circular lawn in front of the house replaced the haunted avenue under the cherry trees. Elms, black walnuts, locusts, maples, horse-chestnuts, ailanthus, and mulberries for silkworms were scattered about. An Irish gardener called Dan laid out new box-edged beds, and from early spring to late autumn there was a succession of bloom.

Flowers from these times have a charming way of reappearing in the grassy hedges—grape hyacinths, with the delicious fragrance that the modern ones have lost, Stars of Bethlehem, Lady's Delights, tall red lily-like tulips, larkspurs, from which the mid-Victorian ladies made little blue wreaths to put in their Bibles and Books of Beauty, daffodils, sweet rockets, flowering almonds and all the old-time roses.

During the years between 1861 and 1865 the garden was neglected, but the last quarter of the century saw it waking up again and distinguished visitors wandering in the shade of the great trees. The poets Longfellow and James Russell Lowell, Helen Hunt, the author of *Ramona*, Sarah Orne Jewett, Sir Richard Jebb, Mrs. Louis Agassiz, Asa Gray, the botanist, and also the Hon. Joseph H. Choate were among those who stayed at the house. Descendants of the old birds sang, the same old-time flowers scented the air, and the same old trees shaded these later guests as they wandered here and there in the quiet sunshine, and

"Still the pine-woods scent the noon; still the catbird sings his tune;
  Still autumn sets the maple-forest blazing.
  Still the grape-vine through the dusk flings her soul compelling musk;
  Still the fire-flies in the corn make night amazing."

LONG ISLAND

LONG ISLAND, which by its fine situation, noble bays and harbours, as well as by its fine lands, may be called the crown province. . . ."[1]

This was written in 1649, while the Dutch still ruled New Netherland. Wiles Wood, in his *Sketch of the First Settlement of the Several Towns on Long Island*, published in 1824, says: "There are numerous facts to prove that at the time of the first settlement of the Island the woods were destitute of underbrush, and that the large trees were so scarce, that it was deemed necessary to take measures for their preservation.

"The first settlers in every town commenced their improvements without any previous clearing. They generally enclosed large tracts of land by a common fence for a planting."

Daniel Denton says of the Island in very early days: "The island is most of it very good soil, the fruits natural . . . are mulberries, persimmons, grapes, great and small, whortleberries, cranberries, plums of several sorts, raspberries, and strawberries, of which the last is in such abundance in June that the fields are dyed red with them."

THE DUTCH AND THE ENGLISH

Numerous settlements had been made in the seventeenth century, by both the Dutch and the English. The eastern part was almost entirely English, the names showing clearly the origin of the first colonists, who still clung lovingly to the Old-World associations, though they had come to America to avoid persecution. Among these first settlements were Easthampton, Southampton, and Southold.

The western part was settled by the Dutch; here we have Flushing, originally Vlissingen, and Brooklyn, which was once Breuckelen, from the Dutch meaning "broken land." The first recorded grant in the latter place was made in 1636. In 1679 the two Labadist monks found the widow Rapalje, called "the mother of Brooklyn," in possession of "a garden and other conveniences which she took care of herself."

The national characteristics were very marked in the types of these early settlements. The English chose the more exposed and bolder situations, modeling their plantations on those of New England, whereas, as T. W. Field says, it was "the invariable practice of the old Hollandish settlers to build in a gentle depression in the ground, where they would be protected from the sweep of the dreaded north winds. These old farmers quietly hid their houses away in the little valleys and turns in the road, much as a cautious fowl creeps into a hedge and constructs its nest for a long incubation."

Even before 1700, Long Island was famous for its fruit trees; many travelers speak of roads lined with cherries. The two Labadist monks said of the profusion of fruits: "It is impossible to say how many peach trees we passed, all laden with fruit to breaking down, and many of them actually broken down. We came to a place surrounded by such trees from which so many had fallen off that the ground could not be discerned, and you could not put your foot down without trampling them."

In 1759 the Rev. Andrew Burnaby wrote:[2] "The soil of most parts [of New York] is extremely good, and particularly in Long Island. It affords grain of all sorts, and a great variety of English fruits, particularly the Newtown pippin.

Before I left I took a ride on Long Island, the richest spot in the opinion of New Yorkers in all America, and where they generally have their villas or country seats. It is indescribably beautiful and some parts of it extremely fertile."

FISH AS FERTILIZER

The fertility of Long Island was evidently not inexhaustible, however. We learn from Timothy Dwight's *Travels in New England and New York* that during the latter part of the eighteenth century the ground had been greatly impoverished because of careless husbandry. But during the fifteen years previous to the date of Timothy Dwight's visit, the farmers had awakened to the necessity of returning to the soil some of the elements which had been taken from it by successive crops. Therefore they began to manure the soil intensively, collecting the fertilizer from their own farms, gleaning it from the streets of New York, New Haven, New London, and even from Hartford, Connecticut. They also used the residuum from the potash manufactures on the shores of the Hudson.

They found, however, that the most effective fertilizer was whitefish, which they caught in Long Island Sound, and spread over the fields. These fish were taken in vast quantities, 150,000 being caught in one haul. This fish fertilizer had a prodigious effect in increasing the fertility of the

Erasmus Hall (1787), in Flatbush, was founded by Dr. John Livingston. The beautiful trees shown in this old drawing were planted by Mr. Jonathan Kellogg, who became principal in 1823 and greatly improved the grounds

land, which in many places rose within a few years to three or four and sometimes six times its former value.

LONG ISLAND NURSERIES

In 1685 a band of Huguenot emigrants settled in Flushing. They brought with them many choice varieties of fruit trees, and even as early as that date engaged to a moderate extent in the cultivation of fruit trees for sale. From then until the present time Flushing has been celebrated for its trees, both in an ornamental and commercial way. Indeed, until about 1840 Flushing had almost a monopoly of the tree-growing industry.[1]

WILLIAM PRINCE'S NURSERY

In 1737 William Prince, who was a lineal descendant of Governor Thomas Prince of Plymouth Colony, started at Flushing the Linnaean Gardens, a nursery which really might

[1]From a Description of New Netherland in 1649 in the Du Simitiere MSS.
[2]*Travels in the Middle Settlements of North America*, by the Rev. Andrew Burnaby, 1759.

[1]*The Trees of Flushing*, by J. W. Barstow.

be included among the botanic gardens, for it exerted a profound influence on the horticulture of the day.

It did not originate as a commercial venture, but grew out of the desire of the first Prince to rear a few trees to ornament his grounds. He found that his first efforts were attended with success, and so turned over part of his lands to the growing of trees for sale. In 1793 the nursery was christened the Linnaean Botanic Gardens, and a catalogue was issued.

The nurseries soon became well-known among the horticulturists of America, and many old English gardens still cherish native American shrubs brought there from the Linnaean Gardens. It is said that the Mahonia, the native Oregon barberry discovered by the Lewis and Clarke expedition and named for Bernard McMahon, was first grown in these nurseries.

New York Historical Society Collections

The Bowne house, Flushing, built in 1661. From a print made in 1828

The Linnaean Gardens remained under the supervision of the same family for five generations,[1] about 130 years, and grew from an original eight acres to sixty acres in 1830 and 116 in 1860.

General Washington visited the grounds, but unfortunately did not comment favorably upon them in his diary; perhaps he failed to find just the type of shrub he was looking for to ornament the gardens at Mount Vernon. During the Revolution Gen. Howe, on entering the town of Flushing after the battle of Brooklyn, respected the planting enough to order a special guard "to protect the gardens and nurseries of Mr. Prince." But in spite of this order, vandals destroyed 30,000 grafted fruit trees, cutting them for hoop-poles.

William Prince was recognized among men of science as a botanist as well as a horticulturist, and enjoyed the friendship of all the celebrated naturalists of his day. The London Horticultural Society named an apple "William Prince" in his honor.

Another important nursery, Bloodgood's, was established in 1798.

THE PARSONS NURSERY

The nursery of Parsons and Co., founded in 1838, soon established a reputation in Europe, and was as well-known in Kew and Versailles as it was in New York. The Parsons nursery also had a non-commercial beginning, and it is to the intelligent forethought of the elder Prince, and to the liberality of the Parsons brothers, that Flushing today owes her great avenue of shade trees, and also her excellent arboretum.

The Parsons Nursery was on the farm where the old Bowne mansion stood. This house was built in 1661 by John Bowne of the Society of the Friends. George Fox, the founder of the Society, stayed in this house, which was the place for the yearly meeting of the whole body in the province of New York, previous to 1690.

ANDRÉ PARMENTIER'S NURSERY

Another pioneer nurseryman, and Long Island's first landscape architect, was André Parmentier, the brother of the horticulturist, Chevalier Parmentier, mayor of Enghien, Holland.

André Parmentier was born in 1780 in Belgium, and came to this country in 1834. He was first urged to take the directorship of the Elgin Botanic Gardens, which had been established in New York City by Dr. David Hosack. Parmentier refused the offer, and bought in Brooklyn a tract of 25 acres, for which he paid $4,000.

The land was very rough and rocky, but Parmentier soon put it in order, using the stones for the enclosing wall. The garden was planted with a great variety of plants, both indigenous and exotic, and under his care became both beautiful and interesting, attracting a great number of visitors.

According to Stuart Gager, Director of the Brooklyn Botanic Gardens, André Parmentier's greatest contribution to horticulture was the introduction into America of the naturalistic type of planting. This was thirty years before Central Park was planned, and there is no doubt that Parmentier and Andrew Jackson Downing prepared the public taste for that style of landscaping.

Downing speaks most generously of Parmentier.

"During M. Parmentier's residence on Long Island," he says, "he was almost constantly applied to for plans for laying out the grounds of country seats by persons in various parts of the union, as well as in the immediate proximity of New York. In many cases he not only surveyed the demesne to be improved, but furnished the plants and trees necessary to carry out his plans. Several plans were prepared by him for residences of note in the Southern States, and two or three places near Montreal. In his periodical catalogue he arranged the hardy trees and shrubs which flourish in this latitude, in classes, according to their heights etc. and published a short treatise on the natural laying out of grounds. In short we consider M. Parmentier's labors and examples as having effected, directly, far more for Landscape Gardening in America, than those of any other individual whatever."[1]

Besides his catalogue, Parmentier issued a large supplement to the *New England Farmer*, cataloguing a great variety of fruits, vines, trees, and flowers. The *Brooklyn Eagle* is authority for the statement that there is a portfolio of Parmentier's drawings still extant,[2] and that they show him to have been a fine draughtsman and an artist of no

---

[1] The importance of the Prince family in the history of American horticulture has been briefly set forth in the introduction to this volume.

[1] *Landscape Architecture*, by A. J. Downing.
[2] The editor has been unable to locate these drawings.

Grouped on this page are sketches of Long Island villas in the first quarter of the nineteenth century. They show the general type of country place planted "informally" in the manner then in vogue, and made popular by Andrew Jackson Downing. The grounds were probably planned by André Parmentier, however

The residence of Benjamin F. Thompson Esq., Hempstead

The residence of Robert W. Mott Esq., at Grove Point, Great Neck

Lakeville House, Long Island

"Casina." The farm of Mr. Woolsey, Hellgate Neck

"Clifton." The residence of W. Cairns, Jr., Esq., at North Hempstead

The residence of George Douglass Esq., at Little Neck Bay

"The Locusts." The residence of J. E. De Kay, M.D.

mean ability. He unfortunately died soon after completing the gardens, and his wife was unable to carry on the business. The land was subsequently sold and cut up into building lots.

GARDEN ORNAMENTS

We find that Long Island, noted as the center of the early nursery business, also had pottery works to supply the demand for garden ornaments.

The *New York Gazette* of May 13, 1751, published the following:

"Any person desirous may be supplied with vases, urns, flower pots, etc. to adorn gardens and tops of houses, or any other ornament made of clay by Edward Annely at Whitestone, he having set up a potter's business (by means of a German family that he bought, who are supposed by their work to be the most ingenious that ever arrived in America.) He has clay capable of making eight different kinds of ware."

OLD LONG ISLAND GARDENS

THE KING HOUSE, JAMAICA

Henry Whittemore in *Long Island Historic Homes* says that the old King manor house is the only one of the homes of famous men who lived on Long Island that is now owned by the public. It was the residence of the Honorable Rufus King, Congressman and Senator from New York and Minister to Great Britain, and of his son, John Alsop King.

The house was built in 1750 and is one of the best preserved of the many Long Island landmarks. Many of the trees surrounding the place were set out during the lifetime of Rufus

King. The pine and fir trees which he planted were sent to him by Mr. Scheaffe of Portsmouth, N. H., and are said to have been the first of these trees planted in that section of the country.

In 1900 there was formed an association known as the King Manor Association for the preservation and care of this property. It is now used for the collection of historical relics of Long Island, and the grounds are used as a public park.

THE GARDEN OF WILLIAM CULLEN BRYANT, AT ROSLYN

The house was built in 1786 by Richard Kirby in the gambrel-roof Dutch manner. The oldest trees were probably planted before 1800.

William Cullen Bryant bought the house in 1825 and added the piazzas. He also changed the old road, and planted many varieties of trees and vines. The box-edged paths and the formal plan were probably originally the work of Richard Kirby. This has today been added to and changed, but the late Harold Godwin, grandson of Bryant, wrote that he knew nothing of the history of the garden. He thought, however, that the grounds were much as they were in his grandfather's time.

"YE BOWERIE OF LADY DEBORAH MOODY," AT GRAVESEND

Lady Deborah Moody, a widow with one son, having had difficulty in England on account of her religious beliefs, went to Massachusetts and was there granted 400 acres of land. As an adherent of Roger Williams, however, she was excommunicated from the church at Salem. She then went with her son to New Amsterdam and was there warmly welcomed by Governor Kieft. In 1643 she and some of her associates went to Gravesend, and in 1645 Governor Kieft issued a patent, with Lady Deborah Moody's name leading the list. This is the only patent extant which is headed by a woman's name.

Gravesend, intended to be a large city, was laid out in the following way:

A favorable site near the center of the town was selected, a square containing about 16 acres of ground was measured off, and a street was opened around it. This large square was afterwards divided into squares of four acres each. The whole was then enclosed by a palisade fence. In the center of each square was reserved a large public yard.

Coney Island was used to pasture the cattle.

Lady Deborah Moody's house, which was called "Ye Bowerie of Lady Moody," was built of cobble stones. It was two stories high, with a frontage of 42 feet, and was said to have been surrounded by a large garden. It was doubtless one of the largest and most conspicuous houses of this little settlement, and consequently was frequently marked off for attacks by the Indians. But Lady Deborah, who enjoyed the confidence of both Governors Kieft and Stuyvesant, seems to have been able to hold her own in those troublous times. She even accumulated a library which has been listed. Among the books was one called "Sylva sylvarum," which we presume was John Evelyn's treatise on arboriculture.[1]

Lady Deborah's high standing and character gave her great influence among the settlers. From a list[2] of articles which she requested to be sent to her, we can see that she lived well on her estate. Among other things she asked for "8 seyths for mowing (I pray let them be very good)."

[1]The principal facts of this account are from Peter Ross's *History of Long Island*, and from an address delivered before the New York Historical Society in May, 1880, by James W. Gerard.

[2]This list is a part of the town records of Salem, Massachusetts.

Views of Long Island about 1840, from Barber and Howe's "Historical Collections of the State of New York"

Western view of Huntington Village

Central part of Jamaica Village

South view of the central part of Riverhead

View of Patchogue in Brookhaven

OTHER NEW YORK STATE GARDENS
AND GARDENERS

SURVIVING GARDENS

THE VERPLANCK GARDEN AT MOUNT GULIAN,
FISHKILL-ON-HUDSON[1]

THE garden at Mt. Gulian was laid out in its present form in 1804 by Daniel Crommelin Verplanck. His portrait as a little boy in a red suit playing with a gray squirrel, painted by John Singleton Copley at the time of the Revolution, still hangs in the old house adjoining the garden.

Originally the garden comprised six acres, but a dowager Verplanck in whose hand the fate of the garden lay cut off two acres; so today it contains but four acres. In this space are to be found fruit trees, vegetables and flowers, formal box-edged beds, pergolas, a sun-dial, and a brook which runs at one side and flows through the woods which bound the

The Verplanck house, built before 1730, at Fishkill-on-Hudson

garden on the south. In these woods an ancestor laid out a wild garden, planting shrubs and trees, many of which belong to a warmer climate. Planted in sheltered places, these plants have lived for a hundred years. For about seventy-five years the wild garden was neglected, but recently this charming spot has been somewhat restored.

The garden has a flat situation which is relieved by two fine specimens of *Magnolia conspicua*. One forgets the flatness when confronted by the fine view of the Hudson River seen from under their branches. The plan of the garden is of the English type, but I do not think that any foreign model was used, or any book consulted—it is so simple. A straight path by lawns and large trees leads from the house to the garden.

On each side of the entrance, shrubs are planted which partially conceal it; there is a myrtle bed at the left among rhododendrons and shrubs, and at the right, beyond the shrub planting, a long row of peonies which forms a low hedge. A few years ago a green wooden fence surrounded the garden. This has been removed. Now two cedar posts with cross-pieces stand at the entrance, and facing you, a little to the left, is one of the fine old magnolia trees—its gray trunk gives the right line as of a column or statue. A small set of formal box-edged beds is laid out at the left, and planted here are some of the old June roses, with old hybrid perpetuals, great clumps of fraxinella and peonies.

[1]Written by Virginia E. Verplanck.

Taking a few steps into the garden from the shrub-shaded entrance along the gravel walk, seven feet wide, which is one of the main arteries of the garden, on the right the principal formal garden is disclosed. It extends fifty feet by fifty feet; the smaller box beds are forty feet by fifteen. The plan of this main box garden begins with a circular bed in the center, from which run out four little graveled paths twenty-one inches wide which divide the formal garden into four large sections, which in turn are subdivided into three beds each, making thirteen beds, all encircled by the narrow gravel walks.

At the corner of the outer beds shrubs are planted to break up the long straight lines—great formal groups of fraxinellas, and interspersed through these beds are early Japanese peonies, herbaceous peonies and tall bushes of June roses. Here are found masses of the old-fashioned lemon lilies and quantities of breeder tulips.

The box, shrubs, peonies, fraxinella, lemon lilies, roses and the quaint old tulips, all belong to the 1804 period. The tulips come in charming shades of purple, lavender, bronze, and almost gray tones, with many shades of reds and yellows. These breeder tulips are found all over the garden, and I am sorry to say that many have been destroyed by too vigorous cultivation and by planting new roses. The fraxinella makes the garden very beautiful in June, blooming before the roses are out. The pointed racemes of white and pink, rising out of the dark green glossy leaves, give an effective formal touch among the masses of white peonies and lemon lilies, blooming at the same time. Think how those masses of fraxinella have been blooming there since 1804!

Yuccas make another planting in the formal beds. It took years to accomplish bloom in all four plantings at once. The yucca plant blooms one season and makes leaves the following year. In order to have a yearly bloom it is necessary to have several plants at each point. These plants belong to the 1804 period. Crown imperial also belong to this period and rise effectively out of eight of the formal beds.

As one stands just within the garden entrance facing the river, with the formal garden on one hand, on the other stretches away a long, long, border of peonies, great bushes planted in 1804—many of them large fine blooms, as fine as modern varieties, while others are poor in bloom and in color. Interspersed in this border are numbers of the fine deep maroon peony, *officinalis, flora plena*.

Beyond the formal beds stands the larger of the *Magnolia conspicua*, a great mass of dark foliage, dominating the garden, and taking away the effect of flatness. Under the low branches which spread across the wide gravel path to meet the border of peonies, one sees the river across rolling fields, bordered with woodlands.

In a spot in the garden old-fashioned Johnny-jump-ups come every year, and nearby is a variety of clematis called in our garden "Old Man's Hat"—a very deep blue single flower. Here too one finds the Georgia crepe flower—so wondrous in perfume, sent by a lover over a hundred years ago to a daughter of the house. Alas! She died before the wedding day. And there is a rose without a thorn from which maidens of the family made wreaths to adorn their heads for a ball. This rose is neither a bush nor a climber, and is planted among shrubbery. When weighted with its bloom it bends over the path to greet us with its charming beauty; then it springs back and is seen no more for another year!

Old-fashioned white sweet-scented violets are scattered

all through the garden. Each spring brings too the daffodils and narcissus, planted so long ago. There is iris of the olden time, and clumps of a large flowering perennial snow-drop which blooms in mid-summer. Grape hyacinths, the lovely deep blue, grow in profusion, even extending into a hay field at one side of the garden. Of the old-fashioned June roses there is a great variety, many of them growing six to eight feet, while the Harrison, the lovely yellow Scotch rose, has attained twelve feet, with a circumference of branches of twenty-three feet. We have a very rare yellow rose, the Austrian Gold Leaf, single, of the sweet-briar family, deepest golden yellow. I think it was a common rose of the olden time, for in rare cases it is found by the ruins of an ancient farm house. It has completely vanished from the gardens. Other old roses are George IV, a deep velvety maroon, at

blooms in autumn as well as June. Its habit is like that of the hybrids of today. It grows on its own roots so there is no danger of its reverting. Most charming and beautiful is the moss rose of our old garden. These roses are so much finer than the modern ones. The moss is longer and the pink a more exquisite shade and to me the perfume seems finer. The Damask is perhaps the most exquisite of the old fashioned roses, having both color and perfume in perfection. One wonders if it was used in the Orient to make attar of roses, its odor is so intense. It was dear to the hearts of the dames of olden times who distilled their petals and made the prized rosewater of our great-grandmother's day. The dried rose leaves formed the basis of the pot-pourri which filled the fine thin china bowl on the drawing room table, giving that sweet elusive perfume which we associate with old portraits, Chippendale

A view of the Verplanck garden at Mount Gulian

times almost black—these bushes grow very tall and stately; the Burnett, like the Harrison, but pink, fading to white; the Shell Rose, a deep pink. Then come a number of roses of shorter growth—a single white, with deep crimson tips and double rows of golden stamens. This rose is very gay, and tiny crimson buds add much color to the bloom. Then there is a small double rose with a most pungent perfume. It is of an exquisite shade of deep rose pink, and every petal has a nip taken out of its edge. This is a very quaint effect; it is as if Dame Nature had got out her scissors and pinked the edges. The name of this rose is lost, but perhaps someone will give it back to me, as they did for Arabella, a small double rose, darker than George IV. Then comes the beautiful cabbage rose, such a pink; no modern rose surpasses it; and the hundred-leaf also. Then we have Pierre de St. Crys, with its velvety texture and tender tint, and the lovely Gloire du Rosamond. The Maiden's Blush with its fragrant odor must not be forgotten. This is the last June rose to bloom, and it seems the favorite haunt of the rose bug.

The Rose of Castile, very fine large variety, of tall growth,

furniture, India rugs and Chinese porcelain. To the family of the Damask Rose belongs the York and Lancaster, a rose of history! It is single and striped white and pink—no two roses alike.

There are one hundred and forty rose bushes of the old varieties in our garden, some of which I have just described, but the names of many others I do not know; I can only love them.

Wide gravel paths cut the nearer part of the garden to right and left of the formal beds. Beyond, the paths are of grass, and in this section the vegetables grow, and some fruit trees. A pergola was built a few years ago, replacing an old trellis, and over its roof Isabella and Catawba grapes extend their shade. These vines are over one hundred years old. The purple bunches of the Isabella hang against the gray rafters and make a charming picture in October.

The main part of the old house was built long before the garden was laid out, some time early in the eighteenth century, previous to 1730. The style is Dutch Colonial, built of stone covered with stucco. This older structure was added to in 1804 at the time the garden was laid out. In this addition is the usual guest room on the ground floor, and this room was occupied by Lafayette in 1824 when he made his visit to this country after his return to France following the Revolutionary War. The style of the 1804 addition is a vivid contrast to the earlier Dutch construction and adds to the interest of the interior of the old homestead.

The land on which the house and garden stand today was bought by an early Verplanck, Gulian by name, from the Wappinger Indians in 1683. He was a partner of Francis Rombout and Stephanus Van Cortlandt, and together they became owners of what was called "The Rombout Patent," a tract of land upwards of eighty thousand acres lying between the Fishkill and Wappinger's Creek, in what is now Dutchess County. From 1683 until today the property has remained in the Verplanck family. This early Gulian was a merchant of some consequence in New York. He had a house

refuge and a home with the Verplanck family. A daughter of the house had taught him to read and write, and during the more than thirty years of his management of the garden, he kept a diary. We have this old record still, written in a fair hand and telling of the weather, of crops and the conduct of his assistants, sometimes white men who now and then were drunk and often lazy! The names of guests in the house are recorded, the date of the opening of navigation in the spring, and names of old steamboats. There are comments on sermons he had heard in the old family church, and remarks on political events.

Old Brown and his wife Julia lived in the garden in a little house that had been part of a greenhouse. Here the old man died in the service of the family and with him passed away the old regime of family retainers. But the garden remains, with many of the old time flowers flourishing in it, as beautiful as it was in 1804.

The garden at The Grove, Rhinebeck, the property of Dr. George Morton Miller

on the south side of Wall Street, then the residential street of the little seaport town of those early days.

This Gulian who made the purchase of the land up the river died in 1751, leaving his property to his son, and I quote from the old will written in the quaint spelling of the day:

"I give and devise to my son Samuel and his heirs forever all that my farm in dutches County, called Mount Gulian, with all the Buildings thereon, and all Slaves, Stocks, household furniture and farming Utenseels. . . ."

It was Samuel's son, another Gulian, who having become sole owner of a third of the Rombout Patent, built the house in the early part of the eighteenth century and named it for his grandfather, Gulian, the purchaser of the land. The term "Mount" was often applied to country houses whether they stood on a hill or not.

This Gulian's son, another Samuel, was the owner of Mount Gulian during the Revolutionary War. He was a member of the Committee of Safety and gave over the house to the Continental Army, and it became the headquarters of Baron Von Steuben. It was here that the Order of the Cincinnati was finally completed. It was here that Von Steuben wrote several important letters in 1782–3 and in the latter year drew up at Washington's suggestion the "Plan for the Disbanding of the Army," which was adopted and carried out at Newburgh where Washington was in that year.

An account of the old house and garden would not be complete without telling of the negro gardener, James Brown, who served the family for many years. He had been born a slave in a southern State, and when a mere boy had run away after slavery had been abolished in New York and had found

THE GROVE, RHINEBECK[1]

The Grove was built about 1790 by Philip J. Schuyler, a second son of General Philip Schuyler of Albany. It was then known as Schuyler Hall, and many notable people of the past have partaken of its hospitality. It remained in the Schuyler family until about 1850 when it was bought by William Starr Miller for his wife, who was a grand-daughter of General Philip Schuyler through her mother, Mrs. Washington Morton (Cornelia Schuyler). At Mr. Miller's death in 1881, Mrs Miller left it to her nephew by marriage, George Morton Miller, who was born here and in whose possession it still is.

The old walnut tree in the front of the house is eighteen and a half feet in circumference. It is supposed to have been planted by General Schuyler. Part of the hemlock hedge in the old garden is over eighty years old, and is still in fine condition.

GRASMERE, AT RHINEBECK[2]

"Rhinebeck House" at Rhinebeck Flats was built in 1775 by General Richard Montgomery and his wife Janet Livingston, who had inherited the place from ancestors who had owned the land through the original Beekman patent granted in 1706. But General Montgomery was killed in the battle before Quebec, and Mrs. Montgomery lost interest in the place, and later it was sold.

[1]This description is written by Mrs. George Morton Miller.
[2]Written by Maunsel S. Crosby.

Two views of the fountain, and the view along a hedge-bordered path in the garden at The Grove, Rhinebeck

The house and the estate, consisting of 900 acres, then became the property of the Livingston family, and during their ownership the name was changed to "Grasmere."

In 1924, "Grasmere" was purchased by Mrs. Earnest Crosby, the present owner, who has designed and planted a modern formal garden, carefully preserving as many as possible of the old oaks, elms, maples and locusts which had been planted by the Livingstons.

Up to 1924 the only pretense to landscape gardening had been an eighteenth-century semicircular walk or "Constitutional," over a quarter of a mile in length, flanked by great maples, chestnuts, locusts and pin oaks with a few ancient lilac bushes here and there. There was also an outline of a path to a vegetable garden. This path had evidently been covered by an arbor, as vines now grow thickly alongside it, but no trace of the arbor is to be seen. Here too, stand specimen ginkgo, catalpa, pink locust and tulip trees, also Norway spruce and scattering beds of plantain and day lilies. There are also the remains of a small shrubbery which must have been part of the first true flower garden of the region, for up to that time flowers and vegetables were planted together.

TROUTBECK, AMENIA[1]

Troutbeck lies in a quiet inland valley in the eastern part of the town of Amenia, in Dutchess Co. For 108 years it was the home of successive generations of the Benton family, the last of whom was the poet-philosopher, Myron Benton.

John Burroughs wrote of Myron Benton: "Planter of trees and vines, preserver of picturesque houses, lover of paths and streams, beautifier of highways, friend of all wild and shy things, historian and portrayer of big trees. . . . He is the practical poet of whom the country needs many more."

The gardens of Troutbeck in Myron Benton's lifetime were of an informal character. The row of superb buttonwood

"There is one spot for which my soul will yearn,
May it but come where breeze and sunlight play,
And leaves are glad, some path of swift return;
A waif—a presence borne on friendly ray—
Even thus, if but beneath the same blue sky!
The grazing kine not then will see me cross
The pasture slope; the swallows will not shy,
Nor brooding thrush; blithe bees the flowers will toss;
Not the faint thistle-down my breath may charm.
Ah me! But I shall find the dear ways old,
If I have leave; that sheltered valley farm;
Its climbing woods, its spring, the meadow's gold;
The creek-path, dearest to my boyhood's feet:—
Oh God! Is there another world so sweet?"

Old buttonwood trees and the sweep of lawn at Troutbeck

trees planted by Benton in 1835 is still standing and is shown in one of the photographs illustrating this article. These trees and the lawn sweeping to them are very fine.

Beyond the lawn there is a spring which has been written about many times. John Burroughs loved it, and said in "Pepacton" that the name Troutbeck was suggested "by the fact that trout came up to dwell in this spring, from the Webetuck. Some of them attained considerable size and with the friendly treatment they received became quite tame, so they would come up and eat out of the hand."

The original house, built in 1796, was destroyed by fire in 1917. It was rebuilt on the same site in 1919 by Colonel Spingarn.

The present garden is modern, and is enclosed by a stone wall. There is also a charming terrace planted with alpines near the house, and a wall garden beyond the brook which flows in front of the lawn to join the Webetuck, the picturesque little river draining the countryside.

One of Myron Benton's poems reveals his great love for his "sheltered valley farm." He called it "The Soul's Return."

[1]Now the residence of Colonel and Mrs. J. E. Spingarn. This description is adapted from an account by Miss Ethel Wodell, of Millbrook.

BLITHEWOOD, AT BARRYTOWN[1]

Blithewood was bought by the late Andrew C. Zabriskie about 25 years ago. Before that it had been owned for many years by John Bard, who in turn had purchased it from Robert Donaldson. Under the guidance of the noted landscape gardener, A. J. Downing, Mr. Donaldson did much to beautify the estate. An earlier owner was Mr. Cruger, who bought the place in 1833 from Commodore John Stevens.

At the entrance stands the gate lodge placed there more than 75 years ago. The avenue, about half a mile long, is of white pines, many of which are more than 100 years old. The place is fortunate in having many fine old trees in good preservation. One of the most remarkable is the very large maple on the north lawn, popularly known as the "All Saints Maple," from its habit of holding its foliage in its autumn coloring until that time.

The house, a Georgian structure, and the walled garden are both modern, having been built 20 years ago by Mr. Zabriskie. The view of the Hudson River and the Catskills which they command is of unusual beauty.

[1]Written by Grace G. Higginson, of the Philipstown Garden Club.

The old gate-house at Blithewood, Barrytown-on-Hudson. Andrew Jackson Downing, the famous landscape architect of the first half of the nineteenth century, did much to beautify Blithewood, which is now the property of Mrs. Andrew Zabriskie

THE FORSYTH GARDEN, KINGSTON[1]

The little garden described in this paper has few features entitling it to special notice. It is a town garden behind an old house; its claims for notice are only its antiquity, and the proof it affords that even a small garden may give its owners, without great labor or expense, lasting pleasure and profit.

The house was built before the Revolution, and partially burned by the British soldiers in 1777, when the whole village was destroyed.

Probably the garden was started before this time, but we have no record of it until it came into possession, about 1820, of the family who still own it. Mr. Severyn Bruyn and his wife came to the house a little more than one hundred years ago. Mr. Bruyn was the son of Jacobus Severyn Bruyn, Lieutenant Colonel in the Continental Army, for three years and a half a prisoner in the hands of the British, having been captured at Fort Montgomery. His wife was Blandina Elmendorf. Their son Severyn married Catharine Hasbrouck, a descendant of one of the old Huguenot "patentees" who received grants of land at New Paltz, in 1678.

Although a professional man, Mr. Bruyn was not too busy to give time and thought to his garden which he loved. This love was shared by his daughter Mary, afterwards Mrs. James Christie Forsyth. From childhood her happiest hours were those spent in the garden, and in watching and tending her plants.

If one opens a heavy old book in the library, very likely from between the leaves will fall pressed poppy leaves thinner than silk, wreaths woven from "spurs" of the delphinium, or faded petals of the Lady Washington geranium, placed there by a child a century ago. Although somewhat altered from time to time, the main plan of the garden is much the same

[1]Described by Katharyn Bruyn Forsyth.

White pines, many of them over one hundred years old, line this avenue at Blithewood for half a mile

The Forsyth garden at Kingston, the property of Mrs. Katharyn Bruyn Forsyth

ders, filled by successive flowers from spring to fall, while vines run over trellises and walls. In earliest spring brave little snow-drops show their tiny bells. There used to be sweet English violets. Next come crocus, little "blue bells," which with wild blue violets spring up here and there at their pleasure. Next come daffodils, white narcissus, hyacinths, bloodroot and May tulips, some rare old varieties. As spring moves on, iris and peonies give color to the scene, till the time for roses comes, the glory of the year: old fashioned roses, Boursault, Madame Plantier, a dark red whose name is lost, the lovely pink "Chancellor"—said to have been brought from France by Chancellor Livingston—, pale Provence, yellow Scotch. Two have unfortunately died, the red-and-white striped York and Lancaster, and a great "double Damask." Now there are modern roses also, including ramblers; as they fade, white lilies and a bed of brilliant poppies take their place. Flowering shrubs and blossoming trees add to the beauty and fragrance, as do white and purple lilacs, horse-chestnuts' stately spires, catalpa, forsythias and spireas.

Like every old garden, this one has fruit trees. There were formerly nectarines and mulberries; delicious little damsons still survive, and green gages, pears, peaches and apple trees. Birds build their nests among these trees, orioles sing among the apple blossoms. The tiny wrens come every year to the little houses built for them. Midway down the central walk is an arbor covered with grapevines, old and new varieties.

There are currant bushes, and formerly there were goose-berries, and a delicate white raspberry I have never seen else-where. The town has spread out too far for the catbirds to visit us, but robins and wrens, chippies, and song sparrows are at home here. Humming birds dart about, and great butterflies fold and open their bright wings.

The birds bathe every day in a hollowed stone, perhaps the oldest "bird bath" in the country. Altogether, this little spot is a joy and refreshment to its owners, from spring to autumn. When summer flowers are gone, clematis blooms on the tall

as formerly. The last of the spicy box which used to edge the walks died not long ago, but the walks are about the same. On one side of the central path are large square beds with wide flower borders. Two of these are given up to vegeta-bles; one is an asparagus bed, the feathery plumes in summer backed by tall hollyhocks. The borders of these beds are filled partly with perennials, with old fashioned annuals, with marigolds, lady slippers, and the mystic four o'clock, which opens its sweet blossoms only at the stated hour. The third large bed is filled with June roses. On the other side of the central path are three grass plats, one formerly a croquet ground, one cut into by oval beds, the third with a tiny cen-tral pool for water lilies, bor-dered by portulacca; a sundial is nearby. On either side against the fence are wide bor-

The garden of Mrs. J. D. McKechnie, at Canandaigua

The garden covers about an acre of ground. The beds are bordered with box. A walk bordered on each side with a privet hedge runs around the en-tire garden. The illustration to the left shows these long privet edges.

The house was built in 1796 by General Peter B. Porter, Secretary of War under President John Quincy Adams. Later occupants were John C. Spencer, Secretary of War under President Tyler, and United States Senator E. G. Lapham.

frames, autumn crocus and hardy chrysanthemums brave the cold, and even in winter, the place is beautiful with evergreens laden with snow, bare branches "rigged inch deep with pearl." Downy woodpeckers and nuthatches trip up and down the trees, while starlings sit far overhead in the topmost branches.

THE GARDEN OF MRS. JAMES ROOSEVELT AND THE GARDEN OF MR. J. R. ROOSEVELT, AT HYDE PARK, DUTCHESS COUNTY[1]

Between Poughkeepsie and Hyde Park on the east bank of the Hudson extends a tract of land known as the Water Lots of the Great Nine Partners Patent, granted by the Crown in 1698. The whole patent included most of northern Dutchess County, but the strip along the river was narrow, and each of the original Nine Partners received one of these Water Lots over four miles in length and with a river frontage of a little over half a mile.

The land now owned by Mrs. James Roosevelt was the river front of Water Lot No. 6. The original grantee in 1698 apparently never lived here. The first authentic records show that the Evertson family was living here about 1760. Their house stood on the site of the present house, and the present garden was started at the same time. After the Revolution the place passed into the possession of David Johnston, a descendant of one of the original Nine Partners, and later into the possession of Mr. James Boorman, who owned the place when he organized and built the Hudson River Railroad in 1848. For some years it was owned and lived in by his daughter, Mrs. Wheeler, and was bought by Mr. James Roosevelt in 1867. The Roosevelt family had lived for several generations at "Mount Hope," two miles further south, but moved after the destruction by fire of the old homestead.

Like so many Hudson River places, the house is located at the end and slightly to one side of a long avenue leading west from the Post Road. This avenue may be called the axis of the place. At its end the house is at the south and the garden to the north. The garden itself has always been surrounded by a remarkable hemlock hedge, and is approximately 300 feet from north to south and 200 feet from east to west. Garden and house stand close to the edge of a high terrace above and about half a mile back from the Hudson River. The view from the house looks down the river for twenty miles, and the garden is protected from the west and north winds by the old trees on the edge of the bank.

The plan of the grounds is substantially the same as it has been for 150 years. One of the principal features of the place is the groups of magnificent oak trees in the two fields on either side of the driveway. Experts place their age at from 250 to 300 years, and their tremendously wide spread proves that they grew in open fields and not under forest conditions. This also is proof conclusive that these broad fields were cultivated by the Wappinger tribe of Indians before the white man came, as the first settlement here did not begin until about 200 years ago.

The adjoining land, owned by Mr. J. R. Roosevelt, was the original river front of Water Lot No. 5. This lot passed through several hands until it was bought by John Crook about 1750. An old map shows that the first "Mansion House" stood about 200 ft. east of the present house, and at the end of another long driveway leading in from the Post Road. The Crook family owned several thousand acres, and because they planted the magnificent trees which border the Albany Post Road, at this point the road was for many years known as "Crook's Lane." The present house—a typical example of the two-and-a-half-story square Hudson River type of architecture, with high porches and a central hall through the house—was built about 1800, probably by Ann Crook who married Colonel William Barber of Revolutionary fame. Later the place was owned by the Broome and

[1]Written by Franklin Delano Roosevelt.

Boreel families, and was bought in 1868 by Mr. James Roosevelt.

As on the adjoining place, the feature is the location of the house and garden at the edge of the high terrace overlooking the river. The garden is south of the house and is protected by another fine old hemlock hedge nearly twenty feet high. The garden is approximately 200 feet wide and runs north and south for a distance of over 400 feet, with a path down the center. This garden also remains in substantially its original form of over 150 years ago. The trees of the main driveway from the Post Road are a noteworthy feature of the landscape. Nearly all of them are the original plantings by the first settlers, while a few old sycamores date back over 200 years and were undoubtedly good-sized trees when the driveway was first laid out.

An interesting tradition is that the British fleet fired many shots at the place during its ascent of the river in 1777, and this was substantiated about ten years ago when several cannon balls were dug up in the garden itself while some re-grading work was being done.

ROSE HILL, SARATOGA[1]

The gardens of Rose Hill have bloomed for considerably over one hundred years. In 1799, Judge James Thompson, then a very young man, and just admitted to the bar, left his father's house in Stillwater and journeyed over to Milton in

Rose Hill, seen from across the pond

Saratoga county, near what is now Ballston Spa, in quest of fortune. His father gave him a horse, a watch, and $65.00 in his pocket as his patrimony.

Shortly after, he bought, on Court House Hill, this farm now known as Rose Hill. In 1805 the house was finished, much as it now stands, and paid for. So one assumes his quest was not in vain.

A garden, of course, followed. The house stood on a hill and there were roses; hence the name!

The plan for the garden was made in 1829 by Mary Stansbury, Judge Thompson's young wife, and she too was the

[1]Written by Harriet L. Carter.

The gardens of Rose Hill, Saratoga

chief gardener, for she was one of those happy individuals for whom all flowers grow as if by magic. In 1845 she remodelled the garden, or rather, further developed the original plan.

The grounds slope down from Rose Hill House to the large round pond, at the foot by the springs. It is shut in on its lower side by willows, now huge and old, and gnarled and broken, but still beautiful. A long path leads from the house to the pond, edged on each side by many rose-bushes, old ones, of old-fashioned sorts: damask, hundred-leaf, Harrison, dark red and others; while the varieties of later years smirk at one with smug satisfaction, but with less charm from the garden beds.

At the left of this path down the hill lies the garden, a very large circular border, broken by eight arches of roses. Inside this round border is a large circle of grass with a superb old elm as the central note. The circular border of perennials and later of annuals is symmetrically intersected by narrow paths, the whole edged with dwarf barberry, replacing the box of many years past.

At the left of the long path a terrace rises about four feet, hedged on top, and so shut in from the lower garden. Here one finds a wealth of annuals, also perennials for cutting, luscious currants on large old bushes and other fruits. Here too, are the hot-beds, and all the paraphernalia necessary to the true gardener.

CEDAR GROVE, AT CATSKILL

On the Albany turnpike, just within the limits of the village of Catskill, lies the estate known as Cedar Grove, with its colonial house and garden on the east side of the road.

The present proprietor is Mr. Theodore A. Cole, son of the Thomas Cole who founded the Hudson River school of

[1]Written by Mrs. Francis J. Higginson.

landscape painters. This artist, wandering through the country, was attracted by the charm of Cedar Grove and sought an introduction to its owner, John Alexander Thompson, who had built the house in 1815. A friendship thus begun led later to the marriage of Thomas Cole to Mr. Thompson's niece, Maria Bartow, who with her sisters inherited the estate at the death of their uncle.

Extending the length of the house, which faces south, is a broad piazza over which climb huge wistarias, honeysuckle and clematis, and in front of which are Missouri apples, ball oleanders and lemon verbenas. Across the driveway, opposite the doorway, stands a massive, wide-spreading thorn acacia tree which has weathered the storms of a hundred and fifty years, and from there stretches the old garden with its beds of flowers separated by grassy walks. In these beds, as the seasons succeed one another, blossom crocuses, hyacinths, daffodils, poppies, roses, lemon lilies, fraxinella, larkspur, hollyhocks, valerian, china asters, and many another old-fashioned flower. To these have been added, without interruption to the general harmony, such novelties as pyrethrum, fringed petunias and the tall and beautiful autumn anemone.

The arrangement of the flowers shows that an artist's judgment has influenced the development of the garden, although the artist himself may have had nothing to do with the actual planting. That Thomas Cole did, however, take more than a casual pleasure in the making of a garden is shown by a passage in his diary describing the ideal color chart for placing flowers. "Blue flowers," he says, "are very fine in the bright sunlight, while in the shade they are of little value. Orange-colored or red flowers, on the contrary, are disagreeable in the glaring sun. They are most beautiful in the shade, which they illuminate with a pleasant glow. In gardening I should place the blue flowers in the light, perhaps intermingled with

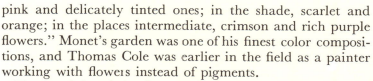

Cedar Grove, the residence of Mr. Theodore A. Cole, at Catskill.
Above are two views of the old garden at Cedar Grove

pink and delicately tinted ones; in the shade, scarlet and orange; in the places intermediate, crimson and rich purple flowers." Monet's garden was one of his finest color compositions, and Thomas Cole was earlier in the field as a painter working with flowers instead of pigments.

To the right of the flower beds at Cedar Grove extends the lawn with shrubbery and banks of flowers in the background. Through the garden runs a gravel path which finally, through trees and shrubs, leads over a rustic bridge to Thomas Cole's later studio.

From the west end of the piazza, looking across century-old lilacs and syringas, may be seen the range of the Catskill mountains. To the east of the house, passing lilies-of-the-valley, yellow roses, iris, peonies, marigolds and chrysanthemums, according to the season, one comes to the first studio of the famous artist, in which were painted well-known pictures: "The Voyage of Life," "The Course of Empire," and "The Cross and The World" series, and his "Dream of Arcadia," which was purchased by the Old American Art Union. Beyond this building, extending to the banks of the Hudson river, is a fine bit of woodland containing oaks, hickories, and pines. Surrounding the Cole dwelling on three sides are orchards which are gardens of bloom in spring and heavily fruited in autumn, adding to the richness of color and variety of effect in the place as a whole.

The present mistress of the old garden is Mrs. Florence Cole Vincent, a great-great-niece of "Uncle Sandy" who laid it out, and grand-daughter of Mrs. Maria Bartow Cole, to whose interest and loving care the garden owed much of its early development, and who was courted among its blossoms. To Mrs. Vincent's devotion and care is due the garden's present order and beauty, and also the remarkable quality of its color.

CONSTITUTION ISLAND

Constitution Island, formerly called Martilaer's Rock by the Dutch settlers, belonged to the Philipse estate, the original title being expressed in the "Great Highland Patent" issued in 1691. Fortifications planned by the First Continental Congress were placed by Washington on this island. It is opposite West Point, and the history of the two is closely interwoven. Benedict Arnold held command at West Point, and had an office on Constitution Island; this small office was in later years incorporated in the Warner home.

The island remained in the Philipse family until 1836 when it was purchased by Henry Warner. The Warner family cultivated gardens and preserved the wild vegetation. Miss Susan Warner and Miss Anna Warner, the former the author

of *Queechy*, were great lovers of gardens and were also well-known gardeners. Miss Anna wrote a book called *Gardening by Myself*.

In 1908 Mrs. Russell Sage purchased the Island from the Warners for $150,000 and presented it to the U. S. Government as a gift from Miss Anna Warner and herself. It then became an addition to the military reservation of West Point, to be for the use of the United States Military Academy forever. The grounds and flowers are now cared for by a committee of the Philipstown Garden Club.

THE ELLWANGER GARDEN, ROCHESTER[1]

The garden of the late George Ellwanger, horticulturist and great lover of trees and flowers, was planned about 1867. It is laid out on a gentle slope on the south side of the house. A gray stone wall encloses it from the street and a high lilac hedge forms the southern boundary.

Among the chief features of the garden are the old pear trees, planted by Mr. Ellwanger, the box-edged paths, flower borders and an old rose bed. On another boundary is a group of fine flowering shrubs and old Japanese yews. The garden is at its best in May when the pear trees, tulips and other spring flowers are in bloom.

[1]Described by Leah C. Ellwanger. This garden, though laid out after 1840, is included here as an illustration of the results of over 60 years of continuous care. A photograph is shown on the following page.

The Ellwanger garden, at Rochester, shows the results of more than sixty years of continuous care

HISTORICAL GLIMPSES OF GARDEN AND TOWN

The diaries and journals of travellers and the writings of historians afford occasional glimpses of New York State towns green with gardens long since obliterated, or suggestions of early plantings, and descriptions of vanished estates laid out on a most ambitious scale. Some of these gleanings from historical sources follow.

NEW ROCHELLE

Very early, the Journal of Madam Knight (1704) gives this good report of New Rochelle:

"We set out for New Rochelle, where being come we had good entertainment. . . . This is a very pretty place, well compact, and good handsome houses, Clean, good and passable Rodes, and situated on a Navigable River, abundance of land well fined and Cleerd all along as we passed, which caused in me a Love to the place. . . ."

ITHACA

A century later (1827), James Stuart's *Three Years in North America* remarks the activity in Ithaca of a former gardener to the Archbishop of Canterbury:

"Public or tea gardens are common in the American towns. In one of the gardens here, kept by an Irish gardener, formerly employed by the Archbishop of Canterbury in the gardens at Lambeth, we saw some fine fruit, especially grapes. . . .

"The American villages are generally announced to you by the spires of their churches peeping through the trees on your approach."

GENESEO

Barber and Howe's *Historical Collections of New York* describes the Geneseo of 1840 and gives an excellent picture of the thriving agricultural district surrounding it.

"Geneseo is pleasantly situated upon a site sloping to the west, and enjoys a delightful prospect, stretching across the valley, and including the town of Leicester. The landscape, embracing an area of perhaps fifteen miles in diameter, agreeably undulated with gentle hills and valleys—rich in garniture of fields, agreeably interrupted with masses of woods, and enlivened with villas, bespeaking the comfortable circumstances of their owners—forms a prospect of matchless beauty. It is rendered still more picturesque by the river, which flows lazily through the valley, but disclosing here and there only a section of the stream, breaking through the bower of trees and clustering vines by which its bright waters are overarched."

An account of Geneseo in the *New York Commercial Adver-*

Barber's drawing (1840) of Geneseo viewed from the residence of James Wadsworth Esq.

tiser in 1840, written by the editor, William L. Stone, speaks of the Wadsworth mansion and garden:

"His [Gen. Wm. Wadsworth's] mansion, the abode of refinement and elegant hospitality, is finely situated at the southern extremity of the principal street of the village, embosomed in groves of ornamental trees, thickly sprinkled, among which are the elm, locust and willow, and looking out on a princely domain of his own, including a broad sweep of flats. . . . Adjacent to the mansion is a large garden, rich with every description of fruit which the climate will allow, and adorned with flowers of every variety and class of beauty."

BEDFORD

Barber and Howe tell us that Bedford was established "in 1681 or 1682, at a place called the hop-ground, on account of its natural product." Chief Justice John Jay made it his home during the latter part of his life. "Here," wrote Timothy Dwight,[1] "he employs his time, partly in the cultivation of his lands, and partly in a sequestered and profound attention to those immense objects which ought even supremely

[1] *Travels in New England and New York.* (1801.)

to engage the thoughts, wishes and labours, of an immortal being." Martha J. Lamb in later years thus described his house and grounds:

"Bedford House, the seat of the Jays in Westchester County was built soon after the Revolution. It stands upon an eminence overlooking a wide extent of rolling country.

"The mansion is reached by a private avenue, which winds

Barber's drawing of the residence of Chief-Justice John Jay at Bedford shows the lindens commented on by Martha J. Lamb

artistically up a smooth elevation, curving and bending about venerable oaks, maple, birches and umbrella elms, passing well cultivated gardens, and finally cuts a circle in a wide velvet lawn, and terminates under the shadow of four superb lindens in front of the dwelling.

"A hall sixteen feet wide extends through the entire build-

A view of Paulding Manor, from "Historical Collections of New York"

ing, the rear door opening upon a background of hill crowned with oaks, chestnut trees, and gigantic willows.

"Creeping over the side of the house is a wistaria, filled with a profusion of blossoms, and honeysuckle climbers adorn the pillars of the wide verandah while rose-bushes peep over the railing. Upon the wooded height in the rear is a pretty

An early drawing of Rochester, showing the central part of Buffalo Street near its junction with State and Exchange Streets

This view of "Rose-Lawn," the one-time residence of Edgar M. Vanderburgh, at Washington, New York, is an excellent example of a gentleman's place between 1830 and 1840, showing residence, greenhouse, grape arbor, tree planting, hedges, and fences. There is an apple orchard to the right, probably locust trees in the dooryard, spruce for a windbreak, and young elms or maples to the right of the greenhouse. The estate is now owned by Mrs. Herman Place, through whose courtesy this drawing is reproduced

school or summer house of stone, which the Chief-Justice built for his children.

"The barns, carriage-houses, and the farm-house of the tenant who has the supervision of the property, are off at a little distance—beyond shrubbery and a clump of locust trees —to the northeast, upon the outskirts of a fine garden."

"Bedford House" is now owned by Mrs. Arthur Iselin, who says that the garden still follows the lines of the original plan.

The residence near Cornwall of St. John de Crevecœur, author of "Letters from an American Farmer," published in London in 1782

A view of Presque Isle, the residence of Wm. Deming Esq., in Dutchess County, from Barber's "Historical Collections of New York"

ALBANY

The regular settlement of Albany may be said to have begun in 1623 when the Dutch established a trading-post and fort there, calling it Fort Orange. It was also called Beverwyck, and not until the conquest by the British did it become known as Albany.

Peter Kalm, the Swedish botanist, visited Albany in 1749. He described the architecture of the town, which he reported as next to New York the principal town in the province. The houses, which he found "very neat," were for the most part "built in the old way with the gable end toward the street . . . of bricks, and all the other walls of planks. . . . The street doors are generally in the middle of the houses; and on both sides are seats, on which, during fair weather, the people spend almost the whole day, especially on those which are in

Albany from Greenbush, from an aquatint in colors, drawn by I. W. Hill, and engraved, printed, and colored by I. Hill

the shadow of houses. . . . The streets are broad, and some of them are paved; in some part they are lined with trees. . . ." Most of the Albany merchants, according to Peter Kalm, had "extensive estates in the country and a great deal of wood." He also described the country between Albany and Saratoga. The farms were "commonly built close to the river, on the hills. Each house has a little kitchen-garden, and a still lesser orchard."

H. D. Eberlein described one of the houses built in 1762, soon after Kalm's visit to Albany:

"The house has massive brick walls and double hip roof, pierced by generous square chimneys. . . . It is an excellent example of the Georgian style of architecture.

"Around the house were gardens and orchards and well-kept borders full of flowers, with ample expanses of lawn."[1]

To Sutcliff[2] in 1803 Albany had "more the appearance of an English town than any I have seen in America. Some of the streets are narrow and irregular and many of the houses are old. On approaching the city . . . the roofs of many of the buildings, from being covered with tin plates instead of slate, exhibit a very singular, glittering appearance in the sun."

The rambling *Memoirs of an American Lady* (1808) by Mrs. Grant include a description of Albany gardens. Mrs. Grant wrote:

"The city of Albany was stretched along the banks of the Hudson; one very wide and long street lay parallel to the river, the intermediate space between it and the shore being occupied by gardens. . . . Every house had its garden, well, and little green behind; before every door a tree was planted, rendered more interesting by being coeval with some beloved member of the family; many of their trees were of a prodigious size and extraordinary beauty, but without regularity, every one planting the kind that best pleased him, or which he thought would afford the most agreeable shade to the open portico at his door which was surrounded by seats, and ascended by a few steps.

"At the other end of the town was a fertile plain along the river, three miles in length, and near a mile broad. This was all divided into lots, where every inhabitant raised Indian corn sufficient for the food of two or three slaves, and for his horses, pigs and poultry.

"In the comparatively barren heights rising above Albany there were several wild and picturesque spots, where small brooks, running in deep and rich bottoms, nourished on their banks every vegetable beauty; there some of the most indus-

The first Manor House in Albany of Jeremiah Van Rensselaer, erected in 1660 and used until replaced by the second Manor House in 1765. From a pencil sketch by Major Francis Pruyn

[1]From *Manors and Historic Homes of the Hudson Valley*, by H. D. Eberlein. The editor has been unable to trace the source of information for the existence of this garden.
[2]Sutcliff's *Travels in North America*, 1803, '04, '05.

trious early settlers had cleared the luxuriant wood from these charming little glens, and built neat cottages for their slaves, surrounded by little gardens and orchards, sheltered from every blast, wildly picturesque, and richly productive."

Gardens in Albany were cultivated by the women. Mrs. Grant says:

"Every one in town or country had a garden; but all the more hardy plants grew in the field, in rows, amidst the hills, as they were called, of Indian corn. These lofty plants sheltered them from the sun, while the same hoeing served for both; these cabbages, and potatoes and other esculent roots, with a variety of gourds grew to great size and were of an excellent quality. Kidney-beans, asparagus, celery, great variety of salads and sweet herbs, cucumbers etc. were only admitted into the garden, into which no foot of man intruded after it was dug in spring. Here were no trees, these grew in the orchards in high perfection; strawberries and many high-

From a watercolor by Major Francis Pruyn

In 1725, Vanderheyden Palace, erected by Johannes Beekman in the old Dutch settlement in Albany, stood on North Pearl Street where the Albany Savings Bank now is

flavored wild fruits of the shrub kind abounded so much in the woods, that they did not think of cultivating them in their gardens, which were extremely neat, but small and not by any means calculated for walking in. I think I see what I have so often beheld in town and country, a respectable mistress of a family going out to her garden, in an April morning with her great calash, her little painted basket of seeds, and her rake over her shoulder, to her garden labors. These were by no means figurative.

" 'From morn till noon, from noon till dewy eve,' a woman in very easy circumstances, and abundantly gentle in form and manners would sow and plant and rake incessantly. These fair gardeners, too, were great florists, their emulation and solicitude in this pleasing employment did indeed produce 'flowers worthy of Paradise.' These though not set in 'curious knots' were ranged in beds, the varieties of each kind by themselves; this if not varied and elegant, was at least rich and gay. To the Schuylers this did not apply; they had gardeners, and their gardens were laid out in the European manner."

Mrs. Grant's *Memoirs* present this description of the residence of Colonel Philip Schuyler:

"His family residence was at the 'Flats,' a fertile and beautiful plain on the banks of the river. The high banks of the Hudson were both adorned and defended by elms (larger than any I have ever seen at any other place) decked with natural festoons of wild grapes.

"There was a large portico at the door, with a few steps leading up to it, and floored like a room; it was open at the sides and had seats all around. Above was either a slight wooden roof, painted like an awning, or a covering of lattice

work, over which a transplanted vine spread its luxuriant leaves and numerous clusters.

"For the accommodation of birds there was a small shelf built around, where they nestled, sacred. . . .

"The house fronted the river, on the brink of which, under shade of elm and sycamore, ran the great road toward Saratoga; a little simple avenue of morello cherry trees, enclosed with a white rail, led to the road and river. Adjoining to this on the south side, was an enclosure, subdivided into three parts, of which the first was a small hay field, opposite to the south end of the house, the next, not so long, a garden, and the third, by far the largest, an orchard. These were surrounded by simple deal fences. These deal fence posts were decorated with the skeleton heads of horses and cattle. These were not mere ornaments either, but a most hospitable arrangement for the accommodation of the small familiar birds.

"From the known liberality of this munificent family, all Indians, or new settlers on their journey, whether they came by land or water, rested there."

Louden's *Encyclopedia of Gardening* (1834) describes the residence of General Van Rensselaer, the wealthiest land proprietor in the United States, as "a mansion at the north end of Albany, with more of the accompaniments of shrubbery, conservatory etc. than is often seen in America; but no great quantity of land is devoted to what we call pleasure grounds, though the estate of the proprietor extends twelve miles in every direction." Louden's source was apparently James Stuart's *Three Years In North America*.

As for the flora of the Hudson River valley in the region of Albany, we have a lush description in the previously quoted poem, "The Hudson," by Ann Eliza Bleecker:

"There, bending low, the waterlilies bloom,
And the blue crocus shed their moist perfume;
There the tall velvet scarlet larkspur, laves
Her pale green stem in the pelucid waves.
There nods the fragile columbine, so fair,
And the mild dewy wild-rose, scents the air.
While round the trunk of some majestic pine
The blushing honeysuckle's branches twine.
There too, Pomona's richest gifts are found,
Her golden melons press the fruitful ground;
The glossy crimson plums there swell their rinds,
And purple grapes dance to Autumnal winds.
While all beneath the mandrake's fragrant shade
The strawberry's delicious sweets are laid."

TWO VANISHED GREAT ESTATES

One of the great land grants was that of "Skenesborough," which has been described as "an eighteenth-century English country estate which happened in the American wilderness."

In 1765 Philip Wharton Skene, born at Hollyards, Fifeshire, Scotland, was granted a royal patent to a tract of about 29,000 acres of virgin land. The grant was formed into a township under the name of Skenesborough. There Skene built mills, forges, a general store, etc., and finally a stone house, 130 feet long, standing as in England it would have stood, in a park, facing across meadows that might be made into lawns, and through a lattice of young oaks and maples that would grow old along with the house.

Skene wrote later: "I only want a few years idly devoted to make a good estate of it."

During the Revolution, however, Skene backed the British side; his holdings were confiscated, and he went back to England. Later he returned to this country and tried unsuccessfully to regain the property.[1]

Another great land grant was the vast domain of Sir William Johnson, of which Mrs. Grant said in her *Memoirs*:

"Sir William Johnson purchased from the Indians (having the grant confirmed by his sovereign) a large and fertile

[1] Adapted from an account by John Pell in the *Quarterly Journal* of the New York Historical Association.

tract of land upon the Mohawk river; where having cleared and cultivated the ground, he built two spacious and convenient places of residence; known afterward by the name of Johnson castle and Johnson hall. The first was on a fine eminence, stockaded around, and slightly fortified, the last was built on the side of the river, on a most fertile and delightful plain, surrounded with an ample and well cultivated domain; and that again encircled by European settlers; who had first come there as architects, or workmen, and been induced by Sir William's liberality, and the singular beauty of the district to remain."

Sir William's active interest in horticulture is attested by the following letter[1] from Jacob Dyckman:

King's Bridge, Mar. 22, 1765

Sir: I wrote you two letters about the trees I sent you but fear Were Miscarried thinking Otherwise I would have had an answer, I wrote you the particulars about them.

I Before told you I would Come and see them safe up but your answer was you thought they would be taken Proper care of which I fear they were not as Mr. Marsh told me [they] Pined very much last summer.

I would always be glad to answer you request About Trees, Plants etc. and I can now furnish you with 100 Grafted pippins, and as many natural trees as you please.

Your Very Humble Servant

JACOB DYCKMAN.

CADWALLADER COLDEN, BOTANIST

Cadwallader Colden, one of our most eminent early botanists, the friend and correspondent of John Bartram, was born in Dunse, Scotland, in 1688. He studied medicine in Edinburgh, and in 1708 came to Philadelphia, where he established himself as a physician. In 1718 he removed to New York State, subsequently holding a number of high govern-

Cadwallader Colden

mental positions. He filled the chair of lieutenant-governor for fifteen years.

During the first years of his residence in New York, Colden lived at Coldenham, near Newburgh, where in leisure hours he studied natural history and natural philosophy. Timothy Dwight says that his botanical knowledge was probably unrivalled on this side of the Atlantic.

In Darlington's *Memorials* of Bartram and Marshall we

[1]Quoted from *Washington Heights, Manhattan: Its Eventful Past*, by Reginald Pelham Bolton, published by Dyckman Institute.

find an account of Colden which shows him with his family at his country place, in about the year 1740.

"About this time that able and sagacious botanist, Doctor Cadwallader Colden of New York, began to pay attention to the natural history of that province; and for a number of years he continued to observe, collect, and describe the indigenous plants in the interesting region around his residence at Coldenham, near Newburgh. He corresponded with the distinguished naturalists of Europe, and communicated to them his discoveries.

"At that sylvan retreat, and in the delightful recreation afforded by botanical research—amid the cares of his public employments, Doctor Colden found a companion and assistant, worthy of special commemoration, in his accomplished daughter."

Miss Colden's botanical accomplishments did not go unappreciated. Doctor Garden, writing to Dr. Colden, Nov. 4, 1754, says, "I shall be glad to hear of Miss Colden's improvements, which no doubt increase every day,—and may we be surprised with more than a Dacier. . . ." And in a letter to Linnaeus, dated London, May 12, 1756, Peter Collinson says, "I but lately heard from Mr. Colden. He is well, but what is marvellous, his daughter is the first lady that has so perfectly studied your system. She deserves to be celebrated." In another letter, dated April 30, 1758, he says, "Last week, my friend, Mr. Ellis wrote you a letter recommending a curious botanic dissertation, by Miss Jane Colden. As this accomplished lady is the only one of the fair sex that I have heard of, who is scientifically skilled in the Linnaean system, you no doubt will distinguish her merits, and recommend her example to the ladies of every country."

Howard Kelly in *Some American Medical Botanists* says that Linnaeus named the genus *Coldenia* for Colden, and as Miss Colden had drawn and described 400 plants, it was suggested that he should name the genus *Helleborus*, "Coldenella."

A quotation from *Family Records and Events*—a letter by Walter Rutherford, a young Scotchman who married one of the daughters of James Alexander—gives a glimpse of Dr. Colden and his truly remarkable family.

"He [Colden] is as gay and facetious in his conversation as he is serious in his writings. From the middle of the woods his family corresponds with all the learned Societies in Europe. Himself on the principles of matter and motion, his son on electricity and experiments. . . . His daughter Jenny is a florist, and a botanist. She has discovered a great number of plants never before described, and has given them properties and virtues, many of which are found useful in medicine and she draws and colors them with great beauty. N. B. She makes the best cheese I ever ate in America."

Colden in the latter years of his life resided at his farm "Spring Hill," at Flushing, Long Island. He died there in 1776.

ANDREW JACKSON DOWNING

The State of New York gave to America her first great landscape architect, Andrew Jackson Downing, who was born near Newburgh in 1815.

The early gardens of Colony and State were modeled on the Old-World style, and were usually laid out by foreigners, or by amateurs with the aid of European books which often gave instructions not at all suited to our climate. But as wealth increased, more and more attention was paid to the artistic development of country places on a large scale, and it was just at the height of the period following the year 1800, which saw a wave of enthusiasm for horticulture and for associations for promoting it, that Andrew Jackson Downing's *Treatise on the Theory and Practice of Landscape Gardening* was published.

This book was the first of its kind written in America. It definitely affected the trend of thought in regard to the planting of large areas of land, and really created in this country the feeling for the so-called "natural" or English type of

The residence of Andrew Jackson Downing at Newburgh

gardening. It was later the inspiration of our next great landscape architect, Frederick Olmstead, who laid out Central Park, New York City, and other municipal park systems throughout the country.

Downing stood for the natural and lasting, as opposed to the stilted, circumscribed bedding system then in vogue. His whole nature was profoundly imbued with the beauty of the Catskills and of the banks of the Hudson. In his writings he expressed, and in his work he put into practice, the great underlying principles of harmony and unity, which give us pleasure as we view a wide-spread landscape or a well-planted lawn.

Downing's *Treatise* was published in 1841, and was dedicated to John Quincy Adams, whose intense interest in horticulture was a great inspiration to the shy young student. The book had a great sale. It was not until 1850, however, that Downing was able to visit England and see there the great estates laid out in the natural style of which he had written. After his return he was chosen to lay out the grounds near the Capitol, White House, and Smithsonian Institute, at Washington D. C., but most unfortunately was drowned as he came down the Hudson on his way to the Capital. The steamer on which he was travelling caught fire, and Downing perished in his efforts to save other passengers. He died at the height of his career, when he was only thirty-seven years of age.

Downing says in the preface to his *Treatise:*

"In the present volume I have sought, by rendering familiar to the reader most of the beautiful sylvan materials of the art, and by describing their peculiar effects in Landscape Gardening, to encourage a taste among general readers. And I have also endeavored to place before the amateur such directions and guiding principles, as it is hoped, will assist him materially in laying out his grounds and arranging the general scenery of his residence."

The cottage of N. B. Warren Esq. at Troy, an example of the work of Andrew Jackson Downing

The contents of the *Treatise* are arranged under the following headings:

"Historical Sketches, Beauties of Landscape Gardening, Wood and Plantations, Deciduous Ornamental Trees, Evergreen Ornamental Trees, Vines and Climbing Plants, Treatment of Ground, Treatment of Water, Landscape or Rural Architecture, Embellishments: Architectural, Rustic, and Floral."

Besides these divisions there is an Appendix which includes notes on transplanting trees, a treatise of exceptional value, and one which might well be placed in the hands of every head gardener of the present day. We quote here a few points.

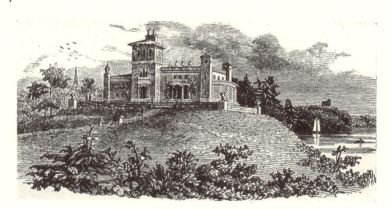

Above are two illustrations from Andrew Jackson Downing's "Treatise," showing examples of his landscape gardening

SELECTIONS FROM DOWNING'S NOTES ON TRANSPLANTING TREES

Transplanting of trees taller than twenty feet is not advisable, in Downing's opinion. He says:

"In this country on account of the hot dry summer climate we should rarely attempt the removal of trees larger than twenty feet in height. . . .

"The first and most important consideration in transplanting should be the preservation of the roots. By this we do not mean a certain bulk of the larger and more important ones only, but as far as possible all the numerous small fibres and rootlets so indispensably necessary in assisting the tree to recover from the shock of removal. The coarser and larger roots serve to secure the tree in its position . . . but it is by means of the small fibrous roots, or the delicate and numerous points of these fibres (root-hairs) that the food of plants is imbibed, and the destruction of such is, therefore, . . . fatal to the success of the transplanted tree.

"To avoid this as far as practicable, we should, in removing a tree, commence at such a distance as to include a circumference large enough to comprise a great majority of the roots. At that distance from the trunk we shall find most of the smaller roots, which should be carefully loosened from the soil, with as little injury as possible; the earth should be gently and gradually removed from the larger roots, as we proceed onward from the extremity of the circle to the centre,

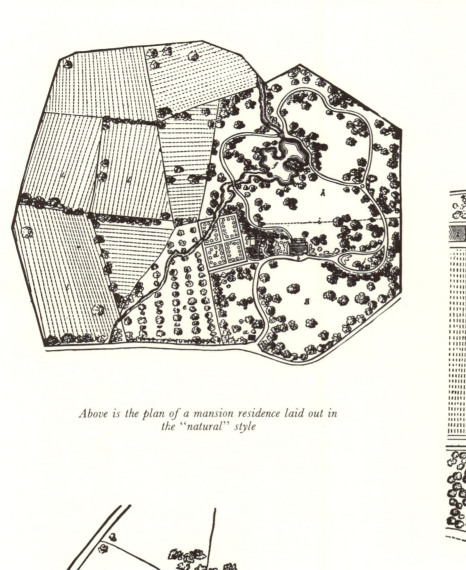

Above is the plan of a mansion residence laid out in the "natural" style

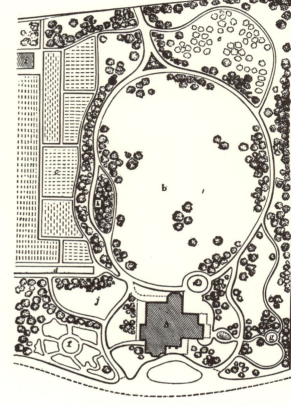

The plan above shows a suburban villa residence

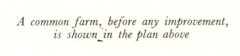

A common farm, before any improvement, is shown in the plan above

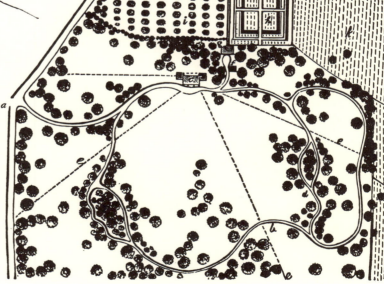

This shows a plan of the grounds of the same farm after ten years' improvement

Examples of landscape design by Andrew Jackson Downing

and when we reach the nucleus of root surrounding the trunk, and fairly undermine the whole, we shall find ourselves in possession of a tree in such perfect condition, that even when of considerable size, we may confidently hope for a speedy recovery of its former luxuriance after being replanted."

Downing then goes on to say that a tree dragged from the ground with a badly mutilated root system will require severe top pruning, so as to make the top correspond in size with the roots. On the other hand, he says, trees dug according to his directions may have the head of foliage left in all its symmetry.

Downing also advises the removal of trees from the skirts of woods or from open and exposed situations rather than the selection of those in the forest. The latter generally have longer trunks and less spread of top, and having been sheltered from frost, sun and wind by surrounding trees, are less hardy and much less able to withstand the shock of transplanting.

A simple machine for removal of trees is described as follows:

"The machine used in removing trees of moderate size is of simple construction; consisting of a pair of strong wheels about five feet high, a stout axle, and a pole about twelve feet long. In transplanting, the wheels and the axle are brought close to the trunk of the tree, the pole is firmly lashed to the stem, and when the soil is sufficiently removed and loosened about the roots, the pole, with the tree attached, is drawn down to a horizontal position, by the aid of men and a pair of horses. When the tree is thus drawn out of the hole, it is well secured and properly balanced upon the machine, the horses are fastened in front of the mass of roots by gearings attached to the axle, and the whole is transported to the destined location.

"In order more effectually to insure the growth of large specimens when transplanted, a mode of preparing beforehand a supply of young roots, is practised by skilful operators. This consists in removing the top soil, partially undermining the tree, and shortening back many of the roots; and afterwards replacing the former soil by rich mould or soil well manured. This is suffered to remain at least one year, and often three or four years; the tree, stimulated by fresh supply of food, throws out an abundance of small fibres, which render success, when the time for removal arrives, comparably certain.

"It may be well to remark here, that before large trees are transplanted into their final situations, the latter [the soil] should be well prepared by trenching, or *digging the soil three feet deep;* intermingling throughout the whole a liberal portion of well decomposed manure, or rich compost. To those who are in the habit of planting trees of any size in unprepared ground . . . it is inconceivable how much more rapid is the growth, and how astonishingly luxuriant the appearance of trees when removed into ground properly prepared. It is not too much to affirm, that young trees under favorable circumstances,—in soil so prepared,—will advance more rapidly and attain a larger stature in eight years, than those planted in the ordinary way, without deepening the soil, will in twenty; and trees of larger size in proportion,—a gain of growth surely worth the trifling expense incurred in the first instance.

"In the actual planting of the tree, the chief point lies in bringing every small fibre in direct contact with the soil. . . . To avoid this the soil must be firmly broken with the spade before filling in, and one of the workmen, with his hands and a flat dibble of wood, should fill up all cavities, and lay out small roots in their natural position. When watering is thought desirable (and we practise it almost invariably), it should always be done when planting is going forward. Poured in the hole when the roots are just covered with soil, it serves to settle the loose soil compactly around the various roots, and thus both supplies a source of moisture, and brings the pulverized mould in proper contact for growth. Trees well watered in this way when planted, will rarely require it afterwards; and should they do so, the better way is to remove two or three inches of the top soil, and give the lower stratum a copious supply; when the water being absorbed the surface should be again replaced. There is no practice more mischievous to newly planted trees, than that of pouring water, during hot weather, upon the surface of the ground above the roots. Acted upon by the sun and wind, this surface becomes baked, and but little water reaches the roots; just sufficient perhaps to afford a momentary stimulus, to be followed by increased sensibility to the parching drought."[1]

[1]Downing should have inserted here the extreme necessity for watering the second summer, as it is then, rather than in the first year, that many transplanted trees are lost.

"Introduction of the Croton Water into New York, celebrated October 14th, 1842." This is a
view of the great fountain in City Hall Park

NEW JERSEY

The ancient catalpa trees at Morven, in Princeton, which were in blossom at the time of the signing of the Declaration of Independence. The history of the garden at Morven is told on page 309

NEW JERSEY

GARDENERS OF FOUR NATIONS

IN NEW JERSEY, as elsewhere, the colonists had their first lessons in the gardening of the New World from the Indians. An old pamphlet printed in 1648, now in the Philadelphia Public Library, contains what is probably the earliest mention of an Indian garden in New Jersey. It thus describes "the retired Paradise of the children of the Ethiopian Emperor," the seat of the Raritan Indian kings:

"A wonder, for it is a square rock, two miles in compass, one hundred and fifty feet high, a wall-like precipice, a strait easily made invincible, where he keeps two hundred of his guard, and under is a flat valley, all plain to plant and sow."

Among the early colonists, the Swedes apparently learned their lesson all too well. In 1749, in the course of his journey through the colonies, the Swedish botanist, Peter Kalm, wrote in his diary: "Quere, Whence did the Swedes here settled get their several sorts of corn, and likewise their fruit trees and kitchen-herbs?" His observation was that the Swedes had brought with them all sorts of corn, fruits and herbs, or seeds of herbs, and that they had at first been forced to buy maize from the Indians, both for sowing and eating; after some years in this country, however, they had extended their maize plantations so greatly that the Indians later found themselves obliged to buy maize from the Swedes.

The term of the Swedish gardeners was but an episode, however, in the early colonial history of the region, for here, as in Pennsylvania, there must have been a succession of gardening methods as one wave of settlement after another would give way before an influx from another nation. New Jersey being originally part of Virginia, which in 1601 comprised all the territory between the southern boundary of North Carolina and the northern boundary of Maine, was therefore English, or at least was considered so by King James. But the first European settlement is believed to have been made by the Danes or Norwegians, who, it is thought, came over with the Dutch colonists to New Netherland in 1618.

"The privileged West India Co." was then formed in Holland, and for some time the Dutch made futile attempts at colonization. These ended shortly after 1630 with a complete abandonment of the country, so that there was no longer a single European on the Banks of the Delaware.

The next colonists were Swedish, and for a time this part of the country was known as "New Sweden." But meanwhile the indomitable Dutch had appeared again, and in 1655 the Swedish authority terminated.

Again the English, founding their claim on priority of discovery, came on the scene. The Dutch were defeated by Sir Robert Carr, and Charles II made a grant of the territory to the Duke of York, Lord Berkeley, and Sir George Carteret. The Duke of York transferred his share to the other two men in consideration of ten shillings and a rent of "one pepper corn," if legally demanded. The bounds of New Jersey were now for the first time defined, and it was known as New Cæsarea in honor of Carteret.

In 1665 Philip Carteret became governor, and from this time until the Revolution, with the exception of a few months in 1673 during the war with Holland, New Jersey was in the hands of the British, and the predominant gardening influences naturally were English.

Two weeks after the general Congress of Colonies had declared itself independent of Great Britain, the provincial congress assumed the title of "State Convention of New Jersey." The first independent legislature convened at Princeton, August 27, 1776, and William Livingston was chosen the first governor.

NOTES ON ONCE–FAMOUS NEW JERSEY GARDENS AND GARDENERS

WILLIAM LIVINGSTON

This same William Livingston who was New Jersey's first governor after the establishment of independence built in 1773 at Elizabeth, then Elizabethtown, a mansion which survives today, though considerably enlarged; in the dooryard stands a horse-chestnut tree planted by Miss Livingston two years before the house was finished. Mansion and tree are shown later in a photograph of the present-day estate of Ursino. What gives William Livingston especial interest in this study of early gardens and gardeners, however, is his consistent interest, throughout a busy political life, in things pastoral. In addition to his political works, he was the author of various essays on miscellaneous topics, writings strongly tinged with a love of nature. In 1747, when he was twenty-four, and but three years out of Yale, he wrote a poem entitled "Philosophic Solitude, or the Choice of a Rural Life," which expresses a revolt of surprising intensity against what we would regard as the comparatively simple city life of the first half of the eighteenth century. We quote a few extracts:

Let ardent heroes seek renown in arms
Pant after fame, and rush to war's alarms;
To shining palaces let fools resort,
And dunces cringe to be esteem'd at court;
Mine be the pleasures of a rural life,
From noise remote, and ignorant of strife;
Far from the painted belle, and white-gloved beau,
The lawless masquerade, and midnight show,—
From ladies, lap-dogs, courtiers, garters, stars,
Fops, fiddlers, tyrants, emperors, and czars.

Full in the centre of some shady grove,
By nature formed for solitude and love,—
On banks array'd with ever-blooming flowers,
Near beauteous landscapes, or by roseate bowers,
My neat, but simple mansion would I raise,
Unlike the sumptuous domes of modern days,
Devoid of pomp, with rural plainness form'd,
With savage games and glossy shells adorn'd.

* * * * *

No trumpets there with marshal clangor sound;
No prostrate heroes strew the crimson'd ground;
No groves of lances glitter in the air,
Nor thundering guns provoke the sanguine war;
But white-robed peace and universal love
Smile in the field, and brighten every grove.

* * * * *

Oft would I wander through the dewy field,
Where clustering roses balmy fragrance yield;
Or, in lone grots, for contemplation made,
Converse with angels and the mighty dead;
For all around unnumbered spirits fly,

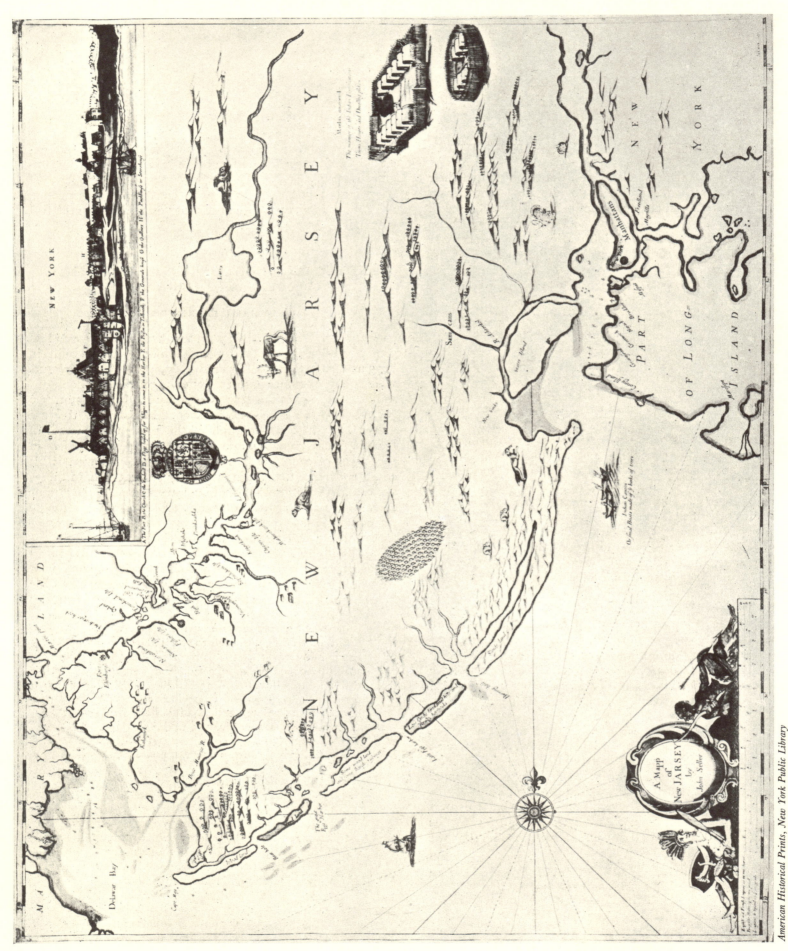

John Seller's "Mapp of New Jarsey," a colored line-engraving which appeared in his "Atlas Maritimus" (London, 1675), was the earliest English map to include a view of New York

Waft on the breeze, or walk the liquid sky;
Inspire the poet with repeated dreams,
Who gives his hallow'd muse to sacred themes;
Protect the just, serene their gloomy hours,
Becalm their slumbers, and refresh their powers.

John Warner Barber's drawing of the William Livingston house as it was in 1838. A photograph of the house today is shown on page 324

ELIAS BOUDINOT

Another eighteenth-century estate in Elizabethtown was that of Elias Boudinot. It is described by Martha J. Lamb[1] as "a great square comfortable structure, with an old-fashioned gable roof, tall chimneys suggestive of forefatherly fireplaces, and a massive door with a brass knocker in the centre of a somewhat imposing front. It stood among lawns and gardens and lofty trees, very much embowered and hidden in summertime with aspiring vines, attractive shrubbery and gay-colored flowers. . . . The house was reached by a private carriage way, from the old road to Elizabethport."

Boudinot evidently took an active interest in horticulture. He wrote to his nephew in London, Judge Samuel Bayard (of Clermont, Bayard Lane, Princeton), on July 15, 1797, a plaint which sounds painfully modern.

"We are much plagued for want of a good gardner . . . Labour is so high that scarcely anything the ground produces will pay the expense of raising it. . . . If a good Scotch or French gardner could be engaged for three or four years for a reasonable rate and without a family, I really believe it would be a good scheme, provided he was really sober and honest.

"We have almost every kind of garden seed imported here from England every spring & sold at reasonable rates. . . . If anything new or out of the common way could be obtained it would be clever to add to our common stock. Extraordinary kinds of Fruit would increase our capital."

Elias Boudinot was president of Congress, and during its sessions made his headquarters in Princeton, at his sister's home, Morven. The present owner of Morven, Mrs. Bayard Stockton, directs our attention to this delightful letter which Boudinot wrote in 1802 to "his Excellency Thomas Jefferson, Private".

"Dear Sir:
"Knowing your fondness for agriculture and everything

[1]From an article in the *Magazine of American History*.

connected with it, tho in a collateral respect, I take the liberty of troubling you with the following. . . . In the Fall I was presented at second hand with a few quarts of an extraordinary wheat from a distant country. . . . I planted them in a good soil at Harvest they turned to be a species of oats of a peculiar nature. Having picked 14 or 15 I laid them on the grass till I gathered more; but in 10 minutes they had disappeared and could not be found. I gathered a number and put them in the centre of a salver with a perforated rim and carefully placed it over night where it could not be disturbed. The next morning I found every grain at the rim of the salver with its head through the holes of the rim. On carefully examining them with a magnifying glass, there appeared a spiral line round the upper part of the leg which I presume is the cause of motion. I have called them animated oats, for indeed they are the nearest line between vegetation and animation that I know of. Many gentlemen both native and foreigners have seen them during the past year, but no one could inform me of their native country."

The "Cottage Residence" of Nathan Dunn Esq. at Mount Holly

GARDENS IN BURLINGTON

Much earlier, Gabriel Thomas in "An Account of West Jersey" recorded this picture of Burlington in 1698:

"There are many Fair and Great Brick Houses on the

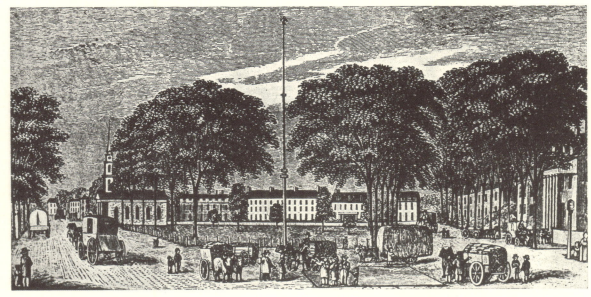

The Lower Green or Military Common of Newark, as drawn by Barber for his "Historical Collections of the State of New Jersey" (1840)

outside of the Town which the Gentry have built there, for their Country Houses, besides the great and Stately Palace of John Tateham Esq. which is pleasantly situated on the North side of the Town, having a very fine and delightful Garden and Orchard adjoining to it, wherein is variety of Fruits, Herbs, and Flowers, as Roses, Tulips, July-Flowers[1],

[1]Gilliflowers (stocks).

Sun Flowers (that open and shut as the Sun Rises and Sets, thus taking their name) Carnations, and many more; besides abundance of Medicinal Roots, Herbs, Plants and Flowers found wild in the Fields."

THE SCHUYLER GARDENS

One of the elaborate New Jersey estates of the eighteenth century was that of Arent John Schuyler, a large stone and brick residence with two fine deer parks in what is now Newark. It was situated "in Bergen County near the Hackensack River a little south of the Belleville road." When Burnaby visited it in 1759 it had passed to Arent's son, Colonel Peter Schuyler. Burnaby wrote in his *Travels Through North America:*

"Immediately after leaving this place [Newark] I travelled seventeen or eighteen miles to the Falls through a rich country interspersed with fine fields and gentlemen's seats.

The "College of New Jersey, Princeton," as drawn by John Warner Barber, showing the grounds and informal planting of 1836

"From thence I returned—and went down two miles farther to the park and gardens of Colonel Peter Schuyler. In this garden is a very large collection of citrons, oranges, limes, lemons, Balsams Peru, aloes, pomegranates and other tropical plants; and in this park I saw several American and English deer, and three elks or moose-deer." Evidently Colonel Schuyler's establishment included a greenhouse for protecting tender plants.

In 1776 the Journal of Lieutenant Isaac Bangs recorded a visit to the Schuyler place.

"Mr. Schuyler's Mansion House is a large, grand, and magnificent building, most beautifully situated upon an eminence on the east bank of the Hackensach River. On the back part of the house is a large neat garden, built partly for ornament, and partly for convenience. At the back of the garden is a tremendous high Hill covered with woods. The scituation of this Gentleman's Dwelling, both for Convenience and Pleasure is the best I have ever beheld."[1]

ANDRE MICHAUX, BOTANIST

The belt of fertile soil which runs northward into New Jersey through Princeton early drew the attention o André Michaux, the French botanist who later established a botanic garden in South Carolina. Mrs. Bayard Stockton, of Morven, at Princeton, has gathered together the evidence of Michaux's first interest in New Jersey. Mrs. Stockton writes:

"As early as March 3, 1786, the Legislature passed an act

[1]Facts from *Some Colonial Mansions*, by Thomas Allen Glenn; Henry T. Coates Co.

enabling André Michaux, 'Botanist, of his most christian Majesty' to purchase a tract of land not exceeding two hundred acres, to be appropriated for the 'sole purposes of a Botanical Garden.' Michaux, as an alien, was unable to hold land except by express act of the Legislature. He was commissioned by the King of France to travel through the United States and 'establish a botanical intercourse and correspondence and to obtain at the King's expense any tree, plant or vegetables that may be wanting, all curiosities which may serve to extend botanical knowledge and increase the enjoyments of the gifts of nature.' Michaux planned to establish a botanical garden of about thirty acres 'in order to make useful experiments with respect to agriculture and gardening, to make a depository not only of French and American plants, but of all other productions of the world which may be drawn from the King's garden in Paris.'

"Old Middlesex County (part of which is now Mercer County) in eastern New Jersey is within the belt or ridge of fertile soil, known to scientists even in colonial times, which runs from North Carolina through Princeton to northern New Jersey. Even today Princeton is famous for its fine old trees and the great number of rare birds who stop to feed, on their migrating pilgrimages both north and south.

"Michaux, so tradition says, stayed long enough in New Jersey to design at least one garden, that of 'Prospect Hall,' the Varick place at Paulus Hook, now Jersey City Heights. Tradition also says that he was the lost Dauphin of France, son of Louis XVI. A diary which he kept, although it has been edited by Mr. C. S. Sargent, Director of the Arnold Arboretum, is somewhat disappointing. He traveled by horseback from Florida and the South to the wilds of Hudson Bay, and from Philadelphia to the Illinois Indian

A drawing of the parsonage in Cranbury in 1833

lands. Here are several entries: 'The 29th. In the evening' (1796) 'crossed the Creeks and slept in the woods—on my deer skin—on account of the rain, at a place where reeds or canes were growing in abundance' (which sounds a far from comfortable bed). 'The 25th. Found that my horse jumped over the fence, and I spent the whole day looking for him'—in spite of which, he seems to have written down the name of every plant, tree and beast that he saw, and in what neighborhood.

"Dr. Benjamin Rush of Philadelphia, famous physician and scientist, who lived for a time at Morven after the close

The Public Square at Morristown in John Warner Barber's drawing of 1836

of the War of the Revolution, writes in his diary: 'This day Mr. Micheaux, a French botanist on a tour through the American woods, drank tea with me, recommended from Charleston. He said he brought the seed of a plum tree from Persea to Charleston which flourished there although no European plums had ever been known to thrive there. He said that the seeds of all plants declined the first year after being transplanted.' "

Michaux finally chose northern New Jersey, and established his garden and nursery in what was then Bergen County; it was popularly known as "The Frenchman's Garden", and was a fashionable recreation spot for early New Yorkers. Its influence in the progress of arboriculture in the United States is said to have been considerable, but no details of the garden have survived. The site is included in the present Macpelah Cemetery, New Durham.

The garden of "Prospect Hall", which Michaux laid out, ran to the waterfront and was an impressive one in its day, containing rare flowers in beds of unusual design. One lengthy avenue of imported plum trees was long remembered. The garden is said to have contained some of the first Lombardy poplars in this country.

"CAMPFIELD HOUSE," MORRISTOWN[1]

In Morristown on Oliphant Lane stands "Campfield House," which, until it was moved years ago, was surrounded by a garden made by one Dr. Jakes Campfield, uncle of Elizabeth Schuyler. In his diary he states that he had "many fair flowers and choice vegetables." It was in this house and garden that "Betsy" Schuyler first met her husband, Alexander Hamilton, when in the spring of 1780 she came from Albany to pay her uncle a visit.

DUTCH GARDENS ON JERSEY CITY HEIGHTS[2]

On Jersey City Heights in what was formerly a part of Bergen County stand two old and memorable houses which once had gardens: the Sip Manor, built in 1666 by C. A. Sip, and Apple-Tree House, where Washington and Lafayette ate under the shade of an apple tree. According to Mr. Mills,[3] the Sip Manor still belongs to one of the direct Sip descendants, "having been held by the families, holding three grants of surrounding land, under Dutch, English and American rule." Unfortunately, the garden has been encroached

[1]Written by Josephine P. Morgan.
[2]Written by Josephine P. Morgan.
[3]*Historic Houses of New Jersey*, by W. Jay Mills. Philadelphia, J. B. Lippincott Co., 1902.

upon and is gone, but the old house with its Dutch air is still standing.

The Dutch grandmothers, like those in Holland, devoted their time to their flower gardens, while the mothers attended to the "Dutch cleansing" of their children. The Dutch gardens of that time were formally laid out in the shape of stars, crescents and circles, bordered by the "gallant box wood." Mr. Mills gives the following account of "An Old Lady of Bergen" who used to work in her half acre "sweet plot" sheltered by a great, black silk calash to preserve her complexion from the bright sunlight of those mornings of yesterday. She once compiled a list of the flowers which flourished in her mother's garden. Besides the beloved tulip, it contained ragged-robins, lady slippers, prince-feathers, Canterbury bells, love-in-the-mist, sweet phœbus, mourning brides, and many other quaintly named flowers of "Merrie England," once to be found in any old fashioned garden. The "Haus bloemen" themselves were the same as those which grew in the neighboring English gardens.

The Sip garden was famous in the annals of old Bergen. Governor Peter Stuyvesant is said to have admired its large variety of flowers when drinking spiced wine under the shade of a willow in its borders, and he knew what a garden ought to be, for he kept a score of negroes at work on his own fine gardens surrounding "White Hall" at the Battery and on his Manor on the Bouwerie. The old willow stood until not many years ago. Lord Cornwallis is said to have hung three spies from its branches the morning he left Bergen after his stay with the Sip family. General Lafayette planted two elm trees near the house, and these stood until recently.

One of the old customs of the Manor was the evening gathering of the family to keep the "Scheravard" or twilight. . . . "While the last light lingered in the sky the old people and the young people would draw the black settle close to the fire and talk over the events of the day."

OLD GARDENS OF TODAY

MORVEN, AT PRINCETON

Mrs Bayard Stockton, in seeking years ago to restore the old garden at Morven to its colonial design, came upon the interesting discovery that the garden of Richard Stockton, signer of the Declaration of Independence, had been modeled on that of Alexander Pope at Twickenham. She has described the effort to restore the garden in a delightful account which she calls

"A Quest for a Garden"

In giving the history of the Morven garden, I mean the "plaisance" about the house, which includes the lawns and planting of trees and shrubberies as well as the actual flower beds or garden, in the American use of the word.

We know that this must have dated back to 1701, when the house was built, but the first tradition we have is that of the planting of the giant French horse-chestnut tree on the north side of the house before 1770. It measures eleven feet around the trunk and at least one hundred feet across from branch to branch. Captain Levis and his brother, Samuel Pintard,

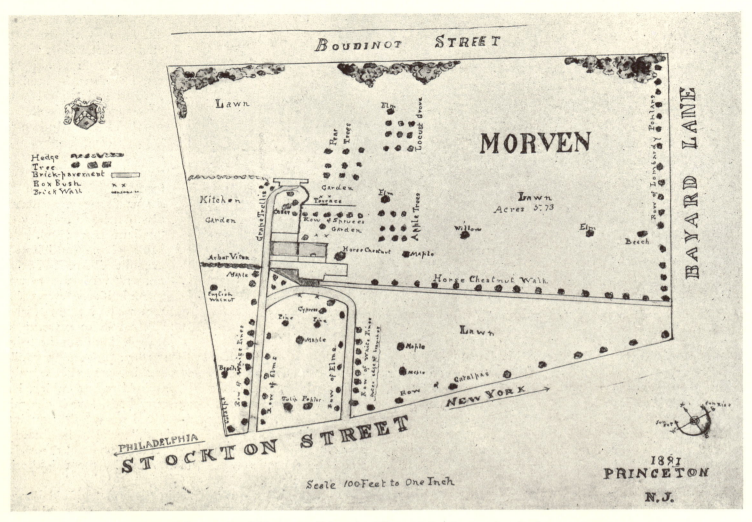

A plan of the grounds of Morven, at Princeton. The row of ancient catalpas is shown on page 304

young Huguenot *émigrés* who had lately arrived from France, came to seek the hands in marriage of Susannah and Abigail Stockton, sisters of Richard the Signer, and in order that he might look with more favor on their courtship, brought chestnuts from the famous tree in the courtyard of the Fortress Château of Loches-sur-Indre in Touraine. From these nuts grew the great tree and those bordering the chestnut walk.

The row of catalpa trees on the King's Highway must have been planted at an even earlier date, as they were in full blossom at the time of the signing of the Declaration of Independence, and from that date have been called the Independence Trees; but the first record is in a letter written from Westminster, London, 1766–67, by Richard Stockton, the Signer, to Annice Boudinot, his wife, which I quote:

"I am making you a charming collection of bulbous roots, which shall be sent as soon as the prospect of freezing on your coast is over. The last of April, I believe, will be time enough for you to put them in your sweet, little flower garden, which you fondly cultivate. Suppose, in the next place, I inform you that I design to ride to Twickenham the latter end of next month, principally to view Mr. Pope's gardens and grotto, which I am told remain nearly as he left them, and that I shall take with me a gentleman who draws well to lay down the exact plan of the whole. In this I shall take pleasure, because I know that it will please you."

In a letter dated February 2, 1766, he writes:

"I send you herewith a little box of flower-seeds and the roots that will do at this season. The seedsman now assures me that nothing but anemonies and rennulus will do to move, as the others are all in the ground and would perish if they were taken up and sent over the sea. I hope these, which are the best of their kind, will please you for the present, but I really believe you have as fine tulips and hyacinths in your little garden as any in England, yet I shall order some of the finest to be sent next July, so as to be set out next Fall. The sensitive plant is a great curiosity—it will stir upon touching as if it were possessed of animal life."

The Signer had plainly not been able to obtain the gardener's plan of Alexander Pope's garden, and the one he had drawn was probably destroyed at the time Lord Cornwallis set fire to the library wing of Morven. So it seemed at first almost impossible for me to find the "exact plan," but in 1899 *Gardens Ancient and Modern*[1] was published, and there at last was a description of it. When Mr. Sieveking was written to, his reply was that the original plan was to be found in the British Museum. This seemed, after five years' fruitless search, victory at last—but four kind friends who offered to go in search of it returned to London empty-handed. It was so prized, and surrounded with such red tape, that no mere American, even armed with a letter of introduction, could get access to it. At last, we procured a copy of it through an Englishwoman. She was not allowed to send a copyist, but must do the work herself between certain hours, under the vigilant eye of an attendant, who returned it under lock and key when the hour sounded. Are the manuscripts of the Vatican more closely guarded?

With this plan and the help of the old Scotch-Irish gardener who had seen four generations at Morven, we were able to trace out the original design—but it takes some imagination. For the Thames River, the highroad between New York and Philadelphia must be substituted. The Chestnut Walk passed from Nassau Street in front of the house crossing; Library Place corresponded to the London Hampton Court Road, which divided Pope's Villa from his garden. The vineyard and the kitchen garden, the groves, fruit trees, were in the same relative positions, and for the "garden house," the slaves' quarters are found.

The cedars, cypress, Spanish chestnuts, yew and elms, were all there. The cypress, which was destroyed in a recent ice storm, was for years well known to American botanists— its only equal being one in the Bartram Gardens near Philadelphia, which is now also gone.

[1] *Gardens Ancient and Modern*, edited by Albert Forbes Sieveking, London, J. M. Dent, 1885; reissued 1899 under the title *The Praise of Gardens*.

Boxwood in the garden at Morven

The great wistaria vine at Morven, from one stem

The Chestnut Walk at Morven, in Princeton

We found a willow grown from cuttings of the historic one at Twickenham, which was said to be the original of all the weeping willows in our European gardens—brought in a basket from the Euphrates by Mr. Vernon, sent by Lady Mary Wortley Montagu to Pope, who planted it with his own hand.

Robert Carruthers' *Life of Pope* says: "Sir William Stanhope sent cuttings of this willow, which fell to the ground 1801, into various parts of Europe and in particular to the Empress of Russia, 1789."

We also found many bulbous roots, grape hyacinths, golden daffodils, narcissus, and a wilderness of tawny-orange day lilies.

After the Revolution, the first mistress of Morven lived alone with her son—a lad of sixteen—on very limited means. Her broad acres had been laid waste by the Hessian troops. One wing of the house lay in ruins; the valuable library, rare paintings and imported furniture, all were gone. The only available funds had been used to alleviate the sufferings of the Signer in the deadly prison ship, an account of which has never been adequately written.

On the anniversary of his death, she wrote of Morven the following quaint lines:

"These fragrant bowers were planted by his hand
  And now neglected and unpruned must stand.
  Ye stately Elms, and lofty Cedars, mourn—
  Slow through your Avenues you saw him borne
  The friend who reared you, never to return."

Not until her son's marriage in 1790 did the work of restoration begin, and then not altogether after the Twickenham Garden, although the general plan has always been retained.

In 1828, the Commodore's day, the fashion had reverted to the formal style. As late as 1865 Morven presented quite a different aspect from that of today. The walk passing in front of the house ended at Senator Stockton's (now Allison House), and was bordered with yellow sweetbriar, damask roses and rare, flowering shrubs—carrying out the old "Desposition of Gardens," that "all trees of your shady walks be planted with sweetbriar, white jessamine and honeysuckle."

In early spring, there was a continued flowering border, brightened with tulips, daffodils and hyacinths, reaching from door to door. Between Boudinot Street and the house were the flower beds, gay with all kinds of old-fashioned flowers, with box edging and trees cut into a perfect menagerie of birds and strange beasts, which the children of two generations had delighted to ride, much to the old gardener's chagrin and apprehension—not for fear of their lives, but of those of his favorite box bushes.

All this had vanished in 1894, when the quest for a garden began—and again with the help of the old gardener, we found the site of the original garden. Here have been planted flowers with a history—sweet-williams from Abbotsford, hollyhocks from Kew Gardens, flowers from the site of the Manor Richelieu, Canada; from Van Rensselaer Manor (Fort Crialo) on the Hudson; from Cliveden (the Chew place in Germantown); from Dow Castle, Ireland; from Sandringham, England; from France, from Holland, from Sweden, and many from nearer neighbors' gardens in Princeton.

When Morven had its two hundredth birthday, October 21, 1901, we marked the day with a white stone, putting a sun-dial where the center of the old garden had been, and carved about the gnomon this motto by Dr. Henry van Dyke:

"Two hundred years of Morven I record,
  Of Morven's house protected by the Lord;
  And now I stand among old-fashioned flowers
  To mark for Morven many sun-lit hours."

H. H. STOCKTON

*   *   *

Mrs. Stockton gives also a list of the old trees, shrubs, vines and flowers found at Morven at the time of the 200th anniversary. The following, then, represent plantings made sometime during the first two centuries of the garden, from 1701 to 1901:

Trees

Populus nigra italica	Fagus sylvatica atropunicea
Platanus orientalis	Liriodendron tulipifera
Salix babylonica	Bride's Trees, "planted at the
Cupressus sempervirens	entrance of the first bride."
Cedrus libani	Æsculus octandra
Pinus strobus	Morus alba tatarica
Picea excelsa	Gleditsia triacanthus
Acer tataricum	Juglans regia
Acer rubrum	Juglans nigra
Acer saccharum	Magnolia acuminata
Æsculus Hippocastanum	Magnolia tripetala
Catalpa bignonioides	Cercis canadensis

Shrubs

Chionanthus virginica	Hibiscus syriacus
Weigela amabilis	Spiræa arguta
Rhus Cotinus	Syringa vulgaris
Forsythia	Syringa chinensis
Calycanthus	Deutzia
Philadelphus floridus	Viburnum tomentosum

Vines

Wistaria sinensis	Lonicera sempervirens
Bignonia radicans	Vitis ("Sweet Madeira grape.")
Lonicera	

Old-Fashioned Flowers

Peonies (pale pink)	Spiræa ulmaria
Harrison rose (yellow)	Hosta (Funkia lancifolia)
Damask rose (pink)	Hosta (Funkia subcordata)
Climbing rose (white)	Hemerocallis fulva
Queen of the Meadow	

PROSPECT: THE RESIDENCE OF THE PRESIDENT OF PRINCETON UNIVERSITY[1]

Two hundred and thirty-six years ago, Prospect was part of a tract of land sold in 1695 to Richard Stockton, whose grandson was the Signer. In 1705, Mr. Stockton sold three hundred acres of this land to Benjamin Fitzrandolph, who handed it on to his son Nathaniel. Nathaniel Fitzrandolph later gave the 48½ acre lot on which Nassau Hall was built. A daughter of Nathaniel's, Sarah by name, married Thomas Norris of Princeton. The property came into her husband's hands, and in 1760 he sold it to Jonathan Baldwin, who in turn sold it on April 1st, 1779, to Colonel George Morgan.

From Colonel Morgan's possession it passed into the hands of his son John, who in 1805 disposed of it to John I. Craig. The latter in 1824 sold it to John Potter, whose son Thomas pulled down the Morgan house and built this present mansion. In November, 1878, it was sold to Robert L. and Alexander Stuart and was added to the University.

For the early history of Prospect, I am indebted to Professor Collins' admirable article in the *Princeton University Bulletin* for June, 1904, entitled "Prospect near Princeton." The first record of interest was during Mr. Baldwin's occupancy, when the history of the place was presumably that of any farm of respectable mediocrity. In 1779 Prospect was sold to Colonel Morgan, gentleman farmer, Indian agent and pioneer western explorer. The farm then took on a style, and enjoyed a reputation which it had never had before.

After Colonel Morgan's coming to Princeton, the story of

[1] Written by Mrs. John Grier Hibben.

his life is that of the finer type of American gentleman of the post-revolutionary period, gravely modest, courteous, hospitable and always chivalrous. One of his ancestors left on a fly-leaf of his family Prayer Book this legacy which his children have never disgraced: "I, David Morgan, gentleman of Wales, bequeath to my descendants in America this comfortable certainty,—they come neither from kings nor nobles, but from a long line of brave gentlemen and women with unstained names."

Prospect, when Colonel Morgan took it, was in a bad state of repair, but he disbursed large sums of money to put it in order, and settled at Princeton to become a scientific farmer. The ground was not terraced, but sloped down to the farm land. Along the College line of the property he planted a row of cherry trees, whose fruit annually offered a welcome relief to poorly fed undergraduates. From the farm, Colonel Morgan sent one hundred Prospect elms for the Square behind Independence Hall at Philadelphia.

The curious bent of Colonel Morgan's mind had not been satisfied with a career as an explorer and an Indian agent. He carried his investigating spirit into the management of Prospect, where he experimented continually now in corn, now in beans, now in methods of pest extermination. He fully deserved the gold medal awarded him by the Philadelphia Society for Promoting Agriculture, the first medal ever given in American agriculture.

The Princeton University Library has in its possession a manuscript, a record kept by Colonel George Morgan, which was given to the University in 1914. This book is a veritable mine of information. I give a few extracts from it:

First Entry, 1780—"I planted a row containing twenty cherry trees on the west side of the land leading from Princeton to the house. These were planted with all their branches a little shortened. Their bodies are at this time all standing, [April, 1780] from 9 to 12 inches round, or from 2½ to 4 inches diameter, one foot from the ground. Likewise a row of twenty cherry trees on the east side of said lane. These were a size larger than the other row and trimmed of all their branches up to the very top so that they look like poles." (An experiment.)

Then follow careful details about the planting of a young apple orchard, "300 trees at 20 feet apart"; of the planting of English walnuts in front of the house; of a row of morello and Kentish cherries; of the bass tree, planted in a line with the above morello trees; of elm trees forming an oval in the front of the house, detached in the inside and planted with thorn and rose.

Second Entry. "I also planted four elm trees forming a square within the oval. The British army in December 1776, having burned and destroyed the farm and most of the apple trees for firewood. They left standing nine large cherry trees which are within the oval of the circus and four others, east of the house with a single one in front and three in a row with one mulberry tree south of the house. These cherry trees within the circus were old ones in the memory of the oldest livers here. They all bear an abundance of cherries."

Speaking of what he is pleased to call "the fruits of the field," Colonel Morgan says, "I sowed wheat, barley, flax, Indian corn, potatoes, buckwheat, turnips, clover, oats, pumpkins, peas, rice, China wheat." And the birds which he saw in the spring of the year 1781 were "Larks, robins, [spelled 'robbins'] blackbirds, rice birds, swallows, pigeons, wild geese, snow birds, blue birds, mocking birds, thrushes, cat birds, gold finches, hanging birds, yellow birds and king birds."

In the Spring of 1799, arrangements were made for a delegation of Delaware Indians to come to Philadelphia and confer with Congress. Colonel Morgan, feeling that city life was not suited to them, had them brought straight on to Princeton and the ten chiefs forming the party camped on the Prospect grounds.

After Colonel Morgan's death, Prospect was owned by

his son, John, who sold it to J. I. Craig, of whom I can find nothing of interest to record. In 1824, J. I. Craig sold it to John Potter. Hegeman says in his history of Prospect: "John Potter moved from Charleston, South Carolina, in 1824, and bought from J. I. Craig that beautiful place now known as Prospect. Here Mr. Potter resided until a short time before his death, when he moved into Morven and lived there with his daughter, Commodore Stockton's wife, until his death.

"Thomas Fuller Potter, youngest son of John Potter, received from his father by will, the old homestead of Prospect

which was built for Judge Field, Mrs. Bradford's grandfather. Prospect is almost unchanged now.

Prospect garden was laid out from Notman's plans by a man named Petry, who was Commodore Stockton's gardener. Mrs. Stockton refers to him in a letter which reads:

"He was among the first to transplant large native trees from the woods to the lawn, and did this quite successfully at Prospect as well as at Morven. After he left the Commodore's service, he went to California where he laid out the streets and planted trees for the then new town of San Francisco.

"He was aided by a man named Noice, who was Judge

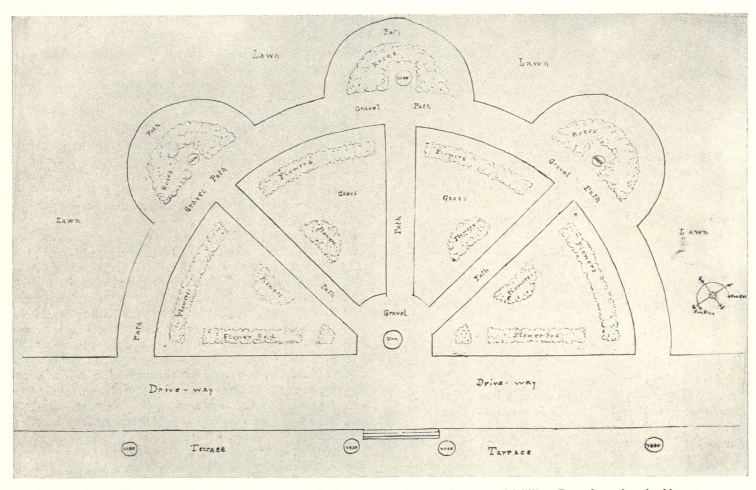

A plan of the garden at Prospect, in Princeton, laid out about 1843 by a gardener named William Petry from plans by Notman

and built the magnificent house upon it, which he lived in until his death, after which it was occupied by his widow."

Thomas Potter was married twice. His first wife died leaving two sons, John and William Potter.

Thomas Potter's second wife was Sarah Jane Hall, of Sunbury, Pennsylvania. To quote again from Hegeman: "A lady of great elegance, dignity and force of character, who admirably graced her position at Prospect. Three children were born to them, one little son, who died at the age of four years, and two daughters, Elizabeth and Alice, who were renowned for their grace and beauty."

It is around Thomas Potter's second wife that many of the interesting stories center. Her pictures show her great beauty and distinction, also her firmness of character. She lived in Prospect in great state and elegance, and it is written that "the younger generation snatched a fearful pleasure when in Mrs. Potter's society, but her few favorites among her many grand nieces who dared go to Prospect, were constantly there in their childhood and youth for long visits."

Mrs. Potter's two daughters were married from this house —Elizabeth, who married Henry Ashurst from Philadelphia, and Alice, who married J. Dundas Lippincott.

The architect of Prospect was Notman, a Canadian, who was then very much the fashion. He built also Castle Point at Hoboken, Alverthorpe at Jenkintown, the Hunniwell house in New Hampshire, and, in Princeton, Alison House and Guernsey Hall, which latter was then called Woodlawn, and

Field's gardener. The greenhouses, I should add, were famed for their camellias."

In the year 1880, two brothers, the Messrs. Stuart of New York, very generously purchased the Potter property for the University.

I do not remember the garden in the days when Dr. and Mrs. McCosh lived at Prospect, for when I came to Princeton to visit as a young girl gardens were not in my mind, but I shall never forget the first time I saw Mrs. McCosh's grave and beautiful face and looked with reverence and awe at her distinguished husband. From her daughter, Mrs. Magie, I have interesting items about Mrs. McCosh's love of flowers and the care she gave the garden. When the grass under the splendid Cedar of Lebanon was cut, she always went out to supervise the work personally and stood there while the gardeners carefully lifted the heavy branches and mowed the grass under it.

In her garden were geraniums, tuberous begonias, anemones, blue canterbury bells, many sweet flowering shrubs, and, in the autumn, salvias. But the most beautiful part of Prospect grounds was the rose garden; many of the roses Mrs. McCosh imported from Belfast, and they were of rare and unusual beauty.

The Prospect gardens have always had a fascination for me from the time that I first saw them twenty-seven years ago. They bore then little resemblance to the present garden. The "Place," as it was then called, began at Washington

Road. Where the '79 Dormitory now stands was a quiet meadow, in which the Patton cows and horses grazed. At one end of it was an old stone barn, and below that, in the space now occupied by the Palmer Physical Laboratory, was a large vegetable garden. We were neighbors of the Pattons at that time, living on Washington Road, and that kitchen garden was a place of joy to the children, Randolph West and Beth, and to me. It was so neat, so flourishing, so peaceful. The long lines of vegetables were always well cared for. There the apple trees blossomed, and the sweet, white violets bloomed in the borders, and there we always found the first

for the picturesque and for proportion, Mrs. Wilson had a group of large cedars planted to form a background. The rose garden was further developed and a long pergola was built at the end of it, covered with climbing roses. An old and graceful sun-dial was placed near the roses, and the setting for the garden was complete. The beautiful peonies, in shade from delicate to deepest rose, peach blossom and cream, the sweet jonquils, the great profusion of iris of unusual coloring —lavender, purple, straw-yellow, cream-yellow, rose and mauve—, and the dahlias all continue to bloom there as when Mrs. Wilson had planted them.

The garden at Prospect, in Princeton

warblers. The garden proper had none of the prettiness of the vegetable garden. In form it was as it is now, but then it was without cedars, the pool or rose garden. In the well-cut grass along the paths were set long and narrow rectangular beds, and in the center, a circular one. These beds were filled each year with undeviating regularity with cannas, geraniums, coleus, ageratum and sweet alyssum. As Lucas says, "those were the days when all the fashionable flowers that we now worship were to be found only in cottage gardens. Gentlemen's places were distinguished by their geraniums. Carpet bedding was the only correct thing. On the edges of the smoothest and greenest lawns, and in circular and oval beds, were the reddest geraniums, the yellowest calceolarias, and the bluest lobelias. Herbacious borders were an eccentricity, —a bid for an odd reputation."

The only things of beauty that redeemed the garden were two large beds of lovely heliotrope. I have always felt that they were placed there by Mrs. Patton's wish.

When Mr. Wilson became president of Princeton University, one of Mrs. Wilson's first interests was the garden, and it was as if a fairy wand had been waved over it, for it became a place of fragrance and beauty. The small narrow beds were broadened and united so that they formed, as they do now, a border for each path. The pool, with its lovely cedars, was placed in the center of the garden, and with a keen sense

For a year and a half Prospect was closed, and the garden went down rapidly. The hedges were untrimmed, the garden unplanted; the pergola, under the weight of tangled roses, rotted and fell; the perennials bloomed, but they were uncared for.

We have made some changes in the garden, in carrying out the plan of having a garden of flowers which should bloom as simultaneously as possible. The roses which occupied two long beds in the main garden were removed, and the beds were planted with flowers maturing about the same time. By June 15th, we have always tried to have a garden in full bloom. This entails considerable loss, for a spring garden is almost entirely sacrificed. Our reward comes, however, at Commencement time, when the garden is a mass of delphiniums, anchusa, sweet-william, canterbury bells, foxgloves, pansies, pinks and forget-me-nots.

The rose garden has again been enlarged, and the sun-dial removed to the middle of the lower lawn and surrounded by beds of Killarney roses and white pansies.

CASTLE HOWARD, AT PRINCETON

Castle Howard is one of the oldest places in New Jersey. The cornerstone bears the date 1685. It was a plantation owned by Dr. Greenland before William Penn granted land to the Stockton family and others in Princeton. It has its vague and enchanting traditions, told in a charming tale— "The Night Call," by Henry van Dyke.

During the Revolution a certain Captain Howard owned it. He was a Whig and his wife was a Tory, and as she was wont to entertain the British officers, he had painted over the mantel shelf

"NO TORY TALK HERE"

Of Castle Howard's grounds and gardens little seems to be known, but today the gardens have been tenderly planned and planted.

Part of the wildflower garden at Castle Howard Farm, Princeton

THE OLD SERGEANT-MILLER GARDEN, PRINCETON[1]

The Hon. Jonathan Dickenson Sergeant, grandson of Jonathan Dickerson, first president of Princeton University (the College of New Jersey, as it was then called), bought the place in 1775 from Mrs. Berrien, widow of the Hon. John Berrien, Colonial Justice of the Supreme Court of New Jersey, who owned Rockingham, later Washington's headquarters at Rocky Hill. Little is known of the garden at that date; whatever was planted bloomed but for a day, for on Jan. 3, 1777, the house was burned to the ground by the Hessian troops, who had taken possession of the town before the battle of Princeton and had turned Nassau Hall and the Presbyterian Church into barracks and stables. Where blushed the rose was now desolation, overgrown and neglected, except for the wildflowers planted by hands unseen.

After the British were defeated at Trenton, Donop retreated to Princeton with his Hessian Grenadiers. On his arrival, he threw up arrowheaded earthworks, surmounted by a cannon, in the old Sergeant garden, which was at the west end of the town, near the junction of Nassau and Stockton Streets. The cannon was left there, and later, when the British marched into Princeton down Maidenhead Road, three or four men fired it off. The British, believing the town to be well defended, were delayed more than an hour by their cautious reconnoitering. After the battle of Princeton, the cannon

[1]Written by Elizabeth Breckenridge Field (Mrs. W. Mason Field).

was again left behind. In later years it had several resting places, but finally the students marked it for their own, and in 1838 planted it in the south campus of the college, the centre of all student activities. "If not all true, 'tis well imagined" and beckons the mind back to stern deeds. I think we may fancy the cannon was a sundial in the old garden with the Greek motto, "The Night Cometh", inscribed upon it.

In 1829, the Reverend Samuel Miller D. D., who had married the daughter of Jonathan Dickenson Sergeant, rebuilt the house as a dignified mansion, and occupied it with his family.

The garden, as we gather from family papers, was at no time a famous garden as we think of gardens today. But if we read between the lines of old family letters, imagination comes to our aid.

A high, white picket fence, with an arch over the gate, enclosed the garden on the front. A madeira vine grew over the porch at the back of the house. In the grounds were a smoke-house and well-house, indispensable adjuncts to every establishment, which brings to us comforting thoughts of good things in time of want and in times of plenty. On the right, leading in from what is now Mercer Street, was a straight entrance driveway, and parallel to it a long flower bed filled with roses and columbines. The roses were not set out in formal state, but mixed with other flowers. We do not know the names of the roses which were planted, but charming visions of color and perfume come to us when we think of our grandmothers' favorite flowers. The white, the damask, the Burgundy, and the Seven Sisters all bloomed at that time.

The real glory of the garden was its beautiful trees. Both shade trees and fruit trees were planted and some of them were rare for their day and generation. There were two large, high trees which had white, bell-shaped blossoms, hanging from gracefully drooping limbs. The name[1] is not known, but they were said to be rare, and the only ones in this vicinity. A magnificent black walnut tree, a rare specimen, known all over the neighborhood, still stands on the property which until recently belonged to Miss Sheldon. There was an English walnut which is said to have borne nuts. There were two tulip poplars, which were laden with blossoms, and a large "white fringed tree," for which no name is given. There were fruit trees of all kinds which bore abundantly, among them two pear trees which were regarded as particularly fine.

An old tradition as to the manner of the planting of a fine, red mahogany, which still stands, is worth repeating. Dr. Miller, a very courtly gentleman of the old school, waiving aside all science, to say nothing of the practice of good gardeners, merely stuck his cane into the ground, and from it grew the present, splendid tree!

After the death of Dr. Miller, the place[2] was purchased by Miss Brown, who planted the box and enlarged the

[1]Halesia?—Editor.

[2]Now the Nassau Club.

Photograph by Rose & Son

The great black walnut tree standing on ground which was once a part of the Sergeant-Miller garden, Princeton

flower garden. The house still remains, and although additions have been made to it, the original can be plainly distinguished. The grounds, however, are much smaller, and but few traces are left of the old garden.

CHERRY GROVE, NEAR LAWRENCEVILLE

Cherry Grove, situated about a mile east of Lawrenceville, New Jersey, on the road through that village from Trenton to Princeton, is believed to be the estate described in the *Penn-*

Houses of New Jersey.[1] In 1854 Cherry Grove passed into the possession of William Scudder and his descendants until 1910.

Another son of the original George Green was Richard Montgomery Green, who later made his home at Harmony Hall in Maidenhead. His daughter Mathilda married Dr. Samuel McClintock Hamill, for fifty years the owner and headmaster of the Lawrenceville School. Their son, Samuel McClintock Hamill, was the husband of the present owner of Cherry Grove, and his children are now living in the house.

The name Cherry Grove comes from the avenue formed

The house and drive at Cherry Grove, near Lawrenceville

sylvania Gazette of September 16, 1756, as "The house and plantation, late the residence of John Dagworthy, deceased, of Maidenhead, Hunterdon County, N. J." Maidenhead was the original name of Lawrenceville. John Dagworthy was High Sheriff of the Separate Government of West Jersey, and a man of means and influence; his son was Col. John Dagworthy.

In 1770 Cherry Grove was acquired by George Green from his uncle by marriage, Jonathan Sergeant, who was actively concerned in the founding of the College of New Jersey, now Princeton University, and was Treasurer of the College from 1750 until his death in 1776. George Green was a grandson of William Green, who came from England and settled in Ewing Township in 1700; he was born in 1738, and was a captain in the American army during the revolution. In the winter of 1776–7, at the time of the battles of Trenton and Princeton, Cherry Grove was seized and occupied by the British, Mrs. Green and her children taking refuge in Bucks County, Pennsylvania. It is said that Hessian soldiers used the bureau drawers as feeding-troughs for their horses. Soon afterwards, however, the family returned. The oldest son, Caleb Smith Green, born in 1770, occupied the house until his death in 1850. The oldest child of Caleb Smith Green was Jane, afterwards Mrs. Thomas Kennedy, who in 1813 wrote from Cherry Grove the letters published in Mills' *Historic*

by two rows of cherry trees which originally led across the meadows belonging to the property, from the old road through Princesville, which bordered the farm on the south, to the road through Maidenhead, on which the house itself was situated. Six of these old trees still survive. The chief beauty of the place has always been its trees, which from the beginning were planted with formal regularity. The most conspicuous of these are two tulip poplars, standing close together where the old foot-path from the front door of the house reached the edge of the lawn at the roadside. Such trees in New Jersey were called the bride-and-groom trees because they were often planted at the front gate by a young couple who built a new homestead for themselves. These particular trees are now of really enormous height, towering above all other trees in the neighborhood. Four box bushes, now grown very large, but still sound, marked the corners of the square on which the house stands. An old smoke-bush remains, immediately west of the front door. Completely protected from the north winds, the smoke-bush has become a tree, reaching higher than the cornice of the house. Behind the house, that is, on the north side, a good many old apple and pear trees which formed the original orchard are still standing.

The original garden was on the east side of the front lawn.

[1] P. 197 ff.

A glimpse of the garden at Cherry Grove as it is today

The straight shafts of the great tulip-trees at Cherry Grove

The flagstone walk across the front of the house led through box borders to the garden gate. A few of the beds and box borders still remain, but most of the old garden had already disappeared when the present owner obtained possession, and the present garden occupies a new site west of the old orchard. Tradition has it that in the old garden the original George Green grew the first tomatoes or love-apples in the vicinity, at a time when everyone else believed that tomatoes were poisonous.

BONAPARTE PARK, AT BORDENTOWN[1]

Within a mile or so of the quaint old town of Bordentown is a great stretch of park and woodland, shady with towering trees and springing undergrowth, green with broad stretches of greensward reaching out to the banks of the Delaware River, which sweeps along to the sea underneath a high bluff.

This place is the famous Bonaparte Park, for many years the home of the exiled King of Spain and Naples—Joseph,

This "view from the hill at Bordentown" about 1820 shows, at the right, a country estate surrounded by the Lombardy poplars then fashionable

A GARDEN ON WOOD STREET, BURLINGTON

The old house and garden at 222 Wood Street, Burlington, are presumably nearly two hundred years old. The date of the building of the house is about 1738.

In 1750, the property came into the possession of Richard Smith and descended to his grand-daughter, Rachel Coxe. It was transferred by her to Daniel Drinker in 1813 and from him descended to Elizabeth Gummere. The property then reverted to Barker Gummere, and remained in the Gummere family until it came to the Hewitt family, the present owners.

James and Eliza Hewitt's youngest son, George, married Anne Barrington, of the North of England Barringtons, and it was under her care that the old garden flourished. It was planted mainly with perennials. In the winter first appeared the winter aconite, peeping out from under the snow; as spring came on, the western end of the garden was a golden mass of daffodils, then the lavender and yellow, and purple and white iris, and the yellow lilies; on the northern side beds of pink and light blue delphinium, with a background of Duchess de Brabant roses, with their delicate fragrance and exquisite but evanescent beauty. Then came the sweetbriar climbing over the lattice on the porch. Later came the delicate pink lilies and forget-me-nots; the phlox, gladioli and asters.

During the first years of Miss Hewitt's life in the old home, a sugar maple tree was planted which has since grown to huge proportions. The old garden bloomed under her care for sixty years, until her death.

brother of the Emperor Napoleon Bonaparte. When Napoleon was unable to make his escape to the New World, Joseph undertook the perilous adventure, carrying with him the records, papers and jewels belonging to the monarchy.

Strange it seems that Joseph Bonaparte should have chosen the neighborhood of this small Jersey town for his refuge in exile, but it is said that for some time before Napoleon's downfall he had indicated just some such location if he were ever obliged to flee to the New World. One day about the year 1816, a gentleman drove over to Bordentown from Jersey's capital with a business agent. It was the Count de Survilliers (Joseph Bonaparte) who had decided to purchase an estate there as a retreat for his persecuted family.

This retreat of an exiled king was purchased from one Stephen Sayre, and consisted of the park of about one thousand acres, which included the portion called "Point Breeze" where Bonaparte's first residence, the Sayre house, stood.

In the course of years, Joseph increased this realty until it included ten farms on the border of Crosswicks Creeks, eighteen hundred acres in all.

A special law was passed in New Jersey to enable the "Count de Survilliers," an alien, to own real estate, and this caused New Jersey to be nicknamed "New Spain." As soon as the law was passed, the Count began remodelling the Sayre house, bringing skilled workmen from Philadelphia to decorate the interior, and gardeners to plan a large park and gardens. The famous Belvidere was erected near the water's edge and the smaller white houses arose. Chief

[1]Written by Miss Clara M. Blackwell, of Trenton.

among these was the Lake House or Villa, built by Joseph for his beautiful daughter Zenaide and her husband, Charles Lucian, Prince de Canino.

The first house was burned down and the new stables were reconstructed for his permanent home. By many alterations these were developed into a very handsome structure. The house was long and low, of brick, covered with white plaster, the most conspicuous feature being a wide carved door opening into a large hall, with reception rooms on one side and dining rooms on the other, filled with a rare collection of pictures, statues and bronzes brought from overseas.

In front of the newly constructed house stretched a fine lawn, and in the rear a large garden of rare plants and flowers with fountains and chiseled animals.

The type of place which Joseph Bonaparte took such pains to develop during the following years not only resembled his own beloved home, Mortefontaine, but followed the natural bent of the French mind in landscape architecture.

Handling large masses was characteristic of the Bonaparte family, and in the course of a few years the Count de Survilliers made Bonaparte Park a veritable wonder, from the point of view of the landscape architect.

It was traversed by nearly twelve miles of drives and bridle paths winding through pines and oaks. On every knoll stat-

A century-old willow tree in Bonaparte's Park, Bordentown

A drawing of Bonaparte's residence and the surrounding park as it was about 1830

uary was placed, and rustic bowers and seats. It had covers for game, and preserves for deer. Over several small streams and gullies rustic bridges were thrown, and all around rose thousands of forest trees.

A strip of marshy ground separated the Point from the wooded heights at the western extremity of the Park; through this flowed a creek, fed by a shallow, winding brook. The Count threw a bridge across the bed of the brook and filled up the hollow, making the marsh into a lake. Here were the garden and villa of the Princess Zenaide. Here she tended her flowers and painted in her studio, while her husband followed his favorite pursuit of ornithology, for which the New World with its strange birds offered a wide field.

The mystery surrounding this villa was greatly en-

The house built by Joseph Bonaparte for his gardener

hanced by a subterranean passage which led from it to her father's mansion. This passage was walled and ceiled with bricks. It was forty feet long, and was said to contain iron doors at intervals, and to be designed as a place of refuge and hiding in case of need. For the Count lived in dread of English and Spanish spies. Be this as it may, the Count insisted that the passage was built only for the convenience of

Another drawing of the Bonaparte establishment at Bordentown

his daughter, so that she might, without fear of inclement weather, pass from her own villa to her father's house.

And now all that remains of the Bonapartes is the great stretch of greensward with one white house (the gardener's) near the road, and the trees that Joseph planted and so greatly loved, still standing, a joy to the passerby.

SUNDERLAND MANOR, NEW BRUNSWICK[1]

In 1783, Miss Mary Ellis, of a distinguished family of Charleston, S. C., had moved with her younger sister, the wife of Gen. Anthony Walton White, to New York. In 1793 they removed to New Brunswick, N. J. There in 1810, some time after the death of Gen. White and shortly after the marriage of his daughter and only child, Miss Ellis bought a farm lying along the Raritan River, about two miles south of New Brunswick, where she took her sister's family to live with her. (After "Oppression Street" was put through her garden.)

Sunderland Manor was named by a niece's husband, Thomas M. Evans, after his birthplace on the Eastern Shore of Virginia, in Accomac County; this place had in turn been named for an ancestral home in England. To the public, however, the charm and beauty of the place was so associated with the name of Miss Ellis that to this day the lovely pine woods along the river are popularly known as "Miss Ellis's Woods."

Adding to its natural beauties of woods and open meadows and river banks covered with wild flowers, Miss Ellis made of Sunderland a place of beauty which soon became noted.

[1]Written by Mabel Evans Kearny.

There were orchards and fields and gardens. There had been a fine peach orchard, the only surviving evidence of its existence being an interesting scrap of paper found with old letters and bills, on which was the signature of Cornelius Vanderbilt, acknowledging the payment of twelve dollars and seventy-six cents for two hundred peach trees sold in 1834.

Miss Ellis sought for the finest varieties of everything she wished to plant, and would send to great distances for specimens. She was looked upon as an authority on all matters pertaining to gardening, and in the quaint old letters of those days there were few who did not mention the delight they enjoyed in remembering their visits to Sunderland Manor. Always especially vivid in their memories were the altogether satisfying vegetable and fruit garden and the luxuriant growth of innumerable flowers; the exquisite perfume of the grape bloom; the flowery snowdrifts of pear, plum and cherry; the flamboyant clusters of the horse-chestnuts, around which was the unceasing murmur of the bees; a snowy-blossomed dogwood rising from a royal purple carpet of violets and an impressive tulip-tree. There were vines bearing fruits and flowers; a magnificent wistaria spread halfway across one side of the house and up over the gable, three and a half stories high to the very chimneys. Up this vine my brothers and I used often to climb to the second story, so strong and gigantic it was. When this great vine was in bloom it almost beggared description.

There was a small garden that I remember, and in it were pyrus japonica, syringa, spirea, bridal wreath, peonies, hare-bells, honeysuckle, bleeding-hearts, roses and many other flowers.

In front of the large rambling house which faced a vista of the river in the distance, and beyond an avenue of grand old horse-chestnuts, there could be found faint traces of what had been probably something like a pleasure garden. This was the site of the original garden planted by Miss Ellis. Growing half wild among the bushes and grass, there sprang up each spring masses of jonquils, daffodils, snowdrops, star-of-Bethlehem, and narcissi, while here and there a red tulip burned like a flame in the grass.

Each year they wandered farther afield, down by the duck pond, and away across the orchard to the edge of the woods.

A tree of especial interest was the *Franklinia*, named in honor of Benjamin Franklin. At the present time it is almost a lost species, there being only about a dozen specimens known. It was discovered in 1765, and since 1790 has not been seen growing in its wild state, though many scientists have looked for it in vain. Very recently an expedition was sent to the valley of the Altamaha River in Georgia, in search of it. The flowers were white with great golden centers and somewhat resembled a water-lily.

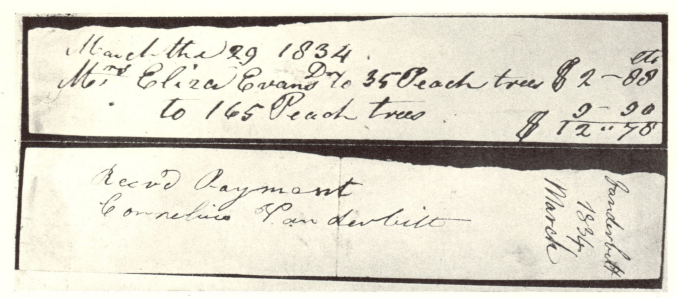
Facsimile of the receipt for the peach trees purchased from Cornelius Vanderbilt for Sunderland Manor, New Brunswick

Near this tree, and probably marking the center of the garden, was a high hedge of box encircling a mound of earth. An opening was cut through and wild tiger lilies grew there. Perhaps in the old days a sun-dial had been placed there.

For twenty-five years the gardens were left to run wild; but even this condition did not detract from their former beauty. Wild roses and blackberry bushes grew in tangles, while here and there in shady places one could find wild red

THE GARDEN AT BUCCLEUCH, NEW BRUNSWICK

Buccleuch was once the official residence of colonial governors. Through the center of the garden ran a broad pathway, for the whole length of the garden, terminating in a large circular bed, and on either side of this walk was a wide flower bed. Here grew mignonette and heliotrope, ladyslippers and petunias, snapdragons and sweet-william, peonies and poppies, shy moss-roses and flaring cockscomb and the

Courtesy of the Jersey Blue Chapter of the D. A. R., New Brunswick

The broad pathway through the center of the garden at Buccleuch

strawberries; their bunches of small fruit looking like a bouquet of flowers, and often, in the deepest shade of low drooping boughs, the white berries were found.

Of enchanting loveliness was the flowering crab-apple tree, the double blossom of pearly pink just doubly more exquisite than its sisters of the orchard. Like near neighbors were a fringe-tree and a tree with little silver bells, hanging in a row on its slender newest branches. In close proximity was a *Magnolia tripetala*, sometimes called the umbrella magnolia, with large, showy white flowers in a wealth of great, green leaves. Its distinctly disagreeable odor, however, withheld entire subjection to its immense attraction.

Beyond these trees, and no doubt edging the lower end of the old garden, was a row of white lilacs, underneath which, spreading further each year, grew lilies-of-the-valley. But as one came into the deep shade of the close-growing lilacs something of awe stole over the spirit, and one stood entranced by their loveliness and marvellous perfection.

Sunderland Manor was the home of Miss Ellis's heirs for ninety-one years, and now for more than two decades it has been in other hands. Some traces of the old garden may yet be seen; the flowers and trees that have endured are even now "carrying on," giving beauty and fragrance and grateful shade.

spicy lemon-verbena, without which no bouquet from that garden was complete. There was a border of dwarf-box, the official guardian and chaperon in all self-respecting colonial gardens. Here there was no running at large, no spreading or trailing of roots, no sprawling in graceful abandon. In its stead were stately dignity, graceful repose and mild frivolity.

The house faced the river. As in most colonial houses, the hallway ran through the middle of the house with an entrance and porch at either end. In front of the entrance, away from the river, stood the sun-dial, in the center of a grass-covered mound. A tall elm tree flanks it on either side and opposite is the arched gateway to the garden.

THE GARDEN OF "URSINO," AT ELIZABETH[1]

The garden at "Ursino" was laid out, with its box hedges and formal beds, about 1795 by Lord[2] and Lady Bolingbroke when they owned the property. They enriched the place by the addition of many shrubs, trees and fruit trees.

Ursino, (then known as Liberty Hall) was built by Governor Livingston in 1773. He had bought the property in 1760, and had sent to England for fruit trees, which he

[1]Written by the late Miss Lucy H. Kean. Ursino is now the residence of Julius Halstead Kean.
[2]George Richard St. John, Third Viscount Bolingbroke.

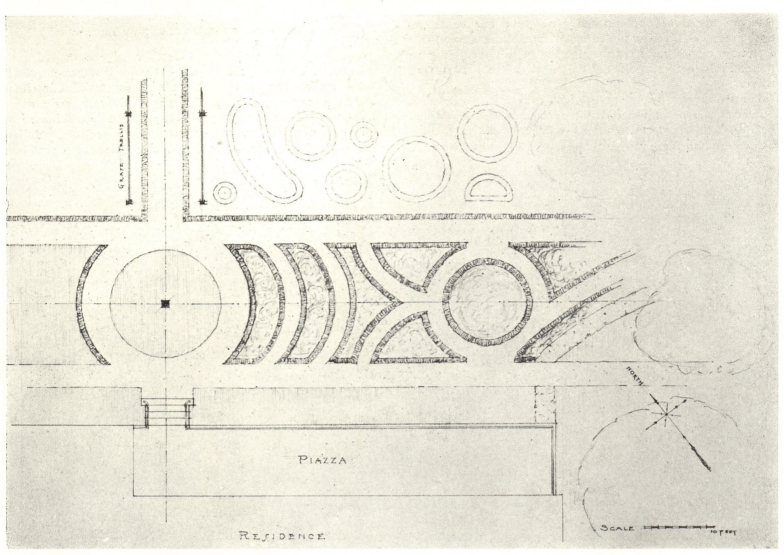

A plan of the garden at "Ursino," Elizabeth, as laid out by Lord Bolingbroke about 1800

The horse-chestnut tree at "Ursino" planted by Miss Livingston in 1771

planted on his newly acquired place. By 1767 the apples were so fine that Livingston sent two barrels of Newtown Pippins to a friend in England.

The horse-chestnut tree in front of the house was planted by Miss Livingston in 1771, two years before Governor Livingston finished the house and moved into it.

In 1772 Alexander Hamilton came from the Antilles and studied with Governor Livingston, going to school to Francis Barber in Elizabethtown, and studying in Governor Livingston's library—what is now the dining-room at Ursino.

In April, 1774, Sarah Livingston was married to John Jay, afterwards Chief Justice of the United States, in the drawing-room at Liberty Hall.

In 1780, during the Revolutionary War, the British raided the house, and tried to get possession of papers which belonged to Governor Livingston. Miss Livingston sat on the box of papers, and they went away disappointed, leaving, however, nicks in the banisters on the staircase which are there to this day.

In May, 1789, Mrs. Washington slept in the house on her way to Mount Vernon. She occupied a bedroom upstairs, which is now very much as it then was.

Governor Livingston died in 1790, after which the house was sold to Mr. Belasis, the name under which Lord Bolingbroke was known in Elizabethtown. He and his lady lived here until 1803, when, on the death of Lady Bolingbroke, they were married in Trinity Church, New York, and returned to England. The lady who had been known as Mrs. Belasis was the Countess von Hompesch, with whom Mr. Belasis had eloped from Germany, where he had passed as an unmarried man. She never knew he was married until after his wife's death.

Mr. and Mrs. Belasis did much to beautify the place. They

"Ursino," photographed from the air

planted many unusual shrubs, and as before said, laid out the garden.

Liberty Hall was sold to Mrs. Niemcewicz about 1803 or 1804. She lived there until her death in 1833, and left it to her grandson, John Kean. When she bought the place Mrs. Niemcewicz changed its name to "Ursino" as a compliment to her second husband, Count Julian Ursin Niemcewicz, a prominent Polish patriot and a friend of Kosciuszko.

During all this occupation, the gardens have always been cultivated. Succeeding generations have worked in and loved the garden at Ursino.

All the old-fashioned roses were in the garden. The rose bushes down the garden walk are offshoots from the original planting.

The lawn is full of narcissus poeticus and daffodils, planted long before anyone now living can remember.

CASTLE POINT, HOBOKEN[1]

The first mention of Castle Point in history is in the diary of the mate of Hendrick Hudson's *Half Moon* which anchored in Weehawken Cove on October 2, 1609. The little party was then trying to make their escape after an attack of the Indians further up the river. In those early days, a small creek connected with the Hudson River to make Hoboken an island.

This island was granted by Governor Stuyvesant in 1663 to a Dutchman named Varlett, the second husband of the Governor's widowed sister, Mrs. Samuel Bayard. She had two children by her first husband who became the ancestors of the Bayard family in the United States. They inherited the

[1]Written by Caroline Bayard Wittpenn (Mrs. H. Otto Wittpenn).

Hoboken property from their stepfather, and it remained in the hands of the Bayard family until the time of the Revolution. William Bayard built a handsome mansion with gardens and orchards at Castle Point. Having been an officer in the King's Army, he decided that he could never fight against his Sovereign, and also that he could not turn against his friends and relatives; so, at the time of the Revolution, he departed rather ignominiously for the West Indies.

In 1780 his house was burnt by a party of patriots, and soon after this the island was confiscated as belonging to a traitor, and became the property of the State of New Jersey. The State decided to sell the island of Hoboken at auction. In 1784, Colonel John Stevens purchased it for some $90,000 and almost immediately built a house on the top of the bluff. This house stood until 1853, when a son, Robert L. Stevens, built the house which is at present in existence.

Castle Point stands on a high, rocky promontory which projects into the Hudson River and from which views extend to the south as far as the Narrows, and to the north as far as Yonkers. The land at the west slopes towards the meadows, which in the old days extended to the foot of the Palisades.

When Colonel John Stevens became the possessor of Castle Point, the land was extremely poor, and the only vegetation consisted of a few scraggly cedar trees. He determined to change his home into a garden spot. He brought from a distance large quantities of good soil, and also planted many trees of various varieties. Unfortunately, these trees have largely disappeared, owing either to the dust and smoke in the atmosphere, or to the fact that their roots may have reached below the good soil.

The flower garden at Castle Point was on the east side, overlooking the Hudson River. There is no record of the

The Stevens house at Hoboken, drawn by W. Birch in 1802. It was built about 1785, and stood until replaced by the present house in 1853

planting in the garden in the eighteenth century, but in the nineteenth century it was laid out in terraces, which are shown in the photograph. The real garden was below the second terrace, and included a border on the extreme eastern side, planted with lilacs, syringa, and other old-fashioned shrubs. Between that and the second terrace there was a large expanse of lawn, broken by beds of flowers. These were laid out in ribbon-like patterns, according to the fashion of the times. Viewed from the upper terrace, their effect was really most attractive. A few flowers for picking were planted along the edge of the second terrace.

Unfortunately, the many demands on the Stevens Institute of Technology, which is the present owner of Castle Point, have made it impossible for the Institute to bear the very great expense of keeping up the greenhouses and gardens. The greenhouses have been torn down, and it is difficult to distinguish the original outline of the garden. The view of the Hudson River is very different from what it was when a beautiful walk skirted the shore of the river, leading past "Sybil's Cave," celebrated by Edgar Allan Poe in the story of "The Mystery of Marie Rôget." Huge docks and great steamers, whose smoke obscures the atmosphere, have taken the place of the picturesque walk which meandered along the river as far north as the Elysian Fields adjoining Castle Point.

THREE OLD GARDENS OF BERGEN COUNTY[1]

Near Hohokus stands the house, marked by the symbols of its English Mason-builders, where dwelt for a time Theodosia Provost, a widow to whom Aaron Burr was paying his court.

The entrance was marked by pointed uprights of sand-

[1]Described by Miss Sarah J. Day, of Englewood.

stone. A stately old black walnut tree still stands, and near it is the long arbor, covered by a wistaria whose branches now travel out, after this century of growth, from a trunk measuring a foot and a half in diameter.

The garden of today, on the site of the old one, lies out in the sunshine beyond the brick-paved wistaria arbor. Poppies and fox-glove and yellow lilies are there, and the bleeding-heart and the pansies and forget-me-nots, as when Theodosia walked down the paths. The ancient syringa bush was there then, but we believe that Theodosia herself may have planted the matrimony-vine which has blossomed year after year ever since.

In 1800 the estate was bought by an uncle of General Rosencrantz. A grand-daughter bearing that name, who lives there today, loving the flowers and ferns, and bringing treasure-trove from the wilds to the old garden, told me these things.

*   *   *

When Washington's troops were encamped on the green before the present courthouse in Hackensack, there stood at a little distance a Dutch-Colonial house. The story is told that one of the General's soldiers, being chased by Hessians, hid himself in a secret recess halfway up the huge chimney.

In the old outer walls you may trace the letters A A (Abraham Ackerman), and the date 1704. Afterwards, a descendant married into the family of the Brinkerhoffs, who came from Holland in 1638, and the house is now known as the Ackerman-Brinkerhoff House, although its rightful name is Linden Hall, from the stately trees about it, trees a century and a half old.

The original garden lay near the house, where ancient white and purple lilacs now bear witness to it. The present gracious owner of the homestead remembers seeing her great-aunt at work among the flowers in that old garden. An aged grape-vine, one of the Isabella variety, also helps to mark the site.

The new garden at Linden Hall has been made in a stretch of ground reclaimed from the marshes, and lies below a terrace bordering the higher levels of the old domain.

*   *   *

When a tribe of New Jersey Indians stole one of the sons

seum at Hackensack) whose deep mark yet remains in the hand-hewn rafters.

Here one finds the distinct remains of a large and once beautiful garden of a stately, formal type. Its great, square enclosure is still surrounded by a stout hedge. Within this an interval of grass had apparently been left, before the flower borders began. The center, we judged, had been occupied by roses —possibly an arbor; beyond these was grass, and then beds

Castle Point, in Hoboken, showing Colonel John Stevens' terraces and gardens of the early nineteenth century, and the house designed by Notman and erected in 1853. It is now the property of the Stevens Institute

of Albert Saborowski (later spelled Zabriskie) who had come to America in 1662, they claimed that they wanted to teach a young white settler their language. In propitiation, apparently, for this high-handed act, they gave the father about two thousand acres of their land in the Paramus Patent. Jakob, the son, returned later well versed in his captors' speech.

Upon these acres one of the Zabriskies made a settlement and home in 1751. A spacious stone-walled barn bears the legend A C Z 1775, and so was finished in time to receive presently the British minie ball (now in the Historical Mu-

in patterns whose borders have left many little tufts of box.

Three magnolia trees were just unfolding their thick, curved petals, ivory-white, with a pinkish tinge, fragrant, and beset by bees. In a corner still grow lilies-of-the-valley whose bells, our cicerone assured us, are double.

Smoke-bushes, wistarias, the inevitable matrimony-vine, still testified to the careful hands that planted them when those boxlines were drawn.

Many of the Zabriskie family are still dwelling in homes near by, although the most ancient homestead has passed into the hands of strangers.

A glimpse down the path through the ancient walls in the garden of The Highlands, the property of Miss Caroline Sinkler, at Ambler, Pennsylvania. The garden is described on page 355

PENNSYLVANIA

John Bartram

1699-1777

The Pennsylvania farmer who became the most important figure in the colonies in botany and horticulture in the eighteenth century. From the portrait by Charles Willson Peale. An account of Bartram's activity is given on page 386.

PENNSYLVANIA

"This fruitful land all plenty doth produce
And never fails to answer human use,
Here yellow Ceres loads the joyful fields,
And golden crops the happy harvest yields."

THIS is the translation of an early Latin poem inscribed to James Logan, William Penn's provincial secretary. And yet, long before the arrival of the mythical Ceres, who presumably accompanied the first white settlers, the land, under the care of the Indian deities, had yielded an abundance to the natives.

A legend of the Lenni Lenapes, the Indian tribe which inhabited the Delaware region, holds that "the Great Spirit descended from the heavens above in the form of a gigantic

that more than a third of the value of all the products raised on the farms of the United States is derived from plants which came to us originally from the Red Man.

Peter Kalm, the Swedish botanist, industriously records in his *Journal* all the information he obtained from the first Swedish settlers in regard to the gardening of the Indians:

"Their hatchets were made of stone. The shape is similar to that of the wedges with which we cleave our wood, about a half a foot long, and broad in proportion; they are made like a wedge, sharp at one end, but rather blunter than our wedges. . . . The chief use of these hatchets was, according to the unanimous accounts of all the Swedes, to make good fields for maize plantations; for if the ground where they in-

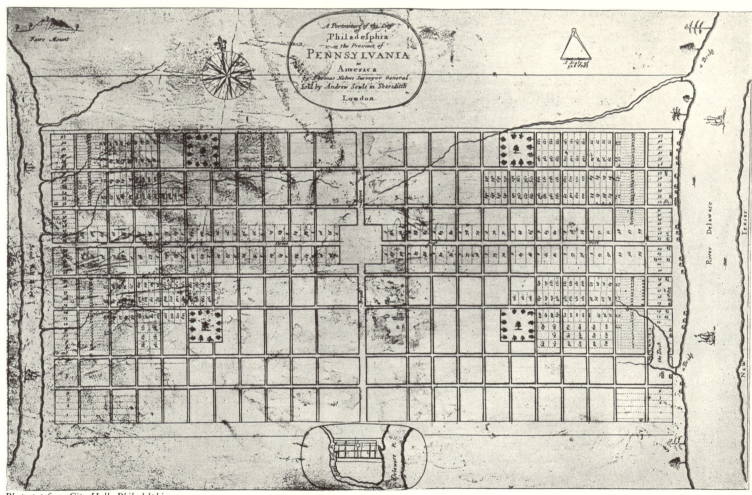

Photostat from City Hall, Philadelphia

The first survey map of Philadelphia, drawn by Thomas Holme in 1683. See page 334

bird and brooded on the face of the waters until the earth arose. Then, exerting the creative power still further, he made the animals, man, and plants."

Thus did the Indians attribute a divine origin to the plants which they cultivated. When America was discovered they were raising maize, beans, and "pompions" or pumpkins, and also "squonter-squash" or squash, and tobacco. They also grew sun-flowers and extracted oil from the seeds. Even at the present time, according to Hodge,[1] we may say

[1] F. W. Hodge, Curator, Museum of the American Indian.

tended to make a maize-field was covered with trees, they cut off all the bark all around the trees with their hatchets, especially at the time when they lose their sap. By that means the trees became dry, and could not take any more nourishment, and the leaves could no longer obstruct the rays of the sun from passing. The smaller trees were then pulled out by main force, and the ground was a little turned up with crooked or sharp branches."

And David Johann Schoepf[1] speaks of the corn-fields:

[1] *Travels in the Confederation.*

"The size of their corn-fields excited astonishment no less than the industry with which they were cultivated. As to both facts an indication is to be had from the statement that troops destroyed corn in the fields to the amount of 160,000 bushels. Still more striking was the number of the fruit trees found and destroyed, and also the size and apparent age of some of their orchards. One time 1500 fruit trees were cut down, and many of them seemed to be very old. To be sure we do not know what varieties these trees were; perhaps the greatest part of them were Indian Plums."

The diversity of the types of gardening in various parts of the state is a reflection of its early colonial history. The Dutch were the first to explore and colonize the region, but gave way before extensive Swedish settlements in the Delaware valley. Later the Dutch, under Peter Stuyvesant, came into dominance again, and most of the prominent Swedish colonists returned to the old country. In 1664 the country became English when Charles II claimed it for his brother James, the Duke of York. In 1681 a large tract was granted to William Penn and was called Pennsylvania in honor of his father, Admiral Penn. In 1682 William Penn established his first colony.

Earlier colonists had been pleased with the new land, and enthusiastic in their reports of its beauty and productiveness. Let us quote[1] from a letter written in 1680 by Mahlon

[1]From Gen. Davis' *History of Bucks County.*

Stacey, who built the first mill on the site of the city of Trenton:

"I have travelled through most of the settled places, and some that are not, and find the country very apt to answer to the expectations of the diligent. I have seen orchards laden with fruit to admiration, planted by the Swedes, their very limbs torn to pieces by the weight, and most delicious to the taste and lovely to behold. I have seen an apple tree from a pippin kernel yield a barrel of curious cider, and peaches so plenty that some people took their carts to a peach gathering. I could not but smile at the sight of it. They are a very delicate fruit, and hang almost like our onions that are tied in ropes. . . . We have from May to Michaelmas great stores of wild fruits—strawberries, cranberries and huckleberries. My brother Robert had as many cherries this year as would load several carts. From what I have observed in this country the fruit trees destroy themselves by the very weight of their fruit."

The foregoing account contradicts Penn's letters to the Society of Free Traders. In these he speaks rather disparagingly of the orchards of the Swedes, as if they had declined to profit by the peculiar fitness of their soils for fruit culture. Yet they must have been the first to naturalize the apple, the cherry, and the peach on the Delaware, and we must give them credit for having anticipated the cherry and apple orchards of eastern Pennsylvania and the Cumberland valley, and the grand peach-tree rows for which the streets of Germantown were famous.

PHILADELPHIA

THE FOUNDING

WHEN William Penn and his followers landed on the shores of the Delaware, Oct. 27th, 1682, bringing with them "all sorts of apparel, utensils for husbandry and building, and household stuff" they found only a few wigwams and about twenty houses in the immediate vicinity. The site which had been selected for the city of Philadelphia was in the midst of a forest, deep but not impenetrable; the size of the trees showed the richness of the soil. There were numerous open park-like areas in which grass grew shoulder-high, furnishing excellent pasturage for the stock of the newcomers.

In the 15th Article of Penn's "Instructions to his Commissioners for settling the Colony of Pennsylvania," he had written:

"Let every House be placed, if the Person pleases in ye middle of its platt, as to the broad way of it, so there may be ground on each side, for Gardens or Orchards or Fields, that *it may be a greene Country Towne, which will never be burnt, and allwayes be wholsome.*"

Arriving in the fall, the settlers were so eager to secure shelter before winter that according to John F. Watson in his *Historic Tales of Olden Times*, some of them dug caves for their first homes. Others, according to Scharf and Westcott, made log cabins, and even primitive lodges such as the Indians used, and so endured the rigors of the first winter.

In the meantime, Penn had not been idle. He wrote to England, "I am now casting the country into townships for large lots of land. I have had an assembly in which many good laws were passed." Then, later: "Philadelphia, the expectation of those concerned in this province, is at last laid out to the great content of those here. Of all the many places that I have seen in the world I remember not one

better seated; so that it seems to have been appointed for a town." And again, in a letter to the Earl of Sunderland in July, 1683:

"I have lay'd out the Province into Countys, Six are begun to be seated, they lye on ye great River and are planted about six miles. The town platt is a mile long and two deep—there is built about eighty houses, & I have settled at least three hundred farms contiguous to it. The Country is in Soyle good, aire serene (as in Languedock) & sweet from the Cedar, Pine and Sarsefrax with a wild mertile which all send forth a most fragrant smell, which every breeze carrys with it to ye Inhabitants when it goes."

That the early settlers had an abundance of fruits, vegetables and flowers very soon after their arrival, the following letter, written in 1683 by Thomas Paskel to J. J. Chippenham in England, will bear witness:

"Our gardens supply us with all sorts of herbs and even some which are not in England. Here are roses, currants, gooseberries, turnips, while carrots and onions are better than those in England, Peaches of three kinds and in such quantity that they let them fall on the ground. . . . They extract from these peaches good spirits—almost every one has a copper boiler in his house.

"There are also pears and apples in great abundance, cherries and apricots, some black and others red, prunes and quinces."[1]

Even under all the stress of laying out a new city, William Penn had time for the appreciation of the native flora. He wrote to Robert Boyle in England:

"Of flowers, I may say, I never saw larger, more variety, or richer colours, in the curious gardens of England. Of them I have ordered my gardener to make a collection against next year."

[1]From *Pennsylvania Magazine of History and Biography*, Vol. VI, No. 3, 1882.

WILLIAM PENN'S LETTERS TO HIS GARDENER

Because of political pressure in England, Penn was unable to remain long in his beloved province. But before he left, construction of his mansion house at Pennsbury had been begun; it was to be quite an elaborate structure surrounded by extensive gardens. After Penn's return to England he carried on an interesting correspondence with his superintendent of construction, and also with his gardener. Extracts from his letters to the gardener show Penn's extreme interest in horticulture, and his desire to make his home in America.

In August, 1684, Penn wrote that he was sending Ralph, his gardener, some walnut trees to set, and some seeds of his own raising, "which are rare good." He urges Ralph to stick to his garden, to get the yards fenced in, and to get doors to them.

Doubtless by this time his grapevines were well established, for they had been sent out with him on his first voyage. He had written to Bordeaux telling his correspondent to send fifteen hundred or two thousand of the vines that bore the best grapes, not necessarily the most.

Later he wrote: "Tell Ralph I must depend on his perfecting his garden—hay dust [hay seed] from Long Island such as I sowed in my court yard is the best for our fields. I will send divers seeds for our gardens and fields. About the house may be laid out fields and grass, which is sweet and pleasant."

Sad news came to him in 1685; he says: "I hear that Ralph is dead." But nothing can deter his gardening spirit. "Let Nicholas then follow the garden diligently and I will reward him." And, "By this ship I intend to send some haws, hazelnuts, walnuts, garden seeds &c."

In another letter he says, "I have now sent a gardener with requisites. Let him have the help of two or three men when needful. He is to have his passage paid and £30 and 60 acres of land at three years, and a month in each year to himself. He is to train me a man and a boy."

And again: "I would have Nicholas have as many roots and flowers next spring by transplanting them out of the woods, as he can.

"Pray let the court-yard be levelled, and the fields and the places about the house be cleanly and orderly kept; so let me see thy conduct and contrivance about grounds and farm accommodations."

He had thought beyond the immediate surroundings of the house. He says: "It would be pleasant to have the old Indian paths cleared up. I would have a walk to the falls, cleared so that two may walk afoot. This fall get twenty young poplars of about eighteen inches round, beheaded twenty feet, to plant in the walk below the steps to the water."

Penn was always appreciative of all that was done for him; he wrote in answer to a report: "I like all that thou hast sent me. I hope they go on with the house and gardens." He then goes on, in the philosophy of the true pioneer:

"I mentioned the kind of outhouses *wanted*. But I know how to shift. I am a man of Providence tost to and fro."

In September, 1685, Penn writes: "I am glad the Indian fields bore so well. Lay as much as you can down with hay dust, and clear away the woods up the river to open a prospect upward as well as downward. Get some wooden chairs of walnut with long backs, and two or three eating tables for twelve, eight, and five persons, with falling leaves to them.

"P. Ford has sent James Reed more trees, seeds, and sciences [scions] which James, my gardener, has here brought. Tell James I would have him lay in a good stock before he parts with anything I send him. I would send free stones for the steps if I had the dimensions. There is gravel for walks that is *red* at Philadelphia near the swamp. Let all be uniform and not *a scu*, from the house. Get and plant as much quick as you can about fields."

In 1686 he writes: "I should like to see a draft of Pennsbury [and so should we!] which an artist would quickly make, with the landscape of the house, outhouses, their proportions and distances from each other. Tell me how the orchards bear. Of what are the outhouses built and how do they stand to the house? *Pray do not let the fronts of the house be common.*"

Penn's interest never waned; again he writes, very evidently thinking of his future home and that of his children: "The trees I sent are choice and costly things, and if I live, and my four children, I shall want enough to transplant to other plantations."

THE RETURN OF WILLIAM PENN

In spite of the constant reports that Penn's agents had sent him, he doubtless was astounded at the growth of his city when he returned to the province in 1699. Gabriel Thomas wrote in 1698: "The Industrious and Indefatigable inhabitants have built a noble and Beautiful City, which con-

The Shippen house, on South Second Street. From a print published before 1800

tains above two thousand houses, all Inhabited and most of them Stately, and of Brick, generally three stories high, after the Mode in London, and as many as several families in each. . . . There are several fine squares and Courts within this magnificent City (for so I may justly call it). As for the particular names of the several streets contained therein, the Principal are as follows—Walnut Street, Vine Street, Mulberry Street, Sassafras Street. Named for the abundance of those trees which formerly grew there."

One cannot resist quoting here also Thomas's comment on the climate, which according to all these old travellers seems to have been a perpetual spring. He says, "The air is very delicate, pleasant and wholesome; the Heavens serene, rarely overcast."

The house of Edward Shippen, to which Penn went while awaiting the completion of his country place, Pennsbury, stood on the west side of Second Street north of Spruce Street. It was called the "Great House," and also the "Governor's House." John F. Watson, in his *Annals of Philadelphia*, says that it was often affectionately called "Shippey's Great House," and that Shippen was distinguished for "the biggest person, the biggest house, and the biggest coach."

Watson also records that the house stood on a small eminence with a row of yellow pines in the rear. Gabriel Thomas, writing at about the time of Penn's arrival, says: "Edward Shippen has an orchard and garden adjoining to his big house that equalizes any that I have ever seen, having a very famous and pleasant summer-house in the middle of his garden, abounding with tulips, pinks, carnations, roses (of various sorts), lilies, not to mention them that grow wild in our fields." *Colonial Families of Philadelphia*[1] says that the spacious lawn, which extended to Dock Creek and on which was maintained a herd of deer, and the orchard of choice fruits were famous in their day.

[1] Edited by John W. Jordan, Lewis Publishing Company, New York and Chicago.

In January, 1700, Penn and his family moved into the Slate Roof House, now known as Letitia House, after Penn's daughter. This house was small but of great individuality. It had extensive gardens enclosed by a high wall, and a commanding aspect. There Penn's son was born, the

Letitia House as it now stands in Fairmount Park

first of his children to be born in America. He was "a comely babe, with much of his father's grace and air," according to Isaac Norris in a letter to a friend in England.

In the spring of 1701 the Penns removed to the manor at Pennsbury. There is no picture of the place in existence, but from contemporary writers we know that Penn spent over £5000 on Pennsbury. The grounds were elaborately laid out, with lawns, vistas, and park-like appointments. We can see that Penn's painstaking instructions to his gardeners had borne fruit. We hear again of the poplars, which were no doubt tulip-trees; they bordered a broad pebble walk which led from the house to the river. Bridges were thrown over Welcome Creek, and steps had been built to a landing and to the boat-house sheltering Penn's barge, which he thought much of, quarreling with his superintendent, Harrison, because the latter used it to transport lime. The gardens and shrubberies were cared for at great expense, gardeners being sent from England for that purpose, as well as all sorts of rare seeds and plants. Trees were transplanted from Maryland, and many wild flowers of the forest were domesticated in the garden. The lawn was seeded with English grasses, and a good deal of the land around it brought under cultivation.[1]

Penn dreamed of settling permanently upon this estate, living there the life of the "lord of the manor." But his wife, and his daughter, Letitia, were ever eager to hurry him away from his rural life in America. They were used to country life, but it was the country life of England, with mansions which looked out on smooth lawns enclosed with hedges of privet and hawthorn, not, as Mrs. Penn may have said, a life on the frayed selvage of the wilderness, with a deep river in front, and behind nothing but insolent bears and wolves and painted savages with scalps hanging at their belts! Mrs.

[1]Scharf and Westcott's *History of Philadelphia.*

Penn and Letitia felt an extreme distaste for colonial life, in spite of the beautifully furnished mansion, surrounded by grounds in which sometimes as many as five gardeners were employed at one time. When, in November, 1701, Penn found it necessary to return to England, his whole household accompanied him.

PUBLIC SQUARES AND GARDENS

The title of the city of Philadelphia to the five public squares within the boundaries of the city, as originally laid out between Vine and Cedar Streets and the Delaware and Schuylkill rivers, derives from a statement made in explanation of a map. If there was a dedication of the ground of the public squares to the use of the city, it was never made by formal warrant or patent.

The earliest known plan is "A portraiture of the City of Philadelphia in the Province of Penna. By Thomas Holme, Surveyor General." The text explanatory of the map says:

"In the centre of the city is a square of ten acres. At each angle are to be houses for publick affaires. There are also in each quarter of the city a square of eight acres, to be for like uses, as the moorfields of London." These statements, made apparently by Holme, are all there is to show that the Centre Square, and the Northeast, Northwest, Southeast and Southwest Squares were dedicated by William Penn to public use. The map is shown on page 331.

CENTRE SQUARE

A meeting house was built on Centre Square. Penn wrote in 1685: "We hope soon to have it up, there being many hearts and hands at work that will do it." How long this meeting-house was in use is not known.

In the following years fairs were held on the square, but about 1698 the "Fair at the Centre" was suppressed.

Centre Square remained without any enclosure for about one hundred years. Gradually the grounds were laid out in circular form, fenced in with wooden pickets neatly painted white. The streets were continued around the enclosure as far north as the line of Filbert Street, and southward to Olive Street. The ground was planted in grass and with trees, and

Wm. Penn's Letitia House (1682-3) on its original site. From an old drawing by W. L. Breton

in 1809 the great attraction of the fountain of the Nymph and Swan was added.[1] It was placed upon a mound of stone in front of the main entrance to the central building.

After the square had ceased to be used as a meeting place by the Friends, it was for many years a mere common, and eventually a race-course. It was also used as a hanging-ground up to the time of the Revolution, and as a training-ground for troops.

In 1829 the name was changed to Penn Square, and Broad

[1]William Rush, sculptor.

Centre or Penn Square, Philadelphia, in 1809

Street and Market Street were carried through the enclosure; numerous large trees were cut down, and the square was thus divided into four small parks, surrounded by picket-fences and having two rows of trees on the sidewalks.

SOUTHEAST OR WASHINGTON SQUARE

This square was first a burying-ground, but this use was discontinued in 1794–5, and the Council ordered that two rows of trees be planted in addition to the row already there. The committee to which the subject was referred made report that in their opinion public walks in a city were very desirable, and therefore the square should be improved.

Before 1816 it was decided that the square should be abandoned as a cattle market, and in 1816 it was resolved that it should be fenced. This was but one step from having it adequately laid out as a public park. The next year George Bridport, artist and engineer, was intrusted with the task of laying out the grounds. Trees were planted, and the place was enclosed with a neat, white, paling fence.

In 1831 a committee of the Horticultural Society of Pennsylvania described Washington Square as follows:

"It is situated south of Walnut and above Sixth Street and contains eight acres. The figure of the whole is as follows: Four diagonal walks, thirty feet wide, leading to a circular spot in the middle, one hundred and twenty feet in diameter. Around this is a walk forty feet wide, and another twenty feet wide intersects the diagonal, making plots thirty feet in diameter, thus forming interesting promenades among fifty varieties of trees, seven of which are European, and forty-three native, a large proportion of which are from distant parts of the Union. Many of the Acers are very handsome trees. Two varieties of Prunus were introduced by Lewis and Clark from the Rocky Mountains. There was also there the Ailanthus and various Pines and Cypress. Hence instruction in regard to our own production is placed before the public, and it is ascertained which trees are best suited to our immediate climate. . . . Recreation is afforded to the assiduous citizen, where he may view four hundred trees in the midst of a populous and busy city. These trees are in a thriving condition, and well-trained by Mr. Andrew Gillespie who is a judicious arborist. The whole is beautifully kept, and well illumined at night with reflection lamps, till ten o'clock, all showing the proper and liberal spirit of our city."

The fountain in Rittenhouse Square in 1852

In 1915 business associations laid out the square on its present lines, planting shrubbery and removing some of the trees.

RITTENHOUSE SQUARE

Rittenhouse Square was originally Southwest Square. It was never used as a burying ground, but from the foundation of the city was a dumping place for street dirt. In 1816 it was fenced. In 1825 it was given the name of Rittenhouse, for David Rittenhouse, the first American astronomer, and Signer of the Declaration of Independence.

In 1852 it was surrounded by an iron fence which has since been removed. At one time three iron fountains were erected, but these are no longer in the square.

LOGAN SQUARE

Logan Square, originally Northwest Square, was named for James Logan in 1825. It was at first bounded by Race,

1837 the square was lighted by gas, and a fine central fountain of marble was built. In 1883 the iron railing was taken down and the grounds were laid out on the plan of Washington Square. This park was originally bounded by Sixth, Race, and Vine Streets, and by the back-ends of Eighth Street lots.

FAIRMOUNT PARK

Fairmount Park began in a humble way. Five acres on the banks of the Schuylkill were first purchased for the enlargement of the city waterworks, and it was not until forty years

A panorama of Philadelphia from the State House steeple, drawn from nature and on stone by J. C. Wild

Vine, Schuylkill Fifth (Eighteenth) and the back-ends of Schuylkill Third (Twentieth), and now contains a little over seven acres. It was once used as a Potter's Field, but by 1842 the mounds had been leveled and an ordinance was passed which read in part that it was an offence punishable by fine for anyone "to climb upon the trees, or to injure the trees or gates in the said squares or to dig up the soil or to injure the grass." Thus we know that by this time Logan Square was under regulation. There was an open paling fence, walks had been laid out, trees planted, and the ground leveled.

FRANKLIN SQUARE

Franklin Square, originally designated Northeast Square, now contains seven acres and three roods.

In 1741, through a warrant issued by Thomas Penn, a portion of it was put to use as a burying ground by the German Reformed Congregation, and it was thus occupied for nearly one hundred years. In 1836 the Supreme Court affirmed the opinion that the land belonged to the city, and some of the bodies were removed.

Park improvements were begun in 1815, by planting trees, sowing grass, and enclosing the ground. The name of the square was changed to "Franklin" in 1825. Improvements had been retarded by possession by the church, but in

later that the idea of a public park was suggested. Then the idea found favor among public-spirited citizens, and the park was created by successive gifts and purchases, eventually spreading over two thousand acres.

The members of the Council who had charge of the construction of the waterworks were fortunately men of taste and discrimination, and after the blasting to make the space for the engine-house was completed, they saw that they had an opportunity for laying out and cultivating a garden, which would be a place of public resort. William Rush, the sculptor, was a member of the committee. When he was appealed to, he brought his figures of the Nymph and the Swan from Centre Square, and placed them on the rocks above the forebay. Later, two other figures by Rush were placed to crown the pediments of the doorways of the wheelhouse.

A pretty garden with grass-plots and trees was planted on the south side of the inclosure, from which steps extended to a paved way lower down, which ran in turn to the dam out in the Schuylkill. Here was constructed a pavilion with seats for the comfort of visitors.

The summit of the sharp acclivity west of the wheel-house was gained by steps and platforms, upon which were resting-places in the form of arbors, from which the most delightful views of surrounding scenery were to be had. The reservoirs

Back of the State House, in Philadelphia. A drawing by W. Birch in 1800

at the top were guarded by an open fence. A path was carried around the mount, which broke away in three terraces upon which shade trees were planted.

These were the Fairmount Gardens when they were opened to the public in 1825. No stranger was allowed to think that he had seen anything of Philadelphia until he was taken to see the Fairmount Water-Works, and this small plot at the southwest limit of the present inclosure was the germ of the Fairmount Park of today.

STATE HOUSE SQUARE

In 1735 the Philadelphia Assembly passed an act that the ground about the State House "shall be enclosed and remain a public green and walk forever."

In 1741 the Assembly ordered that the grounds apportioned to the State House be inclosed by a wooden fence. The brick wall was in an unfinished condition, and some protection was needed before windows could be safely placed in the structure.[1]

One of Caspipina's letters, written in 1771, says, "Mr. F. [Franklin ?] informed me that the plot of ground on which the statehouse stands, and which is one of the squares of the city, is to be planted with trees and divided into walks, for the recreation of the citizens."

In 1785 Col. George Morgan of Princeton presented to the Supreme Executive Council one hundred elm trees, to be planted on the State House Square. This gift was obtained through the influence of Samuel Vaughan of Philadelphia. About the same time a brick wall, some seven or eight feet in height, was built around the inclosure. There was a grand entrance by a central gate on Walnut Street, due south of the State House tower. This portal rose fifteen or

eighteen feet, far above the coping of the wall. It was decorated with a pediment, cornice, entablature and pilasters, beneath which an arched semi-circle in wood, paneled, permitted the narrow paneled wooden gates to open. After this improvement and after growth of the trees, more attention was paid to the decoration of the grounds. Walks were laid out, grass was cultivated, and seats for rest in the shade were placed in various parts of the grounds. The State House Square was really the city's first approach to a little park or square, for though the squares in four parts of the city had been dedicated to public use by Penn in laying it out, they were then under no improvement. The place became a famous resort, and the town poets wrote verses in praise of its rural beauties.

Before planting the square, Vaughan had written to Humphrey Marshall, the botanist, asking him for a list of shrubs and trees, "as it is my wish to plant in the State House Square specimens of every tree and shrub which grows in the several states on this continent."

In 1787 Manasseh Cutler visited the State House Yard. He said it had been laid out but three years, and that the trees were still small, but the walks were well gravelled and rolled hard. He said further that "the painful sameness commonly to be met with in garden-alleys and other works of this kind is happily avoided here, for there are no two parts of the wall that are alike. Hogarth's line of beauty[1] is completely verified."

In January, 1790, the *Columbia Magazine* published the following about State House Square:

"This area, has of late, been judiciously improved, under the direction of Samuel Vaughan Esq. It consists of a beautiful lawn interspersed with little knobs or tufts of flowering shrubs, and clumps of trees, well disposed.

[1]Scharf and Westcott, *History of Philadelphia.*

[1]Simplicity plus variety, William Hogarth's *Analysis of Beauty.*

"Through the middle of the garden runs the spacious gravel walk, lined with double rows of thriving elms, and communicating with serpentine walks which encompass the whole area. These surrounding walks are not uniformly on a level with the lawn; the margin of which, being in some parts a little higher, forms a bank, which in fine weather, affords pleasant seats. When the trees attain to a larger size it will be proper to place a few benches under them in different situations.

"These gardens, if properly attended to, will soon be in a condition to admit of our citizens indulging themselves agreeably in the salutary exercise of walking.

"If the ladies in particular, would occasionally recreate themselves with a few turns in these walks, they would find the practice attended with real advantage."

In 1811 the great brick walls were removed, and in their place was erected a low brick wall, about three feet high, which was coped with marble, with a railing of plain iron palisades, between standards, which resembled three oblong rings on top of each other, and was finished off with a spear point.

The square now appeared more open and attractive than ever from the surrounding streets. A gate of somewhat imposing proportions was fixed on the south, and there were small gates on Fifth and Sixth Streets, about halfway between Walnut and Chestnut.

Watson, in his *Annals of Philadelphia*, says:

"Trees and shrubbery planted in the State House Yard were numerous and in great variety. It soon became a place of general resort. Windsor settees and garden chairs were placed in appropriate places.

"In later years the fine elms planted by Mr. Vaughan annually lost their leaves by numerous caterpillars (an accidental foreign importation), which so much annoyed the visitors, as well as the trees, that they were reluctantly cut down after attaining a large size. . . ."

In 1816 the lot and building were conveyed to the city to be owned by it absolutely.

THE STREETS OF PHILADELPHIA

We may assume that for many years the primeval trees remained standing in some sections of Philadelphia; Sassafras Street, Walnut Street, and Locust Street were named from the trees which once were plentiful in their vicinity. But not until about 1750 do we find any direct mention of street-planting. Then Scharf and Westcott state that "the shade trees which embellished the streets of Philadelphia in those days were the buttonwood and the willow." The Lombardy poplar was introduced from Europe in 1786-7 by William Hamilton.

Watson, in his *Annals of Philadelphia*, says that all the yellow willow in Pennsylvania came from some wicker-work found sprouting in a basket in Dock Creek. It was seen there by Dr. Benjamin Franklin, who took it out and gave the cuttings to the Charles Norris of that day, who in turn reared them at the grounds near the site of the Bank of the U. S., where they grew to great stature.

In 1748 Kalm wrote in his diary: "In most of the streets is a pavement of flags, a fathom or more broad, laid before the houses, and posts put on the outside three or four fathoms asunder." Later, in 1761, we read of a general effort to have all the streets paved.

In the accompanying picture of the Office for Foreign Affairs we see the posts to which Kalm referred, and beside them trees which certainly look like pollarded willows.

In 1821, according to Scharf and Westcott, trees were planted in front of the State House. This planting extended from Fifth to Sixth Street. The trees chosen were ailanthus. In ten or fifteen years the front of the State House in summer was as umbrageous as a forest.

The fire-insurance companies greatly retarded early tree-planting in Philadelphia. One of the first companies adopted this resolution: "No house having a tree or trees planted before them shall be insured or re-insured."

Legislation was then invoked against the objectionable shade-trees and passed by the General Assembly in 1782, only to be repealed a few months later upon the urgent solicitation of tree-lovers. In 1784 there was formed a new company called "A New Society for Insuring Houses from a Loss by Fire." It was stated that a great number of the citizens of Philadelphia found it "agreeable and convenient to them" to have trees planted before their houses, and that this company was being originated in order that this might be permitted. By a curious regulation it was also provided that "all trees planted near houses shall be trimmed every fall in such manner as not to be higher than the eaves of the houses."

The badge or house-mark was a wooden tree on a shield-shaped board, and many of these are still in existence.[1]

PLACES OF PUBLIC RESORT

The first place of public resort fitted up on the plan of the Public Gardens of London was at the Lower Ferry at Schuylkill, known as Gray's Ferry. It was opened to the public shortly after the Revolution, and soon attained a well-merited popularity. Visitors, attracted by the novelty of the thing, were delighted with the tasteful arrangement of the grounds, where shaded walks, beautiful flowers and artistic decorations combined to please the eye, while comfortable boxes afforded places of rest where refreshments of every kind could be obtained. The city poets—the muses have never lacked fervent worshipers in Philadelphia—grew delirious over these beauties, both natural and artificial, and the *Columbian Magazine* more than once admitted into its Poet's Corner "Verses upon Gray's Ferry" and "Lines" and other poetical effusions drawing inspiration from the same source.

Manasseh Cutler in 1788 gives a long and detailed description of Gray's Gardens. For that time they must have presented a remarkable spectacle. Cutler says that there were greenhouses full of tropical fruit, and that the gardens were very large, consisting of detached areas varying in size and form. There were many long alleys, no two alike.

"At every end, side and corner there were summer-houses, arbors covered with vines or flowers, or shady bowers encircled with trees and flowering shrubs, each of which was formed in different taste. In the borders were arranged every kind of flower, one would think, that nature had ever produced.

"At a distance we could see three very high arched bridges, one beyond the other. They were built in the Chinese style, the rails on the side open work of various figures, and beautifully painted.

"We observed a small foot-path; we followed it, and it conducted us along the declivity of a hill which on every side was strewn with flowers in the most artless manner.

"The path directed its course to a stone building over the creek, and at one end there was a fine place for bathing. This building was called the Hermitage. Paths led to an eminence, adorned with an infinite variety of beds of flowers and artificial groves of flowering shrubs.

"On the further side was a fence and a fine view of cascades 70 feet high.

"At the bottom of the Vale is a huge rock, surrounded by tall spruces and cedars. In the top of it is a spacious summer-house. The roof was of Chinese form. It was surrounded with rails of open work and a beautiful winding stair-case led up to it.

"The green-house was quite large, having three stories in front, and two in the rear.

[1] H. D. Eberlein, *Colonial Homes in Philadelphia*, Lippincott.

"This resort was planned by a man by the name of Vaughan, who furnished the owner with an English gardener, who had ten laborers under him."[1]

Gray's Garden ceased to be a place of public amusement about the end of the eighteenth century, although it continued to receive patronage as a place of refreshment. The distance from the city was the principal objection to it, and when equally attractive gardens were established at more accessible points its popularity waned and was gradually eclipsed.

An attempt was made in 1796 by Bates and Darley to establish a popular place of resort at Bush-Hill. For this purpose they leased Andrew Hamilton's mansion with its fine gardens, but their project failed. A few years later, the mansion and grounds were leased to Louzot and Brown, who established there a public ground which they operated profitably.

The Office for Foreign Affairs, showing street planting in Philadelphia in the year 1780

BOTANIC GARDENS AND NURSERIES

Certain nurseries and botanic gardens, although originally established for the cultivation of flowers, trees, and plants, became places of resort in consequence of the elegance of the manner in which they were laid out and the attractions of the gardens and floral splendors.

One of the oldest was that of Daniel Engelman, florist and seedsman. He was a Dutchman from Harlem, Holland, who came to Philadelphia in 1759. At an early date he established his nursery and garden on the north side of Arch Street, between Schuylkill Seventh (Sixteenth) and Schuylkill Eighth (Fifteenth). He was still at his place in 1822. After he relinquished it, about 1826–7, Thomas Smith became proprietor, and reopened it as the Labyrinth Garden.

George Honey, formerly clerk to the County Commissioners, also established a garden at an early period. It was large, containing about six acres and having 495 feet frontage on Race Street, 507 feet on Schuylkill Third, and 556 feet on Schuylkill Second. Thomas Birch, gardener, was established here as early as 1811. John McAran, who for seven years had been gardener for William Hamilton of the Woodlands, and who had laid out and improved Lemon Hill for Henry Pratt, went into business with him as nurseryman, florist and seedsman at the beginning of that year. They remained together until 1822. Birch relinquished the garden about 1824, and it was afterwards kept by August D'Arras.

[1]Manasseh Cutler's *Journal*, 1788.

Another nursery garden was later established by John McAran, who supplied his visitors with strawberries and cream, and fitted out his gardens in a very tasteful style. He built a large high conservatory in which were displayed large plants and trees. His hot-houses were long, spacious, and convenient to walk through. The out-of-door flower beds and the garden, with its little boxes, vines and shrubbery, were all arranged in good taste, and with the occasional display of a rare exotic, and illuminations, the place drew a large and profitable attendance.

McAran's Garden, which contained about four acres, had also a collection of living birds and animals. About 1840 the place became a concert garden and vaudeville theatre.

THE MOYAMENSING BOTANIC GARDENS

The Moyamensing Botanic Gardens, established in 1820 by Alexander Parker, were particularly noted for some box-trees of unusual size which stood near the door. The curious specimens of luxuriant vegetation and horticultural skill were cut and trimmed with fanciful taste so as to represent a square base or pedestal, two or three feet high, upon which rested a huge ball; above this rose a sort of spire, the whole making a very singular figure. Hundreds of visitors came year after year to gaze at these box-trees and wonder how they could preserve the symmetry of their outlines while

This view of the New Market from the corner of Shippen and Second Streets in Philadelphia shows an occasional tree in the streets in 1787

Clarke Hall and Dock Creek, from an early eighteenth-century print

Gardens.' It once filled the eyes and mouths of all passing citizens and strangers, as the nonpareil of the city—say at the period of the Revolution. The low fence along the garden on the line of Third Street gave a full exposé of the garden walks and shrubbery, and never failed to arrest the attention of those that passed that way. The garden itself being on an inclined plane, had three or four falls or platforms. Captain Graydon in his Memoirs speaks in lively emotions of his boyish wonder there, saying of them, 'they were laid out in the old style of uniformity, with walks and alleys nodding to their brothers—decorated with a number of evergreens, carefully clipped into pyramidal and conical forms.' "

THE CARPENTER MANSION

Another interesting garden was made in 1700, when Joshua Carpenter, the brother of Samuel, built a fine mansion on Chestnut Street, between Sixth and Seventh Streets,

perceptibly, albeit slowly, growing larger. The Moyamensing Gardens were on Prime Street (Love Lane) between Eighth and Eleventh Streets. When the extension of the city necessitated the opening of more streets, Tenth Street went through the middle of the gardens, leaving the old house just beyond the line of the sidewalk.

PRIVATE GARDENS AND ESTATES OF PHILADELPHIA

Naturally, the feeling for the improvement of the streets and squares and for the development of public gardens and resorts was only one aspect of the growth of Philadelphia. Good private gardens always keep pace with civic progress. We have now to trace the further development of horticulture through the meagre surviving records of the plans and planting of the grounds surrounding the mansions of Philadelphia and the estates of the suburbs.

CLARKE HALL

In 1694 Mr. William Clarke, a wealthy lawyer, who had been one of the original Council of the Governor in 1682–3, bought a lot at the southwest corner of Third and Chestnut Streets and erected a fine brick house, two stories high, with a double front and a hipped roof. A contemporary drawing of the house and grounds survives, and we find in Watson's *Annals of Philadelphia* a description of the establishment:

"The house was deemed among the grandest in its day; and even in modern times was deemed a large and venerable structure. It was at all times notable for its display and extent of garden cultivation. It occupied the area from Chestnut Street to Dock Creek, where is now Girard's Bank and from Third Street up to Hudson's Alley; the Hall itself, of double front, faced on Chestnut Street...was formed of brick and was two stories high. Its rear or south exposure into the garden, descending to Dock Creek, was always deemed beautiful. In the year of 1704, in consequence of the arrival of William Penn Jun. and [because of] his love of display and expense, James Logan rented and occupied these Clarke Hall premises.

"It was thereafter occupied by some of the earliest governors, and then by Andrew Hamilton, the Attorney General, and at last came into the possession of Israel Pemberton, a wealthy Friend, in whose name the place acquired all its fame in more modern ears as 'Pemberton's House and

The Carpenter mansion, built in 1700

which was at that time a rural spot, remote from what was known as "the city"—one where a citizen might have his country-seat. The grounds were beautifully laid out, and the fruit trees and garden shrubbery for a long time attracted visitors. This house had many associations. Governor Thomas occupied these premises from 1738 to 1747. We are told by Watson that the Governor's amiable lady endeared herself to the young folk by indulging the pretty misses with bouquets and nosegays on May-day, and permitting the boys to help themselves from his fine cherry trees.

At one time the celebrated Mrs. Ferguson, the poetess, granddaughter of Sir William Keith, lived there with her father, Dr. Graeme.

The Carpenter mansion changed hands several times. Finally it became the property and residence of Judge Tilghman, who sold it to the Arcade Company in 1826.

THE CHARLES NORRIS MANSION

One of the handsomest dwellings in the city was that of Charles Norris, erected in 1750, in Chestnut Street, between Fourth and Fifth. A full description of it from the pen of the late Charles A. Poulson records that "in the rear of the kitchen and the house keeper's room, and facing south, was the greenhouse, which contained the best collection of exotics in the province at that period. It was well contrived, for the entrance into its stove was in the corner of the kitchen chimney, and a few hunks of hickory wood put into it betimes prevented any danger from the cold."

We are informed that "the whole house with its balconies and piazzas, was in its appearance altogether singular, and in its days of splendor, with its ample lot extending to Fifth Street, and garden undiminished, was really a beautiful habitation." The account continues:

"The garden yet remains to be described—a spot of elegance and floral beauty. It was laid out in square parterres and beds, regularly intersected by graveled and grass walks and alleys, yet some of the latter were so completely hid by the trees by which they were bordered as to be secluded and rural. A green bank, with flights of stone steps, led the way into the garden, and a profusion of beautiful flowers and shrubs first met the view. The western part was more irregular, and contained on a high dry spot, facing the south, and defended from the north by a high board fence, the hot-beds and seed-house, and led to a very shaded walk, reaching to the extremity of the grounds, with vines covering the fence of the very finest sorts of grapes, and hid on the other side from the rest of the garden by a continuance of espaliers of the finest kind and in the most flourishing condition, and this walk opened into a little spot, separated by a slight railing, and through this path led to a gate opening into the yard of a cottage, which was the residence of the gardener. It was a charming little retirement, and so secluded and quiet it might have been thought to belong to a remote village, although the fence of its enclosure fronted on Fifth Street.

"The garden was plentifully stocked with the finest fruits. An old Swiss gardener was employed in it for over a quarter of a century, and one of the peculiarities of the family was the long time that the same faces composed its household. The coachman lived there as long as the gardener, for in fifty years the family had but two."[1]

Sarah Butler Wister in *Worthy Women of the First Century*, says that the residence with its tiers of piazzas and beautiful garden was more like a villa than a town house. "There were green-houses and hot-houses," she writes, "among the products of which, most unusual for that day, were pine-apples."

Watson also records that the whole front was formerly a garden fence, shaded by a line of remarkably big catalpa trees, and down Fifth Street by yellow willows.

THE BINGHAM MANSION

George Hazlehurst, in *A Part of Old Philadelphia*, is authority for the following:

"About the year 1790 William Bingham built his famous house on Third Street above Spruce. It was designed after the ducal palace of the Duke of Manchester in Manchester Place, London, and no such residence existed anywhere in this country. Its gardens extended to Fourth Street, and along Third Street to the south about half a square. . . . The second floor was reached by a marble stairway wide enough to hold plants and flowers on each side on gala occasions."

Watson in his *Annals* elaborates the description:

"The grounds were laid out in beautiful style, and filled with curious and rare trees; but in the usual selfish style of

[1] From Watson's *Annals of Philadelphia*.

"A Map of Philadelphia and Parts Adjacent" in 1750. Drawn by N. Scull and G. Heap

Graeme Park, near Philadelphia. The house was built in 1722. In 1755 it was the center of a 300-acre tract, 150 acres of which had been cleared of all but tall trees and good young timber, harrowed, sowed in grass, brushed, rolled, and enclosed by a double ditch and double hedge

Philadelphia improved grounds the whole was surrounded with a painted board fence and a close line of Lombardy poplars.

"The house was approached by a circular carriage way of gravel, the access upon both sides of which opened by swinging gates of iron open tracery. A low wall, with an elegant course of baluster upon it, defended the immediate front. The grounds about the house, beautifully diversified with walks, statuary, shade trees and parterres, covered not less than three acres. . . . Its entrance was not raised at all, but brought the visitor by a single step upon the wide pavement of tessellated marble. Its self-supporting broad stairway of fine marble—the first of that description, probably ever known in America—leading to the second story, gave a truly Roman elegance to the passage."

COUNTRY ESTATES NEAR PHILADELPHIA

As Philadelphia grew and became crowded, wealthy citizens began to develop country estates.[1] Thanks to a series of drawings by William Birch, many of which are reproduced in these pages, we have an almost photographic representation of some of the best known country-seats of the eighteenth and early nineteenth centuries. In the preface to his work, Birch says:

[1]Eberlein says: "Many of these country places called 'plantations' were exceedingly unpretentious, for two reasons, first because Philadelphia was still small, and second because of the prejudice against sleeping in the country, for fear of the 'humours' rising from the soil."

"The comforts and advantages of a Country Residence, after domestic accommodations are consulted, consists more in the beauty of the situation than in the massy magnitude of the edifice. The choice ornaments of Architecture are by no means intended to be disparaged, they are on the contrary not simply desirable, but requisite. The man of taste will select his situation with skill, and add elegance and animation to the best choice."

In the early years of the nineteenth century, Sutcliff[1] recorded that "on the banks of the Schuylkill as far as the eye can command one wide spreading Forest was seen, interspersed with farms and sheets of water, which have a little the appearance of lawns and fish-ponds, such as are seen about the seats of our nobility; but upon a scale exceeding all comparison."

This is verification of an earlier statement by Andrew Burnaby, also an English traveler, who wrote in 1759: "I ferried over the Schuylkill, about three miles below Philadelphia; from whence to the city the whole country is covered with villas, gardens and luxuriant orchards."

GRAEME PARK[2]

Governor Keith purchased Graeme Park in 1718. The land lay nineteen miles out of Philadelphia, seeming in that time quite out in the wilderness. It was totally unimproved. The first house was built in 1722, as is shown by a wrought-iron weathervane which bears that date.

[1]Sutcliff's *Travels in North America*, 1804, 1805, 1806.
[2]Thomas Allen Glenn, *Some Colonial Mansions*, Coates and Co., Philadelphia.

In 1737 Lady Keith parted with all interest in Graeme Park to her son-in-law, Dr. Thomas Graeme.

In a letter to Thomas Penn, dated 1755, Dr. Graeme says: "I have endeavored to make a fine plantation. . . . I have a park which encloses 300 acres. . . . It is very good soil—there is now about 150 acres of it clear of shrubs and bushes, only the tall trees and good young sapling timber standing. This I harrow, sow it in grass seed, then brush and roll it. . . . It would have been one of the finest parks for deer that could be imagined. I have double-ditched and double-hedged it in, and as a piece of beauty and ornament to a dwelling I dare venture to say that no nobleman of Europe but would be proud to have it as his seat."

Graeme Park was sold in 1791 by Mrs. Ferguson, daughter of Dr. Graeme, to Dr. Wm. Smith, who sold it to Samuel Penrose.

In front of the old mansion, at about 40 yards' distance, are two great sycamores. They indicate what was in colonial

"The spacious lawn in front is remarkable for being the place of the celebration of the memorable grand procession and fête, on the Fourth of July, 1783, occasioned by the adoption of the Constitution of the U. S. from which event it has obtained the name of Union Green."

BELMONT

Belmont (1745) is one of the old mansions which have been preserved in Fairmount Park. It was the residence of Judge Peters, one of the Founders of the Philadelphia Society for Promoting Agriculture, the first Agricultural Society in America. He was also the first Secretary of War in the young republic.

The surroundings of the mansion were very beautiful. The French traveler, Chastellux, said it was the most charming spot nature could embellish. The garden had clipped hedges, pyramids, obelisks and balls of evergreens and spruce.

"*The Seat of William Hamilton Esq., near Philadelphia,*" a drawing which appeared in the "*New York Magazine.*" The mansion of Bush-Hill, erected by Andrew Hamilton in 1740, has long since disappeared. Note the poplars, said to have been introduced by William Hamilton

days the main approach to the courtyard, where a gateway once existed. Near by is the great "lifting-stone" of Governor Keith. This is a boulder dressed by the stone-cutter into a shape much resembling a mushroom, which Sir William required all applicants for work to lift.

BUSH-HILL

The *New York Magazine* for 1793 speaks of the estate of Bush-Hill.

"The high and beautiful situation of Bush-Hill is perhaps not exceeded by any seat in the vicinity of Philadelphia. It commands a very extensive and grand prospect of some miles around, including the whole city, and the river Delaware and the Schuylkill for a considerable distance above and below the city."

The house at Bush-Hill was erected by Andrew Hamilton in 1740. The estate was a portion of Springettsbury Manor, and contained 153 acres.

The *New York Magazine* continues: "This once elegant villa has not yet recovered from the state of almost total demolition which it suffered from the hands of an inveterate enemy. The gravel walk, and the delightful grove of cedar trees, remain entire. There are also several fine statues of marble still standing.

The *Architectural Record* has printed a restored plan of Belmont, which is here reproduced. Mary G. Kimball writes: "The gardens of Belmont were quite as celebrated as the mansion house. Few others of the period were as elaborately laid out, and there are only one or two instances, such as Mount Airy in Virginia, where sculptured figures are known to have been used as a feature of the garden. Contemporary descriptions mention a Chinese temple and a handsome summer house as objects of interest in the garden, and name the figures of Fame, Mercury, and Diana as the subjects of the sculpture."[1]

Judge Peters had a reputation for wit and repartee, and though he was so intensely interested in the development of agriculture and horticulture, his estate was often neglected. On being reproached for this negligence, he replied:

"How can you expect me to attend to all these things when my time is so taken up telling others how to farm?"

A visit was paid to Belmont on November 15, 1819, by the interesting Deborah Logan. She gives a charming picture of the estate in the hands of Judge Peters:

"The venerable possessor of Belmont judiciously abstains from altering what his predecessors left him. Modern improvements may be furnished by lately acquired wealth, but

[1] "The Revival of the Colonial," by Mary G. Kimball, the *Architectural Record*, July, 1927.

Mount Pleasant, the mansion built by John McPherson on the banks of the Schuylkill in 1761. It was at one time the property of Benedict Arnold

stately trees planted by your ancestors, the furniture they used, and the plate that served them, convey quite different ideas from shrubs and Lombardy poplars, furniture from a fashionable wareroom, or a rich service from Fletcher and Gardiner's. . . .

"But the garden is quite a curiosity from exhibiting a most perfect sample of the taste of Parterres and arbours made of Yew clipped into forms, and beyond this a long avenue of hemlocks, planted close, and arched above, is really very fine, and likewise some trees of the same kind to south of what was formerly a wilderness, very large, and covered to their tops with the finest Ivy which I ever saw; one of them

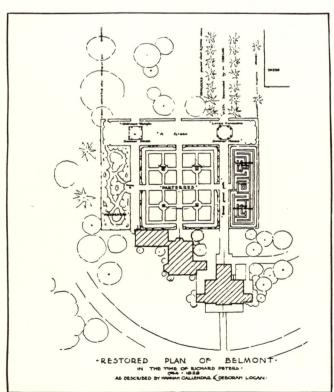

From the "Architectural Record," July, 1927

A restored plan of Belmont as it was in Judge Peters' lifetime

is dead, and the Ivy makes it a vegetable column. . . . But it would be unjust and ungrateful to quit Belmont without noticing the beauty of the Prospect—the Delaware far below it, and the Schuylkill in beautiful breaks at near view. . . ."[1]

MOUNT PLEASANT

That the beauty of Mount Pleasant, now preserved in Fairmount Park, was widely recognized in colonial days is attested by the words of John Adams who dined there in 1775. He said of John McPherson, the founder of the estate: "He has the most elegant seat in Pennsylvania, a clever Scotch wife, and two pretty daughters."

The place later was sold to Benedict Arnold, and by him was settled as a marriage gift on his beautiful bride, the heiress Peggy Shippen, daughter of Edward Shippen, the subsequent Chief Justice of Pennsylvania. When Arnold's treason became known, the State confiscated the life-interest which he had retained in the property. He never himself occupied it, and the name of "The Arnold Mansion" which the house acquired in the nineteenth century is therefore a misnomer.

We quote from an existing description of the grounds in their present state of preservation:

"The house stands well off the highway, and the approach is through a long driveway lined with trees.

"From the lawn surrounding the house, bordered by old lilacs, three terraces descend westward toward the river. Following the old custom, the first of these has been devoted to annuals, in formal beds, bordered with box, the second to perennials in borders, the third to a rose garden. Old-fashioned flowers and varieties have everywhere been used in the replanting. In the center a long gravel path slopes across the terraces, continued doubtless, in the old days, to the river. Across it at the end of the formal garden we may imagine such a Chinese temple for a summer house as Hannah Callender saw in 1762 at Belmont, just across the river. Old trees stand all about. Here, as inside the house,

[1]From the original manuscript letter of Deborah Logan in the possession of the Pennsylvania Historical Society.

all is symmetry, and the spirit of the eighteenth century is summed up not only by the details, but by the general mastery of form."[1]

THE GRANGE

According to H. D. Eberlein, in 1682 Henry Lewis built a substantial stone house on Cobb's Creek, old Haverford Road, Haverford Township. It was far enough from the city to receive the title of "Grange," which was given to it in 1780.

About 1761 Captain Charles Cruickshank, a Scotch gentleman of wealth, purchased the estate. He had a strong bent for gardening, for it was at this period that terraced walks were cut, and the greenhouses and hothouses established and the "natural beauties of the place developed by the appliances of art."

The landscape gardening begun by Captain Cruickshank and continued by succeeding owners has given the Grange a position in this respect unexcelled in all the surrounding country.

Miss Elizabeth Miflin, a grand-daughter of John Ross, gives a description of the Grange, written about 1830:

"Nothing could be more picturesque, beautiful and elegant than this highly favored spot. The gardens, the fountains, the Bath in a private garden with walks skirted with boxwood and the trumpet creeper in rich luxuriance overhanging the door and gateways, where the water was so intensely cold that few entered in. The Green houses and Hot houses, the Dairy, the extensive orchards of every variety of fruit; and then the long dark walk seven-eighths of a mile in extent, shaded by tall forest trees, where the tulip poplar abounded, and where the sun scarcely dared to penetrate.

"Near the beginning of this dark walk Mr. Ross had caused to be constructed, on a spot ten or twelve feet above the walk a seat capable of holding twenty persons and a place

[1]From a booklet copyrighted by the Pennsylvania Museum and School of Industrial Art.

for a table. On the Fourth of July and other warm days of summer he would take his friends there and iced wine would be served. . . .

"No roses or honeysuckle were so beautiful as those from the Grange; no strawberries and Cherries, no pears, peaches, apples and quinces so fine. The place was in the highest state of cultivation . . . and really nothing was left undone to contribute to the beauties and luxuries with which the Grange abounded."

The Grange represents more than a century of growth in the garden.

On every hand great box trees attest the age of the place and the lilacs and syringas grown into trees proclaim the lapse of many summers since they were set out.

SOLITUDE

On the banks of the Schuylkill was the home of Governor John Penn, built in 1789.

William Birch made a drawing of it. We quote the description which he added:

"Here a pleasing solitude speaks the propriety of the title. Upon further research the solitary rocks and the waters of the Schuylkill add sublimity to quietness. The house is built with great skill for a bachelor by the former Governor John Penn since the Revolution."

To this may be added a reproduction of the plan of the estate and the following description[1]:

". . . formality is not wholly banished from the neighborhood of the house. It possessed a circular-ended fore-court, and utility was observed by the thoughtful provisions of bowling green and kitchen garden. The flower garden was distant from the house, reached by a circuitous path which took in as many as possible of the best points of view. For one stretch, where it borders the property, it is flanked by the

[1]From the *Architectural Record*.

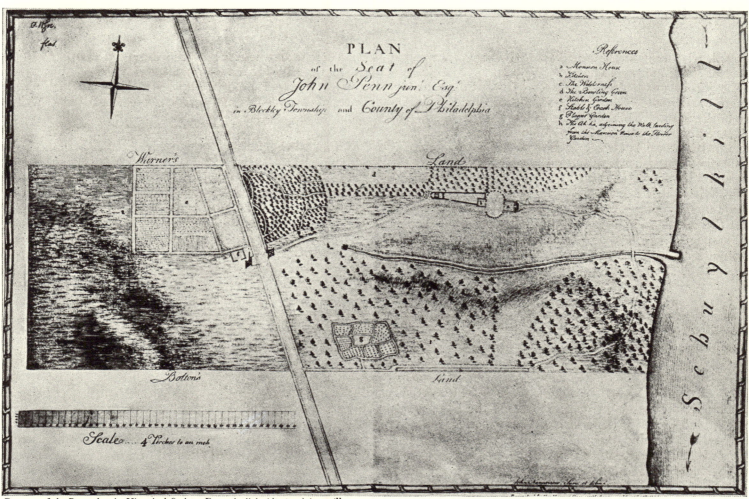

Courtesy of the Pennsylvania Historical Society. From the "Architectural Record"

The original plan of the gardens of Solitude

ha-ha or sunk fence, which since the time of Bridgeman had been the familiar type of barrier in the English landscape garden."

"TOCKINGTON"[1]

The ownership of the land on which "Tockington" is situated dates back to an original grant from William Penn to John Barnes and Sarah Fuller in 1684. Soon, after various transfers of land, John Barnes became the owner of all of Abington Township, and later donated one hundred acres of his land for a Friends' Meeting House, which was built in 1700.

In 1689 part of this tract of land was bought by John

In 1900 extensive repairs were made, restoring the whole building to the colonial type of architecture.

The gardens have remained unspoiled throughout the many changes, each owner respecting the excellent form of the original planting.

PENCOYD[1]

Pencoyd (1791), one of the oldest of the colonial homes which surround Philadelphia, is in the section called the Welsh "Barony" which was settled by Quakers from Wales before 1700. William Penn gave the original grant of one hundred and fifty acres in 1683 to John Roberts, and the land has remained in the same family for eight generations.

W. Birch's drawing of Solitude

Worrell, who built the house called "Tockington," naming it for his wife's ancestral village in Wales.

The garden was laid out in 1740, for at that date the box hedges were brought from England. These hedges now form one of the most charming features of the old garden.

There are other plants of interest there; the old pear trees are the tallest we know of. These trees make a boundary at the foot of the garden, and on a winter's afternoon the unusual form shown in the tracery of their upper branches against the red and gold of sunset makes a picture which arrests the attention of the most casual visitor.

At the end of the garden is a twenty-foot hemlock hedge, and another tall gnarled pear tree. There are unusually large specimens of larch, ash, beech, tulip and buttonwood trees on the lawn. The huge cherries beside the tennis court, dying now alas, are the marvel of arboriculturists.

The remnants of a long avenue of Norway spruces mark the original driveway from Washington Lane, the only road in early days by which "Tockington" and the Abington Meeting could be reached.

In 1896 Mr. David Newport, then seventy-four years old, told us that as a little boy he had often stayed at "Tockington" and that his mother had often reminded him that his three-year-old hands had helped to plant the huge maple trees behind the house. Another of his memories is playing hide-and-seek around the hedges of box where four generations of children have since played.

"Tockington" eventually came into the hands of William West Frazier, the second. His son of the same name has lived there ever since.

[1]Written by Mrs. William West Frazier, the owner of the garden.

There are traditions in the family of a very old garden, but all that now remains is one old brush box tree about twelve feet high, which probably marked the corner of a small formal garden with box-bordered paths and beds.

The present garden was laid out about 1830. It consists of a formal plot about forty feet wide and one hundred feet long, bordered now by a California privet hedge, trimmed fairly low and narrow. The plot itself is then divided into circles and curved beds, edged with box, now three feet high and two feet thick. This box is supposed to have come from the old garden and is therefore over one hundred years old. The beds are planted with old-fashioned flowers.

There is a large stone barn near the house and in its gable is the date 1791. A stone spring-house, over two hundred years old, lies at the slope of the lawn at the foot of a small wood. Large buttonwoods are scattered over the five acres of open lawn. The planting follows no formal plan, the whole place giving the impression of the homelike simplicity of a colonial homestead.

THE WOODLANDS

Among the best known estates of the early nineteenth century was that of William Hamilton. Through records, and the letters of Hamilton written while abroad to his secretary and recently published in the *Magazine of the History of Pennsylvania*, we get a glimpse of the estate of a country gentleman of that time. We have also an excellent drawing of the mansion by William Strickland.

[1]Adapted from an account by Mrs. David E. Williams.

The garden of "Tockington," in Jenkintown, the property of Mrs. William West Frazier

The first Andrew Hamilton had purchased from Stephen Jackson a large piece of ground in Blockley township, west of the Schuylkill, near and south of Market Street, and extending down to the Naganesy (or Mill) Creek. He devised the property to his son Andrew, who, dying six years afterward, devised it to his son, William Hamilton. The property was called "The Woodlands". A comfortable house was torn down sometime before the Revolution, and a magnificent mansion was built on the site. The following description of the grounds of this mansion was written in 1830:

"The grounds are in extent about ten acres, and contain

would be impossible to find a more agreeable situation than the residence of Mr. W. Hamilton."

William Pursh, the botanist, lived at the Woodlands from 1802 until 1805, and introduced plants from all parts of America.

LETTERS OF WILLIAM HAMILTON TO HIS SECRETARY[1]

When William Hamilton visited England, soon after the establishment of peaceful relations with that country, he was so impressed with the pleasing effects resulting from the taste-

Drawn by Wm. Strickland

"The Woodlands near Philadelphia the Seat of Wm. Hamilton Esqr."

a variety of indigenous and exotic plants and trees, chosen for their foliage or fragrance and the scene is diversified by land and water in a very tasteful manner. A winding walk leads through the shrubberies and copses. At one spot there is a charming prospect of the city, at another a large expanse of water is visible. At the descent is seen a creek, overhung with rocky fragments and shade by the gloom of the forest. Ascending from thence the greenhouse appears in view, the front of which, including the hothouse on each side, measures one hundred and forty feet, and contains nearly ten thousand plants. There is surely no city on the continent in whose vicinity more beautiful country-seats can be found than in the vicinity of Philadelphia, and among these the Woodlands are conspicuous for their taste and elegance. The admirers of rural beauty may here find many objects to arrest their curiosity and to invite their observation."

Michaux, who visited Philadelphia in 1802, speaks especially of the collection of exotics at the Woodlands:

"The absence of Mr. W. Hamilton deprived me of the pleasure of seeing him; notwithstanding I went into his magnificent garden, situate upon the borders of the Schuylkill, about four miles from Philadelphia. His collection of exotics is immense, and remarkable for plants from New Holland, all the trees and shrubs of the United States, at least those that could stand the winter at Philadelphia, after having once removed from their native soil; in short it

ful arrangements of shrubbery, shade- and fruit-trees, or in other words, with the natural style of landscape-gardening then coming into fashion, that he wrote, "I shall if God grants me a safe return to my own country, endeavour to make it smile in the same useful and beautiful manner."

Having, therefore, the inclination as well as the means, and being well versed in botany and horticulture, he set to work, on his return, to beautify the grounds of his home at the Woodlands, and allowed no opportunity to pass of adding to his collection of native and exotic plants. Captains of sea-going vessels, friends about to go abroad, and correspond-

[1]From the *Pennsylvania Magazine of History and Biography*, Volume XXIX, January, 1905:- "Some Letters from William Hamilton, of the Woodlands, to his Private Secretary," by Benjamin H. Smith.

From "Colonial Architecture for Those About to Build," by Wise and Beidleman; J. B. Lippincott, Philadelphia

The old colonial barn of the Woodlands provides an excellent model for a garden house

ents in all parts of the world were appealed to for plants, seeds, and cuttings, so that in course of time the Woodlands became famous, not only for the extent and variety of its plants, but also as the best specimen of landscape gardening in the country.

These results were alone attained by the intelligent care and personal supervision of Mr. Hamilton, and naturally, whenever he was called from home by business or pleasure, he was much concerned about the welfare of his valuable collections. This anxiety is very apparent in numerous letters to his secretary, from which the following have been selected, not only as touching upon interesting events of the period, but especially as serving incidentally to record the names of various exotics introduced for the first time to this country, of which only the Lombardy poplar and the curious Ginkgo, from China, have heretofore been credited to Mr. Hamilton.

Only one specimen of the Ginkgo, now the oldest tree of that species in America, still remains in the vicinity of the old mansion; near by are four large trees of *Zelkova crenata*, from the Caucasus, now in their old age, and these, with a few ancient English hawthorns, alone remain to attest the ancient glory of the gardens and grounds at the Woodlands.

Oct. 8, 1784 (Extract).

When you go to Dr. Logan's[1] place, you should ask him for all the seeds he can spare of the pavia. Sow a dozen or two in a warm place & send the rest to me. I desired Bartram[2] to make me up some seeds & gave him a list; they should be asked of him and forwarded.

St. James St., London.
Sept. 30th, 1785.

Dear Sir

. . . For a great while I have wanted to write to you, but from the number of letters I have always had to prepare when any opportunity has offered & a multiplicity of other engagements I have been constantly disappointed in my Intentions. What you have mentioned respecting the plants I sent from hence, gives me satisfaction. I am in hopes they continue to thrive. In consequence of your promise I expected before this to have been furnish'd with a more particular account of their succeeding state, which would have enabled me to supply whatever vacancies may have happen'd by death or otherwise. I flatter myself such a statement of them is on its way hither & will shortly reach my Hands. I shall be at a loss to know what to do in the matter the winter being the best season for transporting plants. I was so particular as to directing you & Mr. Thomson as to the manner of treating those already sent, & you seemed so well to understand me that I can hardly suppose that they have been in any way neglected. I take it for granted that they have not wanted *shade* during the summer nor will go without *shelter* (where necessary) in the coming winter, on which their safety will ultimately depend. When it is recollected how vast has been the expence & trouble of procuring them, I dare to say that no method will be unessay'd that may be proper for their security. . . . To take time by the forelock, every preparation should *immediately* be made by Mr. Thomson who is on the spot, & I have no doubt you will assist him to the utmost of your power. The first thing to set about is a good nursery for trees, shrubs, flowers, fruits etc. of every kind. I do desire therefore that seeds in large quantities may be directly sown of the *white flowering Locust*, the sweet or *aromatic Birch*, the *Chesnut Oak, Horse chesnuts, Chincapins, Judas trees, Dogwoods, Hallesia, Kalmias, Rhododendrons, Magnolias, winterberries, arrow wood, Broom, annonas, shrub St. Johns wort* &c. of crabs, quinces, plums & a quantity of *thin shell'd almonds,* & such others as may occur to you for Beauty or use. I desire also that a large quantity may be collected & put into a nursery of handsome small plants of Elm, Lime, Locust, sweet Birch, white pine, ash-leaved maple, sugar maple,

aspen poplar, Zantoxylon or tooth ache tree, magnolia, arrow wood, nine Bark, cephalanthus or dwarf Buttonwood, Azalea, Kalmia, Rhododendron, Hallesia, Judas tree, Dogwood, Broom, winterberry, clethra, mezerion, morelloes, black Hearts, crabs, quinces (for stocks), raspberries, currants, white and red & and as many as possible of Jasmine & Honey suckles (Jasmines may be had in plenty at Mr. Ross's place & at Woodford and Honeysuckles may be had in great quantities at Mrs. Lawrence's near Frankford & of Dr. Joseph Redman.) Too many of these cannot be propagated. I would likewise have cuttings put into the ground of ye striped althea, Lombardy poplar (if alive) all the kinds of grapes that have throve of those I sent, chicasaw plum, winter haws, Jasmines, Honeysuckles, of that kind of Dogwood that grows in the border on the south side of the kitchen garden on the other side of the valley (which was propagated by cuttings from the only tree which I ever came across, & grows on the point just within the creek's mouth at high water mark & may be easily discovered when in bloom by its corymbous flowers) of paradise apples,[1] red & white currants (particularly the latter) the common raspberry & the twice bearing if it succeeded. Nor should a plantation be neglected of the different hardy perennial plants such as Yuccas, cornflag [Gladiolus] lilie, white narcissus (double and single), pinks, double sweet william, Lychnidea . . . french Honeysuckle, Foxglove, Lily of the Valley (from Bush Hill). . . . Paeonies, Columbines, Hollyhocks, polyanthos, Jonquils (from Bush Hill) Hyacinths &c. I before expressed a desire to have Double oleander & double myrtle encreased as much as possible by cuttings & I would have you in the spring when the azaleas are in flower take particular pains in marking the different kinds & the orchis roots (in the valley) in such a manner as they can be transplanted according to the growth & color. If the season is past for marking the double convolvulus don't let the ground be disturbed until they can be taken care of. The Grape cuttings I sent out last spring are of the most valuable kinds. I saw this season produced on the vines from whence came some of them were taken Bunches of half a yard long, weighing between six and seven pounds. Too much pains cannot be taken to preserve & encrease from them as well as the vines that accompanied them.

I have been frequently pleased in this country with the effect of Ivy in certain situations especially when growing over Buildings and Arches. Suppose you were to plant half a dozen young ones on the east side of the new Bridge over the mill-creek? I dare say no objection would be made by the owner of the ground, for it could do no injury. I recollect giving Mr. Thomson some curious pine seeds that I brought from Lancaster. Ask & let me know what became of them. There was a good deal of asparagus from seed coming forward, when I left home which I trust has before this been put in train for producing crops. I am moreover anxious to know how the perennials of ev'ry kind & annuals have come on. Such of the perennials as have taken, should be transplanted at proper distances and the remainder of the annuals sown early in the spring as well as that of the perennials. Pray were the annuals very fine? What says Madam McCall to them? By the way, *fail not* to make my affectionate compt[s]. to her, altho I bear her a grudge for leaving the Woodlands, I have a very sincere regard for her.

I have great satisfaction in your information respecting the Illinois nut plant[2] and winter Haw. I am afraid to suppose the Bald Cypress has stood it out, for it appear'd a year ago at its last gasp. The Aphernously pines[3] should be particularly attended to. For another plant cannot be obtained in

---

[1]Dr. George Logan, of Stenton.
[2]William Bartram, the botanist.

[1]The tomato, or love-apple, was then cultivated in Spain and Italy for use as a salad, and also as a sauce for soup and meats. Mr. Hamilton mentions it in connection with his kitchen garden plants, and doubtless understood its culinary merits, although it did not come into common use as a vegetable for more than forty years later.
[2]The pecan. In a letter to Humphrey Marshall, May 3, 1799, Mr. Hamilton mentions this tree as "the only one I had which I raised 25 years ago from seed."
[3]*Pinus cembra*, or Swiss stone-pines.

Andalusia, the estate of Mrs. Charles Biddle, as it stands today among its beautiful old trees

England. Those I sent came from the Alps. Altho hardy in respect to cold they may be injured by vermin, poultry &c. &c.

The plants you mention to have sent by Mr. Hill are curious & should not be neglected. Those you describe (as like the Solomons seal) are I imagine of the genus Ruscus. I desired him to secure me some of them from Madeira.

*   *   *   *
*   *

When I sat down to write I did not expect to get further than thro one & I have nearly finished three sheets. So many things have occur'd more than I had any Idea of that I am amazed when I look at what I have written, which I hope however is sufficiently plain in its rough state for you to comprehend as I cannot think of copying it. I have scarce left more room than to conclude with desiring you to accept my sincerest regards & and that you will believe me truely

Your affectionate friend & humble serv^t
W. HAMILTON.

ANDALUSIA[1]

The name Andalusia was given to this place by John Craig, a wealthy merchant, who bought the ground and in 1794–5 built the main portion of the house for a summer residence for his wife and only daughter; the latter afterwards became Mrs. Nicholas Biddle.

The stairway and door of the house are representative of colonial architecture of the south, the residence having been erected about ten years after Washington rebuilt Mount Vernon.

The name Andalusia was selected by Mr. Craig because of his admiration for the Spanish province of that name, and because he had trade with that country. And as it was shortly after the erection of Andalusia that the garden was laid out, the box hedges must therefore be over a hundred years old.

Nicholas Biddle, who married Miss Craig, developed an early interest in agriculture, and before public duties called him to town, spent much of his time at Andalusia. Letters

written in 1816–17 show him engaged in literary labors here, and correspondence from Washington and elsewhere was addressed to Andalusia.

"The Philadelphia Society for the Promotion of Agri-

The gazebo overlooking the garden of Andalusia

[1]Written by Mrs. Charles Biddle.

culture," founded in 1785, was at that time an active force and continued to be for many years afterwards. About the year 1820 Nicholas Biddle was elected president of the Society, and remained at its head until the last year of his life.

Nicholas Biddle and others of his time became imbued with the idea that the grape could be successfully and profitably cultivated in our climate, and later, as a relaxation from his confining duties as president of the Bank of the United States, indulged his taste in this direction.

You will notice about the place the remains of the system of irrigation which was established about eighty-five years ago. At the river bank a pumping plant was built between 1830 and 1835. The water was drawn from the Delaware River and pumped into a reservoir which formerly overlooked this garden.

Looking down one of the box-bordered paths in the garden of Andalusia

This charming old iron seat was made before 1800 for the Andalusia garden

A glimpse through a doorway in the old garden walls at Andalusia

From here the water was conveyed in pipes to the vineyards in the adjacent fields. Some of the old hydrants and pumping stations may yet be seen. These vineyards were persistently maintained and frequently replanted for a number of years. But eventually it became apparent that owing to the rigors of our winters and the general variability of our climate the vines were not destined to flourish.

Mr. Biddle must have then turned his thoughts to the propagation of the grape indoors, for in 1834 we find him busy with the construction of forcing-houses, the walls of which still remain and enclose the present flower garden.

The cultivation of the indoor grape, it is pleasant to relate, proved eminently successful. There are letters extant showing that the Andalusia vineries had not only a local reputation but were considered first rate throughout the State and even beyond its borders. The black Hamburgs appear to have been especially fine.

These forcing-houses were maintained for many years. After the death of Mr. Biddle in 1844, the widow and children continued to live here, and following the death of Mrs. Biddle in 1856, her younger son, the late Judge Craig Biddle, whose tastes were to a marked degree rural, undertook their management. For many years the products of the vine were regularly marketed, but ultimately a falling-off in the demand for hot-house fruit, as well as the added expense due to increased price of labor and fuel, forced the Judge to give up what had been his hobby as well as that of his father.

When a violent hail storm destroyed the glass of the greenhouse, the Judge determined to pull the graperies down, leaving the rear walls standing. This was rather a rude shock to the younger generation who had always felt that there was a certain mystery and attraction about these glass houses, the warm atmosphere heavy with the perfume of the clusters of black and white grapes festooned in clusters from the ceiling. But it was the only feasible plan, and time has gradually obliterated the sense of loss. The walls are now covered with a luxuriant growth of trumpet vine, ivy and wistaria, and contribute to the grace of the garden, serving to shelter it as of yore from the blasts of winter.

The gardens and the surrounding fields were watered from a large reservoir into which the water was pumped from the river. The building holding the reservoir was destroyed by fire several years ago, and the present structure was erected on the old walls. The gazebo replaces the gallery, which ran around the top of the old building, and from which one can now obtain a good view of the garden.

The front part of the "Big House," as it is always called, has a Grecian Portico, and it and the library were built in 1835 by the Nicholas Biddle who married Miss Craig in 1811. He selected for his architect Thomas Hugh Walters, who built Girard College. Mr. Walters had recently returned from Greece and Italy and was an enthusiast upon the beauty of Grecian buildings, as was also Nicholas Biddle, who said that there was nothing true in this world but God and Greek architecture. The portico is an exact copy of the Greek temple of Neptune at Paestum, one of the earliest of the Greek temples built in Italy. The Doric style is followed exactly, showing the guttæ, or drops of water, the truncated cones below the representation of the heads of the bolts holding the beams. These beams are supported by columns which are remarkable for their preservation, not a crack showing after all these years. The inside decorations of the two front rooms correctly represent the Ionic; the familiar egg and dart, the lesbian leaf, and the wild honeysuckle carved in wood at the top of each of the supporting columns are also represented in the marble mantelpieces.

We have no exact information about the planning of the garden. During the many years of its existence there have been times when vegetables were more prominent than flowers, and at one time tobacco was experimented with. We know positively a few of the flowers which were in the first garden for the following list was found written by John Craig on the fly-leaf of an old garden book called *Every Man his own Gardener* by Thomas Mawe, Gardener to His Grace, the Duke of Leeds, John Abercrombie, Gardener Tottenham Court, and other Gardeners, Dublin, Printed for H. Whitestone J. Beatty and R. Burton, MDCCLXXXXIV.

(Memorandum)

Mignonette
Ranunculus
Lupin
Sweet Peas

and several other flower seeds, the last day of April, '97 in pots and in the ground. Mem. a fine rain immediately after.

Monday 6th. May
Mignonette
Larkspur
Scarlet flowers
Sweet peas

and a variety of other flowers sowed in the garden and outer borders.[1]

[1]Memorandum by John Craig, April, 1797.

SWEET BRIAR

Sweet Briar (1797) belonged to Samuel Breck. To quote from his own notes:

"My residence has been, when at home with my family, where it now is, for more than thirty years, on an estate belonging to me, situated on the right bank of the Schuylkill, in the township of Blockley, county of Philadelphia, and two miles from the western part of the city. The mansion on this estate I built in 1797. It is a fine stone house, rough-cast, fifty-three feet long, thirty-eight feet broad, and three stories high, having outbuildings of every kind suitable for elegance and comfort. The prospect consists of the river, animated by its great trade carried on in boats of about thirty tons, drawn by horses; of a beautiful sloping lawn, terminating at that river, now nearly four hundred yards wide opposite the portico; of side-screen of woods; of gardens, green-house etc."

In 1830 the Committee appointed by the Horticultural Society of Pennsylvania to visit gardens and nurseries reported that Mr. Breck had a greenhouse of 54 feet frontage for the preservation of orange, citron, and other tropical trees; all in good order and bearing. "The garden," said the Committee's report, "has been made at considerable expense, and may contain, including the plant yard and shrubbery, about 2 acres."

The mansion of Sweet Briar is now owned by the Junior League of Philadelphia.

BOXLY[1]

William Penn gave the grant of land where Boxly lies to Daniel Francis Pastorius in 1683. The garden was not, however, started at this date, for Pastorius' interest lay in other fields. After many changes of ownership, the property passed in 1803 into the hands of Count Jean DuBarry, a Frenchman to whose love of the gardens of his native land Boxly owes much of its serene Old World charm.

Count DuBarry planned his garden in remembrance of Versailles, importing dwarf box (*Buxus sempervirens var. suffruticosa*), shrubbery and fruit trees; also, in order to have the gleam of white marble against green, he had statues brought from abroad.

The Count was interested in experiments in silk culture—experiments which he hoped would tend to establish a thriving silk industry in America. He planted mulberry trees for food for his worms, and they yet survive in Mulberry Walk, a part of the old garden now incorporated into the new. There also remain quaint square houses, built out along the high stone garden walls. These houses were to have contained the vats in which the silk-worm cocoons were to be boiled.

There was also a picturesque greenhouse, one of the first forms, sunken in the ground to avoid cold of winter and heat of summer. French roses were planted around this building and intermingled with the sprays of trumpet vines.

Count DuBarry sold the place in 1818, and it passed through various hands again, until it was acquired in 1901 by Frederick W. Taylor.

When the place was purchased the garden was sadly neglected, the box having grown into immense billowy masses of green. Mr. Taylor was exceedingly anxious to preserve this box, and yet in order to conform to any plan for remodeling the garden, the plants had to be moved. Experiments were made in order to ascertain the root-growth, and much information was secured. It is known that in box the root-growth for the first twenty or thirty years is straight down like the tap-root growth of a tree. In these old plants the growth had proceeded as usual, but all nourishment directly below having been exhausted, this

[1]Adapted from an account by Mrs. Frederick Winslow Taylor, the owner.

A photograph of the garden of Boxly taken in 1901, showing the mulberry houses and the original garden plan of 1804

A present-day view of Boxly, now the property of Frederick Winslow Taylor, showing the box-bordered walks as seen from the entrance gateway

The old wall at Boxly and one of the quaint, square stone houses, built in 1803, which were to have contained the vats for boiling silkworm cocoons

The century-old box and the gateway in the garden of Boxly, photographed in 1924

The great masses of neglected box which survived at Boxly from the original planting, designed by Count DuBarry.   This photograph was taken in 1901.   Note the figure in the foreground

tap-root system gradually died, and was replaced by a few large roots which ran out to the edges of the bushes, there spreading into a mass of spongy interlaced rootlets, capable of absorbing the needed food. After this information was obtained by experimental observation on one specimen, the immense bushes were moved by means of special machines designed by Mr. Taylor. Twelve hundred feet of hedge were most successfully transplanted, and each year seems to add to the vigor of the century-old box.

Besides the box planted by DuBarry, and now grown from modest borders for his flower beds to such a size that one is hidden when behind it, the old spring-house, dating back two hundred years, is of interest, as is also the great stone wall. This wall so well protects the garden that often the johnny-jump-up blooms all winter and greets the yellow jasmine and snowdrop of February.

THE PATTERSON GARDEN[1]

The Historical Society of Pennsylvania is now in a building on the site of the old Patterson Garden. It is on the block bounded by Thirteenth and Juniper, Howard and Locust.

The grounds of the old Patterson place were landscaped by an Englishman named Mather. They were planned in a formal way, having rectangular walks bordered by beds of brilliant exotics and rare shrubs and trees. These walks led to the great fountain stocked with gold and silver fish and surrounded by aquatic plants, and giant orange and lemon trees.

Two great conservatories held a superb collection of orchids—the finest, it is said, in Philadelphia.

Misshapen Aztec idols guarded the walk to the fountain, while the presiding genius was a marble figure termed Solon.

The grounds were enclosed by a marble and rough-cast wall painted yellow, and in the spring there was a great display of tulips and hyacinths which attracted great crowds.

THE HIGHLANDS[1]

In the White Marsh Valley on the old Skippack Pike along which Washington led his army to Valley Forge, lies The Highlands, built in 1796 by Anthony Morris, the seventh of his name.

The long avenue winds upward under fine old trees and through the park-like fields on either hand to the house, which is of the later Georgian type, stately and simple, with beautiful proportions. An immense white oak stands sentinel beside it, after many years still holding its dignified supremacy, though other trees, rare old balsam firs and pines, keep fellowship with it.

The estate passed in 1813 into the hands of George Sheaff, who developed and beautified it. Despite his evident love and interest in the place, Mr. Sheaff at one time contemplated selling the Highlands, being "desirous of a change of residence," as he himself says. There are preserved several newspaper clippings, faded and discolored, cut from early Philadelphia papers in which Mr. Sheaff advertises his property for sale—sometimes addressing himself to "Foreign

[1]From the *Pennsylvania Magazine of History and Biography*, 1834.

[1]Owned by Miss Caroline Sinkler, Ambler, Pennsylvania.

Photographed by Ph. B. Wallace

A box-bordered grass pathway in the garden of The Highlands, at Ambler. In the background are old locust trees

Photographed by Ph. B. Wallace

The door that leads to the old garden at The Highlands, the estate of Miss Caroline Sinkler, at Ambler

Gentlemen arriving in the United States or others desirous of purchasing an estate"—and speaks of a house with ample accommodations for a family of twenty persons. "The pleasure grounds surrounding the house are shaded with elegant evergreens and very beautifully laid out." He also points out the "advantages of spring house, ice house" (still in the original state) "fish pond, a garden of two acres, orchards stocked with the finest fruit, green house, and grape wall, a stream of water in every field, a daily mail by which Philadelphia and New York papers of the same date are received, and an omnibus passing the gate every morning and evening."

Whether it was that no purchaser offered himself or whether Mr. Sheaff had a change of heart, deciding, to quote his own words in the aforementioned advertisement, "that for beauty, healthful situation and advantages it is not surpassed by any in the United States," suffice it to say that the Highlands remained in his possession. At his death it passed to his son John Sheaff, who lived to be ninety-six years old.

In 1917 it came to the present owner. The garden lies to the east of the house and has been laid out as much as possible on the old lines, though no record of the original plan could be found. There are delightful descriptions of the place and garden written by a visiting Englishman in 1832:

"The farm is three hundred acres in extent, and in the time of DeWitt Clinton was pronounced by him the model farm of the United States. At the present time we know nothing superior to it; and Captain Barclay in his agricultural tour, says it was the only instance of regular scientific husbandry in the English manner, he saw in America. Indeed, the large and regular fields, filled with luxuriant crops, everywhere of an exact evenness of growth, and everywhere free from weeds of any sort, the perfect system of manuring and culture; the simple and complete fences, the fine stock, the very spacious barns, every season newly whitewashed internally and externally, paved with wood, and as clean as a gentleman's stable, these and the masterly way in which the whole is managed both as regards culture and profits, renders the estate one of no common interest in the agricultural as well as the ornamental point of view."

The old crenelated walls still protect the garden and at the two corners stand square garden-houses, with Gothic windows and doors, which in the latter and leaner years were used as dwelling-houses for the old retainers who cheerily raised large families in their picturesque but stinted quarters.

The graperies and orangeries have long since disappeared but the old grass walks are still sheltered by magnolias and boxwood, and flowers and fruit-trees bloom and bear fruit with the changing seasons. Many of the old boxwood borders remain and new ones have been put in where the old lines could be traced. Down a brick path one sees through an opening in the vine-clad masonry a vista across the fields to the deer park—the old wattled fence still holds its straggling lines, but the deer are no longer under the great beeches.

Perennial borders lie on each side of the long grass walk that follows the north wall of the garden; contemporaneous English poets keep sentinel along it, while behind, walled fruit trees and wistaria fling their long branches over the crenelated coping, and pigeons wing their flight from the tower of the garden houses into the perfumed air.

An old sun-dial is recessed in a hemlock hedge, the marking quite defaced with time, but bearing the ancient device of a cross. In the midst of a wide allée of grass lies a long pool

The garden of The Highlands, at Ambler. Looking into the new pool-garden, surrounded by old trees, and backed by the ancient crenelated wall

The garden walk that follows the old grapery wall at The Highlands

The main entrance of the house at The Highlands, seen from beneath the great oak tree

whose still waters reflect the springtime bloom of locust and pear trees which shade it in summer. And the tall spray of a fountain in another allée pleases the eye and gives a sweet cadence to the ear.

A tiny Tudor garden at one side leads through a garden house to the Birdwalk which lies outside the garden. This is a long ravine, tree shaded and full of wildflowers.

On the south side of the house the ground slopes rapidly down the park, and an old path with many worn steps shaded by hemlocks leads one to the Spring House, an octagon room with two wide windows and an old fireplace by which a bath-tub was installed in the early years. A cupboard full of empty jugs discloses that the fireplace was not the only source of warmth and comfort depended on by the occasional bather.

Mertensias and other wild flowers fill the little terrace that surrounds the Spring House; wild grapevines tumble over it and tall sycamores surround it.

No pictures can show the charm, and descriptions give but a dim idea of the elusive beauty of the Highlands. The grounds and gardens are the result of the combined work of sympathetic and trained minds and hands during many years, and make a whole that words fail adequately to suggest.

LANSDOWNE

Lansdowne was beautifully situated on the Schuylkill adjoining Belmont. The mansion was of stone built partially in the Italian style and different from any house standing in Pennsylvania at that time.

The approach to the grounds was by a drive, through a gate, passing a porter's lodge to the west of the enclosure, and through an avenue of trees nearly a quarter of a mile long. The ground was ornamented with busts and statues, and a beautiful garden was laid out. Upon the estate were fine old forest trees. Romantic ravines and valleys opened toward the Schuylkill.

At Lansdowne the utmost hospitality was observed. Washington, Adams and Jefferson with distinguished American statesmen, foreign ministers, and travellers, were guests within its walls.

John Adams wrote under date of June 23, 1795: "Went to Lansdowne on Sunday, about half a mile on this side of Judge Peters'. The place is very retired but very beautiful—a splendid house, gravel walks, shrubberies and clumps of trees in the English style."

In 1816 Joseph Bonaparte, ex-king of Spain, leased Lansdowne for one year.

The mansion burned in 1854. Though the walls were left standing, and the structure could have been repaired, it was utterly demolished by the Park Commission of Philadelphia.

Lansdowne

"Lansdowne lies upon the banks of the Pastoral Schuylkill, a stream of peculiar beauty, deservedly the delight and the boast of the shores it fertilizes. The house was built upon a handsome and correct plan by the former Governor Penn."

American Historical Prints, New York Public Library

Devon, the Seat of Mr. Dallas

"An airy and pleasant situation on the Pennsylvania shore of the Delaware, fourteen miles from Philadelphia. The house was built by Mr. Jos. Anthony."

American Historical Prints, New York Public Library

Fountain Green, the Seat of Mr. S. Meeker

"On the Schuylkill, highly favored by nature, and capable of vast improvement. Upon the half ascent of the bank from the river, the new Canal will pass and if ever finished will be a great ornament to the house."

New York Historical Society Collections

Country estates in the vicinity of Philadelphia, as sketched by W. Birch in the early nineteenth century, and

China Retreat, the Seat of Mr. Manigault

"*An airy and pleasant situation on the Delaware, 17 miles from Philadelphia. The house was built by Mr. Van Braam, late ambassador from Holland to China. It was here that he prepared for the press his account of that embassy. . . . Now the summer residence of the family of Mr. Manigault of S. Carolina.*"

American Historical Prints,
New York Public Library

Sedgley, the Seat of Mr. Wm. Crammond

Westcott's "Historic Mansions of Philadelphia" tells us that "the architect was the elder Latrobe, who drew the plans for the Bank of Pennsylvania. Sedgley was the first attempt made in the neighborhood of Philadelphia to introduce the Gothic style in connection with the country house. . . . It was comfortable and elegant and the grounds were enriched with shrubbery and fine old trees and had every natural advantage in its favor."

American Historical Prints, New York Public Library

Mount Sidney, the Seat of Genl John Barker

"*Derives its honorable name from the patriot Algernon Sidney, who died in the reign of Charles II a martyr to liberty. I.s sylvan scenes mingle with romantic wilds of Sedgley.*"

New York Historical Society Collections

reproduced here with his own descriptive captions. They show the informal planting of the country seats of the period

GERMANTOWN

ALTHOUGH Germantown is now a part of Philadelphia, the circumstances of its founding, its early colonial history, and its distinct and separate influence in the development of gardening in America, demand for it individual treatment.

THE FOUNDING

According to Whittier in the introductory note to *The Pennsylvania Pilgrim*, the beginning of German emigration to America may be traced to the personal influence of William Penn, when in 1677 he visited the continent and made the acquaintance of the intelligent and highly cultivated circle of the Pietists. In this circle originated the Frankfort Land Company, which bought of William Penn, the Governor of Pennsylvania, a tract of land near the city of Philadelphia.

The company's agent in the New World was a rising young lawyer, Francis Daniel Pastorius. In 1683, in company with a small number of German Friends, he emigrated to America, settling upon the Frankfort Land Company's tract between the Schuylkill and the Delaware Rivers. The township was divided into four hamlets, namely, Germantown, Krisheim, Crefeld, and Sommerhausen.

Pastorius, like all the early settlers, was delighted with and amazed at the natural products of the country. He wrote his parents from Philadelphia: "After I had laid out Germantown, and when returning with seven others to this place, we saw on the way, clinging to a tree, a wild grape vine upon which hung about four hundred bunches of grapes. To get the grapes we cut down the tree, and eight of us ate as many as satisfied us."

Under the wise direction of Pastorius the Germantown settlement grew and prospered. The inhabitants planted orchards and vineyards. As a great number of them were linen-weavers, they also grew flax.

In 1692 Richard Frame published in what he called verse a "Description of Pennsylvania" in which he thus alludes to the settlement:

> "The German town of which I spoke before
> Which is at least in length a mile or more"

—and Oldmixon[1] informs us that "in those days of primeval innocence the whole street was fronted with blooming peach-trees."

Edwin C. Jellett in his *Gardens and Gardeners of Germantown*[2] gives many details of the development of the community. He says of early Germantown:

"Here then was an interesting group living and working together as neighbors and plant growers: Pastorius cultivating his garden and raising grapes; Daniel Geissler, farmer and grower of garden truck; Christopher Witt serving as village doctor, and growing plants for his pleasure, edification, and for practical uses."

This garden of Dr. Witt's was, so far as is known, the second garden in America for the study of plants. We have no record of when this garden was planted, but of it Pastorius wrote: "1711, Christopher Witt removed his flower beds to my fence." In 1716 he dedicated a poem to Christopher Witt's "Fig Tree." Pastorius described his own pretty little garden, which grew chiefly cordial, stomachic, and culinary herbs.

Again, we find him writing: "What wonder you then, that F. D. P. likewise here many hours spends, and having no money, on usury lends, t's garden and orchard and vineyard, such time he helps nature, and nature his rhymes, because they produce him both victuals and drink, both medicine and nose-gays, and both paper and ink."

Dr. Rush in his *Manners of the Germans of Pennsylvania* writes: "Pennsylvania is indebted to the Germans for the principal part of her knowledge in horticulture. There was a time when turnips and cabbages were the principal vegetables that were used in the diet of the citizens of Philadelphia. This will not surprise those that know that the first settlers in Pennsylvania left England when horticulture was in its infancy in that country."

Many of the plants which the Pennsylvania German cultivated in his garden and field had been introduced into Germany in 812 A. D. by Charles the Great.

The original order of Charles the Great is translated from the Latin[1] as follows:

"We desire that they have in the garden all the herbs, namely the lily roses, fenugreek, costmary, sage, rue, southernwood, cucumbers, muskmelons, gourds, pole beans, cumin, rosemary, caraway, chick peas, squill, iris, arum, anise, colocyntha, chicory, asumi, laserwort, lettuce, black cumin, garden rocket, nasturtium, burdock, pennyroyal, Alexander, parsley, celery, lovage, sabine tree, dill, fennel, endive, dittany, black mustard, savory, curly mint, water mint, horse mint, tansy, catnip, feverfew, poppy, beet, ginger, marshmallow, high mallows, carrots, parsnips, orachs, amaranths, kohlrabis, cabbages, onions, chives, leeks, radishes, shallots, garlics, madder, artichokes or fulling thistles, big beans, field peas, coriander, chervil, caper spurge, clary.

"And the gardener shall have on his house, the house-leek.

"We desire them to have the following trees; various kinds of apple trees, various kinds of pear trees, various kinds of plum trees, service trees, medlar trees, chestnut trees, various kinds of peach trees, quince trees, hazel nut trees, almond trees, mulberry trees, laurel trees, pine trees, fig trees, big nut trees, various kinds of cherry trees. . . ."[2]

This list of Charles the Great is of the highest importance for the study of horticulture. Its influence is still discernible among our Pennsylvania farmers.

The early settlers of Germantown were thrifty and industrious people; their little community was described by Kalm, the Swedish botanist, when he visited it in 1748, as being in a most thriving condition. He described in detail its distinctive architecture, and mentioned the fact that each house had a fine garden.

Watson says of these gardens: "The small flower bed stood solitary and alone in most family gardens, and sunflowers, and gay and rank hollihocks, and other annual productions were the chief articles for a greater display. Morning glories and the gourd vine were the annual dependence for cases of required shade. None thought of a grape vine for such a purpose."

Shortly after Kalm's visit to Germantown, another observing traveler, Gottlieb Mittelberger, in 1754 wrote most entertainingly of the country generally and of the forest trees. He spoke of the high esteem in which the daisy was held, saying that it was "as rare in Pennsylvania as the rarest and most

---

[1]John Oldmixon, *History of the British Empire in America*, London, 1708.
[2]Published by the Site and Relic Society of Germantown, Philadelphia.

[1]As given in G. H. Pertz's *Monumenta Germanica Historica*, 1835, Vol. III, page 168.
[2]Quoted from *Plant Names and Plant Lore among the Pennsylvania Germans*, by David E. Lick and Thomas R. Brendle.

beautiful flowers in Europe can be, and it is planted in the gardens as a rare flower. . . . Quite as rare are all other European flowers and herbs, and so what is not highly esteemed in Germany is rare and dear in America; and vice-versa, what is not highly esteemed here is precious in Germany."

In 1799 the Reverend John C. Ogden wrote: "The houses in Germantown are very universally shaded with weeping willows, the Lombardy poplar, and other ornamental trees. The gardens are under excellent cultivation with valuable fields to their rear."

Fanny Kemble's first impressions of the country surrounding Philadelphia are in amusing contrast to the enthusiastic

hardly conceive the sort of abomination of desolation which its aspect formerly presented to eyes accustomed to the finish and perfection of rural English landscape.   It will be difficult for those who do not remember the Old York Road and the country between that and Germantown, to imagine the change which nearly fifty years has produced in the whole region."

Early in the development period, as well as in the first period, all the gardens were of the prevailing type—that is, if there was more than a kitchen or herb garden, the additional garden was composed largely of perennial plants in beds, enclosed in borders of box, with walks of gravel or "tan"

Courtesy of the Pennsylvania Historical Society

Cliveden, the Benjamin Chew house in Germantown, built about 1763

This drawing bears out the allusions to a formal garden which contained statuary, but no description or plan of what was evidently an important lay-out have been found. On the doorstep of the house today there are, however, statuary figures preserved from this garden

accounts of almost all these visitors from abroad. She speaks of "the mean-looking scattered farm-houses, and large ungainly barns, uninteresting and uninviting in all the human elements of its landscape, dreary in summer, desolate in winter, and absolutely void of the civilized charm which should have belonged to it."

Contrast this with Manasseh Cutler's remarks in his *Journal*, written somewhat earlier:

"From this place [Bristol] to Philadelphia the land is exceedingly rich and fertile, producing a great quantity of excellent fruit, Indian corn, and finest wheat. . . .

"The farmers' houses are very neat, but not large, generally two stories high, sometimes three and universally painted. Some of them are built of logs, and they are also painted and very handsome. Their gardens are well formed and abound with flowers as well as fruit trees and esculents. There are shady trees at their doors."

Fortunately Fanny Kemble in her *Records of Later Life* gives us a picture entirely different from her first. She wrote:

"One who now sees the pretty populous villadom which has grown up in every direction around the home of my early married years, the neat cottages and the cheerful country houses, the trim lawns and the bright flower gardens, the whole well laid-out, tastefully cultivated, and carefully tended suburban district with its attractive dwellings, could

extending between. Such, with varying degrees of extent and value, were the gardens of Loudon, Toland, Lorraine, Mechlin, Henry, Shippen, Harlan, Conyngham, Handsberry, Baynton, Wister, Deschler-Morris, Vernon, Engle, Morris-Littell, Wyck, Johnson, Pomona Grove, Upsala, Allen, and Schaeffer on Main Street, and other gardens like those of Wakefield, Belfield, Hacker, Spencer, Roberts, Awbury, Gardette, Roset, Rosengarten, Chancellor, Toworth, Wistar, Thomas, Spring Bank, and others upon the side lanes. These are illustrative only, for there are many worthy gardens not here named.

GARDENS AND ESTATES OF GERMANTOWN

WYCK

Edwin C. Jellett in *Gardens and Gardeners of Germantown* says that the most pretentious house of the settlement was that of Hans Millan, built in 1690, and later incorporated in "Wyck."

Wyck is one of the very few properties, if not the only one in Germantown, that has remained in continuous, unbroken possession of the descendants of the original owner.

Caspar Wistar Haines says that Lot 17 on the old plan of Germantown was bought from the Frankfort Company by

"Wyck," in Germantown, the property of Caspar Wistar Haines. This view shows the general design of the garden

A nearer view of the house, showing the large magnolia tree

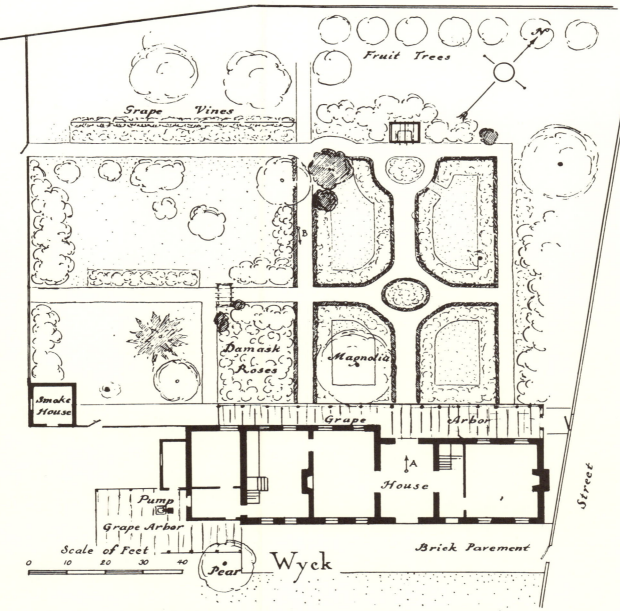

This plan of Wyck, reproduced here by courtesy of Mr. James Bush-Brown, shows the garden as it is today

Hans Millan, who was supposed to have built the house at Wyck. According to family tradition the back part of the house was built first.

The garden is very lovely now, but very little is known of the early planting. The present plan was developed about 1821. Miss Haines writes:

"I believe my old garden was laid out by my mother, Mrs. J. B. Haines, as I have a rough sketch with notes in her hand. I presume it was about 1821–22, as that was the time that my parents removed to 'Wyck' permanently, having previously resided there in the summer. I remember when the asparagus bed, surrounded by currant bushes, still occupied the plot by the street, where the hedge now is. At that time the paths were covered with tan from Engle's old tannery.

"The garden is formal in design, but so cleverly covered by shrubbery, trellises and resting places, that one may wander through its walks without making this discovery. The beds are box-bordered, and present a wealth of wildflowers, hardy plants in variety, roses of 'long-ago,' all flourishing happily together in great profusion."

FAIR-HILL[1]

Fair-Hill was built in 1716. Pastorius referred to Fair-Hill garden as "the one keeping the finest I hitherto have seen in the whole country, fitted with an abundance of rarities, physical, and metaphysical."

Of it Deborah Logan later wrote: "'Fair-Hill,' built and occupied by Isaac Norris, was considered the most beautiful

[1]Information drawn from Jellett's *Gardens and Gardeners of Germantown*.

The southern doorway at Wyck

An old box bush at Wyck

William Bodicker at the Durham Forge, Bucks County, 2nd. month 20th, 1753: 'Send me down, carefully planted in two tubs, two or three handsome Bay trees or board laurels. Let them be straight bodied, about three feet high at most, and about the thickness of one's thumb—not too large in head in proportion to its roots. They should come by water and be often wet by yᵉ boatmen.' And again in 1754: 'Don't neglect sending me some pretty flower roots when yᵉ opportunity offers!' From Reading, Logan's cousin, James Read, sent him laurels and rhododendrons, receiving in exchange fruit trees, shrubs and roses.''

William Logan corresponded with many botanists and nurserymen in England, procuring from them rare plants. Mrs. Wright says:

country-seat in Pennsylvania. The courts and gardens were in the taste of those times with gravel walks and parterres. Many lofty trees were preserved around the house, which added greatly to its beauty and at the time of my remembrance the out-buildings were covered with festoons of ivy, and scarlet bignonia.''

STENTON

Stenton, on the Germantown road, was built as a country home by James Logan, William Penn's trusted provincial secretary.

The mansion was begun in 1728. The family moved into it in 1730, and we can assume, because of James Logan's intense interest in botany and horticulture, that gardening operations commenced immediately.

The following account makes use of excerpts from a booklet on Stenton prepared by Letitia E. Wright.[1]

"Among the colonial gardens the one at Stenton was important; for it was there that men like John Bartram, of Philadelphia, and Abraham Redwood of Newport, received the inspiration which prompted them to establish gardens which became noted the world over. It was at Stenton that James Logan undertook a series of experiments with maize or Indian corn. These he described in letters to Peter Collinson in 1735, which were printed in the *Philosophical Transactions*.[2] As a result of these experiments he wrote a Latin treatise on the generation of plants, published at Leyden in 1739, which was later translated into English (in 1747) by Dr. Fothergill.[3]

"Dr. Pultney in his Sketches of Botany (published 1790) says in regard to this treatise: 'This work was considered and appealed to as among the most decisive in establishing the doctrine of sex in plants.'

"William Logan, the son of James, took great interest in our native trees, shrubs and flowers. He was active in procuring them from the interior of the province of Pennsylvania and from the more distant provinces as well. He writes to

[1]Letitia E. Wright, "Colonial Garden at Stenton, Described in old Letters."
[2]*Philosophical Transactions*, Vol. XXXVI, p. 192.
[3]*Experimenta de plantarum generatione.*

"There were many disappointments and losses on both sides, notwithstanding the great care planned for the plants, bulbs and seeds in their long journey from England to the

James Logan, William Penn's provincial secretary, who founded Stenton and its garden

provinces. In 1749 two large orders for fruit trees from Elias Bland were 'sent to the proper account and risque of William Logan, Merch't,' although at this time his father was still living at Stenton.''

Let us quote one to show the style:

6 named varieties of cherries					
6	"	"	"	Plumbs	*Let them stand*
12	"	"	"	Carnations	*upon the open deck.*

Take care the mise don't Eat them & keep them from stormy whether, you may lett them have gentell Rain but not too Mutch of itt nor too mutch Sun Shine don't lett the Salt Water wash them

Stenton's restored garden of today, a mere pigmy compared to the extensive gardens from which it is descended

Roots of tulips
Ranunculus
Narcissus   *Take care the*
Dutch poppys   *mise don't eat*
Seeds of double Larkspurs   *them.*
Stocks of several sorts
French and African marygolds
Sweet scented peas,[1] with directions
     with them when to be sowed.

William Logan had many difficulties with his orders to Thomas Bincks, seedsman and gardener, who apologizes on May 20, 1751:

"I am sorry that the perennial flowers etc. rec'd such damage, the design of the lids being with a good view & I am apprehensive if due care had been taken would have been of service. For future shall follow thy directions.

"P.S. The charge of the former boxes thou mentioned to dear is the neat expense I paid."

William then tries his inventive faculty on lids:

"Stenton 12m. 17-1754

"Respected Sir Thos. Bincks—Altho' I have had very bad luck with what flower roots and plants I have had from thee, yet I am writing to make one more trial. I think I had nothing to show out of all that came from thee, except's some double hyacinths & jonquils & a very few anemones."[2]

The order enclosed read as follows:

Flower roots to be sent
24 earliest Tulips
30 largest and very best hyacinths sorted
50 double jonquils
100 yellow and blue crocus y^t blow in ye fall of y^e
    year
50 snow drops
24 Persian Iris
12 naked ladies
20 double anemonies (if tuberose roots are plenty
    and cheap send mee some of them dry also)
8 pots of carnations   *Let them be Good and the Potts be*
8 pots of auriculas   *put into a course Rough Box made*
                          with a shelving lid so it may throw
                          ye water at sea when the weather
                          is bad and yet be half open when
                          good so the sun may not come too
                          violently on ye Auricula plants.
Seeds—a few of the *best* Carnations. What I had of
    thee before for such, proved when blown to be
    only common red five leaved pinks. Best
    double Holyhocks various colors.
Several sorts of stocks
Hepatica
Dbl. China Pinks
Snap Dragon
Catipelars & Snales.

The placing of "Catipelars and Snales" among the garden seeds seems puzzling. If you turn to Parkinson's *Paradisus*, published in 1629, you will see among the fancy grasses

---

[1]Sweet peas were not known at the time of Parkinson or Evelyn. They were first cultivated by Dr. Uvedale at Enfield in the year 1713.
[2]This letter was copied from Wm. Logan's letter-book in the possession of the Pennsylvania Society of C.D.A. at their library at Stenton.

"Caterpillars & Snails." Parkinson calls "Caterpillars" *Scorpioides maius* and *minus*, saying, "Under one description I comprehend both these sorts of Scorpion grasses, or Caterpillars, or Wormes, as they are called by Many,—the greatest part of which came to me out of Spain. . . . They have a tart flavor and are cultivated even now in some parts of Europe for 'surprises in salads & soups.'" They are now known as *Scorpiurus vermiculata*.

One of William Logan's most interesting correspondents was John Blackburne (1690–1786), a noted botanist of Orford near Warrington, who maintained an extensive garden, including many exotics. He wrote of plants, their treatment and care, going over in details those he received from Logan, who sent cuttings, seeds, roots and bulbs of native growth.

Stenton is still in existence, and is now owned by the city of Philadelphia, though until very recently it was held by descendants of James Logan.

Painted by Walter M. Aikman in 1909

Stenton, in Germantown

The interior of the house has been restored to its original condition by the Pennsylvania Society of the Colonial Dames of America, in whose custody the house now is. The garden has also been restored under the direction of Mrs. Letitia E. Wright, and follows as nearly as possible the lines of the old planting near the house.

Mrs. Wright says:

"It is but a pigmy compared to the garden it is supposed to represent, which extended beyond the graveyard, with orchards about it, while in its midst were smaller fruits. East of the garden and of the graveyard, which was not built till after the revolution, the ground sloped to a pasture where cattle grazed and through which ran a limpid stream."

Mrs. Sarah Butler Wister, in the sketch of Deborah Logan in *Worthy Women of Our First Century*, gives the following charming description of Stenton:

"Round the house there was the quiet stir and movement of a country-place, with its large gardens full of flowers and fruits, its poultry yard and stables. The latter were connected with the house by an underground passage which led to a concealed staircase and a door under the roof, like the 'priest's escape' in some old English country seats.

"The grounds were adorned with fine old trees. A splendid avenue of hemlocks—which legend would only be satisfied with declaring were planted by William Penn, although the poor man was dead years before Stenton was built—led up to the house."

GRUMBLETHORPE[1]

Grumblethorpe is the name of a substantial plastered stone structure of colonial type, standing on Main Street, opposite Riter's Lane, sometime Indian Queen Lane, now known as plain Queen Street. The house was erected in 1744 by Johann Wister, the second of the Wister brothers to emigrate to America. It was built of stone quarried at "Cedar Hill," and the woodwork was of oak from trees hewn in Wister's wood. The original house differed in certain exterior features from the remodelled house of to-day.

[1]Adapted from a paper by Edwin C. Jellett in *Historical Addresses of the Site and Relic Society of Germantown*, and from an account in Westcott's *Historic Mansions of Philadelphia*.

The dove-cote at Stenton

Grumblethorpe, in Germantown, as it appears today

Grumblethorpe (the name is of comparatively recent origin) was the first house in Germantown to be erected as the "summer home" of a resident of Philadelphia.

The place possessed many rural charms when Johann Wister became the owner. The property stretched over to the east and consisted of field and forest. A portion of this forest survives today and is still known in Germantown as Wister's Woods. After the house was finished, Mr. Wister devoted himself to the laying out of an elegant garden. He had brought with him from Hillspach the German love for fruit and flowers, and it was his pride to adorn the grounds with the finest fruit-bearing trees and floral specimens.

The garden covers an area 188 feet wide by 450 feet long, and is bounded on the east by a vegetable garden, on the north by the barn and pasture fields, the total length of the tract from Main Street to Wakefield Street being 900 feet. It is semi-formal in type, having a central walk ten feet wide flanked by rectangular, semi-circular and angular beds, conforming to lines radiating from the central to two outlying bounding paths, or walks.

Within the garden color and brightness crowd each other, and one viewing its bewildering variety for the first time is hardly able to realize that this enchanting rural gem is situated directly upon the principal business street, and near the centre of modern Germantown.

The garden's central gravelled walk extends from the manor to the barn enclosure, is box-bordered (*Buxus sempervirens var. nana*) throughout its length, and midway arbored; companion walks and interesting links are likewise emerald bound, and at favored points arched by arbors or by latticed trellises clothed by vines.

Upon an elevated square, marking the site of an ice-house built in the year 1809, and the first in Germantown, observable immediately within the garden is an arbored tree wistaria of immense proportions, completely covering its supporting structure.

Grumblethorpe is still in the possession of the Wister family. The house is unoccupied, but the garden is maintained in excellent condition.

CHAMPLOST[1]

Champlost was situated on Fisher's Lane, east of the old York Road. It was one of the oldest and finest estates in Penn-

The Johann Wister house (Grumblethorpe), as it was originally

sylvania. It was brought to its perfection by the Fox family, and was celebrated for its grounds, its gardens, and its magnificent trees.

CLEARFIELD

Clearfield was up on the old York Road east of Stenton. It was occupied by Elizabeth Drinker and family as a summer

[1]Information drawn from Jellett's *Gardens and Gardeners of Germantown.*

The garden at Grumblethorpe, in Germantown

residence. On April 10, 1796, she wrote: "Our yard and garden look most beautiful. The trees in full bloom, the red and white blossoms intermixed with green leaves, which are just putting out. Flowers of several sorts bloom in our little garden."

POMONA GROVE[1]

Pomona Grove consisted of a tract of seven acres lying on the east side of Germantown Avenue above Abington, now Washington Lane. On the lower side it joined the Axe Burying Ground for part of its way, and on the upper side the old Keyser homestead. While Pomona has disappeared, the Keyser house and the Burying Ground remain just as they appeared a century ago.

Pomona homestead was built in 1755, and was large and spacious. During the Revolutionary War it was owned by Christopher Huber, but soon passed into the hands of the Shoemaker family. In 1788 Colonel William Forrest bought it of the Shoemakers. It is told of him that a man came to him in answer to his advertisement for a gardener. The man had an umbrella under his arm, which was such a novelty that Forrest asked him to leave his grounds immediately, as he had no need of a gardener who was afraid of sun or rain.

Colonel Forrest enlarged the house and planted a large number of fruit and ornamental trees, among them the large yew which became so identified with the place. He sold the place to James Duval in 1811. The latter was born in France and came to this country when he was a boy. He was fond of horticulture and devoted his leisure time to improving and beautifying the spacious grounds, which soon justified the name he gave them—Pomona Grove. His constant inter-

[1]Adapted from a paper prepared by Mary W. Shoemaker for the Site and Relic Society, of Germantown.

course with France enabled him to import rare and—for this country—unique plants, for his garden.

Pomona Grove passed through many hands, reaching the height of its glory in 1875 when it was owned by Amos Little. Later Mr. Little sold it to a syndicate, and the estate was cut up into building lots. The grand old English yew, said to have been the finest specmen of its kind in America, was chopped down in spite of the efforts of Thomas Meehan and Edwin C. Jellett to save it.

THE DESCHLER-PEROT-MORRIS HOUSE

In 1772 David Deschler, son of the aide-de-camp to the reigning prince of Baden, and Margaret, a sister of Caspar Wister and Johann Wister, built a home on Germantown Road.

It was built of stone, and was about forty feet square, with a number of back buildings. The front part would have been wider had it not been for a plum tree which Deschler had not the heart to cut down. At the south side lies the beautiful garden, one hundred feet wide, extending westwardly 435 feet. In the garden are box bushes more than a century old.

This was the house occupied by Washington during his stay in Philadelphia. The interior is of unusual beauty of design and finish. The room where Washington breakfasted looked out on the charming garden, and even in that time of stress, it is said that Mrs. Washington had time to raise hyacinths under glass.

THE BUTLER PLACE

To quote from the Horticultural Society's Report of 1830:
"Butler Place is a beautiful place 6 miles from town, on the Old York Road. On viewing this estate our attention was

The Deschler-Perot-Morris house

immediately drawn to the handsome hedges of hornbeam, and *Prunus Canadensis*[?]. We were delighted with the latter, never having seen it before; its fine green foliage contrasts very sweetly with the delicate appearance of the young green shoots. These hedges are pruned periodically and kept in excellent order. The refreshing shade of the numerous walks, all swept as clean as a parlor floor, adds to the charms of this place. Many of these walks are tastefully ornamented with orange, lemon, shaddock, neriums and other exotics; among which we observed a myrtle ten years old raised from seed. It has large ovate foliage, similar to the *Eugenia uniflora*. This myrtle is highly ornamental, and richly deserving of cultivation. Here is likewise a lemon of the St. Helena variety raised from seed. The fruit grows large, of a high color, and much warted. The greenhouse is 45 feet long, the framing ample for early vegetables and flowers.

"Nothing in these grounds pleased me more than the perfect order of the kitchen garden. It contains about two acres, and is indeed a picture of culinary horticulture. There are 4 walks in the length and 9 in the breadth; all intersecting at right angles, and making 24 divisions, besides borders; and these divisions are cropt with vegetables in the finest order; each division having its own crop (not intermixed as we see in most gardens), which is through every stage attended with the utmost regularity. The walks gravelled and edged with box-wood, neatly clipped; and all exhibiting a lovely specimen of art. A half acre of other ground is devoted to flowers and decorative shrubs. On the whole we can assert that there is not a finer kept or better regulated kitchen garden on this continent. Indeed it will bear comparison with European gardens of the highest cultivation, according to its size; and what is exceedingly gratifying is, that the gardener is a native American, and has superintended this place fourteen years, which shows at once capacity and constancy. We are glad to see those born amongst us, begin to relish the minute and orderly labor of the garden and pleasure grounds. Hereto-fore the plough has been preferred by them to the spade, and emigrants alone have adopted amongst us the slow and patient toil of Horticulture."

The foregoing was written while the place was occupied by Dr. James Mease, who had been secretary of the important "Philadelphia Society for the Promotion of Agriculture."

FERN-HILL[1]

Fern-Hill, the first of Germantown's finest and most conspicuous estates, stood upon an elevation, facing the southwestern boundary of the township. In the report of the committee of the Horticultural Society of Pennsylvania in 1830, "it commands a delightful prospect, which extends beyond the city, embracing, of course, in this fine view, the whole of Philadelphia and its suburbs, the whole of their 30,000 dwelling houses, all fresh and in excellent repair, and inhabited by 170,000 people. The country in other directions wears a smiling prospect, corresponding in beauty with that of the city. The garden, green-house and collection of plants rank in the first class. The proprietor is distinguished for his generous encouragement of horticulture, importing, at great cost, rare plants, the best kinds of fruits and culinary vegetables.

"The tea rose flourishes in a superior manner here. Cultivated in frames, it grows as large as any other rose bush in the garden. We saw some covered with flowers. Mr. Clapier possesses, perhaps, the greatest variety of pear trees of any private gentleman hereabouts (except Mr. Girard), many of which he has imported from France. It is almost useless to say that the garden and grounds are in complete order, and stocked with every kind of vegetable and shrub. . . . Tropical fruits and flowering trees surround the mansion and display the richness and variety of flora to the best advantage."

This is a description of Fern-Hill as it was conducted under the direction of Martin Baumann. The standard of excellence first established was always maintained. The estate originally extended from Pulaski Avenue, or "Plank Road," to Wissahickon Avenue, or Lamb Tavern Road, and from Abbotsford Avenue to Nicetown Lane, or Ford Road. Its

[1]Adapted from *Gardens and Gardeners of Germantown*, by Edwin C. Jellett.

owner was Louis Clapier, who was born in France in the
year 1765, came to America in the year 1796, and died in
1838.

Townsend Ward records that "besides a fondness for raising
fat cattle, he had an equal passion for fruit and flowers, and
no visitor left him without a basket of flowers, or of grapes,
should they be in season."

The present Fernhill Park, a section of Fairmount Park, is
part of the original estate of Fern-Hill.

PHI-ELLENA

In 1836 a great garden was established by George Carpenter, the descendant of Miles Carpenter of England, who
came to America when quite young and died in 1791. George
Carpenter purchased 500 acres of land in Germantown,
and erected there a magnificent home called, in honor of his
wife, "Phi-Ellena."

The improvements covered an area of 350 acres, contain-

BELFIELD: THE GARDEN OF CHARLES WILLSON PEALE

When Charles Willson Peale, well known in his day as a
portrait painter and naturalist, had reached the seventieth
year of a life of arduous and unremitting labor, he determined, for his health's sake, to leave his home in Philadelphia
and retire into the country. He therefore bought a farm at
Germantown, more than one hundred fertile acres, well
watered by two mill streams and furnished with a comfortable stone dwelling, "rather old fashioned and in the German stile," with a gambrel roof and an overhanging wooden
balcony along the second story front. Near by were a frame
barn and several other outbuildings.

Problems beset his early efforts to "become a farmer in
the full sense of the word," but eventually he brought his
venture upon a practical footing. With his farm on a sound
basis and under trustworthy management, Peale turned his
attention to a garden. In a letter to Thomas Jefferson, he
says:

"Your favorite pursuit, gardening, I am extending, but in

The entrance to "Phi-Ellena," a vanished estate of 500 acres in Germantown. From a photograph in
the possession of the Pennsylvania Historical Society

ing lawns dotted with a remarkable collection of forest trees,
a deer park, two lakes, extensive driveways, twenty-five acres
of woodland, and extensive flower and kitchen gardens. A
high stone wall enclosed the grounds for nearly a mile in
length on the north.

For many years this place was one of the principal attractions to strangers visiting Philadelphia. The improvements
are said to have been made from plans purchased by Mr.
Carpenter, who directed the work and attended to every detail himself. The gardener, so far as is known, was William
Sinton.

Previous to the city's consolidation, this was the richest and
largest garden in or anywhere near Philadelphia, and through
the beneficence of its owner was regularly open to all who
respected its rules.

BONNEVAL COTTAGE

Bonneval Cottage, on the Old York Road, was built in
1745, and later was occupied by Dr. George De Benneville.
Dr. Benneville loved trees and flowers, and a large buttonwood tree still standing near the house was planted by him in
the year 1768. His garden, in part surviving, was of the prevailing type, box-bordered.

these times especially, gardeners good for real service cannot
be had for any wages."

Peale worked upon his garden with characteristic energy
and enthusiasm. Only the precisely arranged flower beds and
other ornamental evidences of civilization, so characteristic
of the period, were needed, for beauty he possessed already
in "the solemn groves skirting my meadows in majestic
silence and cool appearance, and a spring in the most romantic scenery your imagination can conceive."

The garden he built upon a slowly sloping meadow, with tall
Lombardy poplars and other trees around the lower borders.
Gravel walks wound through it, lined by very low rows of box,
within which grew a profusion of flowers; many of these were
kept in pots that they might, in cold weather, be removed to
his greenhouse. On the slight elevation overlooking the garden and in other appropriate spots he "made summer houses,
so called, roofs to ward off the sunbeams, with seats to rest.
One was made in the chinese taste, dedicated to meditation," and within it he inscribed appropriate sentiments.

Another "has a hexigon base with six pillars supporting a
circular top and dome on which is placed a bust of General
Washington." Again, he made "an obelisk to terminate a
walk in the garden," on the pedestal of which he put mottoes
"to keep myself in a proper temper, and I shall not be sorry
if others, on reading it, receive a useful lesson."

The garden of "Belfield," the estate of Charles Willson Peale. From a painting, probably by Peale

At the termination of another walk he made a pedestal on which were inscribed certain memorable events in history.

More curious was the exercise of his skill as a painter in concealing various unsightly structures by pictorial embellishment designed, as he expresses it, to combine moral sentiment with utility. Wanting a place to keep the garden tools and seed in a part of the garden where a seat in the shade was needed, he built a shed or small room and to hide this "salt-box like structure," he "made the front like a gateway with a step forming a seat, and above, steps painted to represent a passage through an arch, beyond which was represented a western sky, and to ornament the upper part over the arch, I painted two pedistals ornamented with a ball, and on the die of each the explanation of its respective figure."

Finding a spring in the garden, he followed it up the side of the hill until the stream became of some depth, among large stones. There he walled up the hollow, arched it over, and built a neat glazed front; this was his greenhouse. Thence he carried the water by a pipe to a lower part of the garden where he made a round, flower-encircled pool, in the center of which a jet of water shot into the air. This was also his fish pond, containing Schuylkill catfish, which, like his pigeons, became too much endeared to the family to be edible.

An idea of the flowers which Peale cultivated may be had from his description of the view from "the stone steps at the end of the house which lead to the yard in front of the garden. The garden pails are on a stone wall on which grow creepers now in full bloom. They are a fine crimson bell flower in clusters, and an abundance of humming birds are daily sucking the honey. Green Gages, Damson, Quinces, are along this wall and beneath the rose bushes you may discover a long roof which has shelves for bee hives, conveniently situated to get their food from the flowers in the garden. A house between the coachhouse and mansion we call the smokehouse, is so much covered with the elegant creeper that it can scarcely be seen."

Thus, in both farm and garden, "Belfield," came to success. The garden, he says, was so popular as to be in some measure "the Vaux Hall of Germantown. In fact," he adds, "although every precaution was taken to prevent trespass, yet it could not always be prevented where the multitude was admitted at all times. At last I found it necessary to shut the gates on Sundays when the laboring classes were let loose, as it was impossible to restrain them from plundering the fruit."

It had become the pride of the gardener and the admiration of his friends; an old man's source of health and pleasure, and today an antiquarian source on the horticultural taste and fashion of the age.[1]

In 1823 the Peale farm, including the mansion and its elaborately planned flower garden, was sold to William Logan Fisher. Upon the marriage of William Logan Fisher's eldest child, Sarah Logan, to William Wister, the Belfield mansion and garden was given to her as a residence. The gardens and outbuildings, numbering 14 roofs in addition to that of the old house, have been kept as originally planned by Peale to the present day.

Upon the death of Sarah Logan the property came by will to her son, John Wister, and upon his death it was willed to his daughter, Sarah Logan Wister, now the wife of James Starr.

The paths, drains, gardening, etc. adhere to Peale's original

[1]The foregoing has been abridged from a paper written by Charles Coleman Sellers for his mother, Cora Wells Sellers, member of The Gardeners of Montgomery & Delaware Counties.

The garden of Charles Willson Peale, in Germantown

plan. The borders contain many of the old plants. A large quantity of the original box, some of which is now ten feet high, is still undisturbed.

GERMANTOWN NURSERIES AND HORTICULTURISTS

The first nursery in Germantown for the commercial growing of plants was started by Christian Lehman upon Great Road and opposite to what is now Armat Street. This was one of the earliest nurseries in the colonies. He advertised "Hyacinth roots and tulip roots, and most other things in the flower or fruit tree nursery way."

After Christian Lehman's, the first regular nursery established in Germantown was that of Martin Baumann, a native of Alsace. Baumann was a graduate of the school of gardening of Württemberg, and was, if not the first, at least one of the first professional landscape gardeners to come to America. He was first employed in America by Stephen Girard, later leaving the latter's employ to plan the gardens of Fern-Hill for Louis Clapier. As he was known as a skillful garden-designer and plant-grower, in the year 1837 he decided to open a nursery. This nursery was on the south side of Manheim Street, the grounds extending to the line of the present Seymour Street, between the lines of Tacoma Street and Pulaski Avenue. Baumann distributed both garden and hothouse plants, and his growings were regulated to satisfy local needs or demands.

The most important nursery affecting the Germantown of the middle period was that established in the year 1809 by Bernard McMahon upon a lane which found an outlet from the Germantown Road, two miles south of Stenton, the exact and complete site of this nursery becoming "Oakdale Park," now Fotterall Park, Philadelphia. Here McMahon had a notable collection of plants, one of its features being thirty

varieties of native oak trees, among which a specimen of willow-oak was the most conspicuous. He is also thought to have introduced the mock orange.

We quote from an existing record of McMahon's life:

"McMahon, Bernard (about 1775 to September 16, 1816) was born in Ireland and came to America for political reasons, 1796. He settled in Philadelphia where he engaged in the seed and nursery business. He early began the collection and exportation of seeds of American plants. In 1804 he published a catalogue of such seeds, comprising about 1,000 species. He was the means of making many of our native plants known in Europe. He enjoyed the friendship of Jefferson and other distinguished men, and his seed-store became a meeting place for botanists and horticulturists. He was interested in all branches of horticulture. It is thought that the Lewis and Clarke expedition was planned at his house. At all events McMahon and Landreth were instrumental in distributing the seeds which those explorers collected. In 1806 he gave to America its first great horticultural book, *American Gardener's Calendar*, which was long a standard cyclopedic work.

"Nuttall, Bartram and Darlington were among his friends, and Nuttall gave his name in 1818 to the west-coast evergreen barberries which are still known as *Mahonia*."[1]

The preface of the *American Gardener's Calendar*, which McMahon published in 1806, is here reprinted:

"The author of this work takes the liberty of informing his friends and the public that he is constantly supplied at his Seed Warehouse in Philadelphia with a general assortment of Garden Seeds suitable for cultivation in the United States and in the West Indies. Grass seeds of every important and valuable kind, an immense variety of Tree, Shrub and Flower Seeds and roots, procured from the various parts of the world, with which the enterprize of American commerce has any

[1]Bailey's *Standard Cyclopædia of Horticulture*.

connection, as well as from the different States and Territories of the Union; spades, shovels, rakes, Hoes, Reels, Lines, Trowels, Edging-irons, Garden-shears, Watering-pots, Pruning, budding and grafting knives &c. Bulb-glasses, Bass-mats, Glass suitable for hot-bed lights and other forcing departments; seeds for bird-feeding of every kind .

*   *   *   *

"The more effectually to accommodate his customers, he has connected with the Seed Trade, a Botanical, Agricultural, and Horticultural Book Store where a great variety of valuable publications on these subjects, especially the modern works of merit may be had. This with his other business he is determined to extend to the utmost of his ability, and he flatters himself that by his industry, perseverance and punctuality he will be enabled to render this establishment not only useful to himself but of considerable advantage to the community at large."

Planted in the year 1822, about one mile above McMahon's, and upon Germantown Road at the village of "Rising Sun," was the noted nursery and flower garden of Daniel Maupay. It covered seven acres and was given to the growing of roses, annuals, herbaceous, decorative garden, lawn, and hot-house plants. It also contained a miniature flower garden of sufficient merit to attract and receive the commendation of Robert Buist, the well known plant-grower of Pratt's Garden, at Lemon Hill. Samuel Maupay succeeded to the business created by his father.

Dr. Samuel Betton of "White Cottage," situated upon Bockius Lane or Manheim Street, as early as 1830 had a collection of plants of sufficient merit to receive the commendation of Robert Buist. After a visit in that year, the latter wrote:

"We observed a plant of Nandina domestica in full flower —it is the largest we have seen. Here is likewise a plant of Andropogon scheananthus which the doctor says makes a very delicious tea; an uncommonly large plant of Laegerstraemia Indica, that stands the open air; some very fine China Orange trees, and several other valuable plants. The greenhouse is 40 feet; a pit 36 feet; besides framing. The kitchen garden contains one acre, which is judiciously cropt, and well stocked with fruit trees among the latter a very rich cream colored plum, streaked on the side exposed to the sun and very transparent; it is said to be a seedling and of a very rich flavor. A pear orchard of considerable extent is just beginning to bear, and contains 150 varieties. It bids fair to rival some of the old orchards."

Philip R. Freas was the founder of *The Germantown Telegraph*, first known as the *Village Telegraph*. The first number was issued March 17, 1830. This agricultural paper gained a circulation throughout the entire United States.

John Jay Smith, one of the editors of Downing's *Horticulturist*, will be longest remembered for the Laurel Hill Cemeteries of his creation. In the year 1835, following the lead of Dr. Jacob Bigelow, of Boston, he founded, designed, and superintended the planting of North Laurel Hill Cemetery, a project which was for a time looked upon as sacrilegious, but which rapidly emerged from prejudice, and so quickly grew in public favor that "garden cemeteries" were established in many parts of North America. Central, South and West Laurel Hill Cemeteries followed, and the rare trees and shrubs there to be found were planted under the direction of Mr. Smith.

The garden-house of Charles Willson Peale, in Germantown

PENNSYLVANIA IN GENERAL

NATURALLY horticulture reached its highest development around the center of densest population, Philadelphia, and its suburbs. But by the middle of the eighteenth century other parts of Pennsylvania began to be settled, and attempts were made toward road-making, rendering transportation a little less difficult. Still, records are very meager, and it takes a great deal of imagination to picture the countryside between 1700 and 1800. Fortunately

which being green and piled up in rucks cast a very sweet and agreeable smell. The country here is not hilly, nor are the woods very tall or thick. The people in general follow farming, and have very neat brick dwellings upon their farms."

Later David Johann Schoepf in his *Travels in the Confederation* speaks of the region about Pittsburgh:

"In several regions beyond the Alleghany we had occasion to observe the goodness and riotous fertility of the soil in the

"Elm Grove," in Buckingham Township, Bucks County. Now the property of Colonel Henry D. Paxon

we are aided by a few detailed accounts written by owners of large estates, and also by occasional vivid descriptions in the letters or diaries of some adventurous traveler.

Perhaps a few quotations from these early travelers will give us a different feeling about the countryside from that held by Mrs. Penn, who was sure that beyond the cultivated land at Pennsbury lay nothing but dense forests full of ravening wild beasts and savages with scalps at their belts.

Dr. Alexander Hamilton in his *Itinerarium*, written in 1744, speaks of visiting Chester, "a pretty neat and large village. Built chiefly of brick, pleasantly situated upon a small river of the same name."

He speaks also of "the people all along the road making hay

original undisturbed state. The indigenous plants had a lusty fat appearance, and they grew vastly stronger and to greater heights than in their habitat elsewhere. In new-made and unmanured gardens there stood stalks of the common sun-flower which were not less than twenty feet high."

That certainly gives a picture of lush virgin growth in a region now so densely populated and laden with smoke. Schoepf goes on to say:

"Fruit is still a rarity, here as well as throughout the mountains. Near to the Fort was an orchard, planted by the English garrison, but since wholly neglected, and this was the only one for perhaps a hundred miles around. In it were several varieties of the best-tasting pears and apples."

Mrs. Mary Dewee traveled by boat down the Ohio about 1787. One of her descriptions was of a summer-house owned by the O'Hara family, "which," she says, "stands on the bank of the Alleghany river about a hundred yards from the bottom of their garden. It is the finest situation I ever saw. . . . Their house is in the midst of an orchard of sixty acres, the only one at the place."

And elsewhere: "As the sun was setting we rode through Lancaster, a beautiful inland town with some elegant houses in it. I was quite delighted with the view—which at once presented to your sight a sudden rise with houses, trees and gardens, on either side, that has a very pleasant effect."

A later traveler speaks of the valley of the Brandywine as follows:

"The face of the Valley is in no degree uniformly flat but abounds in small and very graceful undulations of its surface—the enclosures are in some places so small and so mixed with orchards and grass lots as to appear nearly like a village of farms, in other places they are spread into extensive fields, and the houses at a distance on eminences—generally ornamented with large trees, give the highest idea of farming wealth and comfort—the copses of wood which are scattered everywhere add greatly to the scene. . . . Chestnut oak and the Buttonwood, the more graceful from their not being planted, but left either by accident or design from the forest which once covered the whole country.

"Along the roads are a number of neat and some elegant houses built and owned by citizens who have once lived in this country or possess connections in it as country seats."

During the short time that William Penn was in America he made many grants of land to settlers. The first land to be taken up west of the Brandywine was a tract of 600 acres, which was granted to George W. Pearce or Peirce, and remained in the possession of the same family until 1906.

Later we read that Thomas and Richard Penn granted a tract to John Page, gentleman, of London. This land was in the Conestoga region, and John Page empowered his attorneys to sell portions of the said tracts to several persons for the rental of "one red rose to be paid on the twenty-third of each June, every year and forever." We wonder how long that "forever" lasted.

PRIVATE ESTATES AND GARDENS

ELM GROVE, BUCKINGHAM TOWNSHIP, BUCKS COUNTY

The garden at Elm Grove is now owned by Colonel Henry D. Paxon, descendant of Samuel Johnson and Martha Johnson, the latter of whom laid out the original garden. This work was done between the years 1786 and 1790. There is no plan of the garden in existence, and it is doubtful if there was one, for the formation of greensward bordered by flowerbeds is so simple that more than likely it was made under the personal direction of the owners, as was the present new West garden.

The long, low colonial house stands as a background and strong barrier between the passing highways and the range

of the north winds. Between the house and the garden a much-used stone walk runs its full length, leading to all four doors opening on the south side. On the southern boundary of the garden, winding around it, is a stream with sloping banks. Beyond this is a meadow reaching southward to fields of pastoral quietness, with here and there a wooded spot, or an old farmhouse.

The garden at Elm Grove is situated on the south side of

In the garden at Elm Grove

the dwelling-house with its groups of quaint little buildings, very low, with interesting gable-ends. The long stone path is divided in the middle with another path which leads to a circular space where there is a sun-dial. Around the sun-dial there are four main squares bordered on all sides by flowerbeds three feet wide. Farther on the garden is divided into beds which conform in shape to the sloping ground.

This dividing path continues through the southern portion of the garden, and is covered with an arbor. At the bottom of the slope it meets another path which bounds the entire southern line of the property, following the edge of a bank sloping down thirty feet to the stream. Here stand old magnolias, part of the original garden. Here also are very old lilacs in irregular clumps, and around their roots cluster white violets, their springtime fragrance part of the association of the household. There are also clumps of old single yellow roses, and a tradition of very beautiful specimens of the flowering crab-apple (*Malus coronaria*). This fragrant native crab-apple was always a part of the gardens of the early Swedes who settled along the Delaware.

These white lilacs and magnolias protected numerous rows of sugarloaf-shaped rows of beehives, and once Samuel Johnson, the first owner, admonished the bees as they worked amongst his flowers

"To mind your ps and qs
Your master loves no kind of drones
But fairly asks his claims and dues."

The special features of the garden are the southern exposure and the seclusion, and the just sufficiently formal arrangement of paths and squares, the central plot with its sun-dial harmonizing with the colonial atmosphere of the house.

This garden has great charm, possessing those qualities of intimacy and repose which go to make a garden a part of the life of the house, and not merely a decorative feature or showspot.[1]

[1]Adapted from a paper by Mrs. Henry D. Paxon, of Philadelphia.

Another view of the garden of Mrs. Henry D. Paxon, at "Elm Grove," in Buckingham Township, Bucks County

CHISWELL—MUNCY FARMS—RESTLESS OAKS

In 1763, the same year that John Penn came to Pennsylvania as lieutenant-governor, Henry Hollingsworth, one of the Pennsylvania merchant princes, built "Chiswell" on Front Street in Philadelphia. The house was named for his ancestral home in Ireland, and no expense was spared on the grounds surrounding the house.

To insure a properly designed garden, Hollingsworth had brought with him from Ireland an expert gardener, Michael McAvoy. McAvoy had in turn brought with him a shipment of box bushes, and also boxes of native soil, native fertilizers, and barrels of real Irish water with which to shower them en route.

These box bushes were planted on this country estate within the city limits, and, out of gratitude for the care bestowed upon them, grew marvellously. They soon made the brick house, set high on a terrace, a landmark, not only to all the city, but to vessels coming up the Delaware.

Lydia Hollingsworth, the daughter of the house, loved this garden, full of lavender, mignonette, larkspur, coxcombs, sweet-williams and moss roses, but she had to leave it to follow her husband, Samuel Wallis, to his clearing, "Muncy Farms," a part of the last Penn purchase from the Indians.

Lydia felt that she could be happy in the wilderness if she could have the one thing she loved the most—a flower garden. So in the fall of 1769 Michael was sent to Muncy Farms, convoying a wagon-train loaded with box-woods and choice garden plants to adorn the new home of Lydia, the great merchant's favorite daughter.

The frontier appealed to Michael, and Lydia persuaded her father that she needed a gardener to stay with her in order to make the wilderness "blossom as the rose."

In a short time the new garden at Muncy Farms, built between the house and the river, bid fair to rival the older garden at Chiswell—grass paths, grottoes, rockeries, hedges, orangeries, and all. McAvoy worked tirelessly, early and late, and as he had brought with him his wife and family, one of his daughters, the auburn-haired Jura, often helped with the weeding. Mrs. Hollingsworth noticed the beautiful child, and often interceded between her and her mother, a stern and severe woman. It was probably misunderstandings over Jura's upbringing which led Mrs. McAvoy to urge her husband to leave Muncy Farms, and take up a claim in the Indian country beyond Tiadaghton. Accordingly, in the spring of 1771 they moved to the vicinity of McElhatton Run, in what is now Clinton County. There they marked out a tomahawk claim, and as soon as enough trees had been girdled to let in the sun, Jura must have a formal garden with rockeries, grottoes and serpentine paths like the one at Muncy Farms, which had been copied from Chiswell in Philadelphia, in turn a replica of the ancestral Chiswell in the old country.

Jura, no doubt mourning for the fair Dresden-China Lydia, worked industriously, setting out not only all the old garden favorites, but sprigs of box, yew, juniper, savin, and specimens of all rare plants and shrubs that she could find locally, including laurel and rhododendron, being particularly successful with the latter.

But after the creative period was over, not even a garden could hold the adventurous spirit of Jura, and she decamped into deeper wilderness with James Logan, the Mingo Indian chief, who had stopped once too often to admire the garden and gardener of the well-named "Restless Oaks."[1]

NEWINGTON[2]

On the 19th day of January, 1786, the Supreme Executive Council of the Commonwealth of Pennsylvania transferred by patent a certain tract of land called "Newington" in Westmoreland County (now Allegheny) to Thomas Shields.

Thus the land was patented into the hands of the Shields family nearly 150 years ago, and immediately a space was selected for a garden. A clearing was made in the river valley open to the rising and setting sun, and protected by a windbreak of trees, listed as "Hoop Ash, Black Oak, White Hickory, and a Sychomore of renown." In 1823 the garden took to itself an air of importance, was framed by a plan; it was fenced and hedged about and gated in.

The French influence was felt in the garden, and it was blocked out in squares and strips, while paths, bordering narrow beds, led to the eastern corner, where we find a formal garden like a huge cut pie.

The little gate which formed the entrance opened on a long and grassy path broken midway by two cedar trees trimmed to look like huge bushes standing like fat sentinels—a home and a protection for the birds.

The garden was outlined by narrow beds of smaller fruits, raspberries, white, pink and red; gooseberries, strawberries—backed by trellised

bloom. In early spring the Star of Bethlehem forced its way through the mass of leaves, and hyacinths and daffodils and the old red peony took their turns. There all the sweet old roses unfurled their petals—the hundred-leaved, the moss, red velvet, and the white and yellow Scotch and sweet briar too. Violets, forget-me-nots, lily-of-the-valley, scented the air, and fox-gloves swayed in the breeze near white and blue Canterbury bells, and blazing marigolds. Overhead jasmine and scarlet cypress stretched their graceful vines.

On the southern exposure grew a flourishing orchard, and in the first row the center tree was a Seckel pear, a seedling from the original found in a fence corner by Dr. Seckel, and to this day the only seedling never grafted. And then, to fix the garden with the ancient times, we find an Indian mound.

The site of Lydia Hollingsworth Wallis's formal garden of 1769, Muncy Farms, Williamsport

The site of Jura McAvoy's garden of 1771, at McElhatton Run

grapes, white and purple, sharing their sunlight with the herb bed, where grew sage and thyme and sweet marjoram, rosemary, and later tarragon. In the midst of the garden flourished all the old-time flowers, growing in a mass of gorgeous

This has been surmounted by a stone-foundationed summer house strong enough to deter marauding hands from disturbing the Indian grave resting quietly below. Beyond this lay the orchard wall above the little Sewickley creek which rippled its sparkling waters to the broad Ohio.

The garden at Newington was very closely associated with the garden at Economy laid out in 1827 by that strange community called Harmony Society, mentioned by Byron in "Don Juan." Plants and trees were exchanged, dahlias being especially remembered as "yust so schoen behind as before."

Preparations were begun in 1813 for building the present mansion. Foresters came from Virginia to select and blaze the oaks to be felled, water-dried, and hewn at the old water-wheel in the flour mill at the entrance on the highway. The bricks were formed and baked from the excavations and in 1816 all was ready to begin. Like Solomon's Temple it was seven years in building. The writer finds recorded in the *Agricultural Alma-*

[1]Adapted from an account by Henry W. Shoemaker.
[2]Adapted from an account by Sarah E. Bissell.

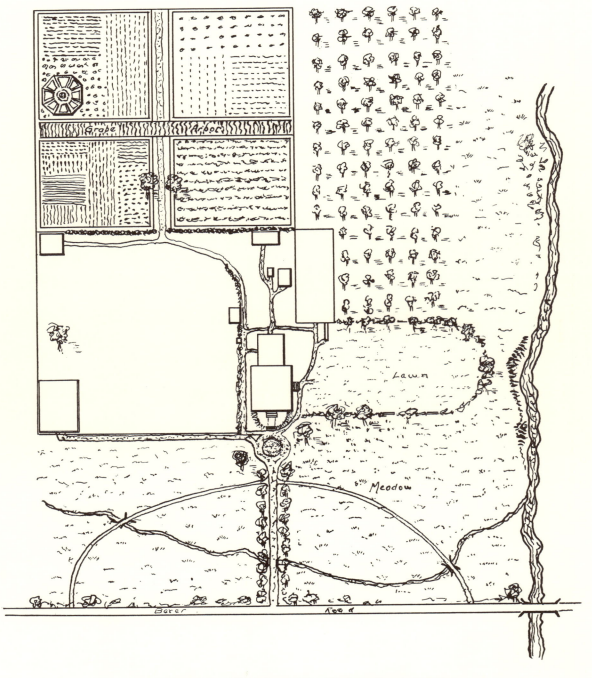

The garden plan of "Newington" in Allegheny County, in 1823

nac, published in Philadelphia in 1823, this notation in the handwriting of the master of the estate: "April the thirteenth, D. and E. Shields and children arrived at Sewickley this day and lodged for the first time in the mansion," and this motto in evidence below, "A.D. 1735. Let us cultivate the ground that the poor as well as the rich may be filled and happiness and peace be established throughout our borders."

BRUNOT'S ISLAND

In the *Western Pennsylvania Historical Magazine* for July, 1926, Annie Clark Miller, in an article entitled "Old Houses and Estates in Pittsburgh," says:

"There was the Great Island Mansion of Felix Brunot, who came to America with his foster brother Lafayette, and remained to practice medicine. A description of this spot is found in an old journal published in 1810, a copy of which is owned by Hilary B. Brunot Esq. The journal is written by F. Cumming, who 'made a tour of the western country and a voyage down the Ohio and Mississippi River.' "

Cumming's Journal says, "Brunot's Island contains three hundred acres, a most luxuriant soil, about half of which has been cleared by Dr. Brunot, a native of France, who adds hospitality and sociality to the abundance which he derives from his well-cultivated farm.

"He has judiciously left the timber standing on the end of the island nearest Pittsburgh, through which and a beautiful locust grove of about twelve acres, an avenue from the upper landing is led with taste and judgment, about half a mile to his house. . . . He has an excellent garden and nursery.

"He has fenced his farm in such a way, as to have a delightful promenade all around it, between the fences and the margin of the river, which he has purposely left fringed with the native wood about sixty yards wide."

Dr. Brunot "collected at home and abroad every plant, leaf and root that contained balm for pain."

View of Pittsburgh

The earliest known view of the city of Pittsburgh, a water-color drawing by Joseph Warren or General Victor Collot

SILVER LAKE

The following is drawn from the Historical Collections of Pennsylvania: "After the Revolution all the lands in the northern part of the state, then a wilderness, became an object of speculation and were taken up in immense tracts by Robert Morris, John Nicholson, Judge Peters and others.

"Among the most eminent in sustaining the Pennsylvania title was Dr. Robert H. Rose from Chester County who came to this county [Susquehanna] while it was yet a wilderness. He was a man of refined taste, a poet and a scholar, of great enterprise and indomitable firmness. He purchased about 100,000 acres of land from the widow Francis and others at a very low price. Dr. Rose after entering with great public spirit into various enterprises for the establishment and improvement of the county erected for himself an elegant mansion on the banks of Silver Lake, surrounded by one of the largest farms in the state. In the cultivation of this farm, in the sale of his lands, and in the enjoyment of an extensive and well-selected library he passed his late years. The town of Montrose in Pennsylvania owes its name to the Rose family . . ."

"Silver Lake, the Seat of Robert H. Rose Esq.," in Susquehanna County

Photographed by Mr. Hartley

An old photograph of Economy

ECONOMY

The first years of the eighteenth century saw the organization of the Harmony Society in Pennsylvania. It was founded by George Rapp, or "Father" Rapp, and his followers from Germany. This group made several attempts at colonization, but at last founded the unique community of "Economy" on the Ohio River, eighteen miles from Pittsburgh. There they built a model town with wide streets, and brick and frame dwellings. And behind the house of the leader was laid out the great garden of Economy, which is still in existence.

Mrs. Agnes Hays Gormly in her booklet, *Old Economy*, speaks as follows of the garden as she found it when Miss Gertrude Rapp was still living:

"We walked between clipped box hedges that guard beds where ranks of Mary lilies stand in the midst of sweet-scented blossoms, with sentinels of great scarlet tulips. Then through another grassy path bordered by stiffly pruned standard roses, each a bouquet in itself, and before us is the pride of Economy—the fish pond. We cross the still water where the goldfish play in schools, by a plank to the island where in 1827 Frederick Rapp built a stone summer house, all set around with green. A winding lattice-enclosed stairway leads to the flat roof, where on Sunday afternoon and holidays the band plays. We pass various sorts of arbors, with many recesses, all vine-clad . . . with secret doors that let you into a cagelike retreat, with benches and tables where the inner man may be refreshed. Beyond is the rough stone wall, ivy-mantled, and crested with a mass of 'hen and chickens' houseleek. . . . A bed of sweet-scented purple and white

violets and lilies of the valley lies under the shelter of the wall. . . . But here we turn to the grotto, built of stone full of fossils and with a door cunningly contrived of bark without sign of hinge or handle . . . the door does swing open and we stand before the big statue of 'Harmony,' once intended as a fountain. In her finger-tips you can see the holes out of which water played upon her lyre. On the walls are tablets recording the founding of Harmony, New Harmony and Economy, and the birth and death of George Rapp. 'Tis an artless place,

The stone-coped path at Economy, as it was originally

The summer-house and fish-pond at Economy

(in every sense), and yet in a way impressive. The narrow path leading to the bakery is bordered always with flowers, snowdrops in early spring, then sweet-scented violets and daffodils, and on in summer succession until tiny button chrysanthemums shine through winter snows."

In time the Society died out, and much of the land reverted to the State. The custody of the properties devolved upon the State Historical Commission, which in 1919 transferred them to the Harmony Society Historical Association.

Not long ago a plan was drawn in which an attempt was made to reproduce the original gardens. This plan has never been carried out, but is valuable as it shows the relative position of the fish-pond, the so-called grotto, and the maze, though it is very doubtful if there ever was a maze, as that form of diversion never appealed to the practical German.

Miss Sarah E. Bissell recollects visiting the garden as a child, and says it seemed to her geometrical and rather harsh, and gave her a feeling of despair because there were no hiding places for the fairies. She also says: "The geometrical forms and lines of the great house were evidently planned and carried out in the garden—small artificial plans brought from Germany: even today one can come across just such gardens on a walk from Koenigsberg to Danzig."

The grotto at Economy

Detail of the summer-house and fish-pond at Economy

One of the headwaters of the Economy irrigation plant, as it was originally

Miss Bissell continues:

"The clipped trees were in the foreground, with the gay beds, brilliant with large coarse German flowers, in front and in the distance meadows encircling it all."

The Allegheny Garden Club now has charge of the grounds, and through their efforts much of the quaint, old-time charm of the garden has been preserved.

THE MORAVIAN SETTLEMENTS

Early in the eighteenth century the Moravian church sent missionary colonies to Georgia and Pennsylvania. Those that went to Georgia afterwards moved to Pennsylvania, where they were joined by other communities. Later Count Zinzendorf, who had befriended the brethren abroad, joined them and brought about the organization of Moravian churches and communities at Bethlehem and Nazareth, and other places in Pennsylvania.

The members of these companies were generally of fine families, who had given up everything in order to come here to convert the Indians. Though their aim was mainly missionary, they planted extensive orchards, and aided greatly in the horticultural development of the regions where they settled.

In 1794 the town of Bethlehem is mentioned in Casenove's Journal as follows:

"The settlement of the Moravians in Bethlehem is situated in a very large valley where the Congregation owns a district

Porch of the Sister House at Ephrata

of about 5,000 acres. It was begun in 1742 and until 1762 the Moravians there were merged into a common family, whose every individual was working for the Community and was kept by it; but since then this full surrender of fortune no longer occurs. Each one of the brothers and sisters keeps his property and is paid for his work."

An old print of the same date shows how extensive and orderly the fifty years of development had been.

A photograph of the doorway of the Sister House at Ephrata shows the simple lines of their style of architecture.

The sisters cultivated flowers at a very early day, and are said to have made charming paintings of them.

"A View of Bethlehem in North America." This old print of the late eighteenth century shows how extensive and orderly the development of the countryside had been in the first fifty years of the Moravian settlement

EARLY BOTANISTS IN PENNSYLVANIA

A NUMBER of men by their intense interest in botany directly influenced the horticultural development not only of America, but of the Old World. William Penn sent many seeds and plants to England, and when he had to leave his province to his trusted provincial secretary and Clerk of the Council, James Logan, the latter, besides looking after the affairs of government most efficiently, found time to interest himself in the world of botany. He was a careful observer, and his papers were always welcomed by European Academies. His name is commemorated in the genus of plants *Loganiaceae*.

Webb in his "Bachelor's Hall" describes a botanical garden which is supposed to have belonged to James Logan:

> "Close to the dome a garden shall be joined
> A fit employment for a studious mind;
> In our vast woods whatever simples grow,
> Whose virtues none, or none but Indians know,
> Within the confines of this garden brought,
> To rise with added lustre shall be taught;
> Then culled with judgment, each shall yield its juice,
> Saliferous balsam to the sick man's use;
> A longer date of life mankind shall boast,
> And Death shall mourn her ancient sceptre lost."

But no one knows if this garden really existed.

JOHN BARTRAM

John Bartram, a most picturesque and interesting character, contemporary with Franklin and Logan, and in constant communication with them, influenced to a very great extent the growth of botanical and horticultural knowledge in this country.

Bartram was born in 1701—the year William Penn left America—at Derby, in what is now Chester County. He was a Quaker. He did not become definitely interested in botany until after he was twenty-four years old. St. John de Crevecoeur[1] gives an account of the simple incident which turned Bartram's thoughts to systematic botany.

One day while ploughing Bartram had stopped to rest; his eye fell on a daisy. "And," he said, "I viewed it with more curiosity than common country farmers are wont to do."

"'What a shame,' said my mind, or something that inspired my mind, 'that thee should have employed so many years in tilling the earth and destroying so many flowers and plants without being acquainted with their structures and uses!'"

From that time on Bartram developed true scientific curiosity, and became enthralled by botany. In 1729 Logan presented him with Parkinson's *Herbal*, thus giving encouragement to the self-taught philosopher. Logan said he was a person worthier of a much heavier purse than fortune had yet allowed him, and "had a genius perfectly well-turned for botany."

In 1727 Bartram bought land at Gray's

Ferry for a botanical garden, and then, being an ingenious mechanic, built himself a house, quarrying the stone and preparing the timbers with his own hands.

Crevecoeur, who visited him here, has recorded the pleasure he found in Bartram's garden; the French agriculturist also spent hours in the study and greenhouse with "this enlightened botanist, this worthy citizen, who united all the simplicity of rustic manners to the most useful learning."

A subscription was started in 1731 to enable Bartram to travel in search of botanical specimens. It was proposed to raise enough to enable him to pursue his travels for three years; he was described as a person who "has had a propensity to Botanicks since his infancy," and "an accurate observer," also a man "of great industry and temperance, and of unquestionable veracity."

The results of these travels were the discoveries of many new and important plants, among them *Rhododendron maximum*, and *Cypripedium acaule*, and two very delightful books by this earliest of American botanists.

Bartram was in constant correspondence with numerous foreign philosophers. Linnaeus said he was the greatest natural botanist in the world, and commemorated his name in the moss genus, *Bartramia*. He was made fellow of several scientific societies of Europe, and finally appointed American botanist to George III. "I believe," wrote Franklin, introducing Bartram to Jared Eliot, in 1775, "you will find him to be at least twenty folio pages, large paper, well-filled, on the subjects of botany, fossils, husbandry, and the first creation."

The Bartram gardens were the first real botanic gardens in America. Those of the Rosicrucians on the lower Wissahickon and the garden of Christopher Witt antedated them, but contained principally medicinal herbs, while Bartram's had from the beginning a most interesting collection of trees and shrubs. The two former gardens passed out of existence, but Bartram's gardens and house have been preserved by the park system of Philadelphia. Many of the trees planted by Bartram's own hands are now alive and flourishing. We may see the Yellow-wood (*Cladrastis lutea*), Silver-bell (*Halesia tetraptera*), Fraser's Magnolia (*Magnolia Fraseri*), the red Horse-Chestnut (*Aesculus rubicunda*), and a Lady Petre pear tree, grown from seed sent over by Lord Petre, a patron.

The residence of John Bartram, built with his own hands in 1730. His portrait is shown on page 330

---

[1] Hector St. John de Crevecoeur, author of *Letters from an American Farmer.*

This tree first bore fruit in 1763. It is now 165 years old and still continues to bear fruit.

In 1787 Manasseh Cutler visited the garden:

"It is finely situated as it partakes of every kind of soil, has a fine stream of water, and a artificial pond, where there is a good collection of aquatic plants. There is no situation in which plants or trees are found here but that they may be propagated here in one that is similar.

"There are in his garden some very large trees. . . . He has also a large number of aromatics, some of them trees and some of them plants. One plant I thought equal to cinnamon. The Franklin tree is very curious. It has been found only in one particular spot in Georgia."

This tree, named for Franklin by Bartram, is the Gordonia, a species of rose bay. There are only a few specimens under cultivation; they have been propagated from cuttings from the original tree.

The two hundredth anniversary of the founding of the Bartram Garden (1730–1930) finds the garden intelligently and carefully restored through the combined efforts of the John Bartram Association, the Pennsylvania Horticultural Society, the Garden Clubs of Philadelphia, the Weeders, the Four Counties Garden Club, and the Civic Club of the City of Philadelphia. The restoration includes the replanting of the shrubbery that marked the boundary of the original garden, destroyed about twenty years ago. There have been large plantings of native shrubs associated with Bartram's early work—rhododendrons, kalmia, azaleas and dogwood. All the planting has been done with material mentioned in Bartram's letters or publications.[1]

Peter Collinson, the English botanist, who took great interest in the flora of the New World

---

[1]A copy of the price catalogue issued by the Bartram Gardens in 1828 is preserved in the Bartram Memorial Library at the University of Pennsylvania.

CORRESPONDENCE OF JOHN BARTRAM AND PETER COLLINSON

Some of the correspondence between Peter Collinson of London and Bartram is here reprinted, as it gives a vivid account of flowers and plants available at that time, and contains most valuable data upon both native and introduced weeds.

Peter Collinson to John Bartram

London, October 20, 1740.

Dear Friend:

Inclosed is the Mate's receipt for a box of bulbs, directed for thee. Make much of them; for they are such a collection as is rarely to be met with, all at once; for all the sorts of bulbous roots taken up this year, there is some of every sort. There is above twenty sorts of Crocus—as many Narcissus—all our sorts of Martagons and Lilies—with gladiolus, Ornithogalums, Moleys, and Irises, with many others I don't now remember, which time will show thee. It is likely some sort thee may have; but I believe there is more that you have not, so pray take great care of them. Give them a good soil, and keep them clear from weeds, which are a great prejudice to these flowers in the spring.

I have several very curious flowers out of the mixed Virginia seeds; in particular a new Jacea, with hoary rough leaves; a very pretty dwarf Gentian, with a large blue flower, the extremity of the flower leaves all notched or jagged. The whole plant is not above three or four inches high; I am afraid it is an annual. But there is a great variety, besides a very pretty Gratiola, and a Dracocephalon,—it is a labiated flower like Snap Dragon, and is very near akin to it. Lord Petre has had the greatest luck, having the largest quantity of seed. He has two or three sorts of fine Chrysanthemums or Sun-flowers; Asters, I have a fine new sort. Your thickets must have a beautiful show in the autumn, with these plants; for I see they must be in great plenty, —for almost every sod has an Aster growing with the various plants that thee sent.

I hope I shall now see Josselyn's Daffodil, or your Dens Canis, with a yellow flower in perfection.

I am much obliged for your account of Mr. Witt's rarities. Thee has unravelled the whole mystery.

Pray tell me, is the plant thee calls a Valerian, with blue flowers, which came in the last cargo, a native of your country? for it has been long in our gardens. We call it Greek Valerian (Polemonium).

Every day I expect thy last specimens from Holland. They have been long delayed by many accidents, but I can't help myself: for Dr. Gronovius is so kind to fix them neatly on fine white paper, that they look as beautiful as so many pictures, and names them into the bargain. Neither my skill nor my time would permit me to do this, so I am glad to comply with his own time; but this will prevent me giving names to the last two quires, till next year. I can tell thee in the next edition of Virginia plants, thee will see Bartramia.

I am thy true and sincere friend,

P. COLLINSON.

Peter Collinson to John Bartram

Now I come to thank my kind friend for his letter of the 28th. of July. I am delighted with his operations on the Larkspur. The product is wonderful. If these charming flowers can be continued by seed, they will be the greatest ornament to the garden in their season of blowing.

John Bartram's notes on weeds in Pennsylvania in 1742, drawn from his letters to Peter Collinson

A brief account of some of the plants most troublesome in our pastures and fields in Pennsylvania; and most of which are brought from Europe.

The most mischievous of these is, first, the stinking yellow Linaria. It is the most hurtful plants to our pastures that can grow in our northern climate. Neither the spade, plough, nor hoe, can eradicate it, when it is spread in a pasture. Every little fibre that is left, will soon increase prodigiously; nay, some people have rolled great heaps of logs upon it, and burnt them to ashes, whereby the earth was burnt half a foot deep, yet it is up again, as fresh as ever, covering the ground so close as not to let any grass grow amongst it; and the cattle can't abide it. But it doth not injure corn as much as grass, because the plough cuts off the stalks, and it doth not grow so high, before harvest, as to choke the corn. It is now spread over great part of the inhabited parts of Pennsylvania. It was first introduced as a fine garden flower; but never was plant more heartily cursed by those that suffer by its encroachment.

The common English Hypericum (H. perforatum, L.) is a very pernicious weed. It spreads over whole fields, and spoils their pasturage, not only by choking the grass, but infecting our horses and sheep with scabbed noses and feet, especially those that have white hair on their face and legs. This is certain fact, as generally affirmed; but this is not so bad as the Linaria. The hoe and plough will destroy it.

Wild Chamomile, called Mathen, is another mischievous weed. It runs about and spreads much, choking not only the grass, but the wheat, more than the other two; but hath not yet spread so generally as they. But this may be killed by planting Indian Corn, or sowing buckwheat on the ground for several years successively. I had it brought many times in dung; but when I find it I burn it root and branch.

Leucanthemum is a very destructive weed, in meadow and pasture grounds, choking the grass and taking full possession of the ground, so that the fields will look as white as if covered with snow; but the hoe and plough will destroy this weed.

The great English single-stalked Mullein, grows generally in most of our old fields, and with its broad spreading leaves, takes up some room in our pastures; but it is easily destroyed with the plough, or scythe, having only single tap roots.

Saponaria is more difficult to eradicate, as it runs deep, and spreads much underground; but it has not yet spread much in the country. With care we may keep it under.

The great double dandelion is very troublesome and in our meadow ground; and difficult to eradicate; but the hoe and plough will destroy it.

Crow Garlick is greatly loved by the horses, cows, and sheep, and is very wholesome early pasture for them; yet our people generally hate it, because it makes the milk, butter, cheese and indeed the flesh of these cattle that feed much upon it, taste so strong that we can hardly eat of it; but for horses and young cattle it doth very well. But our millers can't abide it amongst corn. It clogs up their mills so, that it is impossible to make good flour.

Docks are very troublesome in our mowing ground; and without care they spread much by seed. They stifle the grass by their luxuriant large leaves.

The Scotch Thistle is a very troublesome weed, along our sea coast. The people say that a Scotch Minister brought with him a bed stuffed with thistle-down, in which was contained some seed. The inhabitants, having plenty of feathers soon turned out the down, and filled the bed with feathers. The seed coming up, filled that part of the country with thistles.

*   *   *

Dr. Howard Kelly in his book *Some American Medical Botanists* says that Bartram lamented that a government scheme of exploring Louisiana could not be carried out because the scientists would be exposed to "the greatest savage cruelty of the gun, tomahawk and torture by the Indians." Bartram wrote that on a journey which he made to Pittsburgh, then a frontier post, "an Indian met me and pulled off my hat in a great passion and chawed it all around to show me how he would eat me if I came again."

Bartram was probably the first American to perform successful experiments in hybridization. After his death his sons William and John continued his garden, and for years it was the largest and best collection of trees and shrubs in America. The services of the garden to early American horticulture were very great.

PETER KALM

Peter Kalm, the Swedish botanist, visited America in 1748. He was Professor of Economy at the University of Åbo in Swedish Finland, and a member of the Swedish Academy of Sciences.

He arrived in America in September, and immediately set out collecting seeds and plants. He stayed here three years and eight months, traveling through Pennsylvania, New Jersey, and New York. The majority of the entries in his diary, however, are dated from Pennsylvania. He brought with him a letter to Benjamin Franklin, who seems to have been the first person in America to realize the importance of his visit and to show him kindness.

Kalm's observations and notes, embodied in the form of a diary, make most interesting reading. And as his stay here was much longer than that of the usual traveler, we can conclude that his descriptions of plants and gardens are of real value. His observations of fences and hedges are most valuable from the horticultural standpoint and will be found in the chapter on fencing. We get also from his quaint comments on manners and customs a very good idea of the country as it was before the Revolution.

He says, "The English ladies in general are much inclined to have fine flowers all the summer long in or upon chimneys, sometimes upon a table, or before the windows, either on account of their fine appearance, or for the sake of their sweet scent."

Again: "The orchards contained all sorts of fine fruit. We wondered very much when our leader leaped over the hedge into the orchard, and gathered some agreeable fruit for us. We were still more astonished when no one objected—people in Sweden and Finland guard their turnips more carefully than these Americans do their fine fruits.

"Every countryman, even a common peasant, has commonly an orchard near his house in which are all sorts of fruit, such as peaches, apples, pears, cherries and others in plenty. Peaches grow in such quantity that they could not be consumed—and were frequently given to the swine.

"The ladies make wine from some of the fruits of the land. They also make some of Strawberries. In Maryland a wine is made of wild grape. Raspberries and cherries are also used."

We learn also that the "Virginian Maple" or *Platanus occidentalis* was planted extensively at that time. Kalm states: "It grows for the greatest part in low places, but especially on the edges of rivers and brooks. But these trees are easily transplanted to more dry places, if they be only filled with good soil; and as their leaves are large and their foliage thick, they are planted about the houses and in the gardens, to afford a pleasant shade in the hot season, to the enjoyment of which some seats are placed under them."

Kalm registered one of the earliest comments on the unthinking attitude of the American people toward their forests. He mentions the fact that the houses of Philadelphia were covered with white cedar shingles, and adds:

"Swamps and morasses were formerly full of them [White Cedar], but at present those trees are for the greatest part cut down, and no attempt has been made to plant new ones."

BENJAMIN SMITH BARTON

In 1789 the trustees of the University of Pennsylvania instituted a Professorship of Natural History and Botany and chose Dr. Barton, then but 24 years of age, to fill the chair. He was the first teacher of natural science in the Western Hemisphere. He held the position for twenty-six years.

Dr. Barton wrote the *Elements of Botany*, illustrated by William Bartram, for whose help he was most grateful, saying: "I have loved him for the happiest union of moral integrity with original genius and unaspiring science, for which he is eminently distinguished."

Frederick Pursh and Thomas Nuttall were among those of his friends toward whose success as botanists he contributed very generously. Pursh indeed credited him with having supplied the funds which made possible a botanical excursion through the mountains of Virginia and Carolina. Barton also helped Nuttall finance an expedition in 1810 through the northwestern United States and Canada.

In 1799, Benjamin Smith Barton published a book called *Fragments of Natural History of Pennsylvania*. Dr. Barton at that time was Professor of Materia Medica, Natural History and Botany in the University of Pennsylvania. He made many close and skillful observations on the flora and fauna of Pennsylvania, saying that he could have made the pages more worthy of the reader's notice. "But," he continues, "I want leisure."

He recommends the study of birds in relation to their destruction of insects which feed on useful plants, and says that at that time the study of insect pests was a subject as new as it was important.

· "He was also instrumental in introducing gypsum or calcium sulphate as a fertilizer.

"It was said that he strewed this chemical, also called land plaster, on a clover field, so that when the crop had reached some size the words 'This Has Been Plastered' stood out in luxuriant green plants against the rest of the field.

"Franklin was a frequent correspondent upon agricultural subjects with Jared Eliot of Connecticut, discussing the drainage of swamps, the planting of hedges and many other subjects."

HUMPHREY MARSHALL

Humphrey Marshall was born in the township of West Bradford, Pennsylvania, in the year 1722, and died in 1801.

The residence of Humphrey Marshall, which he built himself, like John Bartram

ADAM KUHN

Adam Kuhn was born in Germantown November 17, 1741. He was educated in Sweden under Linnaeus, and is said to have been the latter's favorite pupil. He practised medicine on his return to America and became the first professor of botany in the Philadelphia College, in fact the first professor of botany in America.

BENJAMIN FRANKLIN

William M. Jardine, former Secretary of Agriculture, writing on "Franklin and Agriculture", says:

"Franklin's 'proposal for promoting useful knowledge among the British plantations in America' was published on May 14, 1743. This paper suggests that an organization to be known as the American Philosophical Society be formed with headquarters in Philadelphia, to collect and disseminate information on a great variety of scientific and practical subjects. Among the subjects listed by Franklin are the following: 'All new-discovered plants, herbs, trees, roots,—their virtues, uses, etc.; methods of propagating them and making such as are useful, but particular to some plantations, more general; —new improvements in planting, gardening and clearing land.' This Society, which traces its descent from the Junto, founded by Franklin in 1727, published many articles on agricultural subjects.

"While Franklin was in England as the agent of Pennsylvania and some other Colonies before the Revolutionary War, he sent home silkworm eggs and mulberry cuttings to promote silk growing in this country.

[1] From *The Amazing Benjamin Franklin*, compiled by J. Henry Smythe, Jr.

With the exception of *Catalogue d'Arbre Arbuste et Plantes Herbacés d'Amérique*, published in Paris in 1783, Humphrey Marshall's *Arbustum Americanum*, or *The American Grove, An Alphabetical Catalogue of Forest Trees and Shrubs, Native to the American United States*, published in 1785, was the first purely botanical work on American trees.

In the same year, the second botanical garden was established by Marshall, on the site of the present village of Marshallton. Even before the definite establishment of this garden Marshall had been employing his leisure time in collecting and cultivating useful and ornamental plants at his paternal residence near the Brandywine.

We quote from a published description of his garden:

"The garden at Marshallton is still in existence, trees and shrubs thriving. Trees planted here at the time of the Revolution now tower high in the air. A Sweet Gum (*Liquidambar styraciflua*), and a Cucumber Tree (*Magnolia acuminata*), have each a girth of sixteen feet. A rare Bartram oak is nearly fifteen feet in circumference. Other old trees of great size are Hackberry (*Celtis occidentalis*), Sycamore (*Platanus occidentalis*), Sugar maple (*Acer saccharum*), Larch (*Larix laricina*), Ailanthus (*Ailanthus altissima*), and Kentucky Coffee Tree (*Gymnocladus dioica*).

"In 1848 the Borough of West Chester named a public square for Marshall, because he was 'one of the earliest and most distinguished horticulturists and botanists of our country, having established the second botanic garden in this republic, and also prepared and published the first treatise on the forest trees and shrubs of the United States, and diffused a taste for botanical science which entitles his memory to the lasting respect of his countrymen.'

"The laudable example of Humphrey Marshall was not

without influence in the community where he resided. His friend and neighbor, the last estimable John Jackson, was endowed with a similar taste for the beauties of nature; and in the year 1777 commenced a highly interesting collection of plants, at his residence at Londongrove, which is still preserved in good condition, by his son, William Jackson Esq. About the year 1800 also, the brothers Joshua and Samuel Pierce, of East Marlborough, began to adorn their premises by tasteful culture and planting; and they have produced an Arboretum of evergreens and other elegant forest trees, which is certainly unrivalled in Pennsylvania."[1]

MINSHALL PAINTER—PAINTER ARBORETUM[2]

Three miles north of Media, the county seat of Delaware County, on a road away from the beaten paths, lies the Painter Arboretum. It consists of five acres of fertile soil, watered by two streams, and is part of an original grant from William Penn.

In 1820, Minshall Painter, then only nineteen years of age, but already an ardent botanist and tree-lover, started this collection. It soon consisted of over 6,000 specimens, including not native American plants only, but many from abroad. The latter were obtained through an exchange of specimens with Kew Gardens, London. Many rare American plants came from the Bartram Gardens.

The seeds and cuttings were planted in nursery rows, and soon on those five acres there was a severe struggle for light and air, resulting in the survival of the fittest, or about half the original planting. Even after the five acres were planted, Minshall's enthusiasm was so great that he planted the hedge rows of the surrounding farm. One of the finest specimens, that of a Sequoia gigantea, stands an eighth of a mile away from the Arboretum upon a hillside. This tree is the gem of the collection and shows such vigor that it will doubtless reach the vast age of its brethren on the Pacific coast.

There are many trees of interest, notably the great cypress which grows at the intersection of the two streams. This tree is a native of the southern swamps, and stands surrounded by outstanding knees, which act as bulwarks against the streams.

Near by grow European and American Yew (*Taxus baccata* and *T. canadensis*), also a large specimen of Osage orange (*Maclura pomifera*), Honey Locust (*Gleditsia triacanthos*), Kentucky Coffee-bean (*Gymnocladus dioica*), and several members of the Magnolia family.

The Paw paw tree (*Asimina*), the Catalpa, the Empress Tree (*Paulownia tomentosa*), are all large thrifty specimens. There is also a fine Franklin tree or *Gordonia*, which every year produces a mass of its magnolia-like flowers.

Other interesting plants of great age grow in the Arboretum. The dwarf box (*Buxus sempervirens var. suffruticosa*) near Painter Mansion was planted by the mother of Minshall Painter in 1790. Near by is a single tea rose of the same age which is still in fine condition. There are also some remarkable specimens of forsythia, berberis, wistaria, spirea, deutzia, calycanthus and azalea. Immediately in front of the mansion is the fine specimen of the Maiden-Hair Tree (*Ginkgo biloba*). There is a well-preserved Cryptomeria of Japan, and a fine collection of American conifers, including hemlock (*Tsuga canadensis*), red cedar (*Juniperus virginiana*), larch (*Larix laricina*), and white pine (*Pinus strobus*).

Minshall Painter never married. He lived with a bachelor brother, Jacob, in the mansion at the garden. He died in 1873 surrounded by his favorite trees, to the care of which he had devoted his life. His epitaph was written by his brother:—

"For thee no more shall vernal spring,
　　Renew the leaves on trees and bowers,
For thee no more shall Flora bring
　　Her choicest gifts of rarest flowers."

[1]From William Darlington's *Memorials of Marshall and Bartram*.
[2]Adapted from a paper by John J. Tyler, who inherited the Arboretum from his uncle, Minshall Painter.

JOHN EVANS—EVANS ARBORETUM

The garden and arboretum planted about 1830 by John Evans, another Pennsylvanian, in Delaware county, about twelve miles west of Philadelphia, contained for many years one of the finest collections of plants in the United States. Evans kept up an active correspondence with Sir William Hooker, the Director of the Royal Gardens at Kew, from whom he received the seeds of many Himalayan and other rare and little known plants. A few only of the trees planted by Evans, who died in 1862, are now alive; among them is probably the largest specimen of the European hop hornbeam in the United States.

A GROUP OF GERMANTOWN BOTANISTS

Dr. William P. C. Barton, the author of *Compendium Floræ Philadelphicæ*, which was published in 1818 and was the first study of the flora of Philadelphia and its surrounding territory, lived on western Manheim Street, the one-time "garden street" of Germantown.

A group of men living in Germantown, by their intense interest in botany and horticulture, aided materially in the development of gardening in Pennsylvania. An article in the *Pennsylvania Magazine of History and Biography* entitled "The Germantown Road and its Associations" gives an account of them:

"Kurtz, a German, owned a large piece of ground on Main Street. He there indulged his strong natural tastes for horticulture and botany. His garden contained every rare tree, plant and shrub of the hardy kind that could be attained. He set his plants without any regard to order, so when he was working in his garden it was with great difficulty that he could be found. He scorned public opinion but respected the views of his scores of friends. He never sold a plant, but gave freely of his riches to all. He died in 1816.

"He had a specially dear friend, Matthias Kin or Keen—contemporary with John Bartram. All around and through Germantown were many trees collected by him. In one place was a very large *Virgilia lutea*, probably seven feet in circumference. In another was a large *Magnolia acuminata*, nine feet in circumference, and eighty feet tall. The choicest specimen was a *Magnolia macrophylla*, a noble specimen, which Kin, it is said, brought in his saddle-bag, wrapped in damp moss, from North Carolina.

"Melchior Meng's Garden adjoined Kurtz's on the north. He had a very fine garden. The immense Linden tree which stood in front of his place was certainly planted by him. Meng's garden was much larger than Kurtz's, and while the latter paid the most attention to shrubs and plants, the former boasted of his very fine lot of trees, which at that time was inferior to none in the country."

BOTANICAL PROGRESS AFTER 1800

After the Revolution for twenty years gardening languished, but as the *Floral Magazine and Botanical Repository*, published by D. and C. Landreth, says in 1839 in regard to the study of botany and culture of plants: "happily a relish for Botanical pursuits has grown with our growth—and we hail the day as not far distant when public liberty shall found a National Botanic Institute at the Capital of the United States."

In 1830 the Pennsylvania Horticultural Society appointed a committee to visit gardens and nurseries. The committee reported that "floriculture has made immense progress within the last ten years, and is now pursued with an avidity that astonishes the European practical visitors. The gardens of the present day are decorated with rarities that money could not purchase a few years ago."

MICHIGAN

The magnificent old French pear trees of Detroit and nearby Monroe (see page 393) are found nowhere else in America. This venerable tree, a hundred feet in height, stands on what was once part of the old Rivard farm and is now the estate of Dr. Fred T. Murphy, at Grosse Pointe Farms. In the background are eleven old French apple trees, several of which are shown in the illustration on page 405. They were called "The Apostles," and the pear tree, which completes their number, was named "The Judas Tree"

MICHIGAN

GARDENS UNDER THREE FLAGS[1]

PREHISTORIC GARDENS IN MICHIGAN

MICHIGAN had gardens before Columbus discovered the flora of the Bahamas—gardens of prehistoric age and origin known as "Garden Beds." In 1748 the explorer La Verendrye reported their existence to the French government; in 1827 Henry Rowe Schoolcraft gave their plans and accurate measurements. With the exception of a few in Wisconsin, the "Garden Beds" were confined to Michigan, where they occupied the most fertile plains in the interior

[1]An account adapted from studies made by Mrs. Henry D. Shelden, member of the executive board of the Garden Club of Michigan and chairman of the committee on historic gardens, and by Dr. Milo Milton Quaife, of the Detroit Public Library, member of the American Historical Association, and the American Antiquarian Society.

Kalamazoo

of the State, their outlines sharply defined by the tough sod of the prairies. These "raised patches of ground," about seventeen inches in height, were arranged in plats or blocks of parallel beds separated by sunken paths, or in parterres having curvilinear figures and scalloped work with ample walks and even avenues between. In extent the plats covered from twenty to three hundred acres, and the beds into which they were divided were laid out with an order, skill, and symmetry which distinguish them from any known operations of agriculture or recognized system of horticulture north of Mexico.[1]

No scientist has been able to estimate the date of the making of the "Garden Beds," but their abandonment is approximately determined by the age of the trees found growing upon them. One of these trees,

[1]*Memorials of a Half Century*, by Bela Hubbard.

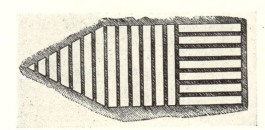

Western Michigan

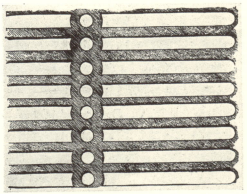

Galesburg

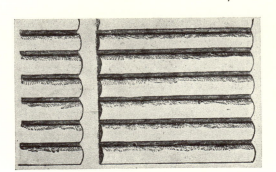

St. Joseph River Valley

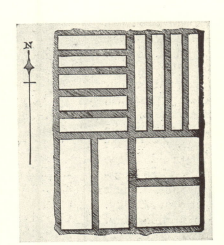

Kalamazoo

Prairie-Ronde

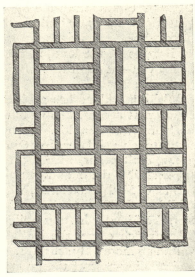

Kalamazoo

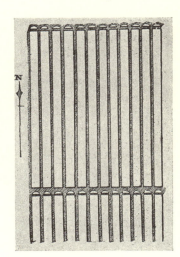

St. Joseph River Valley

Some of the Prehistoric Garden Plats in Michigan

when cut down fifty years ago, indicated by its cortical layers a period as far back as 1500—some years before the coming to this country of the French.

An old Mackinac cottage and garden of about 1750

FRENCH AND ENGLISH GARDENS AT MACKINAC

France ruled nearly the whole continent of North America from 1534 to 1759, and the story of Michigan in its early days is inseparably interwoven with it. Before 1640 the topography of the country was well known, and the maps which were made on royal authority still exist in the national archives in Paris. *Coureurs de bois* and *voyageurs* undoubtedly had penetrated the Straits of Detroit about the middle of the sixteenth century; government records at Quebec record that in the latter part of the sixteenth and early part of the seventeenth centuries Champlain and various others passed the Straits in bark canoes. The priests, however, were the earliest to leave an impress on the land, in the first missions founded in the Northwest—at Sault Ste. Marie, St. Ignace, and St. Joseph.

Michilimackinac has a history as old as any part of our country. It became known to the French before Jamestown, Virginia, was founded, but no settlement was made until sixty-three years later. In 1670 Père Joseph Marquette, the great Jesuit priest, with a company of Hurons, entered for the first time the old Indian village on the south side of the Straits of Michilimackinac, which name it bore. Here he established the first mission and caused to be erected the first fort, the friendly Hurons building one of their own near by. The French came, the Indians increased in number, and within an incredibly short time the town became a stronghold and trading-post of the greatest importance to the Northwest, the rendezvous of trappers, traders, missionaries, merchants, soldiers, *voyageurs*, and Indians. The Straits were the gateway of commerce between the St. Lawrence and Mississippi Rivers, the upper and lower lakes. The fortress was surrounded by high palisades of cedar posts enclosing an area of several acres, within which the Jesuits erected a college—the first institution of the kind in the West. Soon little villages sprang up on the banks of the water—strung along like beads of a rosary—their quaint low houses surrounded by small gardens fragrant with roses, pinks, and sweet grasses.

The North Lake Country is legendary land. Michilimackinac, signifying "Great Turtle," was the Great Manitou of the Indians, whom they worshipped with all the superstition and reverence of an untutored race. Michilimackinac, the island (known today as Mackinac), was so named by the Indians from a fancied resemblance to a turtle as it rises out of the water. The province, straits, and town on the mainland were named for the island.

The Indians considered the island of Michilimackinac sacred, believing it to be the abiding place of the Great Spirit, and they never lightly visited it or made it a permanent home. It was only when touring or going to and from their hunting grounds that they came, and on such occasions whole villages at a time would raise their tepees on the island and devote days to the worship of their god. Then it was that Père Marquette and others of his order would conduct temporary missions there, seeking in friendly ways to convert the savages to Christianity; when the Indians went away the priests went also.

The French never fortified the island or made of it a trading-post. They treated it as a spot sacred to the deity of the Red Men in whose ground they buried their dead.

In 1672 Père Marquette was visited by Sieur Louis Joliet, a priest of the Jesuit order, who bore a commission from Frontenac, Governor-General of New France, empowering him to select Marquette as associate to enter upon a voyage to explore the Mississippi. A year later the two men and their followers accomplished this great enterprise, but Marquette died in the height of his glory on the return journey. His sorrowful followers gave his body temporary burial on the shore of Lake Michigan, but later carried it to the little church he helped to build at St. Ignace, and there, for a hundred years, "Marquette reposed as a guardian angel of the Ottawa Missions." In 1780 the bones of the missionary were transferred to the Indian village of La Crosse, Michigan.

The Province of Michilimackinac was surendered to the

Mission House and School at Mackinac Island. From an old print which appeared in the Quarterly Paper of the American Board of Commissioners for Foreign Missions in 1835

English after the defeat of the French on the Plains of Abraham. In October, 1760, they evacuated the Fort, but it was not garrisoned by the English until the next year, when Captain George Etherington took command. He soon recognized the great strategic advantage of the Island of Michilimackinac, seven miles away from the mainland, and William Johnston called a grand council of the Indians to negotiate for the islands and also for the grants previously made by the Indians to the French for military purposes.

One can reconstruct from the following description a vision of the gardens of the old village of Michilimackinac on the mainland as they must have looked in this period:

". . . The main street follows the beautiful curve of the shore between the lake and cedar-crowned bluff from which the fort looks down in picturesque ugliness that even its white-washing cannot mar. Old-fashioned houses, with terraced yards, where thickets of lilac and snow-ball, and cinnamon roses stand knee deep in the tall grass, range themselves along the street until, towards the eastern end, they drop off into longer distances. Beyond is a common where buttercups and daisies gossip sociably, where sweet-brier grows rampant in the hollows, its perfumed green set thick with exquisite pink of the morning bloom among the paler roses of yesterday; and near the shore rank upon rank of wild flag, so luxuriant in its purple bloom, so lovely in its deep coloring, that one sees it day after day with new fascination. Winding here and there, as if on errands of their own, go narrow, straggling

The fort on Mackinac Island, built by the English in 1779-1780

footpaths to the irregular white buildings of the old Missions."[1]

Governor Patrick Sinclair took command of the Fort of Michilimackinac in October, 1779, and in November sent a detachment of soldiers to live and work on the island. Such of the timbers of the old fortress as could be used again were hauled over the ice that winter to the new fort, which was built on the cliffs, at the foot of which there was a good harbor protected by a water battery. The fort was not formally garrisoned until May 24, 1781.

The deed of Mackinac Island made by the Indians to King George II is dated May 12, 1781, only a few days before the first occupation of the Fort by the English, to whom it was sold "for the consideration of five thousand pounds, New York currency, received from the General Haldimand by the hand of Governor Sinclair."

"Again a new village sprang up at the foot of a new fort," writes an historian, "and among the shabby looking French houses with their roofs of bark, the English built neat white dwellings with red shutters, which have a foreign air with their porches and flights of steps. The better houses stand on the first of the three terraces which are distinctly marked. Behind them are swelling green knolls; before them, gardens sloping down to narrow slips of white beach, so that the grass seems to grow almost into the clear, rippling waves. The gardens are rich with mountain ash, roses, stocks, currant bushes, springing corn and a great variety of kitchen vegetables."[2]

After the War of the Revolution, England ceded the island to the United States. Among the papers preserved in the Pennsylvania Historical Society's archives is the following:

> Report of the nature and State of the Works & Public Buildings at Michilimackinac as delivered over to Major Henry Burdeck of the Artillery of the United States by Lieutenant Andrew Doster of his Britannic Majesty's 24th Regiment of Foot. September 1st, 1796.

Commandant's Garden	is five hundred and forty feet long and one hundred and sixty-seven feet wide, the fences and gates are good, it is in very good order and filled with vegetables.
Subaltern's Garden	is two hundred and forty six feet long and one hundred and seventy three feet wide; the fence is good, it is filled with potatoes.
Government Park	is of an irregular figure about fourteen hundred and seventy yards in circumference, well inclosed, and laid down in grass.

The fur trade had become more important than ever before, the village receiving its greatest support from it, as an outfitting and furnishing place for the great fur companies of the Northwest. It was here that John Jacob Astor, as president and principal share-holder, built up the American Fur Company, whose buildings still stand surrounded with small gardens of beautiful flowers. This trade became extinct in 1842.

Mackinac Island has become Michigan's most beautiful State park, having a remarkable rock formation, old French orchards, tall lilac trees and winding Indian trails through deep forests carpeted with wild flowers, above all of which stands, on the high cliffs, the old fortress of limestone painted white. Its wide ramparts, thick walls, and square blockhouses glisten today against the dark cedars like pearls set in jade, and second only to the fort of St. Augustine in picturesque antiquity.

THE FOUNDING OF DETROIT

In the summer of 1679, the first brigantine sailed the upper Lakes. This was the *Griffin*, built on the shore of Lake Erie by order of Robert Cavelier, Sieur de la Salle. In it went La Salle, Tonti, Father Louis Hennepin and their company. They penetrated to a lake which La Salle named Lake Sainte Claire, for the saint whose feast day it was; then they sailed on through Lake Huron, and found safe harbor at Michilimackinac. Of the shores they passed on their way northward from Lake Erie, on both sides of the Straits, Father Hennepin wrote: "They are covered with primeval forests, fruit trees like walnuts; chestnut and apple trees grow on narrow flower-strewn plains; great pines and cedars; on the high bluffs above and beyond the land is well cultivated."

Eight years later, in 1687, Baron La Hontan, accompanied by Henri Tonti, Sieur Greysolon Duluth and a company of French soldiers, passed through the lakes over the same route that La Salle and Hennepin had sailed in the *Griffin*. La Hontan's impressions of the country through which he traveled, as described by him in a letter dated September 6, 1687, differ very little from those of Father Hennepin.

"You can not imagine the pleasant prospect of this strait and of the little lake, for their banks are covered with all sorts of wild fruit trees. 'Tis true the want of agriculture sinks the agreeableness of the fruit, but their plenty is very surprising."[1]

The first colony on the straits, however, was established by Sieur Antoine de la Mothe Cadillac, who in 1694 was made commandant of the Province of Michilimackinac—the most important post of the Northwest. To obtain permission to

---

[1]*Historic Mackinac*, by E. O. Wood.   [2]*Ibid.*   [1]La Hontan's *Voyages*, Vol. I.

build a fort and found a city on the lower straits, he went to France, where through the kind offices of the Comte de Pontchartrain, Minister for the Colonies, the King not only sanctioned the undertaking but made a deed of gift to Cadillac himself of a large tract of land, to be wherever on the river d'Etroit he might choose.

So it happened that on a summer day in 1701, amidst the acclamations of their compatriots, a fleet of twenty-five birch bark canoes, containing one hundred white men, left Montreal on its perilous journey into the West. Cadillac led the little company in the first boat, at the stern of which floated the banner of France. The voyagers passed safely over the portages, through the rivers and lakes, and arrived on a gorgeous day—the 24th of July—beneath the most commanding bluff on the northwestern shore of the river d'Etroit, where they beached their canoes and landed. Next day after morning mass in the woodlands[1], Sieur de la Mothe Cadillac in the presence of his followers and a large assemblage of Indians took formal possession of the land in the name of King of France and Navarre.

Within two months a strong fortification of earthworks was raised, with high stockades of cedar logs and blockhouses, large houses for Cadillac and Tonti, and cabins for his men. A church was built and named after Ste. Anne, whose feast-day it was, and a house for the priest, in whose garden were grown "herbs for the comfort of parishioners and flowers enough for the altar."

In the autumn of 1701, Sieur Cadillac wrote Count Pontchartrain, for whom he had named his fortified city:

"Fort Pontchartrain de L'Etroit is on a river of moderate breadth and twenty leagues in length, through which the sparkling and pellucid waters of Lakes Superior, Michigan and Huron flow into Lake Erie. The borders are so many vast meadows where the freshness of beautiful streams keeps the grass always green; these same meadows are fringed with long and broad avenues of fruit trees which have never felt the careful hand of the watchful gardener; trees, old and young, bend their branches under the weight of their delicious burden, toward the fertile soil that has produced them. In this land the vine builds a thick roof with its large leaves and heavy clusters weighing down the tops of the trees which receive it. The woods are of walnut trees, white oak, ash, whitewood, and cotton trees; but these same trees are straight as arrows without curves and almost without branches except near the top. They are of enormous size and height."

A historian writes of these first days of Detroit:

"Wild fruit, berries and nuts grew in great abundance, and the people gathered all they could to preserve for the coming winter. When the convoy left Montreal it had carried only sufficient food to last for three months, and food had to be procured from the Indians and from hunting, to enable the people to live until the next harvest time. They had arrived too late to grow any crop for the fall of 1701, but all hands that could be spared were set at work, preparing the soil for wheat, a quantity of which Cadillac had brought along for seed. This wheat, which he called French wheat, was sown on the 7th of October, 1701, and was cut on the

[1]*Landmarks of Detroit*, by Robert B. Ross and George B. Catlin.

21st of the succeeding July. The land was not properly prepared but the crop was good."[1]

The following summer Cadillac directed Tonti, his lieutenant, to have twenty arpents[2] sowed by September 20th, twelve of these to be of Indian corn, which came up eight feet high; 25 acres were cultivated by the soldiers, each with a small garden; larger tracts of land were cultivated by the civilians, "so that in the winter of 1702 there were besides the gardens sixty arpents of wheat. Grapes grew in abundance along the river shore and an arpent of land was set apart, tilled, and set out with the choicest grape vines."[3]

The Indians who formed settlements around the fort cultivated two hundred arpents of land, probably in Indian corn.

And thus were the inhabitants of Cadillac's city provided for. Every man was a hunter and the fish were plentiful in the river and lakes.

"The soldiers were lodged inside the fort, and Cadillac, in order to foster industry, gave them the use of half-arpent spaces outside the enclosure for gardening purposes. These spaces fronted on the east side of what is now Randolph Street, between the River and Fort Street East."[4]

Burton Historical Collections
The Griffin, the first sail vessel on the Lakes, built by order of the Sieur de La Salle in 1679 on the shore of Lake Erie

Madame Cadillac and Madame Tonti came in the spring and were followed by so many would-be settlers that the little community was hard pressed to accommodate them, and in less than a year this frontier post became one of the most delightful towns in New France and "one of the largest in America with a population of six thousand souls." The stockades were enlarged to admit of more private residences.

The French inhabitants were an admirable people. There was much formality in their social life, as their manners and customs were of old France, and their courtesy and urbanity endeared them to the Indians, who greatly preferred them to any foreign race. Because of this friendly relationship the French soon found it safe to take up farms outside the fort. Partitioning the land to the tastes and wishes of the colonists and obtaining grants for the same were among the most difficult tasks that Cadillac accomplished. These grants it was necessary to receive from the King, or from the Governor General at Quebec, and even after this had been done it was often necessary to obtain the consent of the Indian chiefs, who were reluctant to release their claims. For a deed to property the grantee was bound on pain of forfeiture "to clear and cultivate his land, pay a rental of fifteen livres a year in peltries to the crown forever and to aid in raising a May-Pole each May-day before the Mansion House." That each family might have a place with frontage on the river or lake as well as ample acreage for agricultural purposes, the plats were necessarily narrow—usually from one to two arpents wide, though often eighty arpents deep—and hence these places, from their extreme depth as compared to their width, were known as "ribbon farms." Such subdivisions of land were common everywhere in New France.

In 1704, Indians set fire to the town, destroying the houses of Cadillac, Tonti, and many others. Cadillac im-

[1]*Cadillac's Village*, by C. M. Burton, member for Michigan of the Historical Commission, and City Historiographer of Detroit.
[2]An arpent is equal to 192.75 English feet.
[3]*Cadillac's Village*, by C. M. Burton.
[4]*Landmarks of Detroit*, by R. B. Ross and G. B. Catlin.

mediately set about rebuilding the city, enlarging its palisades to afford more space for those who preferred to live within the fortifications. On the site of his burned house he built the largest and most imposing home in the town; it stood on the north side of Ste. Anne's Street (Jefferson Ave.), between the present Griswold and Shelby Streets.[1] A spacious gallery adorned the front of the mansion, overlooking the majestic river and a smooth-cut lawn, in the center of which stood a tall pole from whose top floated the fleur-de-lis of France. Tonti, who became the third of the French governors of Detroit after Cadillac was transferred to Louisiana, also built a larger house on the same point of land where his previous house had stood. Its heavy blinds, doors, and chimney were painted white, and vines were trained over it.

When Cadillac had first come to the "Straits of Lake Erie," he had been received most enthusiastically by the Indians. Quarante Sols, Chief of the Huron village, became a friend of the French and desired that a house be built for him wherein he might live in French fashion. Communicating this wish to the King, Cadillac was commanded to build for the Indian chief a house of oak, forty feet long and twenty feet wide; in 1703 a letter written from Detroit described this house as "delightfully situated on the margin of the river on a little eminence overlooking the Huron Village." Here also was planted a garden like those of the French, in which Quarante Sols received his friends. In 1740 the Hurons removed to the beautiful Bois Blanc Island, and the property was granted to Jean Baptiste Baudry, who received the title from the Governor. When he died the property passed to his son, Jacques Baudry *dit* St. Martin, and thence comes the name, the "Mansion of St. Martin." This house, which tradition assumes to have been the house originally built for Quarante Sols, eventually became in turn the residence of the French and English governors, and of Gen. Lewis Cass (U. S. A.), Governor of the Northwest Territory in 1813.

Jacob L. Ommespron Mersac, an officer of the French army, was given a house inside the fortification and also a large ribbon farm outside. Mrs. Hamlin repeats the tradition that he, "after his retirement from the army, cultivated the land granted him, and that it was his custom always to carry a sword by his side when plowing."

Antoine Forestier, a distinguished physician and surgeon, who came with Cadillac, was also given land which was well cultivated.

It is interesting to note that among the fifty men whom Cadillac brought with him from Quebec, a gardener is mentioned—Pierre d'Argenteuil.

To encourage emigration to his distant province, the King gave to the emigrant a farm of forty acres, needful agricultural implements, and seed enough for the first harvest. Until Cadillac left the town in 1711, the records show the coming of many *voyageurs, coureurs de bois,* artisans and laborers. There also came members of distinguished families in France and Quebec, who were among Detroit's first builders of gardens, and whose descendants still remain. Among the latter were Pierre Boucher; Sieur de Boucheville; M. Jacques Campau, his wife and son Louis; M. Michel Campau and wife; M. Casse; M. St. Aubin and wife; M. Pierre Chene, the founder of the present Chene family; M. de la Foret, captain of the troops of the Marine in this country; M. Charles Farfard; M. Delorme; M. Jacques Godefroy (or Godfroy); François Lamareux, Sieur de St. Germaine; M. Jean LaSalle, soldier of the company of Duluth; M. René le Moyne; M. Claud Rivard, Sieur de Lorange; M. Pierre Robert; M. de Lafontaine, with his wife and children; M. Pierre Morand; M. Joseph Parent, his wife and daughters; M. Jean François Volant, Sieur de Fosseneuve; and Sieur Ettiene Verron de Grandmeuil.[2] They received, in addition to land within the stockade, farms on

the river whose boundaries today bear the names of their first owners. The houses built upon them were of substantial log construction, with wide galleries across the fronts, over which were trained vines brought from the forest or grown from cuttings sent from France. From these embowered verandas it was but a step into flower-filled gardens where tall lilacs, wood lilies, alder and roses grew in enchanting profusion, and paths edged with white stones led down to the water. On the border of the river the *habitants* built their windmills, whose great covered arms, swaying in the breeze, cast changing shadows on the gardens below. There were vegetable gardens planted with borders of lettuce and mint, or currants and gooseberries; behind the houses were cherry trees and vineyards; then came orchards of apple and pear trees, and fields of grain and corn. The *habitants* worked their farms simultaneously, as a precaution against unfriendly Indians as well as for the pleasure of companionship.

In 1709 intrigue and jealousy against Cadillac which had been current in his city and in Quebec reached the court of the King of France. In 1710 Cadillac was removed from his command and appointed Governor of Louisiana. A year later he left Fort Pontchartrain for Mt. Desert, Maine, never to return. Strangely enough, the name of the Sieur de la Mothe Cadillac, owner of the first important house and garden, is almost unknown to the city he founded, and not one of his children inherited an acre of land. The old *habitants* to this day will tell you it was because of an unfortunate encounter he had with the red dwarf, the demon of Detroit—that the creature laid a curse on him that his name should be written in running water forever.

Pierre François de Charlevoix, a Jesuit and a scholar, was the first distinguished man to visit the new colony, arriving in Detroit in 1721, on a tour of the lake country. He wrote of Michigan:

"Nature seems to have denied it nothing which can contribute to make the country delightful; hills, meadows, fields, lofty forests, rivulets, rivers and all of them so excellent of their kind and so happily blended as to equal the most romantic wishes. The lands, however, are not equally proper for any kind of grain, but most are of a wonderful fertility, and I have known some to produce good wheat for eighteen years running without any manure, and besides all of them are proper for some particular use. The islands seem placed on purpose for the pleasure of the prospect, the rivers and lakes abound in fish, the air is pure and the climate temperate and extremely wholesome. The fields are free from weeds and raise a large amount of corn, peas, beans, and wheat."

An old French memoir of these years (1717) gives us an interesting picture of Indian apple orchards on Grosse Isle, below Detroit:

"Grosse Isle, the largest island in the Detroit River, is very fertile and extensive, being from six to seven leagues in circumference. There is an extraordinary quantity of apple trees on this island, and those who have seen the apples on the ground say that they are more than half a foot deep; the trees are planted methodically, and the apples are as large as small pippins. Abundance of excellent millstones are found on this island; all around it are very fine prairies. It was a long time doubtful whether Detroit should not be founded there. The cause of the hesitation was the apprehension that the timber might some day fail."

The eighteenth century brought many French settlers who left a lasting impress on the soil of Detroit.

Robert Navarre, Jr., son of the Robert Navarre who came from France to Detroit in 1730, was well loved by the Indians, and was deeded by the Pottawatomies their village, which was on a beautiful eminence commanding a fine view, and called "Ancient Village." They gave him "this land forever, that he might cultivate the same, light a fire thereon, and take care of our dead."[1] Robert lived on this land in the

---

[1] *Legends of Detroit,* by Mrs. M. C. W. Hamlin.
[2] From a list of property owners up to 1710, compiled by C. M. Burton.

[1] *Legends of Detroit,* by Mrs. M. C. W. Hamlin.

house known as the Brevoort Homestead, in the orchard of which were many fine French pear trees.

Pierre Moran was the founder of the Moran family in America. His son Charles came to establish himself in Detroit some time before the English came in 1760. His family still holds the grant of land given him by the King.

Jean Chapoton was a surgeon in the French army with the rank of major and was ordered to Fort Pontchartrain to relieve Dr. Forestier, the first physician who came to the post. He retired from the army several years previous to the English conquest and settled on the land which he had received as a grant.

Pierre Chene came to Detroit during the time that Cadillac was in command. His homestead was a hewn log structure covered with clapboards. It is said that Pierre Chene held the first deed of land in Detroit. It was given to him by Cadillac. His son Isidore was deeded a tract of land by the Pottawatomies when Robert Navarre, Jr., recived his—a grant confirmed by Governor Hamilton in 1774.

Jean Casse *dit* St. Aubin came to Detroit with his wife in 1710. He owned and resided on the tract known today as the St. Aubin farm.

Michel and Jacques Campau came and settled in Detroit about 1710. Michel possessed much property, which is still in the family; the Campaus and their children were among the most important members of the colony, and were greatly loved by the Indians as well as by the French.

It was outside of the walls of the city that the Military and Naval Gardens were made, also the garden for the mess and the very beautifully planned "Jardin du Roy", fashioned and hedged in formal style with parterres of flowers and grassy paths.

THE FRENCH AS ORCHARDISTS[1]

The orchards were the glory of French Detroit. Bela Hubbard, who settled at Detroit in 1835, records that almost every farm had its quota of fruit trees, while on many were orchards of several hundred. Here originated numerous varieties of apples which were later disseminated widely throughout the Northwest. From here came the famous "Colville"—both red and white; the "Detroit Red"— *Roseau* of the French; the *Pomme de neige*—the celebrated "Snow" apple of America. In addition to these were other varieties of lesser fame.

More distinctive than any of the foregoing were the famous pear trees of olden Detroit. Save at nearby Monroe (to which they were transplanted from Detroit) they are found nowhere else in America, and their origin here is obscure. Local legend (which may or may not be valid) ascribes it to the loving activities of the Jesuit missionaries, and hence they are sometimes called the Mission Pears. Hubbard, writing of a period now almost a century gone, characterizes them as "truly remarkable" for size, vigor, and productiveness. A bole six feet in girth and a height of sixty feet were common. Many showed a circumference of trunk of eight or nine feet, and reared their lofty heads seventy and sometimes eighty feet from the ground. They bore uniform crops, thirty to fifty bushels being often the product of a single tree.

Although time and the exigencies of city growth have together worked the destruction of most of the ancient pear trees, here or there one may still be seen in all its pristine vigor—older than any building or city street, or other living thing of present-day Detroit. Still

> ".... their branches, gnarled and olden,
>   Yield their juicy fruit and golden.
>   Still, each year, their blossoms dance,
>   Scent and bloom of sunny France."

In the latter half of the eighteenth century, when some of the French people of Detroit removed to the Raisin River

[1]Written by M. M. Quaife.

(modern Monroe, Michigan), they carried shoots of their loved pear trees with them. The trees throve in their new home even as at Detroit. One famous tree (cut down in recent years) grew to a height of 125 feet and frequently bore 100 bushels of fruit in a season. About twenty of the old trees still remain in the county, ranging from 50 to 75 feet in height, and all fast approaching their 150th year. Two of them, each over 60 feet high, are on the grounds of the Greening Nursery. "The fruit," writes Mr. Greening, "is of medium size and surpasses the Bartlett pear for canning, being rich, spicy, and juicy. Its superb flavor is retained in all its richness after cooking—the tree is very hardy, and has never been known to blight."

> "Live on, old trees, in your hale green age!
>   Long, long may your shadows last
>   With your blossomed boughs and golden fruit,
>   Loved emblems of the past."[1]

THE ENGLISH PERIOD

France and England struggled long and stubbornly for control of the western continent, but at last came the decisive conflict, the battle near Quebec in 1759, when French power was forever broken. Shortly afterwards a force of British troops under Major Robert Rogers took possession of Detroit. The French troops were sent to Philadelphia, but the colonists were allowed to remain after taking the oath of allegiance.

The Indians never liked the English as well as they had the French and, despite the generous gifts they received, remained hostile—a hostility which culminated in 1763 in the conspiracy of Pontiac.

A diary of the lurid days when the Pontiac war burst upon Detroit discloses at once a hint of the gardens of the period and a hint of the destruction which the hazards of war entailed upon them. The savages were using as a place of concealment from which to harass the garrison the garden of St. Martin, on the Baudry property which had once belonged to Quarante Sols, the Huron chief. Major Gladwin determined to abate this source of annoyance by razing the garden which sheltered them. Accordingly Lieutenant Hay (later Governor Hay) "sallied out at the head of forty volunteers and proceeded to spoil the garden. The fence was of cedar stakes ten feet tall and it enclosed a quantity of fruit trees and a house where the gardener lived, a very great advantage to the Indians. They pulled up the stakes, burnt the house, cut down the trees, and threw them into the river."

England sent out as governors to her new colony distinguished men of prominent families. They occupied the mansion of their French predecessors. Officers who came with them built fine houses and gardens along the river and lake —west and east.

Colonel Knaggs, who accompanied Sir William Johnson in 1761, built in 1790 on the river at Springwells (Belles Fontaines), west of Detroit, a house well known for many years as the "Knaggs House." It was a low, rambling structure, a story and a half high, with steep roof and gables; the front door was shaded by a square portico with seats which commanded a beautiful view of the river in its immediate front, and of a great windmill and pear trees on its point of land. The garden in the rear was planted with flowers, herbs, vegetables and berry bushes.

Commodore Alexander Grant, a descendant of the Lairds of Glenmoriston, built his home and garden at Grosse Pointe, on Lake St. Clair.[2]

In 1771 George McDougall built on Belle Isle a dwelling-house and outbuildings, and cultivated thirty acres of the island as a flower and vegetable garden.

To the English period properly belongs the activity of

[1]From a poem, "To the Old Pear Trees of Detroit," written by W. H. Coyle in 1849.

[2]Further described in the article on Grosse Pointe gardens.

John Askin, who came to America as a soldier, but soon abandoned the military life to embark upon a mercantile career. From 1764 to 1780 his headquarters were at Mackinac, where, along with assured success as a trader, he acquired a comfortable fortune. In June, 1772, he married Marie Archange Barthe of Detroit, and from 1780 until his death in 1815 he was a resident in Detroit[1] and on the Canadian shore opposite Belle Isle. Although a merchant by profession, Askin was always deeply interested in farming. He acquired extensive landholdings in and around Detroit, and about the year 1800 made farming his major activity.

ent communications; By the authority in me vested, as a means of improving the appearances in the front of the Fortifications and grand Parade, by improving and cultivating the ground adjacent bounding the town of Detroit to the North West Do Grant, by these Presents, unto Captain Henry Bird of Kings or eighth Reg. and unto his heirs and assigns forever—a Lot of ground beginning at the N. W. end of St. Honoré Street, and on the east side; continuing in a line with said street as far as the run or ditch which terminates the Grand Parade; then turning toward the East, and bounded by the said run, continues as far as the fence which

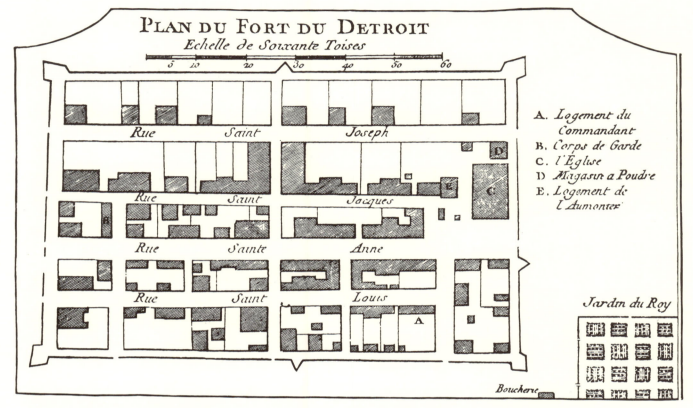

Detroit in 1763, from Bellini's Atlas of 1764. The Jardin du Roy, the beautifully planned formal garden outside the walls, is shown in the lower right-hand corner

Possessed of an active mind, Askin was fond of experimenting, and his papers (now in the Detroit Public Library) preserve frequent evidence of his agricultural activities. He maintained a large orchard, and manufactured quantities of cider which was sometimes marketed at distant Niagara or Mackinac. From Vincennes, cotton seeds were procured for Mrs. Askin to experiment with at Detroit. It is perhaps needless to say that cotton never became a staple of production in Michigan. From Niagara, hemp seed was procured, and Askin was perhaps the first man to test the possibilities of hemp production at Detroit. References in Askin's letters show that besides apples and pears, grapes and currants, a wide variety of fruits and vegetables was cultivated in the family garden. A family so devoted to planting as the Askins would no doubt engage in the cultivation of flowers. No mention of this has been found in the letters, however; possibly the fact that no letters of Mrs. Askin remain explains the omission.

There were made in the English period two public gardens, the King's Garden and the Governor's Garden, delightful plans of which are still shown. One reads of flower beds edged with violets and yellow primrose.

That the English took pride in beautifying the town, the following extract from a deed of land for such purposes would indicate:

"I, Arent Scuyler De Peyster Commanding the King's or eighth Regiment, and the posts occupied by it, on the different

encloses that part of the King's garden occupied by the officers of the eighth regiment: then returning by the side of said fence as far as the King's stables, and following the division in front of said stables as they now stand, to the side of the street—The whole lot containing 2029 square yards more or less."[1]

THE GARDENS OF THE REPUBLIC

Although the war of the American Revolution had been fought and won, it was not until 1796 that the armies of the United States came to claim Michigan.

After the coming of the Americans, the French as well as many of the English families remained, and most of the old French families who had left with the coming of the English returned. During the Indian wars, the French had not been molested, and the Americans found the little village much as it was before the English came.

On the Grand Marais was the farm of Charles Chauvin. The house, facing the river, was made of logs and had great stone chimneys. It was surrounded by gardens wherein bloomed purple spring cress, marsh marigolds and sweet-william, heliotrope, pinks and larkspur; morning glories drooped over the windows. Next the waterfall was a windmill, two orchards of apple trees, and twelve pear trees.

Jean Beaubien, born in 1670 and married to Catherine Trottier in 1692, was the founder of the Beaubien family in Detroit. There were two sons, Jean Baptiste and Antoine.

[1] Until his removal to the Canadian side of the river in 1801, Askin's home was the first farm east of the fort, known today as the Brush farm. The residence was between Brush and Randolph streets, in the vicinity of the Henkel flour mill.

[1] Papers of John Askin, C. M. Burton Historical Collection.

The Beaubien house was built in the southwest corner of Jefferson Avenue and St. Antoine Street; the orchard in the rear "took up nearly one-third of the block. The homestead was a long low structure, in the French style with a row of fine pear trees in front, and between the house and the river stretched a beautiful green pasture, or lawn."[1]

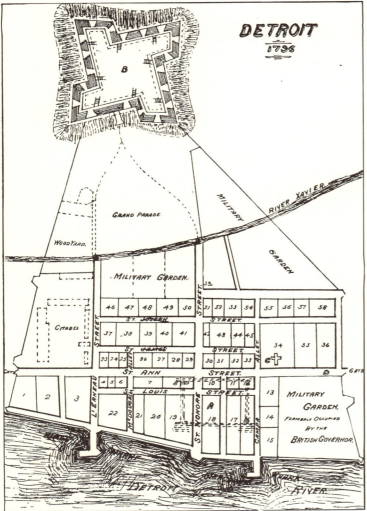

Burton Historical Collection Leaflet

Detroit in 1796

Among the early French settlers who had come to Detroit with Sieur Cadillac was James Campau, whose charming hospitality has lingered in the city's history for over one hundred and fifty years. He had a house inside the stockade next to Cadillac's, and also received a farm outside. One of his descendants was the Joseph Campau whose homestead stood opposite St. Anne's Church, on the south side of St. Anne Street, between Griswold and Shelby Streets. It had a small garden of flowers at its rear and a pear tree.

Jean Baptiste Chapoton, son of the distinguished French army surgeon who had come to Detroit in 1719, had a home surrounded by a beautiful garden.

Solomon Sibley was the first United States citizen to settle in Detroit after its occupation by the United States in 1796. He came from Marietta, Ohio, where he had been a prominent lawyer. He was one of Detroit's most distinguished men, holding many public offices and becoming a judge of the Supreme Court. "In 1827 Judge Sibley built a house at the corner of Jefferson Avenue and Randolph Street, which was well surrounded by shade trees, flowering gardens and extensive shrubs. Later he abandoned this residence and built the house adjoining the Frasers' which was on the southeast corner of Beaubien Street, opposite the cathedral. It was a large, plain, square brick house, and here the Sibley family lived until the Judge died."[2]

The first commandant of Detroit was Colonel John Francis

[1]*Early Days in Detroit*, by Friend Palmer.
[2]*Ibid.*

Hamtramck, a distinguished officer of the Revolution, who was publicly thanked for his splendid services by Gen. Washington. He was appointed by President John Adams in 1799. He built a house on the margin of the river in 1802, "beneath the gigantic elm." James Witherall, Territorial Judge, appointed by President Jefferson in 1807, lived in the house with his family until 1811, when he purchased a farm near the city.

The Territory of Michigan was created by Congress to take effect June 30th, 1805, with Detroit as its seat of government. William Hull, a distinguished officer of the Revolution, was appointed Governor and Augustus B. Woodward, Frederic Bates, and John Griffin, Judges.

On June 11th, 1805, the day before the Governor and the Judges were to arrive, Detroit was destroyed by fire, a calamity which later proved a blessing in disguise, for from the ashes of a picturesque village where houses and gardens had been enclosed by high vine-draped palisades of cedar posts painted white, and whose principal street (Ste. Anne) had been but twenty feet wide, there arose a beautifully planned French city. Congress passed an act directing the Governor and Judges of the new Territory of Michigan to lay out a new town. Major Charles L'Enfant, who had planned the city of Washington ten years before, was at the time in this country, and is thought to have influenced the design.[1] At any rate,

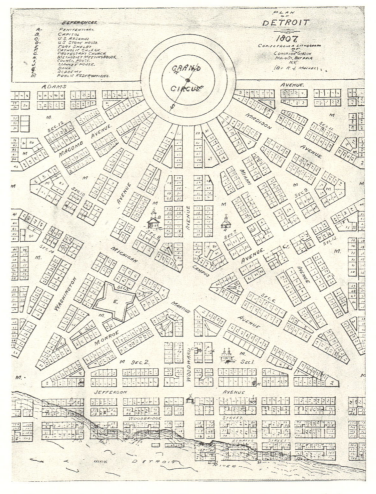

The original plan for the rebuilding of Detroit after the fire of 1805. This plan was rejected

the new plan, under the name of the "Governor's and Judges' Plan" was carried into effect. In its essentials it endures today, with the Campus Martius and Grand Circus Park, the squares and circles from which radiate broad streets and avenues.

[1]Before coming to Detroit, Judge Woodward had been for several years a resident of Washington. He was thoroughly familiar, therefore, with Major L'Enfant's plan for the Capital city, a copy of which he is said to have brought with him to Detroit. Woodward was a man of original genius who could scarcely fail to perceive the unusual opportunity which the destruction of Detroit offered to develop the city on a new and grandiose plan. To what extent he owed his inspiration to L'Enfant must remain a matter for conjecture.

St. Anne's Church, built after the fire of 1805 in the center of a small square

The streets of the old town were widened and a carriage way, twenty feet wide, called the Chemin du Ronde, encircled the town just inside the palisades.

The Mansion House, built in 1805 after the fire, from the chimneys of the burned houses. The grounds were formally laid out and included a summer-house

After the fire the inhabitants found refuge among the farmers and in the fort and barracks outside the town, until houses could be built for them. There was much suffering among those made destitute by the fire.

Among those who proceeded to rebuild at once was Joseph Campau, who erected a new house on the foundation of the old, which was on the site of the officers' Mess House of old Fort Pontchartrain in 1701. A new small French garden was planted. Mr. Campau lived here until his death.

Peter Andrain, Secretary of the Territory, rebuilt his house, as did many others. A stone house was built by Judge James May from the chimneys of the burned houses. It was called the Mansion House, and twenty years later became the leading hotel of the city. It was situated west of Cass Street and its garden with its summer-house and fine trees was much enjoyed by Judge May's friends.

The Commandant's headquarters was a square two-storied house, and in the garden at its rear, near the water, was the Council House, built for the purpose of holding council with the Indians.

One of the oldest houses in Michigan at the time of the fire was that built by Mr. Moran in 1750 in the center of the farm to which his descendants still hold the grant from the King. Its garden, filled with old trees, shrubs, and flowers, ran to the river.

Governor Hull's mansion was built in 1807, and was the first brick house. It was shaded by tall trees, and had extensive gardens of flowers and shrubs.

Again came war with England, and from 1812 to 1813 the land was a battlefield. General Hull surrendered Detroit and all Michigan to Great Britain and left as a prisoner of war, never to return. His house and garden were sold to Major John Biddle. The American victory in 1813, under Commodore Perry and General Harrison, won back the territory. General Lewis Cass was made Governor. He was Michigan's foremost statesman, serving from 1813 to 1860

Governor Hull's residence, built in 1807—perhaps the first brick house

as military commander, governor, senator, cabinet minister and ambassador to France.

Governor Cass took occupancy of the oldest and most famous residence in Michigan, the house on the river which tradition holds was the same one built in 1702 by Sieur de la Mothe Cadillac for Quarante Sols, Chief of the Huron Indians at Detroit. John Hay, the last of the colonial governors, who as Lieutenant Hay had razed the garden in the Pontiac war, had lived there, and was buried in the garden. When the city was turned over to the Americans this house became known as the "White House of the Northwest." Its situation on the immediate bank of the river was very beautiful, and its windmill and great pear trees made it a landmark for

The river front in 1819, showing, at the left, the DeGarmo Jones house; in the center, the mouth of the Savoyard; at the right, the Cass house in its original location. The vessel was the first steamboat on the Lakes

Detroit in 1826. From a water-color drawing by Gen. Alexander Macomb

many miles. Made of cedar logs, clapboarded, with heavy stone chimney, steep roof and gables, heavy blinds and doors, it was both spacious and strong. A wide gallery, fifty feet long, adorned its front. Overlooking the river were smiling gardens and green slopes through which flowed the Savoyard, and on the side was a quaint porch resembling a Chinese pagoda, and a small formal garden. The place was long protected by the walls of the fortress. Governor Cass enlarged and improved its gardens. In 1837 Daniel Webster made one of his notable speeches in the Governor's orchard.

Numerous descriptions of the Cass home were penned by visitors to Detroit. Colonel Thomas L. McKenney, a visitor in 1827, has left a detailed description of the house in his *Sketches of a Tour to the Lakes*. Of the exterior of the home he wrote:

"The position occupied by this relic of antiquity is very beautiful; not on account of the views to it, and from it, only, although these are both fine, but it is sustained on either side and in the background by fertile upland meadows, and flourishing orchards and gardens, which give it a most inviting appearance; and serves to impress one with the idea of old age surrounded by health and cheerfulness. In front are the shores of Canada, with the beautiful river between, and to the right the Huron church, etc., the sound of the bell from which strikes gratefully upon the ear."

The growth of Detroit brought ruin to the old mansion and obliteration to its gardens. A few years after McKenney's visit, the mad boom of the thirties caused a syndicate of promoters to plat the site for city lots. Shorn of its proud associations, the house was removed to another location, where it lived on in humble obscurity for several decades, until it was finally demolished in 1882.

The "Detroit Garden", built in the early nineteenth century, was situated on the northeast corner of Bates and Atwater Streets. It was one hundred and fifty feet by fifty feet in size, and in one corner was a small theatre, the auditorium of which was out of doors under the shade trees. A show was always on when the weather was fine, and the acting was good. The house was a long, low building with dormer windows, set back from the street about fifty feet, the intervening space being filled with trees, roses, and flowering shrubs. Two or three flowered arbors were found on the place.

The "Michigan Garden", on the river corner of Brush Street, was one of the outstanding earlier American gardens. It later became the property of E. A. Brush, on whose farm it was, and after whom the street was named.

A notable garden was that of William Woodbridge, who came to Detroit from Ohio in 1814, having been made Secretary of the Michigan Territory in that year. He was one of Michigan's most distinguished citizens, occupying many positions of trust; he was Governor from 1840 to 1841, and United States Senator from 1841 to 1846. He married Juliana Trumbull, whose father, Judge John Trumbull, author of "McFingall," and called the "Patriotic Poet of the Revolution", lived at the Woodbridge house. Here were entertained Henry Clay, Daniel Webster, John C. Calhoun and other distinguished guests. In 1817 Governor Woodbridge bought two French farms down the river at Trumbull Avenue, and there before his house planted his flower gardens, "fruit yards", and an orchard of two thousand trees. He raised such delicious grapes in his "glass houses" that they were exported to England. He built his house among gardens already grown. The front and rear were covered with lattice work over which climbed vines of roses, grapes, clematis and morning glory. There was a formal garden, semicircular in shape,

The residence of Governor Wm. Woodbridge, torn down in 1873

between the house and the river. The garden was hedged with shrubs beyond which were stretches of lawn.

When the growth of the city at length overtook the Wood-bridge farm, as it had already overtaken that of Governor Cass, Woodbridge opposed in vain the changes which were impending. He regarded the forcible opening of highways through his farm as subversive of his dearest private rights and interests, and he contested the matter long and bitterly in the courts. Himself a lawyer since early manhood, the case proved, according to his biographer, the most annoying one of his entire career. It is interesting in this connection to observe that in his legal argument he placed greatest emphasis upon the injury to his garden which the proposed improvement would occasion. "It is now almost one half of a century," he wrote, "since the complainant bought the place he lives upon; he bought it *as a farm*. It was his purpose as long as he should live, to preserve it and live upon it *as a farm*. Was this a legal, a rightful purpose? And, conceding that the substantial wealth of the State consists in its agriculture, was it not a *meritorious* purpose, and one he might justly claim to be protected in? . . . The measure was deeply regretted, and operated as a great personal injury; for while the 'highway', as such, was of no earthly use to the complainant; *it broke through his garden, destroyed multitudes of grafted fruit trees*, caused the entire destruction of one large barn, and rendered it necessary to remove another. . . ."

Although public necessity may have required the improvement, one cannot withhold the tribute of sympathy for Governor Woodbridge in his fight to preserve his home and garden from destruction. In his case, as in countless others, modern progress strode rough-shod over the dearest possessions of the home-loving individual.

Modern progress had not yet menaced the old gardens of Detroit, however, when in 1818 came the *Walk-In-The-Water*, the first steamboat on the lakes, with a large number of passengers. The descendants of some of them still preserve tiny sealed letters describing the beauty of the landscape as seen from the river, the old gardens and wonderful trees.

Other gardens of the early decades of the nineteenth century deserve mention. Mrs. Deveaux's gardens, which included a nursery of fruit trees, were on the southwest corner of Woodward Avenue and Congress Street. In 1838, at the corner of John R. Street and Woodward Avenue, Thomas Palmer built a commodious house, surrounded by gardens. ". . . Adjoining and including the ground on which the house stood, he owned one or two acres, which were enclosed at the rear and on Woodward Avenue and Grand Circus Park sides by a rail fence, and were devoted to garden purposes."[1]

The widow Savenack lived in an old fashioned French house built around a court on Congress Street. In this court she grew rushes and fleurs-de-lis.

The home of E. A. Brush was on the corner of Brush Street —a two-story wooden structure. It was also the home of a brother, Alfred Brush, whose "chief occupation was horticulture, which he pursued for amusement. In his office in the Michigan or Brush garden, that occupied the square where now the Lyceum Theatre stands, he kept a history of the various trees, shrubs and flowers growing there and entered in a small blank book their daily progress, fruition, etc. The old Brush homestead was . . . situated in the center of a spacious lot that took in the entire width of the Brush farm. The dwelling was surrounded with trees, currant bushes, roses and other flowering shrubs. It was an attractive place and must have witnessed many stirring scenes in the early days."[2]

The dwelling house of William Brown, on Jefferson Avenue near Bates Street, boasted of a very pretty front yard filled with roses, etc.; it also had fine shade trees in front.

Mr. Webster was interested in raising rare plants and flowers; among the latter was the night-blooming cereus.

[1] *Early Days in Detroit*, by Friend Palmer.
[2] *Ibid.*

His specimen was a fine one, and when the time for its flowering approached, he gave notice that on the nights when the plant would be in full bloom, it would be on exhibition in his parlors.

Many of the early homes and gardens of Detroit built between 1820 and 1840 are remembered by the older generation today. Mrs. David Thompson's handsome residence, on the corner of Fort and Shelby Streets, was surrounded by fine old trees and a flower garden in which was an artistic bronze fountain and a summer-house.

Another well known house on the River Road west of the town was commenced by territorial Governor George H. Porter, who died of cholera in 1834 before it was finished. The house was of brick and was among the finest in Michigan. It had a broad veranda with pillars across its front, and its

The John Palmer homestead, at the southwest corner of Griswold and Fort Streets, built in 1829 and removed in 1869

gardens came so close to the windows that one had a feeling that it was literally planted in flowers. This house was later occupied by Colonel Sylvester Larned.

The Lafferte house, built in 1850 on the river in Springwells, was a conspicuous mark in the landscape. It was shaded by an elm which had in 1862 a trunk measuring ten feet in circumference, and a limb-spread of 100 feet.

Father Gabriel Richards, born in France, came to Detroit from Montreal as pastor of St. Anne's Church in 1811. He was greatly loved and revered by the people, who elected him to Congress in 1823, where he served one year. His residence in Detroit was a large unpretentious wooden building with a small garden planted with roses and wood-lilies. During the cholera epidemic from 1832 to 1834 he worked with tireless devotion to relieve the stricken, until he also died from the disease, a martyr to the cause of humanity.

Mr. Bela Hubbard, author of *Memorials of a Half Century*, came to Michigan in 1835. He settled in the town of Springwells, two miles from the western limits of Detroit, occupying the famous old Knaggs home. Near it he built a place called "Vinewood," where he lived all his life. The view from the river in front of his house was beautiful and animating. This fine old house is still standing among its ancient trees and fine old gardens, bounded on its west side beneath the arching elms by the little road once called "Lady's Lane", where the beaux and belles of former years walked in the evening.

The home of Mr. Charles Moran, a fine example of this period, had a garden known for its small flowers, fruits and delicious grapes.

The old Howard House, now occupied by Mr. Henry Haigh, was built at Dearborn, west of Detroit, in 1834. It

The Courthouse or Capitol (1823-28)

had a greenhouse and gardens. The old-fashioned roses, big lilacs, and great trees grown by its original owner still survive.

The Ten Eyck Mansion was built about 1830, and was surrounded with a garden containing beautiful trees and shrubs. Mr. and Mrs. Henry Ford lived in this house until they removed to the one where they now are.

Judge James Abbott, son of the James Abbott who came to Detroit from Dublin in 1768, lived at first in an "old fashioned house among flowers," but later built a fine brick house on the corner of Fort and Griswold Streets. To its garden rosebushes were transplanted from the old home.

Judge James Witherall built a "large house and garden on the Campus Martius," where the Detroit Opera House now stands. He died at his home in 1838.

General DeGarmo Jones came to Detroit shortly after the war of 1812 and built his house down the river "with its front garden, ornamented with a profusion of flowers and two fine pieces of statuary, 'Spring' and 'Autumn'."[1]

On the south side of Jefferson Avenue near Bates Street was Mr. James Connor's residence (built in 1808), with its gardens.

The village "d'Etroit"—that happy, graceful assemblage of all that was best in France and England's adventurous youth, along whose flower-hung streets they played at bowles with the cannon balls of the fortress, and silent-footed Indians trod from one hospitable house to the other—has passed away and in its place stands the fourth largest city in America. The romantic age of the French *habitants*, the English garrison, and the pioneer American are gone forever, and their gardens, like our dreams, are of yesterday.

GROSSE POINTE GARDENS[2]

Old maps in the archives of Detroit show outlines of gardens at Grosse Pointe in the earliest days of its history. French gardens and English gardens—no trace of which remains, except here a description in a faded letter or ancient document, and there an old apple orchard and venerable pear tree.

About ten miles above the center of Detroit, Grosse Pointe projects into Lake St. Clair. This shore is noteworthy for its

[1]*Early Days in Detroit*, by Friend Palmer.
[2]Written by Elsie Sibley Peabody (Mrs. Horace B. Peabody), member of the executive board of the Garden Club of Michigan, Bulletin correspondent, and member of the committee on historic gardens.

stretch of mile after mile of beautiful homes and gardens. These, however, are all modern, for even the oldest dates no further back than the early eighties, when certain Detroiters, desiring the lake air and country quiet for their growing families, gradually bought up the old French farms along the shore of the Pointe.

Grosse Pointe with its "ribbon farms" has always been essentially French, and until forty years ago the houses of the *habitants* occupied the upper banks of the Detroit River and Lake St. Clair, on whose shores stood their quaint gardens and picturesque windmills.

The "ribbon farms" had a water frontage of from one hundred to nine hundred feet and a depth of one to three miles, and the roads which separated them (even far into the city) bore then, as now, the names of the early owners—Dubois, Rivard, Dequindre, Moran and others—, thus distinctly defining the boundaries of these holdings whose land titles go back to the time of the Grand Monarch. "There were thirty-one grants of land on the water given under Sieur de la Mothe Cadillac from 1707 to 1710," says C. M. Burton, "and fifty-seven others from 1734 to 1753 given by the French governor at Quebec. These were all farms."

Seven miles from Detroit is a place once owned by Sieur Joseph Serre, *dit* Saint Jean. His claim is recorded as being "on Lake St. Clair and having an orchard of pear trees and fine gardens of flowers and vegetables." The present owner of this place, Mrs. Dexter M. Ferry, whose house and gardens stand on this long vanished "plantation", possesses the original deed. A mile east on the shore is one of the largest farms, once belonging to the Rivard family, and of its gardens there remains an orchard of eleven ancient apple trees, in whose midst stands a magnificent great pear which, making the twelfth in number, was called the "Judas tree." This is on the property now owned by Dr. Fred Murphy. The Rivard

The James Abbott residence (1835-1881), at the southeast corner of Griswold and Fort Streets, Detroit

farm is divided among four owners today—Mrs. Frederick M. Alger, Doctor Murphy, Mrs. Murray Sales, and Mrs. Hugh Dillman.

Nine beautiful gardens, owned by Mrs. Truman H. Newberry, Mrs. John S. Newberry, Mrs. Paul Deming, Mrs. Frances Dwyer, Mrs. E. H. Butler, Mrs. Dean Ruckes, Mrs. Percival Dodge, Mrs. John Dodge, and Mrs. John Dyar, now stand where once were the farm and gardens of Josette Galignon, who was noted for her roses from France.

The most interesting and pretentious home in Grosse Pointe at this early period was the mansion built there by Alexander Grant some time between 1774 and 1780. This

These beautiful old French apple trees on the estate of Dr. Fred T. Murphy at Grosse Pointe Farms are of the group of eleven apple trees called "The Apostles." In the background is the old French pear tree shown in the illustration on page 392. This was once a part of the Rivard farm

The Dexter house, at Dexter, was built in 1840-43 by Judge Dexter, who was born in Boston in 1792, was graduated from Harvard College, and became a resident of Michigan in 1824. It is recorded of him that his house was so handsome and his grounds so beautifully laid out that they became an example to the neighborhood

house—to which, in a letter to relatives in Scotland, he refers as "a good Mansion House and all other buildings, fine garden and a large orchard,"—was erected on a plantation of 639 acres, a frontage of nine acres on Lake St. Clair and a depth of seventy-one acres.

"The Commodore", as Grant was called, was a great personage in his day. The younger son of a Scotch Laird, he came out to Canada in 1757, and when General Amherst found it necessary to develop some sort of a navy to protect the British interests, he put young Grant, who had seen sea-service, in charge of a sloop of sixteen guns. Later, he was made the first British commodore in Western waters, in command from Niagara to Mackinac, with headquarters at Detroit—a settlement of utmost importance to the English as it was their gateway to all western operations.

Grant married Thérèse Barthe, a well-born French girl, and it was for his wife and ever-increasing family that he built his home on the high banks of the lake and planted his gardens and his orchard.

Life at "Grant's Castle", as the Commodore's home was popularly known, was full of gaiety. Eleven daughters, beautiful of course, attracted the many young naval officers attached to the little fleet stationed at Detroit and the young Army officers on duty at the Fort. The Grants kept open house. Tecumseh, the great Indian Chief, was entertained at the "Castle", as was every other important visitor to the settlement at Detroit. The first harpsichord ever known in the vicinity is said to have enlivened the guests at the numerous festivities of the "Castle."

As Grant's only son died early and left no children, there is no one of his blood who bears the Commodore's name in Detroit today. His estate too, has been divided long since, sold and resold, and no trace of his gardens remains. On the site of his plantation now stand the Convent of the Sacred Heart, the homes of John T. Nichols, of Mrs. Strathearn Hendrie, of the Misses Hendrie, and also lovely "Tonnancoeur," the estate of the late Theodore P. Hall.

Each June during the English occupation, the orchards of the Pointe were filled with Indians, their squaws and papooses, camping there to break their journey to Fort Malden to receive their annual present from the British government. Pontiac had his main camp there during the siege of Detroit, having with him about one thousand braves.

Early in the eighteenth century the Indians gave two thousand acres of land at Grosse Pointe to William Forsythe; he obtained a deed—based on this Indian grant—from the English in 1776. He lived on the farm with his family of six sons. As there is no account of his having an important house or garden he probably was content with the usual home of the *habitant*, a farm and a large orchard of cherry and pear trees, which extended along the lake shore to Moran Road. This is of interest because of the fact that on it now stand modern homes and gardens belonging to Mrs. Cyrus Lothrop, David Whitney, Lawrence Buhl, Charles B. Warren and R. P. Joy. This same William Forsythe bought about the same time land at Grosse Pointe Shores, East of Provençal Road, with three thousand feet on Lake St. Clair and extending back into the country for three miles. This was one of the largest "ribbon farms" and is divided today into four places on which are old trees and delightful gardens now occupied by the homes of Mrs. E. L. Ford, Mrs. Joseph B. Schlotman, Mrs. Henry D. Shelden, Mrs. H. N. Torey, and Mrs. E. D. Speck. Up the shore of the Lake is a tract of land recorded as given to Jean Baptiste de Marsac, whose ancestors were among the first white men to reach New France. On it is now the beautiful modern garden of Mrs. Benjamin S. Warren, which preserves three fine old French pear trees and the original old log house once occupied by the French *habitant*. The house and gardens of Mrs. Harry M. Jewett and the Lochmoor Country Club are also on this original farm.

An early home that remained in the hands of the heirs of the original owner down to present times, was the Provençal homestead. In 1819 a young Detroit merchant named Pierre

The Smith house, Grass Lake. A Michigan home of the dignified type of 1840

Provençal bought a large tract of land in "a place known as Grosse Pointe, on Lake St. Clair." He cleared the primeval forest, planted his garden, and built his house for his wife and himself. For many years no children came to the young couple, so they adopted several, and soon had to erect a separate building on their estate, where they found room, first and last, for twenty-four children, all orphans, of varying ages. This was Pierre Provençal's private charity, and not only did he bring the children up in his home, but when they were ready to go out into the world, he gave to each one a sum of money to start him on his career as a useful citizen. As there was no church in that part of Grosse Pointe, Pierre Provençal made an altar and confessional box and set them up in his home, and a priest came each Sunday and celebrated mass for the scattered neighbors. This is now the property of the Country Club.

The shores of the lake, as well as of the river, were then lined with the picturesque windmills of the French *habitants* and the air was full of their legends and their superstitions. The "Loup Garou" carried off maidens, or, terrified at the sign of the cross, or a touch of holy water, leapt into the open mouth of a giant catfish (which fish was thenceforward anathema to a good *habitant*) or he turned into a stone that is still to be seen at Tonnancœur. The malicious goblin "Le Lutin" haunted the Pointe. He looked like a bristly-haired baboon, with horns and gleaming eyes, and he rode

The house built by Colonel Joshua Howard in 1834 at Dearborn, now the residence of Mr. Henry Haigh. In its early years a small, fenced-in, formal garden lay on each side of the house. The lilacs, roses and trees planted by the original owner still survive

the horses of those who offended him all the night through, and brought them back in the morning, dripping with sweat and trembling with exhaustion. All good *habitants* made the sign of the cross daily on their horses' heads to protect them from this fiend.

Or again they drilled their children to know the day of the month on which Christmas fell, for there was another goblin, "Le Manchon Roulant", who assumed the form of a black muff rolling along the ground. If you met him you must quickly ask, "What day of the month is Christmas on?" He, ignoring the date, would repeat your question, and then, woe betide you if you did not answer quickly, "December 25." A terrible explosion, followed by a vile stench, was the very least of the woes he might inflict on you.

It is a far cry indeed from those Acadian times to the Grosse Pointe of today, with its paved roadway over which automobiles roll, bumper to bumper, a continuous stream for twenty miles. The victims of the Manchon Roulant might find the odor of gasoline fumes reminiscent, but certainly the only feature common to the old Grosse Point and the new is the shape of the various pieces of property which provided the landscape artist with a unique problem—the adequate designing of gardens and grounds on the narrow, disproportionate lots which were once the "ribbon farms" of the *habitants*.

ELSEWHERE IN MICHIGAN

OLD GARDENS IN ANN ARBOR

From *Ann Arbor: The First Hundred Years*, by O. W. Stephenson, is drawn the following account of two old gardens in the town which early became the seat of the University of Michigan:

"James Kingsley came from New England in 1826. He afterwards became one of our most distinguished men. He was the first lawyer admitted to practice, a member of the territorial legislature, Judge of Probate, Regent of the University, and many other things. In 1829 he built a house on the corner of Detroit and Kingsley streets that was so pretentious that it was called Kingsley Castle. . . . Judge Kingsley sold his Detroit Street property in the late thirties to Mr. Colelazer, and it went by his name for many years. It had a large beautiful garden on the Detroit Street side which was terraced. I remember that there was an almond and an apricot tree, besides the flowers, other fruit trees and shrubbery, for I gathered some fruit of both many years after Miss Goodspeed took the place. . . .

"William S. Maynard's fine house was set on a plat of land which extended from Main to Ashley and from Williams Street to Charles Fuller's where Schumaker's hardware store now stands. The garden was tastefully laid out and planted with all kinds of trees, shrubbery and flowers. There were summer houses with seats on which to rest, and lovely peacocks strutting about with extended plumage. It was great fun to romp an entire summer's afternoon in this garden, and eat fruit without stint. This house stood girdled by forest trees. . . . Those good old trees have faithfully served their day and generation, and now, after a lapse of thirty-eight years,[1] still remain an enduring monument to the genius, thrift and remarkable enterprise of that wonderful, active and successful man."

THE COLE HOUSE, AT STONEY CREEK FARM, NEAR ROCHESTER

The old Cole house near Rochester, thirty-two miles from Detroit, now the property of Mrs. Francis Duffield, nestles among trees, well back from the road. Two old spruce sentinels guard the front, which faces the west and looks off over the hills into the sunset; from under the trees at the side, one can catch glimpses of the old mill-pond. The house was built about 1827. Of the "old" garden, only a mock-orange, a yellow rose, a matrimony-vine, and lemon lilies are left, but today old-fashioned flowers have been used, and the old beehives restored, and once more the bees add their lazy, sleepy hum to all the other happy summer sounds.

[1] The book from which this account is drawn was published in 1927.

The Cole house, Stoney Creek Farm, built in 1827, near Rochester, Michigan. From an old print

OHIO

ILLINOIS

The Mills garden as it is today, in Marietta. It was laid out in 1814 and has kept the original plan

OHIO

THE SETTLING OF OHIO

OHIO—the word in the Wyandot signifies "fair river" or "beautiful river"—was originally part of that vast region known as Louisiana which was claimed by France. By the treaty of 1763 it became English, however. The first British settlement of which there is record was a trading post on the Great Miami, established in 1749 and wiped out in 1752. Moravian missionaries were active on the Muskingum as early as 1762. The daughter of one of them is said to have been the first white child born in Ohio.

Since the first real colonizing impulse came after the Revolution, one cannot expect to find in Ohio traces of the French agricultural or gardening influences that are apparent in Michigan.

Following action by Congress in 1785, a large area was surveyed and opened to settlement. Sales of parts of these lands were made in New York, Philadelphia, and Pittsburgh in 1787. In October of that year, the United States sold a considerable tract of land to Manasseh Cutler—who has been encountered earlier in this volume, in the gardening history of several States—and Winthrop Sargent, as agents of the New England Ohio Company. The first settlement in this purchase, and the first permanent settlement in the State, was made at the mouth of the Muskingum, at Marietta, in 1788. That same year saw Gen. Arthur St. Clair appointed as the first territorial governor, and a makeshift government organized. The "Scioto Land Company" was formed. Lands were sold in France, and in 1791 there arrived a group of 218 purchasers from that country; fifty of them settled at Marietta, while the others went on to Gallipolis, which was laid out about that time. Their title to the lands proving defective, Congress in 1798 granted them a tract called the "French Grant," on the Ohio above the mouth of the Scioto River.

From Marietta settlers were spreading into the adjoining country. The tract granted to Virginia for military bounty lands drew many Revolutionary veterans and other settlers from that state. The region between the Miamis, from the Ohio far up toward the sources of the Mad River, became checkered with farms. Connecticut also sent many settlers to the Lake Erie region, into the tract reserved to her.

The first territorial legislature met in 1799. In 1803, Ohio was admitted into the Union.

About 1810 the Indians, who had for some time been peaceably disposed, began to make raids on the farms; one can imagine many an outlying garden laid in ruins. Tecumseh was active in his efforts to unite the tribes against the settlers. The victory of General Harrison in the battle of Tippecanoe, however, effectively put an end to the Indian menace.

MARIETTA

John Warner Barber wrote in the 1840's the following description[1] of the founding of Marietta, Ohio's first permanent settlement:

"In the autumn of 1787, the directors of the Ohio Company organized in New England, preparatory to a settlement. In the course of the winter following, a party of about 40 men,

[1] From Barber's *History of All the Western States and Territories.*

under the superintendence of Col. Rufus Putnam, proceeded over the Alleghanies by the old Indian path which had been opened into Braddock's road, and boats being constructed, they proceeded down the river. On the 7th of April 1788 they landed at the mouth of the Muskingum, and laid the foundation of the state of Ohio.

"The men who laid the foundation were of the highest character. Washington might well say, 'No colony in America was ever settled under such favorable auspices as that which was first commenced on the Muskingum. Information, property, strength will be its characteristics.'

"Soon after landing, Campus Martius, a stockaded fort, was begun on the verge of the beautiful plain on which are situated the Mounds, those celebrated remains of antiquity. The fort was not completed with palisades and bastions until

The Campus Martius, Marietta, in 1791

the winter of 1790-1. It was a square of 180 feet on a side. At each corner was a strong block-house, surmounted by a tower and sentry-box. . . . The area within the walls was 144 feet square, and afforded a fine parade ground. In the centre was a well 80 feet in depth for the supply of water to the inhabitants in case of a siege. A large sun-dial stood for many years in the square, placed on a handsome post, and gave note of the march of time. It is still preserved as a relic of the old garrison. . . . The whole establishment formed a very strong work, and reflected great credit on the head that planned it."

This was Marietta as Barber saw it in 1847:

"Marietta is built principally on level ground, surrounded by beautiful scenery. Many of the houses are constructed with great neatness, having fine gardens, and ornamental trees and shrubbery, which mark the New England origin of its population. . . ."

Fortunately, one of Marietta's earliest gardens survives.

THE MILLS GARDEN

The Mills garden in Marietta, planted in 1814, has been changed from time to time but keeps the original plan. The house stands on a hill, and from the side descends a terraced garden, with beautiful tulips, pansies and other spring flowers in set beds. There is an old-fashioned "summer-house" (*not* pergola), latticed, with an arched top, and covered with roses. The beds are bordered with old box, and there is a sun-dial which is less old.

Below the garden, on another terrace, are trees, evergreen and odd varieties, also red-bud and dogwood. Along the side of the house, on a terrace overlooking the formal garden, is an interesting sky-line, made by house, twin cypresses one hundred feet high, giant hemlocks (native) over one hundred years old, and two silver birches. There are two very decora-

An old drawing of the Blennerhasset mansion on the island twelve miles below Marietta

tive shrubs—oak leaf hydrangea more than sixty years old, and a particularly fine old mulberry clipped to the round. There is also a fine wrought-iron railing made by a local blacksmith in 1855.

Over the side door is an arch of box, made of two bushes, now about ninety-five years old. All borders of flower and vegetable beds are of box.

BLENNERHASSET ISLE, NEAR MARIETTA

The original white owner of the Ohio River island on which Harman Blennerhasset set up his magnificent establishment of romantic and tragic destiny was General George Washington. It subsequently came into the possession of Elijah Backus, and became known by his name, a circumstance which unleashed the wit of an early traveller who wrote: "I soon perceived why this island was named Bacchus. It abounds with vines, which grow to great height and strength but never produce to any perfection."

In 1796 Blennerhasset, born in England of Irish parentage, married the daughter of the Lieutenant-Governor of the Isle of Man, and having become an ardent republican, came in 1797 to America and eventually to Marietta. In 1798 he purchased from Backus for $4500 a tract of 174 acres at the upper end of the island. Here the Blennerhassets lived for a time in a log house until they could erect the beautiful house and lay out the magnificent grounds that made the island the wonder of early voyagers on the Ohio River. On this estate he spent a large part of his patrimony.

"Foreign frescoes colored the ceilings,—the walls were hung with costly pictures, and the furniture, imported from Paris and London, was rich, costly, and tasteful. Splendid mirrors, gay colored carpets, and elegant curtains embellished their apartments. Massive silver plate stood on the sideboard. The drawing-room resembled the richest Parisian *salon* in the heyday of Louis XIV."[1]

An early traveller, Thomas Ashe, alias d'Arville, wrote of his visit to Blennerhasset Isle:

"This island hove in sight to great advantage; a scene of enchantment; a lawn in the form of a fan inverted, with flowering shrubs and clumps of trees, in a manner to convey strong conviction of the taste of the proprietor. The house stands on the immediate summit of the island, is snow

[1]E. O. Randall, *Ohio Archæological and Historical Society Quarterly*, I, 132.

white and furnished with wings which interlock the adjacent trees."

Two or three pages of Ashe's book[1] are devoted to the delights of his stay there. He records that by moonlight, with a torch in the bow of a canoe and his men at the paddles, he took Blennerhasset along the river spearing fish, which they then cooked barbecue fashion. He adds: "This mode of nocturnal fishing was quite novel to the inhabitants of the little insulated world."

Another description speaks of "the original home with its middle house and curving wings, the little landing, the lovely great lawns, the gracefully curving walks and the figures of Blennerhasset and his wife and their doomed children."

Various accounts testify to the cultivation and refinement of both master and mistress of the mansion which was the social centre for Belpré and Marietta. Blennerhasset, it is said, could repeat the Iliad from memory in the original Greek. He was gifted, according to contemporary report, with "all sorts of sense except common sense."

Common sense would perhaps have saved him from his fate. In 1805 he met Aaron Burr, and thereafter lent himself with enthusiasm to Burr's vague scheme for a western empire. His island became a headquarters for the activities of the project. In December, 1806, Virginia militia descended upon him. He escaped, but his property was seized by creditors and the beautiful grounds were used for the cultivation of hemp. In 1811 negroes accidentally set fire to the house and burned it to the ground. Floods completed the ruin of the lawns and grounds.

A great sycamore tree, standing in the midst of a tall clump of elms, is said to mark the foundation of the original mansion. The old well still supplies clear, sparkling water.

Blennerhasset eventually escaped trial when the state failed to convict Aaron Burr of either treason or misdemeanor. His wandering life of disappointments ended in 1831 on the island of Guernsey.

[1]*Travels in America, performed in 1806, for the purpose of exploring the rivers Alleghany Monangahela, Ohio and Mississippi, and ascertaining the produce and condition of their banks and vicinity*, by Thomas Ashe Esq., London and Newburyport. Pp. 149-152.

The old Blennerhasset well

CLEVELAND AND DAYTON

We can cite no records of historic gardens in Cleveland and Dayton, but historians afford us glimpses of cities where gardens must have flourished. In 1838 Cleveland was described as "beautifully located on a gravelly plain elevated nearly 100 feet above the lake. The streets of the city are wide, and near the center of the city is a public square of ten acres. The unusual amount of trees and shrubbery, and park-like grounds surrounding many of the private residences have caused Cleveland to be called 'The Forest City.' It is a spot 'where town and country appear to have met and shaken hands.'"

Settlement of Cleveland began about 1796; its first years were marked by a bitter struggle for existence. In the winter of 1796-7 there were but three inhabitants. Then, in the spring of 1797, arrived James Kingsbury and Elijah Gunn. They and others who followed—the Carters, the Hawleys, Miss Chloe Inches—must have been the first sowers of gardens in Cleveland. In 1798 Major Carter planted two acres of corn on the west side of Water Street. In 1799 the Edwards and Doanes arrived from Chatham, Conn., after a journey of 92 days.

The first permanent settlers in Dayton, arriving in April, 1796, must also have been its first gardeners. The first eighteen to arrive were Wm. Gahagan, Samuel Thompson, Benj. Van Cleve, Wm. Van Cleve, Solomon Goss, Thomas Davis, John Davis, James M'Clure, Daniel Ferrell, William Hamer, Solomon Hamer, Thomas Hamer, Abraham Glassmire, John Dorough, Wm. Chenoweth, Jas. Morris, Wm. Newcom, and Geo. Newcom.

By 1840, John Warner Barber could record that "almost all the private residences are ornamented by fine gardens and shrubbery."

CINCINNATI

Soon after the first settlement in Ohio, at Marietta, several expeditions were organized to occupy and improve a tract of land between the Miami rivers which had been purchased by Judge Symmes. The first, led by Major Stites, laid out the town of Columbia, at the mouth of the Little Miami. The second party, numbering twelve or fifteen and headed by Matthias Denman and Robert Patterson, after much difficulty with floating ice in the Ohio landed on the north bank on Dec. 24, 1788, opposite the mouth of the Licking. The town which they laid out was first called Losantiville, and later renamed Cincinnati. The price of the land on which the present city stands was, according to John Warner Barber, about five pence per acre. A third party, under the guidance of Judge Symmes, established itself at North Bend. For a time there was uncertainty as to which of these three communities was to take the lead, but the scale soon turned in favor of Cincinnati.

The settlers built their first cabins east of and near what became Main Street. The lower level of land was then covered with sycamore and maple trees, and the upper level with beech and oak. Through these dense forests streets were laid out along courses which were marked upon the trees.

In Cincinnati's early years, Fort Washington, which stood

Ohio White Sulphur Springs, seventeen miles north of Columbus, in 1838. "The spring property consists of 320 acres, part of it woodland, handsomely laid off in walks and drives"

between Third and Fourth Streets, was the center of the community. Records of the earliest years mention two gardens. Immediately behind the fort, on the north side of Fourth Street, was the frame house of Colonel Sargent, the secretary of the territory. It had a spacious garden, cultivated with care and taste. On the east side of the fort was the plain frame dwelling of Dr. Richard Allison, the surgeon general of the army. It stood in the center of a large lot which was cultivated as a garden and fruitery, and which was called "Peach Grove." Another garden of that early day was that of the Hon. Willing Byrd.

In 1838, near the close of the period covered by this survey of gardens, John Warner Barber wrote:

"Cincinnati is situated in a beautiful valley of about 12 miles in circumference, surrounded by hills which rise to the height of about 500 feet. This valley is divided nearly in the centre by the Ohio River.

"The greater part of the city is built on two terraces or plains, sometimes called 'bottoms.' The suburbs are very beautiful. For miles and miles the country is disposed in exquisite undulations, with charming country seats scattered here and there."

Several years earlier, Cincinnati had already made an important contribution to horticultural science. In 1835 an excellent *Synopsis of the Flora of the Western States*, by Prof. John L. Riddell of Cincinnati, had been published there.

For the information about gardens in Ohio's early years, and for the accounts of the gardens and gardeners of early Cincinnati and Chillicothe, we are indebted to the Garden Club of Cincinnati, and notably to Mrs. William S. Rowe.

Cincinnati in 1802. From a drawing made by William Bucknell

Mrs. Charles P. Taft's front garden, in Cincinnati

NICHOLAS LONGWORTH, OHIO'S FIRST HORTICULTURIST, AND THE BAUM-LONGWORTH-TAFT GARDEN

As gardens go in the Old World a hundred years is a comparatively short life, but in the Middle West there are very few gardens indeed which, planted a full century ago, still bloom and flourish with all the vigor of youth and all the glory of a long tradition. Such a garden is to be seen today in the heart of Cincinnati behind the old colonial mansion on Pike Street which was the home of the first Nicholas Longworth and is now the home of Mrs. Charles P. Taft.

House and garden alike are now walled in by the tall buildings of a busy manufacturing city, and yet, even amidst these incongruous surroundings, still retain much of their early charm and dignity. Latrobe, the noted architect who planned the house and laid out the grounds originally, could he return today might well be thrilled to see how his work has endured the changing taste of four generations.

The house was originally built for Martin Baum, an early Mayor of Cincinnati. In 1828 it was acquired by "Old" Nicholas Longworth, as he came to be called, the first of that name in Cincinnati and great-grandfather to the late Congressman from Ohio. In 1828 this Old Nicholas was a young

Nicholas Longworth, the first horticulturist in Ohio, and his wife

lawyer whose interest in horticulture was already overshadowing his interest in law. Under the first Nicholas the gardens and park around the Pike Street house were constantly enlarged until they covered many city blocks.

All or nearly all of Mr. Longworth's descendants have inherited from him a love for gardening, and yet it must be confessed that not one of these later gardens, lovely as they are, has ever equaled the old Pike Street garden in extent, beauty, or horticultural importance. The story of Mr. Longworth and his garden would include the greater story of the beginning and the development of horticulture in the Middle West, as well as the story of a tiny settlement on the banks of the Ohio which during the lifetime of Nicholas himself became one of the greatest manufacturing cities in America.

As a penniless lad of nineteen, Nicholas Longworth left Newark, N. J., and landed in Cincinnati from a flat boat in 1802. He came of old Tory stock which had settled in Charleston, South Carolina. The Revolution had swept away the family fortune, and this young son of the house, with true pioneer spirit, pushed westwards determined to build up a new fortune. His immediate ambition was to become a lawyer. With this in view, he associated himself at once with the only judge which the small town of Cincinnati then boasted. By what seems at first glance one of the

merest chances of fate, the young man was
often forced to accept land for his services
instead of fees—vast tracts of untouched
wilderness of little or no value at the moment, but destined in a few years' time, with
the city's amazing growth, to be worth mil-
lions. Is this to be called mere chance? Nicholas Longworth had a passion for the soil
and for every living thing that grew in the
soil. Is this not perhaps reason enough that
land should have come to him as it did?

His first gardens in Cincinnati were laid
out at Rose Lawn on the banks of the Ohio.
After he removed to the Pike Street house,
he began work there on the gardens which
will always be associated with his name.
These were soon the most notable of any in
the Middle West, and visitors came from
near and far to see them. He built many

The Baum-Longworth-Taft house, Cincinnati

stories of his eccentricities; of his love for old
clothes, of his dry humor and his penny
shrewdness, of his dislike for organized charity and his compassion for "the devil's
poor." That is all. Yet not quite all. He
has a secure place in any History of American Horticulture, and he has besides a
footnote all to himself in American Literature. He once sent Longfellow a keg of his
famous vintage, and the poet acknowledged
the gift in the graceful verses entitled, "Catawba Wine."

Mr. Longworth was president of the Horticultural Society for many years. He was
an enthusiastic gardener. Many amusing
stories are told of visitors finding him
working in overalls and offering him fees,

*The driveway and planting at the side of the house, which is now the resi-
dence of Mrs. Charles P. Taft. The buildings on the hill in the distance
stand on ground which was once Nicholas Longworth's vineyard*

greenhouses along his southern boundary, among them one
for a huge *Victoria regia*, another for a famous night-blooming cereus. He had a notable collection of cactus plants and
many camellias. He imported English and Scotch gardeners,
and with them succeeded in raising many exotic fruits, such
as pineapples and nectarines.

His chief interest, however, was in the culture of grapes
and strawberries. Finding the region especially adapted to
the growth of the vine, he made extensive experiments with
as many as forty varieties of foreign grapes. Then he began
testing indigenous varieties and was so successful with the
Catawba that by 1851 his Catawba vines covered vineyards
that aggregated 115 acres. The great wine industry which he
founded attracted vine-dressers and wine-makers from
Germany, France and Italy. These came and planted
vines on all the hillsides about Cincinnati.

Nicholas Longworth founded a mighty industry, but one,
alas, that did not much outlive his own generation. Today
few traces remain of his extensive vineyards, which once
covered the slopes of what is now Eden Park. But the lovely
old colonial mansion on Pike Street still remains, with
hospitable doors still open to the city's distinguished guests,
and behind the old house is still the last remnant of the
famous garden, as lovely now as it was a century ago.

For the rest he is almost forgotten in the city where he was
once the leading citizen. Some few of the old people still tell

*Mrs. Charles P. Taft's side garden. The little church on the hill is a
monastery of the Dominican Fathers. It is on the site of Nicholas Longworth's vineyard*

with the request for an interview with Mr. Longworth. He never enlightened them, but simply said, "Mr. Longworth is too busy at present to see visitors," and went on with his gardening. Much of the ground has been covered with buildings, but Mr. and Mrs. Taft have preserved a flower garden near the house.

After the Revolution the interest in horticulture in America was very marked, and its first sixty years of growth and development were coincident with Longworth's own sixty years of life in Cincinnati.

John Warner Barber's drawing of Nicholas Longworth's vineyard, in Cincinnati

Dr. L. H. Bailey says of him: "He was a leader in the company of horticultural experts and writers which made Cincinnati famous in the middle of the nineteenth century."

THE HOFFNER GARDENS, CUMMINSVILLE

In 1834 Jacob Hoffner, who engaged in business near Cincinnati in 1819, purchased nearly fifty acres of the Hutchinson Farm, and converted the Tavern of the Golden Lamb (built about 1811) into a residence. He occupied the house in 1836.

In time Hoffner beautified about six acres with the finest of landscape gardens. Statuary adorned the walks, the greenhouses were rich in rare exotics, and a picturesque rock-girt pool in front of the house received the waters of the historic spring. The gateways with their sculptured lions and eagles were attractive features and gave to the grounds the appearance of a public park. The lions now mount guard at the

portals of Cincinnati University, and the eagles are in Eden Park.

Hoffner traveled widely and was a great collector of plants, curios, and works of art.

As a leading citizen he was one of the committee to receive Lafayette on his historic visit to Cincinnati. He died in 1894. A public playground now occupies about two acres of the site of the former garden.

THE EMERY ARBORETUM

In 1817 a house was built by a Scotchman named Craig, who had named his 350 acres Cheviot, for Cheviot in Scotland; that is now the name of the little town partly built upon it. Until a few years ago, a very beautiful tract of seven acres was owned by the Tuchfarber family, who preserved its original beauty, and built a noted garden.

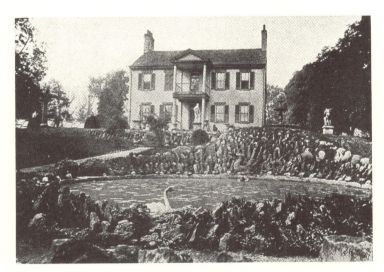

The Hoffner homestead

When Cincinnati, in annexing some of the villages of the hills, took over Westwood, she acquired a botanical garden which for many years had given free and hospitable access to students.

The place was purchased and given to the city by Mrs. Thomas Emery for an arboretum and a sanctuary for birds. As far as possible all our native wild flowers are gathered there and are carefully guarded.

It is known as the Emery Arboretum, and is used by the students of Cincinnati University in their study of forestry and botany.

ALLISONIA

About 1800, the distinguished first physician in Cincinnati, Dr. Richard Allison, had the "Peach Grove" plantation which has been mentioned before. Near by were the fine gardens of two Federal officials, the Hon. Winthrop Sargent and the Hon. Willing Byrd. All these places were close by Broadway and in the vicinity of the historic Lytle home. now Lytle Park, where the statue of Abra-

The Emery Arboretum

ham Lincoln, given to the city by Mr. and Mrs. Taft, is placed.

Dr. Allison's most interesting venture, however, was his project of "Allisonia." He purchased military warrants and entered two surveys of land in Clermont County, one of 434 acres and the other of 441 acres. On May 13, 1815, he laid out a projected town, Allisonia. It was to be a most elaborate and beautiful place, including a number of circular, oblong, and crescent-shaped pieces of ground for purposes of ornament and recreation, and also a market-place. Lots were also set aside for various civic purposes. Allison's death in 1816 interrupted the growth of his new town, however, and it soon lapsed into farm land.

"Adena" property, waiting for the completion of their permanent home.

In 1803, the beautiful mansion of Adena was completed, two miles northwest of Chillicothe, on an eminence which gave a delightful view of the Scioto Valley. The architect was the senior Latrobe, of Washington, who brought the workmen for the construction from that city. The house was built of stone, and was then considered the finest home in the Ohio Valley.

The gardens and shrubbery were set out and cared for by a gardener from England.

Beyond the court at the foot of the steps stretched a lawn, and hedges ran from each wing down to the entrance gate.

"Adena," at Chillicothe, showing the present-day garden, with terraces

CHILLICOTHE

THE GARDEN OF "ADENA"

One hundred and thirty-five years ago, Thomas Worthington, with a band of young men, sons of officers of the Virginia line, came to Ohio on a mission for his guardian, General Darke.

By the Greenville Treaty all lands lying between the Scioto and Little Miami rivers, extending to the Ohio, were secured to Virginia as payment for her troops. The claims of General Darke were considerable. He therefore sent his ward, young Worthington, to establish his ownership in these claims. After a perilous journey through flood and wilderness, this intrepid band in 1796 reached the rude hamlet—consisting of a few huts without windows and deficient in doors—which had been named by the peaceable Indians "Che-le-co-the." The warrants of General Darke lay on the plateau, west of the town. After locating them, Worthington returned to Virginia.

In the following year, 1797, Thomas Worthington married Eleanor Van Swearengen, whose family were, with the Worthingtons, intimately associated with the early history of Ohio. In 1798 Thomas Worthington and his wife and infant daughter were living in a comfortable log cabin on the

The garden lay to the east of the stone house, and was terraced like the garden at Mount Vernon. Rough stone walls held the terraces, and short flights of stone steps led from one level to another.

Many flowers grew in this pioneer garden. Early spring brought crocus and daffodils and fragrant white English violets. In June came the spice roses, and a little rose which the mistress of the house had found in the woods. This was called by her friends the "Worthington" rose; it was double, and as fragrant as sweet briar. By the edge of the terrace grew a long row of yuccas. It is said that Aaron Burr sent Mrs. Worthington the moss roses, the yellow jasmine, and the sweet honeysuckle, to show his appreciation of this garden in the "Wilderness."

At the top of the brown steps was a sun-dial, and at the bottom, in the shade of a pear tree, was a gray stone seat from which one saw the river in the valley.

By the wings of the house was built a terraced court with a curving front, held by a brown stone wall. A flagstone path led straight to the flagged porch before the front door. On either side of the gate of entrance bloomed a Japanese quince, and the walk was hedged with roses, red, pink, and white, in their seasons. Just inside the wrought-iron fence which topped the retaining wall was a privet hedge, neatly clipped, closing in the little plots of emerald turf behind the rose borders.

All persons of distinction who were traveling through the western country enjoyed the hospitality of Adena and visited the garden. Among these people were Bernard, Duke of Saxe-Weimar, Mr. and Mrs. Henry Clay, and President Monroe.

Adena remained in the family of Thomas Worthington until 1900, when it was purchased by Mr. George H. Smith. Mr. Smith renovated the house and grounds, keeping the old lines and traditions.

ZOAR

THE RESTORATION OF THE COMMUNITY GARDEN[1]

The quaint old village of Zoar, five miles from New Philadelphia, was settled in 1818 by 225 German Separatists under the leadership of Joseph Bimeler. In 1824 they organized a communistic society which lasted until 1898. From

[1]Main facts from an article in *Better Homes and Gardens*, May, 1931, by Beulah Canterbury.

the very institution of the community an interest was shown in the art of gardening.

The plan of the Community Garden was drawn from a copy of a supposedly apocryphal drawing of the Garden of the New Jerusalem. At the center of the plan was a Norway spruce, to symbolize the Tree of Life. Beneath was a bower of arbor-vitæ, and radiating from this bower were twelve grass walks, the walks of the twelve apostles, each marked by a clipped Irish juniper. Between these walks were beds planted with perennial flowers and shrubs.

This garden was maintained until 1898, when it was ploughed up and planted in vegetables. Very recently, however, it has been acquired by the Zoar Historical Society, and is now being restored on the exact original lines.

The Society has also leased the King's House, the home of the original leader of the Zoarites. This villa was once set in a stately garden of its own. The members of the Historical Society are petitioning for State aid to maintain the house as a museum, and doubtless to restore its garden.

ILLINOIS

UNTIL 1778 the only settlements in Illinois were French, although the country had been in the possession of the English since 1763. In 1778 and 1779, Colonel Clark's campaigns wrested this part of the country from the British. Emigration into the new land began even before the formal close of the Revolution. The first settlement from the revolting colonies was made in 1781, near Bellefontaine, in Monroe County. The settlers were James Moore, James Garrison, Robert Kidd, Shadrach Bond, and Larken Rutherford; thus we know at least the names of some of the earliest gardeners in Illinois. These pioneers, however, had serious difficulties with the Indians until Wayne's treaty in 1791 established peace.

In 1800, the State of today was still a part of Indiana, but in 1809 the western part of that territory was made into a separate territory bearing the name of Illinois, an Indian name with a French ending; it signifies "real men" and was applied to the Indians who inhabited the banks of the Illinois River. In 1818 Illinois became a State.

An early historian, John Warner Barber, thus described the fertility of the State[1]:

"The surface of Illinois is generally level, and it has no mountains. About two-thirds of it consists of prairies, presenting to view, in some places, immense plains, extending as far as the eye can reach, heavily covered with grass, herbage and flowers. These prairies are generally skirted with woods, and in some places interspersed with groups of trees. For agricultural purposes Illinois is surpassed by no state in the Union. In some of her rich bottom lands the soil is 25 ft. deep."

The various towns and villages of Illinois were pioneer communities until well into the nineteenth century. That the settlers loved flowers and had gardens is certain, but there is little that survives in the records, and, in fact, little in the gardens. We owe the descriptions of several which are presented here to the research of Mrs. William C. Evans, of Evanston.

[1]From Barber's *History of the Western States and Territories*.

Chicago finds no place in this survey, as the horticultural development which has produced its present beauty of parks and gardens came long after the terminal date of this volume. It is, however, perhaps worthy of note that the name Chicago is said to have come from Chi-ka-jo, the word by which the Indians called the wild onions which grew in great abundance on the banks of the Chicago River.

EARLY ILLINOIS GARDENS

The following account by Elizabeth M. Moffat deals with the beginnings of horticulture on the Illinois farms, describing approximately the years at the close of the period covered by this book, and telling especially of the farms near Wheaton.

"On a farm, a small tract, covering an area of one to three city blocks, was surrounded with a chicken-proof fence. This tract was plowed each spring, the surface leveled and used for raising both flowers and vegetables. In many cases the flower seeds were planted in straight rows, these divided into raised beds, the beds often bordered with small stones or shells when these were available. In other gardens, the portion devoted to flowers was not plowed, but the beds were spaded up each spring. In such cases, the beds often were bordered with some low-growing perennial, like clove pink or sweet-william, and in the beds themselves were some of the perennials mentioned in the subjoined list. Somewhat rarely there was an attempt at artistic effect, by having the paths laid out in curves like those of a city park. Even in these there was no harmonious color scheme, the main idea apparently being to have a succession of flowers and plenty of them. Along the fence border were planted shrubs and tall-growing plants like hollyhock and larkspur, while on the porches were morning-glory, matrimony-vine, honeysuckle or Virginia creeper, the two latter being native species brought from the woods. The barns often supported a luxuriant growth of hop-vine. The fruit of this was used in making yeast and certain beverages that were popular in early days but are now forbidden by law.

"In autumn the seeds of annuals were carefully collected and stored for the next season. In a spirit of generosity that is now becoming rare, these seeds were divided among or exchanged with neighbors, so that if some new variety was acquired by one housewife, that variety soon became common in gardens throughout the community.

"The foregoing observations apply to those who came to northern Illinois at an early day and settled upon the then unbroken prairie. My own recollections are chiefly of a garden that my parents had in a small village. They had come from England to Illinois, and naturally my mother cherished the flowers that she had known in her childhood home. Among the species that I recall in her garden were rosemary, live-for-ever, petunia, bleeding-heart, periwinkle, southernwood, bergamot, moneywort, ribbon grass, sweet-william, johnny-jump-ups, larkspur, portulaca, four-o'clocks, hollyhocks and forget-me-not.

"Presumably there were gardens among the well-to-do that were more elaborate than those we knew. My husband recalls one in Elgin. It was directly opposite his parents' home, covered an entire block and was surrounded by a high, tight board fence. The owner was a surly old botanist, and was credited with having in cultivation a very large number of species of flowering plants. No child was allowed to enter the garden, so that it might as well have been on the other side of the world. However, the children did amuse themselves by throwing stones over the fence."

Mrs. Moffat gives this list of species that grew in Illinois gardens fifty years ago, and presumably earlier.

"Phlox (*Phlox paniculata*) vars.; Portulaca (*Portulaca grandiflora*) vars.; Hollyhocks (*Althea rosea*) vars.; Morning Glory (*Ipomoea purpurea*); Ladies' Slipper (*Impatiens balsamina*) vars.; Marigold (*Tagetes erecta*); Buttercup (*Ranunculus acris?*); Scarlet Lightning (*Lychnis chalcedonica*); Grass Pink (*Dianthus plumarius*); Clove Pink (*Dianthus caryophyllus*); Sweet-William (*Dianthus barbatus*); Periwinkle (*Vinca minor*); Moneywort (*Lysimachia nummularia*); Johnny-jump-up (*Viola tricolor*), Britton & Brown say that this has from 40 to 50 common names; Bleeding Heart (*Dicentra spectabilis*); Larkspur (*Delphinium*) Spp; Ribbon Grass (*Phalaris arundinacea*) var.; Blue Flag (*Iris versicolor*); Rosemary (*Rosmarinus officinalis*); Petunias (many varieties, all single); Live-for-ever (*Sedum telephium*); Southernwood (*Artemisia abrotanum*); Button Daisy; Wild Honeysuckle vine; Flowering currant; Flowering almond; Syringa; Lilac; Snowball; Three Peonies (*Paeonia officinalis*, many varieties; *Paeonia tenuifolia*, and *Paeonia moutan*, not common); Rose (Blush, Yellow, and Moss)."

"ELM GROVE" AT JACKSONVILLE, ONCE THE HOME OF GOVERNOR JOSEPH DUNCAN [1]

Joseph Duncan, born at Paris, Kentucky, in 1794, emigrated to Illinois in 1818 and settled on the site of the present city of Jacksonville. He bought land extending over ten square miles, much of it pasture land, with a small amount of woodland.

In 1828 he married Miss Elizabeth Caldwell of New York City, and in 1834 he became Governor of Illinois. It was then that the need of a home somewhat better than the log cabin which had been occupied since the first settlement became apparent. In that same year the new home was built.

There is no record of the architect who planned the home, but he probably came from the East, where the Duncans

had many friends. The house is colonial in style, with the typical large hallway through the center.

As a proper entrance to the home, Governor Duncan planned a semi-circular drive leading from what is now West State Street up to within 120 feet of the house. A wide brick walk leads from the driveway to the doorway. Along the drive were planted elms and sycamores, and elsewhere, trees in naturalistic groups. Governor Duncan also planted lawn trees to shade the house and to frame it. A beautiful elm a few feet northeast of the house has grown very tall and is in very good condition today. Up its trunk—the tree has a high canopy and few lower branches—climbs a grapevine so

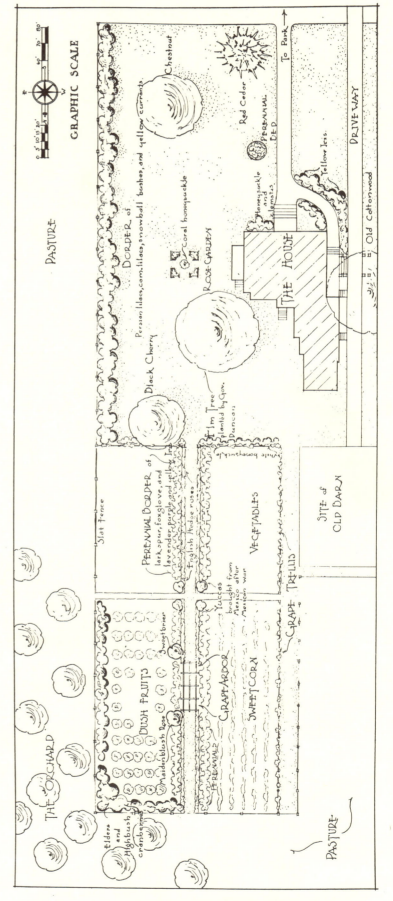

A plan of the Governor Joseph Duncan homestead, at Jacksonville

dense of growth that one cannot easily get nearer than four feet from the trunk.

A number of trees have been cut—their trunks show the great size to which they had grown; one of them, a cotton-wood, has a diameter of six feet. Locust trees also were part of the original planting; they were cut several years ago.

At the back of the house was a large orchard of apples, peaches and plums, which must have presented as beautiful a sight as any flower garden. It is said that the Duncans delighted to stand in the door of the hallway and watch the storms sweep over this orchard and the wide pastures.

Governor Duncan died in 1844, and in 1862 his widow gave a portion of the land to the city of Jacksonville for a park. The entrance driveway was included in this tract.

For many years the old place was neglected, but in 1882 Mrs. Julia Duncan Kirby, a daughter of the Governor, again made a most attractive garden. The garden, patterned after the theory of old-time gardens, was necessarily enclosed. Along the entire west side extended a grape trellis covered with heavy vines; the remainder was enclosed by a slat fence. White honeysuckle covered the south enclosure. The garden was full of the usual old-fashioned flowers, planted from seeds coming from various gardens in Jacksonville made by those who had moved there from the North and the South, bringing with them seeds and slips of the flowers characteristic of the parts of the country from which they had come.

The house and grounds have been saved from the usual city subdivision by the Daughters of the American Revolution, who since 1920 have used the mansion for a clubhouse.

Many of the trees planted by Governor Duncan still survive, serving as a background for his daughter's garden of flowers.

"HAZELWOOD," NEAR DIXON[1]

Some time before 1838, "Governor" Alexander Charters from Belfast, Ireland, a graduate of Dublin College, built a log cabin as the nucleus of a country estate on the Rock River, near Dixon, Illinois. His title of "Governor" was due to his open handed generosity and hospitality, which made him known far beyond the limits of the pioneer settlement.

Margaret Fuller (Ossoli) was a guest of Charters in 1838, and her description of Illinois and of this home and its surroundings gives an imaginative picture of this part of our country in early days.

"The first place where we stopped," she wrote, "was of singular beauty, a beauty of soft, luxuriant wildness. It was on the bend of a river, a place chosen by an Irish gentleman, whose absenteeship seems to be of the wisest kind, since for a sum which would have been but a drop of water to the thirsty fever of his native land, he commands a residence which is all that is desirable in its independence, its beautiful retirement, and its means of benefit to others. . . .

"In front of the house was a lawn, adorned by the most graceful trees. . . . Amid the grass of the lawns with a profusion of wild strawberries, we greeted also a familiar love, the Scottish harebell, the gentlest, most enticing form of the flower world."

The present owner, Mr. E. H. Brewster, has endeavored to preserve the garden as nearly as possible in the form of the original one planned by the open-hearted "Governor" Charters, who, even in that early day, had an English gardener to tend it. There are great banks of hollyhocks, and a number of lilacs which are supposed to be of the original planting.

[1]From information supplied by Florence M. Evans.

Chicago in 1831

FENCES AND ENCLOSURES

The Cook-Oliver house, Salem, Massachusetts. A fine example of gate-posts, gate, and fencing, perhaps designed by McIntire about 1800

FENCES AND ENCLOSURES

NECESSITY dictated protection against the wilderness, wild beasts, Indians, and domestic animals. There is no picture extant of any of the fences or walls of the seventeenth century. The palisados or forts in the early settlements were protected by high fences built of split or whole logs nailed to cross-pieces, which were in turn nailed to posts of heavy logs sunk deeply in the earth; these were made more efficient by digging a ditch a few feet away from the protecting fence.

The importance of fences as a protection and as proof of

Mr. Lamberton's quarter, the Oyster Shell field, the Suburb's quarter, and the Farms."

Throughout the colonies similar regulations will be found, showing that fences were regarded as of such importance to the general welfare that their keep and upkeep became an obligation upon every citizen.

Rhode Island early tried the experiment of allowing each planter to fence his own planting-ground, orchard, garden, and dwelling-house, if he so desired. The stock was permitted to pasture where it would, watched by the herdsman. This

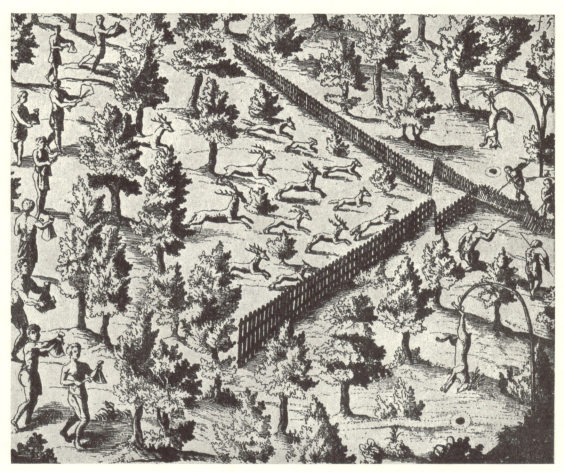

Champlain's drawing of an Indian deer hunt in Canada, witnessed by him before 1620, shows a fence in picket form

ownership of land grants or purchases is reflected in the colonial records by many rulings and regulations passed by the courts. In 1635, at a meeting of the general court in Boston, it was ordered "that John Gallup shall remove his payles at his yard's end."

The court at Boston, on May 10, 1687, provided that "the selectmen shall from year to year appoint Two or more in each Town . . . to view all Common Fences and to Take due Notice of the real defects and insufficiencies thereof, who shall forthwith acquaint the owner of the same." And then follows an explicit ruling concerning the obligations of owners to keep all fences in order, and fines and punishments for infringements of such laws.

At a court held at New Haven in 1645 it was ordered "that those persons whose names are underwritten shall be Viewers of the Fences about the Town ye next Year," and the town is then divided into "Mr. Davenport's quarter, Mr. Browning's quarter, Mr. Evance's quarter, Mr. Gregson's quarter,

proved so unsatisfactory and led to so many quarrels that fencing was ordered to be a "Legal obligation," and the man who did not fence his property under cultivation was fined.

As early as 1635 we know that John Gallup had "Payles at his yard's end" in Boston. This means that a fence built of flat boards or logs nailed close together vertically, and often pointed at the top, was in common usage. There is a record in New Amsterdam of the building of a protecting "paled wall" where the boards were nailed horizontally, as the other and usual method was more costly.

Where stone was plenty and the fields were cleared, laid-up walls of fieldstone were the rule. Thousands of these lovely old walls, so skillfully arranged and balanced without cement of any kind, lasted for more than two centuries; now these beautiful old mossy stones are being rebuilt into houses and more formal walls.

We know from the records that rail fences were early used,

A Connecticut field wall laid up two hundred years ago

A Connecticut wall and stone gate-posts of the early eighteenth century

A section of post and rail surviving in Connecticut in 1930

be above four inches from his fellow, till it come to the rail next under the stakes, and that next under the stakes but ten inches from that above the stakes.

"And for post and rail, it shall be of the same height of the Virginia Fence, four foot and six inches high, and the distance between every rail according to that of the Virginia Fence aforesaid.

"And for Stone Walls, they shall be four foot and six inches high.

"And for a hedge, or a hedge and a ditch, or a ditch only, the sufficiency of any of them shall be judged according to the viewers' judgments. And for that purpose, four men shall be chosen, they or any two of them, to see and view the fences when men shall have occasion to look for satisfaction for damage done by other men's cattle or other men's fences joining upon them, and these four or any two of these viewers to be well paid of those that the damage shall light upon."

Throughout the seventeenth and eighteenth centuries the fields and orchards were fenced with pales made of logs or finished boards, stone walls, post and rail fences, including "worm fences," "water fences" or ditches, and an occasional hedge.

Home lots and gardens were fenced with the same pales as elsewhere, but often finished with care as to placing, and evenly pointed at the top and painted. Stone walls with wooden gates were in common use, and as early as 1720 brick walls handsomely built and often surmounted with fences are mentioned in the records.

Peter Kalm says of rail fences in Pennsylvania:

"The enclosures were not made like ours, for the people here take posts from four to six feet in height, and make two or three holes into them, so that there was a distance of two feet and above between them. Such a post does the same service as two and sometimes three posts are scarce sufficient. The posts were fastened in the ground, at two or three fathoms distance from each other, and the holes in them kept up the planks, which were nine inches and sometimes a foot broad, and lay above each other, from one post to the next. Such an enclosure looked at a distance, like the hurdles with which we enclose the sheep in Sweden."

The History of Byberry, from the Historical Society of Pennsylvania, states that as early as 1682 "it was customary to ditch and plant privet hedges. These hedges were probably introduced on account of the scarcity of rail timber. They made a pleasing appearance to the eye when in

split rails and posts; the posts had two, three, or four holes, into which the rails fitted; these were never painted. They required no gates because the rails were slipped from the posts and removed or lowered when the cattle or the farmer entered or left the field.

Rail fences, in some form, were in common use from the middle of the seventeenth century to the middle of the nineteenth, when the extravagance of such a use of wood discouraged them.

Miss Alice Brayton in her study of the Rhode Island gardens found in the Portsmouth records for the year 1671 the following "rules for fences":

"For a fence called a Virginia fence, it is ordered that it shall be four foot and a half high, staked with stakes, half a foot above the fence plumb up, and that not any of the rails

A Virginia rail or worm fence

Halliday Historic Photograph Co.

This view of the Stevens house, North Andover, Massachusetts (see page 105), shows the laid-up stone fence in common use throughout New England in the seventeenth, eighteenth and early nineteenth centuries

This view near Portsmouth, Rhode Island, shows the construction of a stone wall of the earliest type. The gate was hung by leather thongs and iron bolts thrust through holes drilled in the stone slabs

A laid-up wall at Portsmouth, Rhode Island, showing a modern gate attached to old stone gate-posts, and stone steps used as a stile

The slender rail fence shown in this view across Boston Common toward the Hancock house was erected in the 1760's

This "Farm House in the Back Settlements," from Sutcliff's "Travels in Some Parts of North America," shows a worm fence, early orchards, and the stumps of clearings

The Clark-Frankland house, built on Garden Court in Boston before 1715 and demolished in 1832, had a brick wall surmounted by a handsome wooden fence, and stone gate-posts

Courtesy of Marsden J. Perry Esq.

The fine gate of the John Brown house (1786), in Providence, Rhode Island. Stone posts and marble busts, wooden gates and wooden fence. See also page 202

blossom, and the berries served through the dreary part of the winter for sustenance for the multitudes of wild pigeons. . . . Unfortunately these hedges all died a few years before the Revolution."

Kalm further describes the fences he observed in his travels:

"The inclosures made use of in Pennsylvania and New Jersey, but especially in New York, are those, which on account of their serpentine form resembling worms, are called worm-fences in English. The poles which compose this fence are taken from different trees; but they are not all of equal duration; the red cedar is reckoned the most durable of any, for it holds out above thirty years; but it is very scarce, and grows only in a single place hereabouts, so that no fences can be made of it. It is true, the fences about Philadelphia (which however are different from the worm fences) are all made of the red cedar; but it has been brought by water from Egg-harbour, where it grows in abundance. The supports on which the poles lie, are all made of white cedar, or *Cupressus thyoides*, and the poles which are laid between them of red cedar, or *Juniperus virginiana*. Next to the cedar-wood, oak and chestnut are reckoned best. . . . In order to make inclosures the people do not cut down the young trees . . . but they fell here and there thick trees, and cut them in several places, leaving the pieces as long as is necessary and split them into poles of the usual thickness; a single tree affords a multitude of poles. . . . Thus the worm fences are the most useful kind of inclosures . . . [they] are easily put up again when they are thrown down. . . . Considering how

much more wood the worm fences require (since they run in bendings) than other inclosures which go in straight lines, and that they are so soon useless, one will imagine how the forests will be consumed, and what sort of appearance the country will have forty or fifty years hence, in case no alteration is made; especially as wood is squandered away in immense quantities, day and night, all the winter, or nearly one-half the year for fewel."

We find occasional mention of fencing in the records kept by travelers. In 1783, David Johann Schoepf observed when passing through Pennsylvania:

"Two miles beyond Germantown we came to Chestnut-hill, one of the ranges of hills, all dry and infertile, or, at least, if anything is to be got out of them, requiring more labor and manure than is commonly given.

"Fences certainly are nowhere else to be found of so many varieties as in America, where at any moment the traveller comes on a new sort and cannot but be astonished at the inventive genius of the inhabitants. . . . Commonly the fences are but dead enclosures, either light poles or split logs, bound together in one way or another, laid the one over the other, or it may be upright stakes worked in and across, and so forth. The so-called worm fences are the commonest, and for this purpose, chestnut wood, if to be had, is usual because of its lightness, and because it lasts well, barked. Kalm took the trouble to give drawings of several types of worm fence, but they deserve imitation nowhere.

[1] *Travels in the Confederation*, by David Johann Schoepf.

Halliday Historic Photograph Co.

A double picket fence, with square posts and ball ornaments, in Salem, Massachusetts (about 1800)

"Live hedges are extremely rare; they find planting and attention too troublesome. However, in many regions, it is very ingeniously managed. In order to enclose a piece of land they choose out the youngest trees, and if a sufficiency is not found in the line they plant others so as to fill up the row . . . the trees must all be soft and pliant and stand together as much as possible. Then a deep cut is made in the trunk, several feet above the ground, and the sapling is bent until it lies horizontal, making a right angle with the butt. In this way the row is gone through, one sapling bent over the other; the cut heals, and this part of the trunk becomes a good knuckle for all manner of growth. For the rest the tree thrives, the branches spread, intercross together with the sprouts coming up from the butt, and the roots form a thick and lasting enclosure. This kind of fence is seen in certain parts of Long Island."

In the *New York Magazine* for March, 1793, we find "An essay on the Utility of White Mulberry Trees in making Hedges," written by Mr. De la Bigarre, who read it to the New York Agricultural Society on March 30, 1793. He says:

"The urgent necessity for planting hedges, as the cheapest substitute for our fences, which are proving dearer and more scarce every year, being felt and acknowledged it remains to ascertain the best kind of plant for hedges. . . . White and red hawthorn, elm and birch are reckoned the best plants. . . ." Mr. De la Bigarre then states his preference for the white mulberry, saying that it not only made excellent hedges, but served as food for the silkworm.

A Report of the Horticultural Society of Pennsylvania in 1830 notes that Mr. Butler's country residence six miles out on the Old York Road "had handsome hedges of Hornbeam and Pinus canadensis."

Timothy Dwight, in his *Travels in New England and New York*, writes:

"A great number of the enclosures in the ancient settlements are of stone, the remainder of rails, and of boards. Hedges we have none; all attempts to raise them have hitherto failed of success. In forests and recent settlements, fences are made of logs, raised upon each other; and sometimes trees are felled upon the spot."

Sutcliff's *Travels* makes the following observations about garden walls in 1804-6:

"It is remarkable that I have never seen a garden in America walled round as in England. I believe that one principal reason is the warmth of the climate, and the clear fine atmosphere, which precludes the use of fruit-walls. Besides walls would obstruct the free current of air which would be an objection to them. Yet I have frequently seen gardens fenced around to the height of six or seven feet, with neatly planed boards, painted green or white."

Samuel Breck wrote in his *Recollections* on September 28, 1809:

"We breakfasted at Newport, and set off immediately after through a country but indifferently farmed, although the exteriors of some of the fields offer well-plashed hedges of the American thorn. They are getting into vogue, particularly in the county of Chester in Pennsylvania. I saw them with great delight, and shall set about making one as soon as I return home."

In 1830 the Horticultural Society visited Mr. Samuel Breck's home at Sweet Briar and reported:

"Mr. Breck has taken considerable pains with a hedge of white hawthorn (Crataegus) which he planted in 1810, and caused to be plashed, stalked and dressed by two Englishmen,

Frank Cousins Art Co.

Detail of fence posts and urn from the Cook-Oliver gate, in Massa- chusetts. (See page 422)

Robert N. Cram

The gate and gate-posts of the Peirce-Nichols house (see pages 69-70) in Salem, Massachusetts. A lovely design by McIntire. The fence was re- cently rebuilt, but the gate is old

Robert N. Cram

Wrought-iron fence (1800-1820) with stone posts in front of the house of Miss Mary T. Spalding, Newburyport, Massachusetts

Courtesy of White Pine

A picket fence with moulding mount (about 1800) in front of the Sanford house, Litchfield, Connecticut

who understood the business well. Yet he apprehends the whole of the plants will gradually decay, and oblige him to substitute a post and rail fence. Almost every attempt to cultivate a live fence near Philadelphia has failed. The

foliage disappears in August and the plant itself is short- lived in our climate."

The Horticultural Society also mentions another type of fence at Eaglefield, the seat of Joseph Boni of Philadelphia.

Fence and gates of the Middleton house (1790), Bristol, Rhode Island. See page 237

Halliday Historic Photograph Co.

The Kittredge house (about 1800), North Andover, showing the Massachusetts type of double picket fence

Photographed by Robert N. Cram

Fence and posts of about 1790, at "Elmwood," Cambridge, Massachusetts

The arched gateway (about 1800) at "Silver Creek," in Bristol, Rhode Island. See the arches of the type designed by McIntire for Salem gardens, notably that shown on page 70

Halliday Historic Photograph Co.

A double picket fence with beautifully moulded posts surmounted by urns, in Salem, Massachusetts (1800)

"The house is well built and surrounded by forest trees of large growth and well arranged shrubbery. The lawn is extensive and divided from the house by a handsome chain fence, supported by posts painted green and very neatly turned."

The *Boston News Letter* of November 6–14, 1735, gives us in the following news-item the information that Colonel Dyer had a brick wall about his house in Boston, and a wooden Lion Couchant upon it at his gate post:[1]

"Last Wednesday we were alarm'd at the South End of the Town with the Cry of Fire: and by reason of the exceeding high Wind that blew, many were put into a great surprise by an accident somewhat singular and remarkable:—About one o'clock a pretty high Chimney being on fire, a spark blew therefrom, and entered into the open mouth of one of the carved Lions, couchant upon the Top of the Brick Wall of the House which was the late Col. Dyer's about 100 feet distant from the said Chimney, on the other side of the Street; by the force of the Wind the Fire soon enkindled, and the mouth of the wooden Beast discharging Smoke and Fire, it was presently discovered; and his head being struck at one or two Blows, tumbled into the Street all on a flame, and broke in pieces; and so further Damage was seasonably prevented."

We may safely conclude that brick walls were in use before 1735, and brick walls surmounted with handsome wooden fences were built both by Andrew Faneuil and Thomas Hancock[2] about their homes in Boston.

During the period of great prosperity throughout the colonies between 1700 and the years of disturbance preceding the Revolution, very handsome residences with formal walls and fences were the rule. Few of these survive, but in Boston, Providence, New York, Philadelphia, and Princeton, N. J., and doubtless in many other places, beautifully built formal walls in brick and stone, fine gate posts of stone, brick or wood, and fences in a variety of designs were usual.

After the Revolution the fashion in fencing for the handsome residence continued to be brick or stone walls with fence above, or high faced and finished walls of stone and brick, brick in a variety of forms and stone faced and laid with great skill and beauty. Elaborate fences in wood were everywhere built, and a great many arrangements of pickets, panels and patterns varied them interminably.

Salem, Massachusetts, was noted for its beautiful fences, designed by such architects as Bulfinch and McIntire, and from 1800 to 1840 wrought-iron fences, gates, and balconies were much used for city and large town houses. After 1840 many fences, gates, and balconies, as well as porches and piazza supports, were made of cast-iron. Some of the delightful revival Gothic houses of the 1840 period were fenced with both wood and iron in Gothic pattern, and much of the iron used at the time was well designed.

We cannot give a better idea of the sentiments in regard to fencing in the early nineteenth century than by quoting Downing's chapter[1] on that subject.

"Fences are often among the most unsightly and offensive objects in our country seats. Some persons seem to have a passion for subdividing their grounds into a great number of

[1]From *Art and Craft in New England*, by George Francis Dow.
[2]See illustrations for the Faneuil-Phillips house and the Thomas Hancock house in the Massachusetts section.

[1]From *A Treatise on the Theory and Practice of Landscape Gardening, Adapted to North America*, by Andrew Jackson Downing.

Photographed by Robert N. Cram
Fence and posts of about 1790 at the Vassall-Craigie-Longfellow house, Cambridge, Massachusetts. See also page 37

fields; a process which is scarcely ever advisable even in common farms, but for which there can be no apology in elegant residences. The close proximity of fences to the house gives the whole place a confined and mean character. 'The mind,' says Repton, 'feels a certain sense of disgust under a sense of confinement in any situation however beautiful.' A wide-spread lawn, on the contrary, where no boundaries are conspicuous, conveys an impression of ample extent and space for enjoyment. It is frequently the case that, on that side of the house nearest the outbuildings, fences are, for convenience, brought in its close neighborhood, and here they are easily concealed by plantations; but on the other sides, open and unobstructed views should be preserved, by removing all barriers not absolutely necessary.

"Nothing is more common, in the places of cockneys who become inhabitants of the country, than a display immediately around the dwelling of a spruce paling of carpentry, neatly made and painted white or green; an abomination among the fresh fields, of which no person of taste could be guilty. To fence off a small plot around a fine house in the midst of a lawn of fifty acres is a perversity which we could never reconcile, with even the lowest perception of beauty. An old stone wall, covered with creepers and climbing plants, may become a picturesque barrier a thousand times superior to such a fence. But there is never one instance in a thousand when such a barrier is necessary. Where it is desirable to separate the house from the level grass of the lawn, let it be done by an architectural terrace of stone, or a raised platform of gravel supported by turf, which will convey importance and dignity upon the building instead of giving it a petty and trifling expression.

"Verdant hedges are an elegant substitute for stone or wooden fences, and we are surprised that their use has not been hitherto more general. We have ourselves been making experiments for the last ten years with various hedge-plants, and have succeeded by obtaining some hedges which are now highly admired. Five or six years in this climate, will, under

proper care, be sufficient to produce hedges of great beauty, capable of withstanding the attacks of every kind of cattle; barriers too, will outlast three or four generations. The common Arbor Vitae, (or flat Cedar,) which grows in great abundance in many districts, forms one of the most superb hedges, without the least care in trimming; the foliage grows thickly, down to the very ground, and being evergreen, the hedge remains clothed the whole year. Our common Thorns, and in particular those known in the nurseries as the Newcastle and Washington thorns, form hedges of great strength and beauty. They are indeed much better adapted to this climate than the English Hawthorn, which often suffers from the unclouded radiance of our mid-summer sun. In autumn too, it loses its foliage much sooner than our native sorts, some of which assume a brilliant scarlet when the foliage is fading in autumn. In New-England the Buckthorn is preferred from its rapid and luxuriant growth; and in the southern states, the Maclura or Osage Orange is becoming a favorite for its glossy and polished foliage. The Privet or Prim, a rapid growing shrub, is well fitted for interior divisions. Picturesque hedges are easily formed by intermingling a variety of flowering shrubs, sweet briars etc. and allowing the whole to grow together in rich masses. In all cases where hedges are employed in the natural style of landscape (and not in close connection with highly artificial objects, buildings, etc.), a more agreeable effect will be produced by allowing the hedge to grow somewhat irregular in form, or varying it by planting near it other small trees and shrubs to break the outline, than by clipping it in even and formal lines. Hedges may be obtained in a single season by planting long shoots of the osier willow or by any other tree which throws out roots easily from cuttings.

"A simple and pleasing barrier, in good keeping with cottage residences, may be formed of rustic work, as it is termed. For this purpose stout rods of any of our native forest trees are chosen, with the bark on, six to ten feet in length; these are sharpened and driven into the ground in

Courtesy of White Pine

This view of a house on the lower road at Woodbury, Connecticut, shows the simple type of picket fence in use for many years

From a drawing by A. J. Davis; lithography by Imbert

A handsome iron fence on the interior front at Castle Garden, New York City, built about 1820

New York Historical Society Collections

The Spingler house in New York City about 1800, with its two types of picket fence

Courtesy of Robert Fridenberg Galleries

The American Museum and City Hall of New York about 1820, showing the iron fence. A water-color drawing by Arthur J. Stansbury, reproduced in Stokes' "Iconography"

American Historical Prints, New York Public Library

This drawing of the Parsonage in Cranbury, New Jersey, in 1833, shows picket fencing, rail fences, and paling

An iron fence with stone posts, about 1840, in front of the North Church, Salem, Massachusetts

This "View of the First Beach, Newport, R. I." shows the use of stone wall and finished rail fence as late as 1850

Courtesy of White Pine

A fancy picket fence in the manner of 1840 at the Jabes Bacon house, Woodbury, Connecticut

New York Historical Society Collections

The residence of Joseph Cudlipp, built about 1840 in New York City, had a fence with arrow-shaped pickets

New York Historical Society Collections

This old print of Cambridgeport, Massachusetts, with the old Hovey tavern (burned in 1828) at the extreme left, and the residences of Nathaniel and Isaac Livermore at the extreme right, shows a fence in "palisade" or pale form still in use after 1800

Courtesy of Mrs. Hermann Place, the present owner

This drawing of "Rose-Lawn," the residence of Edgar M. Vanderburgh at Washington, New York, in 1830, shows a delightful combination of styles in fencing—the Virginia rail, the common rail, the tall hedge above a stone wall, and the low hedge

form of a lattice, or wrought into any figures of trellis that the fancy may suggest. When covered with luxuriant vines and climbing plants, such a barrier is often admirable for its richness and variety.

"The sunk fence, or *ha-ha*, is an English invention, used in separating that portion of the lawn near the house from the part grazed by deer or cattle, and is only a ditch sufficiently wide and deep to render communication difficult on opposite sides. When the ground slopes from the house, such a sunk fence is invisible near the latter, and answers the purpose of a barrier without being the least obtrusive.

"In a succeeding section we shall refer to terraces with their parapets, which are by far the most elegant barriers for a highly decorated flower garden, or for the purpose of maintaining a proper connection between the house and the grounds, a subject scarcely at all attended to, or the impor-

tance of which, is scarcely even recognized as yet among us."

It is interesting to observe that Downing put into practice his views as to the desirability of hedges. A visitor to Downing's estate at Newburgh about 1835 wrote[1]:

"I was delighted with the greenness of the hedges, of which I saw four or five kinds growing here, to test their comparative merits in this climate. Every foreigner is justly offended with our unsightly fences—why should we not appropriate to ourselves the beautiful materials which nature seems to have armed with thorns, and decked with foliage, for that special purpose. And then, what a discord between rail fences and green meadows, and what a harmony in live fences and equally verdant fields!"

[1]From "Letters about the Hudson River and its Vicinity," written in 1835-6 by a citizen of New York.

Frank Cousins Art Co.

A cast-iron fence in the Gothic style of about 1840 in front of the Lee mansion, Marblehead, Massachusetts, photographed in 1910

APPENDIX

APPENDIX

PLANTS TO BE USED IN RESTORING OLD GARDENS

A long study of such records as are available has revealed a considerable number of flowering plants actually known to have been in use in colonial gardens. As there is an increasing desire on the part of those interested to preserve buildings and grounds and restore them as they really were, this list of plant material is given. The Garden Club of America is deeply interested in all efforts to preserve the dignified past for the complicated future.

GARDENS BEFORE 1700 ARE KNOWN TO HAVE CONTAINED:

Anemones (what varieties we do not know)
Carnations and clove-pinks
Columbine (the old dark blue)
Crown imperial
Daffodils (the old double yellow)
Gilliflowers (variously considered to have been stocks or double pinks)
Grape flower or Muscary (grape hyacinth)
Hollyhocks (single red and white)
House leeks (*Sempervivum*)
Marigold (double)
Martagon lilies (*Lilium Martagon*)

Moonwort or "sattin" flower (*Lunaria annua*)
Primrose (*Primula vulgaris*)
Roses (called in the records by the following names: Sweet Briar, Blush Rose, *Rosa albida*, "English roses," double and single, undoubtedly the old hundred-leaved rose; and the dog rose, *Rosa canina*)
Scarlet Cross (*Lychnis chalcedonica*)
"Sedum" (several sorts)
Star of Bethlehem (*Ornithogalum umbellatum*)
Tulips (the old variety in red and yellow)
Violets (the small pansy called heart's-ease)
Yellow day lilies (*Hemerocallis flava*)

THE HERBS MENTIONED BEFORE 1700 ARE:

Balm	Five finger	Mustard (single white)	Summer Savory
Belury	Hyssop	Pepper grass	Tarragon
Chives	Lovage	Sage	Thyme
"Clary"	Mint	Sweet Marjoram	Wormwood

FOUR SHRUBS ARE MENTIONED BEFORE 1700:

Flowering peach (known as Double Persica)
Privet (known as primworth and skedge)

White Thorn (*Crataegus*)
Flowering Currant (which we cannot identify)

GARDENS DATING FROM 1700 TO 1750 CONTAINED, BESIDES THE PRECEDING:

Amaranth
Bachelor Buttons
Bell flowers (Campanulas)
"Candy Tuff" (*Iberis amara*)
Devil in the bush (Nigella)
Flower de Luce (Iris, the old dark blue, and *Iris Florentina*)
Fraxinella
Jacob's Ladder (*Polemonium*)

Lilacs (described as blue, white, deep purple and Persian)
Lily-of-the-Valley or May lilies
Peonies (white and red)
Periwinkle (*Vinca minor*)
Southernwood (*Artemisia Abrotanum*)
Spiderwort (*Tradescantia*)
Striped Scotch Rose

GARDENS BUILT FROM 1750 TO 1800 CONTAINED THESE ADDITIONAL PLANTS:

Aloes

Azalea

Balsams Peru

Citron

Clethra

Convolvulus (double)

Dogwoods

Geraniums (five kinds)

Gladiolus

Halesia

Honeysuckle

Hyacinths (double)

Iris (Persian)

Ivy (English)

Judas Trees

Kalmia

Larkspurs (double)

Limes

Magnolia

Manulea tomentosa ("from South Africa")

Myrtle (double)

Narcissus (double white daffodils)

Oleander (double)

Orange

Passion-flower

Pink (double China)

Rhododendrons

Snapdragons

Tuberose

Tulip (double)

Yucca

BETWEEN 1800 AND 1840 MANY NEW PLANTS WERE BROUGHT FROM CHINA,
HOLLAND AND ENGLAND, AND WE NOW ENRICH THE LIST WITH:

Aster (China)

Box

Canterbury Bell

Catalpa

Chrysanthemum

Clematis (*Clematis integrifolia*)

Crocus

Fading Beauty (*Scabiosa*)

Forsythia

Foxglove

Fringe Tree

Fuchsia

Garden Balsam

Golden Chain

Kerria

Lemon trees

Mezerion

Mock Orange

Pea (Sweet)

Poppy

Rose-colored Hibiscus

Siberian Crab

Snowball Tree

Snowberry

"Spirea" (species not known)

Sweet-William or Poetic Pink

Verbena

White Lilies

TWO BOOKS OF THIS PERIOD (1800–1840) MAY BE CONSULTED FOR DETAILS:

Roland Green's *A Treatise on the Cultivation of Ornamental Flowers*, covering soil, sowing, transplanting and general management, which was published in Boston in 1828.

Robert Buist's *The American Flower Garden Directory*, written by a nurseryman and florist and published in Philadelphia in 1839, gives full lists of the flowers in fashion and under cultivation when this study closes.

BIBLIOGRAPHY

BIBLIOGRAPHY

INTRODUCTION

BOOKS

AMHERST, HON. ALICIA; *The History of Gardening in England;* London; Quaritch; 1895.

BAILEY, LIBERTY HYDE; *Standard Cyclopedia of Horticulture;* New York; Macmillan; 1925.

COBBETT, WILLIAM; *The American Gardener;* London; Clement; 1925.

DUCHÉ, JACOB; *Caspipina's Letters;* Bath; reprinted by R. Cruttwell, London; 1777.

FESSENDEN, THOMAS GREEN; *The New American Gardener;* Boston; J. B. Russell; 1828.

GERARDE, JOHN; *The Herball, or Generall Historie of Plantes;* London; J. Norton; 1597.

HUBBARD, HENRY VINCENT, and KIMBALL, THEODORA; *An Introduction to the Study of Landscape Design;* New York; Macmillan; 1917.

JOHNSON, CAPTAIN EDWARD; *Wonder Working Providence of Sion's Saviour in New England;* London; 1654.

KELLY, HOWARD ATWOOD, M.D., LL.D.; *Some American Medical Botanists;* Troy, N. Y.; The Southworth Co.; 1914.

LOUDEN, J. C.; *An Encyclopedia of Gardening;* London; Longman, Orme, Brown, Green and Longman; 1834.

OGILBY, JOHN; *America;* London; printed by the author; 1671.

STUART, JAMES; *Three Years in North America;* New York; Harpers; 1833.

TABOR, GRACE; *Old-fashioned Gardening;* New York; McBride; 1913.

PERIODICALS

New York Magazine, April, 1793.

MASSACHUSETTS

BOOKS AND PAMPHLETS

Adams, John Quincy, Memoirs of; edited by CHARLES FRANCIS ADAMS; Philadelphia; Lippincott; 1874.

BARBER, JOHN WARNER; *The History and Antiquities of New England, New York, New Jersey and Pennsylvania;* Hartford; Allen S. Stillman Co.; 1844.

BENSON, A. E.; *History of the Massachusetts Horticultural Society;* Norwood, Mass.; The Plimpton Press; 1929.

Bentley, Rev. William, Diary of, 1784-1819; Salem, Mass.; Essex Institute; 1905.

Beverly, Massachusetts, Vital Records of; 2 Vols.

BLAKE, FRANCIS EVERETT, compiler; *The History of Princeton (Mass.), 1759-1915;* Princeton; published by the town; 1915.

BOWNE, ELIZA SOUTHGATE; *A Girl's Life Eighty Years Ago;* London; Chapman and Hall; 1888.

BRADFORD, WILLIAM; *History of Plymouth Plantation;* Boston; published for the Massachusetts Historical Society by Houghton Mifflin; 1912.

Breck, Samuel, Recollections of; edited by H. E. SCUDDER; Philadelphia; Porter and Coates; 1877.

BROWN, ABRAM ENGLISH; *Faneuil Hall and Faneuil Hall Market;* Boston; Lee and Shepherd; 1900.

CASTIGLIONI, LUIGI; *Voyage to the United States of America, 1785;* Milano; stampiria di G. Marelli; 1790.

CARVER, ROBIN; *History of Boston;* Boston; Lilly, Wait, Colman and Holden; 1834.

CHAMPLAIN, SAMUEL DE, The Works of; Translated and edited by H. H. Langton and W. F. Ganong; The French texts collated by J. Home Cameron; Toronto; The Champlain Society; 1922.

COUSINS, FRANK, and P. M. RILEY; *The Woodcarver of Salem, Samuel McIntire, his life and works;* Boston; Little, Brown and Co.; 1916.

CREVECŒUR, J. HECTOR ST. JOHN DE; *Letters from an American Farmer, 1770-1780;* New York; Boni; 1925.

CURRIER, JOHN JAMES; *History of Newbury, Mass.;* Boston; Damrell and Upham; 1896.

DAVIS, WILLIAM T.; *Ancient Landmarks of Plymouth;* Boston; Damrell and Upham; 1899.

DEARBORN, H. A. S.; *History of the Massachusetts Horticultural Society, 1829-1878;* Boston; printed for the Society; 1880.

Dexter, Lord Timothy, Life of; edited by Samuel Knapp; Newburyport; John G. Tilton; Boston; 1848.

DOW, GEORGE FRANCIS; *Two Centuries of Travel in Essex County, Massachusetts, A Collection of Narratives and Observations made by Travellers, 1605-1799;* Topsfield, Mass.; The Topsfield Historical Society; 1921.

—— *Arts and Crafts in New England, 1704-1775;* Topsfield, Mass.; The Wayside Press; 1927.

DOWNING, ANDREW JACKSON; *A Treatise on the Theory and Practice of Landscape Gardening adapted to North America;* New York; Wiley and Putnam; 1844; 2nd edition.

DRAKE, SAMUEL; *Old Landmarks and Historic Personages of Boston;* Boston; Roberts Brothers; 1881.

DWIGHT, TIMOTHY; *Travels in New England and New York, 1796-1801;* 4 volumes; New Haven; Timothy Dwight; 1821-22.

EARLE, ALICE MORSE; *Old Time Gardens Newly Set Forth:* New York; Macmillan; 1916.

ELIOT, C. W.; *Charles Eliot, Landscape Architect;* Boston; Houghton Mifflin; 1902.

ENDICOTT, CHARLES MOSES; *Memoirs of John Endecott;* privately printed at Salem; 1847.

FELT, JOSEPH B.; *Annals of Salem;* Salem; W. and S. B. Ives; 1844.

FORBES, ALLAN, and CADMAN, PAUL F.; *France and New England;* Historic Monographs; Boston; State Street Trust Co.; 1925.

GREGG, F. M.; *The Founding of a Nation;* Cleveland; A. H. Clark and Co.; 1915.

HALE, JOHN; *Modest Enquiry into the Nature of Witchcraft;* Boston; J. B. Green and J. Allen for B. Eliot.

HANKS, CHARLES STEDMAN; *Our Plymouth Forefathers;* Boston; Authors Publishing Association, Inc.; 1907.

HAWTHORNE, HILDEGARDE; *Lure of the Garden;* New York; Century; 1911.

HIGGINSON, REV. FRANCIS; *New-Englands Plantation;* Salem; The Essex Book and Print Club; 1908.

Historic Guide to Cambridge; compiled by members of the Hannah Winthrop Chapter D. A. R.; Cambridge, Mass.; 1907.

HOWE, M. A. DE WOLF; *Boston Common, Scenes from four Centuries;* Cambridge; Riverside Press; 1910.

JOHNSON, CAPTAIN EDWARD; *Wonder Working Providence of Sion's Saviour in New England;* London; 1654.

JOSSELYN, JOHN; *New England's Rarities;* Boston; William Veazie; 1865.

—— *An Account of Two Voyages to New-England;* Boston; William Veazie; 1865.

JUDD, SYLVESTER; *History of Hadley;* Northampton; printed by Metcalf and Co.; 1863.

Lothrop, Samuel Kirkland; Some Reminiscences of the Life of; Edited by his son Thornton Kirkland Lothrop; Cambridge; privately printed; John Wilson and Son; University Press; 1888.

MANNING, ROBERT; *Book of Fruits;* Salem; Ives and Jewett; 1838.

—— *History of the Massachusetts Horticultural Society, 1829-1878;* printed for the Society; 1880.

Massachusetts Bay Colony Records.

OGILBY, JOHN; *America;* London; printed by the author; 1671.

PEABODY, ROBERT E.; *Merchant Ventures of Old Salem:* Boston; Houghton Mifflin; 1912.

PEASE, ZEPHANIAH W.; *Life in New Bedford 100 Years ago;* New Bedford, Mass.; George W. Reynolds; 1922.

PERLEY, SIDNEY; *History of Salem, Massachusetts;* Salem; Sidney Perley; 1924.

PLACE, CHARLES; *Charles Bulfinch, Architect and Citizen;* Boston; Houghton Mifflin; 1925.

POWELL, LYMAN P., editor; *Historic Towns of New England;* New York; Putnam; 1898.

Probate Records of Essex County, Mass. 3 vols.; Salem; Essex Institute; 1916.

Probate Court Records for Suffolk County, Mass.

Records of Plymouth Colony.

ROCHEFOUCAULD-LIANCOURT, DUKE DE LA; *Travels through the United States of North America, 1795, 1796, 1797;* London; 1800.

Salem Town Records.

SHURTLEFF, NATHANIEL B., editor; *The Colony of New Plymouth in New England;* Boston; William White; 1855.

SIBLEY, JOHN LANGDON; *Harvard College Graduates;* 3 vols.; Cambridge; Charles William Sever; University Bookstore; 1873.

SMITH, CAPTAIN JOHN; *Description of New England;* Boston; William Veazie; 1865.

SMITH, MRS. E. VALE; *History of Newburyport;* Newburyport; 1854.

STARK, JAMES H.; *Antique Views of ye towne of Boston;* Boston; Ye Photo-Electrotype Engraving Co.; 1882.

STONE, EDWIN M.; *History of Beverly;* Boston; James Munroe and Co.; 1843.

THWING, ANNIE HAVEN; *The Crooked and Narrow Streets of the Town of Boston, 1630-1822;* Boston; Marshall Jones Co.; 1920.

TODD, WILLIAM C.; *Timothy Dexter, Known as "Lord Timothy Dexter" of Newburyport, Mass.; An inquiry into his life and true Character;* Boston; David Clapp and Son; 1886.

TRUMBULL, JOHN; *Autobiography, Reminiscences and Letters, 1756-1841;* New York; Wiley and Putnam; 1841.

UPHAM, CHARLES W.; *Salem Witchcraft;* Boston; Wiggin and Lunt; 1867.

WARVILLE, J. P. BRISSOT DE; *New Travels in the United States of America, performed in 1788;* translated from the French; 1797.

Washington, George, The Diary of; 4 vols.; edited by John C. Fitzpatrick, A.M.; published for the Mount Vernon Ladies' Association of the Union; Boston; Houghton Mifflin; 1925.

WHEILDON, WILLIAM W.; *Sentry or Beacon Hill;* Concord, Mass.; Author's private printing office; 1877.

WILDER, MARSHALL PINCKNEY; "Horticulture in Boston"; in *Memorial History of Boston,* edited by Justin Winsor; Boston; James R. Osgood and Co.; 1880.

WINSOR, JUSTIN; editor; *Memorial History of Boston;* Boston; James R. Osgood and Co.; 1880.

WINTHROP, JOHN; *History of New England, 1630-1649;* James Savage, editor; Boston; Little, Brown and Co.; 1853.

WOOD, WILLIAM; *New Englands Prospect;* London, Tho. Cotes for John Bellamie; 1634.

YOUNG, ALEXANDER; *Chronicles of the Pilgrim Fathers of the Colony of Plymouth;* Boston; C. C. Little and J. Brown; 1841.

PERIODICALS AND PAPERS

American Gardener's Magazine, 1835, 1836.

ADAMS, JOHN QUINCY; two unpublished letters in the possession of the Massachusetts Historical Society.

Bulletins of the Society for the Preservation of New England Antiquities, *Old-Time New England.*

"Catalogue of American and Foreign plants cultivated in the Botanic Gardens, Cambridge, Massachusetts"; published by the direction of the Board of Visitors for the use of Visitors and of Students of Botany. By W. P. Peck, Professor of Natural History in Harvard College, Cambridge; 1818.

Derby Papers; Essex Institute; Essex, Mass.

ELIOT, CHARLES; "Old American Country Seats"; *Garden and Forest Magazine;* 1889.

GILMOR, ROBERT; "Memorandums made in a tour of the eastern states in the year 1797"; Bulletin of the Boston Public Library; April, 1892.

GOELET, CAPTAIN FRANCIS; Extracts from Captain Francis Goelet's Journal relative to Boston, Salem and Marblehead, 1746-50; *The New England Historical and Genealogical Register and Antiquarian;* Vol. XXIV; Boston; published by the Society; 1870.

HALE, COLONEL; papers of; in possession of the American Antiquarian Society; Worcester, Mass.

HIGGINSON, REV. FRANCIS; Journal of the Voyage of; manuscript in possession of the Massachusetts Historical Society.

KIMBALL, FISKE; "Notes on Derby Houses"; from *Architectural Record* and *Pennsylvania Museum Bulletin.*

Ladies' Magazine and Literary Gazette, November, 1830.

Magazine of Horticulture, Hovey's; Boston; 1835-68.

Massachusetts Agricultural Repository.

Massachusetts Historical Society Collections; 77 volumes, 1792-1927.

Massachusetts Magazine; Boston; J. Thomas and E. T. Andrews.

MAVERICK, HENRY; "A Briefe Discription of New England and the Severall Townes therein together with the present government thereof"; *New England Historical and Genealogical Register;* January, 1885.

New England Magazine; "Some Old New England Gardens"; Dec., 1899.

Newspapers; files before 1840 of *Boston Evening Post* and *Boston News Letter.*

Proceedings of the Massachusetts Historical Society.

QUINCY, JOSIAH; Journey of; Proceedings of the Massachusetts Historical Society, Vol. IV, Series 2.

RANDOLPH, ELEANORA WAYLES (Mrs. Joseph Coolidge); "An American Wedding Journey in 1825"; Being the story of the marriage of Eleanora Wayles Randolph and her wedding journey from Monticello to Boston, as gathered from letters in the possession of descendants, and for the most part hitherto unpublished. Edited by Harold Jefferson Coolidge; *Atlantic Monthly,* March, 1929.

SEWALL, JUDGE SAMUEL; Letter Book; Massachusetts Historical Society, Vol. I, Series 6; 1886.

CONNECTICUT

BOOKS AND PAMPHLETS

Adams, John Quincy, Memoirs of; edited by CHARLES FRANCIS ADAMS; Philadelphia; Lippincott; 1874.

BARBER, JOHN WARNER; *City of New Haven, History and Antiquities;* New Haven; L. S. Punderson and J. W. Barber; 1856.

—— *Connecticut Historical Collections;* Hartford; 1836.

CHASTELLUX, MARQUIS DE; *Travels in North America, 1780;* London; Robinson; 1787.

CUTLER, MANASSEH; *Life, Journals, and Correspondence;* published by his grandchildren, Wm. P. Cutler and Julia Perkins Cutler; Cincinnati; 1888.

DAVIS, JOHN; *Travels of Four Years and a half in the United States during 1798, 1800, 1801, 1802;* London; R. Edwards; Broad-Street, Bristol; 1803.

DWIGHT, TIMOTHY; *Travels in New England and New York, 1796-1801;* New Haven; Timothy Dwight; 1821-1822.

ELIOT, JARED; *Essays on Field Husbandry;* Killingsworth, Conn.; 1748-9.

FIELD, DAVID D.; *Statistical Account of Middlesex County in Connecticut;* Middletown; Clark and Lyman; 1819.

"First Settlers and their Homelots," pages 149-171; *History of Ancient Windsor;* Henry Stiles, q.v.

HAMILTON, DR. ALEXANDER; *Itinerarium;* edited by Albert Bushnell Hart, LL.D.; St. Louis, Missouri; printed by Wm. Bixby; 1907.

HURD, D. HAMILTON, compiler; *History of Fairfield County;* Philadelphia; J. W. Lewis & Co.; 1888.

ISHAM AND BROWN; *Early Connecticut Houses;* Providence, R. I.; The Preston and Rounds Co.; 1900.

JENKINS, EDWARD; "Connecticut Agriculture" in *History of Connecticut,* edited by Norris Galpin Osborn; New York; The State History Co.; 1925.

JOSSELYN, JOHN; *New England's Rarities;* Boston; William Veazie; 1865.

LOVE, WILLIAM DE LOSS; *The Colonial History of Hartford;* Hartford; published by the author; 1914.

OSBORN, NORRIS GALPIN, editor; *History of Connecticut;* New York; The State History Co.; 1925.

PETERS, REV. SAMUEL; *General History of Connecticut;* New York; Appleton; 1877.

PERKINS, MARY E.; *Old Houses of Antient Norwich, 1660-1800;* Norwich, Conn.; The Bulletin Co.; 1895.

Public Records of the Colony of Connecticut; Hartford; Brown and Parsons; 1850.

SIGOURNEY, LYDIA HUNTLEY; *A Sketch of Connecticut Forty Years Since;* Hartford; Oliver D. Cooke and Sons; 1824.

STILES, HENRY; *History of Ancient Windsor;* 2 vols.; Hartford, Conn.; Case, Lockwood and Brainard Co.; 1891.

STUART, JAMES; *Three Years in North America;* New York; Harpers; 1833.

TRUMBULL, BENJAMIN; *History of Connecticut;* Maltby, Goldsmith and Co. and Samuel Wadsworth; 1818.

WOOD, WILLIAM; *New Englands Prospects;* London; 1639; Boston; Thomas and John Fleet and Green and Russell; 1761.

PERIODICALS AND PAPERS

"Book of Town Wayes"; transcribed by Timothy Loomis from the original in the Town Clerk's Office, Windsor, Conn.

"Maverick's Account of New England"; Proceedings of the Massachusetts Historical Society; Second Series; Vol. I, 1884-1885.

SHEPHERD, CHARLES UPHAM; an address delivered before the New Haven Horticultural Society; Sept., 1835.

SMITH, HELEN EVERSTON; "An Ancient Garden"; *Century Magazine*, May, 1906.

WELLES, E. STANLEY; "Beginnings of Fruit Culture in Connecticut"; a paper read before the Connecticut Historical Society; May, 1929.

MAINE, NEW HAMPSHIRE AND VERMONT

CHAMPLAIN, SAMUEL DE; The Works of; translated and edited by H. H. Langton and W. F. Ganong; the French text collated by J. Home Cameron; Toronto; The Champlain Society; 1922.

EATON, CYRUS; *History of Thomaston, Rockland, and South Thomaston, Maine;* Hallowell; Masters Smith and Co., printers; 1865.

Maine Genealogical and Historical Register, Vols. I to V.

RANDOLPH, ELEANORA WAYLES (Mrs. Joseph Coolidge); "An American Wedding Journey in 1825"; Being the story of the marriage of Eleanora Wayles Randolph and her wedding journey from Monticello to Boston, as gathered from letters in the possession of descendants, and for the most part hitherto unpublished. Edited by Harold Jefferson Coolidge; *Atlantic Monthly*, March, 1929.

Vermont Antiquarian, Vols. I, II, and III.

Vermont Historical Gazeteer; Burlington; 1867.

RHODE ISLAND

BOOKS AND PAMPHLETS

ABBOTT, J. S. C.; *History of King Philip;* New York; Harpers; 1857.

ADAMS, JAMES TRUSLOW; *Founding of New England;* Boston; Atlantic Monthly Press; 1921.

ANGELL, COLONEL ISRAEL, Diary of, 1778-1780; Central Falls, R. I.; E. L. Freeman Co.; 1899.

AUSTIN, JOHN OSBORNE; *Genealogical Dictionary of Rhode Island;* Albany; Munsell; 1887.

BAKER, VIRGINIA; *The History of Warren, R. I., in the War of the Revolution, 1776-1783;* Warren, R. I.; published by the author; 1901.

BALLOU, ADIN; *An Elaborate History and Genealogy of the Ballous in America;* Providence; E. L. Freeman and Son; 1888.

BAYLIES, FRANCIS; *Historical Memoir of the Colony;* Boston; Wiggin and Lunt; 1866.

BEAMAN, C. C.; *An Historical Sketch of the Town of Scituate, R. I.;* Phenix; Capron and Campbell; 1877.

BERKELEY, GEORGE; The Works of; to which is added an account of his life etc.; London; printed for G. Robinson, Pater Noster Row; and Dublin: John Exshaw; 1784.

BLISS, LEONARD; *History of Rehoboth;* Boston; Otis, Broaders and Co.; 1836.

CAHOON, SARAH S.; *A Visit to Grand-Papa or a Week at New-Port;* New York; Taylor and Dodd; 1840.

CHANNING, EDWARD; *The Narragansett Planters: A Study of Causes;* Baltimore; Johns Hopkins Press; 1886.

CHANNING, GEORGE G.; *Early Recollections of Newport, 1793-1811;* Boston; Nichols and Noyes.

CHAPIN, HOWARD M.; *Days in Early New England;* Providence; T. A. Johnson and Co.; 1920.

—— *Documentary History of Rhode Island;* Providence; Preston and Rounds Co.; 1916.

CHILD, MRS. LYDIA MARIA; *The American Frugal Housewife;* Boston; Carter Hendee and Co.; 1832.

CLAUSON, EARL J.; *Cranston;* Providence; J. S. Hammond; 1904.

COGGESHALL, CHARLES PIERCE; and RUSSELL, THELLWELL: Compilers; *The Coggeshalls in America;* Boston; C. E. Goodspeed and Co.; 1930.

COMER, JOHN, Diary of, 1704-1732; edited with notes by C. Edwin Barrows, D.D.; Philadelphia; American Baptist Publication Society; 1892.

DAGGETT, JOHN; *History of Attleborough;* edited and compiled by Amelia Daggett Sheffield; Boston; Samuel Usher; 1894.

DENNISON, FREDERIC; *Westerly and Its Witnesses;* Providence; J. A. and R. A. Reid; 1878.

DOWNING, A. J.; *Rural Essays;* New York; Putnam; 1853.

Durfee Genealogy; Washington, D. C.; Gibson Bros.; 1902-5.

DWIGHT, TIMOTHY; *Travels in New England and New York, 1796-1801;* 4 volumes; New Haven; Timothy Dwight; 1821-22.

EATON, CYRUS; *History of Thomaston, Rockland, and South Thomaston, Maine;* Hallowell; Masters Smith and Co.; printers; 1865.

ELLET, ELIZABETH F.; *The Women of the American Revolution;* New York; Scribner; 1854.

FERSEN, HANS AXEL VON; *Lettres d'Axel de Fersen a son Père;* Paris; Firmin-Didot et cie; 1929.

FIELD, EDWARD, editor; *State of Rhode Island and Providence Plantation at the end of the Century;* 3 vols.; Boston and Syracuse; Mason Publishing Co.; 1902.

FOWLER, ORIN; *Historical Sketch of Fall River, Mass.;* Fall River; Benjamin Earl; 1841.

FULLER, OLIVER PAYSON; *History of Warwick, R. I.;* Providence; Angell Burlingame & Co., printers; 1875.

GREGG, FRANK M.; *The Founding of a Nation;* Cleveland; Arthur H. Clark Co.; 1915.

GUILD, REUBEN ALDRIDGE; *Life, Times and Correspondence of James Manning and the early history of Brown University;* Boston; Gould and Lincoln; 1864.

Hazard, Thomas B.; Journal of, 1778-1781; The Johnny-Cake Papers; Providence; 1882.

HAZARD, THOMAS B.; *Nailer Tom's Diary;* Boston; The Merrymount Press; 1930.

History of the Ladies' Benevolent Society of the First Congregational Church, 1831-1848; Fall River; J. H. Franklin Co.; 1904.

HOPKINS, CHARLES WYMAN; *The Home lots of the early settlers of the Providence Plantation;* Providence; Providence Press Co.; 1886.

ISHAM, NORMAN M., and BROWN, ALBERT F.; *Early Rhode Island Houses;* Providence; Preston and Rounds; 1895.

JACKSON, ERIC P.; *Early Uses of Land in Rhode Island;* a reprint from the Bulletin of the Geographical Society of Philadelphia, Vol. XIX, No. 2; 1926.

KIMBALL, GERTRUDE S., editor; *Pictures of Rhode Island in the Past, 1642-1833,* by Travellers and Observers; Providence; 1900.

—— *Providence in Colonial Times;* Boston; Preston and Rounds Co.; 1912.

LAMB, MARTHA J.; *The Homes of America;* New York; Appleton; 1879.

LITTLE COMPTON, R. I.; Two Hundredth Anniversary of the Organization of the United Congregational Church, Sept. 7, 1904; Little Compton, R. I.; United Congregational Society; 1906.

LIVERMORE, SAMUEL T.; *History of Block Island;* Hartford; Case, Lockwood and Brainard; 1877.

LOSSING, BENSON J.; *Pictorial Field-book of the Revolution;* New York; Harpers; 1851.

MacSparran, Rev. James, A Letter Book of; edited by the Rev. Daniel Goodwin, Ph.D.; Boston; D. B. Updike; Merrymount Press; 1899.

MANNING, ROBERT; *Book of Fruits;* Salem; Ives and Jewett; 1838.

MASON, GEORGE CHAMPLIN; *Reminiscences of Newport;* Newport; Charles E. Hammett; 1884.

—— *Annals of the Redwood Library and Athenæum;* Newport; Redwood Library; 1891.

—— *Annals of Trinity Church, Newport;* Philadelphia; Evans Printing House; 1890.

MATHER, COTTON; *Magnalia Christi Americana;* in Seven Books; London; 1702.

MUNROE, WILFRED H.; *Picturesque Rhode Island;* Providence; J. A. and R. A. Reid; 1881.

NEWHALL, CHARLES S.; *The Trees of Northeastern America;* New York; Putnam; 1890.

NUTTALL, THOMAS; *The Genera of North American Plants, and a catalogue of the species to the year 1817;* Philadelphia; 1818.

PETERSON, REV. EDWARD; *History of Rhode Island;* New York; John S. Taylor; 1853.

Plymouth Colony, Early Records of, 1633-1698; edited by Nathaniel B. Shurtleff, M.D.; Boston; William White; 1855-1861.

Portsmouth, Early Records of; edited by the Librarian of the Rhode Island Historical Society; Providence; E. L. Freeman and Son; 1901.

POWELL, LYMAN P., editor; *Historic Towns of New England;* with introduction by George P. Morris; New York; Putnam, 1898.

Providence, Early Records of; Snow and Farnham; 1892-1915.

Providence and Rhode Island Plantations; Colonial Records; 10 vols.; edited by John Russell Bartlett; Providence; A. Crawford Greene and Brother; and Providence Press; 1856-65.

ROCHEFOUCAULD-LIANCOURT, DUKE DE LA; *Travels through the United States of America, 1795, 1796, 1797;* London; 1800.

STEERE, THOMAS; *History of Smithfield;* Providence; E. L. Freeman and Co.; 1881.

UPDIKE, WILKINS; *History of the Episcopal Church in Narragansett;* Boston; Merrymount Press; 1907.

Warwick, R. I., Early Records of; Providence; E. A. Johnson Co.; 1926.

WATSON, ELKANAH; *Men and Times of the Revolution;* New York; Dana and Co.; 1856.

WHITEFIELD, EDWIN; *The Homes of our Forefathers;* Boston; Damrell and Upham; 1889.

WILBUR, ISAAC C.; *An address relative to the early history of the town of Little Compton;* Providence; Angell and Co., printers; 1882.

PERIODICALS AND PAPERS

Bulletins of the Society for the Preservation of New England Antiquities, *Old-Time New England:*

Volume VI. No. 2. Serial No. 13. 1916.
" IX. " 1. " " 18. 1918
" IX. " 2. " " 19. 1919.
" X. " 1. " " 20. 1919.
" XVIII. " 3. " " 51. 1928.

EDWARDS, MORGAN; "Material for the History of the Baptists in Rhode Island"; Collections of the Rhode Island Historical Society; Providence; 1867.

FOSTER, WILLIAM EATON; "Early attempts at Rhode Island History"; Collections of the Rhode Island Historical Society; Providence; 1885.

GOOKIN, DANIEL; "Historical Collections of the Indians in New England"; Collections of the Massachusetts Historical Society for the year 1792, Vol. I.

Harris Papers; With an introduction by Irving B. Richman, and a Calendar and Notes by Clarence S. Brighton; Providence; printed for the Rhode Island Historical Society; Vol. X of the Collections of the Society.

HIGGINSON, FRANCIS; "New-Englands Plantation"; London, 1630; reprinted Rochester, 1898; *American Colonial Tracts Monthly,* No. 11.

KOOPMAN, HARRY LYMAN; "The Narragansett Country"; Providence; printed by the General Society of Colonial Wars; 1927.

MORELL, WILLIAM; "New England" (A poem written in 1623); reprinted in Vol. I of the Collections of the Massachusetts Historical Society for the year 1792.

Newport Historical Magazine; Volumes I, II, III and IV, 1880-1884; Newport, R. I.; Newport Hist. Pub. Co.

PARSONS, CHARLES WILLIAMS; "Early Votaries of Natural Science in Rhode Island"; in Rhode Island Historical Society Collections; Providence; 1885.

POTTER, ELISHA R., JR.; "The Early History of Narragansett"; in Rhode Island Historical Society Collections, Vol. 3; Providence; Marshall, Brown and Co.; 1835.

RAND, BENJAMIN; "Berkeley and Percival"; The Correspondence of George Berkeley, afterwards Bishop of Cloyne, and Sir John Percival, afterwards Earl of Egemont, 1709-1753; Cambridge; University Press; 1914.

Rhode Island Historical Magazine; 1880-1887.

Rhode Island Historical Society: Collections, Publications, and Proceedings.

TURNER, HENRY E., M.D.; "The Greenes of Warwick in Colonial History"; read before the Rhode Island Historical Society; Feb. 27, 1877; Davis and Pitman, publishers.

WILLIAMS, ROGER; "A key into the language of America"; first published in 1643; reprinted in the Collections of the Rhode Island Historical Society, Vol. I; Providence, R. I.; 1827.

—— Letters written in 1632-1682; printed in the Publications of the Narragansett Club; First Series, Vol. VI; Providence, R. I.; 1874.

NEW YORK

BOOKS AND PAMPHLETS

ANDREWS, WILLIAM LORING; *The Iconography of the Battery and Castle Gardens;* New York; Scribners; 1901.

BARBER, JOHN WARNER, and HOWE, HENRY; *Historical Collections of New York;* New York; printed for the authors by S. Tuttle, 194 Chatham Square; 1845.

BELDEN, E. PORTER; *New York, Past, Present and Future;* New York; Putnam; 1849.

BLUNT, E.; *Stranger's Guide to the City of New York;* New York; Edmund M. Blunt; 1817.

BOLTON, REGINALD PELHAM; *Washington Heights, Manhattan, its Eventful Past;* New York; Dyckman Institute; 1924.

BOOTH, MARY L.; *History of the City of New York;* New York; Clark and Meeker; 1859.

BROWN, ADDISON; *Elgin Botanic Garden;* Lancaster, Pa.; New Era Printing Co.; 1908.

BURNABY, REV. ANDREW; *Travels in the Middle Settlements of North America, 1760;* London; printed for T. Payne; 1760.

BUSSING, MRS. ANN VAN NEST; *Reminiscences of the Van Nest Homestead;* New York; printed for private circulation; 1897.

CRÈVECŒUR, J. HECTOR ST. JOHN DE; *Letters from an American Farmer, 1770-1780;* New York; Boni; 1925.

DENTON, DANIEL; *A Brief Description of New York, formerly called New Netherlands;* New York; Wm. Gowans; 1845.

DE PEYSTER, JOHN DE; *De Peyster and Watts Genealogy;* Poughkeepsie; printed by Platt and Schram; 1894.

DOWNING, ANDREW JACKSON; *A Treatise on the Theory and Practice of Landscape Gardening adapted to North America;* New York; Wiley and Putnam; 1844.

DRAYTON, JOHN; *Tour through the Northern and Eastern States, 1796;* Charleston, S. C.; Harrison and Bowen; 1794.

DWIGHT, TIMOTHY; *Travels through New England and New York, 1796-1801;* 4 volumes; New Haven; Timothy Dwight; 1821-22.

EBERLEIN, H. D.; *Manors and Historic Houses of the Hudson Valley;* Philadelphia; Lippincott; 1924.

FAY, THEODORE S.; *Views in New York and its Environs;* New York; Peabody and Co.; 1831.

FIELD, THOMAS WARREN; *Historic and Antiquarian Scenes in Brooklyn and its Vicinity, with Illustrations of some of its Antiquities;* Brooklyn; 1868; 110 copies.

FOX, DIXON RYAN; *Caleb Heathcote, Gentleman Colonist;* New York; Scribners; 1926.

FRANCIS, JOHN W.; *Old New York;* New York; W. J. Widdleton; 1865.

GLENN, THOMAS ALLEN; *Some Colonial Mansions;* Philadelphia; Coates and Co.; 1900.

GRANT, MRS. ANNE; *Memoirs of an American Lady;* New York; S. Campbell; 1809.

GREATOREX, ELIZA; *Old New York from the Battery to Bloomingdale;* New York; G. P. Putnam's Sons; 1875.

HALL, EDWARD HAGAMAN; *Philipse Manor Hall at Yonkers, New York;* New York; The American Scenic and Historic Preservation Society; 1912.

HART, ALBERT BUSHNELL, editor; *American History Told by Contemporaries;* New York; Macmillan; 1898.

—— editor; *American Nation;* 27 vols.; New York; Harper; 1904.

HIGGINSON, REV. FRANCIS; *New-Englands Plantation;* Salem, Mass.; The Essex Book and Print Club; 1908.

HUNT, THOMAS; *Historical Sketch of the town of Clermont;* Hudson, New York; privately printed, Hudson Press; 1928.

INNESS, J. H.; *New Amsterdam and its People;* New York; Scribners; 1902.

KALM, PETER; *Travels into North America;* Translated into English by John Reinhold Foster; London; printed for the editor; 1770-71.

KELLY, HOWARD ATWOOD, M.D., LL.D.; *Some American Medical Botanists;* Troy, N. Y.; The Southworth Co.; 1914.

KNIGHT, MADAME; *Private Journal, 1704;* Boston; Small, Maynard Company; 1920.

LAET, JOHN DE; *L'Histoire du Noveau Monde;* Folio; Leyden; 1640.

LAMB, MARTHA J.; *History of the City of New York;* New York and Chicago; A. S. Barnes and Co.; 1877.

LOUDEN, J. C.; *An Encyclopedia of Gardening;* London; Longman, Orme, Brown, Green and Longman; 1834.

Murphy, H. C.; *Anthology of New Netherlands;* New York; Bradford Club publication No. IV.; 1865.

Ogilby, John; *America;* London; printed by the author; 1671.

Rider, Fremont; *New York City—Guide-book for Travellers;* New York; Holt and Co.; 1923.

Rutherford, Livingston; *Family Records and Events;* New York; De Vinne Press; 1894.

Rikeman, A. A.; *The Evolution of Stuyvesant Village;* Mamaroneck, N. Y.; Press of Curtis G. Peck; 1899.

Ross, Peter; *A History of Long Island;* New York and Chicago; The Lewis Publishing Co.; 1902.

Schuyler, George W.; *Colonial New York;* New York; Scribners; 1885.

Smith, Thomas E. V.; *New York City in 1789;* New York; Randolph and Co.; 1889.

Smith, William A. M.; *History of New York;* Albany, N. Y.; printed by Ryer Schermerhorn; 1814.

Steendham, Jacob: A memoir of the first poet of New Netherlands with his poems descriptive of the Colony; by H. C. Murphy; The Hague; The Brothers Giunta D'Albani; 1861.

Stokes, I. N. Phelps; *Iconography of Manhattan Island;* 6 vols.; New York; Robert H. Dodd; 1915-1928.

Stuart, James; *Three Years in North America;* New York; Harpers; 1833.

Sutcliff, Robert; *Travels in Some Parts of North America, in the years 1804, 1805, 1806;* Philadelphia; B. and T. Kite; 1812.

Tabor, Grace; *Old-fashioned Gardening;* New York; McBride; 1913.

Thompson, Benjamin F.; *History of Long Island;* New York; Robert H. Dodd; 1918.

Tuckerman, Bayard; *Peter Stuyvesant;* New York; Dodd, Mead and Co.; 1893.

Van Loon, Hendrick; *Life and Times of Peter Stuyvesant;* New York; Henry Holt and Co.; 1928.

Van Rensselaer, Mrs. Schuyler; *The City of New York in the Seventeenth Century;* New York; Macmillan; 1909.

Williams, Edwin, editor; *New York as it is in 1833; and Citizen's Advertising Directory;* New York; J. Disturnell; 1833.

Whittemore, Henry; *Long Island Historic Homes;* New York and Chicago; Lewis Publishing Co.; 1901.

Wilson, Rufus Rockwell; *New York Old and New;* Philadelphia; Lippincott; 1902.

Winterbotham, Rev. William; *An Historical, Geographical, Commercial, and Philosophical View of the United States of America, and the European settlements in America and the West-Indies;* New York; printed by Tiebout and O'Brien for Jordan Reid, Bookseller and Stationer, No. 106, Water-Street; 1796.

Wood, S.; *Sketch of the First Settlements of the Several Towns on Long Island;* Brooklyn, N. Y.; printed by Allen Spooner; 1826.

PERIODICALS AND PAPERS

Akerly, Lucy D.; "Morris Manor"; an address delivered Dec. 9, 1916; New York; published by the New York Branch of the Order of the Colonial Lords of the Manor in America.

Colden, Cadwallader; Papers; Collections of the New York Historical Society, 1917 to 1923; 7 vols.

Collections of the New York Historical Society.

Davis, Gherardi; "The establishment of Public Parks in New York City"; paper read before the New York Historical Society, April 6, 1897.

Duffield, Rev. Howard; "The Tangier Smith Manor of St. George"; Baltimore, 1921; published by the New York Branch of the Order of the Colonial Lords of the Manor in America; April 24, 1920.

Floy, Michael; "Catalogue of Flowering Shrubs and Fruit Trees, also Garden and Flower Seeds"; New York; 1816.

Francis, John W.; Address before the New York Horticultural Society, Sept. 8, 1829; New York; printed by E. Conrad; 1830.

Gerard, James Watson; "The Old Streets of New York under the Dutch"; A paper read before the New York Historical Society, June 2, 1874; New York; 1874.

Greenlief's *New Daily Advertiser;* Nov. 9, 1798; New York.

Hosack, David; An inaugural address delivered before the New York Horticultural Society, 1824; New York; printed by Seymour; 1824.

Livingston, John Henry; "Livingston Manor"; An address written for the New York Branch of the Colonial Lords of the Manor in America; published by the Order of the Colonial Lords of the Manor in America.

Magazine of American History.

New York Gazette; files from Mar., 1737, to May 13, 1751.

New York Historical Society Collections.

New York Magazine, June, 1790.

Valentine's Manual of the Corporation of the City of New York.

Van der Donck, Adriaen; "Description of New Netherland"; translated from the original Dutch by Hon. Jeremiah Johnson; in Collections of the New York Historical Society; Second Series; Vol. I; New York; 1841.

Year Book of the Holland Society; New York; 1916.

NEW JERSEY
BOOKS AND PAMPHLETS

Baker, A. B.; *Sketch of the First Bishop of New Jersey.*

Barber, John Warner, and Howe, Henry; *Historical Collections of New Jersey;* New Haven, Conn.; John W. Barber for Justus R. Bradley; 1868.

Benedict, William H.; *New Brunswick in History;* New Brunswick, N. J.; published by the author; 1925.

Boudinot, Elias; *Life, Public Services, Addresses and Letters;* Edited by J. J. Boudinot; Boston; Houghton Mifflin; 1896.

Brinckerhoff, Richard; *The Family of Dircken Brinckerhoff;* New York; 1887.

Glenn, Thomas Allen; *Some Colonial Mansions;* Philadelphia; Henry T. Coates Co.; 1900.

Lee, Francis Bazley; *New Jersey as a Colony and as a State;* The Publishing Society of New Jersey; 1902.

Mills, W. Jay; *Historic Houses of New Jersey;* Philadelphia; Lippincott; 1902.

Sieveking, Albert Forbes, editor; *Gardens Ancient and Modern;* London; J. M. Dent; 1885; also published in 1899 as *The Praise of Gardens.*

Woodward, E. M.; *Bonaparte and the Murats;* Trenton, New Jersey; MacCrellish and Quigley; 1879.

PERIODICALS AND DOCUMENTS

Magazines: *Scribner's,* 1880-1881; *Century,* Vol. 24, May 1; *Delineator,* 1905; *American Homes and Gardens,* August, 1913; *Magazine of American History.*

Nielson, Colonel James, Diary of; in possession of Mr. James Neilson, Woodlawn, New Brunswick, N. J.

PENNSYLVANIA
BOOKS AND PAMPHLETS

Bailey, Liberty Hyde; *Standard Cyclopedia of Horticulture;* New York; Macmillan; 1925.

Barber, John Warner; *History and Antiquities of New England, New York, New Jersey and Pennsylvania;* Hartford; Allen S. Stillman and Co.; 1844.

Birch, W.; *The Country Seats of the United States;* Springfield, Penna.; 1808.

Butler, Frances Anne (Fanny Kemble); *Journal;* Philadelphia; Carey, Lea and Blanchard; 1835.

Childs, C. G.; *Views in Philadelphia and its Vicinity;* Engraved from original drawings, 2 vols.; Philadelphia; C. G. Childs, engraver; 1827.

Crèvecœur, J. Hector St. John de: *Letters from an American Farmer;* New York; Boni; 1925.

Cutler, Manasseh, LL.D.; *Life, Journals and Correspondence;* Cincinnati; by his grandchildren, Wm. P. Cutler and Julia Perkins Cutler; 2 vols.; 1888.

Darlington, William; *Memorial of John Bartram and Humphrey Marshall;* Philadelphia; Lindsay and Blakiston; 1849.

Duché, Jacob; *Caspipina's Letters;* Bath; reprinted by R. Cruttwell; London; 1777.

Eberlein, H. D., and Lippincott, H. M.; *The Colonial Homes of Philadelphia;* Philadelphia; Lippincott; 1912.

Faris, John Thomson; *Old Roads out of Philadelphia;* Philadelphia; Lippincott; 1917.

Glenn, Thomas Allen; *Some Colonial Mansions;* Philadelphia; Henry T. Coates Co.; 1900.

Haines, Caspar Wistar; *Germantown History; Some Account of Wyck and its Owners;* Written for the Site and Relic Society of Germantown; Germantown; published for the Society; 1917.

HAZLEHURST, GEORGE; *A Part of old Philadelphia;* Philadelphia; privately printed; G. H. Buchanan Co.; 1913.

JARDINE, WM. M.; "Franklin and Agriculture"; from *The Amazing Benjamin Franklin,* compiled by J. Henry Smythe, Jr.; New York; Stokes; 1929.

JELLETT, EDWIN C.; Historical Address No. 4; Site and Relic Society of Germantown; Germantown; published by the Society; 1909.

—— *Gardens and Gardeners of Germantown;* Germantown; published by the Site and Relic Society; 1914.

JORDAN, JOHN W., LL.D., editor; *Colonial Families of Philadelphia;* New York and Philadelphia; Lewis Publishing Co.; 1911.

KALM, PETER; *Travels into North America;* translated into English by John Reinhold Foster; London; printed for the editor; 1770-71.

KELLY, HOWARD ATWOOD, M.D., LL.D.; *Some American Medical Botanists;* Troy, N. Y.; The Southworth Co.; 1914.

KELSEY, RAYNER WICKERSHAM, Ph.D., Editor; *Casenove Journal, 1794;* Haverford, Penn.; Haverford College Studies, Number 13; Pennsylvania History Press; 1922.

KEMBLE, FRANCES ANNE; *Records of Later Life;* London; Richard Bentley and Son; 1882.

LICK, DAVID E., and BRENDLE, THOMAS R.; *Plant Names and Plant Lore among the Pennsylvania Germans;* Lancaster; Lancaster Press, Inc.; 1927.

McMAHON, BERNARD; *The American Gardener's Calendar;* Philadelphia; printed by B. Graves; 1806.

Mount Pleasant in Fairmount Park; booklet copyrighted by the Pennsylvania Museum and School of Industrial Art.

OLDMIXON, JOHN; *History of the British Empire in America;* London; 1708.

Old South Leaflet, No. 95, Vol. IV; Boston; Directors of the Old South Work; Old South Meeting House.

RUSH, BENJAMIN; *The Manners of the German Inhabitants of Pennsylvania;* written 1789; notes added by Prof. I. Daniel Rupp; Philadelphia; Samuel P. Towne; 1875.

SCHARF and WESTCOTT, *History of Philadelphia;* Philadelphia; L. H. Everetts and Co.; 1884.

SCHOEPF, DAVID JOHANN; *Travels in the Confederation, 1783-4;* Philadelphia; William J. Campbell; 1911.

SUTCLIFF, ROBERT; *Travels in Some Parts of North America, in the years 1804, 1805, 1806;* Philadelphia; B. and T. Kite; 1812.

THOMAS, GABRIEL; *An account of Pennsylvania and West New Jersey;* London; original edition 1698.

TROLLOPE, FRANCES; *Domestic Manners of the Americans;* first edition 1832; reprinted from the fifth edition 1839; London; George Routledge and Sons, Ltd.; 1927.

WATSON, JOHN F.; *Annals of Philadelphia;* compiled by Willis P. Hazard; Philadelphia; E. L. Carey and A. Hart; 1879.

WESTCOTT, THOMPSON; *Historic Mansions and Buildings of Philadelphia;* Philadelphia; J. M. Stoddart and Co.; 1879.

WHARTON, ANNE HOLLINGSWORTH; *In Old Pennsylvania Towns;* Philadelphia; Lippincott; 1920.

WILSON, THOMAS; *Pictures of Philadelphia, 1824;* Philadelphia; Thomas Town; 1824.

WISTER, SARAH BUTLER; *Worthy Women of Our First Century;* Philadelphia; Lippincott; 1877.

WRIGHT, LETITIA E.; *Colonial Garden at Stenton; described in old letters;* copyright by Letitia Wright; 1916.

PERIODICALS AND PAPERS

"Byberry, History of"; *Memoirs of the Historical Society of Pennsylvania;* Vol. II; Philadelphia; Carey, Lea & Carey; Chestnut Street; 1827.

Columbia Magazine, Jan., 1790.

DEWEE, MRS. MARY; "Journal from Philadelphia to Kentucky, 1787-88"; *Pennsylvania Magazine of History and Biography;* Vol. XXVIII; Philadelphia; Publication Fund of the Pennsylvania Historical Society; 1904.

Floral Magazine and Botanical Repository; Philadelphia; D. and C. Landreth; 1832.

KIMBALL, MARY G.; "Revival of the Colonial"; *Architectural Record;* July, 1927.

Logan, Deborah, Original Letters of; in possession of Pennsylvania Historical Society; Philadelphia.

Newspapers: *Federal Gazette,* Philadelphia, Oct. 20, 1800; *Pennsylvania Packet,* Feb. 20, 1781; Sept. 30, 1789; *Pennsylvania Chronicle,* Apr. 12, 1768.

PALMER, T. CHALKLEY; "The Painter Arboretum and Dismal Run; *The Westonian;* Vol. XXXV, Number 4; Westtown, Pa.; The Westtown Alumni Association.

Penn, William, Letters of; in possession of the Pennsylvania Historical Society; Philadelphia.

—— Collections of various pieces concerning; *Pennsylvania Magazine of History and Biography;* Vol. VI, No. 3, 1882.

WARD, TOWNSEND; "The Germantown Road and its Associations"; *Pennsylvania Magazine of History and Biography;* Vol. VI.

Western Pennsylvania Historical Magazine.

MICHIGAN

BOOKS AND PAMPHLETS

BURTON, C. M.; *Cadillac's Village;* Detroit; 1896.

HAMLIN, MRS. M. C. W.; *Legends of Le Detroit;* Detroit; T. Nourse; 1884.

HUBBARD, BELA; *Memorials of a Half-Century;* New York and London; G. P. Putnam's Sons; 1887.

La Hontan's Voyages; Chicago; McClurg; 1905.

PALMER, FRIEND; *Early Days in Detroit;* Detroit; Hunt and June; 1906.

ROSS, ROBERT B., CATLIN, G. B.; *Landmarks of Detroit;* Detroit; Detroit Evening News Association; 1898.

STEPHENSON, O. W.; *Ann Arbor, The First Hundred Years;* Ann Arbor; Ann Arbor Chamber of Commerce; 1927.

WOOD, E. O.; *Historic Mackinac;* New York; Macmillan; 1918.

OHIO

BOOKS AND PAMPHLETS

ASHE, THOMAS; *Travels in America, performed in 1806, for purpose of exploring the rivers, Alleghany, Monongahela, Ohio and Mississippi, and ascertaining the produce and condition of their banks and vicinity;* London; Newburyport, Re-printed for Wm. Sawyer & Co.; E. M. Blunt, State-Street; 1808.

BARBER, JOHN WARNER; *All the Western States and Territories;* Cincinnati; Howe's Subscription Book Concern; 1867.

HOWE, HENRY; *Historical Collections of Ohio;* Norwalk, Ohio; published by the State of Ohio; 1896.

RIDDELL, JOHN L.; *Synopsis of the Flora of the Western States;* Cincinnati; 1835.

PERIODICALS

Better Homes and Gardens, May, 1931; "Zoar Restores Its Century-Old Gardens"; Beulah Canterbury.

RANDALL, E. O.; "Blennerhasset"; *Ohio Archæological and Historical Society Quarterly,* Vol. I, p. 132.

FENCES AND ENCLOSURES

BOOKS AND PAMPHLETS

DOWNING, ANDREW JACKSON; *A Treatise on the Theory and Practice of Landscape Gardening, Adapted to North America;* New York; Wiley and Putnam; 1844.

KALM, PETER; *Travels into North America;* Translated into English by John Reinhold Foster; London; printed for the editor; 1770-71.

Letters about the Hudson River and its Vicinity, written in 1835-7; New York; Freeman, Hunt & Co.; 1837.

SCHOEPF, DAVID JOHANN; *Travels in the Confederation, 1783-4;* Philadelphia; William J. Campbell; 1911.

PERIODICALS

"Byberry, History of"; *Memoirs Historical Society of Pennsylvania;* Vol. II; Carey, Lea and Carey; Chestnut Street; 1827.

INDEX

INDEX